POLITICS AND CHANGE
IN THE MIDDLE EAST

fourth edition

POLITICS AND CHANGE IN THE MIDDLE EAST

Sources of Conflict and Accommodation

ROY R. ANDERSEN
ROBERT F. SEIBERT
JON G. WAGNER
All of Knox College

PRENTICE HALL
Englewood Cliffs, New Jersey 07632

Library of Congress Cataloging-in-Publication Data

Andersen, Roy
    Politics and change in the Middle East: sources of conflict and
accommodation / Roy R. Andersen, Robert F. Seibert, Jon G. Wagner.—
4th ed.
        p. cm.
    Includes bibliographical references and index.
    ISBN 0-13-682840-X
    1. Middle East—Politics and government. I. Seibert, Robert F.
II. Wagner, Jon G. III. Title
DS62.8.A5 1993
320.956—dc20

                                                    92-21592
                                                        CIP

Production Editor: KERRY REARDON
Acquisitions Editor: JULIE BERRISFORD
Cover Designer: CAROL CERALDI
Prepress Buyer: KELLY BEHR
Manufacturing Buyer: MARY ANN GLORIANDE
Editorial Assistant: MILDRED WHITE

©1993, 1990, 1987, 1982 by Prentice-Hall, Inc.
A Simon & Schuster Company
Englewood Cliffs, New Jersey 07632

Printed in the United States of America

10   9   8   7   6   5   4   3   2   1

ISBN   0-13-682840-X

PRENTICE-HALL INTERNATIONAL (UK) LIMITED, *London*
PRENTICE-HALL OF AUSTRALIA PTY. LIMITED, *Sydney*
PRENTICE-HALL CANADA INC., *Toronto*
PRENTICE-HALL HISPANOAMERICANA, S.A., *Mexico*
PRENTICE-HALL OF INDIA PRIVATE LIMITED, *New Delhi*
PRENTICE-HALL OF JAPAN, *Tokyo*
SIMON & SCHUSTER ASIA PTE. LTD., *Singapore*
EDITORA PRENTICE-HALL DO BRASIL, LTDA., *Rio de Janeiro*

To our children,
Brynn, Eric, Kyla, and Joanna;
and to our wives,
Corine, Jan, and Marna

CONTENTS

PREFACE

This book has grown out of the authors' conviction that a proper understanding of present events in the Middle East requires a knowledge of the cultural, social, and economic, as well as the political, background of these events. It is, more specifically, an outgrowth of the authors' attempts to develop undergraduate courses aimed at such understanding. We found that despite the abundance of excellent scholarship on the Middle East, there was a paucity of works that brought together the diverse disciplinary perspectives in a way suitable to our pedagogic aims. This is still the case. It is our belief that this book, with its combination of historical and contemporary materials and its integrated perspective, provides something of value that is not elsewhere available to the undergraduate student or the educator.

Great changes have occurred in the three short years since the publication of the third edition of this book. First, the Palestinian intifadah matured into a genuine movement, challenging twenty years of Israeli occupation. The outbreak of rebellion, its intensity and durability surprised the leadership of both the PLO and Israel. Second, under the leadership of Mikhail Gorbachev, the Soviet Union embarked on a political course that resulted first in the abandonment of its traditional foreign policy, then in the abandonment of its empire in Eastern Europe, and finally in the very dissolution of the Union itself in December of 1991. This change signaled the end of the bipolar world order that had prevailed since the end of World War II, and forced fundamental reappraisals of that world order. These events have also had substantial consequences for the conduct of foreign relations in the Middle East. The emergence of six newly independent republics in Central Asia, with their Muslim majorities or pluralities, is one of the new factors in the international equation now emerging.

Saddam Hussein's ill-advised attempt to annex Kuwait in the summer of 1990 focused these new realities. The invasion resulted in the creation of a coalition of Western and Middle Eastern states that successfully intervened in Kuwait and in the process created other new realities. Among them were dramatic increases in the prestige and the power of the United States, Syria, Saudi Arabia, and Iran—a strange combination of bedfellows indeed. These new realities were at least partially responsible for the change in political atmospherics that resulted in the first serious multilateral peace negotiations between Israel and her Arab subjects and neighbors.

These events have necessitated substantial revisions in the text. In some cases the changes amounted to a straightforward updating. In others, revisions were made so as to give a more thorough background to emerging issues. The chapters on economics and international relations have been updated and considerably rewritten. There are two completely new chapters, one on politics and social life, and the other on the Middle East and the New International Order. The country profiles have been updated, and the glossary expanded. And the book continues to be predicated on the value of using a multidisciplinary approach to examine various facets of conflict and accommodation.

We have directed our writing to an undergraduate audience not specifically acquainted with the Middle East. We have made every effort to avoid disciplinary jargon, arcane theoretical concepts, or other devices that would necessitate a sophisticated background in any of the social sciences. This is not to say that we avoid special concepts or terms, but we introduce such terms but only as necessary and as painlessly as possible.

One of the characteristic problems in writing about another culture involves the use of language. The words used by Arabs, Turks, or Persians to describe institutions and concepts fundamental to their civilization usually have no direct equivalent in English. One is faced with the dilemma of whether to translate them (which necessarily introduces our own cultural bias), or to use "native" terms (which places on the reader the burden of learning a new vocabulary). Added to this problem is the more technical matter of how to transliterate Arabic or other languages into the medium of the English alphabet. Our solution has been one of compromise: We have used foreign words when there is no English equivalent or when the nearest English equivalent would be awkward or misleading. Despite our efforts to minimize foreign words, the text has unavoidably made use of a number of them—especially Arabic terms. Most of these are explained in the text, and whenever possible the explanation accompanies the first appearance of a term, which is indicated by the use of *italics*. As an extra aid to the student we have also included some terms in a glossary. The terms explained in the glossary are in **boldface** the first time they appear in the text. As for the spelling of Arabic and other foreign words, we have omitted the diacritical marks that scholars use to render their transliterations technically correct. We do so on the assumption that the pronunciation of the limited number of terms we use can, for the reader's purposes, be determined without these marks. Nearly all Arabic terms appear in several different English forms in the literature; we have tried to hold to those forms which reflect the most frequent current usage among informed scholars who write for a general audience. In personal names especially, we have often departed from the technically correct forms and employed instead the forms used in English for news reportage and popular historical writing.

Where there is no single established usage or term, we have tried to introduce some consistency. For instance, the 1990–1991 conflict that began with Iraq's invasion of Kuwait is known by a variety of terms including "Desert Storm," the

"Gulf Crisis," the "Gulf War," the "Persian Gulf War," and so forth. With some exceptions that should be clear in their context, we will refer to it as the Iraq–Kuwait War of 1990–1991.

One further matter that deserves mention here is the definition of the Middle East itself. The term *Middle East* raises some problems, for it originates in recent Western military usage and utilizes present national boundaries that cut across historically significant cultural and geographical divisions. Furthermore, the reference to the region as part of the "East" reveals a European bias; from the larger perspective of the whole civilized area stretching from Western Europe to East Asia, the so-called Middle East is located somewhat toward the West and has close cultural ties with the Mediterranean region as a whole. Despite these problems, we shall follow the (more or less) established convention and define the Middle East as the region encompassed on the northwest by Turkey, on the southwest by Egypt, on the southeast by the Arabian peninsula, and on the northeast by Iran. At the same time, it must be remembered that this division is somewhat arbitrary, and that bordering regions like Afghanistan, the Sudan, and North Africa have much in common with their "Middle Eastern" neighbors. For this reason, we shall include them in our discussions whenever appropriate.

The authorship of this book is genuinely a joint affair; there is no "senior" author. The order of our names on the list was randomly chosen. One of the authors is an economist with a long-standing interest in economic development; one is a political scientist specializing in political development in the Third World; and the third is a cultural anthropologist specializing in religion and culture change. Each chapter was largely the work of a single author, but each reflects a dialogue that began long before the book was conceived and has continued throughout its preparation and revision.

We cannot hope to name all the persons and institutions that have made important contributions to this writing. We wish to thank Knox College for its material and moral support, and particularly for maintaining an atmosphere that nourishes interdisciplinary collaboration and teaching. We are indebted to the United States Office of Education, which made it possible for us to observe at first hand the phenomena of social and political change in two Muslim countries, Egypt and Malaysia, during 1976 and 1977. We also thank Dr. John Duke Anthony, founder, director, and driving force of the National Council on U.S.–Arab Relations, under whose sponsorship we have collectively traveled to Bahrain, Iraq, Jordan, Kuwait, Saudi Arabia, Syria, the U.A.E., and Israel and the Palestinian territories it occupies. There are scores of individuals in each of these countries who gave generously their precious time and considerable talents in order that we could better appreciate some nuances of highly complex situations. We also owe thanks to Professor John Woods and the Center for Middle Eastern Studies at the University of Chicago. As always, the staff at Prentice Hall have been supportive and professional, particularly Acquisitions Editor Julie Berrisford and Production Editor Kerry Reardon. We especially wish our erstwhile editor Karen Horton well in her new professional life. The reviewers for this Fourth Edition include Donald S. Inbody, United States Naval Academy and Alain G. Marsot, California State University at Long Beach. Reviewers for previous editions include Jill Crystal, University of Michigan, Michael Rubner, Michigan State University, Marguerite Bouraad-Nash, University of California at Santa Barbara, Donna Robinson Divine,

Smith College, Sanford Silverburg, Catawba College, Jonathan Wilkenfeld, University of Maryland, Eric J. Hooglund, Bowdoin College, John P. Entelis, Fordham University, Nizar Motani, Western Michigan, and Raymond Habiby, Oklahoma State University. Finally, we thank our students at Knox, whose interest in the Middle East, energy, and enthusiasm have given us continued motivation for this work.

Above all, we take this opportunity to express our appreciation to our wives and children for suffering bravely through what is, as every author knows, the seemingly endless task of transforming a set of ideas into a finished book.

R. R. A.
R. F. S.
J. G. W.

INTRODUCTION

Events in the Middle East have captured worldwide attention since the 1970s. Hefty increases in petroleum prices brought about by the efforts of the Organization of Petroleum Exporting Countries (OPEC), the spectacular rise of the Islamic Republic of Iran, the Iran–Iraq war, and conflicts in Lebanon, the West Bank, and the Persian (Arabian) Gulf have riveted the attention of both the regional actors and the world as a whole. Yet only a couple of decades earlier many outside the region saw the problems of the Middle East as largely local affairs that rarely affected the world political arena. Today, the Middle East is properly regarded as crucial to world events, and it will continue to be so regarded in the forseeable future.

The Middle East's geographical position alone, at the junction of Africa, Asia, and Europe, is ample reason for it to command the world's attention. A sign in the Cairo airport proclaims it the "Crossroads of the World," a slogan that rings true for several reasons. Three great monotheistic religions—Judaism, Christianity, and Islam—arose from the same society and culture; the Western and Muslim intellectual heritages have much more in common than is generally recognized. Although some major strands of Western thought can be traced to Greece, much Greek philosophy and science were preserved and transmitted to the West through the writings of Muslim scholars. In fact, the Middle East served as a repository of Greek thought while Europe languished in the Dark Ages. Also during this time, a great intellectual and cultural florescence occurred in the Islamic world. The development of algebra (in Arabic, *al-jabr*), fundamental advances in the sciences of optics and medicine, and many other intellectual achievements originated in the Middle East. Furthermore, concepts from the Far East were melded into Middle Eastern intellectual and cultural patterns. "Arabic" numerals, the decimal system, and the use of zero—all brought to the Middle East from India—paved the way for profound advances in quantitative thinking. The role of the Middle East in trade and conquest, no less than its intellectual activity, made it a crossroads in every way. The Middle East is not a desert devoid of high culture and rich history; the religion of its peoples is not characterized by wild-eyed fanaticism. The Middle East should not be viewed as an exotic area of intellectual inquiry, but rather as integral to our understanding of the world.

A serious study of the relationship of the Middle East to the rest of the world must introduce a broad array of "facts," assumptions, hypotheses, and theories—which might threaten to overwhelm the beginning student. And, although Egypt, Saudi Arabia, Iran, Lebanon, and other Middle Eastern states share a common heritage, particular historic, geographic, and economic influences have produced substantial regional diversity. Thus the Middle East cannot be viewed as a monolithic entity; its constituent regions and entities must be studied carefully in order to identify points of commonality and divergence. The welter of information generated by these complexities can create more confusion than understanding, more tedium than excitement. We have therefore selected two themes—conflict (and its resolution) and social change—to make the task more manageable for the beginning student. Although we focus on political systems in the Middle East, we carry our themes across disciplinary lines into other social sciences. We have not, however, attempted a systematic coverage of Islamic art, literature, science, and theology, even though such coverage would indeed lend richness and subtlety to the topics covered in the text. We encourage the student to explore these topics.

POLITICS AND CONFLICT

The first theme centers around the definition of politics employed: the study of conflicts between groups of people and how those conflicts are resolved in human institutions. Conflict is present in all societies and is caused by competing demands for limited resources. The demand for resources embraces a wide variety of valued things, but may include ordinary things such as money, land, and water, or more abstract things such as deference, prestige, or even claims on cultural and religious symbols of legitimacy. The propensity of human beings to demand such things in greater quantity than the supply allows leads to conflict over distribution or consumption. When formal organizations make socially binding decisions regarding such things, they are engaging in the political resolution of social conflict. To sum up, *conflict* arises out of the inevitable competition for scarce resources; *politics* involves the resolution of these conflicts through the formal and informal processes and institutions that constitute government. We consequently equate politics with the formation and resolution of conflict in social life. Although there are many alternate definitions of politics that could be employed, the one given here is widely used and fits into the major plan of this book.

Conflict and conflict resolution occur at various levels of social organization. For example, conflict over water resources can take place at the local level (which fields are to receive how much water?), or at the regional level (should a dam be constructed in region A or region B?), or at the national level (should a country rely on its existing water sources or explore the feasibility of desalination of ocean water?). Although all of these decisions involve the provision and allocation of scarce resources, the people, institutions, and style of decision making will vary from one level to another. Conflict resolution involving personal discussion among those affected is more likely to occur at the local level than at the regional or national level. The political processes employed depend on the level and arena of conflict.

In this text, we discuss political conflict in terms of the applicable arenas. For example, in a discussion of the elite structure of a given government, we distinguish between the qualities and styles of national and local elites. This is a convenient way of analyzing a nation's political system. However, no nation consists of neatly layered conflict arenas; any given arena interacts with other arenas that are potentially higher, lower, or equal in level. The arenas of conflict in a nation resemble the composition of a multiflavored marble cake in which various colors and flavors dip and swirl irregularly.

As an example, the complex interaction of arenas can be seen in the decisions that led to the construction and operation of the Aswan High Dam in Egypt. Egypt is, as Herodotus said more than 2,000 years ago, the "gift of the Nile." Almost all its arable land lies in the Nile Valley and Delta. Over thousands of years the cultivators of the land have adapted their agricultural techniques and timing to the annual flooding of the river. Regulating the flow of the Nile through the construction of a large dam, it was theorized, would free the farmers from dependence on the caprice of the river, minimize flood damage, and maximize agricultural production.

However, the project brought to light many unanticipated conflicts—some of which had been simmering below the surface of day-to-day events, and some of which were created by the construction and operation of the dam. The major themes of conflict were as follows: (1) The financing and construction of the dam involved superpower interests: The United States had first agreed to finance the project, but backed out of the agreement; the U.S.S.R. then stepped in to fill the breach. (2) The determination of water rights between Egypt and the Sudan had to be resolved, since the lake formed by the dam crossed the border dividing the two countries. (3) Thousands of families had to be relocated from the lake site into existing or new villages and towns. (4) A system for allocating irrigation water to Nile Delta farmers had to be developed. (5) Drainage problems induced by the operation of the dam required individual, village, provincial, national, and finally World Bank intervention. The relationships between various groups involved had to be reworked, sometimes drastically. The Aswan Dam was—and is—the focal point of conflict in several arenas; it is an example of the tendency for solutions in one arena to generate new problems in another, in a complex cycle of cause and effect.

APPROACHES TO SOCIAL CHANGE

Human social life is changing with increasing speed. Certain trends set in motion only a few centuries ago have accelerated and spread until they have profoundly affected most of the world's societies and have drawn nations into an unprecedented degree of interdependence. Westerners, who have benefited in particular from many of these changes, sometimes take them for granted as part of the natural course of human "progress," without much attempt at a deeper critical understanding. Even the social sciences may be subtly influenced by ethnocentric assumptions. For the Western reader to grasp the essence of these changes and to understand their causes without falling into the trap of cultural chauvinism (or its negative counterpart, cultural self-deprecation) is no easy task.

Many Westerners naively assume that the West has been in the forefront of cultural development for thousands of years, a view that is enhanced by grafting European history onto that of the Greeks while placing the Middle East in the vague category of "Oriental" or "Asian" cultures. But, by any objective standards, Western Europe could not be called a leader in world cultural development until very late in history. Even after the Renaissance, Europe was on no more than an equal footing with the older centers of civilization, and it was only in the eighteenth century that it decisively surpassed the Middle East in technology and commercial power.

What is the nature of the unique change that originated in Western society and subsequently influenced the emerging world order, and why did it occur in Europe rather than the older centers of civilization? Marshall G. S. Hodgson, in his remarkably insightful work, *The Venture of Islam*, has characterized this change as one toward "technicalization."[1] A technicalized society is one in which the interplay of specialized technical considerations tends to take precedence over aesthetic, traditional, interpersonal, religious, or other nontechnical concerns—in short, a society structured by the demands of specialized technical efficiency. This is not to imply that nontechnicalistic societies have no interest in technical efficiency or that technicalistic societies care for nothing else, but only that the unprecedented emphasis on specialized technical considerations has played a key role in the development of modern cultures. The process of technicalization and its ramifications can be seen as central to many of the cultural changes that are taking place in contemporary countries, from the poorest to the most affluent. Some of these changes tend to occur repeatedly in different countries because they are directly related to the process of technicalization; others, such as style of clothing or taste in entertainment, are communicated as part of a growing international cosmopolitan culture. Some changes are predictable and others are not, and some may be fundamental to the technicalization process while others are only incidental to it.

Perhaps the most fundamental elements are economic and technological in nature. The rise of technicalism in Europe was accompanied by certain changes that still seem inseparable from it, and central among these is the institutionalization of technical innovation. The ability to adopt efficient technical innovations was the key to success among the competing private business enterprises of seventeenth- and eighteenth-century Europe, and for that reason traditional European social forces that impeded free scientific inquiry gradually gave way before a cultural outlook that took for granted continuous inquiry and innovation. Such an outlook has had far-reaching consequences in noneconomic realms, but its effect on the techno-economic order has been most immediate. It has led to a rapid development of industrial production, the use of fossil fuels, complex machines, standardized mass production, a highly specialized division of labor and knowledge, and a substantial reinvestment of profits in the machinery of production. This pattern of production has been accompanied by a growth of regional interdependence, so that even nonindustrialized regions tend to become part of a growing network for the

---

[1] Marshall G. S. Hodgson, *The Venture of Islam*, Vol. III, (Chicago: University of Chicago Press, 1974), pp. 186–196.

exchange of raw materials and manufactured items. This integration may or may not occur on such terms as to facilitate an increase in economic independence and material well-being for a given society; there is nothing in the creation of a world economic system that assures justice, equality, or a universal advance in well-being.

In addition to its material aspects, the technicalizing trend has had many social and cultural consequences. In society generally, there has been a greater tendency for roles and social status to be achieved rather than ascribed on the basis of gender, age, kinship, or circumstances of birth. The criterion of technical efficiency is applied in politics, where technical competence gradually displaces the more traditional criteria for choosing leaders, while the public becomes increasingly informed and competent in political matters. Mass communication has brought about the possibility of mass public support for political leaders and programs, thus ushering in a new era of participatory politics (or, all too often, active repression of burgeoning popular movements). The institutionalization of change, together with the notion of holding customs and institutions accountable to criteria of technical efficiency, also brings about new attitudes toward societal rules, which are less likely to be seen as absolute and eternal. And, finally, increased communication and interdependence have helped to create a much more cosmopolitan outlook in which an increasing number of people see themselves, if not as "citizens" of the whole world, at least as actors in it.

The historical reasons for the technicalization of the West are difficult to unravel, but they may include some geographical and ecological components. In fact, some of the ecological conditions that retarded European civilization in earlier history may have aided its more recent rise. Among the most significant factors in the rise of technicalism in the West were the unprecedented importance of capital reinvestment and technological innovation, both of which were being built into the commercial institutions of eighteenth-century Europe. It is possible that entrepreneurial capitalism, which supported this competition for technical efficiency, was discouraged in the older civilizations where irrigation-based agriculture promoted the consolidation of a more centralized governmental control. Europe, by contrast, had an economy based on rainfall agriculture that provided less of a basis for centralized control of the economy, and monarchs and central bureaucracies were therefore less able to thwart and exploit would-be capitalists. The West's economic potential in the eighteenth century may have been bolstered by the fact that it, unlike the land-depleted Middle East, still had virgin countryside into which agricultural production could expand. Whatever the historical reasons for the priority of Europe in making the transition, the West's institutionalization of technical efficiency and technological innovation has done much to determine not only the character of the West itself but of the world order as well.

The West did not set out to conquer the world; rather, each European nation sought to extend its political and economic interests and to protect them, not only from local threats but from other European powers as well. Whatever their nationality, Europeans invariably saw themselves as a progressive people ruling and tutoring the backward segments of humankind, and they were able to support this attitude with a technically efficient military force. Sometimes European domination took the form of direct occupation and political rule; but even when it did not, the pattern of domination remained similar. The European powers intervened as necessary to insure that local governments kept sufficient order to protect European interests, but not enough power to pose any challenge to European hegemony. Typically, the economic production of the dominated countries was structured to provide a limited range of raw materials most needed by the dominant power.

In some respects, European cultural domination was just as far-reaching as its political, military, and economic domination. Middle Easterners were classified along with the various Asian peoples as "Orientals," and it was widely held that such people were given to inscrutable peculiarities of thought, blind obedience to tradition, and insensitivity to suffering. Even Middle Eastern nationalism has sometimes been influenced by Western biases in subtle ways; for example, many Middle Easterners have tacitly accepted the classification of themselves as "Orientals," a category that has little meaning except as an expression of European ethnocentrism.

One of the lingering and pervasive effects of Western ethnocentrism is the tendency to confuse "progress" with Westernization, and to hold up middle-class Europe and America as a universal model of "modernity." It is intellectually and morally indefensible to assume that everything non-Western is necessarily backward, especially when much of Western culture comes from a time when Western civilization was less developed than that of the Middle and Far East. Yet it is often tempting, even for the non-Westerner, to equate change with Westernization. The political and economic dominance of the West during the past few centuries has made Westernization a companion of most other changes, so that Westerners and non-Westerners alike sometimes find different types of changes difficult to distinguish from Westernization.

In keeping with the prejudice that Western society sets the course for universal human progress, some Westerners—including certain social theorists—have pictured non-Western societies as stagnant and mired in an unreflective obedience to "tradition." A theoretical view widely accepted a decade or two ago, for example, contrasted the purportedly inflexible and unimaginative conservatism of the "traditional" Middle Easterner with the open-minded, resourceful, optimistic, and empathetic outlook of the "modernized" person. According to this view, the key to progress and affluence in the Third World is a fundamental change in psychological outlook that comes from exposure to more liberated ways of thinking that originate—of course—in the West. Critics of this now outdated view have pointed out, with some justice, that it is more self-congratulatory than illuminating. It ignores the great diversity of outlooks that exist within the "traditional" world and the particular historical conditions that have given rise to them. It also overlooks the possibility that cultural attitudes may be understandable responses to political, economic, or ecological realities that cannot be waved away by a change in attitude—realities that include the Western presence itself.

Perhaps the chief oversight of the "modernization" theory, in the context of this book, is its failure to appreciate the political dimensions of human choice in "traditional" settings. Conflict, political strategy, and calculated choice are found in all human societies, even when they result in the reproduction of a relatively stable system—and few if any societies are ever completely stable. Although the Western observer may be tempted by the romantic notion that every "exotic" custom or idea dates from time immemorial, a closer look at cultural history (especially that of the Middle East) reveals a continuous state of flux. The origin and spread of Islam is one good example of the speed and magnitude of change, even in basic beliefs, that can occur in a traditional society. While people everywhere are inclined to accept the beliefs and perspectives with which they were reared, they are everywhere capable of revising and criticizing these traditions when they no longer seem to fill their needs.

While it is true that a "modern" or technicalized setting may present people with a greater range of possibilities than was previously known, it is important not to underestimate the degree to which rational calculation enters into decision making even when "traditional" values are invoked. Indeed, some of the supposed differences between "traditional" and "modern" outlooks may be largely a matter of rhetorical style. For example, a political leader planning the invasion of a neighboring country may seek to justify it in a variety of ways: He may utilize a rationalistic rhetoric that stresses its benefits ("This invasion will bring peace, security, and good government to all concerned"); he may use a traditionalistic rhetoric that looks to the authority of the past ("These people have always been our subjects"); or he may use religious rhetoric ("God will look kindly on us for subduing the infidel"). All these styles of rhetoric have been used throughout history, but the rationalistic style is relatively fashionable in technicalized societies. The use of such rhetoric does not in itself make one's actions particularly reasonable, any more than the use of a religious rhetoric means that one's actions are divinely guided, or a traditionalist rhetoric proves that a given practice is genuinely traditional. It is a mistake, then, to conclude simply from these differences in public rhetoric that one society's motives and actions are in fact more rational than another's.

The perspective of distance almost always makes other cultures look flat, arbitrary, and deterministic compared with our own. Whether we are getting married or getting dressed in the morning, we see our own actions as guided by reason, filled with subtle meaning, and tempered by personal freedom. The corresponding behavior in another culture seems to us simple, stereotyped, and unreflective. "We" put on neckties because we think, and "they" put on turbans because they don't—or so it seems. Yet, close studies of traditional peoples have shown them to be more critically aware of circumstances and choices than is commonly assumed. Quite often, behavior that appears motivated by blind conservatism turns out instead to be based on a realistic assessment of the alternatives; thus many people are quite capable of grasping the significance of changing circumstances and are able to adapt to them accordingly. Such choices, however, must always be made within the framework of existing institutions, and guided by existing values and assumptions about the nature and purpose of human existence. These values and assumptions are deeply rooted in the cultural heritage of a people; this is as true of the West as it is of the Middle East, and it helps account for the continuing role of religion in both settings. For that reason we have adopted two basic strategies in presenting the material. First, we shall heavily emphasize the historical forces that have shaped the Middle East. To understand what the Middle East is and what it might be requires that one know what it was. The chapters dealing with the history of past centuries, therefore, are best viewed as part of the present landscape and not as a separate story. Second, since the politics of the Middle East are woven together with general social and economic forces, a multidisciplinary approach has been adopted, an approach facilitated by the diversity of the authors' academic training in political science, economics, and cultural anthropology.

Political affairs in the Middle East are treated here as the product of the interaction among social organization, secular values, religion, and the control and allocation of authority and resources at all levels. While the variables must sometimes be isolated for analysis, to remove them permanently from their context is to invite misunderstanding.

TRADITIONAL CULTURES OF THE MIDDLE EAST:
The Cradle of Civilization and Politics

In dealing with "exotic" peoples and cultures, we often form stereotypic images, founded on some grain of truth but containing enough distortion and error to make them at least useless and often harmful. Popular images of the Middle East are a case in point.

The Middle East is no stranger to the Western imagination. It is the setting of the Jewish and Christian holy scriptures. We derive our images of the Middle East partly from these scriptures and the Hollywood images spun around them, and from the news reports of current events. The Middle East is often seen as the primeval wilderness from which our civilization sprang—a wilderness which has since lapsed into timeless stagnation. In the popular imagination it is inhabited mainly by fierce desert nomads who, driven by a childlike attachment to tradition and the fiery narrowness of the barbaric "Mohammedan" faith, spend most of their time menacing each other and impeding peace and progress. With alarming regularity the "Arab" is depicted in film and on television as regressive, sex-crazed, violent, and sinister. News coverage highlights "terrorism," oil profiteering, and other supposed threats, casting Middle Easterners as odious but ineffectual enemies. Thus we form a composite picture of the "Arab" (and all native Middle Easterners are commonly thought by Westerners to be "Arabs") as an evil buffoon. However, the popular notion of the Middle East as a geographical and cultural backwater inhabited by ignorant fanatics is incompatible with even the most elementary knowledge of Middle Eastern culture and history.

Besides the dispelling of these common prejudices, there are several reasons why a look at traditional Middle Eastern culture is useful. For one, it provides a backdrop against which to understand the historical development of innovative social, religious, and political institutions in the region. Furthermore, it allows us to better understand those aspects of contemporary Middle Eastern life that still retain substantial continuity with past traditions. The Middle East today, like any region of the world, has constructed its modern institutions on a base of traditional social arrangements, values, philosophical assumptions, and everyday practices

1

that are deeply rooted in a cultural heritage. And unlike most of the Western world, the Middle East contains regions, or aspects of social life, whose continuity with the lifestyle of two or three centuries ago is in some respects more apparent than are the recent influences of a cosmopolitan, "technicalized" cultural milieu. One must be careful, however, not to fall into the common Eurocentric bias of thinking that all non-Western practices are ancient and lacking in developmental change—a habit of thought encouraged by referring to "tradition" as though it represented some timeless eternality. Except when otherwise clear from the context, we shall use the term *traditional* to refer very generally to patterns of social and cultural life that prevailed in the few centuries prior to the massive incursion of European influence and technicalizing changes into the Middle East. But as we shall see, such cultural features are in many respects part and parcel of historical patterns that reach further back and further forward in time.

Contrary to the above-mentioned Western stereotypes about the region, the most significant historical features of the Middle East were not marginality and simplicity, but centrality and diversity. The centrality of the Middle East in history was partly the product of its strategic location at the junction of the three continents of Africa, Asia, and Europe, and its consequent pivotal role in trade, conquest, communication, and migration. Middle Eastern cultural diversity has been aided by local geography and by the complexities of cultural adaptation in the region. The geographical diversity of the Middle East, which depends largely on the relative availability of water, is striking. Although the "desert" image is correct insofar as the region is predominantly arid, there are sharp contrasts. The Nile Valley, the Fertile Crescent of the Tigris-Euphrates region, and the Mediterranean coast were the sites of the first known farming civilizations and the sources of the images of Eden and the biblical Land of Milk and Honey. These geographical contrasts have also led to diverse but interlocking ways of life suited to different strategies of survival and adaptation.

Another factor contributing to diversity in the Middle East is the region's long and complex cultural evolution. Prior to about 10,000 B.C., all the world's peoples were gatherers of wild foods; the domestication of plants and animals—which set human culture on its path of increasing complexity—originated in the Middle East at about that time. During the ensuing 12 millennia, the Middle East has ranked in the vanguard of social and technological evolution more consistently than any other region of the world. It is from the Middle East that Europe received not only its basic agricultural crops and techniques, but indeed all the most fundamental social and cultural elements we associate with "civilization," including literacy, urban life, and occupational specialization. It is especially interesting, in view of this book's political theme, that the Middle East was the site of the earliest states and formal governments. Due partly to the organizational requirements of irrigation systems, the independent villages of the region were soon encompassed in regional forms of political organization, in which the village-dwelling farmers became "peasants" dominated by a nonfarming urban ruling class. This ruler-producer split was the foundation of the state, since it facilitated, through various forms of taxation, a substantial amount of *surplus production*—that is, production that exceeded the subsistence needs of the farming population. This surplus subsidized the power of the state and ultimately allowed the existence of an urban population engaged in various occupations not directly associated with agricultural production, a necessary condition for the specialized accomplishments of civilized peoples. The necessity of enforcing peasant taxation, protecting the prerogatives of the ruling classes, regulating trade and exchange, and generally mediating social relationships in an increasingly complicated society, gave rise to what we now take for granted as the political apparatus of the state: legal codes, police and military forces, courts, and other instruments of "law and order." The role of the Middle East in political innovation did not end with the early civilizations; the region was also the birthplace of three world religions, each involving unique contributions to social thought. Yet, despite the leadership of the Middle East in political and social development, the region has long been characterized by social conservatism. The everyday lives of most peasants, nomads, and townspeople have until recently been little affected by intellectual and organizational advances in the larger society; instead, these lifestyles have been woven into the fabric of an increasingly complicated plural society.

FOUNDATIONS OF SOCIAL DIVERSITY

While the American "melting pot" ideology views cultural diversity as an accidental and temporary byproduct of history, such diversity has been an enduring and valued part of life in the Middle East. Middle Eastern culture is characterized not only by diversity but also by *pluralism*—the maintenance of diversity as a significant aspect of the social system. The use of cultural diversity, or pluralism, as a structuring principle in society has led some writers to characterize social life in this region as a "mosaic." This mosaic character is particularly difficult to describe because it follows no simple pigeonhole scheme but includes many dimensions, levels, and criteria of variation that often cut across one another. These include six important dimensions of variability and identity that together have shaped much of the character of traditional life in the Middle East: (1) ecological pluralism, (2) regional and local ethnic pluralism, (3) religion, (4) family and tribe, (5) occupational groups, and (6) class distinctions. Although it is sometimes useful to discuss these criteria separately, the reader should remember that in practice they are partly dependent on one another.

Ecological Diversity

Of the many elements that contribute to social diversity in the Middle East, one of the most basic is the relation of people to the land. The vicissitudes of wind patterns, rainfall, and river courses, combined with the effects of irrigation systems, often lead to stark contrasts in the land and its potential uses. In parts of Egypt, for example, a railroad track divides a verdant field producing two or three crops a year from a desert so barren as to discourage even Bedouin herders. Although these arable regions constitute less than 10 percent of the land in the Middle East, their role in the economic and social order of the region has been of the utmost importance since prehistoric times. For several thousand years, since the origin of the state and associated intensive agricultural techniques, agricultural production has been largely dependent on irrigation systems.

The nonagricultural lands that make up the bulk of the Middle East are by no means uniform in character. Some of these are forested mountain slopes; others are arid steppes capable of supporting nomads with their herds of camels, sheep, or goats; still other regions, like the Empty Quarter (Ar Rab Al Khali) of Arabia or Egypt's Western Desert, support virtually no human populations at all. Water is the crucial resource in all these regions, and the utility of a territory inhabited by a group of camel nomads, for example, may change from year to year, day to day, and mile to mile according to variations in rainfall or groundwater. The importance of water is illustrated by the fact that a permanent well, hardly worth noticing in more watered parts of the world, determined the location of the early Arab trading settlement of Mecca, later to become the birthplace of Islam and the spiritual homeland of Muslims around the world.

The geographical division between the desert and the arable lands is a recurrent phenomenon throughout the Middle East, and it has been accompanied by a threefold social division that also spanned the entire region: the division between peasants, nomads, and townspeople. Peasants, who composed as much as three quarters of the population, were engaged directly in agricultural production and lived in the small, simple villages that dotted the cultivable countryside. Nomads were also engaged in primary economic production, based on the husbandry of camels, sheep, goats, or cattle, usually in those regions incapable of supporting agricultural production. Urbanites, on the other hand, were engaged not in primary food production but in other, more specialized occupations traditionally ranging from government, scholarship, or priestly functions to craft work, peddling, and begging, and more recently including modern industrial, service, and other business pursuits.

Nomads

Nomadic herders captivate the imaginations of Middle Easterner and foreigner alike, and often tend to be seen by both (and by the nomads themselves) as the "purest" expression of the region's cultural tradition. In fact, the nomads have been economically and politically marginal throughout most of history, and are becoming more so today. While nomads have traditionally been the sole inhabitants of the region's nonarable land, their population has never been more than a small fraction of the total for the region (in recent times probably less than 15 percent of the population). Nomadic herding was not practiced in the intensive farming regions, and in transitional regions it was combined with village farming. The forms of nomadism varied according to the capacity of the land, which in turn depended on the supply of water. Semiarid steppes supported cattle, sheep, and goats, while the true desert sustained only camel nomads such as the **Bedouins** of Arabia. The camel nomads, for all their aristocratic airs, were confined to the most marginal lands, those unusable to anyone else. Their place in politics has been a complex one. They have traditionally been admired for their independence, virility, and simple virtue; and the fourteenth century Arab sociologist Ibn Khaldoun took note of their role in periodically taking over and revitalizing the leadership of Islamic states, drawing on their qualities of military discipline and tribal solidarity. It is also true, however, that the political influence of nomads was only sporadic, and that much of the time they were peripheral to the sources of state power. In recent decades, national governments have tried to control nomads by promoting their settlement in sedentary communities.

The ruggedness and apparent simplicity of nomadic life have led to the widespread misconception that it was the oldest and most primitive lifestyle of the Middle East and that it involved complete independence from the more settled and sophisticated life of the cities and villages. This was not strictly true, for nomadic herders traditionally depended on settled communities for manufactured items and agricultural products, which they obtained by trading their animal products, and prior to the control of the modern state, by raiding the villages. When drought made herding less feasible, some nomads were liable to shift temporarily or permanently to a more settled life in the city or village. The camel nomadism of the desert has existed only since the introduction of the camel in about 2000 B.C.; even the herding of sheep and goats, which originated much earlier, depended to some extent on the existence of settled populations and probably did not predate them as a general stage of development.

Of all the nomads in the Middle East, the Arab Bedouin has occupied a position of special significance. The Bedouins are Arabian camel nomads who constitute only one of the many nomadic groups in the Middle East, yet they have played a unique role in the cultural consciousness of the region. Prior to the birth of the Prophet Muhammad, the Arabs (that is, the original speakers of Arabic) were a collection of tribes occupying central Arabia. Many were camel nomads, and the others were sailors, caravaneers, and townspeople who traced descent from nomadic herders. Islam facilitated the spread of Arabic as the daily language of much of the Middle East and the holy language of all Muslims, and with it came some measure of identification with the Arab Bedouin heritage. Thus, despite the ambivalence that urbanites and villagers have often felt for the fierce and "lawless" inhabitants of the desert, the Bedouins were at the same time acknowledged as the "truest" Arabs. (In Arabic the term *Arab* refers, in the strictest usage, only to the Bedouin.) A Cairo shopkeeper might underscore his business integrity by referring to his (literal or figurative) Bedouin heritage, and the desert outside modern Riyadh is periodically dotted with the tents of Saudi urbanites celebrating their recent Bedouin past with weekend campouts.

Peasants and Urbanites

Despite the common perception of pastoral nomadism as the primeval Middle Eastern lifestyle, peasants and traditional city dwellers carried on an equally old and well-established pattern of life, one with roots in the early civilizations of Egypt and Mesopotamia. We have pointed out that the historical relation between village-dwelling peasants and urbanites depended on a political organization that taxed the village-dwelling farmers, thus subsidizing the ruling class in particular and the non-farming urban populations in general. The development of the state, then, entailed two divergent ways of life, the urban and the rural, each of which existed as a result of the other. (In this context, "city" and "urban" refer to permanent settlements of any size whose populace consists primarily of nonfarmers—as opposed to a rural peasant "village" whose inhabitants walk daily to their farms.)

From the perspective of the traditional Middle Eastern state, the peasant village existed for the purpose of delivering its tax quota in the form of agricultural produce, money, labor, or some combination of these. For their taxes the villagers rarely if ever received such government services as police protection, education, or public works. As long as the village headman delivered the taxes, the village was left to govern itself. Internally, the village was relatively homogeneous, consisting of peasants who exercised little influence on the politics of the state that governed their lives, and who had few if any opportunities for social mobility.

Although modern Middle Eastern states are generally committed to changing these conditions, life in peasant villages retains a continuity with the past. Many villagers are still small landholders, sharecroppers, or landless laborers. Each village is divided into families and blocks of related families, and is headed by a patriarch of the most influential family, whose authority is shared with other village elders. Like the nomads, the peasants have been led by the conditions of their lives to a distinctive world view. Unlike the nomads, whose traditional values emphasized militant independence, peasants were typically fearful of authority, distrustful of the world outside the village (and often of their own neighbors), and pessimistic with regard to social change. The unenviable position of peasants led traditional urbanites and nomads alike to despise them as "slaves of the soil" while continuing to depend on them for the production of basic foodstuffs.

If popular conceptions of the Middle East give undue attention to the nomads because of their romantic image, historians are liable to place great emphasis on the towns and cities as the locus of rulers and their "high" culture, the source of written documents on which historical scholarship largely depends. Traditional urban life in the Middle East does not lend itself easily to general description, because urbanites were involved in a great variety of occupations and modes of living. The traditional Middle Eastern cities were, among other things, seats of local and regional government. As such, they were the home to political elites and their retinue, including military commanders, civil and legal authorities, government bureaucrats, and religious leaders. In addition to those involved in government, traditional urban life also involved a middle class of merchants, artisans, professionals, and petty officials. The least affluent and prestigious urbanites were peddlers, laborers, and sometimes beggars. In addition to its role in political and religious leadership, the city has traditionally been a center of crafts and trade, with the **suq**, or bazaar, serving as a distribution point for manufactured wares as well as the products of the farmers and nomads. Many traditional cities also became producers of wealth in their own right by virtue of their profitable involvement in the trade between Europe, Asia, and Africa.

Although many aspects of traditional Middle Eastern urban life were as ancient as the lifestyles of the village and desert, *ancient* does not imply *simple*. Life in Middle Eastern towns and cities reached a high degree of sophistication and complexity millennia ago. Some urban centers, such as Jericho and Damascus, were already ancient in biblical times. Others, like Baghdad and Cairo, were founded over a thousand years ago as seats of government and represent landmark achievements in urban planning. Today, of course, Middle Eastern cities are also hubs of modern industrial and commercial activity; yet in many ways the old continues to exist alongside the new.

Ethnic and Religious Diversity

The ecological pluralism of nomads, peasants, and townspeople was only one dimension of traditional cultural diversity, the other dimensions being ethnic, religious, familial, occupational, and social class distinctions. Ethnic differences, or differences in historical descent and cultural heritage, have existed both between and within regions. Vast regions of the Middle East are set apart from others by their distinctive language and culture, the most prominent example being the divisions between the speakers of Turkish, Persian, and Arabic. Each of these groups occupies a major contiguous portion of the Middle East, and each correctly conceives of itself as having different cultural roots. The extent of their historical divergence is suggested by the languages themselves, which are classified into different families and differ from one another more than English does from Persian. These regional groups have also exhibited differences in values, outlook, social organization, and sometimes religion.

The ethnic diversity of the Middle East would be relatively easy to discuss if it were confined to regional divisions, but the vicissitudes of history have brought about a more complex situation, since migrations have created much cultural diversity within regions. It is difficult to say whether the Middle East has seen more migrations than other regions or whether these are simply better documented due to the region's long tradition of literacy. Waterways and seafaring, land trade, the nomadic ways of some of the inhabitants, and the existence of organized states bent on conquest have all contributed to the physical mobility of peoples. We find, for example, the Sumerians appearing rather suddenly more than 6,000 years ago in the lower Mesopotamian region, creating the world's first literate civilization, and then fading from the scene to be displaced and eclipsed by peoples of other backgrounds. The Jews historically occupied several parts of the Middle East, including Egypt and Palestine, and then many dispersed from the region only to return in this century. During the long career of the Islamic state, Arab ruling classes spread their influence from Spain to Persia; Egyptians were ruled by resident Turks; and much of the region found itself under the sword of Asian Mongols, while the ethnically diverse elites of the Islamic world sought refuge in Muslim India. While such migration resulted in a considerable amount of cultural assimilation, it also gave rise to multiple ethnic communities within regions.

What is especially striking about local ethnic diversity, from the viewpoint of the outsider, is that these ethnic differences have been institutionalized as a stable feature of traditional Middle Eastern life. One reason for this is that ethnic distinctions have often been reinforced by other kinds of traditional diversity, such as religion, occupation, and social status.

Descent, Occupation, and Social Stratification

The traditional importance of family, kinship, and common descent in the Middle East is difficult for a Westerner to appreciate. While the European or American considers the individual to be the basic functioning unit of society, the individual has had relatively little autonomous importance in the traditional

Middle East, or for that matter in most traditional societies. Instead, the individual's status, privileges, obligations, identity, and morality were inextricably tied to the descent group. Traditionally the minimal descent unit was the extended family, whose structure we shall discuss in the following section. The extended family was part of a larger group of related families, the lineage (in Arabic, *hamula*). The families of a nomadic hamula pitched their tents together, and among sedentary villagers the hamula was (and is) likely to be represented by a clustering of residences. The hamula has served, among other things, as a political unit that resolved internal disputes between families and represented their interests to the outside world. Sometimes the lineages were further united into a "tribe." Each of these units was based on the notion of shared ancestry from some patrilineal founder. The idea of common descent remains important in the contemporary Middle East, and as in the past it extends to larger groupings: All Arabs consider themselves as having a common descent, and for that matter the Jews, Christians, and Muslim Arabs together are thought to share common ancestors in the biblical patriarchs. The more specific and immediate the common descent, the more relevant it is to one's personal obligations and identity. It is hardly surprising, in view of the practical importance of descent, that ethnic groups within a particular region are in no hurry to obliterate their distinctive ancestry.

Another important factor in maintaining ethnic distinctions has been their connection with occupation. In the traditional Middle East, one's occupation was quite often determined by family background. Of course, the matter of occupation was relatively simple for the child of a Bedouin or peasant family, but scarcely less so for the son of an urban artisan. Membership in organizations that controlled crafts and trades was frequently passed from father to son, as was the requisite training. Since occupation was largely ascribed rather than achieved, it frequently became associated with certain ethnic groups. The continuing relationship of descent to occupation was dramatized in practical terms when, after the formation of Israel, the exodus of the Jewish population of Yemen left that country virtually bereft of blacksmiths, bricklayers, and practitioners of certain other trades served by this ethnic group.

As the above example shows, ethnic differences have often been associated with religious affiliation, reflecting differences both within and between the three major religions of the Middle East. Whole regions may be characterized by a predominant religion, as in the concentrations of Shia Islam found in Iran and parts of Iraq. Many minority religions are also concentrated in specific regions, as with the Christian Copts of Egypt. The integrity of the non-Muslim groups has been reinforced on the local level by the traditional Muslim practice of allowing minority religious communities protection and self-government in return for their recognition of Muslim hegemony.

A final type of social diversity is the division of socioeconomic classes. Since the origin of the earliest states, Middle Eastern society has been stratified into classes that enjoy varying degrees of privilege and wealth. These distinctions are relatively subdued in the countryside, but quite apparent in the cities, where lifestyles span the extremes from poverty to opulence. Distinctions of class are of course tied in various complex ways to family background, ethnicity, occupation, and ecological situation.

The Patchwork of Pluralism: Two Historical Examples

Traditional Middle Eastern society, we have argued, was a complex tapestry in which ecological, ethnic, family, tribal, occupational, and class factors were interwoven. The complex way in which these dimensions intertwined can be seen in two different examples of traditional life: the city of Mecca in Muhammad's day, and the Bedouin camp.

The city of Mecca as Muhammad knew it in about A.D. 600, forms the backdrop of major historical events that we shall discuss in the following chapter. It had been founded two centuries earlier by a tribe of Bedouins who had shifted from nomadism to trading and had located their settlement at the site of a permanent water supply and the junction of two major trade routes. Their social organization and world view still bore the stamp of Bedouin life, yet even this budding town had begun to manifest a more urban sort of complexity. The formerly egalitarian founding tribe had differentiated into richer and poorer divisions, and the more favored displayed the trappings of aristocracy. Some families of this tribe had begun to control and monopolize religious worship, in which shrines played a large role. Attached to the ruling tribe were subordinate "client" groups, and below them were slaves. The range of occupations was considerable, and many were interwoven with specific ethnic backgrounds. One author makes reference to "Syrian caravan leaders; traveling monks and curers; Syrian merchants; foreign smiths and healers; Copt carpenters; Negro idol sculptors; Christian doctors, surgeons, dentists and scribes; Abyssinian sailors and mercenaries."[1] It should be kept in mind that Mecca was at this time a relatively new and modest-sized trade settlement, a mere upstart in comparison with the more established seats of Middle Eastern government.

Even the traditional Bedouin camp was hardly the simple affair one might expect. In fact, such a camp was liable to include representatives of as many as half a dozen non-Bedouin groups, each performing a separate function as defined by various criteria of descent and cultural tradition. While the Bedouin extended family owned the livestock, the camel herders themselves might have come from another, less "noble" group which lent its services as a form of tribute to the Bedouins, who in turn took the responsibility of fighting to protect the herds from other Bedouin raiders. Members of another ethnic group, the Sulaba, whom some anthropologists recognize as the most ancient inhabitants of the desert, served as desert guides, coppersmiths, leatherworkers, and in various other specified functions. The Sunna, members of a group said to be of partly African origin, served as blacksmiths. African slaves were also part of an affluent Bedouin household; well dressed and well fed, they were reputed to be fierce fighters in defense of their masters' herds. Two sorts of traders were also likely to be found in the Bedouin camp. One of these was the Kubaisi, an ambulatory shopkeeper who supplied the camp with a variety of merchandise; the name is derived from a town on the Euphrates from which at least some such merchants traditionally came. Finally, the 'Aqaili, usually a member of the tribe of 'Aquil, bought camels on behalf of urban firms in return for cash and rifles. In this complex scheme, the Bedouins served

---

[1] Eric R. Wolf, "Social Organization of Mecca and the Origins of Islam," *Southwestern Journal of Anthropology*, VII (1951), 336–337.

primarily as soldier and protector, engaging in raids against other Bedouins, defending the group against such raids, and granting safe conduct across their territory.[2]

UNITY IN DIVERSITY

As we have seen, the cultural pluralism of the traditional Middle East was set in a context of unity and integration. The ties that bound diverse segments of society into an integrated whole were based on two principles: the functional interdependence and complementarity of unlike parts; and certain overarching similarities of culture, social organization, and religion.

Traditional nomads, peasants, and urbanites were by no means autonomous groups, nor were they necessarily set apart by competition, although conflicts of interest certainly have occurred between them. Bedouins have depended on peasants for agricultural products and on townspeople for manufactured goods. In the past, they often exacted tribute from peasant villages, sold protection to caravans, and acted as middlemen in trade. The existence of cities and villages was a further convenience when climate or other factors forced Bedouins into settled life, just as the opposite movement often occurred when conditions were reversed. Although prior to the twentieth century the Bedouins were rarely subject to the sort of constraint and taxation the state would have liked to impose, neither were they entirely exempt from state control. Peasants, on the other hand, were always under direct state rule, which set the conditions that governed their lives. Despite internal village self-government, peasants were expected not only to fill their tax quotas but to obey all laws of the state, over which they had little say. The peasants were also, as noted above, subject to raiding and tribute demands from nomads. It is difficult to say in what ways the peasants benefited from others, since exchanges between them and urbanites or Bedouins were typically out of their control and somewhat in their disfavor. Just the same, the towns did provide manufactured items and markets where certain of the peasants' needs could be provided for. The state also provided military protection against outside invaders.

Because they were not engaged directly in food production, urbanites were in a sense the most dependent of all. Like all urban populations they ultimately depended on the rural production of food and raw materials directed into the towns through taxation and trade. In the Middle East, the situation was complicated by the presence of the Bedouins, since the urban marketplace served as an intermediary between two modes of rural production. Clearly the divisions among occupational specialties, like those of ecological situations, have been characterized by economic interdependence and complementarity.

We must also not forget that the Middle East possesses overarching cultural similarities that in some measure unite all its people. If one's identity as an Arab, for example, implies separation from Persians, Turks, Berbers, and Kurds, it also implies a unity of outlook and identity with many millions of other Arabs. Cultural similarity, however, transcends even these broad regional and ethnic groupings;

---

[2] Carleton S. Coon, *Caravan: The Story of the Middle East* (Huntington, NY: Robert E. Krieger, 1976), pp. 191–210.

significant features of culture and social organization have traditionally united all Middle Easterners. A list of these features would be very long and would range from the threefold ecological system mentioned above to particulars of material culture like the use of the black hair tent among nomads throughout the entire region. Most significant, however, are similarities in traditional social organization and cultural values that underlie the region's diverse social types.

Family, Kinship, and Marriage

Throughout the Middle East the traditional family has had a similar structure and function. It was patrilineal—that is, it traced descent principally through the male line. Wives were expected to take up residence with their husbands after marriage. The traditional family was strongly patriarchal, remaining intact until the death of the father, at which time each of the sons became a family head. Typically, then, such a family consisted of three generations of men and their wives, and any unmarried daughters or sisters. The traditionally preferred form of marriage among Muslims is between a man and his father's brother's daughter. Although there are conflicting reports on the actual frequency of such cousin marriages, Muslim marriages do tend to favor patrilineal relatives. The Middle Eastern family has long served as the basic unit for holding property in the form of farmland, herds, or smaller business enterprises; it thus acquired a fundamental economic significance.

The importance of kinship in traditional society did not end with the family. Peasant villagers, townspeople, and nomads alike recognized larger kinship groupings among related families. Among the nomads and their recent descendants, these groupings have often been extended to a tribal organization. Tribes varied in size from a single band to a powerful and influential group encompassing numerous bands. Relations among the men of each tribe were relatively egalitarian, leadership being based on the "first among equals" principle. There were frequently, however, marked differences of social standing, or "nobility," among tribes, to the extent that marriage to members of lesser tribes was sometimes forbidden. Today as in the past, it is in the nomad and nomad-derived groups and their tribal organizations that one finds the strongest development of blood feuds, collective responsibility, group honor or "face" (in Arabic, **wajh**), and strict rules governing hospitality and sanctuary. (These will be discussed further in the following chapter.)

Traditional marriage and sex mores have shown considerable persistence in much of the Middle East. Despite recent trends to the contrary, marriage is still often arranged by parents, being seen more as a relationship between kin groups than between individuals. An effort was usually made to match mates in terms of social prestige and background. The traditional position of women was, on the whole, one of subordination to men. Compared with the West, a greater emphasis is still placed on female chastity, purity, modesty, and even complete seclusion and veiling. As in the past (but now for somewhat different reasons), veiling and seclusion tend to be practiced most often among urban elites. The conduct of women has generally been thought to reflect on the honor of the patrilineal family, and men are vulnerable to dishonor by the conduct of their daughters, sisters, or wives. Muslim law permits as many as four wives, but while multiple marriages are a sign of affluence, they have always been infrequent in actual practice. Traditionally,

Muslim males could initiate divorce more easily than women. But despite the patriarchal bias that it shares with other Middle Eastern religions, Islamic law has allowed remarriage of divorced women, insured women a share in the inheritance of property, and protected their right to own property separately from their husbands. Today, traditional ideas about marriage, the family, and the position of women are being modified in some quarters in response to new interpretations of Islam, as well as secular ideas of individualism, women's rights, and romantic love.

Religion

Of all the factors that unify Middle Eastern culture, none is so fundamental as religion. The Middle East is the birthplace of the three major monotheistic religions: Judaism, Christianity, and Islam; the vast majority of Middle Easterners today, however, are Muslims, or adherents of Islam. This is significant not only because of the unifying influence of one ubiquitous religion, but also because that religion has a remarkably pervasive influence on social and cultural life. Islam permeates the daily life and social norms of the vast majority of the Middle Eastern population that is Muslim. It is a religion whose stated aim at the time of inception in the early seventh century was the unity of all people into a single social and spiritual community, and it succeeded to a noteworthy degree. Islam brought unprecedented political, intellectual, and spiritual unity to the Middle East and made the region a hub of world power for a thousand years. How and why this happened is the subject of the following chapter.

THE FOUNDATIONS
OF ISLAM

Through the dusty streets of a middle-class residential neighborhood in Cairo echo the sounds of dawn: The first vendors are calling their wares, their chants accompanied by the clopping of hooves and the rattling of cart wheels. Blended with these is a more haunting but equally familiar sound, a singsong of Arabic from the loudspeakers on the minaret of a small local **mosque**:

> God is most great.
> I testify there is no deity but God.
> I testify that Muhammad is the Messenger of God.
> Come to Prayer;
> Come to Salvation...

It is the same message which five times daily has called the faithful to prayer in Cairo and its predecessors for more than 1,300 years. That same message, in the same Arabic, emanates from mosques as far away as West Africa and Indonesia, calling one fifth of the world's population (only a minority of whom are Middle Easterners or Arabs) to pray toward their spiritual homeland in Mecca. The religion of Islam, signified by this call to prayer, is central to an understanding of the Middle East's most salient features—its historical and contemporary influence on other parts of the world, the unity of belief and commitment that counteracts some of its bitterest political divisions, and the religious vitality that infuses every aspect of its social, cultural, and political life.

Ninety-five percent of all Middle Easterners are Muslims, followers of the faith of Islam. For them, religion is not a matter separable from daily life or confined to certain times and places; it is the foundation of ethics, morality, and family—ultimately, the blueprint for a righteous and satisfying life. Dismayed by the secularism of both the capitalist and the communist ideologies, Muslims see Islam as an essential element that gives direction to their social aspirations and saves them from the dissipation and immorality they see in the West. They are also keenly aware of Islam's success as a world religion, a religion that has always aimed at the social unity of the entire community of believers, that has led the Middle East to a position of considerable historical influence, and that has provided the foundations of a civilization which for many centuries surpassed Europe.

CENTRAL BELIEFS OF ISLAM

For the Muslim, Islam is at its root nothing more nor less than the complete acceptance of God and submission to His will. The very word *Islam* means *submission*; and *Muslim* means *one who submits*. The most important step toward this submission is the recognition that there is only one God, the God of Abraham and Moses, of Christians and Jews as well as Muslims, whose name in Arabic is *Allah*. Muslims believe that they alone have accepted God completely, and that all their beliefs follow from this acceptance. According to the teachings of Islam, a complete acceptance of God entails recognition of His absolute oneness; a Muslim must reject not only other gods but all alleged "associates" of God, including offspring and other semidivine personages. Christians, they feel, have compromised their monotheism by mistaking one of God's prophets for the "son" of God. The acceptance of God also requires belief in all of God's messages through all His appointed messengers, including not only Jesus and the Old Testament prophets, but also—and most significantly—the seventh-century Arab prophet Muhammad. It is through Muhammad, the "seal of the prophets," that God has sent His final and most comprehensive revelations, placed on the lips of Muhammad by God and recorded in the holy scripture, the **Koran**. Since true belief in God means acceptance of His final revelations, the Muslim declaration of faith (the **shahada**) testifies that "There is no God but Allah, and Muhammad is His prophet." Such a declaration is sufficient to make a person a Muslim, but the conscientious pursuit of the faith demands much more.

The Five Pillars of Islam

Muslims recognize five fundamental ritual obligations that make up the "pillars" of their religion. The first and most important of these is the declaration of faith mentioned previously. The second is prayer, which ought to be performed five times a day (before dawn, at noon, in late afternoon, just after sunset, and in mid-evening), facing in the direction of the **Kaaba**, the holy shrine in Mecca. Prayer may be performed anywhere, but the preferred situation is with other Muslims in a special place of worship, the mosque. Prayer involves a complex series of preparations, prescribed movements, and phrases. The most important prayer time is Friday noon, when Muslims participate in a formal service under the direction of a prayer leader (*imam*), who reads from the Koran and may also deliver a sermon and discuss matters of public interest.

The third pillar of Islam is the giving of alms, either in the form of **zakat**, a fixed amount used to meet the needs of the religious community and provide for the welfare of its members, or as a voluntary contribution (**sadaqua**), which brings religious merit to the donor.

The fourth pillar of Islam is fasting during the daylight hours of the month of **Ramadan**. While Islam is not an ascetic religion, Muslims view the abstention from food, liquids, smoking, and sexual relations as a celebration of moral commitment, healthy self-discipline, and religious atonement. Since Ramadan is a lunar month, it rotates through the seasons; and the abstention from food or water from dawn to dusk of a summer day is no small sacrifice. At the same time, it is typical of Islam's relatively practical orientation that the very young, the elderly, the sick, and even the traveler are exempted, at least temporarily, from this obligation.

The fifth and final ritual obligation of Islam, the pilgrimage to Mecca, falls only on those members of a Muslim community whose health and resources permit them to fulfill it. It is a great honor to make the **hajj**, or pilgrimage, and those who have done so carry the honorific title of **hajji**. The center of the pilgrimage is a shrine in Mecca said to have been founded by Abraham. The pilgrimage draws together, both physically and spiritually, persons from various national and cultural backgrounds who represent the farthest reaches of Islam. During the pilgrimage, however, all participants shed the marks of their nationality and social position and don the plain white cloak that signifies the equality of every Muslim before God.

The Koran and the Hadith

The ritual obligations of Islam, important as they are, are only the outward expressions of the system of belief that underlies Muslim life. When Muslims accept the oneness of God and the validity of Muhammad's revelations as the word of God, they also accept certain sources of authority for religious truth. Foremost among these is the written record of Muhammad's revelations, the Koran. The Koran is said to be the exact word, and even the exact language, of God. Approximately as long as the New Testament, the Koran is composed of a series of chapters, or **suras**, of varying length. If we were to compare it with the literary forms familiar to the American reader, it more closely resembles a book of poetry than a narrative or a continuous essay. In fact, the Koran in the original Arabic (the form in which Muslims of all nations know it) is regarded as a masterpiece of poetic literature as well as religion. Its subject matter ranges from terse warnings about the Day of Judgment to long discourses on marriage, inheritance, the treatment of non-Muslim minorities, and the duties of each Muslim in spreading the faith. Of the Koran's message on these points we shall have more to say later in this chapter.

A second source of divine authority is the collection of sayings and practices attributed to the Prophet. The Prophet's personal utterances were not, like the Koran, a direct recitation of God's words, but they are thought to have been informed by the Prophet's divine inspiration. Muslim religious scholars recognize that not all these reports (**hadith**) about the Prophet are equally reliable, and much effort has been devoted to tracing their sources and evaluating their accuracy. Even so, there exist various hadith that can, like the holy texts of other religions, be used to support widely differing positions on many issues. There are several recognized schools of Muslim law that differ on the degree to which analogy, scholarly interpretation, social consensus, and established custom might be used to supplement the Koran and the hadith, but all agree that the latter are the most fundamental basis of the Muslim social and legal code (**Sharia**). In principle, they apply to every life situation that a believer might encounter, and provide a guide for every sort of decision.

The Ulema

Since Islam teaches the equality of every believer before God, there is, at least in orthodox **Sunni** Islam, no clergy to act as intercessors with the divine. On the other hand, the emphasis on written texts has given rise to an important class of religious scholars, the **ulema**, who collectively advise the community and its political rulers according to God's word. To the extent that most traditional education in Muslim societies is religious in nature, the ulema have filled the role of academics and teachers; to the extent that Islam recognizes no ultimate division of religion and state, the ulema have been not only legal and political thinkers but a political force in their own right. This is true in the contemporary Muslim world, where Cairo's Al-Azhar, the center of Muslim high scholarship, is also an international forum for the discussion of contemporary issues of Muslim politics and social values.

Unlike most Far Eastern religions, which generally try to divorce themselves from the flow of historical events, Islam resembles Judaism and Christianity in its explicit involvement with society and history. Although it is the ultimate concern of individual Muslims to prepare themselves for the Day of Judgment, that preparation takes worldly form in the pursuit of a just and righteous social life. Perhaps even more than Judaism and Christianity, Islam is intimately concerned with specific social relations and institutions. Our discussion of Islam will therefore take the form of a historical account. Islam arose in a particular social setting, and it directly addressed social problems related to that setting. One of the paradoxes of Islam is that while it goes beyond most other religions in specific references to the cultural institutions of its original setting, it has spread to encompass an astonishing variety of peoples and cultures without sacrificing the relevance of its original precepts. In so doing it has followed a remarkable path of adaptiveness balanced with continuity, operating in some contexts as a revolutionary force and in others as a source of stability and cohesion, or, when its practitioners have seen fit to use it so, as a source of deep conservatism. None of these uses is inherent in the religion itself, but each is the outcome of particular human communities applying Islam to particular historical situations. Because Western readers are likely to see Islam as an essentially conservative ideology, let us consider the radical transformations that Islam brought to its original social setting.

PRE-ISLAMIC ARAB ETHICS

Unlike the Persian, Byzantine, and other empires that were the heirs of thousands of years of urbanization and central government, the Arab urbanites of Muhammad's time were in a process of transition to settled life, and their society was still organized on the ethical principles that had served their nomadic Bedouin forebears. It is this traditional Arab ethic, or rather the conflict between it and urban life, that provided the backdrop for Muhammad's teachings. Islam at its inception constituted both a revitalization and a radical reform of the old ethic. For these reasons, it is worthwhile to take a closer look at traditional Bedouin society.

As is usually the case with nomadic peoples, the Bedouins did not have a centralized government or political authority. Such authority would have been impossible to maintain, not only because no centralized power can easily impose itself on peoples of such mobility, but also because there was no economic foundation to support one. Yet the Bedouins were by no means isolated in the desert wastes; they were in frequent contact with other Bedouin and non-Bedouin groups, and had need of some measure of political order to regulate cooperation and resolve conflict. In such situations, political organization tended to be built from the bottom up—that is, groups were arranged in a hierarchy of levels that acted to deal with whatever conflicts or common interests were at hand. There is a saying attributed to the Arabs, "I against my brother; my brother and I against my cousin; my brother and cousins and I against the outsider." The saying signifies a hierarchy of loyalties based on closeness of kinship that ran from the nuclear family through the lineage, the tribe, and even, in principle at least, to an entire ethnic or linguistic group (which was believed to have a kinship basis). Disputes were settled, interests were pursued, and justice and order maintained by means of this organizational framework, according to an ethic of self-help and collective responsibility. If a member of one nuclear family was injured or offended by a member of another family, it was the right and obligation of all members of the injured family to settle the score. If the disputants were members of different lineages, all members of both lineages became involved (in varying degrees, depending on their closeness to the offended and offending parties). In the same way, a whole tribe or alliance of tribes might have been moved to defend its interests against another group. The collective duty to take up the disputes of a kinsman meant also that someone might legitimately be killed in atonement for the crimes of a relative. An "even score" might take the form of a life for a life or a theft for a theft, or it might be sought in a negotiated settlement. An inherent weakness in the system emerged, however, when the disputing sides were unable to agree on what constituted an even score; and the situation developed into a blood feud that involved whole tribes and their allies and lasted for generations.

Yet the revenge ethic was not the unbridled play of impulse, but a system designed to keep a modicum of order in a society without centralized legal authority. Since the individual's kin group answered collectively for his transgressions, it exercised considerable power of restraint over impulsive acts by an individual. Restraint was required even in revenge, which if excessive could initiate a new cycle of offense and counter-revenge. Revenge could, as already noted, be mitigated through an arbitrated settlement that preserved both the system of order and the honor of the disputants while keeping violence to a minimum. In the end, however, it was the ever-present threat of violent reprisal that acted as the chief deterrent against crime.

Every form of social organization requires a particular kind of value commitment, and the central value of the Bedouin ethic was (and still is) the honor and integrity of the various groups, or rather the concentric circle of groupings with which the individual identified. Group honor was often referred to as "face" (wajh), the maintenance of which was a central concern of every member of a given group. (It is, incidentally, the enduring concern for the purity of the group through its patrilineal kinship line, and the belief that sexual misconduct of its women is one of the greatest blows to a family's honor, that contributes today to the seclusion of Arab women.) The other side of the Bedouin's fierce unity against outsiders was his hospitality toward those who entered his domain with permission and were therefore under his protection. Hospitality, as much as revenge, was the measure of a group's willingness and ability to protect its interests and those of its allies, and was thus a reflection on its honor.

Despite its harshness, the Bedouin ethic had its benign side as well. Not only was hospitality highly valued in Bedouin society, but so was generosity. Arab traditions point to the existence, from pre-Islamic times to the present, of a strong belief in the virtue of generosity and sharing, even toward strangers. Generosity to outsiders was a gesture of hospitality that reflected favorably on the strength and honor of the group. The sharing of wealth within the kinship group provided for the needy, reinforced the sense of general equality and cooperation essential to the members' mutual commitment, and supported the leader's prestige by emphasizing his benevolence.

Although the Bedouin Arab's system of law and politics was based on the patrilineal kinship group, it could be extended in various ways to adapt to varying circumstances. Alliances could be established between tribes, and genealogies might consciously or unconsciously be altered to reflect the new relationships. Other pseudo-kin relations were, in pre-Islamic times, established through adoption. Through the payment of tribute and obedience, one group could become the protected client of another, a status which connoted social inferiority and was therefore undertaken only when necessary. Slavery, a widespread practice throughout the ancient Mediterranean and Middle East, provided yet another set of human relationships that supplemented the family and tribe, and which carried its own set of customary regulations.

In sum, then, the Bedouin system of political and legal organization centered on kinship groups and their dependents. Ultimately it depended not on authority imposed from the top, but on the individual's sense of honor, which was invested in an ever-widening series of kinship groupings. While such a system was well adapted to the needs of a decentralized society, it resulted in a relativistic morality, which placed loyalty to the group above all abstract standards guiding human conduct. A deed was evaluated in terms of kinship loyalties rather than absolute ethical merit; even the deities were often tied to territories and groups, and thus provided no means for moral transcendence. The outlook thus created has sometimes been called "amoral familism" because it equated ethics with family interests; it might be better thought of, however, as a coherent moral system centered on kinship, a system which was functional in certain circumstances but carried with it some severe limitations in uniting people under a more inclusive morality.

We have examined the pre-Islamic Bedouin social ethic in such detail for several reasons. It is important to realize that the organizational and moral aspects of the system have persisted not only among Bedouins but also to some extent among settled Arabs to the present time, and that this ethic has influenced Muslim society in a number of ways. It is even more important to realize that the ministry of Muhammad revolutionized the Arab society of its time by subordinating the old familistic ethic to a transcendent system of morality, facilitating a moral and political transformation in Arabia and beyond.

THE SOCIAL SETTING OF MECCA

At the time of Muhammad's birth in about A.D. 570, Arabic-speaking peoples occupied the central Arabian peninsula; they were subject to the influences of several powerful empires. Most Arabs were either Bedouin nomads or their settled descendents who occupied themselves with trade and agriculture. Agriculture in the area did not compare with that of the more fertile regions of the Tigris-Euphrates to the north and the Mediterranean coast to the northwest, or of the Yemen[1] to the southeast. Consequently, neither the wealth nor the political organization of the Arabs matched that of their neighbors. At that time Syria (the traditional name for the fertile part of the Middle East bordering the Western Mediterranean) was under the control of the Byzantine Empire, while the Iraq (the farming region along the Tigris and Euphrates) was controlled by Byzantium's principal antagonist, the Sassanian Empire with its ties to the Iranian highland. The Yemen, home of an urban agricultural and trading civilization, was losing its former power and was under the threat of domination by the Christian Abyssinian Empire in Africa, which had already intervened in the region on one occasion. Placed in a delicate situation between several more powerful forces, the Arabs were gradually developing their own urban economy and their own political strategies. Arab groups near the areas of Byzantine, Sassanian, and Yemeni influence benefited from an arrangement in which the empires sponsored and subsidized them as "kingdoms" in return for military protection of their borders against the rival empires and their Arab clients. Away from these "buffer" Arab kingdoms, equidistant from the contemporary superpowers, most Arabs remained nomadic while some others were beginning to develop a different source of strength.

Located astride some of the most important trade routes that connected Europe, Africa, and Asia, Arabia moved much of the world's long-distance trade. For several centuries prior to Muhammad's time, Arabs had been assuming an increasingly active part in the trade that crossed their region. The Arab tribe of **Quraish** had founded the trade settlement of Mecca in the **Hijaz** (the mountainous region of Arabia's Red Sea coast) at the juncture of several major trade routes.

Although the Meccans were relatively sophisticated urbanites who were several generations separated from Bedouin life, their society was essentially structured by the Bedouin ethic, with some modifications. The backbone of Meccan organization was the Quraish tribe and its constituent lineages, which had successfully managed to avoid blood feuds only by emphasizing tribal loyalties over more divisive ones. The leadership of the community was vested in the tribal elders, who, as among the Bedouins, had limited powers of enforcement. In order to insure the much-needed security of the regions through which their trade passed, it was necessary for the Quraish to enter into alliances with surrounding desert tribes, alliances which obliged them to take part in costly disputes with their allies' respective enemies. Meccan trade was sanctified and protected by pagan religious practices, particularly by the Meccan holy shrine of the Kaaba, which drew pilgrims from much of Arabia. By establishing times and places of truce connected with religious observances, the Meccans were able to protect trade from the threat of feuds among the tribes. Thus through the selective use and modification of Bedouin organization, the Meccans established a viable urban-mercantile economy. The system brought considerable affluence to the Meccans and allowed them

---

[1] The terms "*The* Yemen and *The* Iraq" distinguish the historically recognized regions from the modern nations of the same name, Yemen and Iraq.

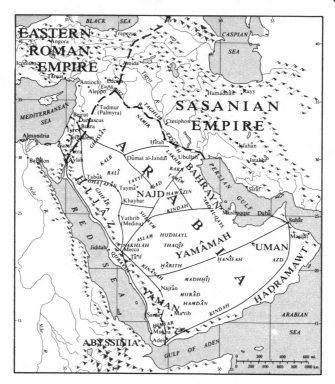

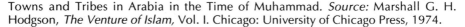

Towns and Tribes in Arabia in the Time of Muhammad. *Source:* Marshall G. H. Hodgson, *The Venture of Islam,* Vol. I. Chicago: University of Chicago Press, 1974.

to win influence and respect among other urbanites and merchants in the Yemen and Syria as well as in the Hijaz.

Even so, the Bedouin ethic as applied to an urbanized mercantile society was beginning to show its limitations in Muhammad's time, with accompanying strains on Meccan life. Economic inequality had increased between the various lineages of the Quraish, leading to a conflict of vested interests and a growing social stratification that was difficult to reconcile with familial unity. Non-Quraish minorities who had become clients of the Quraish were now reduced to little more than debt-slaves. The town of Mecca held a wide range of occupations practiced by several resident ethnic groups, including Copts, Syrians, Africans, and Jews; these also did not fit comfortably into a social structure based primarily on kinship, pseudo-kinship, and slavery. In addition to the problems of inequality and diversity, the Meccans were faced with the ever-present threat of feuding should the unity of the Quraish become disturbed; there was no binding, authoritative central leadership. Located between warring empires and in the midst of feuding tribes, the Meccans lacked convincing assurances that their military strength could always be concentrated against outside threats rather than internal squabbles. In adapting the Bedouin social ethic to their needs, the Meccans were straining it to its limits.

The Confessional Religions

At this time, the religious as well as the social life of Mecca was hovering on the brink of significant change. The previous centuries had seen the rise from Asia to Europe of a variety of religious traditions that, unlike their more ancient counterparts, "looked to *individual* personal adherence to ('confession of') an explicit and often self-sufficient body of moral and cosmological *belief...*which was embodied in a corpus of sacred *scriptures*, claiming *universal* validity for all men and promising a comprehensive solution to human problems in terms which involved a *world beyond death.*"[2] Although these "confessional religions" included such widely divergent traditions as Christianity and Buddhism, the forms native to the Middle East exhibited some general similarities. The Zoroastrianism of Persia resembled the major Semitic religions, Christianity and Judaism, in its belief in the oneness of God and of transcendent truth, a single universal standard for righteous conduct, a historical struggle between good and evil, the necessity of practical social action and individual responsibility, and a final divine judgment that holds every person accountable for the actions of his or her lifetime. The implications of such religions are quite different from those of a pluralistic, relativistic, kinship-centered paganism.

These confessional religions had political implications as well as spiritual and intellectual influences. The major political entities of the time were associated with confessional religions—the Persians of the Sassanian Empire with Zoroastrianism, the Byzantines and Abyssinians with Christianity, and the Yemeni with both Christianity and Judaism. These last two religions in particular had been making inroads in central Arabia, and some Arab groups had already converted to them. The cohesiveness that these religions offered was an attractive alternative to pagan pluralism, and it might have seemed in A.D. 600 that many more Arabs would eventually become Jews or Christians.

Inner developments as well as outer pressures were moving the Meccans toward religious change. The Meccans had found it expedient to promote the centralization of worship in pilgrimages to shrines, such as that of the Kaaba, and that custom carried with it the seeds of a more fundamental religious transformation. In Arab tradition, the minor deities of places and social groupings had been the most important forces in daily life. Allah, the God presiding over relations between tribes—and therefore over intertribal pilgrimages, shrines, and truces—began to assume a greater importance as the intertribal character of worship developed. In Muhammad's time the Kaaba was associated primarily with Allah, but the Meccans still recognized a plurality of gods, rites, and cults that separated them from the monotheistic religions by a wide gulf.

MUHAMMAD'S MINISTRY

Muhammad was born into a minor but respectable branch of the Quraish. His father died shortly before his birth, and in keeping with the custom of some

---

[2] Marshall G. S. Hodgson, *The Venture of Islam*, Vol. I (Chicago: University of Chicago Press, 1974), p. 125.

Meccan families he spent the first few years of his life in the desert under the care of a Bedouin wet nurse. Muhammad's mother died when he was six, after which he was placed in the care of his uncle, Abu Talib. The young Muhammad tended sheep and sold goods in the marketplace, and by the time he reached adulthood he had gained a reputation as a capable businessman and a person of good character (in Mecca he was known as *al-Amin*, "the trustworthy"). At the age of twenty-five he married Khadija, a wealthy widow fifteen years his senior, for whom he had been managing business accounts. She remained his only wife until her death some twenty-five years later. During their marriage she bore him three sons, all of whom died before reaching adulthood, and four daughters.

Had Muhammad been an ordinary man he might have settled into a life of secure prosperity, but he was extraordinarily preoccupied with the moral and religious problems of his time. Like many of his contemporaries, Muhammad was dissatisfied with the religious climate around him. He often went into seclusion in a cave on the outskirts of town, where he meditated. It was during one of these retreats that he received the first of a series of visions in which the Angel Gabriel called upon him to become the Apostle of God. According to his biographers, Muhammad at first doubted the visions, but then accepted his calling after Khadija and a Christian relative of hers pronounced them genuine. These first visions came in about A.D. 610, but it was several years before he began his public preaching. Khadija became his first convert; she was quickly followed by Ali, a younger cousin being raised in his household, and Zayd, a former slave of Khadija. During the first few years of his ministry, Muhammad's converts were to span the social scale from slaves and tribeless persons to wealthy merchants; for the most part, however, they tended to be young men occupying the less favored positions within the more respected families.

When Muhammad began his public preaching, his revelations were simple and direct: there is but one God, Allah the Creator, and those who ungratefully turn away from Him to the pleasures of this world will be held accountable on the Day of Judgment. Wealth and social position will count for nothing in the Final Judgment, whereas justice, piety, and righteousness will count for everything. Every person is equal before God, and righteousness is a matter between the individual and God, not a striving for power and position among kinship groups. Pride, the mainspring of the Bedouin ethic, was a vice to be replaced by humility before the Creator.

It seems that another central theme in the earliest revelations was the Meccans' excessive pride in wealth and their unwillingness to share with those in need. Through Muhammad, God accused the Meccans:

> ...you honor not the orphan, and you urge not the feeding of the needy, and you devour the inheritance greedily, and you love wealth with an ardent love.
> (Koran, 89:18-21)

There is no evidence that Muhammad supported a communistic system in which all wealth was to be made public, but only that he advocated more compassion and sharing, and less stinginess and pride, than was common among the Quraish. In this, evidently one of the earliest ethical messages in Muhammad's preaching, there is considerable continuity with the Bedouin ethic. The most favored Meccan families had succeeded in cornering a growing portion of the community's wealth and privilege, and they had all but abandoned the traditional obligations of sharing. By attacking the Meccans' greed and calling on them to share their wealth, Muhammad was reasserting a moral principle recognized in the Bedouin tradition, but now in a new context and with new ramifications. In a mercantile society where success depended more on opportunism than kinship, the power of the kinship group over the individual was often too weak to enforce such sharing. But in the Koran, this obligation to share came to be represented as a sacred duty for which the individual will answer to an all-powerful God on Judgment Day. In this way, Muhammad's reassertion of a traditional value had a radical twist.

In some respects the revelations of Muhammad were perfectly in tune with the developmental course of Meccan society. As has already been pointed out, the Meccans were in need of a unifying moral-religious system not only to serve their need for internal cohesion, but also to meet the challenge of the other monotheistic religions and the political forces with which they were confronted. Yet in other ways, the teachings of the Prophet ran against the grain of the prevailing cultural beliefs and the vested power interests in Mecca. In particular, the Quraish saw in Muhammad's budding sect a challenge to the values that legitimized their own power, and a denunciation of the religious observances that they had so carefully structured to serve their political and economic interests. Furthermore, the Prophet himself, as God's appointed leader of the righteous, appeared to be making a personal bid for power that might encroach on their own. Not too surprisingly, the Quraish led the way in persecuting Muhammad and his followers to the extent that part of the Muslim community (but not the Prophet) sought temporary asylum in Abyssinia. Relations between Muslims and non-Muslims were tense in Mecca, and became more so as the Muslims made it increasingly clear that they sought the conversion of all Meccans. The tide seemed to turn against Muhammad in 619 when his wife Khadija, his most intimate personal supporter, and his uncle Abu Talib, who had insured the support of his lineage against the rest of the Quraish, both died.

The Hijira

Muhammad's followers were saved from an increasingly threatened existence in Mecca by what was to become a turning point in the growth of Islam. In 620 the Prophet was approached by a handful of converts from the town of Yathrib, 200 miles to the north of Mecca. Yathrib had been founded (or revived) as a farming oasis by several Arab Jewish clans, who had later been joined by other families of pagan Arabs. The problems of family ethics in the city had eventually reached a level of crisis, in which blood feuding was so widespread that the community had little peace. The Muslims, and others at Yathrib, saw in Muhammad an arbitrator whose religious commitments and sense of justice would serve them well; therefore the Muslims and the others at Yathrib promised obedience to Muhammad and safety for the Muslims who came with him if the Prophet would agree to relocate in their city. After negotiating during the two following years with a growing delegation of Muslims from Yathrib, Muhammad and the main Muslim community emigrated to Yathrib in the year 622.

The year of the migration, or **Hijira**, subsequently became the first year of the Muslim holy calendar, and the city of Yathrib became thereafter known as

Medinat al-Nabi ("city of the Prophet") or simply Medina ("the city"). There is more than a ritual meaning to the Hijira date as a demarcation. It was in Medina that the Muslims, cut off from previous kinship ties, established their independent political existence based on the principles of Islam. It was also in Medina that Muhammad was presented with the opportunity to construct a new Islamic social order among his followers. If Mecca was the birthplace of Islam as a religion, Medina was its birthplace as a state and a way of life.

The Koran's Social Regulations

The social problems of Medina had some parallels to those of Mecca, but the differences were considerable. Medina was based on farming rather than trade, and the kinship groups there were still relatively strong. Unlike Mecca, where the domination of the Quraish had given some measure of unity and had helped avert blood feuding, Medina was torn by violent strife among its many kinship groups. The predominantly Arab population of Medina was not entirely pagan and included a substantial and influential Jewish faction, a fact which was to complicate Muhammad's ministry there. While some of the most basic ideas of Islam—including the oneness of God, Final Judgment, humility, and generosity—were preached at Mecca, the longer suras containing the most detailed social regulations came to Muhammad while he was judge-arbiter at Medina, and were first addressed to the people of that city.

For the most part the social regulations of the Koran do not define political institutions as such (even the leadership of the Muslims after the Prophet's death was left unprovided for), but they do emphasize the moral responsibility, autonomy, and dignity of the individual by providing detailed rules by which the righteous could guide their daily lives with a minimum of dependence on the old sources of authority, particularly the tribe and lineage. The required abstention from pork, wine, and gambling was, for example, a matter to which any individual believer could adhere without outside support or resources, thereby placing himself in the community of believers and setting himself apart from tradition by these simple and very personal acts of choice. The blood feud, one of the most sacred duties of the old order, was outlawed; in its place equal penalties were set for specified crimes, regardless of the social status of the parties involved. Similarly the *zakat*, the alms tax collected by the Muslim community on behalf of the needy, transferred certain duties and powers from the lineage and tribe to the religious leadership, and at the same time gave the powerless a more secure status independent of their kinship groups.

Many of the Koran's social regulations concern marriage and the family, and here again the tendency was to favor the rights of the individual and the immediate family over those of tribe and lineage. Numerous forms of marriage prevailed in Arabia prior to Islam, some of which were nothing more than casual relationships in which each partner remained under the control of his or her respective family, and others which made wives little more than slaves. The status of marriages and their participants was determined more by family connections, power, and social position than by any universal rules. The Koran universalized marriage forms and family obligations; it discouraged casual forms of quasi-marriage and gave equal status in law to all marriages between free persons. The Koran limited the number of wives a man may take to four, and counseled that all wives must be treated equally. Inheritance remained within the immediate family rather than becoming diffused into the larger kinship group. The rights of the husband-father (including the right to divorce) were strengthened, not so much at the expense of the wife (who had never enjoyed much power) as at the expense of his and his wife's lineages. The husband's rights included the ultimate custody of children after divorce.

In tune with the theme of personal autonomy and responsibility, the Koran showed its recognition of individual rights in other ways. For example, the right to life was affirmed in the prohibition against infanticide, a practice that had often been used to eliminate girl babies. The Koran held strongly for individual property rights, urging respect for the property of even the most vulnerable members of society, including women and orphans. The bride wealth traditionally paid by a husband to the wife's family was to become her personal property, and a woman's property was protected from appropriation by the husband during marriage and retained for the wife in the event of divorce.

Slavery was a firmly entrenched practice in the Middle East (and, until recently, in many other places where economic factors favored it). Nevertheless, the Koran allowed slaves greater rights than those granted slaves in, say, nineteenth-century America, and it taught that it is meritorious to free a slave. Muhammad set an example by freeing his own slave, who later became a prominent Muslim.

It has been suggested by some writers that the conception of fairness, individualism, and equality implied in Koranic teachings is derived more from the cultural outlook of the marketplace than from the temple or the palace. If this is true, it may be more than coincidence that such an innovation originated not in the older and more civilized centers of power, but in the new mercantile communities of the Hijaz. In any case, it is difficult to deny that Islam was, in the context where it originated, a major step toward the forms of morality most widely recognized in the modern world.

The Spread of Islam

While Muhammad's position in Medina was that of judge-arbiter and did not necessarily depend on the conversion of the populace, the pagan Arab population of the city increasingly became Muslim. The pressures to convert came from several sources, including not only the attractiveness of the teachings and the prospect of inclusion in a cohesive social entity, but also an increasingly aggressive self-identification on the part of the Muslim community.

A central concept in the Koran is that of the **Umma**. Originally the term referred to the people to whom a prophet is sent, but it soon came to refer to the believers in Islam as a community in themselves. It is to this community that a Muslim's social responsibilities were ultimately directed, and loyalty to the Umma came to be seen as inseparable from loyalty to God. The idea of the Umma expresses Islam's radical departure from the past in a most fundamental way, for membership in this community of believers cut across all traditional distinctions of family, class, and ethnicity. In principle, the Muslim owed allegiance unconditionally to another Muslim, even a foreigner or a person without social standing, and against even a sibling or parent if they were unbelievers.

It does not seem that Muhammad at first had in mind the creation of a new religious community to oppose Judaism and Christianity. Rather, he saw himself as a reformer of those religions, who in the tradition of previous prophets would lead Jews, Christians, and pagan Arabs out of error and thereby revitalize the religion of Abraham. Muhammad at first prayed in the direction of Jerusalem and observed the fast of the Jewish Day of Atonement. He was soon to be disappointed, however, by the unwillingness of most Medinese Christians and Jews to convert to Islam. During the Medina period the religion of Islam came to be defined in a manner increasingly distinct from the other monotheistic religions. Muslim prayer was reoriented in the direction of Mecca, where the Kaaba was eventually to become the central shrine of Islam. The fast of the Day of Atonement was replaced by fasting during the month of Ramadan. The Koran also required that Muslims strive to convert nonbelievers. If the message of the Prophet is God's holy word, it applies equally to all who will accept it. Because of Islam's emphasis on the creation of a divinely guided community whose religion is expressed in ethics and justice, the dedicated Muslim cannot rest content with personal enlightenment or salvation.

Jihad and the Djimmi System

The extension of the faith is a holy duty and a struggle from which a conscientious Muslim should never retire. The struggle is represented in the concept of **jihad**, or holy war. Just what is entailed in the Koran's support of jihad has always been subject to various interpretations by Muslims, but the Koran did make it clear that Christians and Jews were "people of the book" who, though in error, ought not to be converted against their will. As long as they did not oppose the hegemony of the Muslim community in Arabia, they were to be placed in the status of protected communities, or **djimmis**. Following the Arab traditions of client-patron relationships, these communities were expected to pay a tribute tax and to show deference to the Muslims; but they were protected from harsh treatment, exploitation, and attack by either outsiders or Muslims. The pagan Arabs were a different case: Muhammad was above all a prophet sent to them, for they had strayed the farthest from God. The conversion of all pagan Arabs, including not only most Meccans but also most Bedouin tribes, was so important that it was to be implemented by whatever use of force proved necessary.

The conversion of the Arabs proceeded apace during the Medina years. After the Hijira, Muhammad and his followers began to attack the Meccan caravan trade and to clash in a series of skirmishes and battles with Meccan forces. The success of some of these early engagements, sometimes against unfavorable odds, was widely interpreted in Arabia as evidence of divine favor toward the Muslims. Muhammad offered all converts a share in the booty of war, and the Muslims began to gather a following of Arab tribes that posed a growing threat to the Meccans and their own Arab allies. Under Islam, much of the amorphous realm of the Arabs was crystallizing into a community united by a divine purpose and a sense of community.

The Meccans had been obliged to make so many concessions to the growing power of the Muslims that when the Prophet's army reentered the city, some eight years after the forced emigration, it encountered only token resistance. Muhammad was a benign conqueror, so much so that his veteran followers complained of the material rewards granted the Quraish in return for their support. Mecca became a Muslim city almost overnight. The Kaaba, following the destruction of pagan idols and its "restoration" to Allah as Abraham's temple, became the focal point of Muslim prayer and pilgrimage.

Two years later, in A.D. 632, Muhammad, the messenger of God, died. Unlike most prophets, he had lived to see the basic fulfillment of his mission. The word of God had been delivered and heard, and the pagan tribes of Arabia had at least nominally converted to Islam. The religion of Muhammad's childhood had become virtually extinct. Islam was established as a coherent set of beliefs, ritual practices, and social ethics that had swept much of the world known to Muhammad. This in itself is a remarkable enough accomplishment, and it is unlikely that Muhammad could have anticipated that Islam was to spread its influence farther and more deeply than did the Roman Empire, or that within four generations people from Spain to western China would be praying toward Mecca.

FIVE POPULAR MISCONCEPTIONS ABOUT ISLAM

According to popular notions widespread in the West, Islam is an exotic religion of the desert nomad, a religion characterized by fanatical intolerance of the "infidel," spread "by the sword," and dedicated to an ultraconservative view of human social existence. Such a picture is founded on misconceptions about the nature of Islam and of its historical role in Middle Eastern society.

Islam as an Exotic Religion

Viewed from the perspective of Jews and Christians, Islam is by no means an exotic religion. Each of these three religions embodies many of the same notions of society, history, divine will, and personal responsibility—especially compared with the nonhistorical, otherworldly orientation of many Eastern religions. Each recognizes the same God, the same early patriarchs, and most of the same prophets; and each originated among Semitic-speaking peoples of the Middle East. There are differences, to be sure, but in the perspective of cultural history the three religions must be seen as very closely related. In some respects the Muslim might see more continuity among the three religions than does the Jew or Christian, since Muhammad's prophecies are believed to be merely an outgrowth of the same tradition that encompasses Jesus and the Old Testament prophets. Muhammad had come into contact with Jews and Christians and was familiar with their verbal renditions of their scriptures. While there is no direct written connection between Judeo-Christian and Muslim scriptures (Muhammad was said to have been illiterate), and certain scriptural events have become altered and elaborated in the Koran, there can be no question that Islam views itself as the culmination of the Judeo-Christian religious tradition.

Insofar as Muhammad was an apostle to the Arabs, and the Arabs identify ultimately with their Bedouin heritage, there is some truth to the picture of Islam as a "religion of the desert." In fact, Islam draws selectively on certain ancient Bedouin values, such as sharing wealth and caring for those in need. Nevertheless, at its core Islam is an urban and cosmopolitan religion that in its day undermined the tribal system of ethics and religion and replaced it with a rationalized, universal set of beliefs. Its main thrust is at one with the other confessional religions, and not with "primitive" religions centered on nature and the family. Therefore to represent Islam as merely an extension of the Bedouin outlook, as is so often done, is fundamentally false.

Islam as a Militant Religion

One often encounters the assertion, even among some historians, that Islam is a particularly militant and intolerant religion, and that it was spread mainly through the use of force—or as the phrase goes, "by the sword." Historically, Islam no more deserves such a reputation than does Christianity. It is true that the scriptures of Islam do not advise believers to turn the other cheek, and that the Koran actually praises those who go to war in defense of the faith. The very concept of jihad, the holy struggle against the unbeliever, seems to the Westerner to suggest a program of ruthless suppression of other religions. It should be kept in mind, though, that the concept of jihad is a complex one for Muslims, and that the idea of struggle can be interpreted and implemented in various ways. In some sense, the duty of spreading the faith and the idea of universal brotherhood and equality before God are but two sides of the same coin. If the message of God is good for all people, then one does humankind a disservice by leaving the infidels to their disbelief. This, however, does not and never has meant that the Muslim community sanctions random acts of aggression against non-Muslims. On the contrary, the djimmi system protected the rights of religious communities that rejected Islam entirely.

As for conversion "by the sword," the Western accusation against Islam has an exceedingly weak foundation. The Koranic stand on forced conversions is ambiguous, and one can find hadith that seem to forbid it as well as those that seem to support it. Muhammad took a hard stand toward pagans, the nonmonotheistic Arab tribes, but opposed the forced conversion of adherents of the other confessional religions in Arabia. In later times, other communities, including the Hindus in India, were extended formal protection as djimmis. As we shall see in the next chapter, the millions who converted to Islam did so for a variety of reasons. Even the pagan Arabs probably converted more often for the sake of various material, social, and spiritual advantages than out of fear. The Muslims of Asia, whose population today exceeds that of the Muslim Middle East, were generally converted through the influence of peaceful merchants. The reader should not forget that despite the teachings of Jesus, Christianity was spread at the point of a sword in much of Europe and the Western Hemisphere. We suspect that if the historical record is examined carefully, it will show that the spread of Islam depended no more consistently on the use of force than did the spread of Christianity.

Islam as an Intolerant Religion

As for religious intolerance, it is instructive to compare the attitudes of Christians and Muslims toward the Jews, who were a religious minority in both the Muslim and Christian worlds. Tensions have often existed between Jewish communities and the politically dominant Muslims or Christians. One reason for this tension lies in the very nature of the Jewish existence as a religious and cultural minority, with all the conflicting loyalties, suspicions, and persecutions that frequently accompany minority status. Second, the presence of an unconverted population seems to thwart the universalistic claims of both Islam and Christianity. Finally, the historical connections of both Christianity and Islam with Judaism have given rise to more speciflc allegations against the Jews: Christians have traditionally blamed them for betraying Christ, while Muslims have accused them of spurning Muhammad's ministry. Indeed, tension between Muslims and Jews became severe even at Medina, where early attempts to convert the Jewish Arabs of that city came to nothing. The Prophet eventually expelled two of the major Jewish clans and sanctioned a bloodbath against the third for their alleged intrigues against him. During this period, the Koranic revelations upbraided the Jews for their supposed errors and their lack of faith in God's Prophet.

Despite the ever-present potential for conflict, the actual history of Jewish minorities in both Christian and Muslim worlds has been quite variable, and it would be difficult indeed to portray the differences in terms of Christian love versus Muslim intolerance. While interethnic relations in both contexts had their ups and downs, the Christian and Jewish minorities under Islam ultimately enjoyed the status of protected communities as defined in the Koran. To be sure, this djimmi status carried obligations of civil obedience, special taxation, and a limitation of political independence, but it also exempted these minorities from the requirements of jihad and zakat. It can be argued that Jewish minorities in Christendom labored under equally severe restrictions and held a less secure legal status. It is interesting to note that when the Muslims were expelled from Spain in the twelfth to fifteenth centuries, the Jewish communities which had previously thrived under Muslim rule were subjected by the conquering Christians to persecution, forced conversion, and banishment. Putting aside the ecumenical spirit that has recently appeared in the Christian world, there is little in the historical record to support the Western image of Islam as an essentially fanatical and intolerant religion compared with traditional Christianity. Neither is there much support for the idea that active enmity between Muslims and Jews (or Christians) is inevitable.

Islam as an Ultraconservative Religion

Many Westerners believe that Islam is a more socially conservative religion than is Judaism or Christianity. Some have even referred to the recent revival of religious commitment in Muslim countries as a "return to the seventh century" (as though, unlike Christians and Jews, a Muslim must choose between religion and modern life). It is true that Islam's scriptures are notable for their detailed pronouncements on the conduct of social life, a fact that poses a special challenge to the Islamic modernist. However, Judaism and Christianity are by no means lacking in specific social rules; and the scriptures of these religions date to an even earlier period than the Koran. The social ideas presented in the Koran were in many respects radical departures from the prevailing customs of the time, and must be seen in their historical context as innovative.

Islam as a Sexist Religion

Since Islam's position on women's rights has sometimes been used as an example of Muslim conservatism, let us examine this subject as a case in point.

Like Judaism and Christianity, Islam reflects the patriarchal character of traditional Middle Eastern society. Many of its social regulations presuppose a family in which the male is the chief authority and economic provider, as well as a descent system traced through the husband and father. We therefore find a variety of sexually differentiated rules; for example, men but not women may take more than one spouse, a woman receives only half a man's share of an inheritance, and divorce is easier for a man than a woman to initiate. In each of these matters, however, Islam may not be as conservative as it first appears. Plural marriage was permissible among pagans, Jews, and Christians until long after Muhammad's day, and the effect of Islam was therefore not to originate plural marriage but to regulate it, to set limits upon it, and to define the rights and obligations of each partner. Under Islam a man is allowed no more than four wives, and only one if he is unable to treat several wives equally. Men are counseled to treat their wives with kindness, and hadith even criticize men who behave selfishly in sexual intercourse. The Koran advises those with marital difficulties to seek arbitration by representatives of both the wife's and the husband's families, indicating not only that the preservation of a marriage is desirable but also that a woman's grievances ought to be taken seriously. As for property and inheritance, the most significant innovations of Islam were in securing for women the right to inherit property and to receive the bride wealth formerly paid to the bride's family by the husband, and in protecting her full rights of property ownership even in marriage and divorce. This right of a woman to control her own property after marriage, established by the Koran in the seventh century, is still being sought today by women in some parts of the Western world.

The veiling and seclusion of women, for which Islam is often criticized, is more a matter of folk practice than an intrinsic part of Islam. While the Koran advocates sexual modesty on the part of women, it makes the same requirement of men. The social custom of keeping women veiled or behind closed doors is not specifically Muslim, but reflects traditional Middle Eastern concerns. The purity of the women in a family guaranteed its honor and insured the integrity of the male line. Furthermore, the impracticality of keeping women in extreme seclusion has caused the practice to be concentrated in, and symbolic of, the traditional urban upper classes (including many Jews and Christians). It is the traditional public opinion in favor of female seclusion that, contrary to the practice of Muhammad and the early Muslims, has kept women out of the mosques and away from active religious practice. Over the past century, many Muslim intellectuals have objected to the seclusion of women on the grounds that it is contrary to the tenets of Islam.

The Koran echoes the sentiments of traditional Middle Eastern society and of Judeo-Christian thought in saying that "men are the managers of the affairs of women, for that God hath preferred in bounty one of them over the other" (4:5–52). However, Islamic scriptures do not go as far as the Christian in asserting the moral inequality of women and men. We do not find in the Koran anything corresponding to Paul's pronouncement about the "shame" of women for having brought sin into the world (in the Koran both Adam and Eve are tempted equally), or the Christian idea that man is the image and "glory of God" while woman is "created for man." If anything, the Koran goes out of its way to emphasize the moral (as distinct from social) equality of the sexes. Repeatedly it makes clear that its pronouncements stand alike for every believer "be you male or female."

If we can separate the essential religious teachings from social customs that have grown up around them, we will find in Islam no more basis for sexist attitudes than is present in the scriptures of Judaism and Christianity. It is true that a relatively large portion of Muslims retain close ties with the customs of a premodern age, while many Christians and Jews living in the West have all but forgotten some of the more conservative social customs upheld in their scriptures. Nevertheless, there is no reason to assume that Islam is inherently less compatible with modern life and change than its sister religions. Many Muslim modernists, in fact, view Islam as an essentially progressive religion with regard to sex roles and other social issues, and they chide conservative Muslims for allowing custom and prejudice to distract them from the true principles of their faith. We shall have more to say on this subject in a later chapter.

In this chapter we have endeavored to portray Islam as a religious faith and as a product of human history. In so doing we have introduced the reader to the interplay between religion and society. At any given point in history the relationship between religious thought and social practice is likely to be a complex one, with religion acting as both a conservative force and an invitation to social change. As a society develops through time, that relationship is subject to constant revision and reinterpretation, sometimes in differing ways by different members of society. While every religion has fundamental themes and values that ultimately guide its development, the range of possible circumstances, applications, and interpretations is often astonishing.

A fundamental challenge to any religion is to address the universal problems of human existence in a way that transcends the narrow limits of time and place, while retaining enough particularity to give its message substance and social relevance. Islam originally addressed the problems of a very specific society in an exceptionally particular and detailed way, and yet it has subsequently presided over a dozen centuries of cultural development among peoples spanning three continents. While readers should be sensitive to the unifying features of Islam, they should also keep in mind the many contradictions and conflicting interpretations that have occurred within other religious traditions as they adapted to varying circumstances and interests, and expect no more consistency from Islam than any other living religion.

THE POLITICAL LEGACY
OF ISLAM, A.D. 632–1800

Accustomed as Westerners are to the ideal of separating politics from religion, it is easy to overlook the extent to which political thought and action throughout history have been expressed in religious terms. In traditional Christianity no less than in Islam, questions of justice, public obligation, class privilege, and even revolution have been inseparable from religious issues. Some writers see this as evidence that until recently humankind was driven by religious urges at the expense of practical considerations; others have concluded that the religious impulse is nothing more than a cloak for self-interest. A more moderate interpretation, which we prefer, is that religion has provided the concepts and the language by which human beings have pursued their immediate interests and defined their ultimate values. For this reason, a religious outlook never remains static. It is, indeed, a continuous dialogue; and the form of that dialogue bears the stamp of general human concerns, the changing circumstances of history, and the special qualities of vision that characterize the particular tradition.

While the social thought of Islam is in itself neither more nor less important than that of other world religions, it is especially significant for the study of Middle Eastern politics. Islam has had a decisive influence on state politics throughout the region since the death of Muhammad, and today the Islamic heritage is present in new ways. To be sure, Islam is not immune to the influence of contemporary events, and its current political role is different from the one it played in previous centuries. Nevertheless, Islam has a personal and social significance that most contemporary Middle Easterners take seriously, and there is no doubt that the present restructuring of Middle Eastern societies and their interrelations will continue to be based on a common Islamic cultural heritage. Even those who wish to minimize the role of religion in politics must pursue their programs with an acute consciousness of the Islamic milieu.

The revelations of Muhammad introduced a new framework within which to work out the problems of social life. Yet no matter how consistent a statement one makes about the human condition, the attempt to apply it to actual conditions will always lead to contradictions and conflicts, and to resolutions that raise new problems in turn. The difficulties are compounded even further as a religious tradition encounters cultural variation and historical change. As human communities over the past thirteen centuries have explored the implications of the Islamic vision, they have uncovered numerous conflicts and paths of resolution. No simple generalization can do justice to this rich heritage of thought, nor is it possible to catalogue fully the many outlooks that have developed under the auspices of Islam. It is possible, however, to sample some of the issues that Muslims have most often raised, and to indicate the characteristic ways in which these issues have been approached within that tradition.

The ministry of Muhammad had a dual character that arose from his role as a civic leader and a religious visionary. Muhammad made it clear that Islam can be realized only by the creation of a religiously guided community, the Umma. At the same time, such a community exists only insofar as it is defined by Islam. Thus, neither the religion nor the Umma can exist except in terms of the other. Islam requires, by its very nature, a social order that is both politically sound and divinely guided. But the requirements of political efficacy and divine guidance are not always easy to reconcile, at least in the short run; and the problems arising from this contradiction have stimulated much of the political dialogue in Islamic thought. This problem of mediating the demands of faith and politics has manifested itself in more specific conflicts such as power versus justice, privilege versus equality, guidance by the community versus the conscience of the individual, and the need for adaptive innovation versus the enduring vision of Muhammad's model community.

THE ESTABLISHMENT OF THE ISLAMIC STATE

The teachings of Muhammad, concentrating as they did on individual obligations, left unanswered a great many questions vital to the future of his community. Most pressing was the question of leadership, for which Muhammad had made no provisions. After the Prophet's death, the community at Medina made preparations to choose its own leadership and expected the Meccans to do the same. Many Bedouin "converts" considered themselves to be personal clients of Muhammad and believed that their obligations ended with his death. At this critical moment in history, the initiative was seized by Abu Bakr and Umar, two of Muhammad's closest associates who were to become the first two **caliphs**, or representatives, of the Prophet. Under their strong leadership, the unity of the Muslim community was aggressively asserted. They declared that there would be no prophets after Muhammad, and that the Umma must unite under a single authority. Bedouins slipping away from the Islamic fold were brought back by force in the **Riddah** (Wars of Apostasy); and even as these campaigns were being completed, the energies of the newly united Arab armies were turned against the faltering empires of Persia and Byzantium, thus launching Islam on its fateful course.

The Muslim campaigns against the neighboring empires were phenomenally successful. Weakened by decades of indecisive warfare against one another and by internal strains, the exhausted, stalemated Sassanian and Byzantine empires encountered the greatest threat where they had least expected it. The old Arab buffer states, no longer subsidized by the empires, joined with the Muslim Arab conquerors; other local populations, often religious minorities long persecuted by the established state religions, were less than enthusiastic in defending the hegemony of their old masters. Under Umar's guidance (634–644), the terms of conquest were lenient, even attractive. Establishing a pattern for subsequent conquests, Umar allowed life to go on, protected and undisturbed, in those cities that submitted willingly; they were subject only to a tax. These taxes, along with revenues from lands won in battle and one-fifth of all other booty, went to the Muslim state, which in turn distributed much of it to its soldiers. Under Umar's leadership Egypt, the Fertile Crescent, and much of Iran came under Muslim domination; the Sassanian Empire was toppled, and the Byzantines were driven back into Anatolia.

The Muslim Empire, as it took form in the early period, was an Arab military state. Using Bedouin military experience and turning its energies from internal raiding and feuding toward fighting the infidel, the Muslim state rapidly gained power. Under capable administrative leadership, the Arab conquerors instituted an orderly process for collecting revenue and for distributing it by means of the army register, or **diwan**. Conquered people were guaranteed their civil and religious freedom as djimmis in return for their submission to Muslim rule and taxation (often a more attractive arrangement than the older empires had afforded). The Arabs themselves lived in garrison towns segregated from the conquered populace; they had no intention either of blending into the local life or of inviting their new subjects to become like them. Forced conversion of the djimmis was rarely an issue, since the Muslims considered their religion, their Arab background, and their privileged status as conquerors and tax recipients as inextricably connected. In order to promote religious unity and to safeguard against any possible deviations from the faith, Umar did much to establish the forms of worship and to promulgate knowledge of the Koran in the garrison towns. The center of social life in such towns became the mosque, and the military leader himself emphasized the religious character of the community by personally leading the people in prayer.

The caliph Uthman (644–656) continued Umar's policies, but with less success, for the Muslim community was now confronting some of the social and moral problems arising from the transition of a religious movement into an organized state. Many malcontents saw Uthman as a symbol of what they thought was wrong with the community: a turning from faith to secular power. For them it was particularly galling that Uthman's kinsmen, the **Umayyads**—who unlike Uthman himself had long opposed Muhammad—were now being favored in administrative appointments. Opposition to Uthman was particularly strong in the Iraq at Kufah, and in Egypt. In 656, Uthman was murdered by a group of his opponents from the Egyptian garrison, and the Prophet's cousin and son-in-law Ali was immediately proclaimed caliph. The rebels, who supported Ali's accession, claimed that Uthman had betrayed Islam and that his murder was therefore justified; Uthman's supporters and others horrified by the killing accused Ali of condoning it, and demanded that he punish those responsible. The situation quickly developed into civil war, with Ali's supporters in the Iraq pitted against Muawiyah, the Umayyad governor of Syria. After initial successes, some of Ali's men persuaded him to submit to arbitration as demanded by Muawiyah, whereupon a faction of Ali's army, the **Kharijites**, turned against Ali for abandoning the cause. His supporters' loyalties were now split, the arbitration was indeed damaging to his position, and Ali's fortunes declined until his death at the hands of a Kharijite in 661.

The death of Ali was a turning point for Islam. The last of the Prophet's close personal followers was now gone. The initial unity of Islam was forever shattered, and the issue was raised—an issue which was to trouble Islam until the present—of whether civil order within the Umma is more important than the divinely mandated legitimacy of its leadership. The accession of Muawiyah established a dynasty of rulers whose ultimate recourse was to secular power, and the religious idealists took on the function, which they have generally had ever since, of a moralistic oppositional force.

THE GOLDEN AGE OF THE CALIPHATE

If Islam had lost some of its purity in the eyes of its more idealistic adherents, it was also entering into its own as a civilization and an empire. Under the Umayyads (661–750), Islam spread across North Africa to Spain; in the East, it spread to the Indus Valley. The structure of the empire remained essentially that of an Arab conquest state, in which Islam remained primarily the religion of a segregated Arab elite. Other trends, however, were beginning to appear.

Despite the ethnic biases of the Arabs, the universalistic, cosmopolitan facets of Islam were beginning to surface as the empire embraced highly sophisticated peoples who were both willing and able to take an active part in Muslim civilization. At first, non-Arab converts to Islam were given only marginal status as *Mawalis*, or clients, of influential Arab families. Indeed, their existence posed economic problems since the empire was set up on the assumption that Arab Muslims would collect taxes from their subjects on the basis of religious affiliation. In practice, non-Arab converts to Islam often found themselves excluded from Muslim economic privileges despite their conversion. But the forces of change were at work. The Arabs with their Bedouin and mercantile backgrounds were now heirs to the traditions of the centralized agrarian state, and the conditions associated with agrarian life came to have more and more sway over them. The Arab ruling class came increasingly to look like any other local gentry, and the caliphs took on the aspect of semidivine emperors ruling at their court in Damascus.

Throughout the period of Umayyad rule, a gathering variety of factions promoted a growing antigovernment spirit. Some disliked the favoring of Syrians over other Arabs; some opposed the distinction of Arabs from other Muslim converts; and some disliked the centralized control over the distribution of revenues, which they felt worked to their disadvantage. Many Arabs despised the pretensions of the caliphs and chafed under the spirit of imperial rule, so incompatible with traditional Arab values. Whatever the specific sources of discontent, the criticisms tended to converge on the accusation that the government was impious, that it had made irreligious "innovations" instead of following the way of the Prophet, and that it had forgotten its communal obligations in favor of material advantages for the few. What was needed, they agreed, was true Islamic

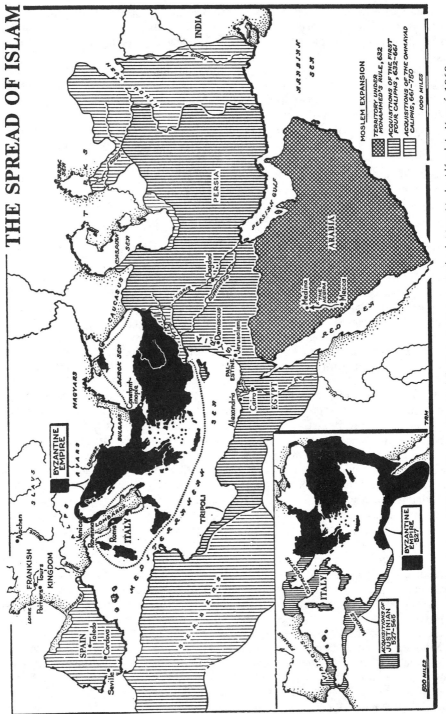

THE SPREAD OF ISLAM

MOSLEM EXPANSION

TERRITORY UNDER MOHAMMED'S RULE, 632

ACQUISITIONS OF THE FIRST FOUR CALIPHS, 632–661

ACQUISITIONS OF THE OMMAYAD CALIPHS, 661–750

1000 MILES

ACQUISITIONS OF JUSTINIAN 527–565

BYZANTINE EMPIRE 527

500 MILES

The Spread of Islam. *Source:* Sydney Nettleton Fisher, *The Middle East: A History*, 2nd ed. New York: Alfred A. Knopf, 1969.

guidance for the community. In the 740s a coalition of interest groups and sects, including the **Shia** (the "party" of Ali, which still bore a grudge against the Umayyads), launched a civil war that ended with the establishment of the **Abbasid** dynasty in 750.

Many of those who had supported the overthrow of the Umayyads were soon to be disappointed. It is true that the bases of the empire were considerably broadened by the change, for the new order with its capital at Baghdad was much more open to the participation and influence of the Iraqi Arabs and especially the non-Arab Persians. Some writers have even gone so far as to characterize the change as one from Arab to Persian domination, because of the decisive participation of Persians at the highest levels of government as well as the increasing influence of Persian language, literature, and culture. Yet in these changes lay the seeds of bitter disappointment for the old opposition. Far from a return to charismatic rule by Ali's inspired descendants, as the Shia had hoped, or even a return to a purer life modeled on the early Umma, as others had advocated, the caliphate continued on its evolution toward agrarian absolutism. Under the Abbasid caliphs, the power of the court reached its peak, with the caliph exercising his own law at his whim, which was enforced on the spot by his ever-present executioner.

The city of Baghdad, which the Abbasids built for their capital, symbolized the trends in government. Unlike the Arab garrison towns located on the edge of the desert, Baghdad was built on the Tigris River on a site that commanded key agricultural land in the Iraq and principal trade routes. It was laid out in a circle; and instead of emphasizing Arab tribal divisions, as the garrison towns had done, the entire city was oriented toward the government complex and the caliph's huge palace. The court of the caliph was the center of an aristocratic high culture marked by strong Persian influences, and Baghdad came to play a dominant economic, political, and cultural role reminiscent of the older Persian and Mesopotamian seats of government.

While absolute despotism was as repugnant to the Bedouin and the ulema as it is to modern taste, it by no means hindered Abbasid civilization itself. Such a monarchy protected the powerless—especially the peasants—against the more grotesque abuses frequently visited on them by decentralized oligarchies and competing petty rulers, and it also brought a degree of order that set the stage for unprecedented material prosperity in the Muslim world. Trade and agriculture flourished, banking and communications were effectively organized across the empire, and government was carefully regulated under a *vizier* (comparable to a prime minister) and an established bureaucracy.

This was the Golden Age of Muslim civilization, to which Muslims in later times would look for inspiration. Muslim power was unparalleled anywhere in the world, while Islamic art, architecture, literature, and poetry—drawing on Arabic, Persian, Greek, Indic, and other traditions, and supported by the courtly high culture—reached their peak of development. Arabic works from this period on mathematics (*algebra* and *logarithm* are Arabic-derived words), chemistry, optics, and medicine put these sciences at such a high state of development that Europeans were still consulting the Arabic works five hundred years later. The Crusaders who entered the Middle East at the end of the eleventh century, after the decline of the Abbasid caliphate, were seen with some justice as uncultivated barbarians.

Ironically, the Golden Age of Islamic civilization also signaled the beginning of the decline of the caliphate. For reasons not altogether clear, the Abbasid caliphs began to lose their hold on the vast empire after their first century of rule. In an attempt to bolster their own power against competing factional loyalties, the caliphs by 850 had begun to use private armies. These guards were usually slaves obtained from the Turkic-speaking nomadic tribes of the Eurasian steppes; they were kept totally dependent on the caliph and were loyal, presumably, only to him. The caliphs, however, soon found themselves at the mercy of their own palace guards; by the mid-to-late ninth century, most caliphs were puppets of a Turkish soldier class that was in one form or another to dominate most Middle Eastern Muslim States for the next thousand years. In the ninth century, some provinces started to assert their independence, and the empire began to devolve into a decentralized civilization with the caliph as figurehead. Under various dynasties, multiple centers of power developed, and their political control decreased with distance; in some areas there was little more than local civic government. Yet the social unity of the Umma and the norms that governed Muslim life did not depend on a central government and therefore did not decline with the caliphate. Instead, the political disintegration of Islam was accompanied by the continued development of a common, international pattern of Muslim social life that was based on Islamic Sharia law and was overseen by the formally educated ulema.

MONGOL DESTRUCTION AND THE REBIRTH OF EMPIRE

The period from the mid-tenth to the mid-thirteenth centuries saw the militarization of political power. This tendency was brought to an extreme by the Mongol conquests and afterward in the period of the Ottoman and other late empires. Before the thirteenth century, the overall tendency toward decentralized rule by local Muslim rulers, called *emirs*, was reversed only a few times—as in the case of the Seljuk Turks during the eleventh century. The Mongols, however, were able to consolidate pure military power on an unprecedented level. The Mongol invasions were joint efforts involving Turkic-speaking armies recruited among the nomadic tribes of the Eurasian steppes and a Mongol military elite originating in Asia. Due to a complex of historical and technological factors, during the thirteenth and fourteenth centuries the Mongols and their armies were able to conquer most of the civilized world from China to Eastern Europe and place it under the centralized administration of military chieftains. With the fall of Baghdad in 1258 and the execution of the last Abbasid figurehead caliph, political control passed into purely military hands. Although non-Muslim in origin, the Mongols and their Turkish forces converted to Islam; subsequently some of the severest Mongol campaigns under Timur (Tamerlane) were fought in the name of Islamic purity. Destructive as their terrorist techniques were, once established, the Mongols became patrons of Islamic high culture and rebuilders of public works. One of their most enduring influences, however, was the establishment of efficient, highly organized states based on the army. In these states, ultimate control was in the hands of a supreme military ruler whose succession was determined by armed contest within the ruling dynasty; the army organization included not only combat troops but the entire governmental apparatus. So centered on the army were these empires that their capitals were wherever the army and its supreme leader happened to be, and government records were carried into the field on campaigns.

Eventually the effects of Mongol conquest gave way to more homegrown military empires, which in some respects benefited both from the destruction of the old order and from the Mongol military system. Equally important in these new empires was the use of gunpowder, which favored the technologically advanced urban populations over the Eurasian nomads and allowed greater concentrations of power to develop. The most important post-Mongol concentrations of power in the Middle East were the Safavid Empire, centering approximately in what is now Iran, and the Ottoman Empire, originating in what is now Turkey. Each arose and achieved much of its glory during the sixteenth century, and each was dominated by a Turkic military elite but used Persian or Turkish as a literary language and Arabic as the religious language. Each followed somewhat similar paths of development, but it is the Ottoman state that is of the greatest interest here, partly because it most directly confronted the growing power of Europe, and partly because it continued as an active force in world politics until the twentieth century.

The Ottoman Empire

The **Ottoman Empire**, named after its original ruling family of Osman Turks, had its roots in Anatolia during the pre-Mongol period. Located on the frontier of the Byzantine Empire, the Ottoman state had long been associated with the continuing struggle against the infidel; accordingly, it held a prestigious position within Islam and attracted many would-be **ghazis**, or defenders of the faith. A turning point for the Ottomans came with the long-sought conquest of Constantinople in 1453, which they renamed Istanbul and made their capital. Ottoman power grew rapidly as Islamic territories expanded into Hungary and even to the gates of Vienna, which the Ottomans unsuccessfully besieged in 1541 and again in 1683. To the south, Ottoman power encompassed the Levant, Syria, the Iraq, the Hijaz, and Muslim North Africa as far west as Algeria. Rivalry between the Ottomans and Safavids took on religious overtones as the Safavids became more militantly Shia and the Ottomans increasingly Sunni, a conflict that has left the Middle East religiously divided to this day along former Ottoman-Safavid boundary lines.

Like other Muslim empires before it, the Ottoman Empire developed features of an agrarian state with its social stratification and its absolute monarchy, but the Ottoman form remained distinctive. A military ruling family presided over a vast army of *Janissaries*, slaves who were loyal only to the rulers. These slaves were obtained as children from non-Muslim populations, often Christian, and were brought up and trained as Muslims. They formed a class that made up not only the military component of the state but the bureaucracy as well. At first they were not allowed to marry. When marriage was permitted, the offspring of slaves were freeborn and therefore were disqualified from government service, thereby assuring that there was little opportunity for the formation of privileged classes or loyalties at odds with Ottoman interests. The machinery of Ottoman government was remarkably efficient. Furthermore, the Ottomans accomplished what few Muslim governing powers had done before them: They successfully allied themselves with the ulema. Ottoman success with the ulema was related to the

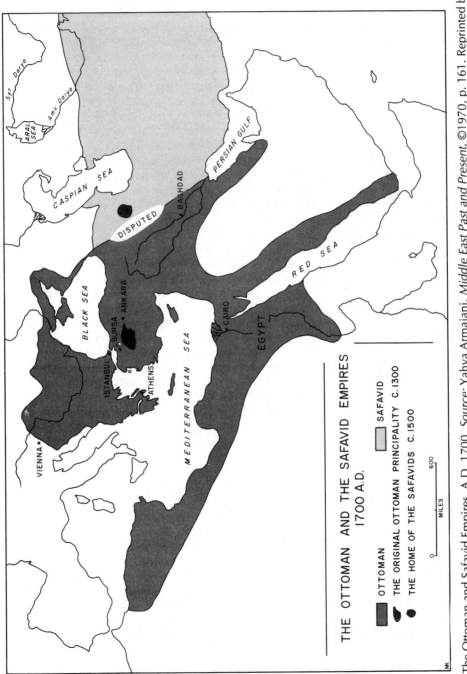

THE OTTOMAN AND THE SAFAVID EMPIRES
1700 A.D.

SYR DARYA

AMU DARYA

ARAL SEA

CASPIAN SEA

DISPUTED

BAGHDAD

PERSIAN GULF

RED SEA

EGYPT

CAIRO

BLACK SEA

ANKARA

BURSA

ISTANBUL

ATHENS

MEDITERRANEAN SEA

VIENNA

◼ OTTOMAN

⬮ THE ORIGINAL OTTOMAN PRINCIPALITY C.1300

● THE HOME OF THE SAFAVIDS C.1500

SAFAVID

0   600

MILES

MK

The Ottoman and Safavid Empires, A.D. 1700. *Source:* Yahya Armajani, *Middle East Past and Present*, ©1970, p. 161. Reprinted by permission of Prentice-Hall, Inc., Englewood Cliffs, NJ.

empire's origin as a ghazi state and its devotion to defending the faith against not only the Christian powers but the Shia Safavids as well. It should also be kept in mind that a career as a religious scholar was one of the few paths of prestige open to the freeborn sons of the military-bureaucratic slave class. Under the Ottoman system, the ulema relinquished much of their traditional oppositional role with regard to the ruling powers, and came instead to identify with those powers. In return, the government supported the ulema's authority and that of Sharia law, and submitted to some token checks on its power; for example, the ulema could in theory depose the Ottoman sultan if they judged him unfaithful to Islam.

A certain amount of pluralism was built into the Ottoman system. The djimmi communities, or **millets**, were allowed military protection, religious freedom, and self-government under their own chosen leaders, subject as always to a kind of second-class citizenship in the Muslim state. Ottoman provinces relatively distant from Istanbul, such as the Hijaz and North Africa, were also allowed some degree of self-government. For example, the **Mameluks** of Egypt, a Turkish slave class that had ruled Egypt from 1250 until their defeat by the Ottomans in 1517, were allowed to continue in power under minimal Ottoman supervision.

By the eighteenth century, the empire had long since stopped increasing its territories and was beginning to take note of the rapidly growing European threat. Some attempts were made to modernize the Ottoman army, but these were thwarted by more sweeping problems that plagued the empire. The military ruling class had gradually become civilianized, had suffered a loss of discipline, and had begun to lose even its former structural integrity (army bureaucrats, for example, began to pass their status on to their children). Corruption and demoralization became widespread in government, a condition which many Western observers of the time assumed to be a universal trait of "oriental" governments. When the Western powers began in earnest to move in on the Middle East around the turn of the nineteenth century, they found the Ottoman Empire ill prepared to resist them.

GROWTH AND DECLINE IN THE ISLAMIC STATE

Many observers have noted that Muslim civilization and Muslim political power seem to have gone through an early period of phenomenal growth and vitality that was followed by a long era of "decline," or "stagnation," ending finally in Western dominance. Often, the rapid growth is attributed to military force driven by religious fanaticism, while the "decadence" that followed is said to reveal the defects either of the "oriental mind" or of Islam itself, both of which are often accused of authoritarianism and resistance to innovation. Such a view is misleading not only because there is no such thing as an oriental mind, but also because the problem of "growth" and "decline" is much too complex to lend itself to such easy generalizations. The Muslim world, like any civilization that endures for centuries or millennia, experienced many different kinds of growth and decline. Indeed, what is decline from one point of view may be growth from another; for example, the decline of centralized government was accompanied by a strengthening of Muslim law that reached across political boundaries. Furthermore, decline in one local region may be offset by growth in another.

The original growth of Islamic civilization actually involved two processes that reinforced one another: the spread of Islam as a religion, and the extension of Muslim political rule (or ties with the centers of Muslim power). The reasons for the spread of Islamic influence varied with the circumstances. In Medina, conversion to Islam was a matter of civic convenience as well as personal conviction. Among the Bedouins of the Arabian peninsula, political advantage and later the threat of force encouraged conversion. The subjects of the Sassanian and Byzantine empires yielded to a well-organized conquering army, but at the same time they were attracted by the promise of being better off as djimmi communities than as Sassanian or Byzantine subjects. Under the Umayyads, non-Arabs converted despite Arab discouragement in order to benefit from the advantages of Muslim social status. In India political conquest preceded conversion, while conversion itself resulted more often from the attractiveness of Muslim institutions and the personal appeal of **Sufism** (Muslim mysticism) than from the threat of force. In Southeast Asia, which now includes a large segment of the world's Muslim population, Islam spread peaceably as part of an international mercantile culture, again aided by the appeal of Sufism.

The difficulties encountered by the various Muslim political powers after their establishment were due to a variety of causes, but none of these involved turning away from Islam as such. It appears that the Middle East may have been suffering from some long-term adverse effects on its ecology, as a result of the ancient and intensive agricultural exploitation of the land. Many Islamic governments followed a policy of assigning "tax farms" as rewards to the military; these temporary revenue assignments were often exploited with little regard for the welfare of the peasants or the condition of the land and irrigation works, thus contributing to the decline of productivity. Coupled with the Mongol invasions and the Black Death during the thirteenth and fourteenth centuries, these trends may have reduced the vitality of agriculture, urban life, and even trade. There is some indication that population may have declined and that nomadism may have increased during the age of the Muslim empires. In addition to the economic factors, certain political processes seem to involve an inherent dynamic of growth and decline. In agrarian societies, an existing order tends to accumulate vested interests, tax exemptions, and special privileges to the detriment of the overall functioning of the polity, until at last the weakened governmental power is overthrown and the accumulated commitments wiped away (as happened in the Arab conquest of Byzantine and Sassanian domains). This and other political processes may have contributed to cycles of political disintegration and revitalization both before and during the age of Muslim power.

As for intellectual development, it appears that the creative exploration of new ideas reached a peak during the Abbasid caliphate; afterward, the legal, moral, and theological conceptions of the ulema prevailed and became increasingly hostile to innovation, especially after the ulema were integrated into the Ottoman order. While some see this as further evidence of the stagnation of "oriental" civilizations, one could just as easily see it as the natural consequence of the refinement of the Sharia, and particularly of its institutionalization in the **madrasah** schools where the ulema were trained—features that in turn provided much of the resiliency of Islamic law. The spirit of conservatism that prevailed after the collapse of the caliphate did not in itself cause political decline, nor was it very different from the conservatism that prevailed in Europe before the eighteenth century. The pattern of peaks and valleys in political power and social strength has been common to both regions throughout most of history.

LEGITIMACY IN GOVERNMENT

As stated earlier, the teachings of Muhammad stressed the righteous community that was structured to realize the demands of justice and piety. Since the early caliphate, a central problem in Islam has been to reconcile the demands of political reality and those of faith. The champions of Islamic values needed a workable government in theory, but rarely approved of what they found in practice. The Islamic governments needed the approval of Islam to make them legitimate, but while the Muslim rulers were devout men, they were willing to make only limited concessions to Islamic ideals in government.

In some respects, the first caliphs were able to avoid many of the inherent difficulties of legitimizing Islamic political power. They were personal followers of the Prophet who were intimately acquainted with his words and deeds and ruled largely by virtue of that knowledge. Like traditional Arab leaders they also depended largely on their own personal qualities and reputation, and on their close acquaintance with the community (that is, with the core of Muhammad's following). They also acquired much legitimacy through their military leadership (Umar preferred to be called the "commander of the faithful" rather than caliph), a role well established in Arab tradition, and which carried with it the notion of leadership among men who were essentially equals.

The Political Role of the Ulema

Under Uthman a gap began to develop (or to become apparent) between Islamic ideals and the realities of political power and privilege. The issue of Uthman's murder and Ali's accession became symbolic for Muslims of the conflict between communal loyalty and religious purity. Although the Umayyads won on behalf of political solidarity, they had to face renewed challenges first from Ali's sons and later from a coalition of factions who wished to see Islamic government guided by uncompromising religious ideals. When this coalition failed to reverse the tendency toward secular power, Muslims were obliged to choose between remaining loyal to the protest against government or remaining loyal to the powers that governed Islam regardless of their faults. While the Shia took the former course, the bulk of the community, later called Sunni, chose in favor of the political unity of the Umma. As the pious, learned men of the Islamic world began to form into a coherent body of ulema, this body became a kind of loyal opposition, aloof from and critical of the government but not overtly disloyal to it. The ulema generally recognized the legitimacy of the caliphs, even while criticizing their ways. As the caliphs became powerless, they were still invested with theoretical legitimacy as the arbiters of any affairs concerning all Islam, and as the source of authority to the various local emirs. After the fall of the caliphate, the ulema were inclined to grant at least some legitimacy to the emirs on the grounds that they provided the political order necessary to the community. This trend culminated in the Ottoman theory that whoever can rule the Muslim community according to the Sharia is entitled to be considered the caliph. The Ottoman interpretation completes the transition from the original theory in which secular power is derived from religious legitimation, to one in which religious legitimation is derived from secular power.

The unique political role of the ulema in Islam deserves special comment. Many traditional agrarian societies had a priesthood, a privileged group of religious practitioners who mediated ritually between the common people and the supernatural, and who tended to be intimately connected with—and supportive of—the political ruling class. The Muslim ulema, however, are scholars rather than priests, and their training in subsidized institutions has been open, in theory, to anyone showing promise. Under the protection of Islam, the ulema have traditionally presented a voice of opposition that attempted to hold political figures accountable to the principles of Islam, principles opposed to privilege and self-indulgence. Even today this heritage influences the relations between the Muslim religious leadership and the politicians. The ulema in Saudi Arabia, for example, retain the right to declare a king unfit to govern, and they exercised this right in 1964 when they approved the deposing of King Saud.

THE SHARIA LAW

The Koran did not provide a complete guide for social life, and after the death of Muhammad the question arose as to how it was to be interpreted and how Muslims should deal with problems it did not directly anticipate. It soon became evident that the secular values of the conquered agrarian states, not to mention the old Arab ways, might reassert themselves unless Islam provided more detailed codes. By gradual steps, religious scholars developed a complex, cumulative set of guiding rules for Muslims that came to be known as the Sharia. At the core of the Sharia is the Koran, but it was necessary to supplement the Koran with reports (hadith) about the sayings and practices of the Prophet and his community. Later, as Sharia thinking attacked more complex problems, the Koran and the hadith were extended by means of the principle of analogy, by reference to the consensus of the Umma (or more specifically, its recognized religious leaders), and by reference to the welfare of the Umma. The relative importance of these various avenues of **fiqh**, or understanding, was debated by leading scholars, and by the ninth century several major schools of legal thinking had developed. Each of these was accorded equal validity, and although they differed somewhat on the methods of arriving at legal codes, their results were similar. Muslims were expected to adhere consistently to one or another of these schools, usually according to the common practice of the locality. Today there are four such recognized schools in Sunni Islam.

Formal training in Sharia law became institutionalized in the madrasahs, Islamic schools supported by privately endowed religious foundations (**waqf**, plural *awqaf*) where any capable person could study free of charge. Such schools helped to determine who was qualified to interpret the tradition, and to standardize the Sharia against indiscriminate reinterpretation. They also made it possible to broaden the Sharia beyond the strict limits of the Koran and hadith without sacrificing its coherence or throwing it open to uncontrolled change. The Sharia, thus broadened and codified, provided a universal law that applied to every Muslim and to diverse aspects of life ranging from the settlement of political and business disputes to the regulation of family life. The application of this code and the qualifications of its administrators were valid in all Muslim nations regardless of political boundaries, which allowed Islam to prosper as an international social order even in times of political decentralization.

Based on the mercantile and Arab values of Mecca and Medina, the Sharia embodied a social philosophy that was opposed to social class or other privilege; it tended to support individual rights and individual social mobility and to protect the weak against the strong. Along with an uncompromising concern for Islamic principles of social justice, however, went a distrust of innovation and of the deviant or the outsider—an inclination that became more and more established in the madrasahs after the fourteenth century. In the madrasahs the methods of teaching became extremely conservative and were aimed at discouraging innovation. Any question that had once been decided upon and accepted by the ulema was no longer open for discussion, and new issues were to be resolved insofar as possible in exact accordance with previous decisions. Even the number of errors was determined—there were six dozen false sects of Islam, and every new heresy could be classified with those already known. Yet, without this careful regulation the Sharia probably could not have served its vital function in Muslim life.

The sway of the Sharia was never absolute. Because monarchs often found the Sharia incomplete, irrelevant to certain questions, or excessively "soft" on criminals, they typically established their own courts and legal codes. The peasants and townspeople, on the other hand, sometimes found it in their interest to follow customary law, even (as in the case of some inheritance rules) when it contradicted the Sharia. Despite these auxiliary legal systems, however, the Sharia stood as the supreme expression of legitimacy. It was the core of Islamic social life, to which every Muslim ultimately owed allegiance. Safe from random innovation, local cultural influence, and the tampering of political interest groups, the Sharia provided a means of integrating an international civilization.

THE SHIA

The conflicting demands of political unity and religious purity, which became apparent so early in Islamic history, gave rise to the great sectarian split within Islam—that between the Sunnis and the Shia. While the majority of Muslims are Sunnis, who place loyalty to the established order of the Umma above religious disputation, the Shia, a substantial minority, believe that only a divinely inspired political leadership is worthy of a Muslim's loyalty. The historical split between the two groups is difficult to discuss because the key events of the past have been imbued subsequently with complex symbolic significance. At the time of his death, Ali stood for the protest against the supposed corruptions of Uthman's rule, and his defeat was viewed by many Muslims—particularly those in the Iraq—as an unfortunate triumph of worldly power over true Islamic piety. Those loyal to Ali and to what he stood for, came to be known as the *Shia* (party) of Ali.

A turning point in the history of the Shia was an insurrection in 680 against the Umayyads under Ali's son Husayn, in which Husayn, abandoned by the bulk of his supporters, was killed. With the rise of the Abbasids in 750, Shia hopes that the new political unrest would lead to a reinstatement of Ali's line were dashed, and the Shia assumed the posture of a minority opposition to the political establishment.

Under the Abbasids the division between the Shia and the Sunnis became more distinct. The Sunni position, even among those who sympathized with Ali's protest and despised Uthman and the fallen Umayyad dynasty, was that devotion to the solidarity of the Umma and obedience to its recognized leadership should transcend religious dissension. By the tenth century, the Shia had developed into a distinct and very influential group which proposed, in opposition to the Sunni view, that Muslims should follow only those authorities who were rightly guided. In the Shia view, this gift of divine guidance (what sociologists call "charisma") was possessed only by a small number of the elect, descendants of the Prophet through his daughter Fatima and his son-in-law Ali. While Husayn was the last of these to make an open bid for power, the Shia believed that secret knowledge and divine inspiration had passed through Ali's line to a succession of rightful leaders. The Shia movement eventually split over differing interpretations of this line of succession. The largest faction was the "Twelvers," who believed that the twelfth imam in the succession had gone into hiding from the wicked world, where he would remain until his eventual return as the **Mahdi**, or Muslim messiah. In Twelver Shiism, which predominates in Iran, it has occasionally been possible for religious leaders to claim sweeping powers as representatives of this "Hidden Imam." Another major faction, the **Ismailis**, part with the twelver line in disputing the identity of the seventh Imam. They came to emphasize the esoteric knowledge of a secret religious elite, a knowledge revealed to pious individuals only by degrees as they ascend in the religious hierarchy. Ismaili Islam reached the peak of its influence in the Fatimid dynasty in Egypt (969–1171), which was renowned for its achievements in government, commerce, art, and learning.

The Shia came to see the majority of Muslims as betrayers of their faith, and temporal power as essentially illegitimate. In this atmosphere of resistance, they developed the practice of denying their true beliefs in public when necessary, as well as the idea that the inward truth of the Koran (as opposed to its outward or superficial meaning) is unknown to the community at large and must be interpreted by the Imams or their agents. (The use of the term *imam* can be confusing, since it can refer to a variety of roles ranging from a leader of Muslim prayer to—in Shia thought—a leader of all Islam. Generally, we have capitalized Imam only when it refers to the latter or to a specific historical personage such as the Imam Ayatollah Khomeini.) Another strong current in Shia thought is the tragic view of the fate of the righteous man in an unrighteous society, and a deep sense of guilt over the betrayal and martyrdom of Husayn. Once a year, during the month of **Muharram**, Husayn's martyrdom is commemorated in an outpouring of grief, self-flagellation, and resentment toward the Sunnis. If the ulema of Sunni Islam looked askance at the political establishment, the Shia simply regarded it as illegitimate, to be tolerated only for the time being. Despite the differences in outlook, Sunni and Shia Islam actually developed remarkably parallel institutions, parallel Sharia codes, and even parallel debates over similar issues. Mystical Sufism, which was largely a Sunni phenomenon, developed its Shia counterpart in a particularly inward-turning brand of personal devotion to Ali and Husayn.

Even in Ali's day the Iraq was a center of proto-Shia resistance. It remained so under the Umayyads as part of the protest against Syrian power; and even after the fall of the Umayyads, Shiism remained strong in the old Sassanian domains— so much so that some historians characterize Shiism as a Persian movement against Arabism. Shiism was even more radically localized, however, during the rivalry between the Sunni Ottomans and the Shia Safavids, when nonconforming minorities in each domain were persecuted or driven out. Today Shiism is largely confined to the Middle East, where more than a fourth of the Muslims are Shia, most of whom live in Iraq or Iran.

SUFISM

If the Sharia was uncompromisingly oriented toward history, justice, and practical responsibility, other elements of Islam addressed very different facets of religious life. Mysticism, that brand of religious awareness that emphasizes the clarifying and enlightening inward experience over conventionalized and verbally communicated ideas, is pervasive in human cultures and was well established in the Middle East before the rise of Islam. Like Christianity and Judaism, Islam has developed its own distinct tradition of mysticism. In early times the mystically inclined Muslims, or Sufis, were a small minority hardly distinguishable from other Muslims, but after 1100 they became more prominent and influential. The Muslim philosopher-theologian Ghazali (d. 1111), though not a Sufi himself, aided the rise of Sufism by arguing that it was not only consistent with the Sharia but was a valuable complement to it.

Sufi mystics used classic techniques of posture, breathing, meditation, music, and dance to induce states of extraordinary awareness that they regarded as closeness to God. In their philosophical writings they emphasized love and cosmic unity, even posing Jesus as the ideal Sufi. Like the Sharia, Sufism was populistic— it took little notice of traditional lines of privilege and was open to all who would pursue it. Unlike the ulema, who were oriented strongly toward the Sharia, the mystics tended to be tolerant of local cultures and customs, of human weakness, and of different levels of understanding. They viewed the Islamic concept of jihad, often translated in English as "holy war," as an inward struggle for enlightenment. Even so, Sufism had its outward, institutional side. After the tenth century, Sufis began to organize themselves into separate orders, or **tariqahs**. Each of these recognized a different line of communication of mystical knowledge, beginning with the private communications of Muhammad to certain followers, and going through a known line of teachers (*pirs*). One could become a pir only by studying under another recognized pir, so that the body of knowledge within each order was preserved and controlled. These Sufi orders had social and political uses, for they often became the organizational cores of guilds, young men's military clubs, or even some governmental organizations. One ambitious caliph, shortly before the Mongol invasions, even sought to restore the power of the caliphate through the judicious use of Sufi tariqahs.

Because of Sufism's tolerance, its association in folk religion with local "saints" and their tombs, and its abuse by wandering charlatans or extremists who considered themselves outside the Sharia, the ulema often took a dim view of Sufism. However, despite occasional outbursts of anti-Sufi reaction, as in the thirteenth century, Sufism was established as legitimate by the Sharia principle of consensus. Some ulema scholars were Sufi pirs themselves, and Sufism came to dominate the inward side of religious life in Islam, especially among the Sunnis. The personal appeal of Sufism supplemented the social appeal of the Sharia and contributed greatly to Islam's spread as a religion, and thus indirectly to the political sway of Islam. Furthermore, Sufism remained another potential counterbalance to the outward authority of any "Islamic" government.

ISLAM AND RADICAL POLITICS

Muhammad's ideal of religiously based law and government contained the seeds of religious support for the status quo, and also for religious opposition to it. The tradition of religious opposition is represented in one way by the ulema, and in quite another by the many radical movements in Islam's history. It is not possible to mention all the major movements that have arisen in Islam, but a few examples will suffice for illustration: the Kharijites, the Ismailis, the Sudanese Mahdi, Twelver Shiism, and the Muwahiddun movement.

The Kharijites

Islam's first civil war began with an insurrection of Egyptian soldiers who murdered the caliph Uthman and justified the act with the accusation that he had departed from Islam and was therefore a usurper. Ali's supporters accepted this line of reasoning, while his opponents accused him of condoning the murder of a believer and of attempting to disrupt the community. When Ali agreed to submit the issue to arbitration, his most extreme supporters turned against him to become Kharijites ("seceders"). The Kharijites embodied a radically anarchistic interpretation of Islam, in which personal piety was held to be not only the sole measure of a person's right to lead the community, but the only criterion for membership in the Umma itself. Thus, the impious Uthman was not only a false caliph, but an unbeliever falsely professing Islam; it was therefore the duty of a believer to kill him. In Kharijite eyes, anyone who had committed a "grave" sin was excluded from the Umma, and the most extreme Kharijites did not hesitate to kill non-Kharijites indiscriminately when the occasion presented itself. Even among the Kharijites themselves, on principle no leader was to be trusted, and their "caliph" could be deposed for the slightest transgression. Ali found it necessary to suppress the Kharijites by force, and he was eventually assassinated by one of them. There were more than a score of Kharijite rebellions during Ali's and Muawiyah's reigns, and small Kharijite communities have continued to exist down to the present. In their extreme approach to the issue of piety versus political order, the Kharijites severely crippled their own political strength and assured themselves a marginal role in Islamic society.

Ismailis and Qarmatians

The Shia went in a direction opposite to that of the Kharijites by elevating the charismatic leader to an exalted status, the Ismaili Shia going to the furthest extreme. Their central belief was that a highly esoteric knowledge of the all-important inner meaning of Muhammad's teachings was transmitted through secret communication from the Prophet to certain elect followers. The Ismailis gave rise to a number of movements, but none more fascinating than the **Qarmatians**. Originating in the desert between Syria and the Iraq in the late ninth century, the movement designated its leader as an emissary of God. The Qarmatians were dedicated to the overthrow of the wealthy and privileged, and the Bedouins and peasants who joined the sect apparently held all goods in common. After its suppression by the Abbasids, the movement reappeared in Bahrain, where it became established as an egalitarian, communistic state that lasted well into the eleventh century. It is said that the Qarmatians spurned the Sharia and orthodox forms of worship, and that one of their leaders who was thought to be the Mahdi, or the Muslim messiah, set himself above Muhammad (this, however, may be hostile propaganda). In any case, the Qarmatians seem to have regarded other Muslims as unbelievers, and in 930 they succeeded in temporarily abducting the Black Stone from the shrine at Mecca, on the grounds that it was an object of idolatry.

The Mahdi

The Qarmatians were by no means the only Muslims to believe in a Mahdi. Running sporadically throughout Islam is a chiliastic orientation, which holds that the world will eventually be delivered from its wickedness into an age of justice and piety, and the wicked will suffer vengeance from the righteous. The idea of a deliverer, or Mahdi, appears repeatedly in this chiliastic thinking. Of the many persons hailed as Mahdis, one of the most recent and striking examples is the Sudanese Mahdi of the late nineteenth century. Arising in opposition to the inroads of the modernizing Egyptian ruler Ismail, whose stated intention was to make Egypt part of Europe (and the Sudan part of Egypt), the Sudanese Mahdi drove the Egyptians out of the Sudan and preached a program of Islamic moral reform, not only for the Sudan but for all Islam. The Mahdi appointed his own caliph. Publicized among pilgrims at Mecca, his program seemed to many Muslims an attractive alternative to the weakened and discredited Ottoman leadership, until the British finally succeeded in crushing the movement in the 1890s.

Twelver Shiism

Of all the Shia movements, Iranian "Twelver" Shiism has the greatest contemporary relevance. Although it shares with the other forms of Shiism a basic emphasis on esoteric knowledge vouchsafed through the lineage of the Prophet, Twelver Shiism has shown itself to be a persistent factor in the political arenas of the Middle East, alternating between active and passive political activity. Whereas the Ismaili Shia held substantial power only during the Fatimid reign, the Twelver

Shia have held dynastic power a number of times, always in the area of present-day Iran and Iraq.

As a consequence of its substantial dynastic experience, Twelver Shiism has developed elaborate doctrines regarding the relationship between faith and the state and between the ulema and the governor. These theories saw contemporary expression during the "Tobacco riot" protests against the Qajar dynasty near the turn of this century, during the nationalist protests against the shah of Iran in the immediate aftermath of World War II, and most recently in the successful movement against the shah and in the design and implementation of an Islamic republic in Iran. Recent scholarship indicates that a critical turning point in the movement against the shah was Ayatollah Khomeini's successful invocation of the activist symbols of Twelver Shiism, thus effectively transforming Iranian Shia religious activity from quiet protest to political confrontation. In so doing, Ayatollah Khomeini of necessity invoked symbols and myths from the earliest days of Shiism, thus showing anew the relevance of the past to the present.

The Muwahiddun Movement

In Arabia during the late eighteenth century, a former Sufi teacher, Muhammad Ibn Abd-al-Wahhab, came under the influence of the conservative Hanbali school of Sunni Muslim thought, which rejected the role of ulema consensus in the interpreting of the Sharia. He called for the purification of Islam from the influence of evil innovations, which he believed were responsible for the decadence of the Ottoman world. With the aid of Ibn Saud, a local ruler who had converted to the movement, Ibn Abd-al-Wahhab set about to promote an extremely puritanical reform of Islam, which opposed all forms of Sufism and pre-Islamic custom and denounced most Muslims as idolators and infidels to be killed. Even after decades of Ottoman attempts to suppress the movement, Ibn Saud's grandson was able to seize Mecca and Medina, to destroy many of Islam's holy shrines, and to massacre the residents of these cities. The movement was temporarily suppressed in 1818, only to reappear in the twentieth century, again championed by members of the house of Saud. This "Unitarian" or **Muwahhidun** movement (a designation preferred by its followers over the more frequently encountered term, **Wahhabi**) was to become the foundation of the modern state of Saudi Arabia.

Thus the deep-lying conservatism of contemporary Saudi Arabia, far from being a continuation of some ancient local heritage as Westerners often assume, is actually the result of a relatively recent political-religious movement that by usual Muslim standards can only be regarded as unusually conservative and puritanical.

As these examples show, Islamic political-religious movements have a long history and can take many forms. Like similar movements in Christianity, they tend to adopt a "restitutionist" outlook—that is, they see themselves as restoring the original purity of the religion. The exact nature of that restoration, of course, tends to be partly a projection of the values of the reformers. Despite their unswervingly religious tone, such movements tend to display an acute consciousness of social problems, and to support political programs—some more practical than others—to remedy them. Some such movements bear significant political fruit, as in the case of Muwahhidun influence in Saudi Arabia. The sociology of religion shows that such religious movements often center around charismatic leaders who are thought to have special knowledge of transcendent order and purpose, and they often arise in times of cultural, social, political, and economic upheaval. It should not be surprising, then, if the close of the twentieth century sees a succession of charismatic religious movements within Islam, propounding various avenues toward the revitalization of the faith, and providing the vehicles for an assortment of social and political reforms. We shall have more to say about Islamic revivalist movements in Chapter 7.

DIVERSITY IN ISLAMIC POLITICAL THOUGHT

The Ayatollah Ruhollah Khomeini, leader of Iran's 1979 revolution, was quoted as saying, "We Muslims are of one family even though we live under different governments and in various regions." While the statement is an accurate reflection of the Muslim ideal of a united Umma, it should not be taken to mean that Islam represents a single, monolithic bloc with a fixed perspective on every significant issue. The recent upsurge of Islamic revival can only be expected to revitalize discussion and controversy among Muslims on the many issues that have always occupied the dialectic of Islamic thought. It is not easy to say, once and for all, what constitutes the Islamic vision of society, law, and government. Almost from its beginning, Islam has had its factions, particularly the Sunnis and the Shia. It has manifested an inward, mystical side as well as an outward set of codes and institutions. Muslims have tried to mediate between the heritage of Middle Eastern civilization, with its despotism and social privilege, and the principles of social equality enunciated in the Koran. Islamic civilization has been deeply influenced in various times and places by diverse cultural traditions, secular philosophies carried on from the Greeks, the aristocratic high culture of the royal courts, and the folk practices that preceded Islam and were independent of formal theology. Cosmopolitan and universalistic in its core outlook, Islam has had to deal with those who chose not to join the brotherhood of Islam. Each one of these conflicts has engendered not one but numerous solutions, depending on historical circumstance.

Yet it would be misleading, despite the change and adaptability of Islam, to see it as entirely amorphous or plastic, lending itself indifferently to every possible interpretation. Throughout the Islamic dialogue run certain recurrent themes that have their roots in the fundamental principles laid out in Muhammad's ministry. One of these is the interdependence of religion and the sociopolitical order, which is built more deeply into Islam than in most world religions. It would be harder for a serious Muslim to accept the separation of church and state than for a traditional Christian, even though the possibility of such a separation was suggested by Egyptian President Sadat's admonition that there should be "no religion in politics, and no politics in religion." Furthermore, Muslim law involves a detailed pattern of everyday life that regulates such matters as alcohol consumption and marriage. Such personal moral regulations existed more informally in traditional Christianity, but in Islam they are part of a literate tradition that will be relatively difficult to change or to separate from political issues. The Sharia is not easily circumvented;

strictly speaking, it is open only to interpretation, not legislation. The forces that gave the Sharia and the ulema such independence in the past will probably continue to insure Islam's role as an active challenge to the political status quo. Westerners observing the dialogue in contemporary Islamic political thought may mistakenly assume that Islam is "waking up" and examining these issues critically for the first time, but nothing could be further from the truth. Whatever the solutions toward which Muslims move, they can be expected to show the influence of previous dialogue within the tradition, a dialogue that will continue to allow for diverse possibilities.

WESTERN IMPERIALISM, 1800–1914

Imperialism is a familiar word that seems at first to have a clear and straightforward meaning, but on closer inspection its meaning becomes blurred and indistinct. It may mean any one of three relationships in which a relatively powerful country dominates the political, economic, or cultural affairs of a weaker one. In political imperialism, the powerful country controls the major governmental decision making of the weaker, either directly or by proxy through pliant, cooperative officials of the weaker country. Economic imperialism denotes a situation in which a weaker country becomes dependent on stronger countries for income. Cultural imperialism means a situation in which a weaker country adopts the language, manners, and lifestyle of the stronger.

All three kinds of imperialism occurred in the Middle East in the nineteenth century. It is difficult to assess the full consequences of these relationships since many aspects of them have not yet been fully played out and are still active today, but most writers feel that the negative effects of imperialism outweigh the positive. The study of imperialism, however, contains many difficulties in concept, definition, and measurement, and a final assessment is far from certain. For example, it is often difficult to say whether certain commercial transactions between weak and powerful countries benefit only the powerful or whether they work to the mutual benefit of both. And while a weaker, less-developed country may chafe over being dependent on a stronger one, its very dissatisfaction may spur it to make some positive reforms that it might not otherwise have made. The effects of imperialism on the weaker country may be shallow or deep. One country may survive a period of imperial stewardship and keep most of its social, cultural, and economic fabric intact. Imperial domination in such a case is only a kind of veneer. In other cases, imperial domination may deeply disrupt a country's social, economic, and political structures.

Nationalism, like imperialism, is another term that most people understand immediately, but on closer study find difficult to apply exactly. Nationalism is not just a matter of simple patriotism born of deep loyalty to an ethnic group, religion, homeland, leader, or set of institutions, although nationalist movements frequently contain a mixture of all these elements. Nationalistic movements give the appearance of solidity because they are often bound together by resentment toward the imperial power. Once the imperial power is removed, however, the seemingly solid and cohesive nationalist movement often disintegrates into perhaps scores of factional conflicts. We must study such root factions and forces if we are to gain a deeper understanding of a particular country or region.

In this chapter we shall examine how European imperialist powers penetrated the Middle East in the nineteenth century, just before the various nation-states in the region emerged. The Europeans did so in a series of powerful, deep-reaching thrusts, and we shall examine how certain areas responded to such battering.

SETTING THE STAGE

For thousands of years, most areas of the world were fairly equal in technology and economic well-being. Major inventions and technological innovations occurred at irregular intervals and in widely separated regions. An innovation that arose at a certain time or in a certain region had little influence on a technology that was being developed in another place or time. It took centuries, even millennia, for ideas and innovations to become uniformly diffused over the large areas of Asia, Europe, and the Middle East. Regions that were late to adopt a particular innovation or bit of technology from abroad had a comfortably long time in which to achieve parity with other regions before the next innovation came along.

During the period from about A.D. 1400 to 1700, however, a set of institutions and cultural forms was developed in Europe that promoted and regularized the flow of innovations. The most important advances occurred in organization and administration, weaponry, and communications. The process of how these innovations were accepted and how a continuing need for them was institutionalized is still not well understood. The result, however, is clear: Technical innovation became a continuous, irreversible, accelerating process. The process of regaining parity because of slow diffusion was at an end; Western Europe achieved technological dominance over the rest of the world, and other regions had no time to catch up.

It is difficult to say just when the West began to penetrate the Middle East or when it finally achieved political and economic dominance. One very important date, however, is 1498. It was in this year that the Portuguese navigator Vasco da Gama sailed around the southern tip of Africa to India, thus opening an important new trade route to the East. Although Europeans had gradually taken control of the Mediterranean sea trade for the past two hundred years, the opening of this new ocean route to India now assured them of total control over most of the world's maritime trade. The Middle Eastern overland trade routes began to decline. European control of the Mediterranean had already begun to shift the middleman functions from the Arabs to the Venetians and Genoese. Furthermore, Western technical and manufacturing innovations were resulting in the production of better products. As a consequence, Middle Eastern handicraft production, especially that found along the south and east Mediterranean coasts, also began to decline. These developments tore wide rents in the economic and social fabric of the region. Middle Eastern handicraft production was loosely organized in guilds—groups of craftsmen whose taxes provided a source of revenue for the various local governments, and whose presence contributed vitally to the social life of the area. Many of the ulema were either guild members or were supported by guilds. Therefore, a decline in the well being and consequent leadership role of the religious establishment directly followed the decline in handicraft industries. European dominance in commerce and production was accompanied by advances in military technology. European armies became powerful instruments of national will. After centuries of successful expansion, the Ottoman Empire began to lose territory to the Europeans.

Some writers claim that the Europeans' technological superiority also gave them a sense of moral superiority. While this may or may not be true, Europeans, in their quest for control of the Middle East, often clothed their political and economic motives in the vestments of religion. A belief in the inherent decadence and wickedness of Islam provided generations of Europeans with a strong rationale for imperialistic ventures in the Middle East, and this belief had a strong impact on the various cultures with which they associated.

THE OTTOMANS

By 1800, the decline of the Ottoman Empire was well under way and was to accelerate over the next hundred years. Western technology and military power were having an increasingly powerful impact. The Ottoman elite, long used to thinking that Western knowledge was not worth having, realized that it could no longer maintain its sense of superiority. An early sign of this change of attitude is the so-called Tulip Period (1718–1730), during which the Ottoman elite succumbed to a fad for everything Western. It built French-style pleasure palaces, wore Western clothes, sat on Western chairs, and cultivated Western gardens. It developed a mania for tulips and sent the price of tulip bulbs to absurd heights, high offices being sold for particularly exotic strains.

Aside from these extravagances, the period also saw the tentative beginnings of a new intellectual atmosphere; previously rejected reforms were now being seriously entertained. Most of them were shallow and aimed only at making institutions in the existing framework—especially the military—more effective. Selim III (1789–1807) attempted more fundamental reforms; and while most of these failed or were partially successful, they did lay the groundwork for later reforms in the nineteenth century. Once antireformist resistance was overcome, particularly that from the traditional military corps (the Janissaries), reform activity quickened, culminating in the **Tanzimat** period. The Janissaries represented the most important group of the nonmodernized army. They viewed the building of a modern army and bureaucracy as a threat to their power and, therefore, were at the forefront of the coalition resisting reform. But Sultan Mahmud II (1808–1839) cleverly built a new coalition loyal to him and had the Janissaries killed when they rebelled in 1826. This event is called the "Auspicious Incident" because it allowed the sultan to initiate a period of significant reform. The Tanzimat period is the name given to the reform period.

The Tanzimat Period (1839–1876)

The Tanzimat reforms were achieved with no clearly defined master plan other than a mostly unstated desire for greater government centralization. During previous centuries, the empire had expanded successfully by means of policies that favored extreme decentralization. By giving local governments large measures of autonomy, the millet system had kept the provinces reasonably satisfied. However, the military in remote areas had begun to look more to its own interests than those of the empire. Within limits, local authorities had the power to tax the population as they saw fit, as long as they remitted a negotiated amount to the central government; the sultan consequently had little control over the size of the royal treasury. As the empire declined and the booty of conquest stopped flowing into the capital, the Ottoman sultans tried to make up the difference by increasing taxes. However, the provincial authorities, having become used to self-rule for several generations, felt no great loyalty to the sultans and firmly resisted them. The sultans therefore saw that it was crucial to reorganize the empire around a strong central authority.

The Tanzimat reforms were many and far-reaching. Ministries were established to impose uniform regulations all over the empire. The military was completely reorganized along Western lines, and its incentive system was restructured to create greater commitment to the empire. The tax collection system was streamlined to allow revenues to flow directly to the royal treasury; local governments had their powers reduced.

Although many Tanzimat reforms failed and many others did not work out exactly as intended, they marked a turning point in Ottoman history. And although the empire continued to lose territory in the nineteenth century, the reforms were a sign of considerable lingering vitality. The Ottoman Empire was far from being the "sick man of Europe," as was said at the time and as was commonly believed into this century. To be sure, the empire was beset by internal and external difficulties of massive proportions, but there was also substantial positive change. The entrenched powers were understandably opposed to the reforms, but in time they were either accommodated or suppressed. Modern organizational forms and military technology spread to other areas, especially in the areas of communications and education.

Although the reforms' impact on cultural life was not a central concern during the early years of the Tanzimat period, they had a pervasive and enduring result. Many reforms required that administrators undergo specialized training and education. A new generation of technocrats arose who began to respect the West, for it was there that the needed knowledge was stored. Along with technical knowledge, this new class also absorbed the political philosophies of nationalism and democracy. The lack of qualified personnel within the empire, and the increasing encroachments of European governments and commercial interests, also brought an influx of powerful and active Europeans to the center of the empire.

The Tanzimat reforms were surrounded by international intrigue. England, France, and Russia (and later Germany) had vital interests in the Middle East which they tried to protect and enlarge. For most of the nineteenth century, the Ottoman Empire had to defend itself against European powers who were pushing and shoving among themselves for competitive advantage. Europe generally did not want to see the Ottoman Empire collapse; the scramble for spoils afterward would have certainly ended in a blood bath and much destruction. So, first one European power and then another supported the empire. But while the Europeans wished the Ottoman Empire a long life, they did not want to see it strong. On the contrary, they chipped away at its edges and blunted many of the effects of the Tanzimat reforms. There is no question that nineteenth-century Ottoman administration was corrupt and inept, but it is questionable whether a smoothly functioning modern organization would have done much better. The European powers had the empire pinioned. The Tanzimat reforms were a significant attempt to adapt to technological realities, and they represented a skillful attempt to resolve the empire's internal conflicts while playing off European interests. But in the end, the Ottomans could not escape the debilitating entanglements imposed on them by Westerners.

As the European powers increased their leverage, responsible parties in the empire grew increasingly dissatisfied with the course taken by the sultan and his inner circle. Various changes of policy were demanded, the most important being representation in legislative bodies, the adoption of a constitution, and the formation of an Ottoman ideology. Some favored a wholesale adoption of European ways, some sought a return to a past era of Islamic purity, and others advocated a host of intermediate positions. The restive attitude of the new technocrats and the role of the Western powers presented the sultan with a problem common to most reforming autocrats—how to control the demands of a new class of people who possess the technical knowledge on which the empire depended. Since the military and commercial presence of the competing Europeans prevented any return to past ways, and since the Europeans could not be expelled, a long series of struggles and partial accommodations took place; this process resulted in the granting of a constitution in 1876 by the shrewd Sultan Abdulhamit (1876–1909). The constitution was suspended shortly thereafter, but was reinstated with significant changes in 1908.

The Young Turk revolution (1908), which prompted the sultan to reconvene the legislative body and activate the constitution, had its ideological roots in various sources of discontent. A significant pan-Islamic and then pan-Ottoman movement, supported by the sultan, arose in the last third of the nineteenth century. The pan-Islamic movement championed the rights of all Muslims. The pan-Ottoman movement was broader; it called for more or less equal rights for all (including non-Muslim) subjects of the empire. But these movements contained many contradictions. Increasingly, waves of ethnic and geographical nationalism developed in reaction to Ottoman hegemony at the same time the sultan was reaffirming the equality of all his subjects. This led to discontent among the military forces who were asked to support the call for equality while being attacked by the supposed beneficiaries of the call. The ideological reaction was pan-Turkism, the notion that the ethnic identity of the empire deserved first consideration. Turkish greatness and the virtues of the Turkish people were celebrated in a large number of literary works.

By the turn of the century, the calls for a Turkish nation, military discontent, millet terrorism, and European pressures put Sultan Abdulhamit in an increasingly defensive position. He responded with many repressive measures. He paralyzed the bureaucracy by insisting on personally approving the smallest changes in policy. Finally, a financial crisis sparked a widespread revolt, and the revolution of 1908 forced the sultan to agree to demands for a constitution and representation.

The period after World War I was particularly devastating for the empire. The positive effects of some of the modernizing reforms had been undone by a series of crippling conflicts. Furthermore, the Ottoman Empire had aligned itself with the Central Powers during the war; when they were defeated, the empire was dismembered. The Allied forces divided the empire among themselves and imposed a particularly harsh rule on Turkey. But the Turkish nationalist forces who had been successful in 1908 rose to defend the homeland. Led by Kemal Ataturk, they repelled the Europeans and established an independent Turkish state. A remarkable series of reforms followed that would ultimately transform and secularize Turkey.

EGYPT

Long-standing corruption and generally ineffective rule had led to centuries of decay in Egypt. But the power of this weak Ottoman province was to change markedly during the nineteenth century. For the Ottomans of the nineteenth century, Egypt was something to be both feared and imitated.

In the last decade of the eighteenth century, the French were looking on Egypt with increased interest largely because of their struggle with the British. Egypt could be France's granary, and its possession could control Middle Eastern military and commercial traffic, providing a base from which to threaten the British in India. Napoleon invaded Egypt in July 1798, and with remarkable ease destroyed the Mameluk forces who ruled Egypt under loose Ottoman control. Napoleon presented himself to the Egyptians, and especially the ulema, as a liberator from foreign rule. But his call for cooperation went unheeded, and he was forced to quell a rebellion in Cairo in October 1798.

As all rulers of Egypt knew, control of the Levant was vital to Egyptian security. Consequently, Napoleon invaded Palestine and Syria in 1799. He met with failure, however, as Ottoman forces halted the French advance and the British navy attacked the French fleet. Since the security of Egypt could not be maintained, Napoleon quickly reassessed his position and quit Egypt in August 1799. The last French forces withdrew by 1801.

The brief French presence in Egypt gave advance warning that European powers would be drawn into Middle Eastern affairs on a much larger scale than before. It also served as a lesson to the Ottoman rulers and to the future Egyptian ruler, **Muhammad Ali (Mehemet)**, that European organizational and technical skills were superior to those of the Ottoman Empire—so superior that the rulers would have to adapt quickly if the empire was to remain secure.

Muhammad Ali had fought against the French in Syria. Born in Albania, and serving in the Ottoman army, this "selfish, illiterate genius" slowly eliminated his Ottoman rivals in Egypt and assumed control in 1805. He was to rule Egypt until his death in 1849. The lessons of French military superiority were not lost on him. He also realized that the key to building a similar kind of force required a fundamental reordering of the Egyptian economy; the material requirements of a strong military depended on an economy that could supply the needed goods. Although officially confirmed as governor in 1806, it was only after beating back a halfhearted British invasion in 1807 and massacring the last serious Mameluk rivals to power in 1811 that Muhammad Ali achieved a secure hold in Egypt. He then began in earnest to modernize Egypt's military. Egyptians were sent to France to learn modern military technology; and foreign advisors, particularly French, were brought to Egypt. Technical knowledge was diffused throughout Egypt by means of training institutes and translations of technical treatises.

Because a strong military was necessary for retaining and expanding power, much of the early effort was directed to meeting its basic needs. An army of over 100,000 men, if it were to be modern, needed munitions, communication systems, clothing, and food. Since there was no established industrialist class in Egypt, the government financed and managed its own factories. European industrialists and financiers were invited to provide capital and expertise to supplement the effort. In addition, Egyptian soldiers—drafted into military service in 1823 for the first time in centuries—were "forced" to learn technical skills. To guard against foreign domination of key positions, European factory managers and technical personnel were required to train their Egyptian counterparts.

To mount this ambitious drive, the government needed a strong financial base. The 1811 massacre of the Mameluks gave the state control of their vast land holdings. All land rights were subsumed by the government, and the system of tax administration was altered. The traditional system had allowed local leaders to pay a sum to the government in return for the right to tax the **fellahin** (peasant); under the revised system, the government collected the taxes directly. The government also assumed control of most agricultural marketing, especially export crops. These policies increased revenues, lessened the power of reactionary local leaders, and partially circumvented an Anglo-Ottoman treaty that limited import and export taxes to 3 percent.

Long-staple cotton was introduced to the Nile Delta in 1821. Although this superior strain of cotton stimulated local textile production, it also tied Egyptian economic fortunes to the vagaries of the international market. Cotton soon became Egypt's leading export, accounting for 75 percent of all receipts by 1860. The Delta, capable of producing a food surplus from a variety of crops, was transformed into a cotton monoculture designed to sustain the textile mills of England. Egyptian dependence on cotton earnings forced more and more land to be turned over to its production, and the country that Napoleon had seen as a granary for France was now forced to import food.

Muhammad Ali grew increasingly independent of the Ottoman authorities. The empire saw little harm in this during the early years of his rule. Before Muhammad Ali, Egypt had been a corrupt and militarily weak entity and of little value beyond the taxes paid by Cairo to the Ottomans. Under him, Egypt seemed to be undergoing constructive change and developing a credible military force. Muhammad Ali's armies waged various campaigns under the Ottoman banner, the most important being the successful campaigns against the Wahhabis, the conservative expansionist tribal movement in Arabia.

Muhammad Ali's independent actions finally led to a crisis in 1832. Under the pretext of insufficient payment for Egyptian aid in the empire's unsuccessful attempts to stem the Greek rebellion, Muhammad Ali invaded and occupied Syria—making Egypt an all but independent political and military force. In 1838, he declared his intention to become king of Egypt. The antiquated military force that the empire sent to displace the Egyptians from Syria was no match for

Muhammad Ali's modern troops. After defeating the empire's forces, he toyed with the idea of invading Anatolia proper, but European interests, especially the British, defused the crisis. The British did not want to see Egypt, an ally of France, grow powerful; nor did they relish the possibility of Russia dominating a weakened Ottoman Empire. When the Ottoman Sultan Mehmut II died in the midst of the crisis, it seemed that Russian influence in the imperial court would be expanded significantly. The admiral of the Ottoman navy sailed the fleet to Alexandria to be put in the service of Muhammad Ali rather than run the risk of having the fleet controlled by the infidel Russians. As it was, the empire weathered this "Russian threat."

British and Ottoman pressures effectively halted the reformist and expansionist actions of the Egyptian ruler. Muhammad Ali retained his role as governor of Egypt and was given the right to hereditary rule, but he lost much in the bargain. He relinquished the Ottoman fleet, pulled out of Syria, reduced the size of the army from 130,000 men to 18,000, and accepted the 1838 Anglo-Ottoman Commercial Code. The 1838 Commercial Code enlarged the preferential treatment afforded to foreigners doing business in the Ottoman Empire and made state monopolies illegal. The aggressive economic policies of the preceding thirty years had changed the face of Egypt. Some ventures had been successful, but many operations were wasteful and inefficient. Although Egypt may not have been able to sustain these new ventures at such a pace, it was unquestionably shaking off its moribund status of the previous centuries. Acceptance of the 1838 Commercial Code both sealed the fate of Egypt's economic experiment, and assured foreign control of most Egyptian commerce and industry.

The story behind the building of the Suez Canal under the direction of the remarkable Ferdinand de Lesseps illustrates European dominance in a spectacular fashion. The terms of the contract to build the canal (set in 1854), the methods used to construct the canal, and the subsequent European actions serve as a model of imperial deceit and connivance at its worst. Essentially, Egypt supplied all of the labor (about 20,000 men) and gave the shrewd de Lesseps free access to the Egyptian treasury through various contract provisions, bribes, and bullying. In return, Egypt retained seven-sixteenths ownership but surrendered most of its rights to the profits until the canal was completed (1869). Other smaller ventures proposed by Europeans and accepted by the weakened heirs to Muhammad Ali's governorship were similarly one-sided. The granting of concessions to Europeans ended in a financial crisis that opened the way to total European control.

The financial chaos that engulfed Egypt in the 1870s was not, however, due exclusively to European chicanery. The Civil War in the United States brought a trebling of cotton prices and also deprived English mills of cotton grown in the Southern states. The Egyptian governor of this period, Ismail Pasha, in an attempt to Europeanize Egypt, constructed a large system of canals, railroads, bridges, harbors, and telegraph facilities, and he brought over a million acres of land back into cultivation. He did much of this on the assumption that cotton prices would remain high. Many of the contracts with foreign construction firms were made with highly unfavorable terms for Egypt, the Egyptian administration being very corrupt. The spending extravaganza, coupled with the end of the U.S. Civil War and the consequent dive of cotton prices, put Egypt in an impossible position. The external debt of Egypt had reached over £70 million by the time the Suez Canal opened, as opposed to about £3 million six years earlier. Thus, an increasing proportion of the government's revenue went directly to foreign debt repayment—about 60 percent in 1875. In that year the British government bought the Egyptian shares in the Canal for £4 million, in what amounted to a liquidation sale. Egypt was now bankrupt and faced with foreign ownership of the Suez Canal. By 1876 British and French officials were overseeing Egyptian and Ottoman finances in order to protect European interests.

To improve Egypt's finances, the puppet governor Tawfiq imposed an austere fiscal policy that led to an army rebellion in 1882. This gave the British ample excuse for drastic action to protect their investments. At the "official request" of Tawfiq, British forces invaded Egypt, crushed the rebellion, and settled in for the next seventy-five years. The official British position in Egypt was awkward, however. Although they had been invited to enter at the governor's request, they nevertheless owned the Suez Canal, which in turn was situated in a province of the Ottoman Empire. This ambiguous situation was to persist until Egypt was declared a British protectorate in 1914.

Britain had an excellent reason for wanting to control Egypt: The Suez Canal shortened the route between England and India by 4,000 miles. The occupation of Egypt, however, burdened the English with the usual geopolitical anxieties. The security of the Red Sea, and thereby the Arabian peninsula, became vital. The Levant and the Sudan also had to be dealt with if security was to be assured. The latter two problems were solved by convincing the Ottoman sultan to cede the Sinai peninsula to Egypt (1906) and by establishing a joint Anglo-Egyptian force to reimpose rule over the Sudan (1898). Britain entered the twentieth century with a firm foothold in Egypt.

THE LEVANT

Muhammad Ali's control of the Levant during the 1830s forms a watershed in the history of the area. The reforms introduced and the subsequent European penetration have been aptly called "the Opening of South Lebanon." In the decades before the Egyptian incursion, the population of the interior, if not the coast, looked eastward when they were looking outside their immediate area at all. European trade had been on the decline, and Europeans were treated with a xenophobic hostility when they did manage to gain access to the area. The area had a relatively sparse population (about 1.3 million), rapacious Ottoman governors, and a highly insecure hinterland. However, the urban population, about half of the total, had learned to live with the situation by developing a relatively closed system of production and distribution.

The modernized, Western-oriented Egyptian army radically altered this situation. Security of travel was greatly enhanced; life in the cities became more secure; and, most important, a wave of European commercial interests quickly entered and dominated economic life. By the time of the Egyptian withdrawal, Syria was looking to the West for trade; the indigenous craftsmen had to shoulder the brunt of the change because their nonstandardized, low-quality, high-priced goods could no longer find a local market. This process continued after the Egyptian departure.

Western ascendancy was given a further boost in 1858 when the **Maronites** created a crisis in Lebanon by declaring it a republic. Under Ottoman rule, the Druze, Sunni Muslims, and Maronite Christians had achieved an uneasy balance. The Tanzimat declaration of equality for all non-Muslims in the empire had already aroused Muslim antipathy. In 1860 the situation worsened and erupted into large-scale religious massacres. Because they had long-standing interests there, the French landed troops under the pretext of giving aid to the Ottomans and calmed the situation. An autonomous Lebanon, limited to the mountains and not including the coastal areas, was established. A Catholic Christian governor was to administer the area and maintain a local militia. The Ottomans maintained only titular control and effectively abandoned the area. Thus the French, and a host of Christian missionaries, gained a base of operations in the Middle East.

THE ARABIAN PENINSULA

In the history of the world's major religions, circumstances occasionally allow strong revivalist movements to form and flourish. The Middle East in the nineteenth century provided the right circumstances for Islam. The **Sanussi** movement in Libya, the rise of the Mahdists in the Sudan, and the Wahhabi movement in Arabia were three of the most important.

Muhammad ibn Abd-al-Wahhab (1691–1787) spread his message during the latter part of the eighteenth century. He was convinced that the strict, austere Hanbali law was superior to the other three sanctioned Sunni schools of law, and that Islam had deviated from its true path. He criticized especially the Sufi (and pre-Islamic) custom of venerating saints by worshipping at their tombs, which he thought to be idolatry. Abd-al-Wahhab spread his word throughout the Najd region of Arabia; in time he converted a powerful tribal ruler, Ibn Saud, who spread the doctrine and his rule over great stretches of Arabia.

The Ottomans long had controlled the coastal Hijaz and the holy cities of Mecca and Medina. From there, Ottoman rule arched out over what is now Jordan and extended south to the al-Hassa area of Arabia on the Persian Gulf. It is likely that the Wahhabis would have been left undisturbed in the great desert areas if their religious beliefs had allowed them to adhere to geopolitical boundaries. But this was not to be the case. They declared that those who practiced the idolatry of saint worship were infidels and, as such, deserved death. By 1803 the grandson of Ibn Saud controlled the Hijaz, including Mecca and Medina. The tombs were destroyed, and many worshipers were put to death. The Ottoman authorities, of course, could not tolerate a renegade force holding two of the most holy cities of Islam, but lacked the means to expel them. It was not until Muhammad Ali consolidated his strength in Egypt that an attempt was made to beat back the Wahhabi movement. The first Egyptian forces were dispatched to Arabia in 1811; however, the armies of Ibn Saud were not pushed deep into the interior until the Egyptian campaign of 1818–1820.

For the remainder of the century the interior of Arabia passed back and forth between the authority of the Ottoman-backed Rashids and the forces of the Saud family. It was only in 1902 that a small band of Saudi forces raided Riyadh, the seat of Rashid power, and began to assume control of most of what is now Saudi Arabia—with the exception of the Hijaz, which remained under Ottoman control. Saudi power was more or less consolidated by the beginning of World War I.

Nineteenth-century European interests in the Arabian peninsula centered on trade and communications; therefore, they concentrated on securing the safety of the coastal areas. The British were seeking greater control in the area in order to defend India from possible encroachments by the French, Russians, and Germans.

Napoleon's invasion of Egypt in 1798 brought a swift reaction. In addition to Nelson's destruction of the French fleet off Alexandria, the British took Perim Island (1799), which lies between Africa and Arabia in the narrow southern inlet to the Red Sea. Because they lacked supplies, especially water, they were quickly forced to abandon the island and withdraw to Aden, a port area long known and used by the British in their East India dealings. The British reluctantly made Aden a permanent outpost as event after event dictated their presence; they would retain control of Aden until 1967.

What Westerners call the Persian Gulf (and the Arabs call the Arabian Gulf) came under British control with the taking of the Straits of Hormuz in 1622. (A glance at a map reveals that whoever controls the Straits of Hormuz controls all traffic in and out of the Gulf. Since at the present time a substantial percentage of the world's petroleum passes through the strait, the area is vital.) To the British in the seventeenth century, the security of the Straits of Hormuz and the ability to insure safe passage through the Gulf were important because the British needed a quick line of communications to India. The route around the Cape of Good Hope was long and risky, and the Red Sea was to be under uncertain Ottoman control until the British intervened in Egypt in 1882. The next best route from India to England was to sail to what is now Kuwait and then travel overland through Basra and Baghdad.

By the 1830s the British had largely suppressed piracy on the Persian Gulf through military forays and treaties with the coastal powers. Later in the century they thwarted other European trade schemes in the Middle East by entering into treaties with local rulers that prohibited trade or other dealings with any other foreigners without British approval. The most notable of these agreements was the one made with Kuwait in 1899.

In the nineteenth century, then, British Gulf policy changed from simply establishing a line of communications within the British Empire to defending it. British control of Egypt and the Suez Canal relieved them from having to penetrate the interior of Iraq in order to protect their communication lines. German influence in the Ottoman Empire gave them reason to go on the defensive. The Germans gained a concession in 1899 to build a railroad through Ottoman territories in the Middle East. By the beginning of World War I, the Constantinople-Baghdad portion of the line was complete. But by early 1900, the ruler of Kuwait, in accordance with the recent British treaty, had refused the Germans permission to build a railroad terminal on the Gulf.

Events, however, finally forced the British to push into Iraq. In 1907 petroleum was discovered in the Abadan area of Iran, and there was some evidence that nearby Iraq would hold equally important fields. Another chapter of Middle Eastern history was beginning to unfold.

IRAN

Although all of the nation-states in this area are special cases in many ways, Iran stands apart. Because of its political, social, and cultural differences, and because of its geographical position, Iran's relationship with the Middle East proper has waxed and waned over the centuries.

During the eighteenth and nineteenth centuries, Persia was subject to less European influence than Egypt or the Levant. European commercial interest, of course, had become well established during the preceding centuries, but the full-scale economic, military, and philosophical thrusts of the West had not yet penetrated to the heart of the Persian system. Yet Persia's nationalist sentiments—generally reactions against foreign domination that are expressed in mass movements—in some ways presaged those in other parts of the Middle East. Although the reasons for this presaging are not fully understood, it is clear that Persian nationalist reactions depended on an interplay of forces such as official social classes, power relationships designed to increase insecurity and mistrust, and the central place of the Shia clergy.

From Sassanian times on, the social structure of Iran consisted, with some exceptions, of four major groups: (1) the royal family, (2) the political and military bureaucracy, (3) the religious establishment, and (4) the masses. Although some outstanding individual cases helped promote a popular belief in easy social mobility, shifts from one class to another were relatively infrequent. Widespread belief in the possibility of upward mobility, of course, enabled the ruling class to promise the less fortunate a chance to enjoy a better life. But in such a system, downward mobility is just as possible; favored positions were therefore jealously protected. Desirable posts were usually procured by some form of money payment, or bribe, indicating that accumulated wealth was generally a prerequisite for entering and retaining a high position. Since the accumulation of wealth depended on having a good position, the system not only reduced mobility but promoted class tensions. The bureaucracy also suffered, since considerations of individual merit were often set aside. The shah presided over this system that was full of class rivalry and predatory competition. The ruling class could move social inferiors about with relative ease and frequency, as if they were chess pieces, thereby limiting any individual's or group's power and influence.

Iran had long had a Shia majority. Traditionally, the Shia had opposed any secular authority because of their belief that the betrayal of Ali had given rise to a series of illegitimate rulers. While waiting for the return of the Hidden Imam, who would set the world on the correct path again, the Shia believed that the clergy had an obligation to examine all secular actions and make them consistent with Islamic thought. Since interpreting the correct path of state and religious affairs depended on specialized scholarly wisdom and knowledge, a loose hierarchy of clerical authority developed in Iran that was lacking in Sunni Islam. Since most secular authorities are unwilling to submit to higher authorities, an understandable tension developed between government officials and clergy. And since the clergy had the ear of the masses, any secular ruler had to be careful and restrained in dealings with the clergy.

Bazaar merchants have traditionally been important sources of discontent and have led opposition movements in the Middle East, but in Persia they were subject to the same insecurities that shackled the bureaucrats and the military. The clergy (through their spokesmen, the **mujtahids**, who were learned religious leaders with successful ministries) was the only group not under the shah's direct control.

The Qajar Dynasty

The Qajar dynasty (1779–1925) came to power about fifty years after the fall of the Safavid Empire. At first, the Qajars were extremely brutal in their attempts to consolidate power. Once they had established a reasonable degree of control over the various tribes, however, they then had to face the emerging threat from the West. By the 1850s, two major Western actors—England and Russia—had forced Persia into the arena of Western politics. The British feared that a Russian advance southward would ultimately threaten India. The Russians had long desired access to the Indian Ocean.

The Qajars seem to have seen the need for radical bureaucratic and military reforms, but their actions were no more than superficial palliatives. Shah Nasiruddin's rise to power (1848–1896) roughly marks the beginning of the reform movement; the Persian elite began to realize that the Western powers could not be banished but would have to be accommodated. The last half of the nineteenth century saw numerous intrigues between the British, Russians, and occasionally the French, as they entered into agreements over their respective roles in Persia, broke the agreements, and then hammered out new ones. The shah, meanwhile, in order to maintain Persian independence, was attempting to play off one power against the other and create a stalemate between them.

To accomplish this, and to build up the treasury, the Qajar rulers during this period began to grant concessions to Europeans. In essence, a European adventurer-entrepreneur would pay a sum of money to obtain a monopoly in some sphere of economic activity. The concessionaire would then return home to sell shares in the new company to speculators and thereby turn a profit. The rulers granting these concessions welcomed European money because it absolved them from having to impose heavier taxes on an already restive population. They also hoped that they could check European power by granting concessions to individuals of different nationalities. The Qajars reasoned that the Europeans would see the need for political security and stability in Persia so as to protect profits, and they hoped that the Europeans would introduce some industrial development to boot. To be successful, such a policy called for a finely tuned balance of forces. The concessionaires, however, often played fast and loose with contracts, and the ruling elite were increasingly concerned with shoring up royal revenues.

The 1872 concession granted by the grand vizier to Baron Julius de Reuter, a British citizen, is a spectacular example of the sorry state of Qajar affairs. The concession gave de Reuter a monopoly over railways, mines (excepting precious metals and stones), irrigation construction, all future factories, telegraph lines, road construction, and (for twenty-five years) the proceeds of customs collections. In return, the royal purse was to be increased by a small flat payment and a share of the profits of the various ventures. In short, the country had been sold, and sold very cheaply. The reaction against this outrageous concession was swift in coming. Protests erupted from the Russians, members of the Iranian royal court, the clergy, and nationalistic groups. The combination of international pressure and internal discontent forced the shah to cancel the concession, basing this decision on a technicality.

This was not the end of concession granting, however. The British continued to make inroads, the most significant being the acquisition of the rights to form a national bank, to navigate the Karun River, and to run a tobacco monopoly. The tobacco concession (1890), following on the heels of the bank and river navigation concessions, was to be complete—from the growing of the tobacco to export sales. Again, Russian reaction was strongly negative. Internal reactions led by a domestic coalition (which was to surface periodically throughout the twentieth century) signaled the beginnings of the drive for a constitution.

Under the inspiration of the remarkable **Jemal al-Din al-Afghani**, who was active all over the Middle East as a proponent of pan-Islamic policies, a coalition was formed of merchants, clergy, and intellectuals, many of the latter having a Western orientation. The intellectuals and mujtahids were able to set aside their fundamental disagreements in the face of their common hatred of what they viewed as the selling of Persia. The Russian government gave material and moral support to the coalition.

As the dissatisfaction grew into a countrywide protest—ironically coordinated through the use of the British telegraph system—and tottered on the brink of revolution, it became clear that the reaction against the tobacco concession was part of a larger hatred toward all foreign concessions and, thereby, the policies of the Qajar regime. Facing the prospect of revolution, the shah canceled the tobacco concession in 1892.

The "tobacco riots" and the cancellation of the tobacco concession had far-reaching implications for the subsequent history of Persia. For the first time, a nationwide protest against the policies of the regime, spearheaded by the relatively independent and very powerful clergy, had immobilized the government. After many years of quietude the clergy took an active role. The internal coalition formed the backbone of the movements that later resulted in the granting of the 1906 constitution and the overthrow of the Pahlevi dynasty in 1978–1979. More immediate effects included a decade of Russian ascendancy in Persia, the slowing of concession granting to foreigners, and the beginnings of the same kind of disastrous debt policy that had brought so many woes to Egypt and the Ottoman Empire in previous decades.

The shah was forced to pay a sizable compensation to the tobacco concessioners. Because he lacked requisite funds, the British provided a loan. The Russians, fearing a reassertion of British influence, also provided loans, thereby tightening the financial noose. In this respect, Persia was closing the gap between it and other Middle Eastern countries by the beginning of the twentieth century. While Westernization had brought with it a few plusses, Iran received little true benefit from foreign intrusion due to the conditions of the intervention, the corrupt, obsolete government structure, and the relationship between the various social classes.

Further British inroads were made with the award of a petroleum concession in 1901, the discovery of petroleum in 1908, and the British government's purchase of most of the shares in the resulting oil company (later to become British

Petroleum) a few months before the beginning of World War I. The weakness of the Qajar dynasty, and growing fears of expansionist Germany, also led the British and Russians to formalize an often-breached agreement that divided Persia into spheres of influence: The Russians were to have the north and the British the south, with a neutral strip in between.

The Qajar dynasty limped along until the conclusion of World War I, but its power rested on a weak base. Riots in 1905–1906, led again by the mujtahids with the support of modernizers and merchants, forced the granting of a constitution (1906) and the formation of a consultative assembly, the Majlis. Although the assembly initiated a series of reforms, intrigues by the rulers and international powers, internal dissension within the Majlis, and economic recession militated against a full-blown democratic and modernizing movement.

During World War I the Allies viewed Persia as a vital conduit through which to supply materiel to Russia. Due to the success of the Russian Revolution of 1917, the Bolsheviks renounced the tsarist claims in the 1907 Anglo-Russian agreement. The British then moved northward and assumed almost total control of Persia. Shortly after this, they withdrew from the Caspian Sea area, and the Soviets invaded the port of Enzeli. The Iranian Soviet Socialist Republic of Gilan was then formed in 1920, but the Soviet Union withdrew its support for it less than a year later and the republic failed. In this chaotic swirl of events, Reza Shah came to power.

Reza Shah led the Russian-trained Cossack Brigade, one of the few, if not the only, effective military units in the Persian army. He assumed power on February 26, 1921, named himself commander in chief of the military, and appointed an intellectual ally as prime minister. As Reza Shah gathered more power, he dismissed the prime minister in 1923. In 1925 he ascended to the throne and took the ancient and kingly Persian name of Pahlevi.

Reza Shah was an extraordinary modernizer and autocrat who faced the formidable tasks of establishing internal order, lessening foreign domination, and establishing Iran as a modern nation. The Majlis continued to function under his rule (indeed, Reza Shah's taking of the Peacock Throne was confirmed by a vote of the Majlis and by an amendment to the constitution), but the Majlis failed to fulfill the hopes of those opposed to autocratic rule in that it merely rubber-stamped Reza Shah's policies rather than evolving into an independent legislative body. The shah promoted divisiveness among those on the periphery of power. This created insecurity, fragmented the opposition, and convulsed the machinery of government. Acting along the lines of Muhammad Ali in Egypt a century earlier and his contemporary Ataturk, the shah developed a series of reforms to lessen the power of the clergy and to increase his own. He also laid the foundation for a modern economy by constructing an improved communications network and by instituting educational reforms.

Because of the shah's flirtation with Germany during the 1930s, culminating in his refusal to join the Allied cause at the outset of World War II, the 1907 Anglo-Russian accord was renewed, the British protecting their petroleum interests in the South and the Russians controlling the North. Facing a serious challenge to his power and wishing to save the throne, Reza Shah abdicated to his son, Mohammed Reza Pahlevi, in 1941.

CONCLUSION

Nineteenth-century Middle Eastern history was dominated by the tidal wave of European power that swamped and distorted every society it touched. Although the procedures and timing of European penetration differed in the specific countries, there were some common features of this penetration throughout the region.

First, most Western inroads were made with reference to European geopolitical rivalries. It was not until the twentieth century that the Europeans (and the Americans) seriously considered the economic prizes to be gained from the Middle East. During the nineteenth century the various European powers generally tried to avoid the financial and political headaches associated with direct rule; rather, they sought to establish client relationships.

Second, the general process of Western dominance had a certain inevitability due to the technical superiority and advanced organizational structure of the West. The technical revolution had been largely institutionalized in the West after centuries of cultural and scientific preparation. Military might was the most obvious manifestation of this superiority, but it was perhaps no more important than the organizational and cultural modifications that supported the technical revolution.

Third, European involvement in Middle Eastern affairs dramatically disrupted the area's society and culture. Some countries attempted to adopt Western ways; others rejected all Western influence. All countries, however, generally recognized the technical superiority of the West and tried to avoid Western domination; however, they all failed. The peoples of the Middle East fought a rear-guard action; their policies and pronouncements tended to be protective, not affirmative. Much of the history of the Middle East in the twentieth century can be viewed as an unraveling of the consequences of nineteenth-century European domination.

THE RISE
OF THE STATE SYSTEM,
1914–1950

The period after World War I saw the decline of Western political hegemony in the Middle East. However, many events during the preceding decades paved the way for this development. For example, the defeat of the Russians by the Japanese in 1905 was greeted with much satisfaction in the non-European world. A Western power had been humiliated at last by an Asian power. The news of the Russian defeat, together with other events, provided a needed catalyst for action in the unsettled Middle East. In Persia, the revolts of 1905–1906 severely weakened the Qajar dynasty and resulted in the establishment of a consultative assembly. In Turkey, the Young Turk revolution of 1908 sealed the fate of the Ottoman rulers. In Egypt, an incident in 1906 sparked a nationalist movement.

Each change in Ottoman policy over the decade—from pan-Islam to pan-Turkism—had a strong impact on Arab lands. After 1908, the ethnic nationalism of the Turkish leaders became openly imperialistic. Under the millet system, an individual's nationality was not defined by geographic boundaries. An Ottoman Muslim could identify equally with all Muslims of the empire—members of his own millet. Ottoman Muslims did not consider themselves to be Turks, Iraqis, or Syrians: these words existed as historical terms or identified administrative districts. As pan-Ottomanism and then pan-Turkism weakened identification with the empire, and as Western influences filtered into the Middle East, the Arabs of the provinces began to search for a new set of symbols on which to base their identity. The Ottoman Middle East, then, was in a state of political and intellectual flux at the onset of World War I.

The strong ties between Germany and the Ottoman Empire that had developed over the preceding quarter century led to an alliance in war. The Allies had good reason to fear Ottoman entry into the war: The Ottoman military forces were reasonably strong and the truncated Ottoman Empire still posed a considerable threat to what the Allies, especially the British, perceived as their national interests. The Suez Canal and the petroleum fields of Persia were of particular importance.

Egypt was still nominally part of the Ottoman Empire until the outbreak of the war, even though British forces had occupied the country since 1882. Egypt was made a British protectorate in 1914, after England declared war on the Ottoman Empire. There was little fear for the security of Egypt from the west and south. Libya (then Tripolitania and Cyrenaica) had been invaded by the Italians in 1911 and declared a possession of Italy. However, the Italians faced continual tribal resistance, especially after their entry into the war on the Allied side prompted the Central Powers to aid the Libyan guerrillas. When members of the Sanussi, a largely rural religious movement, were beaten back after moving to attack Egypt, the fractious Libyan resistance became ineffective. The Sudan had been administered by the joint Anglo-Egyptian condominium since 1898–1899 and caused little concern.

The Arab lands of the Hijaz and (Greater) Syria posed the most significant threat to the security of Egypt and the Persian (Arabian) Gulf. Two basic concerns faced the Allies: the Ottoman military threat and the closely related, but distinct, question of the attitudes of the local Arab leaders.

The military concern was realized early on both the Egyptian and Persian Gulf fronts. By early 1915 Ottoman forces had reached the Suez Canal and Ottoman supporters had disrupted the flow of petroleum from Persia. There followed a long and bitter struggle by the British to beat back the enemy. After sustaining very heavy losses the British entered Baghdad in March 1917. The British also pushed through Palestine, taking Jerusalem in December 1917. An armistice was reached only in October 1918. By then the British had pushed toward Homs and Aleppo. The "sick man of Europe" had waged a brave and tenacious battle.

With the military balance in doubt until the end of the war, the Allies sought aid from every available quarter. This led to a series of secret agreements and overt pledges that helped swing the outcome in their favor; but these same pacts contained fundamental contradictions, some of which have not yet been resolved.

THE McMAHON-HUSEIN CORRESPONDENCE

At the onset of the war an immediate Allied concern was how the people in the Ottoman provinces would react to the coming call for a jihad against the Allies by the sultan-caliph. Obviously, an Arab revolt against the Ottomans would aid the Allied war effort in the Middle Eastern front. There were reasons to suppose that conditions were ripe for such a revolt. The key figure to be won over was Sherif Husein, sherif of Mecca and emir of the Hijaz. The British high commissioner in Egypt, Sir Arthur Henry McMahon, contacted Husein, hoping to persuade him to sever his already strained relationship with the Ottoman Empire.

The McMahon-Husein correspondence (July 14, 1915 to January 30, 1916) set the terms for an Arab revolt. In return for entering the war on the Allied side, Husein was assured that a large stretch of Ottoman-Arab territory would be made independent under his leadership at the conclusion of the war; it included the Hijaz and what now is Syria, Iraq, and Jordan. He had first demanded that other territories be included, but allowed his claims to lapse on what now is the non-Hijaz portion of Saudi Arabia, Lebanon, and areas extending northward into Turkey. The fate of Palestine was left somewhat ambiguous in the correspondence, and after the war the British seized this ambiguity to press their claim that Palestine was not part of the agreement.

Husein's silence to the call for a jihad was transformed into a call for an Arab revolt. Although the revolt did not produce anything resembling a mass movement, it brought relief to the Allies. The crack Ottoman troops stationed in the Yemen were isolated in Medina and between the Hijaz and British-dominated Aden, and the people of Syria found cause to retaliate against the brutality of their Ottoman rulers.

The British also made an agreement with Ibn Saud that recognized his rule in the non-Hijaz area of what is now Saudi Arabia and allowed for a formal recognition of Kuwait. The British also entered into agreements that essentially called for the Persian (Arabian) Gulf peoples to cooperate with the British without forcing them to take up arms in the actual conduct of the war.

British success in promoting the Arab revolt by promises of independence did not prevent them from completing negotiations with the French and the Russians (who later repudiated the tsarist claims after the 1917 revolution) that created a new division of Western influence in the Middle East. The Sykes-Picot Agreement (1915–1916) allowed the French control of the Levant coastal area and the right to oversee the interior of Syria. The British were to receive what is now most of Iraq and Jordan. Palestine was to become an international zone. The terms of this agreement were revealed to Husein by the Russians during the war, but the British managed to calm his fears by minimizing the document's importance. However, this agreement formed the basis of the postwar division of British and French areas of domination. The Allies entered into other agreements that defined areas of influence or rule throughout the rest of the region. As with the Sykes-Picot Agreement, the Allies were able to dictate terms in these agreements that would expand their influence after the war. These agreements were to cause much frustration and bitterness among the Arabs.

The Balfour Declaration

Although the disposition of Palestine was unclear under the McMahon-Husein agreement, it seemed most likely that it would become an independent Arab state. The Sykes-Picot Agreement called for Palestine to become internationalized. After the British issued the famous Balfour Declaration on November 2, 1917, the fate of Palestine remained unclear. The declaration, sent by Lord Balfour to Lord Rothschild, must be quoted in full:

> I have much pleasure in conveying to you on behalf of His Majesty's Government the following declaration of sympathy with Jewish Zionist aspirations, which has been submitted and approved by the cabinet:

> His Majesty's Government view with favor the establishment in Palestine of a National Home for the Jewish People, and will use their best endeavors to facilitate the achievement of this object, it being clearly understood that nothing shall be done which may prejudice the civil and religious rights of existing non-Jewish communities in Palestine, or the rights and political status enjoyed by Jews in any other country.

I should be grateful if you would bring this declaration to the knowledge of the Zionist Federation.

The carefully constructed ambiguity of the statement was designed to elicit Jewish support for the Allies without alienating the Arabs. It succeeded in the former but failed in the latter, and thus added another layer of misunderstanding to the growing dilemma.

Palestine, the Holy Land of the Bible, had always had Jews among its population. But it was not until the last two decades of the nineteenth century that substantial numbers emigrated to Palestine from Europe. Many European Jews were motivated by the ethnic nationalism that had spread throughout Europe in the nineteenth century and was now beginning to take hold in other areas. But wherever they lived, the Jewish people were a small minority, a minority that had frequently endured extreme physical brutality and systematic social and economic discrimination and persecution. While their situation was not always desperate in Christian Europe, it was always insecure. Whether or not the Jews could or should be assimilated into their European countries of residence, therefore, was a central question for Jewish leaders. Many of them began to believe that the Jews were entitled to self-determination. However, to enjoy this, the Jewish people would have to have their own political entity, a separate state. The trickle of Jews who settled in Palestine before the turn of the century came primarily from Russia and Poland (the great majority of Jewish emigres from these countries fled to Western Europe and the United States). Those who emigrated to Palestine did so for many reasons—religious, secular, socialistic, and personal. All, however, sought a better life.

The World Zionist Organization

The idea of creating a special homeland for the Jewish people was popularized by Theodor Herzl (1860–1904). After covering the Dreyfus trial (1895) as a correspondent, Herzl became convinced that as long as they remained a minority people, Jews would always suffer periods of deprivation. His book, *The Jewish State* (1896), aroused enough interest to warrant calling the first World Zionist Congress, which was held in Basel, Switzerland, in 1897. The congress created the World Zionist Organization and called for the formation of a Jewish homeland in Palestine. The movement spread quickly throughout Europe. However, Palestine had not been a unified area under the Ottomans; rather, it had been divided into two provinces, with the area around Jerusalem enjoying a special status.

During the nineteenth century, millions of Europeans were emigrating to new lands in various parts of the world; the Jewish call for a homeland in Palestine was therefore not unique in that regard. Zionist leaders, however, believed mistakenly that hardly any local people would be displaced since most of Palestine was relatively empty. Moreover, they believed that what people were there were of such a low culture that they could only benefit from contact with sophisticated Europeans.

The World Zionist Organization financed and organized a substantial wave of immigration into Palestine in the decade before World War I. By 1914, about 85,000 Jews were living in Palestine, three times the number that had lived there thirty years earlier; however, they constituted less than 15 percent of the total population. Jews were still a small minority even in Palestine, but they were a highly organized and growing minority. A settler's life was often difficult, and a number of settlements failed for lack of farming experience and because of harsh agricultural conditions and a host of other conditions. But the settlements generally succeeded. It should be remembered that, however loosely it was controlled, Palestine was still part of the Ottoman Empire, and the settlers were subject to Ottoman law and administration. For example, Ottoman law did not always allow noncitizens to own land. A complex system of third-party land ownership had to be worked out. Also, Russian Jews were often singled out for harsh treatment because Russia was an Ottoman enemy.

With the beginning of World War I, the Ottomans imposed systematically harsh treatment on all Jews in Palestine. Wartime dislocations and a failed harvest compounded the woes of all residents—Muslims, Christians, and Jews alike. By the time of the Balfour Declaration, the Jewish population had declined to about 55,000. Given these deteriorating conditions, Zionist leaders saw their vision of an independent Jewish state rapidly recede. The war posed difficult problems for them. Jewish leaders were not sure that supporting the Allied cause would improve the position of world Jewry or further the goal of creating a Jewish homeland. Germany, in fact, had recently improved conditions for Jews and created a better environment for them than had any other country in Europe. Seeing that Jews would have a difficult time wherever they lived, and seeing widespread anti-Semitism in the Allied countries, the Zionist leaders gave the Allies only halfhearted support.

The Allied powers, however, were facing enormous difficulties during the war and needed support. Dr. Chaim Weizmann, a Manchester University chemist with connections to high-ranking officials in England (due to his war-related research) and a Zionist leader, pressed the Zionist cause with the British. Zionists in other Allied countries were doing the same. Finally an agreement was reached that culminated in the Balfour Declaration.

THE MANDATES

The Allies were well aware that the contradictory agreements made during World War I were going to be difficult to resolve. After the war, the Americans (with some British support) urged the formation of a commission to ascertain the wishes of the local populations. The French, however, rejected the idea and insisted that the Sykes-Picot Agreement be carried out. The British suspected the French of wanting to establish a firm foothold in the Middle East and tried to change the terms of the agreement. An understanding was reached in September 1919: Mosul would eventually be appended to Iraq rather than Syria, Palestine would come under British control, British troops would leave Syria, and the French would be compensated with a share of the Turkish Petroleum Company.

Syria and Lebanon

A son of Husein, Faisal, led the Arab revolt against the Ottomans and helped to capture Damascus near the end of World War I. He correctly foresaw France's intentions in Syria, but underestimated the extent to which Palestinian nationalism had flowered during the war. He was more concerned with the French than the Zionists. Consequently, he entered into negotiations with the Zionist leaders, seeking their aid in thwarting France; in return he accepted the legitimacy of Zionist aspirations. The French accord with the British placed Faisal in an impossible position. Since his agreement with the Zionists was conditional on the granting of Syrian independence, he repudiated the pact and was declared by the Arab Congress to be king of Syria and Palestine in March 1920. The French protected their claim to Syria by seizing on Faisal's failure to reply to an ultimatum calling for the acceptance of the mandate; the French brought in troops from Lebanon and routed Faisal. Faisal had, in fact, sent a telegram of capitulation to the French, but it did not stop the troops.

The Syrians of the interior were quite hostile to the French invasion; France responded with firm political and military action. To win over the Lebanese elite, France quadrupled the area of Lebanon. To fragment the anti-French nationalistic movement, Syria was split into separate autonomous administrative districts. Although Syrian administration was centralized after about a year, the French found that this cosmetic remedy did not solve their problems. The hostility of the Syrian population required France to maintain a military presence and suppress all political activity. Damascus was shelled on several occasions. Direct French rule was also imposed on Lebanon. Although there was considerable opposition in Lebanon, it did not rival that in Syria. However, the new, enlarged Lebanon now included areas dominated by Muslim Arabs; the delicate balance of political, ethnic, and religious groups was upset, and tensions between the various indigenous groups occasionally spilled over into violence.

During World War II, British and Free French forces invaded Lebanon and Syria in 1941 to wrest them away from Vichy France. When it appeared that the French would renege on their promises of independence at the end of the war, the British forced them to withdraw. Lebanon and Syria finally achieved political independence.

Iraq and Transjordan

The expulsion of Faisal from Syria in 1920 left the British in a particularly delicate position. The wartime promises made to Faisal's father, along with Faisal's widespread (albeit thin) popular support, spelled increased instability and a loss of British influence. The British responded by engineering the election of Faisal as king of Iraq and by creating another area, Transjordan, where they installed Faisal's brother, Abdullah, as emir. The government of British India had supplied troops and administrators to Iraq during World War I. When the League of Nations gave Britain a mandate over Iraq instead of granting independence to Iraq, widespread insurrection broke out. After a particularly bloody campaign to restore order, the British sought to install a friendly ruler and selected Faisal in July 1921. In 1922, Iraq was given a special status, and in 1932 it was granted nominal independence, with a continuing British military and administrative presence. The British, however, retained their prominent position in Iraq for another quarter century.

Transjordan had been carved out of the new British mandate of Palestine. Abdullah had been made emir to mollify Husein and to keep Abdullah from invading Syria in revenge for his brother's defeat. By splitting the mandate, the British hoped to defuse Palestinian nationalism. In fact, British policy won the enmity of both Arabs and Zionists who were seeking control of Palestine. Transjordan was an extremely poor and sparsely populated country and did not have a strong current of nationalism. It attained formal independence in 1946, but remained dependent on British and American aid. It was, in short, a client state.

Generally, Britain's policy of indirect rule in Iraq and Transjordan better prepared those countries for independence than France's direct rule in Syria. This is not to imply that British policy was particularly farsighted; although they were swayed by Wilsonian notions of self-determination, the British were weary of war and no longer wished to continue the heavy financial burden of direct rule. But by staying in the background, the British allowed the area's indigenous people to educate themselves for self-government and adapt to technological change. On the other hand, the French, ever fearful of increasing local power, kept their subjects politically and technologically ignorant.

A national consciousness determined by the boundaries drawn by Europeans began to form during the interwar years in Syria, Iraq, and Transjordan. The people who had for so long traveled between Baghdad, Damascus, and Amman with no sense of being in foreign cities were now beginning to observe the new international borders. However, passports were not the only things that kept Iraqis, Syrians, and Jordanians estranged from each other. Iraqis and Syrians learned different European languages, worked with incompatible technologies (the electrical system being a prime example), and started to perceive themselves as being of different nationalities.

EGYPT

The longtime (1883–1907) British consul general of Egypt, Lord Cromer, brought financial order and economic progress to Egypt by establishing a highly effective administrative system and by major projects such as the first Aswan Dam. The nominal Egyptian rulers (and their even more nominal Ottoman rulers) were at the mercy of the British, but they had little reason to complain. Although the British controlled Egypt, they viewed their stay as temporary, brought order out of chaos, and prevented the nationalism of the urban intellectuals from gathering much steam. But a 1906 incident in which British officers shot one villager and hanged three others touched off deep nationalist and anti-British feelings, and the British then began to make very limited concessions to nationalist demands for political representation and participation. These all but stopped when Egypt became a British protectorate in 1914.

Immediately after World War I, Saad Zaghlul, a nationalist and a respected administrator, asked the British for permission to circulate a petition for Egyptian independence. After they refused, he organized an independence movement. The British arrested and deported him in 1919. Riots followed, and after a time the British began to relent on some issues. Because of the weakness of the official puppet government and the considerable size of Zaghlul's following, the British decided to negotiate with him personally. But their concessions did not satisfy him or the other nationalists. After negotiations broke down, the British tried to main-

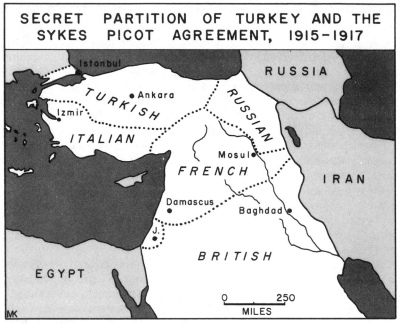

Secret Partition of Turkey and the Sykes-Picot Agreement, 1915–1917.
Source: Yahya Armajani, *Middle East Past and Present,* ©1970, p. 304.
Reprinted by permission of Prentice-Hall, Inc., Englewood Cliffs, NJ.

The Mandate System, 1920. *Source:* Yahya Armajani, *Middle East Past and Present,* ©1970, p. 304. Reprinted by permission of Prentice-Hall, Inc., Englewood Cliffs, NJ.

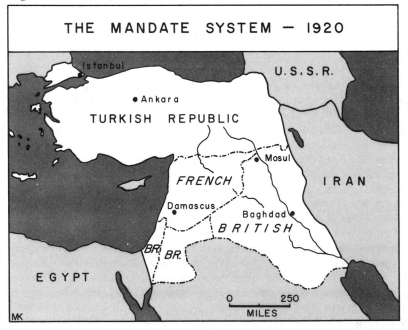

tain civil order by unilaterally declaring Egypt to be independent on February 28, 1922. The declaration contained, however, four "absolutely reserved" clauses in which the British retained control over areas they deemed vital to their interests: (l) the Sudan—and with it, the Nile River, (2) all foreigners and minorities in Egypt, (3) the communications system, and (4) Egyptian defense.

After returning from a second British-imposed exile, Zaghlul saw his Wafd party win, in September 1923, a sweeping victory for seats in a parliament that had been recently declared by the king. Zaghlul was then asked to form a new government. Because the British then refused to back down on any of their four conditions, he saw no point in organizing a government. More riots followed. The assassination of a key British official, Sir Lee Stack, prompted fierce British reprisals, and the nationalist movement declined. By the late 1920s, the movement was in disarray. In 1936, the Egyptian government signed a treaty with Britain based on the 1922 declaration of independence and a revision of the four clauses: The British high commissioner would leave, British troops would be restricted to the Suez Canal Zone, and the capitulations (regarding the special status of foreigners) would eventually end. The 1936 agreement was prompted by British and Egyptian fears arising from Mussolini's invasion of Ethiopia (1935), the death of King Faud, the accession of King Farouk (a quiet and ambivalent nationalist sympathizer in those days), and the relatively quiescent state of the nationalist movement.

With the beginning of World War II, the British felt it necessary to reassert their control over Egypt. The country virtually became an Allied base for the duration of the war. Since many of the Egyptian political elite had pro-Axis leanings, the British intervened in Egyptian politics, especially in the selection of political leaders. The local Egyptian authorities were reluctant to take up arms against Britain's enemies, for the British had humiliated the Egyptian nationalists, whereas the Germans and Italians had not. As with the conclusion of World War I, Egyptian nationalism entered the post–World War II era with renewed vigor.

The Egyptian political struggles since 1882 had been three-sided and unevenly matched. Basically, the aspirants to political power, the nationalists, were strong enough not to be ignored, but weak enough to be manipulated between the British and the Egyptian monarchy. The position of the king was delicate. Sometimes he supported the nationalist cause of independence, telling the British that the elite of the monarchy would control the nationalists and prevent them from implementing anti-British policies; on the other hand, he opposed the nationalist cause when it seemed to be getting strong enough to threaten the monarchy. For their part, the British discouraged nationalist causes that the king advocated, yet encouraged the causes when the king seemed to be getting too much power. The nationalists made only modest gains for several reasons: They advocated reform, not revolution; they were mostly members of the middle class; and various factions had been weakened by being played off against each other.

The first modern nationalist movement in Egypt had resulted in the 1882 British invasion. The nationalists had been jolted into action then by the financial collapse of the Egyptian government and the exploitative policies of Britain and France. Nationalists had gathered strength during the following decades, only to see their gains swept away by the British takeover during World War I. They again pressed their claims immediately after the war, gained some measure of self-rule, but then fell victim again to imperialist power. The trauma of World War II, another event that was basically a European affair, alerted the nationalists to the insufficiency of their past gains.

The Wafd Party and the Muslim Brotherhood

The nationalist groups in Egypt during the interwar period were of various persuasions, but they all saw the British as a common enemy. The two most important movements were the Wafd party and the Muslim Brotherhood. The popular Wafd party of Zaghlul was a secular reformist movement, one which basically accepted British ideas of representative government and, thereby, could accuse the British of perverting their own stated ideals. The Muslim Brotherhood, founded in 1928 by Hasan al-Bana, expressed its hatred of British domination by calling for a return to Islamic fundamentals, including the formation of an Islamic government. Estimates of its membership in the late 1930s ranged up to a million. The message of the Brotherhood was disarmingly clear: The wretched condition of the masses, the venal behavior of the elite, and the general degradation of their common heritage were due to the acceptance of Western ways. The solution to the situation was equally clear: Get rid of the Westerners and their puppets and establish an order that would make the Koran the constitution of the country. Although the Wafd party had considerable influence with the middle-class voting population, the Brotherhood laid out a straightforward message that appealed to the masses. The Muslim Brotherhood's strident message was feared by the establishment. Because of this perceived threat, and because of occasional assassinations by Brotherhood zealots, it frequently had to operate in a clandestine way. An assassination attempt on Nasser in 1954 drove the group underground, and it was declared illegal. It remains a force, although the leadership of Egypt viewed it as a minor irritant until the assassination of President Sadat in 1981.

The Muslim Brotherhood represented an early twentieth-century attempt to establish a new Islamic identity after two centuries of Western exploitation. The economy of Egypt was mangled, divisions among social classes widened, and secularism was on the rise. Many observers think that the Muslim Brotherhood is naively fighting a rear-guard action that it will ultimately lose. While these prognostications may yet prove true, it is now clear that the success of the Brotherhood in the 1930s helped similar political forces to coalesce in such far-flung countries as Syria, Libya, Iran, Pakistan, and Indonesia.

Egypt after World War II

After World War II, socialism gained widespread popularity in the Third World. Nationalists of all persuasions were quick to adopt current socialist slogans and formulate grandiose programs. Most socialist creeds were not based primarily on Marxism or any other intellectual system. Rather, they were more a reaction against the Western private enterprise system and commercial domination. Socialist programs called for an end to the gross income disparities in society. The misery of the masses was apparent enough, and the cause of their misery was attributed to the selfishness of the local elites, who were allies of the imperialists. As young intellectuals and technical specialists absorbed these ideas, nationalist movements began to gather momentum. Broad-based nationalist parties then attempted to draw in the masses, especially those in cities, who were more sophisticated than those in rural areas.

The situation in Egypt after World War II reflected these trends. When the British resisted the Egyptian government's demands for a troop withdrawal and a renegotiation of the 1936 treaty, popular sentiment erupted into major riots in Cairo. The situation was complicated by the desperate economic conditions and the failure of the Egyptian army to prevent the formation of the state of Israel, which many Egyptians regarded as another outpost of Western imperialism. On January 26, 1952, a month after forty-three Egyptian policemen had been killed in a pitched battle with British troops in Ismailia, rampaging masses burned many Western-owned buildings in Cairo. Six months later, on July 23, 1952, a group of young army officers, including Gamal Abdel Nasser, Anwar Sadat, and Muhammud Neguib, staged an almost bloodless coup and forced King Farouk to abdicate and leave Egypt three days later. The monarchy was abolished the following June.

SAUDI ARABIA

After capturing the Rashid stronghold of Riyadh in 1902, Ibn Saud began to consolidate his rule over the interior of the Arabian peninsula. He and the Wahhabi forces defeated the last Rashid forces in 1921. The British were divided as to what to do about this growing tribe of religious zealots. During World War I, it had looked as if Husein would not be able to control the important Hijaz region against the hostile Wahhabi forces of Ibn Saud. The British decided to back both Husein and Ibn Saud on the condition that British financial support would be withdrawn from whatever side first attacked the other. The strategy worked through the war years but crumbled after the last Rashid power had been destroyed. For it was then that Ibn Saud could turn his attention to the birthplace of Islam.

By 1924 Husein was in a particularly vulnerable position both at home, because of poor administration, and abroad, because he unilaterally declared himself caliph after Ataturk had abolished the title in Turkey in March 1924. Ibn Saud's forces struck and in short order forced Husein to abdicate in favor of his son, Ali. Ibn Saud then established a protectorate of sorts over the Hijaz. In 1926 Ibn Saud was proclaimed king of the Nejd, the central area of Arabia, and in 1932 of Saudi Arabia (incorporating the Hijaz). Thus a small band of Wahhabis, led by the Saud family, had spent the whole of the nineteenth century warring for temporary power in an "inhospitable and unimportant" area and had now achieved statehood. Given the region's chronic instability and poverty, one can forgive the British and others for their inability to see Ibn Saud's potential as a leader or the significance of the nation he created.

Saudi Arabian political stability was achieved through a combination of centralization and wise leadership. Ibn Saud extended the traditional system of Bedouin rule to the nation by demanding that all significant power flow through him, by carefully adjudicating complaints, and by ensuring that those who came under his rule were treated with magnanimity. As power was consolidated and the flow of petroleum started to transform life in Saudi Arabia, an essentially ad hoc system of government evolved. Although the line separating national from local power is still ambiguous, the council of ministers that was established in 1953 clarified the areas of responsibility and took over some of the powers of the king. The system has undergone continuous revision and adjustment, with the king and royal family incrementally losing power.

The evolution of Saudi Arabia's administrative system, however interesting, pales in importance when compared with the history of its petroleum revenues. In the 1930s Ibn Saud used the first trickles of oil money to subsidize and calm tribes that were reluctant to stay within the nation, and to strengthen the weak financial base of the kingdom. After a time, the trickle of oil revenues became a torrent. But the kingdom still had financial troubles because there was no system of accountability. By 1962 an alarmed council of ministers (and other powerful notables) had convinced the weak King Saud, son and successor to Ibn Saud (who died in 1953), to submit the country's finances to modern budgetary procedures. By this time, the activities of some members of the royal family seemed to be based more on the visions of grandeur in *The Thousand and One Nights* than on the strict tenets of Wahhabi fundamentalism. Prince Faisal became king in 1964 when King Saud was forced from power by family pressures. It is important to recognize that the term "king" is somewhat misleading when applied to the leader of Saudi Arabia. He is better described as a leader chosen from and by the core elites of the country.

TURKEY AND IRAN

The two large non-Arab countries of the Middle East, Iran and Turkey, emerged from World War I in chaos. In each country reforming autocrats came to power—Mustafa Kemal (later named Kemal Ataturk) in Turkey and Reza Shah (later Reza Shah Pahlevi) in Iran. Each gathered power and brought order to his respective country during the interwar period. Each instituted secular, nationalist, and developmental reforms. Each country became aligned with the West, especially with the United States, after World War II. Each, however, followed a distinctively different path: Turkey moved unsteadily and tentatively toward Western-style democracy, while Iran continued to be ruled by one family.

The policies of secularization—both substantive and symbolic—had definite political aims: to lessen the power of the religious establishment and create a new set of allegiances. In Turkey, the new allegiance was to be to the nation and democratic institutions. In Iran, the shah became the locus of power and the central symbol of the nation.

Turkey

Ataturk had a habit of ramming programs through the legislature and not tolerating any significant opposition, a habit that conflicted with his populist ideal of involving the masses in political life. He encouraged opposition movements, but suppressed them as they gained strength. Since his reforms often involved "radical" secularization, they were sure to be opposed and cause populist ideals to be temporarily shelved. Indeed, Ataturk considered the policies of his party—which controlled the Grand National Assembly—to be the only correct and permissible ones. However, Ataturk was far more than a simple autocrat. He had a considerable influence on the development of democracy in Turkey. He set up democratic institutions, broke the power of the old ruling elite, patched up Turkey's international relations, brought a sense of nationhood to the country, and laid the groundwork for positive economic gains. In short, he lived up to the name bestowed on him—Ataturk, "father of the Turks."

When Ataturk died in 1938, Ismet Inonu, a long-time ally, was the natural choice of the Grand National Assembly to be the second president of the republic. With the autocratic Ataturk gone, a pent-up desire for reform gushed forth. But the reformers had to bide their time as Inonu negotiated Turkey through the years of World War II, declaring war on Germany only in 1945, when it was quite clear that the threat of a German invasion was practically nil. Turkey emerged from the war in near economic collapse and under the threat of Soviet expansion southward. Under the Truman Doctrine of 1947, and other pacts, the United States gave Turkey (and Greece) significant military and economic aid in order to thwart perceived Soviet intentions. American aid also put Turkey firmly in the Western camp.

The clamor for reform after a quarter century of rule by the same political party proved too great for Inonu to overcome. The 1950 elections resulted in a stunning upset when the opposition party gained a legislative majority. The election marked a turning point in Turkish politics; a change of government had come about by popular vote. While the military had not intervened in the election, it remained a formidable force in Turkish politics. Indeed, the internal financial troubles that had beset rapidly developing Turkey brought a military takeover in 1960. But the military leaders respected the role of political parties in Turkish life. Their stated goal, which they carried out within a year, was to return Turkey to civilian rule once a reasonable degree of social and economic order was established. The military staged another coup in 1971; again they promptly turned the reins of power back to the civilians once order was reestablished. As if running in ten-year cycles, the military reluctantly took power once more in 1980. Civilian rule was partially in place two years later.

Iran

The 1950 elections and the later military coups in Turkey contrast sharply with events in Iran. In 1951 the Iranian prime minister, Dr. Mohammed Mossadegh, a long-time nationalist, led an unsuccessful battle to nationalize the British-owned petroleum company. The Iranian legislature, the Majlis, was dominated largely by those interested in maintaining the status quo and had gained considerable political power in the previous decade. In 1941, the Allies had forced Reza Shah Pahlevi to abdicate because of his flirtation with Germany and his refusal to accept Allied demands to redivide Iran into British and Soviet spheres of influence. His young son, Mohammed Reza Shah Pahlevi, ascended to the Peacock Throne. During the 1940s the new shah had his hands full simply remaining on the throne as both internal rivalries and Allied actions sheared power away from him and transferred it to the Majlis. Dr. Mossadegh then convinced the members of the Majlis that it was in the national interest and their personal self-interest to vote for nationalization of the British-owned petroleum company.

Nationalization with due compensation was an established point of international law, but the Mossadegh-led Majlis met with British-led Western intransigence. The Western powers boycotted Iranian petroleum. World petroleum supplies were abundant enough to absorb the loss of Iranian production, especially since the region's other major producers did not support the Iranian nationalization and continued to sell their petroleum to the West. If they had cooperated, it is possible that Iran would have won the day and the course of Middle Eastern history would have changed. As it was, the economic toll of the boycott mounted and support from the Majlis dwindled; its members' nationalistic zeal fluctuated with the size of their purses. The Majlis's consequent rejection of Dr. Mossadegh's oil policy in the face of Western pressure reconciled it to the power of the shah, for whom a nationalist victory would have meant a loss of power. Dr. Mossadegh and his group of supporters became isolated. He could either capitulate or take his case to the streets. He chose the latter course and won a short-term victory; the outpouring of nationalization sentiment was strong enough to topple the throne. But in 1953, with the active support of the U. S. Central Intelligence Agency, the military intervened, arrested Mossadegh, and restored power to the shah and the equally conservative Majlis. A revised agreement with the petroleum company was then drawn up; this new agreement changed the terms of the previous agreement but allowed for continued Western ownership. Those pressing for economic independence—the clergy, the communists, and a growing group of reformers—had lost the battle. Within a year Iran entered into a military pact with the United States and put itself firmly in the Western camp for the next quarter century. As Turkey struggled with a highly imperfect representative rule, Iran saw all its political and economic power become increasingly centered in the person of the shah.

By the early 1960s, the shah had promulgated the White Revolution, the goal of which was to hasten the industrialization of Iran and to better the lot of the peasants through a land reform program. It is no accident that the White Revolution shifted power away from the clergy and the restive urban technocrats and intellectuals. While it promoted economic growth, the White Revolution also promoted insecurity among the opposition and concentrated more power in the hands of the ruling elite. As the growing petroleum revenues enabled the shah to transform the Iranian economy, they also made his continued tight control of all political processes increasingly problematic. The same social forces that had coalesced in the 1890 tobacco riots were again finding a common bond. There is some irony to the fact that the shah's decisive support of the quadrupling of petroleum prices in 1973–1974 accelerated this process. As the shah immediately spent the riches that poured in, he began to lose control over the flow of events. The careful balancing of interests demanded by the informal Iranian political system degenerated into an indiscriminate bludgeoning of the opposition, as the SAVAK (the Iranian secret police) and its network of informants struggled against widespread resentment. The system was running amok.

FROM PALESTINE TO ISRAEL

By 1920 the forces that were to create the dilemma of Palestine for the remainder of the century were in place. The basic issue was, and remains, which group has the right to control the area.

The British were aware of the potential difficulties even before they were granted the mandate for Palestine. The Zionists clung to the idea of a national homeland for Jews as proclaimed in the Balfour Declaration. The Arabs demanded the same self-determination that had been promised to other contiguous Arab lands. Over the next twenty-five years, British responses to the situation clearly reflected the policy dilemma but did little to bring about an acceptable resolution. They issued periodic white papers that outlined the extremely low probability of a peacefully negotiated settlement, but formulated no coherent policy. The British momentarily cooled the passions of first one side and then the other without resolving the source of the conflict.

Nationalism had infected both the Arabs of Palestine and the Zionists by the end of World War I. Self-determination was the goal of each group. The British military administration and the British civilian mandate government allowed Jewish immigration on a limited scale and made it easier for Jews to acquire property. Arabs and Jews were involved in several incidents in 1920, and in 1921 Arabs had made several significant attacks on Jewish settlements. The British promptly suspended immigration for a month until tempers subsided and then put the old policy back into force, temporarily acceding to violence and then continuing business as usual. They ignored the King-Crane Commission of 1919, which was organized by Woodrow Wilson, and British committee reports that indicated that there was little room for compromise.

Winston Churchill, then colonial secretary, stated in 1922 that the phrase "national home" in the Balfour Declaration did not mean that all of Palestine was to become a Zionist nation, but that a national home for the Zionists could be created within Palestine. The British also separated Transjordan, first created in 1921, from the Palestinian mandate, thereby shutting off Jewish settlements there. The Zionists viewed these policies as attempts to thwart their movement and abrogate the Balfour Declaration. Arab leaders saw the policy as working within the confines of the Balfour Declaration in that it simply redefined the specifics, and they therefore rejected the "clarifications." Indeed, for the next two decades, Arab policy was based on the premise of the illegitimacy of the Balfour Declaration. They therefore could not acknowledge Britain's repeated attempts to modify the declaration. Indeed, the Arabs rejected Britain's attempts to have Arabs and Jews sit on a joint consultative body in Palestine for the same reason; to sit in the same chamber would give legitimacy to the Balfour Declaration and, thereby, to the Zionists.

Although the Zionist community was composed of several competing factions, its government was solidly organized and well structured, and it could depend on British support for its major concerns. The Arabs of Palestine stood in stark contrast: While most politically aware Palestinian Arabs wanted self-determination, they had no effective political organization. Their rejection of the Arab-Zionist consultative bodies had its logic, but it was politically unwise because it deprived them of a forum in which to air their grievances.

The Arab Executive, a committee formed by the Third Arab Congress in December 1920, was the most important Palestinian Arab organization during the first years of the 1920s. Since Syria had been occupied by the French earlier that year, the idea of Palestine becoming part of southern Syria had faded. The new Arab strategy was first to unify the Palestinians, second to protest British moves that facilitated Zionist settlement in Palestine, and third to prohibit the League of Nations from forming a mandate on terms unfavorable to the Arabs.

Although the Arab Executive managed to hold the various Palestinian Arab groups together for a couple of years, it split apart in 1923. In September of that year, the League of Nations finished drawing up the provisions of the mandate. Thus, one of the major forces for unity was lost. The Arab Executive was divided over what strategy to use. Should it lodge official protests and try to negotiate and persuade, or should it simply not cooperate at all? Some advocated not paying taxes, but landowners feared that this would lead to property confiscations. At the same time, some elite families revived their long-standing feuds. The Sixth Arab Congress (1923) was to be the last for five years. The Palestinian voice became muted.

Official negotiations ceased, and the Jewish and Arab (Muslim and Christian) communities became more isolated from one another. The Zionists prohibited Arabs from leasing or even working on land purchased by the Jewish National Fund. And Histadrut, the General Federation of Jewish Labor, was insisting that Jewish-owned establishments hire only Jews. Outside of Jerusalem and Haifa, where Arabs and Jews lived side by side, the two peoples lived and worked apart in an atmosphere of growing hostility.

Arab fears went beyond becoming a numerical minority in their own land. Most Zionists, after all, were Europeans, and however separated they had become from the mainstream of European society, they nevertheless were steeped in Western ways. In 1930, over 90 percent of all Jewish males in Palestine were literate, as opposed to only 25 percent of all Arab males. About 75 percent of the Jews were urban residents, as opposed to 25 percent of the Arabs.

The relative calm that prevailed during the mid-1920s belied a growing sense of frustration and bitterness. The Jews made up about 10 percent of the total population of Palestine in 1922 (the remainder consisted of 10 percent Christians and 80 percent Muslims). Their numbers grew at a moderate rate through immigration, except in 1925 when a relatively large number entered. Due to a harsh recession more Jews left Palestine in 1927 than entered. It seemed to the Arabs that the Zionist cause had lost its appeal, and that the Arabs would remain a firm majority. But 1927 proved to be an anomaly. By 1930 Jews constituted about 16 percent of the population. It was clear that Zionism was alive and vigorous.

The Seventh Arab Congress convened in 1928. Encouraged by the 1927 decline in Zionist immigration, the congress sought to present a united front to press Arab claims. The new Arab coalition sought legislative representation as a first step toward self-determination. But events were to severely weaken the coalition and lead to its dissolution in 1934. A few months after the meeting of the Seventh Congress, Zionists demonstrated at the Wailing Wall in Jerusalem by raising the Zionist flag and singing the Zionist anthem. There were clashes with Arabs. By August of 1929, full-scale rioting broke out, resulting in 740 deaths (472 Jews and 268 Arabs). The cautious, elite-dominated Arab Executive was losing its grip on its base of power. Arab politics in the 1930s was fragmented at the top and radicalized at the bottom.

The British sent an investigating team to Palestine after the Permanent Mandate Commission of the League of Nations, in response to the 1929 riots, issued a report outlining Arab-Jewish tensions. The subsequent British white paper recognized the seriousness of the situation and called for an immediate temporary end to immigration. Arab satisfaction from the position taken in the Passfield white paper was short-lived. In England, the Zionist reaction was quick and vehement. An open letter from the British prime minister to Chaim Weizmann, the highly influential British Zionist, repudiated the latest immigration policy. This "black letter," as the Arabs referred to it, indicated to some Arab leaders that they could not hope to negotiate with Britain for independence. Britain was henceforth to be regarded as an enemy. An Arab boycott followed. Although they had succeeded in having immigration reinstated, the Zionists were also troubled by British actions. While the British had acceded to Zionist pressures, it was quite clear that they had no clear commitment to the Zionists' ultimate goals. The British, then, were faced with hostility from both camps.

The rise of Nazi Germany in 1932 produced a steady stream of Jewish immigration to Palestine. The Jewish population of Palestine increased fourfold from 1933 to 1936; by 1936, Jews composed over 27 percent of the total population. The Zionist resolve to accommodate Jews fleeing the horror of Nazi Germany aroused intense Arab bitterness. In April 1936, terrorist violence broke out between the two communities. The Arab leadership, somewhat united by the crisis, called for a general strike. Within a month the strike became a civil war. The dispatch of 20,000 British troops and mass arrests halted the general strike and the civil war by the end of October.

Another British investigating commission arrived in Palestine in 1936. The British accepted the report of the commission and issued another white paper calling for the partition of Palestine into Jewish and Arab sections with an international corridor extending from Jaffa to Jerusalem and beyond. The plan was rejected by most significant (but not all) factions of both sides, and fighting broke out again in September 1937. At one point the British had put several thousand Jews under arms to help quell Arab hostility. The arrangement broke down after the British hanged a convicted Jewish terrorist in June 1938, setting Jewish terrorist groups off on a rampage of reprisals.

The adverse reaction to the 1936 white paper advocating partition prompted the appointment of a commission to reconsider the exact boundaries. Although the report of the commission, which was published in 1938, contained three potential partition plans, it also pointed out that the notion of partition was impractical.

A conference in London followed in 1939. The participants worked for a peaceful resolution, but they failed to gain acceptance from either side. The only interesting result was that the British government made the McMahon-Husein correspondence public for the first time. After the conference, the British decided unilaterally that within ten years a united Palestine would receive a constitution that would guarantee Arab representation and protect Arab land rights. Jewish immigration was first to be reduced and then to cease after five years. Jews demonstrated their anger by burning and sacking government offices in Palestine and by launching terrorist attacks on the British.

Eight thousand Arabs and 21,000 Jews from Palestine served in the British armed forces during World War II. Hostility to the British in Palestine, however, continued. The Jews were especially active because they considered the British policy to be a virtual death warrant for those fleeing the Holocaust. By 1946 the unofficial army of the Jewish Agency (the new name for the World Zionist Organization, that had been adopted in 1930), the Haganah, numbered 60,000. Various terrorist groups, most notably the Irgun (of which the later prime minister Menachem Begin was the leader) and the smaller Stem Gang, complemented this force. The Zionists had taken the initiative in attacking the Arabs and the British. The weaker but numerically dominant Arabs attacked the Jews and the British. The war-weary British attempted to quell the violence, which was now out of control. As more and more survivors of the Holocaust illegally entered Palestine, the British desperately grabbed for a solution. In 1946 an Anglo-American committee devised a variant of the partition proposal that again was rejected; a 1947 British proposal calling for a five-year British trusteeship met with a similar fate. The British were totally frustrated and angry over European and, especially, United States support of Zionism; the United States, however, had refused to allow mass Jewish immigration to its shores. The British then washed their hands of the affair and turned the problem over to the fledgling United Nations.

A subsequent United Nations commission found what all previous commissions had noted: The demands of each side were understandable, inflexible, and irreconcilable. In November 1947, the United Nations called for the partition of Palestine. The mandate was to end May 1, 1948, and the two states were to be established on July 1, 1948. The Arab states began to rally their forces in support of the now disorganized Palestinians who had rejected all aspects of the plan, but it was too little too late. A Zionist offensive resulted in victories as the British pulled out. On May 14, 1948, David Ben-Gurion announced the formation of the state of Israel. The Zionists had Palestine, or at least a portion of it. Subsequently, Egypt administered Gaza militarily, and Transjordan announced the annexation of the West Bank of the Jordan River not under Israeli control (1950).

However, the formation of Israel did not give the Zionists complete security. The Arab population that had remained in Palestine, along with the sizable number who fled as the fighting became particularly vicious, viewed Israel as illegitimate, and the Zionists as a foreign power. Further, the Arab countries that had been defeated by the highly efficient Israeli army in the war following the declaration of independence suffered a deep humiliation. Although the Arab states surrounding Israel had a substantial numerical advantage, they were militarily weak. Their armies were ill trained, badly equipped, and lacking in dynamic leadership.

According to the Arabs, Israel was just another outpost of Western hegemony. Various Arab leaders vowed that they would not rest until the state of Israel was destroyed. According to the Israelis, British vacillation, the Nazi Holocaust, and the refusal of the Western countries to accept large numbers of persecuted Jews proved Herzl's 1896 argument that only in their own sovereign state could Jews expect to be safe and secure. To the age-old Jewish dictum, "Next Year in Jerusalem," was added the cry "Never Again."

There was no ground for accommodation on the issue of Palestinian rule. Both sides were desperate and bitter: the struggle had been waged for a third of a century, and almost every long-time resident knew someone who had been killed or attacked. The "freedom fighters" of one side were considered to be brutal "terrorists" by the other.

CONCLUSION

Most countries of the Middle East had achieved political independence by 1950. Few, however, had achieved self-determination. The Western powers had substantial economic and strategic interests in the area that they were determined to protect.

The new alignment after World War II of Western powers into Soviet and American camps set the stage for renewed attempts to carve out spheres of influence. The American-led group sought to establish client relationships with the northern tier of nations—Turkey, Iraq, and Iran—in order to thwart Soviet aspirations. To the south the United States sought to protect Persian Gulf (Arabian) oil and the Suez Canal. Since overt outside control of local political systems was quickly becoming a relic of the past, the great powers tried to maintain their influence by other means. They gave economic and technical assistance and military aid to muffle revolutionary impulses. The primary aim of the United States and the Western European powers was to stop Soviet expansion, not to develop independent economies and military forces. To strengthen Middle Eastern countries against revolution, the Western powers helped build a military and economic apparatus that was effective and resilient but still dependent on Western support.

The postwar economic and military position of most Middle Eastern countries was extremely weak. The political elite of these countries generally wanted to avoid fundamental reforms. In this, they had much in common with the United States: They both sought political stability. The extent of military and economic dependency was the major point in question. However, the growing militant nationalism in the Middle East complicated the matter.

The need to achieve economic independence and strengthen the indigenous cultures began to be appreciated by those concerned with self-determination: Political independence would not suffice. Those who saw economic dependence as the major impediment to self-determination found socialism particularly attractive. It was, after all, Western private enterprise that had transfigured and dominated the economies of the Middle East. A restructuring of the local economies to meet local needs was going to be necessary; but this would be almost impossible in a system dominated by foreigners and serving foreign markets. Furthermore, if the foreign private enterprise system controlled the course of local economic events, it could also be blamed for the continuing misery of the masses. (Leaders of private enterprise systems seldom have been noted for placing at the top of their political agenda concerns for a more equitable distribution of income: Socialists, on the other hand, generally do.) Not all modernizers shared these thoughts, nor were their ideas set out in a neatly framed system. Rather, the sentiments more often than not arose from a sense of dissatisfaction—a growing awareness that a fundamental reordering of society had to occur before full self-determination could be achieved, and that the restructuring could not take place as long as foreigners remained dominant.

Another source of dissatisfaction came to the surface during this period: It appeared that continued Western domination was stripping away the cultural fabric of Arab (and especially Islamic) society. Calls for an indigenous cultural renaissance had been made throughout the century, but the pulse of the movement, led by disaffected religious leaders, gained momentum in the postwar era. As with the secular modernizers, the clergy also called for an end to the current order. They sought a return to Islamic fundamentals rather than a culture heavily laden with Western values, whatever form of economic independence was achieved.

Middle Eastern political leaders thus faced a difficult choice. Accepting Western aid would enhance their economic and military strength and possibly mute some of the discontent caused by the "revolution of rising expectations." But this alliance would meet with resistance by those who perceived continued Western economic or cultural domination as a barrier to self-determination. The situation was complicated for several Arab countries because the American-led bloc supported Israel, a country which the Arabs generally thought of as a Western colonial settler state.

THE DRIVE
FOR SELF-DETERMINATION

Most of the major nations of the Middle East achieved independence by 1950. However, for some independence was neither permanent nor even meaningful. Superpower, regional, and internal struggles were still in the process of shaping these countries (and being shaped by these countries). While the postwar decline of direct European political control was bound to change Middle Eastern political relationships, it was an open question of whether those relationships and government institutions would be altered in a fundamental fashion. Amid this uncertainty came the growing recognition that attaining political independence was not the same as achieving self-determination. The latter was not likely to occur in a state if its economy was dependent on that of another, nor if the population looked to imperialist powers for cultural sustenance. Many false starts, program reversals, and policy contradictions occurred. There was no readily available blueprint for action, no clearly defined and agreed-upon analysis of the problems and solutions. All parties were feeling their way through a minefield of political dangers.

The very difficult task of building nations from states became more complicated after 1973. The petroleum price changes of the 1970s significantly changed many relationships between and within nations. The 1980s were dominated by another series of shocks; moral, societal, political, military, and economic. Finally, three fundamental events during 1988–1991 changed the very playing field on which the game was being contested.

First, Palestinians in the territories occupied by Israel since 1967 rebelled. The **intifada** brought increasing domestic and international pressure on the Israeli government to finally resolve the "Palestinian issue." Israeli defense forces acted to suppress the rebellion, but to little avail even though more than a Palestinian per day was killed over a period of several years.

Second, the collapse of the U.S.S.R. as a superpower competing against the United States ushered in a series of dramatic changes in official ideology, demography, and international political alignments. Those states that had received aid from the U.S.S.R., notably, Syria, Iraq, and South Yemen, were cut adrift financially. The Soviets also announced during this period that they would allow immigration of large numbers of Jews—maybe 1 million people would be involved. Israel faced the prospect of having its Jewish population increase by 20 percent in a couple of years, enhancing their position as a Jewish state, but also presenting them with an immense financial burden. The rise of nations with majority Muslim populations from the ashes of the Soviet empire also meant that westward leaning Turkey, the more religiously-oriented Iran, conservative Saudi Arabia, and others, scrambled to forge new alliances.

Third, the 1990 invasion of Kuwait by Iraq, and the subsequent war, shook the foundations of the area. Indeed, the combination of the collapse of the Soviet empire (and the Soviet Union itself), the intifada, and the Iraqi invasion, signalled changes so deep-seated that they rivaled in importance the mandate system that gave the basic geopolitical boundaries to the region.

In the early morning of August 2, 1990, Iraqi forces invaded Kuwait, and within a couple of days were dug in at the Saudi border after having an easy time with the totally outmatched Kuwaiti defense forces. Six months later, an allied force, led by over a half million U.S. troops, and supplied with a stunning display of high-tech weapons, liberated Kuwait and crippled the Iraqi military and economic infrastructure. The military victory came with surprising ease: The campaign was over in about a month with very low allied losses. The effects of the invasion and war, however, will take decades to play out. In the immediate aftermath, Saddam Hussein was still in power, had crushed a Shia revolt in the south, and bargained an uneasy and unstable compromise with the Kurdish resistance in the north. Jordan, a nervous supporter of Iraq after the invasion (partially due to the domestic popularity given to Iraq's call for the liberation of Palestine as part of their overall plan) suffered a loss of Western and Persian Gulf financial aid, and now dealt with the burden of several hundred thousand Palestinians who had been forced to flee from Kuwait. On the other side of the war front, about 1 million Egyptians working in Iraq had returned home after Iraq expelled them. Several hundred thousand Yemeni workers were evicted from Saudi Arabia because the Yemeni government "supported" Iraq. Syria, a crucial ally of the United States in the coalition against Iraq, gained the ability to reinforce their control over Lebanon. Israel suffered missile attacks from Iraq during the war, and faced increased pressure to settle with the Palestinians after the conflict. The Middle East had changed forever.

The intifada, the breakdown of the U.S.S.R., and Iraq's invasion of Kuwait combined to change the face of the Middle East in a fashion that no analyst could have predicted only a couple of years earlier. Because of the state of flux that now exists, there have been wildly different interpretations as to the future. The evolution of meaningful national independence in a setting of increasing global interdependence is not well-understood in the best of cases: It is further muddled in the Middle East. Some of the major concerns will be mentioned in this chapter, and some will be sprinkled throughout the text.

The major sections in this chapter deal, respectively, with the impact of an ideology, the effects of a change in economic well-being, and the analysis of a particular arena of conflict.

The first section deals with the role of Egypt generally, and Gamal Abdel Nasser particularly, with respect to self-determination and Arab unity. Although the complexity of internal and regional politics denies a neat encapsulation of events and trends, it is clear that the visions held by Nasser were widely shared, that there has been universal difficulty in effecting solutions, and that there has been widespread disagreement on what package of policies would best serve to realize the vision.

The general impact of petroleum prices forms the basis for the second section. OPEC-initiated actions in 1973–1974 and 1979–1980 increased the nominal price of petroleum tenfold—to about $30 a barrel. In 1985–1986 prices crashed to $12. Prices soared to $40 in the immediate aftermath of Iraq's invasion of Kuwait and then settled back to $20 a few months later. The petroleum-exporting countries are in profoundly different situations now than before the first wave of price increases. The resulting income disparities within and between countries are a potential source of future instability.

The third and longest section is given to an analysis of Israel and Israeli-Palestinian-Arab state tensions. The reader should not infer from the length of this section that these issues dominate the Middle Eastern landscape. It is quite clear that they are only dimensions of the larger scene and that most of the fundamental issues of conflict and accommodation would remain in force if the antagonists in this arena settled their differences. There are three major reasons why an extended discussion is in order. First, Israel has a unique place in the Middle East. The heritage of its people and the origins of its statehood differ in significant ways from other nations of the region. Second, the Israeli-Palestinian-Arab state issues have had a high degree of international visibility that often has been translated into simplistic notions of "good guys and bad guys." While it is difficult not to get passionate when millions of lives hang in the balance, it would be foolhardy to ignore the complex reality and, thereby, throw reason to the wind. Third, this arena serves as an enduring example of the difficulties involved in conflict resolution.

THE NEW ARAB NATIONALISM

The 1952 Free Officers' coup in Egypt is a good example of a transition in the Middle East. The leaders of the coup represented a new force in Egypt in particular and in the Middle East in general. Typically (but not exclusively) they were from nonelite families and had been among the first generation of their class allowed to rise in the ranks of the military. They viewed traditional regimes as preserving the status quo and maintaining the division between the haves and the have-nots. Their revolution was premised on the belief that a continuation of the existing political order would consign the majority of the population to permanent impoverishment. They also thought that widespread political corruption and indifference to national needs were responsible for Egypt's humiliating defeat by the Israelis in the 1948 war. It is clear that the Free Officers had no clear plan for their new postrevolutionary society; rather, they saw the new society rising like a phoenix from the ashes of the old regime.

Gamal Abdel Nasser emerged in 1954 as the leader of the Revolutionary Command Council (RCC), the name adopted by the Free Officers after taking power. Three years after the revolution he wrote of his disillusionment with the notion that a new social order based on equality and justice would evolve naturally.

It became clear to him that the various groups competing to influence the reordering of Egypt were generally concerned with enhancing their own well-being without much regard for truly national concerns; he perceived them as attempting to change the actors in the political and economic hierarchy without changing the structure. He believed, therefore, that Egypt needed a transition phase between the old order and the new; he called this transition "guided democracy," and the RCC was to be its guide. Nasser and his associates felt that individual competition had to be channeled if it were to result in positive change. In practice this meant that a just and democratic society could be attained only by temporarily limiting democratic action. With no clear definition of ultimate objectives and means, and given the day-to-day pressures of political life, Nasser and the RCC developed policy through experience and perceived necessity.

The Arab League was formed in 1945 in recognition of the power of collective action. The League did not provide much more than a forum for debate during the first decade of its existence, but events centering around Egypt during 1955–1956 highlighted the need for cooperative action and provided an impetus to engage in fresh efforts to attain collective action. The historic Bandung Conference of 1955 brought together for the first time a large group of Third World leaders who wished to develop a nonaligned status. They clearly expressed their desire to be free of American and Soviet entanglements, the presumption being that the superpowers were unreliable allies who would manipulate Third World countries for their own interests. The superpowers generally discouraged notions of nonalignment, and each sought to exploit situations that would at least keep the nonaligned countries from being wooed by the other side. Nasser emerged from the conference as a leader of the movement. The United States was particularly alarmed by what it saw as Egypt's drift away from the Western bloc; it reasoned that if the Soviets vaulted the northern tier of U.S. allies—Turkey, Iraq, and Iran—American vital interests would be challenged.

The Suez Canal Crisis and the Israeli War (1956)

The United States decided to deny military assistance to Egypt on the grounds that such assistance would promote an arms race in the Middle East (irrespective of American arms sales to Israel). This decision provided the impetus for the decade-long Soviet ascendancy in Egypt. Nasser purchased arms from the Soviet bloc in 1954–1955 in return for promised future deliveries of Egyptian cotton. When the United States countered in 1956 by withdrawing proposed financial assistance for the construction of the massive Aswan High Dam on the Nile, Nasser nationalized the Suez Canal. Egypt and Britain had negotiated an agreement in 1954 that called for the end of British military presence in the canal but allowed Britain to use the military installations in the area of the canal in time of crisis. Nasser's nationalization action thereby weakened Britain's position. Nationalization itself was not contrary to international law as long as just compensation was paid to the owners of the property. However, military actions took place before issues of compensation could be settled. About three months after the nationalization, Israel invaded Egypt and captured the Sinai peninsula and the Gaza Strip, stopping short of the Suez Canal. Israel claimed that it needed to disrupt Egyptian-based guerrilla raids into Israel, that Egypt's blockade of the Straits of Tiran severely compromised its vital interests, and that a three-day-old Egyptian-Jordanian-Syrian defense pact, accompanied by verbal declarations to destroy Israel, constituted an immediate threat to its security. A couple of days after the Israeli invasion, British and French forces attempted to capture the Suez Canal. Their objective failed, a cease-fire was quickly arranged through the United Nations, and all three invaders subsequently quit Egyptian territory. United Nations troops were placed in Gaza and at the head of the Gulf of Aqaba. The Soviet Union then offered to provide financial assistance for the construction of the high dam at Aswan. The United States now had more reason than ever to believe that the Soviets were jumping the northern tier of U.S. allies. However, Nasser's policy of nonalignment prevented Egypt from joining the Soviet camp.

Nasser emerged from the Suez crisis as an Arab hero, and Egypt's long history of leadership in the Arab world was reaffirmed. Along with the status accorded Nasser was a recognition that Arab unity could help meet major Arab goals, victory over Israel being high on the list. Nasser and the RCC had, of course, realized that it was worthwhile to cooperate with other "progressive" Arab states on some matters and with all Arab states against Israel, but Arab unity now began to assume a new meaning: Instead of an end in itself, it came to be seen as a means to Arab victory in Palestine. Events in Syria were to provide Egypt with its first opportunity to exercise leadership under the banner of pan-Arabism.

Syria

In contrast to the relative ethnic and religious homogeneity of Egypt, Syrian society is characterized by considerable heterogeneity. Sunni Muslims form a majority of the population and are in an economically preferred position. However, minorities play vital roles. Particularly important are large numbers of relatively prosperous Christian merchants and landholders, and the **Druze** and the Alawites, who dominate the senior ranks of the military, partially due to the successful preindependence French policy of fragmenting power and to the unwillingness of the Sunni elite to encourage their sons to enter the military as a career. Syria spent its first three years of independence, 1946–1949, under ineffective civilian rule; a coup in 1949 ushered in the first of many military governments.

In 1954 the Arab Socialist Resurrection Party, or **Baath**, gained considerable influence in the government, influence that it held through 1958 and that figured prominently in the 1958 drive to form a political union with Egypt. Baath ideology combines socialist thought with visions of past Arab unity. The Baathists argue that the unity of the Arab peoples will evolve naturally as the individual states move along a socialist path. Baathist influence in Syria in the 1950s, however, was far from being uncontested. From the right they faced the growing hostility of conservative elements who saw Baathist policies of income redistribution and nationalization as simple expropriation. On the left the relatively strong communist party was seeking closer ties with the Soviet Union, a country which the Baathists considered to be imperialist. The threat of a communist takeover of Syria occurred at a time when the Baathists were suffering a loss of prestige and power; the Baathists felt compelled to act forcefully to lessen the chance of Syria falling under Soviet hegemony. Nasser's immense popularity as an antiimperialist and his growing enchantment with broad socialist principles helped promote the union between

Egypt and Syria. Such a union fit neatly into the Baathist ideology of Arab unity, while it offered the Baathists a hope of maintaining their own position in Syria.

The United Arab Republic

The United Arab Republic, U.A.R., was formed in 1958 following a relatively brief period of negotiation and a hasty working through of the mechanics of formal acceptance in each country. As opposed to Muhammad Ali's expansionist motives in the capture of Ottoman Syria in 1832, Nasser's aims were limited and were more a result of Syrian persuasion than of any enthusiasm within Egypt. While the union undercut communist influence in Syria, Egypt's growing control of the Syrian bureaucracy and its sometimes heavy-handed implementation of previously legislated but largely ignored income-leveling policies led to Syrian dissatisfaction with the union. Since the Baathists were the driving force behind the union, they suffered a corresponding loss of prestige. The experiment ended when the Syrian army forced the Egyptian high command to leave the country in September 1961. Nasser accepted the decision rather than engage Syrian forces. A nonsocialist government was formed in Syria, but it was ousted from power in early 1962. A military Baathist group staged a coup in 1963; the Baathists had managed to regain a share of power.

The next round of power shifts resulted from a split within the Baathist party into two groups: a moderate faction led by people with political experience in Syria, and a progressive faction led by younger men, generally army officers, who represented the minorities. Animosities between the two groups culminated in a 1966 coup in which Alawite officers played a prominent part. In 1970, another coup took place and the Alawite position became more firmly established under the leadership of Hafez al-Assad. He has led Syria since. This long continuous rule was accomplished through the establishment of tight organizational control of the armed forces and bureaucracy, and the suppression of local opposition. Although there is little argument that the rule of Hafez al-Assad has brought a measure of domestic stability and prosperity to Syria, there is the question as to whether the transition to another leader will be smooth. Beyond instability that can be caused by "palace politics," the substantial heterogeneity of the population and the unevenness of power sharing must be considered. There have been times when elements of the population were restive. Especially noteworthy are the actions against civilian uprisings in Aleppo (1980) and Hamma (1982). It was necessary to dispatch regular forces to quell the disturbances. Much blood was spilled.

Syria assumed an ever more important role as regional power broker. Especially important was the role it played in Lebanon, a country which holds immense strategic value to Syria. Besides having troops in Lebanon since the mid-1970s, President Assad positioned Syria as the only national body that could guide, but certainly not direct, affairs in Lebanon.

Syria's role in Lebanon specifically and the Middle East generally was enhanced during and after their participation in the coalition that expelled Iraq from Kuwait. The Syrian economy suffered during the 1980s because of inefficient state-run enterprises, a cumbersome system of economic controls, heavy defense expenditures, an extended severe drought, and significant cutbacks in Soviet-bloc military, economic and educational aid. During the last couple of years of the

1980s, Syria worked hard at satisfying the major demands of the United States by being more supportive of private enterprise and free trade, being more flexible toward convening a peace conference with Israel, and dealing with the nettlesome issue of "state-sponsored terrorism." Although they made some progress repairing relations with the United States, they were still in a very delicate position until the Iraqi invasion of Kuwait and the subsequent need of the United States to build an alliance that included important Arab nations. Syria received substantial benefits from joining the alliance. They received tacit permission to rid Lebanon of (Christian) General Aoun, who had rejected a peace formula for Lebanon agreed to by most other actors in the area. Syria's intervention helped bring peace of sorts to Lebanon, while enhancing Syrian power and prestige—some would say hegemony. Syria also received substantial financial aid from the Gulf states. Finally, increased U.S. pressure was put on Israel to join a peace conference.

Jordan, Lebanon, and Iraq

The 1958 formation of the United Arab Republic helped to trigger significant events in Jordan, Iraq, and Lebanon. Jordan and Iraq were still ruled under separate Hashemite kings who had been installed by the British after World War I. However, the monarch in each country, King Hussein in Jordan and King Faisal II in Iraq, was in considerable difficulty by the time the United Arab Republic was formed.

Jordan. Jordan was a client state of Britain. It depended on Britain for military assistance and subsidies to prop up its weak economy. The nationalists of Jordan saw British aid in particular and Western actions in general as part of a new imperialism. For example, they viewed Britain's 1954 Suez agreement with Egypt as a dangerous compromise since it allowed for reoccupation whenever British national interests were at stake. In 1955, Britain formed the Baghdad Pact with Turkey, Pakistan, Iraq, and Iran. Jordan was pressed to join, but nationalist reactions led to rioting in January 1956. King Hussein, then twenty years old, responded to the crisis by expelling the British military command from the country, including General Glubb, who had been in Jordan for twenty-five years. This popular move brought temporary respite to the monarch, but elections in October brought a pro-Nasserist and socialist majority to parliament. The British-French-Israeli invasion of Egypt a month later led the Jordanian government to sever ties with Britain, thereby ending the subsidy. Hussein began to receive financial support from the United States in 1957, but he faced considerable political opposition even though he had suspended the parliament. When Egypt and Syria formed the U.A.R., there was much local popular sentiment for Jordan to join. In order to counter this, and with advice from the United States, Jordan and Iraq hastily established an Arab Union. But in July 1958, a revolution in Iraq ended Hashemite rule there and brought an end to the short-lived Arab Union. Hussein then was granted his request for 2,000 British troops to be stationed in Jordan to help save the throne. Military and economic aid was also given by the United States to help the young king. Contrary to the expectations of most informed observers, the dynasty has survived not only that scrape but also several other crises through the decades. Indeed, King Hussein is now regarded as a much stronger leader than most observers would have imagined possible a few decades ago. For example, he made significant initiatives with respect to Israeli-Palestinian issues and partially patched up longstanding contentious relations with Iraq.

   Lebanon.   The rise of pan-Arab sentiments during the 1956–1958 period also had far-reaching consequences in Lebanon. The National Pact, an understanding rather than a formal document, went into effect in 1943 and guided Lebanese political life for a third of a century. The pact formally recognized the religious and cultural heterogeneity of Lebanon and divided the major governmental posts between the different groups who were to share power. It also stipulated that the Christians would not look to France for support, and that the other Lebanese Arabs would abandon their hopes of affiliation with Syria. The formula for political rule was based on the results of the 1932 census, which indicated that no single group constituted a majority of the population: Of the three largest groups, the Christian Maronites constituted 29 percent, the Sunnis 21 percent, and the Shia 18.5 percent. Since the Muslim birth rate exceeded the Christian, the Sunni-Shia Muslim population gained majority status in the ensuing decades, and the Shia have became the largest group. However, because all parties doubted that a new pact could be worked out, the population figures of 1932 remained in force; no subsequent census was taken in Lebanon.

   The government that came to power in 1943 lasted until 1952 when the president, Bishara al-Khoury, became isolated by a coalition of disaffected politicians of different religious affiliations. The government fell when the army refused to follow a presidential order to break up a protest demonstration. This change of government, called the Rosewater Revolution, brought Camille Chamoun to power. The coalition that brought the government down and elected Chamoun, the Social National Front, started to split into factions as soon as its source of unity, opposition to the former government, was removed.

   The carefully managed balance of religious forces tended to support the status quo; any fundamental reordering of the system ran the risk of upsetting the balance in unpredictable ways. The Christian leadership had an added incentive to resist change, for Christians held more economic power than non-Christian citizens. But there were also forces calling for significant changes. For example, the Druze leader Kamal Jumblatt supported a package of reforms aimed at liberalizing the political structure and equalizing the income distribution. The Muslim population saw Chamoun leaning toward France as pan-Arab sentiments swelled. When Chamoun did not take a forthright stand against the 1956 Anglo-French-Israeli attack on Egypt, his image as a pro-European was reinforced. Discontent became more widespread and seemingly more dangerous for the Christian leadership as Muslims were swept into the pan-Arab movement.

   By the time of his 1958 visit to Damascus in conjunction with the formation of the U.A.R., Nasser was more than a popular hero: to many people he symbolized the drive for Arab self-determination. Muslims from Lebanon flocked to Damascus to hear him speak. The event catalyzed Lebanese discontent. Many called for a new census to rid the country of its fictitious Christian majority; some suggested that Lebanon join Syria in the U.A.R.. President Chamoun responded to this slow but inexorable wave of discontent by imposing piecemeal controls on political expression.

Lebanon was on the brink of civil war from May to October of 1958. A massive demonstration and general strike took place in May in response to overall conditions; it had been triggered by the assassination of a pan-Arab publicist. The pan-Arab Muslims were joined by a loosely organized group headed by the Druze leader Kamal Jumblatt and several prominent Christian leaders who saw Chamoun's policies leading to failure and, thus, a victory for the pan-Arab forces. In mid-July, Hashemite rule in Iraq ended by revolution. As King Hussein of Jordan received British troops, President Chamoun called on the United States to send help under the Eisenhower Doctrine. Troops from the United States landed on the beaches of Lebanon before the end of the month. It is difficult to say what effect these troops had. Their presence probably cooled passions sufficiently to allow the Lebanese to forge a compromise out of an intractable situation. Although Chamoun was replaced by the end of July, fighting along communal lines continued on a sporadic basis. A cabinet that would endure was pieced together in October; it contained equal numbers of Muslims and Christians, thereby partially recognizing the changed demography. U. S. troops left Lebanon by the end of the year.

Although the Lebanese managed to avoid full-scale civil disorder until 1975, maintaining the fragile peace became increasingly difficult. First, calls for Arab unity and later for pan-Islamic unity were met with sympathy by a significant portion of the Arab population, thereby putting the system under direct attack. Second, the Western bias of Lebanon's free market economy put Lebanon out of step with most other Arab nations and drew corresponding criticism. Third, there were periodic incidents with Israel. Lebanon managed to avoid conflict with Israel during the 1956, 1967, and 1973 wars without being completely ostracized by the Arab community of nations. But border problems with Israel led to the civil war of 1975, the entry of Syrian troops into Lebanon, a deepening schism between the religious communities, and the Israeli invasion of 1982.

The Palestinians who were living in Lebanon did not pose a serious problem for the government until the mid-1960s. To be sure, having more than 200,000 Palestinians in loosely supervised camps administered by the United Nations caused much worry. But it was not until the rise in power and popularity of the Palestinian Liberation Organization (PLO) that the situation threatened to get out of hand. As Palestinian forces struck Israel, Lebanon suffered reprisal raids. The Lebanese government was in a difficult position. To suppress the PLO would anger the sizable and passionate anti-Israeli groups in the country and, most probably, lead to civil war. To allow the Palestinians to operate freely would result in further crippling reprisal raids from Israel.

By late 1969 an agreement between the Palestinian and Lebanese leaderships was reached with the help of President Nasser. Essentially it gave the Palestinians the right to rule the refugee camps and to move freely through the country in return for a promise of cooperation with the Lebanese government. After King Hussein of Jordan defeated a PLO army in Jordan in September 1970, the situation started to deteriorate; Lebanon became the only base from which the Palestinians could mount attacks on Israel. During the first few years of the 1970s, PLO attacks on Israel increased, and Israel responded with reprisal attacks.

Civil war broke out in April 1975. A peace was hastily constructed, but it fell apart in August and fighting raged again. The army of Lebanon intervened during the first few months of 1976, but some units joined the forces favoring the Palestinian position. Things had irrevocably fallen apart.

It would be inaccurate to characterize the Lebanese civil war as divided strictly along communal lines. While communal divisions were certainly present, many Christian Arabs supported the Palestinian cause. In any case, the Palestinians and their allies gained the upper hand and threatened the largely Christian strongholds. Israel announced that it would decisively counter the present danger. When the Syrian army then sent forces to Lebanon to bring some order to the situation, Syrian President Assad was put in an extremely delicate position. The overriding immediate aim of Syrian policy was to defuse an explosive situation. The Palestinians and their supporters had to be held in check, but this meant that the Syrians would have to support the Christians. The irony was made complete by the open secret that the Christians were also supported by Israel.

The tragic conflict, which eventually claimed at least 60,000 lives, gradually subsided as the Syrians stabilized the Christian areas. A coalition of Arab nations originally led by Saudi Arabia hammered out an agreement with the parties and installed an Arab Deterrent Force in Lebanon. The force was predominantly Syrian; it consisted of about 22,000 Syrian troops and about 5,000 troops from the other participating nations. Lebanon limped through the remainder of the 1970s with a largely powerless government, the Syrian army controlling the countryside, a growing Christian army, armed private militias, a restive Palestinian population, the economy in shambles, and the future uncertain.

Understanding events in Lebanon has always demanded an unusual attention to detail: The coalitions essential for order were based on the intricate intersections of many forces. A change in the position of one group necessitated adjustments by all others if political coherence was to be maintained. While it is apparent that the 1975 civil war started the unraveling of the delicate political web that held the country together for one-third of a century, the aftermath of the 1982 Israeli invasion made it clear that a reconstruction of the old web was impossible; a new order had to be established.

On June 6, 1982, Israeli forces invaded Lebanon. Israel had been ever more frustrated by PLO actions. An assassination attempt on the Israeli ambassador to Britain served as the official reason for the invasion. Israel's stated goal was to establish a 40-kilometer *cordon sanitaire* so as to blunt terrorist attacks on northern Israel. Another primary goal, unstated at the time, was the destruction of the PLO. In rather short order, Israel destroyed the Syrian air force located in east-central Lebanon and had Syria accept a cease-fire. This allowed Israeli troops to move up the coast directly to Beirut to do battle against PLO forces concentrated in several large "camps." Aerial bombardment of the camps preceded the Israeli troops.

Two months later an arrangement was made whereby PLO forces in and around Beirut would quit Lebanon. The removal to several different locations was supervised by a multinational force, which included a relatively large contingent of U.S. troops. The multinational force left Lebanon by September 10, shortly after the evacuation. In the midst of this Bashir Gemayel was elected president of Lebanon. He was assassinated one month later (September 14). Two days later Israeli forces allowed the Christian militia to enter the Palestinian camps of Sabra and Shatila. During the next three days many hundreds of Palestinians were massacred. A few days later Amin Gemayel, brother of Bashir, was chosen to be president. Shortly thereafter the multinational force returned to Beirut. Amin Gemayel remained in office until his term expired in 1988. The presidency remained vacant until 1991.

By 1983, then, the situation in Lebanon had changed dramatically. Syrian forces remained in large parts of eastern Lebanon, the army of Israel occupied the western part of the country north to Beirut, and the PLO was in some disarray due to the exit of 8,000 of its troops from Beirut. In addition, the superpowers moved ever closer to direct involvement. The Soviet Union poured a massive amount of military aid into Syria in order to replace and upgrade the equipment destroyed by Israel. Soviet technical advisers were on hand to assist the Syrians. U. S. marines, part of the multinational force, were in barracks at the Beirut airport. Their stated task was to assist the regular Lebanese army. Since no significant militia recognized the legitimacy of the government, the goal of the U.S. forces lost meaning.

Internal security deteriorated markedly through the next two years. There were numerous battles between the various militias, and between the militias and the Israelis. U.S. forces and mountain-entrenched militia exchanged artillery fire. In addition, urban terrorism increased. It became somewhat commonplace to have a bomb-laden vehicle explode in this or that quarter of the city, killing scores at a time. Selected foreigners, especially Americans, were killed or kidnapped. The most spectacular action against Americans, who were generally perceived as allies of Israel and/or the Christian-dominated government, was the bombing of the air-port barracks, killing 241 marines and prompting the United States to leave Lebanon shortly thereafter (February 1984). The bombing seems to have been a direct response to a U.S.-brokered (and subsequently forgotten) peace agreement (May 17, 1983) between Lebanon and Israel.

In late 1983, rejectionist PLO units forced a second evacuation of PLO forces loyal to the PLO leader Yasir Arafat, this time from the northern port city of Tripoli. The rebel units, initially aided by Syria, acted because of their distaste for a conciliatory attitude Arafat was taking toward a proposal to establish a Palestinian "entity associated" with Jordan. Israel finally quit Lebanon in mid-1985, although its forces continued to indirectly control the southern portions of the country.

While the Christian leadership was unwilling to yield its position of preeminence, the Shia plurality was "awakened" and found political voice. This awakening of the Lebanese Shia is a complex social phenomenon. However, a few convenient benchmarks can be mentioned. First is the appearance, success, and (somewhat) mysterious disappearance of a prominent and charismatic religious leader, Musa al-Sadr. He disappeared while on a trip to Libya and fragmentary evidence suggests that he was assassinated by official Libya. The disappearance elevated his already considerable stature as the symbol of new Shia assertiveness and served as a rallying point for the Shia of Lebanon. Before his disappearance he organized the Shia of southern Lebanon and guided the formation of AMAL ("Movement of the Deprived"), a political and later military force that bypassed traditional Shia leadership. Second, the success of the Iranian revolution gave inspiration and material aid to many of these self-described "disinherited" Shia muslims. Third, the successive dislocations of the Shia population of southern Lebanon by the Israeli-supported Christian army, Palestinian militia, and the Israeli army in the aftermath of the 1982 invasion increased the need for the Shia to act.

AMAL advocated a Lebanon free of confessional politics, a policy that, not surprisingly, would strip power from the Christians and give power to the Shia. AMAL was not ideological in that it did not call for the complete overhaul of the organization of Lebanese society: it merely sought a larger share of the pie in a peaceful Lebanon. Thus, it was in substantial, if unstated, agreement with the apparent goal of Israel and Syria. The leadership of AMAL reflected this "reformist" attitude in that it was largely middle-class.

AMAL, however, had to contend with another potential champion of the Shia, **Hizbollah** (Party of God). Hizbollah was led largely by clerics, financed by Iran, and it was strongly ideological in that it advocated the formation of an Islamic republic. It seems that grass-roots loyalties to each group were rather ephemeral, depending on particular and immediate material conditions rather than deep-seated ideological beliefs. Therefore, the popularity of Hizbollah has been linked to the desperate state of the Shia of Lebanon and the perceived inability of AMAL to effect a solution. The spectacular rash of hostage-taking in the 1980s was often alleged to have direct links to Hizbollah or some associated group.

The formal Lebanese government and its army were powerless as the various communities became more insular and desperate. Each of the major confessional groups, with the exception of the Druze, splintered into smaller factions and retreated into a vicious and fluid communal bloodletting. Lebanon was less a country than a tribal battlefield. Yet it continued to survive.

Amin Gemayel's presidential term was to end in September 1988. Efforts to find a new power-sharing arrangement and a new presidential candidate failed. The United States and Syria (generally in opposition to each other) were involved in the search for a new president (and also in the veto of certain candidates). The search for an acceptable candidate failed and the office of the president was vacant. Before leaving office, Gemayel appointed (Christian) General Aoun to head a military caretaker government that was to yield power once a new agreement on power sharing and an acceptable candidate was found. However, General Aoun refused to accept a proposed government headed by (Sunni) Prime Minister Hoss, and an Arab League attempt at compromise failed. General Aoun, supplied with weapons by an Iraq wanting to curb Syrian power, tried to wrest power through the ouster of Syria. Finally, an Arab League initiated effort resulted in the Taif accords in November 1989. The accords were produced when the Lebanese parliament (elected in 1972) was convened in Taif, Saudi Arabia. They agreed to a new power-sharing agreement. The number of seats in the parliament was to be expanded (to 108), equally divided between Christians and Muslims, instead of the old ratio of six Christians to every five Muslims. The powers of the (Christian) president were trimmed and the (Sunni) prime minister enhanced. Further, the Lebanese "special relationship" with Syria allowed Syrian troops to remain in Lebanon so as to help the government disarm the various militias. The clear winners from these arrangements were the Lebanese Sunni and the Syrians.

General Aoun rejected this new government. He was finally removed from power in October 1990, under the fire of Syrian forces—and at a time when the United States needed Syrian participation in the coalition against Iraq, thereby causing the United States to give a diplomatic "green light" to Syrian plans. As the new government assumed more control, and as the various militia were disarmed (of their large weapons), the average Lebanese citizen enjoyed more peace than in the preceding fifteen years.

Lebanon, however, remained in a difficult position. The Syrians held sway in large parts of the country. The Israelis and their Christian clients occupied the south. The Bekka valley harbored several thousand Iranian militia, and the Palestinians also remained

Iraq. The July 1958 revolution in Iraq, led by General Abdul Karem Kassim, brought death to many of the country's traditional rulers, including King Faisal II and the veteran prime minister, Nuri al-Said. The coup was originally supported by an assortment of nationalist and leftist groups. The alliance, however, began to unravel soon after the revolution. The Iraqi Baathists urged joining the U.A.R., but, unlike the Syrian Baathists, those in Iraq were not sufficiently powerful to force the decision. Rather, Kassim played off the pan-Arab Baathists against the communists. The nationalist group, the National Democrats, gained early favor with Kassim but lost most of their influence within a year. A highly turbulent five years followed; the communists tended to gain in power as a group but individuals had to remain vigilant because of Kassim's frequent purges of top government leaders. Kassim was finally killed in a 1963 *coup.*

General Abdel Salam Aref then came to power. Aref had been an original member of the 1958 group that had destroyed the monarchy, but he had also been purged from the government in 1958. Aref brought Baathists into the government, but they were again purged within a year. When General Aref died in a helicopter accident in 1966, he was succeeded by his brother, Abdel Rahman Aref, the prime minister at the time, who held office until the 1968 coup, which brought General Ahmed Hassan al-Bakr to power. Again the Baathists returned to a position of prominence, but it was a Baathist party stripped of its pro-Nasserist fervor. By 1968 the pro-Nasserist and communist elements were widely distrusted in Iraq. Part of the strength of General Hassan al-Bakr's rule stemmed from the fact that many of his associates came from the same area in Iraq (indeed, many came from the same village). One of these associates was Saddam Hussein, and when illness caused al-Bakr to resign in 1979, Saddam Hussein took power. As vice-president for a decade, Saddam Hussein assumed an ever-greater proportion of strictly presidential roles for the aged and ailing al-Bakr.

The decade of the 1970s in Iraq can be characterized as one of economic growth, fueled by petroleum price increases, and political consolidation of power, through brutal repression and also genuine progress in forging broad-based alliances with some major Kurdish and Shia groups. The 1980s were dominated by the horrifically bloody war with Iran (1981–1988). It is important to note that Iraq was able to continue quick economic growth through loans and grants given by the Arab Gulf states and well as through credits extended by a variety of Western creditors. Indeed, Baghdad had enough money to have about 2 million foreigners working in the economy as Iraqi men fought and died at the front. Although generally not mentioned, the war with Iraq also had a potentially profound effect on the role of women. During the war they filled jobs heretofore reserved for males; and after almost a decade of employment in a wide variety of posts it was clear that the clock could not be turned back.

Iraq entered the 1990s with several pressing economic problems. First, the Gulf states stopped providing financial aid once the war with Iran was concluded, and the debt-servicing payments on loans contracted during the decade were becoming a heavy burden. Second, petroleum prices were sagging. Third, Iraq's major port, Basra, was going to be closed for an indefinite time because the Shatt al-Arab, the waterway from the Gulf to Basra, was filled with sunken ships, unexploded ordinance, and silt. Beginning in the early months of 1990, official Baghdad articulated its grievances. They lost about $1 billion per year for every $1.00 per barrel decrease in the price of petroleum. They claimed that certain members of OPEC, notably Kuwait, were exceeding their quotas of oil production, thereby depriving Iraq of badly needed revenue. Kuwait's action was particularly galling since it had arguably the world's highest per capita income and was earning more from interest earnings than petroleum sales. Iraq also charged that Kuwait was cheating Iraq in that they were pumping more petroleum from a shared field than had been agreed to. Further, Kuwait would not discuss yielding to Iraq two islands that were vital to protect Umm Qasr, Iraq's only sizable port after the closure of Basra.

Iraq also realized that the winds of change were blowing in the conservative monarchies of Arabia. For example, Kuwaiti elections in April of 1990 were roundly criticized as a sham, and were effectively boycotted by groups of Kuwaitis calling for significant democratic reform.

Finally, there did not seem to be a military counterforce in the area that would prevent an Iraqi takeover, and it was quite clear that most governments were not particularly sympathetic to Kuwait.

On a larger scale, the Iraqi leadership seems to have thought that it was poised to assume the mantle of leadership in the Arab world. One would have expected Iraq to be war weary in early 1990; it was not. Rather, they were aggressively proud that they had survived a war against an enemy with three times their population, that they had experienced economic growth through the period, and that the Kurds and especially the Shia did not heed Iran's calls to revolt. Words, actions, and visual symbols of the upbeat attitude abounded, one of the most startling being a billboard showing in profile Nebuchadnezzar and Saddam Hussein.

The invasion of Kuwait in August 1990 was the first in a series of Iraqi miscalculations. The United States quickly responded to a request from Saudi Arabia for protection from Iraq. Iraq (10 percent) and Kuwait (10 percent) controlled about one-fifth of world petroleum exports. If Saudi Arabia were added, the figure would rise to more than 40 percent. After two months the U.S. build-up was revised to include an offensive capability; this was possible after the United States had gathered European and Arab nations (especially Egypt and Syria) into a coalition against Iraq. On the international diplomatic front, the United Nations passed a series of resolutions against Iraq, and the Arab League condemned the invasion while seeking an all-Arab solution.

Although the Iraqi position became increasingly hopeless, they did not move. Finally, the coalition forces attacked in January 1991, killing many thousands of Iraqis, devastating the infrastructure, and liberating Kuwait. Saddam Hussein remained in power, however, as the coalition forces stopped short of a full-scale occupation. In the immediate aftermath of the Iraqi defeat, the Shia and the Kurds were in open revolt. They were quickly crushed by the remnants of the army. United Nations postwar sanctions against Iraq proved to be troublesome. The Iraqis were not forthcoming with U.N. inspection teams who were charged with locating and destroying the nuclear, biological, and chemical military capabilities of Iraq. On the other side of the ledger, the U.N. sanctions against Iraq had brought suffering and death to thousands of average Iraqis who could not receive medicine, spare parts to repair the destroyed water systems, and so on.

The difficulty of governing Iraq has been complicated by the pressure of communalism—the attempts of the various religious and ethnic communities to assert their power on the nation. Although Sunni Muslims are a minority, they have had a far greater hand in ruling the country than their numbers would indicate. The Shia Muslims in the southeast form the largest bloc of citizens, about 60 percent of the total, but they had been largely excluded from power. It was with some concern, then, that official Baghdad viewed revolutionary Iran's calls to the Iraqi Shia to overthrow the government; their numbers were large and they had some basis for discontent. The other large minority, composing nearly 20 percent of the population, is the Kurds. They are non-Arab Sunni Muslims with their own language and culture, and they have been extremely tenacious in their almost continuous struggle for autonomy against the governments where they are a sizable minority—in Iraq, Syria, Turkey, and Iran.

Although the Treaty of Sevres (1920) called for the establishment of an independent Kurdistan, this plan was not carried out. Kurdish leaders still seek an independent status, and the governments of Iraq, Iran, Syria, and Turkey have had long-standing difficulties trying to assimilate the Kurds. The Kurds have numbers large enough (about 20 million) to be a constant threat, but they are few enough in any one country so that they never have had enough power to break away to form an independent state.

Generally, Kurdish fortunes take dramatic turns during times of regional conflict as the major actors selectively lend support to Kurdish resistance groups in the country of their antagonist. Thus, the shah of Iran supported Iraqi Kurds in their battle against Baghdad until a 1975 Iran-Iraq agreement was reached. In the early years of postrevolutionary Iran, the Kurds of Iran were supported by Iraq. By the mid-1980s Iran had forged an alliance with some Iraqi Kurdish groups. The 1988 Iranian capture of a strategically important city in Iraq brought a particularly brutal Iraqi response: It dropped chemical weapons on the city, reportedly killing 5,000 Kurdish noncombatants who were also Iraqi citizens.

Although the fractious Kurdish resistance had continued through the decades following World War I, partially due to aid delivered by one or more of the regional antagonists, the prospects for an independent Kurdish state remained dim because it was not in the interest of any nation to have the Kurdish movement become too successful. Indeed, regional cooperation on the issue started in 1984 when Iraq and Turkey agreed on joint action against Kurdish rebels. In 1987 Turkey and Syria agreed to "cooperate" on Kurdish security questions. After the 1988 cease-fire between Iraq and Iran, the Iraqi government launched a series of major attacks against the Kurds, driving many thousands to refugee camps in Turkey and Iran. On a more positive note, Turkey initiated a substantial economic development program in the Kurdish areas of Turkey in an attempt to woo Kurdish loyalties; however, Kurdish independence movements continued in Turkey and elsewhere.

After the 1991 war, the prospects of the Kurds continued to follow this decades-long pattern, albeit in a more spectacular fashion. The Kurds captured the attention of the world for a couple of weeks following the end of the war as television crews recorded poignant scenes of hundreds of thousands of civilian refugees walking through snowy mountain passes to escape the advancing Iraqi army, only to be met by Turkish border guards refusing sanctuary. In contrast, Iran accepted more than 1 million Iraqi Kurds. Concerted coalition action led to an arrangement where Iraqi troops would stay out of specified Kurdish areas. Major Kurdish leaders then entered into negotiations with Baghdad concerning the form and extent of Kurdish autonomy within Iraq. As the talks dragged on without conclusion, the international media became bored and the Kurds once more were forgotten by the larger world, except for an occasional media blurb showing their desperate condition. And as the world stopped paying attention, the Iraqi military again moved against the Kurds.

PETROLEUM AND THE GULF

A substantial percentage of world petroleum supplies come from the Gulf countries by tankers through the Straits of Hormuz or by pipelines overland to various ports. Since the industrial power of the West and Japan is critically dependent on Gulf petroleum exports, any threatened long-term disruption of supplies from the area invites intervention from the great powers and thereby runs the risk of starting a global conflict.

The Iran-Iraq (1981–1988) war was a central concern through the 1980s. As each of the antagonists attempted to disrupt the petroleum-exporting capabilities of the other, the remaining Gulf nations and the great powers stood by nervously. The stakes were raised in 1987 when the United States responded to a Kuwaiti request for protection of vessels from Iranian attack. The ships were protected by "reflagging"—having ships sail under the U.S. flag and offering them safe passage as they plied the Gulf. Within a year there were several limited engagements between U.S. and Iranian naval units. There also were a couple of disastrous mistakes, including an Iraqi air attack against a U.S. naval vessel, which killed 37 personnel, and a U.S. ship-based missile attack on an Iranian civilian airliner, killing 290.

Iraq's invasion of Kuwait brought renewed concerns over Gulf shipping safety. Environmental concerns became much more important during this episode. Massive amounts of petroleum were dumped into the Gulf during the conflict. Besides the potentially disastrous effects on the fragile environment of the shallow Gulf, the slicks for a time threatened to foul desalination plants in Saudi Arabia and to ruin significant fisheries.

The Iranian Revolution

It is a somber irony that the Gulf's economic growth, which was made possible by the West's need for petroleum, generated instability. For example, the checks and balances that the shah of Iran employed to discourage any gathering of power outside of his control became ineffective with economic growth. By the middle of the 1970s, the modified traditional Persian system of creating insecurity among the potentially powerful had broken down. The shah, especially through

SAVAK, the large secret police organization, responded by applying more overtly repressive measures. It was as if the shah had traded his rapier for a meat axe. Much has been written about the heavy-handed role of SAVAK—originally trained and supervised by the CIA of the United States and Mossad of Israel—and how popular reactions against it helped to bring the downfall of the Pahlevi dynasty. However, it is also important to understand why those in power thought that these actions were necessary. As the old system of controls was breaking down under the weight of its own complexity, the shah was faced with the choice of accepting a loss of power or redoubling his efforts to stamp out opposition. He chose the latter course but lost the gamble.

The apparent inability of the U. S. government to interpret the danger signals emanating from Iran during the shah's decline was dramatically illustrated when President Carter toasted the shah on New Year's Eve, 1977, with the remark that Iran was "an island of stability." The view from the palace, however, was not the same as the one from the streets of Tehran. By New Year's Eve of the following year, the U.S. government urged all of its citizens in Iran, some 40,000, to depart. The shah left Iran for a "vacation" on January 16, 1979. He was to die in an Egyptian military hospital a year and a half later, never having returned to Iran.

The young, politically alienated urban technocrats joined the antigovernment movement in a manner surprisingly similar to the 1890–1892 tobacco riots. Again, it was the clergy who led the revolt. They had two deep sources of disagreement with the shah. First, the policies of "modernization" introduced by the shah were unabashedly secular in design. Second, some policies, land reform for example, were designed, partly, to woo peasant support away from the religious authorities and toward the shah. Ayatollah Ruhollah Khomeini was exiled from Iran in 1963 because of his opposition to the rule of the shah. He mostly stayed in Iraq during his exile. In 1978 he was expelled from Iraq as part of an agreement between Iran and Iraq designed to patch up their contentious relations. Iran sought to have Ayatollah Khomeini out of the area because his continued calls for the ouster of the shah were finding widespread acceptance in Iran. Iraq had its own reasons for wanting the powerful leader out of the country. Shia Muslims make up a majority of the Iraqi population and are concentrated in the southeast of Iraq. The Kurds, who are Sunni Muslims but not Arabs, account for about 20 percent of the population and live in the north. The Sunni Arabs of central Iraq have controlled the government and have generally been in an economically advantageous position. For obvious reasons, the government of Iraq preferred not to harbor someone of Khomeini's stature and ideology. The banishment of Ayatollah Khomeini from Iraq did not lessen his influence against the shah. As the leaders of the tobacco riots had used the telegraph to coordinate their actions, so Ayatollah Khomeini directed the Iranian revolution by telephone from Paris, until his return to Iran on February 1, 1979.

The streets of Tehran ran with blood during 1978 as demonstrations, many of them peaceful, were repeatedly met with brutal force by the shah's troops. By December 1978, it was apparent to most observers that the shah's time was limited.

The Iranian Revolutionary Government

Khomeini's return to Iran brought a massive outpouring of popular approval. The last government appointed by the shah before he left Iran fell on February 11,

1979. Revolutionary Iran appointed a government headed by Mehdi Bazargan, but the civilian government was subject to the dictates of the Revolutionary Council headed by Ayatollah Khomeini and found it extremely difficult to conduct day-to-day business. Prime Minister Bazargan tendered his resignation several times before it was accepted (November 6) by the Revolutionary Council. The Revolutionary Council ruled until the outlines of a new constitution could be drawn and a new president elected. Abolhassan Bani-Sadr was elected president in February 1980, and the new parliament, the Majlis, was elected in May 1980. The first Majlis of the new republic was dominated by the Islamic Republican Party—a group led by many of the country's most important religious leaders. The president, Bani-Sadr, although closely aligned with this group when both were in opposition to the rule of the shah, was generally considered to have a more secular orientation than the clergy.

Although the particular twists and turns of events in postrevolutionary Iran were impossible to predict, the revolution followed a familiar pattern in that once the glue of common discontent toward the policies of the shah was removed, the fundamental differences between the various opposition groups surfaced. The enduring lessons are that successful revolutions are those which hold the important factions together once the old government has been removed, and that success or failure must be measured in terms of what has happened to the country some decades after the seizure of political power by the revolutionaries.

While the transition from one form of government to another is always problematic, Iran faced a very unusual set of circumstances. First, it was attempting to establish an Islamic republic in a form apparently quite different from other governments adopting that label. A particularly difficult initial point involved the conflicts of authority between the president and the religious leaders. During the early days of Bani-Sadr's presidency, Ayatollah Khomeini directed the government to reverse its decisions on several occasions. It would have been difficult for the government even in the easiest of circumstances to decide on the limits of religious authority in matters not strictly religious, but the charismatic power of Khomeini was such that the issue was never in doubt: The government was forced to accede to his directives.

The crisis of authority deepened throughout the presidency of Bani-Sadr. In early June 1981, Ayatollah Khomeini stripped the president of his role as commander of the armed forces. The Majlis then declared Bani-Sadr politically incompetent, clearing the way for Ayatollah Khomeini to dismiss him as president on June 22. The role of president was to be filled by a three-person commission until a new president was elected. The three individuals, all members of the Islamic Republican Party, were the chief justice, the speaker of the Majlis, and the prime minister. Violence between the country's various political factions had been increasing in the months preceding the ouster of Bani-Sadr. The strife intensified, culminating in an explosion in Islamic Republican Party headquarters in Tehran, killing seventy-four, including the chief justice (Ayatollah Beheshti), several cabinet ministers and subministers, twenty members of the Majlis, and other party leaders. The course of the Iranian revolution became highly problematic: Bani-Sadr was in hiding and being sought by the government, the political leadership was in disarray, and groups again were taking to the streets. The crisis of political authority was but one of the major issues faced by the new government. There was considerable diversity of opinion concerning the economic role of the state, the proper extent of limitations to be placed on private enterprise, the ideologically correct nature of contracts, and so on.

The revolutionary government survived the near chaos of these years through a consolidation of formal political power by the clerics, a systematic suppression of some important opposition forces, such as the Tudeh (Communist) Party, the reestablishment of a functioning bureaucracy, and so on.

The new government also had pressing international problems, especially with respect to the United States. It was commonly believed that the U.S. Central Intelligence Agency (CIA) had brought the shah back to power in 1952. Would the United States attempt to do it again? The leaders of the revolution knew that they were in a stronger position than the 1952 nationalists, but they also knew that thousands of SAVAK and military personnel loyal to the shah would take up arms at the bidding of the United States. Although the United States government tried to distance itself from the shah, its messages to Iran were mixed and were received with skepticism. As a positive step, the United States announced on October 5, 1979, that it would resume the shipment of some military replacement parts to Iran. Most of Iran's immense arsenal of military hardware had come from the United States, and the United States had been supplying parts more or less on an "as needed" basis. Without an adequate supply of spare parts, Iranian military capability would be at a disadvantage. The promised parts, however, were not to be shipped because of events that ensued during the next month, November 1979.

On October 22, 1979, the deposed shah entered the United States to receive medical treatment for cancer. The U. S. government had been told repeatedly that the entry of the shah into the United States would only inflame Iranian passions, increase suspicions about the United States, and endanger U.S. citizens still in Iran. On November 4 the United States Embassy in Tehran was occupied by individuals identified only as "students." About sixty embassy personnel were taken as hostages. In the following weeks many furious words were hurled about without much action. However, some points seemed clear: Those holding the hostages were following the dictates of Ayatollah Khomeini, and the United States would refuse to meet Iranian demands to return the shah to Iran.

The government of the United States worked to bring diplomatic sanctions against Iran in the United Nations; it also imposed economic sanctions of its own and encouraged its allies to do the same. It used intermediaries not generally thought of as being in its camp to try to negotiate the release of the hostages. These United States actions did little to cool Iranian hostility. However, it is questionable what difference a conciliatory tone would have made, for Iran was full of conflict and contradiction. In April 1980, President Carter ordered military units to attempt a rescue of the hostages, but the mission was aborted when several problems made it impossible for the attack force to advance beyond a desert landing point south of Tehran. Given the apparent high odds against success, the fact that it was attempted at all indicates the president's overpowering need to end the crisis. As it was, the United States was forced to take a more patient stance. The hostages were released in January 1981. But the war with Iraq had started a couple of months earlier.

The Iraq-Iran War: 1980–1988

The new republic faced the nettlesome problem of dealing with the minorities in Iran. The Kurds of the north, a Sunni group, had begun to agitate for independence. The Iraqi government supported Iranian Kurds in their efforts, just as the shah had supported Iraqi Kurds before a 1975 agreement with Baghdad but had temporarily ended that support. The government also faced challenges from the Baluchis of the southeast and the Azerbaijanis of the northwest. For its part, Iranian radio was exhorting the Iraqi Shia to overthrow their government. Other Gulf countries, all with sizable Shia populations, were understandably nervous. Even Saudi Arabia had cause for worry; its relatively small Shia population is located in the petroleum-rich northeast, and was receiving the same message that was being sent to their Iraqi counterparts.

Iraq revoked its 1975 agreement with Iran that had ended Iranian support of the Kurds in Iraq in return for the settlement of a long-disputed border in the Gulf area in Iran's favor. The agreement had set the border between the two countries along the Shatt al-Arab thalweg (middle of the navigable portion of the waterway), Iraq's only major route to the Gulf and thus the only sea route for imports and exports from their port city of Basra. Iraq apparently wanted to regain control of the entire waterway—the pre-1975 (disputed) convention had given Iraq sovereignty to the Shatt al-Arab to the Iranian shoreline. The initial Iraqi assaults were verbal and attempted to foment trouble among the substantial Arab population in Iran's petroleum-rich Khuzistan area. Open warfare broke out on September 22, 1980. Iraq scored initial victories by taking some Iranian territory along the Shatt al-Arab and by damaging the important port and refinery city of Abadan. Iran responded by bombing Baghdad on several occasions and by making a considerable effort to hold Abadan.

The war droned on. There were times of relative quiet, furious offensives, deliberate bombings of civilians, the use of poison gas (by Iraq), and attempts to widen the war. There was little movement toward resolution, militarily or diplomatically. Indeed, official Tehran said on several occasions that there could not be peace as long as the government of Saddam Hussein held power. The war may have strengthened the power of the Iraqi government in ways it did not perceive when it initiated the conflict. For example, the government found it worthwhile to work to placate the country's Shia majority in order to counter messages from Iran calling for an Iraqi Shia revolt. Also, the receipt of Gulf financial aid and the use of Jordanian transport routes served to strengthen ties with a couple of important Arab neighbors. Finally, at the close of 1984 the United States resumed diplomatic relations with Iraq, ending a seventeen-year break. The benefit to Iran was nil except for the possible internal unity gained from facing such an active external threat.

A cease-fire was arranged in mid-1988. Earlier in the year each side had terrorized the population of the enemy's capital city by lobbing missiles into civilian areas—a phase of the conflict dubbed "the War of the Cities." Then Iraq scored a series of major battlefield victories. Both countries were war weary.

The very fact that Iran accepted a cease-fire pointed to changes in the course of the revolution. Early in the conflict Iranian leaders proclaimed that a theological imperative directed their efforts: Iran would not yield until the "infidel" government in Baghdad fell. The world stood by nervously during Iran's "moment of enthusiasm" in the immediate postcoup years. Calls for the export of the revolution gave pause to conservative governments of the area. While the cease-fire did not quiet all fears, it did signal that revolutionary fervor was lagging in an Iran increasingly ready to be guided in its internal and international affairs with the cold calculations of the pragmatist rather than the passion of the religious ideologue.

After Khomeini's death in 1989, the pragmatists strengthened their position. Khomeini was succeeded in the faqih-ship by Hojatoislami Ali Khamenei, a prominent cleric and ally of speaker Rasfanjani, the leader of the pragmatists. Rasfanjani was elected to an enhanced presidency later in 1989. Iran stood aloof from the Iraq-Kuwait affair and the Gulf war in 1990–1991 and apparently was instrumental in the piecemeal freeing of all of the U.S. hostages held in Lebanon— the last being released in December 1991.

The subsequent elevation of title of Hojatoislami Ali Khamenei to Grand Ayatollah in 1991, signalled another vector of the power of the "pragmatists." Khamenei's new title was met with substantial displeasure by more than one hundred members of the Majlis. They stated that Khamenei did not have the theological background to assume the role of successor to Ayatollah Khomeini. The semiofficial conservative press summarily dismissed the complaints. It is also interesting that they did not champion Khomeini's son, Ahmad, as a worthy alternative. This further hints that the revolution was becoming institutionalized, and that dynastic succession was not to be the rule. Elections to the Majlis in 1992 further strengthened the hand of the pragmatists.

Saudi Arabia's Political Stability

On November 20, 1979, the day after "extremists," whose motivations were initially unclear to the outside world, took over the Grand Mosque in Mecca, the United States came under attack in widely scattered parts of the Islamic world. The attacks seem to have been sparked by a radio broadcast in which Khomeini implicated the United States in the Grand Mosque seizure. United States embassies were attacked in Calcutta, Dacca, Istanbul, Manila, Rawalpindi, and Lahore. The American embassy in Islamabad, Pakistan, was burned down; two Americans were killed and several others narrowly escaped death after waiting hours for the local authorities to intervene.

Until the attack on the Grand Mosque, Saudi Arabia's political stability had been shaken only slightly. When King Faisal was murdered by a nephew in 1975, there was some speculation that it was a political act, but the assassin seems to have been mentally unstable. Faisal was succeeded in orderly fashion by King Khalid. Partly because of his weak health, he was to yield many major state responsibilities to Prince Fahd. Fahd assumed the throne on the death of Khalid (1982). Since Saudi Arabia's massive petroleum output and low population had allowed it to accumulate enormous financial reserves, the West was particularly fearful of political instability in Saudi Arabia; its petroleum was essential to the West and it could severely disrupt world financial markets by moving its reserves from country to country. But the monarchy was politically cautious and conservative, and the Western countries viewed it as a moderate, "sensible" nation. Likewise, Saudi Arabia's adherence to strict Islamic ideals blunted criticisms of its monarchical form of government by the most "progressive" Arab nations. Given this position and the desire to assume a greater leadership role in the Arab world, the Saudis promoted and developed a reputation as conciliators.

Saudi Arabia's public image of tranquillity and stability, however, concealed as much as it revealed. Saudi society was undergoing massive and rapid change. Its per capita income was one of the highest in the world; it was one of the world's leading financial powers; and it had begun countless expensive construction projects. Only a few decades earlier, central Arabia had been one of the poorest areas of the world. Social change, however, has not yet occurred on as dramatic a scale as the change in income. However, the tens of thousands of Saudis who have studied in the United States and Britain are not likely to completely accept their country's traditional political culture nor its Islamic austerities. The seizure of the Grand Mosque in Mecca may have been an isolated event, but it is possible that such disturbances will begin to occur more regularly as the popular desire for more political participation increases.

The Iraqi invasion of Kuwait, and the military action that followed shook Saudi Arabia to its core. First, it was clear that the Saudi military could not stop Iraq if Iraq's ultimate intentions were to overrun Saudi Arabia. The Saudis wondered if the Iraqis would cross the border. They decided that this was quite likely. Then they had to determine the proper response. While the Arab world generally opposed the invasion, many called for an "Arab solution" to the problem. But they were not ready to defend Saudi Arabia—at least not quickly, and time was not on the Saudi side. They knew that the West thought well of them, if for no other reason than that they supplied vital petroleum on a regular basis. But requesting the West, specifically the United States, to intervene would run counter to a host of important considerations: The Arab governments would not view Western intervention favorably; worldwide Muslim sentiment would not favor the keepers of the holy places of Mecca and Medina when they allowed infidels on their soil; and, finally, the influx of Western forces could upset the delicate interplay between religious austerity and material wealth. In the end, the Saudis had over one-half million allied forces in their country. Although they weathered the crisis, it is difficult to imagine that Saudi Arabians were not changed in the process. Indeed, one such manifestation was the 1992 announcement of the intent to form a (appointed) consultative assembly.

The collapse of petroleum prices in the mid-1980s gave rise to a different set of tensions faced by the Saudi government. In the early 1980s, Saudi Arabia earned over $100 billion per year through petroleum sales. The figure had fallen to under $20 billion by the last years of the decade. At first the government ran deficits financed from previous earnings; then it was forced into the politically unpopular act of slashing expenditures.

Another potential cause of instability concerns the "awakening of the Shia." For example, in December 1981, Bahrain authorities arrested and subsequently convicted seventy-three individuals for plotting a coup. Bahrain charged that the *coup* was part of a larger effort, one that was designed to bring about the fall of Saudi Arabia, and that the plotters had direct ties with Iran. During the hajj of 1987, Saudi authorities clashed with demonstrating Iranian pilgrims in Mecca. More than 400 Iranians were killed. Shortly thereafter, the Saudi embassy in Tehran was overrun by Iranians. Relations between the two countries reached an all-time low, although diplomatic relations were quickly restored.

TABLE 6-1. SHIA POPULATION IN THE GULF

COUNTRY	NUMBER (x 1,000)	PERCENT OF TOTAL
Qatar	11	16.0
U.A.E.	45	18.0
Oman	28	4.0
Kuwait	137	24.0
Bahrain	168	70.0
Saudi Arabia	440	8.0
Iraq	8,100	60.0

Source: James Bill, "Resurgent Islam in the Persian Gulf," *Foreign Affairs,* Vol. 63 (Fall 1984), 120

As Table 6-1 indicates, the Shia population in the Gulf is substantial. What is not indicated are the particulars of the population, which tend to give it potential influence beyond that predicted simply by the strength of numbers. For example, Shia in Saudi Arabia represent 8 percent of the population but are concentrated in the petroleum-rich northeastern part of the country. The Shia of Oman and the United Arab Emirates are concentrated in specific businesses. Those of Bahrain make up 70 percent of the population and are the poorest and least educated of the country. Therefore, the governments of the Gulf countries, all ruled by Sunni elites, have to be especially sensitive to Shia concerns.

Yemen

North and South Yemen affected a surprisingly quick and smooth unification, which was ratified in May 1990. As opposed to several other ill-fated attempts at unification in the Arab world, there was a strong logic to this move. During the past several decades North Yemen (actually, it is geographically to the east of South Yemen) was evolving away from its 1,000-year-old theocratic and xenophobic state. Meanwhile, South Yemen was losing its radical zeal.

The Peoples Democratic Republic of Yemen, generally called South Yemen, attained independence in 1967 when the British pulled out of Aden. In 1970 it became a Marxist state. As the only long-standing nonconservative government in the area, South Yemen was involved in many political battles in the Arabian peninsula. It received aid from the Soviet Union, East Germany, and China. Although any state in this volatile region must be taken seriously, it was tempting to regard South Yemen as the neighborhood's bad boy. It continually was in somebody else's backyard, but when dealt with sternly, it was dissuaded from doing much damage. However, this analogy does not illustrate its potential importance in the region. (Ethiopia, Djibouti, and Somalia are all in the strategically important Horn of Africa across the Gulf of Aden.), South Yemen has been involved with rebels in Oman, and it supported Iraq during the Iraq-Kuwait affair and the Gulf war.

There were several impulses for the unification of North and South Yemen, including a civil war in South Yemen in 1986, the collapse of the Soviet-bloc, and the discovery of significant petroleum reserves in both countries.

The Gulf Cooperation Council

The Gulf Cooperation Council (GCC) was formed in 1981 by the conservative Gulf states—Saudi Arabia, Kuwait, Bahrain, Qatar, the United Arab Emirates, and Oman—partially in response to the perceived threat from revolutionary Iran, and partially in recognition of some of the more obvious economies of scale to be garnered through cooperation. They proceeded slowly with respect to the establishment of joint security arrangements. They made somewhat more progress on the economic front. Customs duties were eliminated on a wide range of products manufactured or grown in the member countries, and skilled labor was allowed to take employment in any of the states.

The GCC also tried to build a common educational system. The most ambitious effort in the area was the establishment of the campus for the Gulf University in Bahrain. The campus, however, now has no students: The squeeze on petroleum-based budgets in the late 1980s directly led to a forced fiscal austerity by the GCC.

Although the accomplishments of the GCC have been modest, it remains an important body in that it has provided a forum for collective political and economic ventures. This became obvious during the 1991 threat from Iraq. Cooperation and coordination was much smoother than it otherwise would have been in confronting the Iraqi aggression.

ISRAEL

The Jews of Palestine were not able to bask in the glory of victory after the state of Israel was formed in 1948. Their turbulent history has been dominated by war and the threat of war. Indeed, it was not until President Anwar Sadat of Egypt set foot on Israeli soil in November 1977, that any Arab leader officially recognized that Israel was a permanent entity in the Middle East. Even then, President Sadat's act of conciliation toward Israel isolated Egypt in the Arab world for several years.

More than most nations of the world, much of Israel's daily life is directly, consciously, and openly affected by international events. It is no exaggeration to say that virtually every long-time citizen of Israel has known someone killed in war. The Israeli "siege mentality" has been born of experience and is firmly based in reality. Israel has been under siege since its inception. It has heard numerous calls for its destruction over the years, it has lost many of its sons and daughters in military action, and it has witnessed its enemies' tremendous growth in financial power and military capability. This is not to say that all Israelis agree on how to resolve Israel's almost continual crisis. On the contrary, Israeli public opinion on most vital issues reflects the considerable heterogeneity of Israeli society.

The Political Setting

Israel's prime minister is the de facto head of government: The position of president is largely ceremonial. The prime minister is chosen from the members of parliament, the Knesset, and is instructed to put together a cabinet. Members of the Knesset are elected through countrywide proportional representation. The voters choose between "lists," each list representing a political party or coalition of parties. The 120 Knesset seats are divided between the lists according to the percentage of the national vote garnered; for example, a list gaining 10 percent of the vote receives twelve seats. Any single list must gain a minimum of 2 percent of the vote to be eligible for a seat. If the government is to function effectively, of course, it must maintain the support of a legislative majority on at least the key issues of the day. Realizing this point is essential for an understanding of Israeli politics; coalition politics has dominated the system because no single party has ever gained a clear legislative majority.

Although Israeli citizens have been presented with a wide range of lists in each general election, they generally select from three prominent groups: the labor-dominated left-center, the right-center, and the religious parties. The Labor list formed the governments from 1949 through 1977. The right-center put together the ninth and tenth Knessets (1977–1984). The religious parties have generally gained between 10 and 20 percent of the vote and have been the group that the other two have turned to in order to form a legislative majority. Therefore, they have had an influence beyond their voting strength.

The Labor list itself is a coalition of several distinct parties that unite for election purposes. Generally, these parties have espoused a socialist ideal in domestic affairs. The most powerful Labor group, the Mapai, held the loyalties of many Israelis through its control of the Histradut, the pervasive labor organization. Since the Mapai drew its leadership primarily from the Histradut, it has become identified by many as the group that in the past provided temporary relief to immigrants, helped them secure housing, and gave them employment. Other major Labor groups were more strident in their socialism, more willing to subsume nationalist aspirations and identify with the working classes of all nationalities. The Labor parties were able to garner a plurality of Knesset seats until 1977; they constructed their legislative majority by taking the religious parties into the fold.

The religious parties, as the name suggests, are concerned primarily with religious issues—for example, the notion that Israeli Jews have the right to settle in all biblical lands irrespective of the modern-day existing political boundaries.

The Labor alliance started to lose power during the 1960s partially and ironically because of its past success. Because it could not manage to win a majority of Knesset seats, and because the Labor bloc itself was an amalgam of parties and viewpoints, it had to broaden its political position to accommodate more of the electorate. But in so doing, the political focus became blurred, and dissension within the bloc grew. A host of other factors contributed to its inability to gain a majority, including the changing profile of the voters (rural to urban, older to younger) and voter disillusionment with incumbents who had failed to ensure peace and security.

The performance of governments based on coalitions is always problematic. The Labor bloc was large enough to prevent a quick succession of governments; but it had to depend on other parties and found it difficult to move away from the status quo. The status quo, however, meant insecure national borders and a large military budget.

Although there had been defections of important figures from the Mapai during the 1960s, it was only after the 1973 war that the coalition began to face serious challenges to its premier position. The 1973 war resulted in heavy Israeli casualties, no military victory, and a psychological shock to the populace. In June 1974, the government of Prime Minister Golda Meir was forced to step down in favor of another set of Labor-bloc leaders headed by Itzhak Rabin. However, the new government also faced a rocky road. Israel was becoming more and more isolated internationally; the military budget grew larger and more burdensome; and the economy faced high rates of inflation. Since the Rabin government was forced to adopt the amorphous policies of its predecessors, it had difficulty in resolving vital issues. Finally, in 1977, a series of financial scandals involving Rabin and some cabinet ministers eliminated the government's remaining strength.

The Democratic Movement for Change (DMC) then emerged as an important new coalition party. It was a single-issue party that advocated changing Israeli electoral laws to rid the Knesset of debilitating factionalism. The leadership of the DMC was drawn from a wide ideological spectrum, although much of the platform resembled that of the labor bloc. Their apparent aim, in return for a promise of electoral reform, was to gain enough seats in the Knesset to help form a majority. The results of the election dashed their hopes.

The Labor Alignment had its number of Knesset seats reduced from fifty-one in 1973 to thirty-two in 1977. Since the National Religious party, holding twelve seats in 1977, no longer desired to unite with the Labor Alignment, it proved impossible for the Alignment and the DMC (fifteen seats), along with the other smaller parties, to form a majority in the Knesset. The big winner in the 1977 elections was the Likud bloc, which emerged with a plurality of forty-three seats. After a month of negotiations, a government was formed (June 1977) that aligned the Likud bloc with two religious parties (and later with the DMC, which reserved the right to disagree on questions including religion and the occupied territories). Menachem Begin, the leader of the Likud bloc, became the new prime minister. The new government was conservative in domestic issues and aggressive in foreign policy: It advocated a selective dismantling of socialist policies in favor of private enterprise, and the settlement of Israelis on former Arab lands occupied by Israel during and since the 1967 war, known as the *occupied territories*. Indeed, Prime Minister Begin referred to the occupied area as being "liberated." As the new government became established, it remained unclear whether the basic shift away from Labor-bloc positions would continue. Analysis of the 1977 election indicated that Israelis voted against the Labor Alignment rather than for the Likud coalition.

The Likud coalition fell apart in early 1981. The results of the June 30, 1981 election gave Labor and Likud forty-nine seats each. The smaller parties generally lost seats but gained in bargaining power since both Labor and Likud eagerly sought their favor in hope of forming the needed sixty-one seat majority. Likud finally patched together a fragile coalition and Begin continued as prime minister. The coalition fell apart in two and a half years, and another election was held in July 1984. Israel was in the midst of a particularly difficult set of circumstances. Especially important were the heavy psychological, financial, and human costs exacted by the continued Israeli presence in Lebanon, which they had invaded in 1982 to quell the Palestinians. Contributing factors included domestic and international antagonisms generated by the accelerated pace of settlement in the West Bank, and by an unusually harsh economic climate.

Prime Minister Begin dropped out of political life well before the election— he did not even campaign for or publicly endorse Likud candidates. Election results again yielded a stalemate (forty-four seats for Labor, forty-one for Likud). After prolonged negotiations, Likud and Labor joined forces to form a "National Unity Government." The Labor leader, Shimon Peres, was prime minister for the first two years, while the new Likud leader, Yitzhak Shamir, filled the post of foreign minister. Then Shamir switched positions with Peres. If nothing else, this unique arrangement of power sharing indicated the impossibility of either party forming a coalition government by bringing the increasingly contentious smaller parties into its fold. Analyses of the election indicated that there was a hardening of attitudes among the voters, and that voting by ethnic blocs increased (for example, Ashkenazi voted for Labor, Orientals for Likud).

The 1988 elections yielded the same sort of stalemate. However both Labor (thirty-nine) and Likud (forty) won fewer seats than in the previous election. The religious parties gained seats, but both Labor and Likud were unwilling to adopt certain religious party issues in order to form a coalition. Therefore, Labor and Likud again formed a "unity" government. During the campaign both blocs had agreed that this cumbersome power sharing was to be avoided: Israel needed decisive action on several pressing issues, and a "unity" government essentially meant that any such action would be blocked by one of the blocs. But the postelection realities dictated another round of power sharing. The obviously debilitating results of an electoral system based on proportional representation were not ignored, and electoral reform became a serious issue again.

The coalition fell apart in March 1990, and a new government was formed in June. Labor failed to form a new government; Likud gathered the needed majority by hammering out an agreement with the religious and right-wing parties. In the interim, there was a rally of 100,000 in Tel Aviv calling for electoral reform. However, the call went unheeded.

The government fell apart again in January 1992, when two religious parties bolted from Likud. Israel had suffered through a tough year during 1991: It was forced to sit on the sidelines during the Gulf War, had failed to settle Soviet immigrants in a coherent fashion, was rebuffed by the United States when it requested a $10 billion loan guarantee to aid in the process, had initiated a furious but socially disruptive pace of settlement on the West Bank, and was pressured into the beginnings of a peace conference with the Arabs. If nothing else, the Israeli political process points to the dangers of having an electoral system that rewards fringe parties in a setting of social heterogeneity when core values are at stake.

Likud suffered a stunning defeat in the June 1992 election, winning only 32 seats. Labor won 44 seats and, importantly, liberal lists gained seats, allowing Labor to form a coalition without yielding to the demands of the ultra-nationalist and religious parties. Labor Prime Minister Rabin acted quickly to reinvigorate the peace process that had stalled under the Likud government.

Social Setting

The coming to power of a non-Labor government in 1977 was in many ways the political expression of the social change that had been occurring since 1948. The composition of the Israeli population in 1950 was markedly different from what it had been two years earlier. Estimates (open to some question) made by the United Nations team that drew up the 1947 partition plan showed a total population of 1.8 million, two-thirds being Arabs. By the end of 1949, the Arab population had fallen to about 160,000 and represented one-eighth of the total; the Jewish population had roughly doubled to 1.2 million. The Arabs had become a minority. Jewish immigration continued to be heavy through 1952. Thereafter, natural rates of increase and immigration contributed equally to the population growth. By 1990 the population of Israel was 5 million, 85 percent being Jewish. Also by 1990, Israel was receiving large numbers of Jews emigrating out of the Soviet Union (due to the general Soviet relaxation of restrictions). Israeli authorities were quick to embrace these people, but they faced the prospect of financing the absorption of up to 1 million new citizens within a couple of years, a daunting task. Although the influx of these people was substantial, the changing character of the Soviet Union meant that it was impossible to predict how long the flow would continue.

Israeli society is a complex amalgam that nevertheless invites categorization and, thereby, oversimplification. Perhaps it is easiest to begin with a three-way ethnic breakdown: European Jews, Oriental Jews, and Arabs. The European (**Ashkenazi**) group also includes Jews who immigrated to Israel from North and South America, and South Africa; the major distinguishing factor being the common parental or cultural lineage with European Jewry. The great majority of Jews who came to Palestine during the five preindependence waves of immigration were from Europe: The first four waves were primarily from Russia and Eastern Europe; the fifth wave included a considerable number of Jews fleeing the Holocaust. The leaders who emerged from the first four waves set the ideological tone for the young state, a blend of socialism and Zionism that emphasized the virtues of working the soil. The fifth wave came to Palestine largely out of desperation. These people faced death in Nazi Germany and had been denied adequate refuge in the Allied countries. Their motivation was survival, and they did not necessarily have the socialist-Zionist pioneering spirit that had guided former immigrants. Although their impact on Israeli society should not be overemphasized, many of these immigrants were urban, middle class, skilled, and more closely in touch with Western European culture than those from Eastern Europe and Russia. Their numbers were large and their votes had to be counted. Nevertheless, immigrants of the first four waves headed every government save one—that of Rabin, a *Sabra* (a native-born Israeli). The postindependence wave of Eastern European immigration was largely over by 1952.

In the first few years following independence, many Jews from Asia and Africa immigrated into Israel as Arab governments acted in increasingly unfriendly ways and as local Arab populations sometimes vented their anger at Israel by attacking Jews who lived near them, but who, by and large, had nothing to do with Israel. During the first twenty-five years of independence, Israel absorbed 750,000 of these immigrants, the largest group, 255,000, coming from Morocco. The effect on the social structure of Israel has been profound. Jews of African-Asian origin, called imprecisely either **Sephardic** or Oriental Jews, came to Israel to escape hostility and did not share the Western values and orientations of the Ashkenazi Jews. Their shared Jewishness was all that bonded them with their fellow Israelis. Although there are notable exceptions, the Oriental Jews of Israel generally have a substantially lower than average per capita income, have had less education, hold less significant government posts, have less desirable housing, and are viewed in a somewhat disparaging light by many of their fellow citizens. They are the soft underbelly of the Jewish population of Israel. The most notable exceptions to these generalizations are the Sephardic Jews who were the longtime residents of Palestine. The Sephardic Jews of Palestine were totally conversant with local Arab culture and had an articulated social structure in place well before the Zionist movement started. This small Sephardic elite tended to view all Jewish immigrants with some disdain.

Although many Sephardic Jews of Palestine found government posts under the British mandate, neither they nor the Oriental Jews of more recent arrival shared fully in Israeli political life after independence. Their numbers swelled during the first decade of statehood until they became the Jewish majority by the 1970s, and the Ashkenazi-controlled major political parties had to woo their votes. The scene was complicated by the rise in numbers of another identifiable Jewish group, one that cut across Ashkenazi and Oriental distinctions: Sabras, or native-born Israelis. Although generally associated with their parents' group and marrying within that group, Sabras started to form another social force and comprised over half the Jews in Israel by 1977, most of them of European parentage. The immigration of Soviet Jews into Israel will further complicate this mix.

If the Oriental Jews are the underside of Israeli Jewish society, many Arabs are in the position of belonging to a different culture, yet also being citizens of Israel. The flight of Arabs out of Palestine from 1947 to 1949 was motivated largely by a concern for personal safety, the same concern that brought many Jews to Palestine. Since the fighting in Palestine in 1947–1948 was largely between Jewish and local Arab forces, it is not surprising that various Jewish groups actively sought to rid the fragile state of the hostile Arab population. The most famous—or infamous—terrorist act of this early period was the massacre in the village of Deir Yasin, where 250 Arab men, women, and children were killed. While the political leaders of Israel officially opposed the act, they did not proceed in a forceful manner to end terrorism by the armed bands that cooperated with the military.

Arab migration from (and within) Israel destroyed any semblance of order and coherence in the remaining Arab population. The two sources of leadership, the urban professional elite and the traditional leaders of the villages, had generally fled. Of the major cities of Israel, only Nazareth maintained a large Arab population; only a few thousand remained in the other urban centers. A wide-open and often bitter competition for power took place in many rural areas. There was no center around which the Palestinian Arabs could rally. They were further divided along religious lines: 70 percent were Muslim, 21 percent Christian, and 9 percent Druze and other religions. In the immediate postwar years, Palestinian Arabs had no political leadership and suffered extreme economic deprivation.

Neither Zionist theory nor past political policy gave the leaders of the new state a clear formula on how to deal with an Arab minority in a Zionist state. Indeed, some Israelis hoped for a time that the problem would solve itself—that the flight of the Arabs would continue until none were left. In any case, the fledgling state had other pressing problems to deal with in order to survive. The economy was in chaos, the machinery of government was incomplete, and thousands of indigent, relatively unskilled immigrants were flowing in. The ad hoc policy toward Palestinian Arabs was mainly concerned with the maintenance of state security.

The geographical concentration of the Arab population made administration somewhat simple. A few months after Israel was formed, the army units that had occupied Arab-populated areas were formally charged with administering them. Since most of the Palestinian Arabs lived in areas that were Arab under the U.N. partition plan, a military administration was logical in that Israel was an occupying force. However, the military administration was to continue until 1966, well after the annexation of these areas. Regardless of its other policy measures, the emplacement of what essentially was an army of occupation defined the basic attitude of the state toward these "part-citizens." However, even within the military administration the principles of administrative action were not clearly spelled out; security remained the only articulated goal.

Security would be enhanced if the Arab population were fragmented geographically and politically, if their economic power were limited but not desperately low, and if their emerging leadership were placed in a dependent situation and co-opted. Many of the Israeli government's policies can be connected to one or more of these aims. For instance, land use and land right policies consistently had the effect of stripping land away from the Arab population, especially in those areas the government deemed necessary to place under full Jewish control. Travel restrictions made it difficult for Arabs to reestablish political unity; and other policies established tight control over the Arab labor force. Occasionally the policies of the military administration resulted in spectacular displays of violence. In October 1956, for example, forty-nine residents of the Arab village of Kfar Kassim were killed for disobeying a curfew order of which they were unaware. The growing tensions surrounding the 1956 war and the need for absolute control led to the tragedy. That the responsible officers were given relatively light sentences confirmed the Arab's view of the Israeli government's attitude toward them.

By the mid-1970s the Arabs of Israel began to express a sense of nationalism, but it was not until the 1988 uprising in the occupied territories that they moved to build a unified political base with strictly Arab concerns at the forefront. Their formidable task was complicated, however, by the increasingly severe restrictions the government had placed on their political activity.

Israel and the Border States

Following the May 14, 1948, declaration of statehood, Israel immediately was engaged in war by Egypt, Iraq, Lebanon, Syria, and Transjordan. The initial round of fighting lasted for a month and was followed by a month-long truce administered by the United Nations. Ten more days of fighting was followed by a second truce. Sporadic fighting and truce arrangements occurred throughout 1948. Finally, the British government declared that it would act on the 1936 treaty with Egypt that allowed British troops to enter Egypt to protect vital British interests. This announcement, and pressures from the U.S. government on Israel, helped bring about a series of bilateral armistice agreements between Israel and its neighbors.

The war and the armistice agreements increased Israeli territory by more than 30 percent beyond what was allowed for in the partition plan. The Israeli army, although outnumbered substantially, mounted a series of crisp and well-coordinated attacks on the various Arab armies. However, the Israeli success was due at least as much to the ineptitude of the Arab armies and the lack of coordination between them. While various Arab leaders charged that Israel had won because of Western support, several Arab nationalist spokesmen expressed their dissatisfaction with the kind of leadership that resulted in such humiliation. Terrorist activities ripped through Egypt in the latter part of 1948 and throughout 1949; the Egyptian prime minister was assassinated. The winds of discontent in Egypt continued to blow until the Free Officers' revolution in 1952. Three coups occurred in Syria during 1949–1950; none of the new leaders, however, engaged the public's imagination. King Abdullah of Jordan was assassinated in July 1951. The shame of the 1948 defeat resulted in more Arab reprisals against their own governments than against Israel. Their anger was well placed, but it would take another quarter century before Arab armies could begin to match Israeli forces.

The task of creating and maintaining stability in newly created states generally has proved to be a formidable task. Israeli leaders had their job complicated by continued hostile relations with Arab states and by Israel's special population and economic problems. The flood of Jews coming from Europe after the close of World War II and from Arab countries during the late 1940s and early 1950s put the new state under tremendous strain. Israel, after all, was to be the homeland for all Jews. Indeed, the Israeli declaration of independence implied, and subsequent legislation (the Law of Return) granted, this right. Therefore, all immigrants had to be accepted. On the other hand, the economic and social system was put under an enormous burden—so enormous that many feared Israel would collapse. In 1952, the Jewish Agency, the organizers and financiers of most of this immigration, in an attempt to ease the crisis, introduced certain financial criteria for immigration. However, the new criteria for immigration did not solve other pressing problems. For instance, many immigrants did not adhere to the Zionist-socialist ideology on which the early settlers had founded Israeli society, and the flight of Arab farmers and the cessation of agricultural trade with Arab states had caused a food shortage that assumed crisis proportions.

Many immigrants had to be settled on the land, but most were not ideologically suited to life on a kibbutz (a form of collective farm developed by earlier settlers), nor life in the cooperative agricultural villages, the moshav. The government had placed many immigrants in farming villages under the supervision of instructors who gave technical information, executive direction, and ideological guidance. Ideally, the villages were to be located behind the border settlements and evolve into autonomous cooperatives. This process was carried out by fits and starts, with some successes and failures.

The first several years of statehood, then, were difficult. However, the population, food, shelter, and state security problems were adequately solved by the mid-1950s. A considerable amount of ingenuity and hard work had been required, but the job was eased considerably by a large amount of foreign aid flowing into the country that made it possible for Israel to cope with the situation. Immediately after independence the ratio of the value of exports to imports was about 15 percent; that is, for every $1.00 spent on imports only $.15 was earned from exports. The ratio climbed to 60 percent in the 1970s, but the absolute value of the gap had increased. The gap between international spending and earning was covered by international remittances—gifts and loans from governments and individuals. About $15 billion was received during the new nation's first twenty-five years: 25 percent came from Jewish Fund collections, 25 percent from German reparation and restitution payments, 9 percent from bond sales, 13 percent from direct, unilateral transfers (generally from individual to individual), 13 percent from U.S. government loans and gifts, 7 percent from direct private investment, and 8 percent from various short and medium term loans. Much of Israel's economic growth was due to these sources.

The economic successes of the first couple of decades of statehood were not to be sustained. Israel's international debt position deteriorated considerably. Per capita external debt ranked among the highest in the world by 1980, and debt service payments became increasingly onerous, averaging around 20 percent of the value of export earnings in the 1980s. Growth slowed, inflation sometimes topped 100 percent,[1] and the extensive social welfare state constructed in the first two decades did not allow for a flexible response by the government. Solutions to these problems required a strong government; as it was, Israel went through most of the 1980s and early 1990s with coalition governments unable to reach agreement on crucial policy issues.

The 1956 Arab-Israeli War

As Israel steadied its economy and settled its immigrants, the Arab nations limited their anti-Israeli activity. They generally did not have firm control over their own internal political situations and, therefore, shied away from full-scale conflict. However, Nasser's success in nationalizing the Suez Canal aroused Israeli fears of Arab unity. A few years earlier Israel had initiated its policy of severe military reprisals against any government that allowed its territory to be used as a base for attacks on Israel. The policy was designed to discourage further attacks by making the punishment exceed the transgression. Although Israel was censured by the United Nations on several occasions for implementing this policy, it nevertheless held firm. Israel and the West were deeply concerned with the pan-Arab sentiment that was growing under Nasser's leadership and Egypt's drift toward the Soviet bloc. Israel was also concerned with the increasing number of raids from Egyptian territory, and Egypt's refusal to allow Israeli ships through the Suez Canal and especially the Straits of Tiran. In response, Israel invaded Egypt on October 30, 1956. Within four days, Israel was in control of the Sinai and the Gaza Strip. One day after the start of the Israeli invasion, the British and French announced a joint expedition to seize the Suez Canal, an action that the United States opposed. When the fighting ended a few days later, the British and French held Port Said at the northern terminus of the canal. An eventual settlement called for the removal of the invading forces from Egyptian soil and the stationing of United Nations troops along the Egyptian-Israeli borders (primarily in the Gaza Strip and along the important Straits of Tiran, through which Israeli shipping could reach the port of Aqaba and thereby avoid the Suez Canal).

The Arabs henceforth considered Nasser a hero. He had turned back Israel, France, and Britain, and had earlier rebuffed U.S. attempts to limit Egyptian military strength. Israel had scored an impressive military victory but found itself in a

---

[1] It should be noted that the disruptive effect of the enormous rate of inflation is ameliorated considerably because the economy is indexed—that is, wages rise automatically with inflation, thereby lessening the usual kinds of redistribution of income generally associated with inflation.

more delicate position than before, as Nasser's influence and the pan-Arab movement gathered momentum after the invasions. During the decade following the 1956 war, Nasser remained the undisputed leader of the Arab world, although he had to share some of his prestige with Ahmed Ben Bella of Algeria after the success of the Algerian revolution against French colonial rule. He was also concerned with the situation in Yemen, and sent 70,000 troops to support the republicans against the Saudi-backed royalists.

The 1967 Arab-Israeli War

From 1956 to 1966 Israeli-Arab tensions remained just below the boiling point as a host of large and small issues—including important disputes over water rights in the Jordan River, changing relative military strength, and shifting Arab alliances—threatened to fan the conflict again.

For two years the Syrian government had permitted Al-Fatah, a military arm of the fledgling Palestine Liberation Organization (PLO), to use Syria as a base for raids into Israel. In May 1967, various Arab leaders became convinced that Israel was about to launch a massive reprisal attack against Syria. As a visible display of Egypt's willingness to go to war, Nasser had Egyptian troops march through Cairo on their way to the Suez Canal. This action sounded like a battle cry in the Arab world, which then called on Nasser to crush Israel. Since his popularity had begun to wane, Nasser needed to be firm and decisive if he were to remain the leader of the Arab world. Confrontation politics are always dangerous, but especially so when each side has developed a "worst case" scenario. On May 19, 1967, Egypt requested that UN troops be withdrawn from Egyptian territory. The United Nations complied promptly—too promptly to suit many observers. On May 24, Nasser announced that the Straits of Tiran were closed to Israeli ships. The die was cast. The Six-Day War started on the morning of June 5. The Israeli air force destroyed most of the Egyptian air force while it was still on the ground. Quickly and efficiently Israel pressed the advantage it had secured by air; within a week it had taken the Sinai and Gaza from Egypt, Jordanian territory west of the Jordan River, and the Golan (Quneitra) district of Syria, commonly referred to by the Israelis as the Golan Heights. In contrast to the postwar agreements of 1956, Israeli troops continued to occupy territory in which well over a million Arabs lived. The war was another crushing humiliation for the Arabs, and Nasser offered his resignation.

Israel gained a clear military victory and established three buffer areas it considered vital to its security. But it also had to control well over a million additional Arabs at a time when the Palestinian movement was gathering steam. Israel's occupation of Arab territories put it in a difficult position in the United Nations. The Security Council of the United Nations responded by adopting Resolution 242, which required Israel to withdraw its forces from occupied territories, and also required Arab states to recognize Israel's right to exist, among other things.

The 1973 Arab-Israeli War

The end of the 1967 Arab-Israeli war did not bring peace. Israel continued to hold the occupied territories and even to build Jewish settlements on them. It faced a line of hostile Arab states, especially Egypt, and was burdened with an enormous defense budget.

By 1973, Egypt's President Anwar Sadat had three years of experience in office. He had ceased to be viewed as a weak, sometimes comical, figure and had begun to assert his own brand of leadership. The 1967 war had been devastating to the Egyptian military and economy. Because the economy had already been extremely weak (partially due to the abrupt and untimely way in which Nasser nationalized many industries in the early 1960s) and because there was a high rate of population growth, the capacity of the average Egyptian to endure hardship was being severely strained. But the Soviet Union was reluctant to give President Sadat the military aid he needed, probably because of the possibility of upsetting the movement toward detente with the United States. In July 1972, President Sadat ordered the immediate departure of 40,000 Soviet military personnel and their dependents from Egypt. The oil-rich Arab states were already supplying Egypt with considerable aid, but could not be expected to deliver military hardware. If Egypt had allowed the status quo to continue, the minimal demands of its military would have worsened the already dangerous economic situation. The government of Israel, seeing Egypt's plight, then set down more stringent conditions for peace, obviously hoping that President Sadat would accede. But acceptance of the Israeli position would have endangered Egypt's aid from the oil-rich Arab states and possibly triggered a coup. President Sadat then embarked on a fruitless international diplomatic offensive as a last step short of war. Because he saw no other way out of the stalemate, Sadat and President Assad of Syria then planned a joint attack on Israel for October 6, 1973. The war, called the Ramadan or Yom Kippur War, was launched on time. Carefully trained Egyptian forces managed to penetrate Israel's defenses with the objective of seizing a strip of the Sinai east of the canal. However, Israeli forces crossed the canal at another point and isolated the Egyptian army. A cease-fire, sponsored by the United Nations with the encouragement of the great powers, took effect on October 24. It took until the following May for terms to be worked out on the Syrian-Israeli front.

The Israeli army had again proved capable of meeting the Arab threat. It had recovered from the initial forays of the Egyptian army and mounted its own offensive; it also beat back Syrian attempts to regain the Golan Heights. But the results of this conflict were different from the earlier wars on at least a couple of counts. First, the cost of the effort in terms of money and men was staggering. It was obvious that neither side could afford many more such ventures. Second, the Egyptian army performed as a tough, skilled unit. Although it did not in any sense win the military battle, it was obvious to many that a limited Egyptian victory was well within the realm of possibility.

It seems that President Sadat's gamble in initiating the war had paid off. The Egyptians had mounted a successful limited strike and then invited the great powers to help Egypt find a way to break the stalemate with Israel. It was a high-risk strategy, one which came dangerously close to forcing direct military involvement by the United States and the Soviet Union. But the stalemate was broken as the U.S. secretary of state, Henry Kissinger, took the lead in promoting a new settlement. In the months after the war, Dr. Kissinger and a number of other interested parties flew repeatedly from one capital to another in what was called "shuttle diplomacy." After a time, terms of peace were established between Egypt and

Israel. President Sadat had put much stock in efforts of the United States to bring the needed settlement. The Syrians, still engaged in combat against the Israelis, and unable to win back any territory, were understandably upset by Egypt's separate agreement with Israel. Sadat's actions were considered to be a form of appeasement, and Egypt became isolated in the Arab world. Syria's President Assad assumed the leadership of the front line states. Nevertheless, President Sadat continued his efforts to bring a lasting peace to Egypt. His most spectacular move was to go before the Israeli Knesset in November 1977. Although the major issues between Egypt and Israel were not resolved by this dramatic initiative, it did set the stage for further negotiations, the most important being the Camp David talks between Prime Minister Begin, President Sadat, and President Carter. This resulted in a formal peace treaty and diplomatic relations. Egypt and Israel continued their sometimes fractious negotiations through the remainder of the 1970s, resulting in a gradual Israeli withdrawal from the Sinai and a partial normalization of relations between Egypt and Israel. Israeli withdrawal was completed in April 1982.

Egypt's partial accommodation with Israel continued to alienate it from Syria, its supporters, and the Palestinians. It was charged that Egypt forgot the Palestinians in a selfish and shortsighted attempt to gain temporary security. Sadat's dismantling of Nasser's socialist economy was seen as further evidence of his Western bias.

Syria, the new claimant to Arab leadership in the struggle against Israel, was caught in an ironic swirl of events. As noted earlier, Syria had found it necessary to place troops in Lebanon to control Palestinian activities and to avoid Israeli reprisal attacks. By 1982, Christian separatist forces controlled a sizable strip of southern Lebanon, with the help of Israeli materiel and military aid. Syria effectively controlled the rest of Lebanon (not including parts of Beirut and some mountainous areas), which included the Palestinians.

The 1982 Invasion of Lebanon

The 1982 Israeli invasion of Lebanon profoundly changed the character of several key political relationships in the Middle East. It has been argued that the 1967 war resulted in an Arab moral crisis: It became clear that visions of Arab unity were pure illusion; Nasser's dream was dead. In the same light, the invasion of Lebanon marks a profound moral cleavage in the Israeli polity. Israeli opponents to the invasion tended to view it as brutal aggression that undermined Israel's moral foundations. Israeli peace groups gained new life; a protest demonstration in Tel Aviv drew several hundred thousand participants. Supporters of the government, of course, saw the action as necessary, arguing that the last PLO foothold had to be destroyed. Political divisions hardened.

The 1982 invasion of Lebanon, of course, did not occur without reference to Israeli security on other borders. Israel's separate peace with Egypt culminated with the April 1982 withdrawal of Israeli forces from Sinai. The process of withdrawal was aided by the presence of a multinational peacekeeping force. Included in the agreement were scheduled (and continually postponed) talks that were to lead to eventual autonomy in the Gaza Strip.

Withdrawal from the Sinai necessitated that Israelis be removed forcibly from their illegal settlements. This threatened the fragile domestic coalition that depended on the support of those members of the Knesset favoring virtually unlimited settlement in occupied territories. Prime Minister Begin weathered the storm, partially due to prior decisions on the rapid settlement of the West Bank, and partially because of the extension of Israeli civilian law (December 1981) into the Golan, an action which translated into de facto annexation.

In early May 1982, the Knesset formally supported Prime Minister Begin's statement that Israeli settlements would not be dismantled as part of any peace negotiations, and that Israeli sovereignty over the West Bank should be established once the interim arrangements called for in the Camp David accords had run their course. During the first several months of 1982 there was considerable unrest in Gaza and the West Bank.

Israel apparently thought that if the PLO were crushed in Lebanon, and if Syrian forces were neutralized, it could establish more secure borders to the north and east; the agreement with Egypt had provided breathing space to the south. The invasion and occupation of Lebanon (1982–1985) accomplished some objectives—the PLO in Lebanon was severely weakened, and time was afforded for the continued rapid settlement of the West Bank. But it carried substantial liabilities, including the weakening of Christian power in Lebanon, an ultimately more powerful Syrian presence there, a rapprochement between the PLO, Egypt, and Jordan, and considerable domestic unrest.

These adverse conditions, however, were but surface manifestations of deeper seismic rumblings caused by the war. Of prime importance was the subsequent regrouping of the PLO, and its 1985 acceptance of the "Jordanian option." While it is dangerous to draw specific long-range implications, it is quite clear that there are straightforward connections between the 1982 invasion and the Palestinian uprising.

THE PALESTINIANS AND THE 1988 UPRISING

The Palestinian diaspora that resulted from the Israeli victory of 1948 was largely to Arab countries. In 1950, about 900,000 Palestinian refugees were in camps operated by the United Nations in Lebanon, Jordan (and the West Bank), Syria, and the Gaza Strip. The plight of these people was deplorable. The United Nations relief effort was minimal; the food ration was limited to 1,600 calories a day, and housing often consisted of scraps of material loosely thrown together to form primitive shelters. No national Palestinian leadership had arisen before the establishment of Israel, and refugees grouped together on a traditional village basis. Throughout the 1950s the outside world heard little about the refugee camps, except for occasional news shorts showing their humiliating and stultifying living conditions. The rest of the world seemed to wish the Palestinians away; the Palestinians were unable to generate any coherent response to their plight. On the few occasions when they protested their conditions, they were suppressed by the host Arab governments, the most notable early example of this being Egypt's actions in the Gaza Strip in the 1950s.

Organized resistance eventually did develop, beginning with the formation of Al-Fatah in the late 1950s, and the creation of the Palestine Liberation Organization in 1964 through an initiative of the Arab League. It was apparent to the various national leaders that the festering discontent in the refugee camps was being used to form effective paramilitary units dedicated to the overthrow of Israel. These groups took heart in the success of the Algerians in thwarting the best efforts of France through a combination of tight organization, urban guerrilla terrorist activity, and tenacity. Palestinians began to think that they too could bring a Western power to its knees. However, there were significant differences between the two situations, one difference being that the bulk of the Palestinians and the heart of their resistance movement were outside Israel. Israel's reprisals against any nation from which anti-Israeli actions originated, coupled with its military superiority, deterred the Arab League. The League thus decided to control the Palestinian activists. It thought that the PLO could serve as a Palestinian umbrella organization and at the same time be subject to the League's control. Al-Fatah, under the leadership of Yasir Arafat, however, remained active.

With the end of the 1967 war, Palestinian fortunes began to rise. For most of the 1960s, Palestinian leaders had disagreed with Nasser's dictum "Unity Is the Road to Palestine," preferring instead "Palestine Is the Road to Unity." The outcome of the 1967 war made it clear to them that their hopes for nationhood would be dashed if they followed Nasser's proposition. The Palestinians believed that only *they* could and would act to defeat Israel. Therefore, they ignored Arab pleas for unity. The various "frontline" nations, bordering Israel, however, faced the prospect of having independent Palestinian armies in their territories, armies bent on destroying an enemy that the nations themselves were not prepared to attack. The PLO could no longer be expected to control the different Palestinian groups or obey the wishes of the Arab League. Each country therefore gave tacit support to a particular Palestinian organization, supported its growth, and tried to control its activity. Well over a dozen sizable groups and a bewildering array of splinter groups formed between 1967 and 1969. In 1969, Yasir Arafat of Al-Fatah became the head of the PLO. Apparently the thinking in Arab capitals was that Arafat's successful organization would be controlled more easily if he were given a new mantle of authority as leader of the PLO.

King Hussein of Jordan tended to view the Palestinians as potential citizens of Jordan rather than aspirants to a separate nation. Since the PLO had between 30,000 and 50,000 troops in Jordan by 1970—forces better described as a conventional army than as guerrilla fighters—and since the fractious liberation movement was demanding more and more autonomy in Jordan, the king could either sit back and watch his country being dismantled or take decisive action. Black September is the name the Palestinian movement gave his response: in September 1970, Hussein ordered regular Jordanian troops against the PLO. Thousands of Palestinians were killed, and Palestinian power in Jordan was broken. The only remaining sanctuary close to the Palestinian homeland, Lebanon, absorbed large numbers of refugees and found itself traveling down a dangerous road. The Palestinians were in decline, but they remained a force to reckon with.

The PLO was not significantly involved in the 1973 Arab-Israeli war except for promoting strikes in the occupied West Bank. In November 1973, the Arab heads of state declared the PLO the sole legitimate representative of the Palestinian people. To Arab leaders, the move made sense for several reasons: Jordan's King Hussein had been discredited as a representative of Palestinian interests due to the events of Black September; it was necessary to include the PLO in any peace negotiations; and the PLO now seemed to be more flexible than before on many issues.

In November 1974, Yasir Arafat addressed the United Nations and saw that body pass resolutions declaring the right of Palestinians to seek independence and granting the PLO permanent observer status in the United Nations. The PLO had attained international legitimacy. But it was not recognized by Israel and, therefore, could not enter into direct negotiations. Nor was it accorded more independence of movement by the Arab nations. Its fortunes took a turn for the worse during 1975 when Lebanon fell into civil disorder. The PLO had been hinting that it could accept the continued existence of Israel if Palestinians were granted an independent status on West Bank territory. Israel indicated that it could accept a Palestinian "entity" on the West Bank only as long as that entity was formally part of Jordan and as long as Israel was allowed to maintain defense forces in the area. While these positions were far apart, they at least allowed the participants room to negotiate and continue the slow process of finding a mutually acceptable solution. But the moderating forces in the PLO lost ground to the "rejectionists"—those who saw the elimination of Israel as the only possible foundation for a Palestinian state. Since the PLO could not control rejectionist activities during the collapse of Lebanon, its claim to preeminence was compromised.

Events following the evacuation of PLO forces from Lebanon in the aftermath of the Israeli invasion of 1982 point to a couple of facts. First, the PLO is a multinational organization; it did not collapse due to the evacuation. Rather, the organization simply changed the primary locus of activity away from that country. In addition, those evicted from Lebanon were afforded considerable prestige in parts of the Arab world because of the tenacity of their forces in the face of the clearly superior firepower of the Israelis, and they gained a more cordial relationship with several important Arab governments, especially Egypt and Jordan. The well-established organizational structure of the PLO, and the financing offered by several Arab governments (along with a Palestinian income tax), indicated that the PLO would be a force to reckon with for some time.

Second, Al-Fatah continued to be the most powerful group within the PLO, and Yasir Arafat maintained his position as head of both Al-Fatah and the PLO. Rejectionist forces and breakaway Al-Fatah groups failed in their attempts to wrest power away from this now clearly dominant group. The most prominent of these rejections of Arafat's leadership occurred after the first PLO evacuation from Beirut. Rejectionist Al-Fatah forces located close to Syrian positions in Lebanon took up arms against their brethren when the PLO (and the mainstream Al-Fatah forces under Arafat) was seen as entertaining notions of compromise that would have yielded considerable territory to Israel. The rejectionists, with Syrian support, wrested control of large camps around Beirut.

Third, the PLO strategy for the struggle for Palestine allowed more accommodation. In the 1970s the PLO abandoned the notion that Israel needed to be destroyed if Palestine were to exist; that is, it moved from a military to a political strategy. By the 1980s they were giving strong indications that the establishment of a Palestinian "entity," which need not include all of the territory occupied by Israel, would be acceptable if assurances could be given for eventual independence. King Hussein of Jordan and Arafat held discussions on these matters a little more than a decade after Black September: Irreconcilable differences have a transient quality.

The Intifadah

The widespread Western, and especially American, view of Israel as a beleaguered David struggling against an Arab Goliath was shattered in 1988. Television screens around the world showed confrontations between stone-throwing Palestinian youth, of Gaza and the West Bank, and the Israeli Defense Forces (IDF). Palestinian teenagers took on the persona of the stone-throwing David, while the Israeli crack troops with sophisticated weapons appeared as Goliath. Television cameras revealed instances of the inevitable excessive use of force by the IDF. As the 1982 invasion of Lebanon had thrown Israel into moral crisis, so the Palestinian uprising intensified it and laid to rest notions of a beneficent Israeli military occupation.

An auto accident in Gaza in December 1987 provided the spark that ignited the uprising, popularly called intifadah by the Palestinians. Apparently all of the principals were surprised by the strength, depth, and spread of the initial stages of the rebellion. The PLO was among those surprised, and quickly scrambled to coordinate the civil disorder. Although the auto accident provided the catalyst for the intifadah, the discontent had been growing for some time.

The 1967 war had resulted in Israeli occupation of Gaza, the Sinai, the Golan, and the West Bank (including East Jerusalem). Each of the areas presented Israel with different opportunities and problems. The Sinai, of course, provided a massive buffer against Egypt. A decade later this land was traded for peace as part of the Camp David Accords. The Golan district was earmarked for permanent control by Israel almost immediately after the war's conclusion. Because Israel feared Syria more than any other belligerent neighboring Arab state, this strategic border area would not be relinquished. The task of maintaining control was eased because close to 90 percent of the prewar population had fled.

Gaza had been militarily administered by Egypt since 1949. Although it lost between 15 and 20 percent of its population due to the 1967 war, it still contained about a third of a million residents in a very small area. Furthermore, a large percentage of these families were refugees from the 1948 war, still openly hostile to Israel. Consequently, Israeli policy in Gaza was dominated by police action rather than settlement.

East Jerusalem was claimed as Israeli territory shortly after the war. It was a piece of property that Israeli politicians for religious, historical, and cultural reasons could not contemplate giving back. The West Bank was more problematic. Immediately after the cessation of hostilities in 1949, King Abdullah of Jordan hastily convened a conference of West Bank Palestinian notables who gave their blessings to the formal annexation of the West Bank by Jordan. The international community never accepted the result, but it did allow the de facto administration of the territory by Jordan. However, the majority of the Palestinian population never accepted Hashemite rule. The disputed status of the West Bank allowed each interested party to frame arguments and policies consistent with its most convenient premise. For instance, Israel held that it could negotiate only with the government of Jordan, while the PLO claimed that it alone represented the occupants of the occupied territories. After six months of the intifadah, and some forty years after the annexation announcement, Jordan formally renounced any claim to the West Bank.

The West Bank lost about a quarter of its population in 1967. Especially important was the fact that over 90 percent of the population of the west Jordan Valley, located between the Jordan River and the western mountains of the rift, fled to the East Bank or other nearby places of rural refuge. Only 10,000 Palestinians remained.

Israel's Allon Plan, although never formally accepted as official policy, provided the basic blueprint for Israeli action during the first decade of occupation. The plan called for settlement of (1) the Jordan Valley rift from the northern Israeli border to just north of the Dead Sea, and (2) an area from Jerusalem south past Hebron to the border, and from Jerusalem to the Dead Sea in the east. This meant that the Palestinian area of the West Bank was divided into two parts, which the Israelis have called Judea and Samaria. The northern enclave (Samaria) had a corridor that joined Jordan at the northern end of the Dead Sea. The areas marked for Israeli settlement (including a strip west of Samaria and one running along the Sinai border) were designed primarily with defense in mind.

While the Allon Plan served defense interests, it did not satisfy the increasingly popular goal of establishing settlements throughout the West Bank—including the religiously important and heavily Palestinian-populated central areas ignored by the Allon Plan. The Likud bloc victory of 1977 extended the settlement policy to include Judea and Samaria. In 1977 Prime Minister Begin declared that the "Green Line" (the 1967 borders) had "vanished." To the Labor government's security rationale for settlement, the Likud government added a theological imperative: The land had been promised to them by God. Although believing in the same God, the Palestinians did not receive the same message. Nevertheless, Israeli colonization proceeded apace.

By 1990 about 100,000 Israelis had settled in the occupied territories, mostly on the West Bank, mostly in bedroom suburbs of Jerusalem and Tel Aviv. The bulk of these settlers were not religious zealots, but middle-class Israelis trading a crowded urban environment with scarce and expensive housing for newly constructed subsidized units only fifteen minutes from the city center. These units also served a military purpose. Called "fortress settlements," they are generally multistory apartment complexes that are built on high ground and close to each other (or interlocking) so as to prevent enemy penetration. They have other defenselike features, such as narrow windows with metal shutters. Jerusalem is virtually surrounded by these fortress settlements. The 1991 acceleration of settlement, as guided by the Minister of Housing, Ariel Sharon, largely followed this policy by "thickening" these urban clusters and nearly doubled the number of Israelis living in the occupied territories.

A substantial number of settlers in the earlier years went to newly constructed towns throughout the West Bank. In order to build these settlements, land rights had to be secured, transport and power grids constructed, and water systems put in place. By 1988 half of the West Bank's land had been ceded to Israelis through the application of a wide range of measures. A road network was in place, connecting the cities, bypassing Arab towns, and preventing the development of ribbon settlement of Palestinians next to the roads. Access to water, especially for agricultural use, became increasingly difficult for Palestinians. Although the placement of some settlements was dictated by the desire to control a particularly important religious site, the overall pattern was designed to isolate the Palestinian towns.

Israelis opposed to the settlements complained about the expense of the program in times of economic hardship. They also argued that annexation would undermine Israel's stature as a Jewish state if the Palestinians were given full citizenship rights, or destroy the democratic character of the state if they were denied citizenship. But colonization continued and de facto annexation took place.

Many of the Palestinian refugee camps were forty years old at the time of the uprising. The tents of four decades ago had been replaced by concrete block structures which had rooms added to them as the camps took on more the character of permanent settlements than places of temporary refuge. Some camp residents owned autos, many homes sprouted television antennas, and an articulated economic order brought increases in material well-being. Some material conditions, however, remained appalling—for example, open sewers draining into disease-ridden, fetid pools of filth. Residents were reminded daily of their occupied status: The men of Gaza gathered every morning to get transport to Tel Aviv for regular jobs or day labor. Israel demanded that they return to the camps every night or have identity cards that permitted their stay in Israel. The usual colonial pattern of discrimination against Palestinians in terms of wages and the types of jobs available for them prevailed. More than 100,000 Palestinians of the occupied territories worked in Israel. Economic dependence for them was not limited to the labor market or the camps. For example, the agricultural produce and industrial output of the occupied territories were denied ready access to Israel when they would compete with Israeli-produced goods. In addition, licenses to produce goods in potential competition with Israel were denied, water rights were curtailed, and so on. The military plan for maintaining civil order was called the "Iron Fist": long-term detentions without charge or trial, collective punishment, deportations, and the strict control of basic political expression. When this is placed in the context of a systematic loss of land rights and increased economic dependence, it is not surprising that the Palestinian population became more embittered and desperate.

The widespread nature of the rebellion meant that a decisive response by the IDF would result in unacceptable levels of carnage. As it was, the limited response still resulted in an average of one Palestinian death per day. As Israel groped for solutions, the revolt continued. In addition to some widely reported excesses of the military, there were several largely symbolic statements and actions by Israeli officials that fanned the flames. Prime Minister Shamir at one point said that the troublemakers were mere "grasshoppers" and would be dealt with as such. Ariel Sharon, early architect of the settlement policy on the West Bank and planner of the 1982 invasion of Lebanon, moved his residence to the Muslim quarter of the old city of Jerusalem. Some members of the Knesset called for the forcible removal of all Palestinians from the West Bank. Substantive actions supported these symbolic acts. In April 1988, Abu Jihad, the supposed PLO coordinator of the uprising, was assassinated in Tunis by a team widely assumed to be associated with official Israel. Deportations, detentions, and other restrictive measures increased, but the rebellion continued. Israel was a few months away from elections, and the Palestinian National Congress was preparing a declaration of independence.

It was no surprise that the 1988 election campaign in Israel was vicious. Israel's position in the occupied territories was increasingly precarious, and international opinion was increasingly sympathetic to the Palestinian position. The crisis of conscience brought to center stage by the 1982 invasion of Lebanon intensified. The Labor bloc advocated (with many provisos) the convening of an international conference that would trade land for peace. Likud was not so disposed. The always important religious parties hardened their positions.

The religious parties gained seats in the November 1988 election. Likud won forty seats and Labor thirty-nine seats. A coalition was put together after six weeks of negotiations. Likud, which was called on to form a government, initially negotiated with the religious parties, but finally found the positions of the religious bloc to be unacceptable. Particularly controversial was the policy proposed by religious conservatives that called for the redefining of the Law of Return so that only converts converted by Orthodox rabbis to Judaism would be eligible for "return status." Many Jews outside Israel, especially in the United States, expressed deep shock and hinted that acceptance of this policy would change their attitude toward Israel. Also, after the election and before the formation of the new government, the Palestinian National Congress declared an independent Palestinian state (November 15, 1988), a move that received warm worldwide support. A month later Yasir Arafat addressed the United Nations. In the address, and in subsequent clarifying remarks in the next several days, the PLO stated its recognition of the state of Israel and renounced terrorism. A few days later, and after much diplomatic dancing, the United States opened official discussions with the PLO, something it had not done for thirteen years.

The new coalition in Israel again joined Likud and Labor in a "marriage of inconvenience." Before the election, all parties had agreed that the policy paralysis of the last such government should not be repeated. However, there were differences in the composition of the new government, the most important being that Likud would hold the posts of prime minister and foreign minister throughout the coalition (instead of the Labor-Likud split and midterm switching, as had occurred before), but many of the debilitating aspects of power sharing remained. The major actors of the new government declared agreement on their unwillingness to talk with the PLO and on the need to end the intifadah. They disagreed on most other important matters. As stated earlier, the coalition fell apart by 1990. The subsequent Likud-religious party government met a similar fate in 1992.

The formation of a Labor government after the June 1992 elections gave new hope for the peace conference. Likud had used the peace conference to buy time; to "create facts on the ground," especially through its ambitious settlement policy in the occupied territories. The peace negotiations were all but dead at election time. The Labor government brought a new attitude to the negotiating table: They saw Israel's best interests served through a series of compromises with the Palestinians. Instead of attempting to construct new realities through colonization, they offered to give the Palestinians a measure of autonomy.

TURNING POINTS

The August 2, 1990 invasion of Kuwait by Iraq, along with the subsequent political and military responses, signalled a significant turning point in modern Middle Eastern history.

Almost every border in the Middle East was initially defined by European powers—by way of the Balfour Declaration, the mandate system, and various territorial realignments thereafter. Arab governments, almost without exception, railed, orally if not through policy, against the artificial nature of the imposed borders. Arab unity, they said, would be denied as long as the borders remained. Through the last decades of the twentieth century, however, these same governments actively sought to build and strengthen loyalties to the nation-states described by the hated European-imposed boundaries. They succeeded in their efforts to various degrees, but the ideologically convenient dream of Arab unity continued to be part of the required rhetoric until the invasion of Kuwait by Iraq.

The invasion was universally condemned as an illegitimate exercise of state power. Several actors (Algeria, Libya, Jordan, the PLO, Sudan, and Yemen) contended that an "Arab solution" would be the only acceptable solution. But those countries of the Arabian (Persian) Gulf (except Yemen) disagreed; they called for U.S. military intervention. Egypt and Syria were persuaded to accept this view and, most important, to contribute troops to the effort.

It is difficult to overstate the enormity of these actions. The invasion of Kuwait marked the first time that a modern Arab state invaded another. The Arab world was quick to point to the sanctity of the borders. Then the United States, a long-time staunch supporter of Israel, along with ex-colonialists France and the United Kingdom, were invited to Saudi soil to do battle against fellow Arabs.

The Arab allies in the war against Iraq consisted of the petroleum-rich and population-poor countries of Arabia (minus Yemen), Egypt, Syria, and distant Morocco. Actually, Egypt had struck its basic bargain with the notion of Arab unity a decade earlier in the Camp David accords when they had reached a separate agreement with Israel, thereby ignoring the Israeli occupied territories, except to the extent that reference was made in the accords to vague and unworkable linkages concerning negotiations for the formation of Palestinian "autonomy." By 1990, Egypt was in a very difficult economic situation; a situation eased after their participation in the allied cause by U.S. and Gulf economic aid and significant debt forgiveness. Syria faced the same general economic malaise: a burdensome defense outlay in Lebanon, continued Israeli occupation (and settlement) of the Golan territory, and cutbacks in aid from the Soviet bloc. They needed the United States as an ally; the crisis in Kuwait provided a convenient entre.

At the conclusion of the war there were a series of pronouncements that called for a "new order" in the Middle East. The GCC countries along with Egypt and Syria were to provide for regional military security on a cooperative basis, thus providing a vehicle for dissuading further invasions. However, the Gulf states apparently feared the brawn and long-term intentions of Egypt and Syria. Consequently, they started to back away from the agreement immediately. For their part, Egypt and Syria were not ready to engage in significant military expenditures and risk the possible loss of life without receiving substantial compensation, a compensation not being offered by the Gulf states.

It also was widely recognized that the extreme disparity in wealth between the haves and have-nots could not persist (or widen) without the threat of increasing significant instability. Therefore, various actors dreamed up schemes that allowed for petroleum-inspired Gulf charity to infuse the income-poor and population-rich nations. But the petroleum-producing countries would have difficulty in the best of times satisfying the needs of Syria and, especially, Egypt. Also, the Gulf countries felt betrayed by the eventual support of Iraq by Jordan, Yemen, and the PLO during the Gulf war. It would be quite extraordinary, then, if large-scale income redistribution took place. Rather, it is more likely that the rich states will continue to write checks to pay for defense and to otherwise defuse the desires of a particularly nettlesome neighbor. The basic military and economic fragmentation is likely to remain.

Although the allied forces crippled Iraq quickly and easily, Saddam Hussein remained in power after the conflict. There are a couple of reasons the allies did not press their advantage until he fell. First, although Iran generally watched the spectacle from the sidelines and had shown signs of considerable political moderation, neither the United States nor the Gulf states wanted to see the postwar Gulf dominated by Iran, an event which would be more likely if Iraq fell into prolonged chaos. The removal of Saddam Hussein would likely have assured such a case since his brutally repressive regime had decimated opponents and thereby rid the country of an identifiable alternative leadership. The communal nature of Iraq— the Shia of the south and the Kurds of the north—meant that it was likely that the country would crumble without a strong central authority. And without a center holding the country together, the allies, especially the United States, would have had to settle in for a long-term military occupation. This was rejected out of hand. As it was, the Shia and Kurds revolted against Baghdad anyway. The Shia were quickly and savagely repressed by Saddam Hussein as the allied forces sat less than fifty miles away. However, thousands of Shia continued the revolt despite increasingly energetic campaigns by the Iraqi military.

The Kurdish revolt of the north took longer to sort out, partially because of the organized Kurdish resistance and the flight of millions of Kurds into Turkey and Iran. As has been the case, since the 1920s the Kurdish resistance has briefly gained the sympathy of the wider world. As always, the world soon grew bored with news clips of the Kurdish plight. And, as always, those countries with substantial Kurdish populations, most notably Iran and Turkey, were not particularly anxious to see the Kurdish independence movement succeed. The Kurds of Iraq were given some protection through the application of measures designed by the United Nations to keep Iraq's military from unleashing its full force on the Kurds. Official Iraq viewed these (and other) measures as a violation of its national sovereignty. While Saddam Hussein's government pressed for greater access to the Kurdish areas, the Kurdish opposition supplied the world with documentation to support their claim that even before the war the Iraqi government engaged in a policy of systematic extermination of the Kurds.

United Nations sanctions against Iraq, and Iraqi reluctance to meet the terms of the U.N., kept tensions high. Iraqi citizens were suffering terrible consequences from the sanctions, but the government of Iraq refused to fully cooperate with the U.N., thereby keeping the sanctions in force and straining the nerves of all parties. Particularly nettlesome was the issue of the United Nations inspection teams charged with finding and disarming Iraq's stockpile and production facilities for weapons of mass destruction. On several occasions the teams were denied access to Iraqi facilities. In July 1992, a standoff resulted in the United States threatening military action and moving up the timing of joint military exercises with Kuwait. Although negotiations finally broke the impasse, all concerned parties expected that more confrontations would take place.

The implications of the war for Israel were secondary in the physical sense, but emotionally and politically profound. The intifada was droning on at the time of the invasion, enervating all parties. After facing a universal diplomatic firestorm during the first week of the occupation of Kuwait, Saddam Hussein announced that Iraq would withdraw if Israel quit the occupied territories and if Syria withdrew from Lebanon. Despite Saddam Hussein's past indifference to the Palestinian cause, the PLO embraced him and the Palestinian population took heart. When faced with such threats in the past, the Israelis had responded with a preemptive strike. However, they were constrained this time; the allies needed Arab participation in the war effort, and it would not happen if Israel were to strike Iraq. Therefore, Israel was pressured to sit back—they even maintained this stance during the war when Iraq lobbed psychologically devastating and physically ineffective Scud missiles into Israel. Israelis went through the war donning their gas masks at every air raid warning; it was feared (but not realized) that the Scuds would be armed with biological or chemical warheads. Palestinians "danced on the rooftops" as the Scuds sped toward their targets. Not surprisingly, Israeli attitudes toward the Palestinians hardened, and the already dispirited Israeli peace movement collapsed. Ironically, the June 1992 Israeli elections resulted in a government that was closer to meeting the goals of the Israeli peace movement than any government since the territories were occupied in 1967.

Israel also was affected by U.S. agreements with other members of the coalition. First, Syria was given a "green light" to root out Christian General Aoun from his fortified Beruit position. He had denied the implementation of a new power-sharing agreement since he saw it as bringing grief to the Christian population of Lebanon. Syria quickly routed Aoun, saw the new government installed, had the new government request Syrian help in disarming the various militia, and signed a Treaty of Brotherhood, Cooperation, and Coordination, insuring a very strong Syrian voice in Lebanon. A united and Syrian-dominated Lebanon placed Israel in an awkward position: For more than a decade they controlled much of southern Lebanon directly and through the proxy of a Christian militia. Withdrawal would remove a buffer for the northern Israeli border and weaken their position in the Golan. To remain meant that they would face increasing international pressure. They remained. On their part, the Syrians agreed to withdraw their forces from all of Lebanon except in the Bekka valley by late 1992. In mid-1992 they engineered the approval of elections in Lebanon to take place before the Syrian withdrawal; the apparent Syrian aim was to insure that there would continue to be a Lebanese legislature friendly to Syria.

After the conclusion of the conflict the United States placed considerable pressure on Israel to come to a peace conference. As the only superpower, and with newly forged ties to important Arab governments, the United States apparently thought that it was in a unique position. After a considerable amount of posturing by all sides, initial meetings were held during the last portion of 1991 and into 1992. Although true peace was still in the distant future, it marked a significant turning point in the long history of the Arab-Israeli conflict—at least the involved parties were talking. After the Labor victory in mid-1992, the prospects for peace increased.

Kuwait was pillaged and torched by Iraq. Not long after the invasion, Iraq announced that Kuwait was properly (historically speaking) part of Iraq. Since the Iraqis planned to stay in Kuwait, structural damage to buildings was initially limited. But anything moveable was potential booty. For example, the University of

Kuwait lost its 700,000 book library and all of the computing facilities. Office buildings were systematically cleared of furniture, autos were stripped and burned, the national museum was looted, medical supplies were taken, and so on.

After the war, the physical reconstruction of Kuwait City happened quickly—after all, the Kuwaitis had a fortune in international reserves to pay whatever was needed. But there were tougher "reconstruction" projects with uncertain futures. First, the more than one-third of a million Palestinians living in preinvasion Kuwait had to leave; their perceived pro-Iraqi stance made the Kuwaiti bitter. Along the same lines, Kuwait decided to reduce its prewar population (2.2 million) by one-half. Second, although Kuwaiti voices calling for democratic reform were muted during the frenzy of reconstruction, it is highly probable that this is an issue that will surface again. Indeed, all of the Gulf states with traditional leadership were facing this issue to varying degrees.

Finally, there are the Kuwaiti oil fields. Previously, the world never had more than five wells burning at one time. Iraqi forces torched 640 at the time of their retreat. Nobody has a clear notion of the short- and long-term ecological damage that these fires may cause. As with many such events, the media provided immediate footage of the spectacular fires. Then coverage all but stopped; it quickly became old news. The U.S. government did not discourage this lack of coverage; after all, there were significant portions of the U.S. population who had counselled against war and for continued economic sanctions against Iraq as an alternative. A reminder of the damage would not work in the administration's favor. To the surprise of all observers, the last oil fire was doused in nine months (December 1991), instead of requiring the two-to-five years originally estimated. The ecological cost remains unknown.

CONCLUSION

The nations of the industrialized world have had many decades to develop their forms of government, economic structures, and cultural perspectives. Most countries of the Middle East have not had time to gently sift and winnow such weighty ideas. Rather, they have been thrown headlong into the race for modernity and are still in the process of defining their identities. We can expect to see many changes in the Middle East in the last years of this century, although we can identify only the broad contours of these changes.

Many of the important issues in the Middle East are connected to the drive for self-determination. Although most of these countries had gained formal political independence by 1950, they still faced the tasks of establishing effective governments, charting independent economic courses and settling on coherent cultural identities. Their tasks were complicated by the acceleration of worldwide technological and organizational revolutions that acted to make the world more interdependent. Greater world interdependence meant that one nation's policy changes could easily conflict with the interests of other nations, and that each nation would have to make a greater number of decisions between mutually beneficial and harmful interdependencies. Statements of many Third World leaders reflect the dilemma; they have generally been quick to point to the difficulties, but have not been able to arrive at affirmative policies. However, some guides to the future are identifiable from the decisions of the past.

First, none of the powerful countries of the world can feel sure of having this or that bloc of Middle Eastern nations in its camp. The nations of the Middle East are now able to act more independently. It also seems likely that the various regional relationships will continue to be fluid. For example, Libya sought political union at times with Egypt and the Sudan, but has had hostile relations with these nations at other times. It also strongly backed the "progressive" government of Iraq during some periods and strongly opposed it at other times. The rise of independent Muslim republics in the southern reaches of the former Soviet Union in the early 1990s led Iran and Turkey to scramble into new regional alliances. The changing alliances and relationships reflect that the actors are still in the process of searching for fundamental common interests that will transcend transitory conflicts.

We also know that the Middle East's dominance of world petroleum markets will continue to have a major effect on regional and global politics. For example, Gulf tensions regularly bring statements of neutrality from Western governments along with warnings that the West will not tolerate actions that might close the Straits of Hormuz. Such pressures on the Middle East are certain to continue. Furthermore, the financial strength of the petroleum-rich countries will continue to alter regional relationships between have and have-not nations. Conflicting interests will also continue to surface between the have nations; for example, Iran, which has low petroleum reserves, can be expected to have an attitude toward petroleum pricing different from Saudi Arabia, which has large reserves.

Perhaps of greatest ultimate importance, Middle Eastern societies will continue to change at a rapid pace. Rapid change has stimulated a search for a new sense of identity that is bound to take different directions across countries and through time. The most arresting manifestation of this search has been the resurgence of Islam as a regional, national, and personal symbol of identity. It is difficult to know whether this resurgence will act as a vehicle through which social tensions will be played out, serve as a causal agent itself, or create its own dynamic. In any case, the Islamic resurgence promises to continue to be a significant political force.

THE POLITICS OF RELIGION, CULTURE, AND SOCIAL LIFE

I n recent years the roles of religion and culture in Middle Eastern politics have attracted increased attention. However, few aspects of Middle Eastern politics are as difficult to understand without introducing our own cultural biases and distortions. Try as we may to transcend ethnocentric prejudices and pursue a deeper insight, the goal remains elusive. In our introduction we cautioned against certain popular but misleading assumptions, including the conception of non-Western cultures as inherently stagnant and of non-Western persons as unreflective and unimaginative with regard to the choices facing them—the sort of view reflected in one Western writer's condescending depiction of "The Arab" as "a child of tradition." Western journalists frequently portray a renewed commitment to Islam as an unthinking "return" to some irrelevant and regressive past, while Christian or Jewish renewals in the West tends to receive a more nuanced and tactful treatment and to be placed in a richer explanatory context.

We have also mentioned the limitations of the sort of modernization theory that attempts to explain social change in developing countries as the result of adopting a more rationalistic cultural outlook. According to certain modernization theorists, people achieve "modernity" when they trade in their unthinking obedience to tradition for a set of attitudes more appropriate to life in a changing, cosmopolitan world. While each theorist has a slightly different list of "modern" attitudes, these purported traits tend to draw a distinction between "modern" and "traditional" people that is as self-congratulatory to the former as it is unflattering to the latter: "modern" people are empathic, mentally flexible, ambitious, rational, democratic, egalitarian, open to change, punctual, hard-working, and so forth. Implicit in much writing about modernization is an unstated premise that "modern" equals "Western." While some modernization theorists have been more cautious and sensitive than others, this general approach has some inherent faults apart from its frequent descent into outright ethnocentrism. First, it tends to understate the diversity, the dynamism, and the critical awareness that may exist in "traditional" cultures. Second, by treating such a broad range of social transformations simply as the product of an attitude adjustment, this type of analysis ignores (among other things) relationships of political and economic inequality central to the colonial and postcolonial order, implicitly recasting colonialism as an educational outreach program. This politically self-serving interpretation clouds our understanding of the complex historical processes that have led to current political realities. This brings us to a third flaw in modernization theory, to which we shall return momentarily: its failure to shed much light on the resurgence of Middle Eastern religious and cultural values so central to the contemporary scene.

These "modernization" theories are based on an element of truth: Certain ways of living and thinking are becoming more widespread, especially among people in urban-industrial settings and those whose social circles are the most cosmopolitan. In our introduction we characterized many of the emerging traits of contemporary life in terms of Marshall Hodgson's relatively value-neutral concept of *technicalization*, a social trend in which the demands of specialized technical efficiency come to play a more central role than they did in preindustrial and precapitalist societies. Throughout this book we have used the terms *modern* and *modernizing* to refer to the complex set of changes that accompany the technicalizing trend. We do not mean to suggest that these developments are necessarily desirable or that they define the inevitable direction of social change; in fact, they have sometimes raised moral questions and provoked negative reactions in the West as in other parts of the world.

No discussion of the politics of cross-cultural understanding, especially as regards the Middle East, would be complete without a look at the work of the prominent literary and cultural critic Edward Said. In *Orientalism* and other works, Said discusses the intricate web of assumptions by which Westerners characterize Muslims and Middle Easterners in terms of timeless, exotic essences.[1] Such depictions, Said argues, have more to do with our need to define ourselves by contrast with an imaginary "other" than with any genuine traits, interests, or motives of the depicted people. In fact, Said maintains that the "Orientalist" (whether the classic colonial sort or the modern "expert") shows surprisingly little interest in how actual "Orientals" view themselves or in what they have to say on their own behalf. In Said's view, loose generalizations about such things as "the Arab mind" provide all-too-convenient substitutes for a deeper look at the common human motives, historical developments, and specific concerns that motivate flesh-and-blood people.

While it may be argued that Said himself is guilty of overgeneralization, the problem he describes is very real. Some of these pitfalls may be unavoidable whenever different peoples try to understand one another—especially when trying to do so from a distance. But if we want to demystify the motives of Muslims and Middle Easterners and to understand them in plausible human terms, it is in our interest to move beyond wholesale characterizations and to examine the maze of challenges, strategies, and interests that characterize Middle Eastern politics. This is especially difficult when we turn to such emotionally charged issues as cultural identity, religion, and social values.

[1] (New York: Pantheon Books, 1978.)

THE POLITICS OF CULTURE

It is often suggested in the Western press that Middle Easterners must either side with the forces of growth and progress (rashly equated with Westernization) or remain in the clutches of the "dead hand" of tradition. This view is based on a notion of non-Western cultures as static and unreflective, stifled by authoritarian doctrines and an unchanging consensus on social, moral, and intellectual issues. The hand of tradition, however, turns out to be more animated (and more manipulated) than one might suppose. Even in the most stable societies, cultural consensus is partially offset by ambiguities within the traditions and by diverse strategies of interpretation.

Social theorists have come increasingly to view cultural tradition not so much as an inert body of rules and beliefs as a battleground of shifting, contested meanings. Tradition is a perpetually unfinished project; how people comprehend their traditions and apply them to practical situations is subject to constant negotiation. In complex situations such as that of the contemporary Middle East, the process of interpretation is complicated by conflicting—and often disguised—power interests at various levels ranging from the individual, communal, class, and ethnic arenas to the international and intersocietal arenas. The range of acceptable cultural interpretations within any given community is defined as much by their relation to social forces as by any logical justification or compatibility. In keeping with our broad definition of politics as the conflict and accommodation of competing demands for control of limited resources, the struggle over authoritative definitions of cultural meaning can aptly be called a *politics of culture*. In the arena of cultural politics, power interests assert competing claims to the labels, ideals, and symbols that a community holds in high esteem.

The Politics of Culture in Islamic History

We have seen that Islamic civilization was characterized from the start by a complex cultural and political dialogue. The ideal of a religiously inspired social order has always embroiled Islam in the politics of cultural belief and everyday social practice. To begin with, there was the question of how impeccable the religious credentials of the Umma's leadership must be, with the Shia insisting on leadership in the Prophet's genealogical line and the Sunnis more inclined to accept any overtly Islamic leadership able to govern effectively. Beneath this rift lies a deeper concern shared by Sunni and Shia alike: the danger of apostasy, of falling away from true Islamic guidance. The time before the Prophet is viewed by Muslims an age of great wickedness and barbarity (**jahiliyya**), but the original Muslim community under the Prophet's leadership (and in a different way, the great age of the caliphate) was a golden age, an exemplary time that later societies will never excel but can only hope to emulate. Since Muhammad was the Seal of the Prophets and his revelations completed God's message to humankind, there will be no future prophecies and no improvements on the rightly guided life of the Prophet's community. To turn away from that model is to renounce God and to slip backward into the darkness of jahiliyya. Innovation (**bida**), in the sense of forsaking the essential elements revealed by Muhammad and practiced in the Islamic golden age, is the slippery slope to apostasy. The early Islamic period was also an era of unequalled cohesion and expansion, a fact which reinforces the association of political success with piety, and of political decline with apostasy.

Because Islam has been grafted onto a variety of local cultural traditions and has spanned long periods of social change, the question has often arisen as to how far everyday practices may depart from those of the Prophet's community without subverting Islam. To compound the problem further, there is plenty of room for disagreement as to just what is authentically Islamic and what is innovative. Ordinary people in past-oriented societies have tended to project their own practices back in time, so that any custom may appear to be validated by tradition and, in the case of Muslim societies, to merge with Islam itself. The high ulema have despaired of this tendency and sporadically denounced folk practices as innovations, even though they may not always agree among themselves on what deserves this sort of condemnation. Is the seclusion of women, for example, a tenet of Islam or is it really a folk custom that departs from the practices of the Prophet and the original Muslim community? Is the veneration of the Black Stone in Mecca a central part of Muslim worship as most Muslims believe, or is it, as some purists have claimed, an example of idolatry? Islamic civilization displays an in-built tension over such issues of social and cultural correctness, a tension that has energized and shaped much of its political dialogue. Over the whole of Muslim history one can see cyclical periods of sociocultural "decline" followed by zealous revitalizing movements, often led by charismatic warriors under the banner of a purified Islam. While these movements were deeply intertwined with the play of secular power factions, their capacity to mobilize support often depended on their claim to cultural, and ultimately religious, authenticity.

Colonialism and Cultural Politics

The confrontation with the West has added a profound dimension to cultural politics in the Muslim Middle East. Prior to the colonial career of the West, Christian Europe represented an external military threat and a challenge to Islam's universality, but it also reinforced the Muslim perception of the unbeliever as uncivilized and insignificant. All this was to change radically with the rapid rise of European influence, a cultural and political explosion unequalled since the expansion of early Islam. It was not until the seventeenth and eighteenth centuries that Europe, which had previously lagged behind the Middle East, decisively surpassed the Islamic world technologically. By the end of the nineteenth century, however, Europe had established its power throughout the Muslim Middle East. This came as a bitter blow to a civilization that, despite occasional setbacks, had remained the most powerful and cohesive force in world politics for more than a millennium.

The relation of colonialism to economic and formal political hegemony has been discussed in previous chapters, but it is also important to consider the profound cultural meanings that colonialism had for both the colonizers and the colonized. Whatever their material motives, the colonial powers generally thought of their efforts as part an inexorable pattern of universal progress, in which culturally advanced peoples acted as benevolent protectors and teachers of the "backward" elements of humankind. From the colonial point of view, acquiescence seemed a small price to pay for the generous tutelage of a higher culture, and those who resisted seemed obtuse and ungrateful. In recent decades, Western influence has

shifted from overt political rule to various modes of cultural and economic hegemony, supported less by a conscious ideology of domination and more by a set of
cultural assumptions that make Western preeminence seem a natural consequence
of living rationally in the modern world. The latent ethnocentrism of this neo-colo-
nialist outlook, cloaked in the seemingly neutral language of reason and modernity,
can be more seductive and threatening than was the older, cruder ideology of colonial subjugation.

In addition to the effects of domination, colonialism has brought about a special set of problems with regard to sociopolitical identity. The Middle East, particularly under the Ottoman Empire, was an intricate mosaic of linguistic, regional,
and religious groupings, the balance among which was disturbed by colonial intervention and the ensuing political changes. The impulse to assert local identity
raised such questions as: Who are we first and foremost? Are we citizens of the
Ottoman Empire, or Arabs, Turks, or Persians; or are we Egyptians, Iraqis, or
Syrians; or are we Muslims, Christians, or Jews; or are we Shia or Sunni? The
problem of local identities was also compounded by the drawing of modern national boundaries, most of which reflected the concerns of colonial powers rather than
those of the peoples contained within—or divided by—those boundaries.

The confrontation with Europe has also posed some philosophical problems
for Muslims. As mentioned above, Islam has generally looked to the past—the
Islam of the Prophet and the splendor of the caliphs—to define its ideals. The post-
Enlightenment, Western secular worldview, by contrast, embraced the idea of
unlimited human progress through reason. Although the presence of a progress-
oriented ideology is neither a necessary nor a sufficient condition for the actual
improvement of the human condition, it lent Western ascendancy a philosophic
dimension that challenged orthodox Muslim thought and invited some kind of
response. Muslims had to find a way of reconciling profound social changes with
their own cultural conceptions of a golden age.

THE CONTEMPORARY POLITICS OF ISLAM

One of the most dramatic shortfalls of classic modernization theory was, as we
have suggested, its failure to anticipate the phenomenal resurgence during the
1970s and 1980s of Islam as a political force. In order to understand the Islamic
revival, it is not enough to place it within the simplistic dichotomy of reason versus
tradition; we must relate it to the specific problems of Middle Eastern societies and
the diverse tactics that have been employed to address them. We have already
noted the internal dynamic of Islamic civilization as it struggled to maintain political and social viability over the centuries, and the important role that religious
renewal has played in this internal process. In the modern global context, Muslim
civilization must not only contend with these perennial problems of internal cohesion and growth, but also with the threat of being overwhelmed by economic,
political, and cultural forces from the outside. The response to these challenges
since the beginning of the last century has embraced a wide range of possibilities.
Some movements or leaders have tried to align the Middle East culturally with the
"modern" world by the wholesale adoption of Western practices and values in
many areas of social life. Others have used Western ideas more selectively, aggres-

sively asserting national identities and goals at odds with some Western interests while embracing "modernizing" technical and social reforms that seem to further those objectives. Still others have supported a reassertion of Middle Eastern social and religious ideals, in some cases rejecting "modern" social values as inimical to Islam, or at other times claiming Islam to be compatible with (or even uniquely supportive of) such "modern" ideas. The past two centuries have seen these diverse strategies combined in various ways to form a rich internal dialogue in the Muslim Middle East, a dialogue in which cultural values and historical symbols—both local and imported—are interpreted in conflicting ways. The Islamic revival is a part of this discourse, and it must be understood in relation to the other parts.

The phenomenon to which we refer has been variously labeled Islamic resurgence, Islamic revival, Islamic renaissance, the Islamic revolution, Islamic fundamentalism and radical Islam, among other terms. We shall use *Islamic revival* or *resurgent Islam* to refer to the whole spectrum of movements whose aim is to strengthen Islamic influences in political, economic, and social life. The Islamic revival is real and pervasive and raises challenges to most forms of constituted authority, whether modern bureaucratic, charismatic, democratic, or authoritarian.

Not all Islamic revivalists share the same vision. The conservative revivalist wants to see the prevailing version of Islam taken more seriously, but does not envision any radically new interpretations or any purging of accepted religious practices. The Islamic radical or fundamentalist, on the other hand, advocates a return to what is perceived as a lost purity in religious practice, which may entail not only the reimposition of the Sharia law and Koranic education, but also a rejection of many locally accepted traditions of belief and ritual that do not strictly agree with the vision of a "pure" and uncorrupted Islam. Fundamentalists often take a dim view of cultural values and social practices originating in the West, although they may be quite accepting of technical innovation.

While the Western press has given considerable attention to the fundamentalists, who seem to exemplify Muslim fanaticism, it has less to say about another kind of Islamic revival. **Islamic modernism** is predicated on the belief that Islam can be adapted to the circumstances of modern life without losing sight of the fundamental truths of Muhammad's revelations. In opposition to the fundamentalists who see the Koran as a strict, literal, and unvarying prescription for righteous behavior, modernists wish to preserve the spirit and intent of Islam in a modern social context. Modernists begin with some of the same premises as the fundamentalists, including the need to cleanse Islam of accumulated man-made innovations that depart from the original purity and intent of God's revelations. Unlike the fundamentalists, however, the modernists locate the core of Islamic truth in its liberal ideals of justice and reason, arguing that Islam is entirely compatible with modern life—or at least, with a version of modern life that steers away from the godlessness, hedonism, social injustice, and abuse of power that they see in many developed nations. While modernism and fundamentalism can at times lead to radically different positions, they may at other times be rather difficult to distinguish. We shall illustrate some of the differences and convergences of these two positions later in this chapter.

One of the ironies concerning the modernist wing of the Islamic revival is that it achieved considerable visibility long before the modern fundamentalist movement rose to prominence. Modernist arguments were articulated in the well-known writings of Jemal al-din al-Afghani (1838–1897), who traveled widely in the Muslim world, and by his pupil Muhammad Abdu (1849–1905), whose ideas contributed to social reforms in Egypt, Turkey, and elsewhere. Islamic modernism has had a considerable following among educated and liberal-minded Muslims and still has its influential advocates. But while this kind of moderation may prevail in the end, the mildness of the modernist position does not seem to make for good political drama and news headlines, and, more important, it may not address forcefully enough the concerns of the average Muslim in times of social upheaval. We do not suggest that the Islamic revival is entirely dominated by fundamentalists. Whether the majority of Muslims today are fundamentalists (as opposed to conservatives or modernists) is hard to say, but it is the fundamentalist faction that seems, for the moment, to be the more active and visible political force.

The contemporary Islamic revival springs from a number of political and historical sources. First and foremost, the movement attempts to address the current predicament of the Umma: the subjection of Islam to foreign control; the apparent falling away from simple pious faith, particularly among the urban intelligentsia and ruling elites; the Western technological challenge to time-honored social conventions; and the fall of Arab and Islamic influence to an all-time low. All this can be explained, say the revivalists, as the consequence of turning away from the true and uncorrupted revelation of Islam. Implicit in the movement, then, is the expectation that a return to Islamic purity will restore the Umma to its rightful place on earth and bring Allah's beneficence once again to his people.

Prior to the Iranian revolution, none of the successful Middle Eastern political movements of the twentieth century had been driven primarily by the sort of religious concerns that had remained important to the average person. The Egyptian revolution, for instance, first seized power and only later turned its attention to the formulation of a program of justification. Baathism, despite its origin among Levantine intellectuals, has never clearly specified what sort of society it was trying to mold. Similar criticisms could be made of the shah's White Revolution in Iran or the Turkish revolution under Ataturk. More significantly, they all subordinated Islam to a broader secular framework, excluding it from a central place in their ideology and policy. Thus they denied the connection of Islam with political practice—thereby failing to address some basic concerns of the pious masses and neglecting a powerful source of political legitimation.

Modernization in the Middle East in the 1960s and 1970s became increasingly a program of Westernization and technological development, lacking any consistent social or moral vision responsive to public sentiments. In the educational systems, religious schools were replaced by secular government-controlled institutions. From the perspective of its fundamentalist critics, Westernization brought increasingly immodest dress, promiscuous sexual behavior, the consumption of alcohol, and "corrupt" entertainment (including motion pictures, television, pornography, and rock music). The growing wealth of the cities enhanced this image; as the political and social elites consumed Western products more extravagantly, the pious folk became more and more estranged from the elites of their societies.

The growth of urban wealth, concentrated in the elites, has given rise to perceptions of a widening economic gulf between the rich and the poor. Such a gulf is particularly obnoxious to the pious Muslim who takes seriously the Koranic injunctions regarding charity. The failure of elites to support a more equitable distribution of national resources has become a rallying point of the revivalist Muslim opposition that demands social justice. In this setting, the Islamic resurgence draws on the radical egalitarian and democratic impulse associated with Islam in its earliest forms. Thus, a particular interpretation of values rooted in the Islamic tradition has been used to express dissatisfaction with existing patterns of social relations, and with existing political authority.

The notion of the West as a source of moral degeneracy is in some respects a reaction to the humiliating colonial doctrines of Western cultural superiority, but it is also moved by specific opposition to certain Western-inspired social trends. The Islamic revival often calls for the rejection and expelling of Western influences depicted as "Satanic" in origin. Many proponents of Islamic revival profess to see little difference between the social systems of capitalism and communism, a view increasingly popular among secular Middle Eastern leaders as well.

The existing tension between the worldviews of Muslim fundamentalists and Western modernists found a fine focus in the controversy that followed the 1988 publication in England of Salman Rushdie's *The Satanic Verses*, a novel that includes in its narrative a thinly disguised interpretation of Muhammad's revelation. The novel, although strongly critical of the moral decay and the racism of colonialism and the modern Western societies, also contains material relating to Islam that many Islamic religious authorities, particularly in the Shia clergy, found overtly blasphemous. On this basis, Iran's Ayatollah Khomeini pronounced a sentence of death on Rushdie and announced a bounty of $5 million for whomever carried out his "execution." Western governments were initially incredulous at this and ultimately outraged. Muted criticism of the decision was also heard from the less fundamentalist Sunni ulema, suggesting that the Islamic world did not universally share this judgment. Nonetheless, most other countries with substantial Muslim populations banned the book, if only to head off communal conflict (a major consideration in India's decision). The author condemned the censorship, expressing surprise over the reaction and protesting that he only wanted to present a "secular humanist view of the creation of a religion." That such a view would be unacceptable to anyone believing in divine revelation seems obvious. But whatever the author's intent or readers' judgments, the controversy has expressed forcefully the divergent assumptions upon which we predicate our views of the world. Even within the Muslim world there is evidence of differing views, and some Muslims have defended the author's freedom of expression despite the book's offensiveness to them.

Groups espousing an Islamic revival have gained political power in Iran, Sudan, Libya, and Pakistan. They contend for power in Lebanon, Morocco, Afghanistan, and Algeria; and they figure in the politics of every Middle Eastern nation. They are actively, if irregularly, advocating the inclusion of Islam in government, even promoting an Islamic Republic in which the Sharia would be established as the law of the land. Their progress has been uneven to date, and the obstacles to their programs are serious. Nevertheless, these movements have gained in strength over the past two decades.

The phenomenon of Islamic revivalism cannot be treated in isolation from the larger dialogue of which it is part. This dialogue includes not only religious issues but also the problems of cultural identity, the challenges of serious moral, social, and economic problems, and the quest for collective self-esteem and self-direction. The resulting discourse brings up diverse and often conflicting perspectives from which to address the challenges of a changing world. The examples of Turkey, Egypt, Saudi Arabia, and Iran illustrate some of the complex forms this dialogue has taken.

TURKEY: RADICAL WESTERNIZATION AND THE DURABILITY OF ISLAM

Turkey's unique historical circumstances have placed it in an ambiguous position with regard to Western Europe. At the height of the Ottoman Empire, Turkey had functioned as a frontier state that directly confronted, and at times threatened, the Christian West. Europe itself was regarded as a less accomplished civilization, and Christian Europeans were among the subject peoples within the Empire. At the same time, Turkey's proximity and long commercial association with the West, its cultural distinctiveness from other Muslim peoples, and its political strength compared with other Middle Eastern nations in the colonial period, allowed for an exceptional policy toward the West. No other Muslim nation has so explicitly committed itself to the project of cultural Westernization, and Turkey's experience reveals the limits of a Westernizing strategy.

The tanzimat reforms of 1839–1876 (see Chapter 4) were aimed not at fundamentally changing Turkish culture or society but at strengthening its military and government structures. Nevertheless, these reforms helped to shape the attitudes of a generation of middle-level government officials, who developed strong sympathies toward Western humanitarian and libertarian ideals. The liberalizing trend found strong expression in the Young Ottoman movement of the 1860s. Far from leading to an acceptance of colonialism, liberal ideals were linked with the project of casting off foreign control and pursuing the sort of self-determination achieved by the European nation-states. Thus, the liberals viewed with extreme distrust the sort of "Westernizing" elites who collaborated in European domination. The liberal movement emphasized the potential contributions of Turkish national culture to modern life; for example, the florescent Turkish literature of the time emphasized a more colloquial language and democratic idiom than the classical forms, and expressed the ideals of the liberal intelligentsia. In this setting, there flourished a modernist interpretation of Islam that located the core of Islamic tradition in its liberal values. According to this interpretation, Islam's pure monotheism, its commitment to freedom and social justice, and its opposition to superstition make it the most rational of world religions and therefore the most compatible with modern life. Such an interpretation not only validated Islam, but it suggested that the reversal of fortunes lately suffered by the Muslim world might only be temporary. It gave a traditionalist mandate for rooting out, in the name of a purified (that is, rationalist) Islam, the "superstitions" and customary practices associated with Islam by the common folk and the conservative ulema.

During the period of 1876–1909, modernizing changes continued not under the auspices of liberalism but under the authoritarian rule of Sultan Abdulhamit, who suspended the recently adopted constitution and ruled by means of a despotic police state. Abdulhamit's use of religious legitimation was different from that of the Young Ottomans. Initially appealing to the conservative ulema against the liberal modernists, he soon turned to a new brand of pan-Islamism, pressing his claim (contrary to existing Islamic interpretation) as "caliph," not in the restricted capacity of overseer of the Sharia and the Muslim community, but as political ruler of an Islamic empire. Abdulhamit's project of building a Hijaz railway to carry pilgrims to Mecca, symbolic of his attempt to unify the Umma, drew material support from Muslims the world over. Despite his restrictions on freedom of expression, he continued to develop modern schools, build literacy, and promote Western science and technicalization.

The Young Turks rebellion of 1908, which restored the constitution and eventually forced Abdulhamit from power, had to face anew the confusing question of Turkey's identity. Should Turks align themselves with the Muslim world or with Europe? Should they form a Turkish nation based on a common language and culture, or unite with other Muslims under the banner of pan-Islamism, or try to maintain control over a religiously diverse Ottoman realm, even as Christian and other fragments of that Empire seemed intent on going their own way? Military conflicts over territory gave the Young Turks little respite, and events connected with World War I soon put an end to the Ottoman Empire and, very nearly, to Turkey itself. Turkey struggled for its very life, and Mustafa Kemal, who emerged in the 1920s as the hero of that struggle and "father" of the Turks ("Ataturk"), was in a uniquely powerful position to make sweeping changes in Turkish society.

Ataturk's vision of the Turkish nation was influenced by European nationalist romanticism by way of the Turkish social theorist Ziya Gok-Alp. Arguing against the pan-Islamic and pan-Ottoman ideologies popular at the beginning of the century, Gok-Alp had promulgated a vision of a strictly Turkish, Westernized nation-state. Humankind, he argued, is naturally divided into "nations," each marked by a distinctive language, culture, and folk "spirit." Thus, Turkey could adopt whatever outward forms of government and elite culture that were most progressive at the time without compromising its immutable national character; the ascendent Western cultural forms could serve Turkish development as a world power in the twentieth century, just as the Persian-Arabic civilization had served the same purpose centuries earlier. Gok-Alp adopted a liberal modernist view of Islam, arguing for its place in Turkish national culture, but not in a capacity that would damage Turkey's aspirations as a modern Westernized state.

This vision of the Turkey as a modern state in the Western mold was resolutely implemented by Ataturk. In a series of measures from the mid- to late 1920s, Islam was disestablished as a state religion: Sufi orders were officially abolished and their property seized by the government; the madrasah schools were closed and the state-sponsored training of the ulema came to an end; the Sharia law was replaced in its official capacity by a slightly modified version of the Swiss personal law. The interplay of symbolic and pragmatic elements is dramatically evident in certain of Ataturk's policies. In 1928 he abolished the use of Arabic script, decreeing that Turkish must be written with occidental letters; this was not only a symbolic alignment with Western culture, but in practical terms it cut succeeding generations off from the literary heritage of Ottoman civilization. Similarly, the purging of Persian and Arabic elements from the Turkish language celebrated the language of the ordinary Turkish people at the expense of the classical Persian-Arabic high culture. (When non-Turkish roots were necessary for certain words, preference was often given to Latin and French). The Muslim call to prayer, heard the world over in Arabic, was now said in Turkish.

Perhaps Ataturk's most deeply symbolic political gesture—and the one that prompted the most riots—was the 1925 ruling that adopted the Western brimmed hat and outlawed the fez and all other brimless headgear. The various hats, caps, and turbans had distinguished the many traditional ethnic groups, religious orders, and statuses within the Islamic community while serving the common practical function of allowing believers to touch forehead to ground during the performance of Muslim prayer. Thus, as Hodgson observes, Ataturk's policy

> ...served...several functions at once. It symbolized the rejection of the Perso-Arabic and the adoption of the Western heritage (in itself the brimmed hat was not particularly modern—for instance, it was not particularly efficient—but it was very explicitly Occidental). More substantively, it [abolished] for the whole population the old distinctions of status which headdress had marked and which were incompatible with the interchangeable homogeneity which a modern nation-state presupposes; and it particularly reduced the visibility of those religious classes whose prestige and influence Kemal had to eliminate if the secular Republic were to survive. Finally, it served as a psychological coup. Even in language, "the hatted man" had meant a European, and "to put on a hat" had, as a phrase, meant "to Europeanize"—that is, "to desert Islam, or the state" (which came to the same). Kemal was demanding, if effect, that every Turkish man own himself a traitor to all that the Ottoman state had stood for. It was one of those blows which forces people to come to an inner decision: either they must resist now, or acknowledge defeat and henceforth hold their peace. Those most so minded did resist and were crushed; the rest now had overtly to admit Kemal's authority, if not his wisdom, and found themselves implicitly committed to whatever more might be implied in Westernization.[2]

Ataturk's policies helped to strengthen Turkey's educational system and its industrial economy, as well as to promote economic and social reforms associated with modernizing societies. Turkey has moved toward a closer association with the West, but the movement has not been as all-encompassing as Ataturk might have envisioned. His policies themselves departed so radically from popular sentiments that he could ill afford to promote the kind of political freedoms that might have brought Turkey closer to the political ethos of the West. And despite his veneration of the common people, Ataturk's policies went against the current of popular religious commitments.

The Kemalists never intended to abolish Islam, but rather to guide it toward a more personal, rationalized, Westernized form, similar to Protestantism. To some degree, however, the closing of the madrasahs had the contrary effect of reducing the influence of educated (and modernist) ulema and promoting the more folk-oriented versions of Islam. Despite the Kemalist ideas taught in the school systems, local imams continued to compete for the loyalty of most villagers. Sufism, far from being crippled by the dismantling of the tariqahs, was somewhat purified by it and flourished at the grass-roots level. The growth of religious freedom after World War II saw the return of formal religious training and of the tariqahs, and in this atmosphere some factions became openly dedicated to undoing Ataturk's policies. Turkey today, while still officially adhering to the fundamentals of Kemalism,

[2] Marshall G. S. Hodgson, *The Venture of Islam*, Vol. III, (Chicago: University of Chicago Press, 1974), pp. 264–265.

is characterized by a wide array of positions on Islam and Westernization, from secularism and Islamic modernism to Islamic fundamentalism aimed at reestablishing Sharia law. The reemergence of Islam in Turkish national politics is likely to have far-reaching consequences; in a country where secular Western values were so vigorously promoted, it must stand as a testimony to the durability of Islam.

EGYPT: THE LABYRINTH OF POSSIBILITIES

Egypt's brush with French colonization at the beginning of the nineteenth century dramatized its need for an effective strategy of self-definition and self-determination. Its unique position in the Middle East suggested a number of particular qualities, needs, and possibilities. Egypt possessed an ancient pre-Islamic urban and agrarian heritage, and its long history of urban culture had helped it to become one of the premier centers of learning and culture in the Islamic world; al-Azhar in Cairo was the recognized center of Sharia scholarship. Located at the fringes of Ottoman control, Egypt was semi-independent and a ripe target for European colonization. During the nineteenth century the European powers, particularly Britain, established a strong social, political, and economic hegemony in Egypt that fell just short of outright colonial rule and which was to last until the middle of the twentieth century. At the same time, Egypt could and sometimes did define itself as a legitimately Western nation, pointing to its active role in the classical Greek and Roman world at a time when Western Europe was still at or beyond the periphery of Western civilization.

In the first half of the nineteenth century, Muhammad Ali tried to bring Egypt into the modern world on a basis of cultural and material strength. His program of selective assimilation of Western ideas stressed military technicalization, economic development, and modern forms of education and government. Even at this early date, rural Islamic-oriented resistance to these modernizing changes posed a significant challenge, leading Muhammad Ali to attempt control of the Sufi orders by manipulating and co-opting their leadership.

Islam, however, was not only a conservative force. The Persian scholar Jemal al-Din al-Afghani (1838–1897) traveled throughout the Muslim world, including Egypt, promoting ideas foundational to much of twentieth century pan-Islamic, Islamic nationalist, and Islamic modernist thought. Like other restorers of the faith, he held that Muslims should return to the example set by the first caliphs and the early Muslim community. At the core of al-Afghani's teaching was the natural affinity of Islam with science and reason, the unity of the Umma as against local and ethnic loyalties, and the need for a unifying political leadership modelled on the pious early caliphs. His student Muhammad Abdu (1849–1905) became the chief religious authority of Egypt and a seminal spokesman for Islamic modernism as a model for Egyptian sociocultural development. Like al-Afghani, he rejected the wholesale adoption of Western ideas in principle, preferring instead to use the disciplined methods of reasoning developed by certain prestigious early Islamic scholars, and employing established ideas from Sharia interpretation such as the principle of *maslahah* (preservation of the public welfare). He saw reason as given by God to protect humankind from either excess or adulteration in religion. Abdu placed more emphasis than did the Persian al-Afghani on the glories of classic

Arab civilization and on Egypt as an exemplar of Arab culture. But, like Afghani, he saw Islam as providing a superior basis for social justice, moral cohesion, and intellectual progress—a vehicle for outdoing Europe even in the areas of its greatest strength, while at the same time retaining the moral-religious virtues of Islamic civilization and the full benefit of local cultural integrity.

Some of Abdu's scholarly disciples interpreted his ideas of *salafiyya*, or the true wisdom of the pious ancestors, in a manner sympathetic to the conservative Muwahhidun ("Wahhabi") movement of Saudi Arabia. But for the majority of the urban middle and upper classes, a loose interpretation of Islamic modernism became a license to adopt secular and Western ideas at their convenience without the stigma of religious apostasy. This is not to say that Islamic modernism eliminated the role of Islam either as a personally meaningful element or as a symbol of Egyptian identity. Nor did it make conflicts over cultural identity any less troublesome. While foreign-sponsored schools taught European ideas in European languages, a native flowering of Arabic literature struggled to reconcile the vastly different worlds of the classical Arabic language and literary forms, the local Arabic vernacular and popular literary culture of the Egyptians, and the foreign literary genres that expressed "modern" individualistic conceptions of the self. Meanwhile, the discovery of the tomb of King Tutankhamen in 1922 renewed a popular interest in the glories of pre-Islamic Egypt that coexisted uneasily with the sentiments of either Arabism or Islamic renewal. In short, Egyptians faced a bewildering smorgasbord of different, and partly incompatible, cultural symbols and identities.

The first half of this century saw a growth of specific social problems in Egypt besides those of economic and political self-determination referred to in previous chapters. Social changes were creating new sources of discontent including, for example, uncontrolled population growth, migration into urban areas that greatly outstripped economic development and resulted in endemic unemployment, and a highly unequal distribution of land, capital, and other social resources. The effect of growing inequality was worsened by the breakup of communal village holdings and a weakening of familial and other networks of support for the destitute. These structural problems were accompanied by the growing prominence of films, popular songs, and sundry entertainments that, according to their critics, extolled individualism, romantic love, and other harbingers of hedonistic immorality.

Although Gamal Adbel Nasser rose to power in 1952 by seizing a political opportunity, he became the first Egyptian leader in many decades to develop doctrines addressing a broad spectrum of his country's social problems. Eschewing the "borrowed ideologies" of the capitalist west and the communist bloc, he employed Islamic slogans and vocabulary in support of policies whose ultimate objectives were essentially secular. Nasser's ambition to bring the Arab world together under Egyptian leadership was based on a doctrine of Arab nationalism, which promoted the idea of a single Arab nation united by language, culture, and historical achievements. (Arab nationalism gained by its representation of Israel as a Western colonial settler state, and of the Palestinian cause as a symbolic rallying point for Arab resistance to foreign domination.) The pursuit of social equality in the form of "Arab Socialism," oriented toward state control of the means of production and the redistribution of income and land holdings, was linked with the Islamic concepts of equity, the care of the needy through zakat (alms), and the ideal of the unity and common good of the Umma. Nasser reformed the great mosque school of al-Azhar to resemble more closely a modern university, and he persuaded the high ulema to issue religious decrees, or *fatwas*, in support of such government policies as birth control. "Islamic" organizations and publications were organized and sponsored by the Nasser government to legitimize official policies at home and abroad. Although Nasser did much to reintroduce Islam into Egypt's political rhetoric, his use of Islam was selective and was essentially a means to other ends. By this time, however, a far more serious movement for the Islamic redemption of Egyptian society had been gathering strength at the grass roots.

The Muslim Brotherhood was founded in 1928 as a Muslim young men's association promoting personal piety, but by the 1940s it had become a radical, sometimes violent, political faction highly critical of Egyptian government, society, and culture. Drawing its membership largely from the ranks of educated and professional people—traders, teachers, engineers, and the like—it advocated the restoration of Islamic law and government as an antidote to the decadence it saw everywhere in Egyptian life. Sayyid Qutb, a modernist literary critic whose two years in America had helped to turn him against Western lifestyles and modes of thought, led the Brotherhood through some of its most radical years, until his execution in 1966. At first sympathetic to Nasser and the Free Officers, the Brotherhood soon parted ways with the government on a variety of issues.

Like the modernists, the Muslim Brotherhood sought a return to the roots of Islam in order to create a more just and decent society, hoping to reopen the process of *ijtihad* (Sharia interpretation) and reapply the values of the past to the problems of the present. But the Brotherhood's vision of Islamic values drew on different traditions of Sharia interpretation, resulting in a fundamentalist ideology that contrasted starkly with the liberal-rationalist Islam of the modernists. They opposed democracy and Marxism alike as incompatible with Sharia rule, questioned the teaching of Western philosophy and modernist Islam in the schools, and opposed the formal separation of religion from government. They had less tolerance than the modernists for religious minorities, Sufism, or folk religious practices. They targeted for criticism a broad array of "anti-Islamic" values and decadent practices that they associated with modern life—from exploitation, domination, materialism, and bank interest to "entertainment," consumerism, romantic song lyrics, popular women singers, mixing of the sexes, and birth control. While they opposed Nasser's Arabism as an anti-Islamic attempt to draw distinctions within the Umma, they nevertheless criticized the lack of attention to classical Arabic—the language of the Koran and of high Islamic culture—in the schools and media. Where Abdu and the modernists had chided the ulema's hidebound conservatism, Qutb's Muslim Brotherhood attacked them for their timidity in defending Islamic traditions.

So vehement was the Muslim Brothers' opposition to the Nasser government that they considered resistance to it a higher cause than the struggle against Israel. In the political rhetoric of the Brotherhood, Nasser was equated with every enemy of Islam from Crusaders, Jews, and Mongols to Turkey's Kemal Ataturk. Almost from the beginning, the Brotherhood was divided between those (including Qutb) who shunned violence and those who were willing to use assassination and other forms of terror. The latter gave the government an excuse for suppressing the Brotherhood by force.

Both the Brotherhood and the establishment used symbols and concepts from Islamic history to revile one another. Qutb drew on the writings of a prestigious medieval Islamic thinker, Ibn Taymiyya, to press the argument that any Islamic leader who fails to apply a significant part of the Sharia has thereby abandoned Islam. The Brotherhood equated the state of Egyptian society with jahiliyya, the period of utter wickedness before the coming of Islam. The pro-Nasser faction, speaking through sympathetic ulema, countered that the concept of jahiliyya properly applies only to a specific historical time, and reversed the charges of apostasy by labeling the militants as *Kharijites* (the fanatical sect which, claiming "sinners" to be outside the Umma, assassinated the prophet's son-in-law, Ali), thus contending that it was actually they who had left the Umma.

After Nasser's death the fundamentalists were at first encouraged by Anwar Sadat's apparent interest in Islam. Sadat began and ended his speeches with Muslim benedictions; he declared the Sharia as the basis of all legislation (a matter more of labeling than of substantive reform), and his 1973 "Ramadan" war against Israel (code named "Badr" after one of the Prophet's famous victories) employed the Muslim battle cry "Allahu Akbar" ("God is Great"). He encouraged Muslim student associations in order to combat residual Nasserite Arab socialism. But Sadat wanted it both ways, declaring the separation of religion and government and instituting in 1979 family laws that liberalized women's rights in divorce, alimony, and child custody. His assassination by Jihad, a militant army cell including some former members of the Muslim Brotherhood, was a sobering lesson for Sadat's successor Hosni Mubarak.

The Muslim Brothers stand out less as radicals today than in Nasser's time. The 1980s saw the growth of widespread popular interest in various forms and degrees of Islamic revival. The vast majority of Egyptians in all walks of life continue to be devout Muslims, and the visible expressions of that faith became more evident during the decade following the Iranian revolution. Muslim student associations earnestly promoted Islamic morality, politicians debated whether Egyptian laws are in keeping with the Sharia, and television shifted away from such fare as the American-made "Dallas" toward a greater emphasis on religious programs. Attendance at mosques increased. Merchants and bureaucrats were more likely to interrupt official business for daily prayers. The government, responding to both international and domestic Muslim pressures, prohibited the sale or consumption of alcohol except to non-Muslim foreigners. A movement toward quasi-traditional forms of "Islamic" dress, especially for women, not only symbolized an interest in Muslim norms of sexual modesty but also asserted local resistance toward Western fashions while subduing the display of differences in wealth and social status. Bearded men and veiled women were more often seen in the streets of Cairo. The label "imported ideas" became a common expression of disapproval, and rationalist interpretations of Islam were often stigmatized as irreligious innovations (bida). Despite recent signs of a liberal reaction, the symbols of Islamic resurgence mentioned above are no longer the exclusive province of radical fundamentalism, but are often associated with popular, middle-of-the-road conservatism.

A number of social forces have conspired to encourage cultural nativism and religious conservatism in modern Egypt: a succession of modernizing leaders who underestimated the importance of popular religious sentiments; the failure of modernizing secular policies to deal with internal social and economic problems; the humiliating defeat by Israel in the 1967 war, interpreted by some Muslims as a divine punishment; the example of the 1979 Iranian Revolution; pressure from Saudi Arabia to adopt stricter laws as a condition for aid; the example of Sadat's assassination; the critique by Third World intellectuals of Western cultural domination; and, perhaps, even the West's own disaffection with some aspects of modern life.

Egypt illustrates many of the diverse cultural issues and possibilities facing modern Muslim nations. Although the interpretation of cultural tradition lends itself to manifold possibilities, it is no longer prudent for political leaders to ignore popular religious and cultural values on the assumption that they will soon fall before the juggernaut of secular Western ideas. Not surprisingly, President Mubarak's public policies and personal lifestyle show an astute sensitivity to the politics of religious and cultural symbolism in contemporary Egypt.

SAUDI ARABIA: AN ISLAMIC CAMELOT?

It is hard to imagine a nation commanding more of the symbols of Islamic legitimacy than does Saudi Arabia. Its roots lie in an Islamic purification movement begun by Muhammad Ibn Abd al-Wahhab in the mid-eighteenth century and carried forward by the Saudi family, which unified the present nation in 1932 under the leadership of Abdulaziz ibn Saud (1879–1953). Inspired by the strict Hanbali school of Sharia law, Ibn Wahhab's teachings (whose adherents prefer the designation Muwahhidun ["Unitarian"] over the popular term, "Wahhabi") embraced a puritanical version of Islam that today forms the core of Saudi Arabia's religion, politics, society, and culture. Saudi Arabia is formally dedicated to the ideal of jihad, or struggle on behalf of the faith: Its flag displays the *shahada* (declaration of faith) and a sword.

Saudi Arabia had from the beginning what many Muslim fundamentalists elsewhere still struggle for: the Sharia as virtually the sole law of the land. When King Khalid ascended to the throne in 1975, he reaffirmed that "Islamic law is and will remain our standard, or source of inspiration, and our goal." (His homage to the Sharia was astute, since the consent of the ulema is needed for all transfers of power and was instrumental in the deposition of the dissolute King Saud in 1964.) Lawyers are scarce in Saudi Arabia, for Sharia religious courts decide all legal cases excepting certain commercial actions and suits against the state (the latter are adjudicated by appointees of the royal family). This strict interpretation of the Hanbali legal code, with its provisions for beheadings and amputations, has become for most Westerners (and for many non-Saudi fundamentalists) a vivid symbol of zealous Islamic justice.

American troops stationed in Saudi Arabia during the Iraq–Kuwait War of 1990–1991 were surprised at the strictness of Saudi social norms. Saudi women wear full facial veils in public; non-Saudi and even non-Muslim foreign women may be publicly upbraided for failing to cover their hair. Men too must dress modestly and would not, for example, appear in public wearing tank-tops or shorts. The ubiquitous semiofficial "religious police" (**mutawwa**) patrol the streets ready to rap the exposed ankles of immodestly dressed women, ensure that shops are closed promptly at prayer times, enforce the fast of Ramadan, and generally scold or even detain persons behaving in a manner that strikes them as un-Islamic. Mingling of the sexes in public is considered inappropriate; schools and universities are segregated; and even foreigners caught in the company of women who are not their spouses may find themselves in trouble. Possession of alcohol is a serious criminal offense. American forces in Saudi Arabia during the Iraq–Kuwait War were obliged to rename chaplains "spiritual advisors," avoid religious insignia, and go through the motions of concealing the nature of Christian and Jewish religious services (ironically, the enemy regime in Iraq not only tolerated but even subsidized Christian worship).

Saudi Arabia is unique among Muslim nations in being the birthplace of the Prophet and the site of Islam's holiest places. The Saudi royal family makes much of this; King Fahd's official title is "Guardian of the Two Holy Mosques" (that is, Mecca and Medina). The government has gone to great lengths to provide facilities and services for pilgrims during the hajj, and Fahd himself may be seen participating in the yearly ritual cleansing of the Mecca's holiest shrine, the Kaaba.

In many respects, then, Saudi Arabia might appear to be an Islamic fundamentalist's Camelot, confidently enforcing strict Islamic norms while occupying a place of privilege in Muslim ritual and history and wielding the power of a premier oil-producing state. But beneath this apparent self-assurance one may detect a certain precariousness and insecurity in the position of the Saudi elites. So far, the regime has been reasonably successful at pursuing three potentially incompatible goals: (1) the maintenance of a credibly devout Islamicism, safe from fundamentalist challenges; (2) the pursuit of a permanent place in the modern global economy; and (3) the preservation of the Saudi monarchy. The third element, Saudi rule, is important not only from the viewpoint of elite self-interest, but also because it has so far tried to head off a direct collision between the first two aims. However, the strategies used so far to reconcile these diverse ideals could eventually shatter along the fault lines of inherent contradictions and double-edged political tactics.

The Prophet Muhammad is reported to have said, "The princes will corrupt the earth, so one of my people will be sent to bring back justice." In November of 1979, on the first day of the Muslim year 1400, several hundred followers of a man claiming to be the Muslim messiah, or Mahdi, produced weapons from under their cloaks and seized the Grand Mosque at Mecca. Securing the permission of the ulema, Saudi forces retook the mosque after many days of combat during which more than 200 soldiers, hostages, and rebels (including rebels' family members) lost their lives. Most of the rebels were Saudis, some of whom were driven by old political grievances with the government. But their stated complaints had to do with the erosion of religion and the breakdown of morals in the kingdom, as evidenced by working women, Western entertainments, the surreptitious consumption of alcohol, and so forth. At the root of their protests were issues of religious purity, Western influence, and the alleged moral corruption of the Saudi rulers. While the Saudi populace and the Muslim world were appalled at the audacity of these rebels, their claims resulted in a number of symbolic gestures toward increased moral strictness. The incident dramatized before a world audience the vulnerability of Saudi prestige.

The Saudi public takes a certain pride in its royal family, for it symbolizes the lofty, independent spirit of a people who have never submitted to foreign rule, as well as the immense progress that the nation has made from the isolation and poverty of only a generation ago. At the same time, however, the notion of monarchy is not in strict accordance with Koranic ideals of equality before God, nor is it in keeping with the contemporary fundamentalist preference for rule by popularly chosen religious experts. Thus, the monarchy is at pains to show that its rule is dedicated not to its own aggrandizement but to the welfare of the Umma. However, the huge influx of oil wealth in the past few decades has enabled the royal family (which has thousands of recognized members) to lead lives of privilege and self-indulgence, provoking criticism throughout the Muslim world, especially among the poor and the devout. The display of privilege and materialism is not only unseemly, it is unjust and un-Islamic. On the other hand, the Saudi rulers make an important ritual gesture toward traditional modes of public access by holding royal audiences where the humblest citizens can bring their troubles to be adjudicated.

Not all the problems facing the house of Saud involve questions of lifestyle; some have to do with the conflicting requirements of the society. For example, the Saudi government has declared that the Saudi educational system is, above all, Islamic in its intent. However, another important goal of the Saudi state is to establish an economy that can continue to develop and be self-sufficient without dependence on the single, exhaustible resource of petroleum. In doing so it must emphasize high-tech industry, communications, and international commerce, for which a religiously oriented educational system is not particularly well suited. Thus the Saudi universities must place religious goals in the background if they are to compete with the best Western institutions (where many Saudi royalty are still educated); but to turn away from traditional educational goals is to incur the wrath of religious critics.

Saudis are sometimes led to inconvenient or inconsistent practices by the contradictions of a society that is highly technicalized in some ways but which hopes not to compromise moral norms developed in a very different social context. Because women are not allowed to drive, for example, a male professional might have to leave work to take his wife or child to the doctor (or entrust them to a male chauffeur, who is usually a foreigner, and sometimes an infidel). While alcohol is legally forbidden, it is a mark of prestige and hospitality among certain affluent, cosmopolitan Saudis to offer a guest fine Scotch whiskey worth hundreds of dollars a bottle on the black market. This nation of great affluence, with sophisticated information technology, submits every imported videotape to rigid censorship: The Muppets do not pass the censors because one of the characters is a pig, and pork is forbidden under Islamic law. Trivial enough in themselves, these examples point to the coexistence of very different social values within a single system. All societies involve significant contradictions; whether those in Saudi society will continue in their present form or resolve themselves in some consistent direction, only time will tell.

Saudi relations with the United States pose something of a dilemma for the Saudi leadership. Radical Islamic fundamentalists of the past few decades have been adamant in their opposition to communism, but the United States is equally disliked in some circles, not only because of its power and its secular materialism, but also for its role as Israel's closest ally. Saudi Arabia's educational, commercial, and military security needs—to say nothing of its prestige in the West—are well served by friendship with America. Yet, the social policies required to promote one's image in the United States are sometimes the opposite of those needed for a nation aspiring to Islamic legitimacy, and any concessions to foreign influence are certain to arouse fundamentalist antagonism. Even as American troops went into battle the Iraq–Kuwait War of 1990–1991 defending Saudi interests, religious fundamentalists abused Saudi women's rights advocates by calling them "American sympathizers."

The issue of Saudi Arabia's image in the West was highlighted by its official opposition to the 1980 British-produced television documentary, "The Death of a Princess." Broadcast in the United States and Britain, the program dealt—somewhat loosely, its critics say—with the execution of an adulterous Saudi princess and her commoner lover. The program, which the Saudis tried to prevent from airing, outraged Saudi honor by making public the shame of the royal family and by going so far as to suggest that Saudi princesses cruised the desert in limousines looking for sex. Whatever its factual basis, the "documentary" reveled in Western stereotypes of Islamic justice and Saudi extremism. In the end, some stations chose not to air the show and others followed it with a panel discussion including Arab (but not Saudi) speakers. Although the program reached only a small audience, the incident suggests the degree to which even conservative Muslim nations are sensitive to the way they are perceived elsewhere in the modern "global village."

There seems to be a growing worldwide consensus on human rights and essential freedoms (even though many nations prefer to make exceptions in their own cases), and international prestige and internal order appear to be increasingly linked to certain criteria deemed necessary for human rights in all nations. However, the rights and freedoms widely accepted in the modern world may not always be compatible with the demands of the Muslim conservatives and fundamentalists whose opposition the Saudi government wishes to avoid. For example, the country's Shia minority is economically and politically underprivileged—and ripe for agitation from Saudi's arch-rival, the revolutionary Islamic government of Iran. Several disturbances have already occurred, including one indirectly related to the Grand Mosque incident of 1979. But for the Saudi government to assuage Shia demands for improved rights and economic conditions would be to inflame Sunni fundamentalist sentiments of the sort that provoked the Mosque takeover. Indeed, any move toward equal rights for women and religious minorities, freedom of worship, or certain other rights recognized in the West and elsewhere, is likely to incite radical Islamic opposition that could conceivably unseat the government. Having taken the road of Islamic legitimation, Saudi Arabia has not only tapped a powerful force in its favor, but it has also limited some of its political options.

Saudi Arabia's self-cultivated role of world Islamic leadership poses serious challenges and problems that also partially offset the rewards of national prestige. While the guardianship of the holy places gives the Saudi regime a high religious standing, it also puts it under the burden of maintaining the ritual purity of Saudi soil; the presence of American troops in Saudi Arabia during the Gulf conflict was seen by some purists as a desecration. And while the exposure of pilgrims to Saudi Islam may sometimes help promote it as the normative model for world Islam, interregional contact during the hajj also keeps alive the dialogue of diverse possibilities for Islamic culture. Saudi Arabia's sponsorship of countless international Islamic conferences has had a similar effect, bringing forth both liberal and ultra-fundamentalist perspectives potentially critical of Saudi practices.

The Saudi Arabian ulema, like the royal family, are in a delicate position. While they enjoy exceptional power in government and the courts, their co-optation by the monarchy has led them to relinquish much of the oppositional function historically exercised by the ulema in Muslim society. Should they become too closely allied with the ruling elite, they could lose their credibility among the more stringent Muslim factions, and with it their usefulness to the monarchy. On the other hand, if they express too much opposition to government policies, they could find their influence in government diminished. Saudi monarchs have already shown a willingness to circumvent the conservative members of the ulema with rulings designed to win international credibility, as when King Faisal mollified President Kennedy by abolishing slavery and permitting television in private Saudi homes.

The Iraq–Kuwait War drew international attention to Saudi Arabia: its social and political order, its problems and its political restrictions, and its dissenters. In March of 1992, after years of lobbying from a coalition of Saudi liberals and religious conservatives, King Fahd announced the formation of a long-promised *Majlis Asshura*, or consultative council. Accompanying the announcement was a carefully worded decree spelling out the regime's doctrines of political legitimacy and answering a number of implicit questions about Saudi rule. It asserts that the announced changes are not innovations, but simply the continuation in a new form of religiously mandated practices that have always existed in the kingdom. The principle of "mutual consultation," which is mentioned in the Koran, is said to have been present all along in various arrangements for consultation with the ulema. The decree also pledges to "ensure the rights of individuals and their freedom and refrain from any action that will affect these rights and freedoms except within the limits stipulated in the laws and regulations." Protection of property and freedom from illegal search, arrest or imprisonment are affirmed. Concerning the monarchy, the decree states that the Sharia "identifies the nature of the state, its goals and responsibilities, as well as the relationship between the ruler and the subjects." The king notes that this relationship is based on "fraternity, justice, mutual respect, and loyalty," and that "there is no difference between a ruler and a subject. All are equal before the divine laws of Allah." Above all, the decree declares unequivocally that the Sharia is the law of the Saudi state, and that "The Kingdom's constitution is the Holy Qur'an [Koran] and the Sunnah (sayings) of the Prophet."

King Fahd's astute attempts to clarify the basis of Saudi political legitimacy show a keen understanding of political forces, but not everyone will be satisfied. Because the council is appointed by the ruling family rather than elected, and would therefore place no real limitations on royal authority, it falls short of the hopes of either the liberals or the conservatives. Each of these groups favors popular election and freedom of speech, but this apparent agreement of goals may conceal deeper divisions that could surface if the base of participation broadens. The recent experience of Algeria shows that religious fundamentalists may envision democracy and freedom of speech as means rather than as ends, employing them to establish a strict reign of religious and cultural authoritarianism along fundamentalist Islamic lines. An opening up of Saudi political processes may reveal a deep rift between the long-term objectives of the fundamentalist and the liberal wings of the opposition. The liberals, for example, might see reform as leading to greater rights for women and the Shia minorities, while religious conservatives might envision democracy as a process of installing pious ulema who would protect the community from just such changes.

By commanding the Islamic symbols of legitimacy so effectively, Saudi Arabia's elites have managed to forestall many of the complex debates and issues that have troubled Egypt, Turkey, and most other Muslim nations. How long they can continue in this way is another question.

IRAN AND THE ISLAMIC REPUBLIC

Iran's Twelver Shiism is based on the premise that, until the reappearance of the Hidden Imam, no earthly government is truly legitimate. This philosophy is well suited to an oppositional role, but the rise of the Shia-based Safavid Empire in the fifteenth century prompted a modification of this theory: Although the Hidden Imam is the only true ruler, the Shia ulema can and should lead the people in his absence, and their guidance can legitimatize secular rule.

At the beginning of the present century, there were two factions vying for control of the government—those advocating active guidance from the ulema according to the rationale stated above, and those pressing for a modern constitutional government. In 1906 these factions reached a compromise that provided for constitutional government, but with guarantees as to the Islamic nature of the government and a stipulation that all laws would conform to the Sharia. This compromise was set aside, however, with the ascendence of the Pahlevi dynasty in 1925. As he moved away from the representative government provided by the constitution, Reza Shah paid little attention to Islamic values and did much to suppress the visible manifestations of Islam. A split between secularizing and Islamic factions began to grow. With the forced abdication of Reza Shah and the partial return to democracy in the 1940s, a renaissance of Islam led to the reappearance of veiling, religious garb, and public ritual. Thousands of pilgrims were issued passports for the hajj, and a number of Muslim organizations—including some that were violent and extremist—appeared on the scene.

The young Muhammad Reza Shah was at first allied with the moderate religious establishment. During the 1950s, however, the United States colluded with him to eliminate the popular nationalist prime minister, Dr. Mohammed Mossadegh, and the shah moved steadily toward autocracy. Aided by American assistance and growing oil revenues, he launched a program of modernization that he dubbed the "White Revolution." His programs included much that was potentially beneficial, including land reform, industrialization, and the advancement of public health and education. However, he had little appreciation for the social and cultural context of these developments, forcing a pace of change that was self-defeating and which brought severe social upheavals. Land reform stripped power from the clergy, and it moved faster than the ability of the people—including its peasant beneficiaries—to adapt to it. Ships loaded with goods arrived to find no docking facilities; thousands of cars and trucks sat idle without adequate roads or trained drivers; millions of dollars of oil revenues went for imported goods rather than the development of home-based manufacture, while urban migrants from the countryside looked for employment. The shah refused to listen to competent advisors, Muslim clergy, or popular sentiment, ruthlessly suppressing all dissent with brutal police state tactics. Despite important contributions to the material standard of living, the shah's policies resulted in a political condition that was more repressive and less promising than in 1906 when the first Iranian constitution had been adopted.

Perhaps looking for a source of legitimation that would not bind him to the authority of the Shia clergy, the shah turned to the political symbolism of the pre-Islamic Persian Empire. He was not the first to think of this; during the nineteenth century, certain critics had attributed the decline of Iran to the dilution of Persian culture by Arab and Turkish influences, and some even blamed Islam itself. Thus, they had advocated turning away from these influences to a renaissance of Persian culture. The shah's regime chose this strain of nationalism: He dubbed himself the "Sun of the Aryans" and had his wife Farah crowned empress—the first since A.D. 632. Although the shah's "Peacock Throne" ideology did not renounce Islam, it dismantled a long-standing balance between nationalist and Islamic definitions of political authority and turned Islam from a potentially powerful source of legitimation into a lethal weapon for the opposition.

Although the opposition to the shah included a broad spectrum of religious, secular modernist, Marxist, and other viewpoints, the shah's brutal tyranny tended to unite them and to make their differences seem less significant. The opposition ideology derived much of its character from the negation of the shah's excesses: his denial of human rights and free speech, insensitivity to popular opinion, submissiveness to American interests, and so forth. Whatever their diverse social ideals, the dissenters were brothers and sisters in suffering, and a bravely resisting figure such as the Ayatollah Ruhollah Khomeini seemed in some sense to speak for the common cause of the disaffected. In the case of the Iranian revolution—as in so many others—it proved easier to unite in opposition to evil than to join in a vision of the good. The Iranian Revolution of 1979 was followed by a reign of terror in which thousands were executed, beginning with the minions of the old regime and proceeding gradually to the leftists, other out-of-favor elements among the dissidents, social misfits, and ethnic or religious minorities.

At the core of the revolutionary ideology was the total institutionalization of Islam in government. The revolutionary "Council of Experts" articulated a theory of government by "the jurist" (faqih), a religious figure chosen to represent Islam; Khomeini was, of course, the jurist. Ironically, the traditional Shia opposition to worldly rule has elements that can be used to legitimize forms of political-religious leadership that make Sunni political authority seem humble by comparison. The chiliastic concept of a Hidden Imam who will eventually appear to redeem the world and punish the wicked, and who may send a deputy to rule in his name until his arrival, led many to see Khomeini as a divinely appointed spokesman for the Imam, or even as the Imam himself. (It should be noted that most of Iran's Shia clergy have opposed such extremes, and that many reject involvement in worldly politics both on theological and practical grounds.)

Postrevolutionary Iran is steeped in "Islamic" values and symbols. The educational system is aimed at purging Western influences and making people better Muslims, and college entrance examinations stress religious education and attitudes. "Islamic dress" is the norm. The language of politics and the mass media is rich in religious symbolism. Chiliastic imagery and the Shia idealization of martyrdom figure prominently in patriotic rhetoric, and major political announcements may be timed in accordance with auspicious dates in the Muslim calendar. As a reaction against the shah's choice of cultural and historical symbols, "nationalist tendencies" are eschewed as contrary to Islam: Persian literature and poetry are in disfavor, and it was even suggested that the Persian Gulf be renamed the "Islamic Gulf," at once symbolizing the unity of the Umma and rejecting the celebration of a pre-Islamic cultural identity.

The identification of the United States as "Number One Satan" expresses a number of themes in the revolution. To begin with, there is a secular political grievance: The United States supported the shah and helped to depose Mossadegh, a charismatic popular leader who might have changed Iranian history for the better. SAVAK, the shah's notoriously cruel secret police force, was organized and trained with the help of the FBI and CIA to search out "internal enemies." But the United States also functions in radical Iranian Shia thinking as a potent symbol of the powerful, antireligious, worldly oppressor—as a force against the oppressed, righteous, martyred victim who will triumph with God's help in the end. The United States is associated in political rhetoric with the satanic figure of Caliph Yazid, the historical caliph who martyred Ali's son Husayn. Thus, symbols of American or Western influence, such as clothing and entertainments, are excoriated as anti-Islamic. Any victory in the conflict with the Great Satan is claimed as evidence of God's favor, while a defeat may be seen in light of the perennial martyrdom of the righteous. Of course, it is not only Iran that uses common enemies to promote internal unity, and it is not only the United States that is demonized in Iranian political rhetoric—Iraq, for example, also symbolizes the irreligious oppressor. Furthermore, it should be kept in mind that not all factions in Iran are comfortable either with the extremism or the international isolation that this militant rhetoric entails.

Khomeini's political philosophy placed great emphasis on the conflict between the oppressor and the oppressed. The oppressors included both the West and the former communist bloc, as well as assorted local and internal villains. The regime has expressed its commitment to Iran's poor, favoring them for rationed goods and offering them government employment. It has also endeavored to raise their living conditions through rural development and nationalization of private commercial assets.

The Islamic Republic

One way in which the revolutionary government of Iran has attempted to address "oppression" is by exporting its style of Islamic revolution to other Muslim countries. The direct appeal of Iran's strategy is greatest where there are substantial Shia populations, as in Iraq, Lebanon, and the Gulf States. But even non-Shia Muslim militants may be inspired by the success of the Iranian revolution, and the decade following 1979 was one in which the whole Muslim world reverberated with the concept of "the Islamic Republic."

The concept of an Islamic state has an understandable appeal for Muslim activists accustomed to being on the defensive. However, the Islamic Republic raises a new set of troublesome issues. While it is clear that the Koran regulates social life in a variety of ways, it makes no provision for government as such:

Nothing is said about leadership, succession, or the structures and institutions that make up a system of government. Indeed, some Islamic modernists have argued that it was not the intent of God's revelations to establish any particular system of government, and that whatever their moral and religious responsibilities, governments are entirely human creations. If one does accept the notion that the Koran requires an Islamic government, the exact form of that government must rest on elaborate, and potentially debatable, interpretations of the Koran and Sunna. The body of preexisting interpretation in the Sharia is concerned mostly with personal conduct in ritual, family, and business matters—and of course, it does not refer to uniquely modern situations and problems. While the Sharia cannot in principle be modified, its application to contemporary legal and political affairs would require considerable extrapolation. It could be argued that the extension of Islam and the Sharia into highly contested social and political applications might weaken it by tying its fortunes to the vagaries of politics. The same kind of issue arises with regard to the role of the ulema. Historically, participation of the ulema in government has tended to weaken their oppositional role (as in the Ottoman and Saudi cases), and thus potentially to diminish their status as an independent moral force. Furthermore, strong links with governing factions or structures can quickly become liabilities when the tide of politics turns against them. For these reasons, many ulema are wary of excessive direct involvement in politics.

The supporting ideology of the Islamic Republic parallels in many respects the doctrines of Third World liberation—as in, for example, the emphasis on social justice, dignity, and empowerment for the common people, the rejection of foreign domination, and the celebration of indigenous spiritual and cultural values. At the same time, the Islamic Republic is theoretically incompatible with one of the classic elements of most Third World movements, namely, nationalism. There is but one Umma and it includes all believers in Islam. Any less inclusive Islamic Republic that pursues its own national interests in opposition to the rest of the Umma can expect its status as an Islamic Republic to be contested. The pursuit of a single, universal Islamic Republic offers little hope of success in the contemporary world scene, but the existence of competing Islamic Republics is a contradiction in terms.

Democracy also poses a problem for the Islamic Republic. As long as the will of the people is suppressed by a non-Islamic establishment, it is easy enough to use the demand for popular participation as a blanket concept for a variety of different and incompatible goals. Islam has a long history of populist thought that defines popular participation largely as participation by the ulema, insofar as they embody accepted religious ideas and apply the Sharia in a manner consistent with social justice and equality before God. This is quite different from the Western conception of democracy, and it raises urgent practical issues, including the right of dissent, the political rights of religious minorities, the limits on suffrage and representational government, and the constraints on legislation. The Islamic concept of unity, or **tawhid**, refers not only to the oneness of God but to "unity" in a variety of other meanings including the political. While tawhid is part of the ideal Islamic state, it is difficult to reconcile tawhid with the actual plurality of ethnicity, political views, culture, and religion encompassed within any modern state. Although Islamic-based governments like Saudi Arabia and Iran have tried to equate the will of God with the will of all the people, it is inevitable that one or the other will be compromised to the detriment—in someone's eyes—of the regimes' legitimacy.

What is the future of the concept of an Islamic Republic? Has it already had its day, or will it continue as a serious option for Muslim states? High ideals can become tarnished—sometimes unfairly—when they are obliged to confront the complications, compromises, and intractable problems of the political arena. The problems of Middle Eastern nations are sobering enough, and the Islamic Republic raises some of its own. Some observers detect a strain of disillusionment within Iranian society, and the success of the moderate Rafsanjani faction in the elections of April 1992 may indicate a move toward a more pragmatic and less ideologically ambitious definition of Islamic government.

SEXUAL POLITICS

Throughout this book we have treated politics as a dynamic process of conflict and accommodation, a process that connects in complex ways with cultural, societal, religious, and economic factors. We have referred to arenas and levels of conflict and resolution that dip and swirl irregularly, so that issues on one level may have ramifications on other levels. More specifically, we have identified *cultural politics* as the arena of conflict that centers on conflicting definitions of cultural norms, categories, and symbols. Few problems better illustrate these kinds of conflict than male-female relations in the Middle East. These relations deserve to be termed *sexual politics*, not only because of their potential for conflict and resolution, but also because of their relevance to the struggle for power and authority in domestic, community, national, and international contexts, and their multifaceted relations with other political problems discussed in this book.

Sexual Equality in Islam: The Modernist Interpretation

Despite Western stereotypes to the contrary, there is a case to be made for Islam as a liberating and egalitarian influence in opposition to rigidly sexist traditions. This case has been made by a variety of Middle Eastern Muslims and non–Middle Eastern apologists since the middle of the last century, in an attempt to free Islam of the taint of "backward" folk traditions and reconcile it with modernizing trends. The view that many of the standard, prevailing interpretations of Islam are actually un-Islamic, and that the true, original Islam is more compatible with modernization than those pseudo-Islamic social traditions is characteristic of Muslim modernism. There is much in the historical record to support a modernist interpretation of Islam as regards sex roles. Few would deny that the Koran ended a number of abuses against women or that it established inheritance and property rights that were extremely liberal by the standards of the time; one Muslim feminist refers to these provisions of the Koran as a "feminist bill of rights." Beginning with Muhammad's wife Khadija, the women of the early Muslim community were active in public life, even to the occasional extreme of serving as warriors or of instructing men in religion. After a delegation of women converts questioned the Prophet about the male-oriented language of his earlier revelations, certain key Koranic verses used a "he or she" locution similar to that of modern "nonsexist" writing. As we noted in Chapter 2, the Koran seems relatively free of the intimations of spiritual and moral inequality that one may find in parts of the Christian Bible.

The modernists have rightly pointed out that many of the "Muslim" customs that outsiders criticize as sexist are not necessarily Islamic in origin. We have already noted that the veiling of women existed in pre-Muslim times as a symbol of social status. Koranic references to the veil are ambiguous, and can be read merely as prescribing modest dress in public. Similarly, many modernists deny that the Koran provides any general support for the custom of secluding women in the home. The exclusion of women (until recently) from public worship in the mosques is also said to be a reflection of folk tradition that is directly at variance with the practice of the Prophet and his early followers. Muhammad's admonition against a man taking a second wife if the husband doubts that he can treat them equally, together with the Prophet's statement elsewhere as to the impossibility of equal treatment, is offered as evidence that Islam really meant to rule out polygamy. Besides, others have pointed out, polygamy is mentioned in the Koran only in connection with certain special and unusual circumstances, and is not necessarily endorsed as a general practice. The Koranic basis for the rule of evidence in Islamic courts—that a woman's testimony is worth only half that of a man's—is also noted as applying to certain (perhaps obsolete) social circumstances and is not, the argument goes, intended to be universal. Modernist writers have also pointed out that some antifeminist sentiments commonly attributed to the Prophet are based not on the Koran but on the less reliable hadiths.

Furthermore, the apologists point out, even unequal institutions may sometimes be better than they appear. Seclusion in the harem, for example, accustomed women to a considerable degree of freedom and achievement in a predominantly female world; thus women physicians, for example, were (and are) surprisingly common in the Middle East, as are all-female work groups in the contemporary mass communications industry and elsewhere. Similarly, polygamy is sometimes said to have relieved the burden on the traditional wife while providing sororal companionship. The fact that the Koran allocates to women only one-half the man's share of inheritance must, it is said, be balanced against the recognition that men are required to provide for women but not vice versa, and that the dowry paid by the husband at marriage becomes the wife's personal property.

Perhaps the strongest point on behalf of the egalitarian interpretation, however, is that a major thrust of the Koran is the elimination of injustice and the protection of the weak from abuses by the strong. If one accepts this as an overriding message of Islam, even customs once considered as Muslim might be superseded in the name of this ultimate Islamic principle.

Sexual Inequality in Islamic Tradition

The above arguments notwithstanding, there are certain historical realities that even the most devoted modernist is obliged to recognize. To begin with, the social regulations of the Koran do portray a world in which public affairs were handled mainly by men, a world in which women usually moved in a domestic sphere circumscribed by male authority. The inequality recognized in the Koran is social rather than spiritual in nature, entailing a number of sexually asymmetrical regulations, such as the difference in inheritance shares, the fact that only men can take more than one spouse, and the ability of men only to obtain a divorce without publicly showing cause. Although the outlook of the Koran is probably no more male-oriented than that of Jewish and Christian scriptures, the Koran is explicit in its regulation of domestic life, and its detailed implementation in Sharia law leaves little latitude for interpretation.

There is no mistaking the trend in sex roles after the Prophet's death. Conservative views arising both from folk tradition and from the practice of the Persian and Byzantine upper classes led to consistently antifeminist interpretations of the Koran and the accumulation of antifeminist hadiths attributed to the Prophet. By the time Sharia law had taken its definitive form in the ninth century, these conservative interpretations had taken on the authority of divine command. For example, the Sharia gives legal force to the husband's right of unilateral divorce, but it leaves up to the man's judgment the fulfillment of the Koranic requirements that he have good cause for divorce and that he first seek reconciliation. Similarly it gives legal status to the Prophet's permission to marry up to four wives, but leaves up to the husband the fulfillment of the Koran's clearly stated precondition of equal treatment. The Sharia occasionally even sanctifies customs that cannot be documented in the Koran and seem at odds with the Prophet's attempts to strengthen the family; particularly the custom of *triple divorce*, in which a husband can divorce his wife simply by saying "I repudiate thee" three times in succession. In most schools of Muslim jurisprudence this divorce is binding and cannot be rescinded even at the husband's will. Most ulema, while disapproving of the practice, must recognize its legality as an established part of the Sharia. It must be kept in mind that the Sharia, technically at least, is not subject to modification; thus its explicitly conservative interpretations of sex-role issues pose an inconvenience to the modernists.

Equally problematic is the tendency of rank-and-file Muslims and even the ulema to imbue traditional practices and attitudes with the sanctity of Islam. Whether or not the Koran actually insists on traditional female subordination, ordinary people may feel that they are defending Islam whenever they resist innovative, especially Westernizing, influences in favor of retaining their own traditions. There is even a basis for this in Islamic theology, since the Prophet is reported to have said that God will not let His people agree in an error; hence, Muslim jurisprudence recognizes consensus (that is, the consensus of the ulema) as one criterion of religious truth. Thus, traditional attitudes about women and sexuality achieve a quasi-religious status despite their lack of any direct basis in scripture or theology. Important among these attitudes is the notion that female unchastity is the most potent threat to family honor, and that women's sexuality threatens the social order. It is taken for granted that men will be possessive and protective of the women in their own families and opportunistic toward others. Women are thought of not as self-controlling but as being controlled by others; a good woman submits to the control of her father, brothers, and later her husband, whereas a bad one submits to the predatory stranger. Women are not to be trusted but rather contained—confined within the circle of male overseers, within the veil, and, whenever possible, secluded and protected in the women's quarters of the household. Many Muslim men may see this private patriarchal domain as their last bastion of authority in a world otherwise dominated by exogenous forces. A sense of helplessness in the face of other changes might even lead to a retrenchment of this miniature polity within the home.

The Struggle for Reform

Much of the modernization of sex roles in the Middle East has stemmed indirectly from international politics. Turkey and Egypt, as the two main centers of Middle Eastern Muslim power in the early nineteenth century, were the first to feel the threat of the Western incursion. Their response in each case was a judicious attempt to modernize the military and other sectors of society that might help stave off foreign rule. These programs of modernization, implemented by Western-educated cadres, led to a general fascination with, and grudging respect for, Western culture. Colonialism was, of course, as much a cultural as a military onslaught, and Middle Easterners were faced with a significant challenge in the West's claims of cultural superiority. It was in this context that the first Muslim modernists began their attempt to rediscover Islam, purified of its misguided "folk" interpretations, as the progressive religion par excellence. By the turn of the century the Egyptian modernist scholar Qasim Amin had produced Arabic books on *The Emancipation of Women* and *The Modern Women*. Decades ahead of their time, these works set out such modernist arguments as those discussed above, for which they were publicly condemned as un-Islamic. Amin argued that full equality of the sexes was required by Islam, and also that it was necessary for Egypt's national development. Although such ideas were unpopular, they provided a basis for a more active wave of feminism. In 1923, educated Egyptian women formed the Feminist Union, publicly cast off their veils, and began to campaign for legal reform. The same year saw the establishment of the Republic of Turkey under the leadership of Kemal Ataturk, the ardent modernist reformer. Building not only on his role as founder of the modern Turkish state but also on nearly a century of reform in women's status and other social issues, Ataturk instituted sweeping reforms that eliminated legal distinctions between the sexes, abolished polygamy, and allowed women to vote and stand for office. Although he did not outlaw the veil and could take no direct action against the deeper attitudes that gave rise to it, he never missed an opportunity to dramatize publicly his support of sexual equality. Yet although he replaced the Sharia with the Swiss Civil Code, Ataturk claimed to be purifying Islam of its latter-day misinterpretations.

In 1956, Habib Bourgiba, after leading Tunisia to independence, initiated a process of reform that placed his country alongside Turkey and Egypt in the vanguard of sexual egalitarianism. Unlike Ataturk, who disestablished the Sharia as the law of the land, Bourgiba based his program on his own radically modernist reading of the Sharia. His reforms, generally similar to Turkey's, banned polygamy, required informed consent of a bride as a precondition of marriage, set a minimum age for marriage, gave the sexes equal rights in divorce and child custody, and provided equal educational opportunity. Justifying these changes in the name of purifying Islam and catching up with the West, Bourgiba even went so far as to provide free abortions to married or single women without the need of a husband's or guardian's permission.

If Ataturk and Bourgiba succeeded largely because of their favorable political positions; reforms in some other countries have failed for equally political reasons. In Algeria and Morocco, for example, schooling for girls and other egalitarian reforms were sponsored by the hated French colonial regime and became associated with the taint of cultural imperialism. Despite the important role played by women in the war of independence, postcolonial Algeria and Morocco deliberately adopted a conservative interpretation of Muslim women's roles as part of the repudiation of Western culture. These sentiments, along with a fear that working women would add to the severe male unemployment, have led to policies aimed at keeping women in the home. In Saudi Arabia, where political legitimacy rests on Muwahhidun conservatism, the veiling and segregation of women are actively enforced and have encountered only weak opposition. An organized demonstration during the 1991 Iraq–Kuwait War, in which Saudi women defied the rule against driving automobiles, resulting in widespread denunciation not only of the women involved but also of the American influence on which the protest was blamed.

Most Middle Eastern countries, however, lie between these extremes and are characterized by a dialogue between the forces of conservatism and change. Modernizing economies, urbanization, a greater variety of role models, and women's education provide the foundation for fundamental, though often very slow, changes; in the meantime, legal reforms gradually accumulate.

Women in the Islamic Revival

Since the mid-1970s, the plodding pace of social and legal reforms in women's roles has been overshadowed by a more dramatic turn of events: a widespread popular movement devoted to a restoration of "Islamic" behavior and dress. If this movement were simple conservatism among the traditionally oriented rural population, it would hardly be surprising; it is understandable that even fifty years after Ataturk's reforms, rural Turkish villagers still continue in the patterns of marriage, dress, and sex roles that prevailed in the old days. Paradoxically, however, the most self-conscious reassertion of "Islamic" roles for women is found in those places where Westernization, social reform, and education have proceeded the farthest. Again ironically, the protest is often most evident among educated middle-class women, the daughters and granddaughters of the women who boldly cast away their veils and campaigned for legal reforms. In Egypt, women university students have taken increasingly to wearing various forms of modest "Shari" dress, some go veiled in public, and a few have even elected to seclude themselves in their homes. In Tunisia, where reforms of family and divorce laws had gone particularly far, educated women clad in veils publicly confronted President Bourgiba to protest his liberalizing policies and reaffirm the value of traditional feminine roles. These events reflect more than mere inertia against change; they constitute a political phenomenon in their own right.

A comparison between the Middle East and China with regard to sex role changes might be instructive. In postrevolutionary China, the ideal for sex role change was clearly and unequivocally portrayed: The old patriarchal order was to be abolished and replaced by sexual equality. Of course, changes in behavior have not entirely lived up to the ideal, nor have they been painless. Nevertheless, the degree of change within only a generation or two has been remarkable, especially in comparison with the Middle East, when one considers the strength of patriarchal attitudes and institutions in Chinese tradition. Of course, the Middle East as a whole has not experienced anything like the upheaval of the Chinese Revolution, but there are other differences as well. The role of Islam in establishing the cultural and social forms of the Middle East, in placing it so centrally in world history, and in structuring a centuries-old competition with the Christian West, all contribute to the importance of Islam as a vehicle for the political response to Western domination. The Middle Easterners' struggle for self-determination, in other words, is expressed in the need to be Muslim. But Islam, as we have seen, is uniquely concerned with marriage and family life, and thus the domestic arena becomes, in a sense, a setting in which the drama of international domination and resistance is symbolized and is acted out.

Seen in this context, the West's vocal concern over the plight of Middle Eastern women is itself an example of cultural politics—another blow in the age-old rivalry over "who is more civilized than whom." Western feminists may add to this sense of rivalry by unconsciously equating Westernization with progress—a habit of thought that tends to muddle the issues and to divide those who could be united by deeper common interests. In this setting of cultural and political rivalry, departure from traditional family and sex-role patterns in favor of those prevailing in the West—even when sponsored by popular nationalist leaders or justified in the name of purified Islam—is widely seen as a capitulation to foreign domination.

The case of Iran aptly illustrates the interplay of sexual politics with the national and international arenas. Interest in greater opportunities for women began during the nineteenth century among the Western-oriented middle class, and by the early decades of this century women were involved in forceful public demonstrations in support of nationalist and democratic causes. In the 1920s, some educated women braved persecution in order to operate private schools for girls. The cause of sexual equality was, however, unwittingly sabotaged by the policies of the Pahlevi rulers. Reza Shah, who came to the throne in 1925, pursued a program of Westernization that included public schooling for girls, forced abolition of the veil, and other changes in family life. Reza Shah's high-handed methods fostered an ulema-led opposition that, after his abdication in 1941, led to a dramatic backlash against his policies. Legal reforms were reversed, and the ulema publicly called for a return to the veil. During the 1960s and 1970s Muhammad Reza Shah attempted another program of legal changes, including women's suffrage and the Family Protection Laws of 1967 and 1973, which modified in women's favor the prevailing practices regarding polygamy, divorce, child custody, and related matters. It seems, however, that the shah valued these changes more as symbols of "modernization" than as actual advances toward equality. In a much-publicized interview with an Italian journalist he scorned "Women's lib," pronounced women inferior to men in ability, and remarked that "women count only if they are beautiful and graceful...."

Authoritarian in his methods and reliant on the United States for support, the shah came increasingly to be seen not only as an agent of cruel outside oppression, but more specifically as a harbinger of Western-style profligacy, whose "feminism" was really nothing more than an attempt to turn women into painted playthings. Through an ironic twist of politics, a strong ulema-led opposition to the shah's policy of women's suffrage became (for some, at least) an important rallying symbol of popular empowerment. The movement against the shah appealed to people's sense of social justice, personal freedom, national pride, and religious piety. The appeal was equally felt by both women and men, and both participated actively in the revolution. As often happens, the success of the revolution of 1979 brought rude surprises for some. While perhaps many women had never aspired to a growing personal freedom or equality with men, others felt betrayed by the repeal of the Family Protection Laws and the attempt to return women to their traditional roles. Some women who had worn veils as symbols of protest against the shah felt differently when the new government began to require "Islamic" dress. Beneath the apparent unity of post-revolutionary Iran lies a great diversity of assumptions and opinions about the direction of progress. Iran's religious leaders claim that it is they who truly respect women's equality with men, while the chief threat to women is those who would plunge them into Western-style "immorality." While many women appear to accept this claim, others see it as a rationalization for reactionary, sexist policies that amount to a betrayal of their trust.

The changes in Iran, though dramatic, are not entirely unique. In Egypt, modest "Islamic" dress has been voluntarily adopted by a growing number of young women, often from the educated middle class. Liberal family and marriage laws championed by Mrs. Sadat were later repealed following repeated protests by veiled Egyptian women, and a leading Egyptian feminist and film director was pressured into self-exile by opponents who labeled her a "foreign agent" for her feminist views.

We have argued that these reversals against women's rights are in part a spinoff from the Islamic resistance to Western domination. This is aided by the inevitable tendency of any culture to form inaccurate and ethnocentric stereotypes about another—in this case, exaggerated notions about the supposed promiscuity, materialism, and breakdown of family life in the West. It may be more difficult for the Westerner to see, however, that some elements of the Islamic "revival" may also stem from informed reflection, women's self-interest, and intelligent cultural criticism. Middle Eastern women directly familiar with Western culture have pointed out its flaws as a model for women's fulfillment: Accustomed to moving in a segregated women's world, they see Western women as obsessed with dating, pairing, and heterosexual attraction. While criticizing the traditional Middle Eastern domination of women within the domestic setting, they are shocked and repulsed by what they see as the tasteless public exploitation of women and femininity for hedonistic and commercial purposes. In this light, veiling and other forms of neo-Islamic dress take on still another meaning: Islamic dress is for many women an assertion of personal choice, a way of preserving one's privacy and dignity in a public or work setting, and an affirmation of one's cultural pride in the face of a smug and domineering West.

As the above example shows, it is not always easy to distinguish reactionary elements from modernist ones. Although one might expect fundamentalist and modernist Islam to be irreconcilable opposites, the two may at times be almost indistinguishable. The writings of Ali Shariati (1933–1977) provide a case in point. Educated in sociology at the Sorbonne, Shariati endured two decades of imprisonment, surveillance, and exile from his native Iran because of his opinions. As an articulate defender of Islam and critic of Western society, Shariati became a spokesman for the anti-shah movement and a veritable saint of the Iranian revolution following his death. His writings continue to provide guidance for Muslim revivalism in postrevolutionary Iran and elsewhere. Shariati, however, was an

Islamic modernist in the tradition of Muhammad Abdu, Qasim Amin, and al-Afghani; while he defended Islam in the face of Western secular thought, he was equally eloquent in his attack on the traditionalists who "confuse being old-fashioned with being religious." He blamed tradition for depriving women of their rightful place in Muslim society, for excluding them from religious life, and for ranking them in social standing "at the level of a washing machine." To the discomfort of many Shia ulema, Shariati flatly proclaimed the equality of the sexes and advocated their equal participation in social life. His ideal, however, was not the "superficial" modernity of the Western woman. Instead, he offered as his ideal woman the Prophet's daughter Fatima, the perfect wife and mother, exemplar of courage and social responsibility, and leader in the protest against the materialistic trends in the religion of her time. Was Shariati a modernist or a traditionalist? The very fact that this question is so difficult to answer may suggest that, in the end, the meaning of modernity must be framed within the terms of each society's historical experience.

CONCLUSION

We have defined politics as the process of conflict and resolution involved in the pursuit of limited good, and we have suggested that this good may include the privilege of defining the symbols and values by which people live. Political behavior everywhere follows patterns that, if not always strictly rational, display a more or less intelligible logic once the underlying premises are understood. Those premises, however, are invariably rooted in cultural values and symbolic relationships that cannot be reduced to pure rationality. This is not a situation that peoples and nations are likely to outgrow in the forseeable future; perhaps not ever. Religious and cultural symbols are both a defining source of social goals and a reflection of historical striving toward those goals. Thus in our discussion of the Islamic revival, for example, we have steered away from explanations that would reduce religion and its associated values to the status of mere political devices; or on the other extreme, explanations that would make politics simply the tool of religious dogmas. History shows a dynamic, evolving relationship between social life and changing interpretations of religious and cultural heritage. To see one as a mere puppet of the other, or to reduce either to nonhistorical essences, is to pursue a comforting simplicity at the expense of genuine understanding.

POLITICAL ELITES

The study of political and social elites has been extraordinarily rewarding to social scientists. Among the reasons for this is the fact that most complex societies have well-defined elites. These elites are prominent; they are easily identified and studied. Elites are intimately involved in the processes that produce and resolve group conflict over the allocation of resources; they exist in all of the arenas of conflict, whether they be local, regional, national, or international; and elites prompt or resist or reflect changes in the social, economic, and political processes.

In all but the most simple societies, certain people perform political functions; they make the binding decisions of the society. These people, the elite, can be distinguished from those who do not exercise substantial power, the public or the masses. In other words, at one level or another, and with varying degrees of effectiveness, an elite is composed of those people who decide "who gets what, when, and how." And since those decisions are going to both satisfy and disappoint members of that society, especially since allocations take place in an environment of relative scarcity, the activities of the elite both resolve and generate conflicts. For example, a decision to transfer land from traditional landowners to the previous tenant farmers will satisfy the demands of the tenant farmers but will motivate the landlords to seek some form of compensation for their losses. Thus, the elite in its action creates new demands on the system as it attempts to reconcile existing conflicts.

Members of an elite tend to represent the interests of the societal group from which they spring. A member of an elite whose ancestors were small farmers can be expected to represent the interests of those with similar backgrounds *to a predictable degree*; and an elite member whose ancestors were landless peasants would be expected to represent a substantially different point of view, especially on those problems that directly involve the conflicting interests of landholders and tenant farmers.

If members of the elite represent their own groups of origin with some predictability, then the composition of the elite can reveal much about the state of politics in a given society. For example, the overrepresentation of one segment of society in the elite would imply that disproportionate shares of that society's produce were going to that group. And on the other hand, the absence of a potentially important elite group—the educated professional class, for example—would imply that the group was being disproportionately penalized by the actions of government. Thus, the composition of the elite is of great importance to the society attempting to modernize, for a modern society attempts to involve most or all of its citizenry in the pursuit of a new social and political consensus. Consensus is not built by excluding large or important groups from the political process or the elite. Thus, the general representativeness of the elite is an important indicator for anyone attempting to understand the political process in a given country or region.

The analysis of the elite in a transitional society—and most of the systems under study here are in a transitional state between the traditional and the modern—will generally reveal an elite of changing composition. In particular, we should be alert to changes in the elite that indicate an expansion of the elements of society participating in political decisions, and to evidence that indicates traditional opposition to that change. It is axiomatic that established elites will oppose such changes, since those changes involve a dilution of the elites' past influence. Conflict is implicit between those elements of the elite proposing and supporting technical modernization and those elements of the elite opposing such changes. In most of the countries of the Middle East, this process expresses itself in terms of a religious elite opposing the modernizing efforts of the bureaucracy, professional classes, and the military. Since World War II and the nominal political independence of the nations of the area, this conflict has occurred between the traditional religious elite of the Middle East—the ulema—and the government, usually dominated by the military bureaucracy.

Although we have discussed the peculiarities of the ulema in earlier chapters, it is important to recall some of its primary characteristics, particularly since it complicates our analysis. First and foremost, the ulema is unusually diffuse; it has no clear hierarchy, or rules of membership, or formal organization. Existing independently of the political order, it has nonetheless historically penetrated and influenced that order, reflecting the pervasiveness of Islam in general. The ulema is consequently difficult to pin down in sociographic terms. But there is no denying its existence and no denying its desire to maintain its authority, which it derives from sacred or religious sources. And it is the ulema's maintenance of sacred sources of authority and knowledge that brings it into conflict with the focus of modernization. For modernization, as it developed in the West, recognized the authority of man, not God. Thus, the ulema, as the frontline bastion against secular authority, often finds itself in fundamental opposition to the secular values of Western-style modernizers. As we shall see, this opposition takes various forms in the political systems of the Middle East. Historically, the ulema has sought to influence and advise government rather than serve formally as officers of the state. They have further preferred to exercise moral vetoes over unacceptable policy. There are indications that this policy may be changing in Iran, Saudi Arabia, Libya, and the Gulf states; but basically the political power of the ulema has been negative—oppositional power rather than the power of positive influence or accommodation.

A prominent exception to this situation involves the Shia community in Iran. Here the clergy, more formally organized than in Sunni-dominated areas, has taken direct control of the government for the purposes of implementing an Islamic republic. Although this experiment is important, it is also important to remember that the Shia account approximately for only 10 percent of the world's Muslims. In the main, the ulema still keeps its distance from government, seeking to exert moral or oppositional influence in contrast to the direct exercise of political power.

By contrast, the modernizing forces in the Middle East can be described as adopting the opposite of the political style of the ulema. The forces generally supporting technical modernization in the Middle East are the governmental entities that gained political power in the aftermath of independence. Although nominal power at that time was held by hereditary monarchs (such as Farouk in Egypt and the Hashemite monarchs in Jordan and Iraq), more actual political power was held by the bureaucrats and military officer corps of those governments. And as the political pressures of independence grew, the actual formal political power of these elites grew, ultimately displacing the hereditary traditional authorities in countries such as Egypt, Iraq, and Libya. In other countries, such as Saudi Arabia, Iran, and the U.A.E., a system of shared powers between the traditional and the bureaucratic-military elites developed.

It is not surprising that the technically modernizing elements in the political elites of the Middle East should so often come from the bureaucratic and military cadres, for the preceding colonial regimes tried to create a capable, modernized bureaucracy *without* an attendant modernized, independent political structure. Thus, at independence, those elements that had been most exposed to the logic and philosophy of secular modernity were the bureaucrats and the military.

Consequently, we expect to find the elite structures of these Middle Eastern political systems in a state of flux, reflecting the low level of consensus in the society as a whole. The historical traditional order preceding the transitional stage to modernization was characterized by relatively high levels of consensus and elite congruence, and presumably the emergent modern order will be as well. Just as predictably, the intermediate transitional state will reflect the growing conflict over the objectives and basis of sociopolitical organization.

During those periods in a country's history when elite consensus and integration predominate, the leadership of the country can be indifferent or undistinguished without great cost, for the widespread agreement upon processes, institutions, goals, and the like will provide adequate direction to even the most unimaginative regimes. But when elite conflict and competition are evident, and consensus absent, the resources, imagination, and capability of the individual head of state become of great consequence. Since the Middle East finds itself in just such a transitional situation, we will spend some time in the following chapter analyzing the emergent styles of political leadership in the region. We will attempt to show the political and social consequences of varying political leadership styles, including styles that we shall call traditional, modern-bureaucratic, and charismatic.

TRADITIONAL, TRANSITIONAL, AND TECHNICALLY MODERNIZING ELITES

Figures 8-1, 8-2, and 8-3 present models of the elite structures of traditional, transitional, and modern Middle Eastern societies. Before discussing each of these elite categories, a few remarks on the diagrams themselves are in order.

In these models, we distinguish between three levels, or strata, of society: the elite, represented by the smallest group of circles in the center of each diagram; the ruling class, or those groups from whom the elite is regularly recruited; and the mass public, those members of society with considerably fewer resources and influence, who make up the majority of the society. The broken lines surrounding the ruling class vary in the three diagrams; they are intended to indicate the ease with which movement from the mass public to the ruling class can occur. If there is real opportunity for persons of demonstrated merit or capability to move from the mass public to the ruling class, we describe the society as having open, or permeable, boundaries; and if there is little possibility of an individual moving from one class to another, we label the society closed, or impermeable. The quality of permeability is of great importance to a society's ability to adjust to the changing demands of modernization.

Another feature of our model reflects the degree of cohesion, or consensus, in the elite. In this model, the closer the elite elements are, the higher the degree of consensus among them. You will notice that two of the identified elite models have relatively high degrees of association, whereas the transitional model indicates a high degree of bifurcation and internal conflict. Finally, while these models describe national elites, they can also apply to regional and local elites as well. All countries in this area are, in effect, mosaics of elite structures.

The Traditional Elites

In many respects, we have already discussed the traditional elite structure in the preceding chapters dealing with classic Islamic social organization and the early stages of modernization. We need, however, to put that knowledge into the context of elite competition in the contemporary world. A short review of the main components of each elite is appropriate here, however, and we shall begin with the center of the traditional elite, the monarch (caliph, sultan, bey, or sheikh) and his immediate subordinates (traditionally, the diwan).

In most classic Islamic states, the ruler perpetuated his control largely on the basis of the elite's acceptance of his traditional right to rule. Particularly in Sunni political systems, a very high priority was placed on the maintenance of the established rule, with many theorists claiming that even tyrants should be obeyed until the very structure of the Islamic community itself was threatened. Shia communities were less disposed to accept established authority, but even in these communities, established authority had high credibility. In most traditional Islamic states, the head of state ruled on the basis of a widespread belief that such rule was correct and, moreover, divinely determined.

The bureaucratic apparatus that supported the monarch, however, was subject to greater vagaries. The *diwan*, drawn primarily from privileged families in the nobility and ruling class, were much more subject to being removed from office, not uncommonly at the caprice of the hereditary monarch. In some traditional systems, notably the Turkish Janissary corps and the Egyptian Mameluks, rulers and high ministers might come from slave origins, devoid of family connections. Such arrangements were designed to minimize family or clan-related court intrigues, but often succeeded only in substituting one form of intrigue for another.

The diwan, and their aides and staffs, administered the kingdom; they collected the taxes and maintained the appropriate records. The record keepers, the **katib**, provided the source from which many of the ministers of the diwan were recruited, and they exerted much influence on the matters of court. The caliph, diwan, and katib, combined with the caliph's favorites, constituted the bulk of the court in a traditional Islamic state.

Also of the elite, but not so regularly or intimately a part of courtly life, were the wealthy merchants of the capital city, large-holding landowners, military officers, and the higher ulema. All of these elements had a restraining role on government: practically, in the merchants' and landowners' reaction to taxation; and morally, in the higher ulema's criticisms of policy. The ulema, in particular, limited the role of government by deciding what questions should be resolved by the caliphate, and what questions were in the exclusive domain of the Islamic community—essentially the greater and lesser ulema. The relationship between caliphate and ulema was periodically rocky, and many a traditional authority defied the moral sanction of the ulema, formally and informally, successfully and unsuccessfully.

Many of the conflicts between the caliph and the higher ulema in Sunni states centered on religious opposition to efforts at "modernization" or changes in the social and political structure of the state. One major exception to this pattern has been the continually strained relationship between the monarchy and the Shia

FIGURE 8-1. The Traditional Elite.

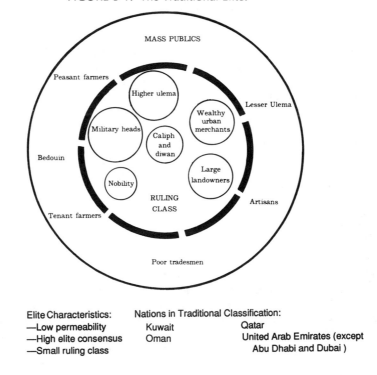

Elite Characteristics:	Nations in Traditional Classification:	
—Low permeability	Kuwait	Qatar
—High elite consensus	Oman	United Arab Emirates (except
—Small ruling class		Abu Dhabi and Dubai)

higher ulema in Iran. In this case, the Shia mistrust of political authority (see Chapter 3) has resulted in the higher ulema's espousing a strong form of constitutionalism as a basis for government. In this restrictive sense, the Iranian ulema has been among the forces striving for a more "modern" political system, fomenting conflict with the authoritarian aspirations of the Iranian shahs. This conflict has persisted down to the present day in Iran. However, in other areas of life, such as the liberalization of women's roles or secular education, the Iranian Shia ulema's position is nearly indistinguishable from that of the Sunni ulema.

The military hierarchy has also been a persistent element in the ruling class and the elite of the Islamic state and of traditional political authority. There is no Islamic tradition separating military authority from political, social, or religious authority. Moreover, military life has traditionally been a means of social access and upward mobility. Particularly in linking outlying Bedouin military forces with the urban caliphate and elite, the military has played an important role in the integration of the traditional elite. And as we shall see, the military is an important force in both the transitional and modernizing elites.

Generally, the traditional elite has a very low permeability—that is, the ruling class is very stable and outsiders move into it only with great difficulty. With the exception of the ulema (particularly the lesser ulema) and the military to some degree, social mobility was largely unknown in the traditional elite. Elite circulation was historically confined to the established ruling class and resulted in considerable unresolved tension. Indeed, many of the theorists of Islamic society, including the well-known Ibn Khaldun, attributed the decline and fall of the caliphates to the increasing restiveness of the mass publics (peasants and Bedouins), and the inability of the ruling class and elite to respond to them. The very cohesiveness of the traditional elite, its homogeneity and small size, contributed to its ultimate demise.

The weakness of the traditional state becomes most obvious when conflicts arise. In the traditional Middle East, political control, as a rule, declined proportionately as the distance increased from the political center. With the ruling class and elite centered primarily in the capital city, it was but a matter of time until the periphery suffered from neglect or exploitation. Common causes of provincial unrest came from such factors as deteriorating irrigation systems, increasingly exploitive taxes, and the failure of the government to protect farmers and merchants from banditry and other forms of predation. As opportunists perceived the possibilities deriving from these growing demands, the power of the central authority would dwindle to a point of crisis. If the traditional authority was lucky or aggressive, the threats might be laid to rest. If not, new elites and political structures, often drawn from restive elements within the ruling class and not from the mass publics, would be constituted.

In the late nineteenth and early twentieth centuries, these traditional Middle Eastern political systems—notably the Ottomans and their client states—came under heavy pressure from the national systems of Europe. The traditional political elites found themselves hard pressed to respond adequately to superior European political, military, and economic power. As the threats became real dangers and Europeans finally took control, some traditional elites adopted a new, European technical world view. These new claims on power, and the horrified traditionalist response to them, are the primary features of the next elite system, the transitional.

However, some countries resisted the pressures of modernization. Many of these nations could more properly be labeled *imminently pretransitional,* since they have been unable to resist the pressures of rising revenues and regional politics. Also, there is a pronounced unevenness of development within the group; Abu Dhabi, for instance, shows many signs of rapid transformation to a transitional form of elite structure, while Fujaira still lingers on the periphery of the Middle Ages. Such regimes would appear to be particularly vulnerable to change. Their ownership of, or proximity to, substantial petroleum reserves will make them increasingly subject to external and internal pressures for change. Most of these systems will in the near future become transitional political systems. Contemporary Yemen, formed from the combination of traditional North Yemen with the People's Democratic Republic of Yemen, emerged almost overnight as an advanced transitional state.

The Transitional Elites

The consequence of elite disagreement over the basic forms and derivations of authority produces a type of structure called *transitional.* The term is most often used to denote the stage between the disruption of traditional authority and the triumph of technical modernization; however, it might just as easily occur prior to an aggressive reassertion of traditional leadership, although this is unusual. It does seem to apply to the turmoil afflicting contemporary Iran and the rise of conservative Islamic political parties.

The transitional elite model (see Figure 8-2) has a dotted line separating the elite and ruling class into two polarized and contending groups. Although the specific composition of the elite can vary from country to country, certain groups or elements are likely to have a prominent role. For instance, wealthy landowners who owe their prosperity to the support of the traditional leadership still participate in political decisions. The military, often the first group to be systematically exposed to the influence of secular modernity by reason of their education, can be usually counted upon to support modernizing programs. The bureaucracy, trained in the science of public administration by a prior colonial administration, will also tend to support modernizing change. Those elements of the traditional elite with hereditary power can be counted on to cling to that power, by and large. And most of the greater and lesser ulema can also be counted upon to take sides in the issues at hand, although their decisions can frustrate both traditional and modernizing elements in the elite.

The transitional elite is generally composed of (and represents more) social groups than the traditional elite, in spite of the transitional elite's disagreement over the means and ends of political, social, and economic life. Internal conflict in the elite can produce irregular policy, wavering between the demands and desires of a fragmented society. This may often lead to frustrating inconsistencies that produce growing dissatisfaction from both traditional and modernizing elements. Thus, transitional societies are subject to growing internal pressures that demand resolution. Not uncommonly, these pressures build up to political violence—assassinations, demonstrations, and the like. On a more positive note, such behavior short of violence bespeaks a broader level of political participation and is one of the early signs that the pressures of change are building. The transitional society

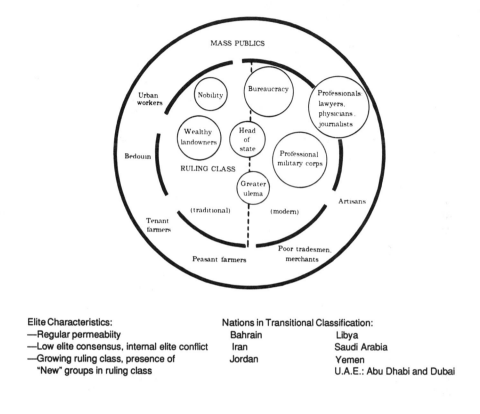

Elite Characteristics:
—Regular permeabiity
—Low elite consensus, internal elite conflict
—Growing ruling class, presence of
  "New" groups in ruling class

Nations in Transitional Classification:

Bahrain	Libya
Iran	Saudi Arabia
Jordan	Yemen
	U.A.E.: Abu Dhabi and Dubai

FIGURE 8-2. Transitional Elite.

and its elite—as disorganized and chaotic as they sometimes seem—carry the seeds of a new social order based on greater participation and wider social consensus.

Oil has been a major factor affecting the prominence of transitional elites in the Middle East. Two relatively large and influential oil producers—Iran and Saudi Arabia—are transitional in character, as are two smaller but also influential countries: Kuwait and Libya. In combination they account for the bulk of oil production and reserves in the Middle East—indeed, in the world. As a group, these countries also exhibit radically different political styles: modernizing monarchies, and two variants of the Islamic republic.

The transitional elites in the Middle East have provided the arenas for some of the most important political changes in the entire region. The fall of the shah of Iran in 1979 is, of course, the most dramatic of these changes and in some respects the most important. But the style of politics and elite organization in Libya, Kuwait, and Saudi Arabia have been equally as important and deserve some mention here.

The fall of the shah can be directly related to the strains placed on his political authority by a failure to accommodate new groups in the political elite and by a parallel failure to maintain the support of the more traditional groups in Iran. For example, the newly emergent professional middle class was largely uninfluential in the shah's autocracy. Since this group holds a near monopoly of modern technology and skill, it can be ignored only at the ruler's peril. Ironically, the ambitious technical modernization program of the shah simultaneously enhanced the size and potential power of the middle class at the same time as it alienated them. Thus, disaffected professionals found it advantageous to join with the forces of the traditional Muslim leadership against the shah. The opposition of the Shia ulema, again ironically, was based on the disruptive and secularizing influence of the shah's modernization program. The combination of traditional and modern opposition was too much for the shah's primarily military base of support, and he was forced to leave the country. The results of the change—particularly the attempt to establish an Islamic republic—are now clear.

The initial political coalition that governed Iran during the transition from the shah's rule to the new republic can be characterized as a "temporary pluralism" dominated by the Shia clergy under Ayatollah Khomeini. Indeed, the new government organized by Mehdi Bazargan was heavily populated with ministers representing the urban professional and secular political groups that had combined with the Shia opposition against the shah. As the design of the new republic became apparent, Bazargan's secular-professional government was replaced by a government under Bani-Sadr, a government dominated by nonclergy Shia leaders committed to the implementation of the Islamic Republic. Under Bani-Sadr's stewardship, and partially responsive to the strains of the U.S. hostage crisis, the Shia clergy began to play a growing political role in the government. By the early 1980s, after the fall of Bani-Sadr, the clergy consolidated their power, assuming most of the important positions in the Islamic Republic. The Iranian elite is now dominated by the politically active Shia clergy, at the expense of the urban professional classes and important ethnic and religious minorities. This narrowing of the Iranian political elite is likely to cause future conflict.

The last months of the Iran-Iraq war placed the Iranian government and elite under terrific strain. As a consequence, Iran's governing elite was divided between the poles of the Iranian moderates, led by then Speaker Rafsanjani, and more conservative groups committed to even greater levels of Islamization and further prosecution of the war. The stakes in the controversy included the right to nominate the successor to Ayatollah Khomeini as the "religious expert," the faqih of the Islamic Republic. Reports from Iran in late 1988 indicated the execution of a number of the members of the leadership of the most conservative factions of the ruling Islamic coalition, particularly among the followers of Ayatollah Montazeri. Commentators equated this action with the consolidation of power within the elite by the Rafsanjani faction, empowered by Khomeini's public stand in favor of ending the war. Ultimately this version proved to be true, with Rafsanjani and his followers consolidating their control over the Republic's institutions.

The complexity of Iranian politics was exemplified in the political ramifications of Khomeini's reaction to the novel, *Satanic Verses*, written by Salman Rushdie, an Indian citizen living in London. This novel, found blasphemous by many Shia mullahs, prompted Khomeini to sentence Rushdie to death and place a price on his head. Ayatollah Montazeri opposed this action, and in the process questioned the direction of government generally. Khomeini responded by demanding and receiving Montazeri's resignation as the faqih-designate. In a related move, Khomeini attempted to kick Speaker Rafsanjani upstairs to a more ceremonial post as president of the republic. Other commentators have assumed that these actions indicated the increasing influence of the uncompromising conservative faction within the governing coalition.

Two other equally plausible explanations deserve consideration, however. First, this may be just one more example of a charismatic leader finding it difficult to relinquish power, a common phenomenon in the later stages of charismatic rule. Secondly, Khomeini may have been concerned that the revolution was losing ideological momentum and, like Mao Tse-tung in the Great Cultural Revolution in China, sought to institutionalize the ideological-revolutionary fervor of his movement. In truth, all of these observations may be appropriate.

Since the end of the war with Iraq and Khomeini's death, the Rafsanjani faction has consistently consolidated its power. The elevation of Ayatollah Khamenei to the position of the faqih further increased the moderates influence, since Khamenei lacked the prestige of his predecessor. Under the leadership of President Rafsanjani, the government of Iran has adopted relatively moderate foreign policies. Iran's neutral posture during the Iraqi invasion of Kuwait improved its prestige and positioned it as one of the influential states of the Gulf region. But the conservative factions are not totally excluded from power; and leftist revolutionary groups also began modest terrorist operations against the government in the early 1990s.

By distinct contrast, the elite changes taking place in Saudi Arabia have been occurring more *within* the ruling family and its coalitions. As princes and retainers of the monarchy have received substantial educations in the elite institutions of the West—at Oxford, Cambridge, M.I.T., Harvard, and the Sorbonne, for example—they have become increasingly aware of the need to adapt to the pressures and advantages of modern social organization. Indeed, the organization of OPEC has been often attributed directly to just such influences. The Saudi elite appears to be attempting to modernize the economic and technical facets of Saudi society without making corresponding changes in the political and social facets. This is a very difficult maneuver, for as the experience in Iran suggests, the educated and professional classes begin to desire power and influence. Ordinarily, analysts would be inclined to predict failure in this effort and disagree only on the timing of the ouster of the monarch and his ruling family. But the extraordinary wealth of Saudi Arabia, combined with its relatively small indigenous population, may allow for unusual and unanticipated developments. It is clear at this point, however, that the Saudi system has gone from traditional to transitional elite politics in a fairly short period of time, largely within the framework of the hugely extended royal family. The abdication of King Saud in favor of his more progressive brother, Faisal, and the publicly emerging differences of opinion between the royal princes under King Khalid provided evidence of both the changes and the relatively short time frame within which they occurred.

Rivalry within the royal family has come down recently to competition between three branches: the Sudairi, led by King Fahd, includes many of the technically trained and sophisticated bureaucrats; the Jilwa, led by Prince Abdullah, head of the National Guard, which is the branch traditionally concerned with the cultivation of the tribal loyalties that have supported Saudi rule; and the religious branch of the family, descendent from the Wahabbi reformers of the nineteenth century and the dominant force in the ulema. The death of King Khalid in 1982 and the resulting transfer of power to King Fahd consolidated the power of the Saudi modernist factions in the elite, but not completely at the expense of the opposition.

The Saudi elite has conceded extensive social power to the religious branch of the family, with the result that Saudi Arabia maintains one of the most conservative social atmospheres in the Middle East. The quasi-official religious police, the **mutawwa**, are responsive to leadership from the religious branch of the royal family. They are responsible for maintaining the codes of propriety in dress and worship. In the aftermath of Desert Storm, this branch of the royal family has complained publicly about declining standards of personal conduct, demanding even more restrictive rules and punishments. At the same time, other elements in Saudi society encouraged the creation of a consultative assembly, and King Fahd has announced his intention of doing so, appointing a national and other local assemblies. Many observers connect the demands for political liberalization and opposing demands for greater conservatism with the catalytic presence of foreign troops during the confrontation with Iraq. All in all, the political elite of Saudi Arabia finds itself under considerable political strain in the early 1990s. Nonetheless, intrafamily adjustment to political realities continues to characterize Saudi rule in the 1990s. Saudi pragmatism, combined with its great wealth, should allow it more latitude for maneuver than most monarchical regimes.

Developments in Kuwait in the early 1990s were traumatic and violent. The brutal, and largely unanticipated, invasion of Kuwait by Iraq in August of 1990 threatened to terminate Kuwait's long-standing monarchy. The diplomatic and military response to the occupation are discussed in detail in following chapters. But from an elite perspective, the results of the events were significant.

Returned to power by an international coalition led by the United States, the Kuwaiti royal family was widely expected to institute long-awaited democratic reforms. Unfortunately, they did not materialize. Instead, the government of Kuwait embarked on a program of reestablishing the traditional government and increased "nativization," an attempt to ensure security by drastically reducing the guest population in Kuwait. Hundreds of thousands of foreign nationals—particularly but not exclusively Palestinians, Jordanians, and Iraqis—streamed out of Kuwait. Many held important positions in the government and in the professions. A series of public trials of those accused of collaboration with the Iraqi occupiers contributed to an already negative environment for foreign workers. Both collaborators and noncollaborators were expelled or fled. As a result, the political elite of Kuwait has actually narrowed in the months since Desert Storm. Democratic reforms have been promised, but not implemented. Whether or not this reassertion of more traditional elite domination will work remains to be seen. It is not clear that there are enough native Kuwaitis willing or able to man the offices of a complex modern bureaucracy. But like Saudi Arabia and the other Gulf monarchies, the vast oil wealth of Kuwait gives it more possibilities than less affluent regimes.

The prevailing situation in Libya is in stark contrast to that found in Iran and Saudi Arabia. In Libya, the change from traditional to transitional status came with the elimination of the monarchy in 1969. In its place has developed a unique blend of Muslim puritanism and radical Arab nationalism, personified by Qadaffi, a charismatic leader. The Libyan regime is run largely by its military bureaucracy, within which there are recognized competing factions. And there are some contributions from a small professional elite and an equally small traditional ulema. Libya, one of the major oil exporters of the region, is particularly uneven in its development. Thus, changes within the transitional elite structure of the country can be anticipated, although constrained by the erratic influence of Colonel Qadaffi. Qadaffi's attempts to replace regular bureaucratic organization with democratic people's delegations have confused the situation in Libya substantially, and he plays this confusion to his own benefit. Elite consequences are sure to follow from these innovations and strains, but their character and direction are uncertain.

In the past, Libya's substantive support of radical and terrorist groups, including the Palestinians, brought substantial benefit to these movements. However, the U.S. raid on Libya in April 1986 seems to have somewhat reduced Libyan predilections for international intrigue or the support of terrorist movements. Nonetheless, Libya continued to pay for its past sins. Early in 1992, Britain and the United States accused two Libyan diplomats of directing the bombing of Pan Am flight 103 over Lockerbie, Scotland. Both countries have demanded the extradition of the two, and, uncharacteristically, the Libyan government at one point conditionally agreed to such a surrender, only to reverse its position later. For whatever reasons, internal or external, the Libyan elite seems more focused on its internal problems and less interested in staking out an international role.

The Jordanian political system has few substantial economic resources. In fact, Jordan's major economic asset had been the West Bank of the Jordan River, now an occupied territory of Israel and renounced by Jordan as its territory. Jordan is apparently one of the least viable of the nations of the Middle East, and its continued survival is due to substantial foreign aid. What modern, middle-class elements it does have are largely foreign, and largely Palestinian at that—a fact leading to the bloody confrontation between Palestinian guerrillas and the Royal Jordanian Army in 1970–1971. This confrontation, important for both the Palestinian and Jordanian elites, was caused by a growing recognition of both parties that political power was slipping increasingly into the hands of the Palestinian-dominated bureaucracy. Relying primarily on the bedouin-dominated Arab Legion, King Hussein managed to expel the most militant of the Palestinians at that time, who fled to southern Lebanon and elsewhere.

It had long been recognized that one possible solution to the Palestinian problem—namely, the integration of the West Bank and Gaza Strip into Jordan, or some other form of federation—held great risks for the existing Jordanian elite, as great numbers of well-educated Palestinians unsympathetic to the Jordanian regime would become politically active and legitimate. Moreover, the relationship between King Hussein and the PLO has been a turbulent one, oscillating between periods of cooperation and outright conflict. Nonetheless, King Hussein's announcement in July 1988, abdicating political and administrative responsibility for Gaza and the West Bank, surprised many observers, particularly in Israel and the United States, where fanciful hopes for a "Jordanian solution" had been kept alive. Hussein's action, while distressing to those seeking a "moderate" solution to the Palestinian problem, was probably of positive consequence to the Jordanian political elite, removing the major threat to its continued existence and eliminating many, although not all, Jordanian-Palestinian officials from its ruling class.

From 1988 to 1990, political liberalization appeared in Jordan. Elections to the legislature provided a substantial broadening of the political elite. Men and women from a variety of parties and professions gained office. The king and his counselors appeared willing to accept the practical limitations on monarchical power implicit in such changes. The future for democracy appeared much brighter. But events since 1990 have prompted King Hussein and his advisors to rein in the legislature, limiting its role and purging some of its membership.

Earlier gains were put at risk during the events of Desert Storm. Jordan, highly dependent on its trade with Iraq, attempted to maintain a neutral posture. Neither side would tolerate such diplomatic niceties and as a result Jordan paid a high political price for its attempted independence. American and Gulf state aid virtually disappeared; and Jordan found itself diplomatically isolated and the subject of great suspicion. Street demonstrations in support of Saddam Hussein and Iraq did little to dignify King Hussein's argument that he was attempting to broker a negotiated settlement between the parties. During Desert Storm and its aftermath, Jordan became the terminus of a massive migration of its nationals from Iraq, Kuwait, and the Gulf states. A near doubling of the refugee population in Jordan further strained the already inadequate resources of the state while at the same time remittances from workers abroad declined.

Jordan's emerging democratic institutions and its changing elite will be severely tested. But there are encouraging signs on the horizon. Jordan proved to be a willing participant in the peace talks between Israel and the Arab states begun in Madrid in 1991. As long as they continue to muddle forward there is some basis for hope that a solution to the regional conflicts endangering Jordan might emerge. Jordan has as much or more to gain as any state in the region from the solution of these long-standing problems.

All of the transitional regimes of the Middle East are important to the region and to the larger world community. As indicated earlier in this chapter, these regimes are all in an incipient state of change. They thus constitute much of the kindling for the Middle Eastern tinderbox—and the general direction of their change will have profound implications all over the world.

The Modern Elites

In contrast to the transitional elites, the modern elite is one whose day has come. In the modern elite situation, the traditional elite has been either excluded from rule completely or had its influence substantially reduced. Emergent groups who represent larger sections of the population now hold sway. These new groups find themselves in the heady but unaccustomed position of being able to exercise real political power. The political experimentation following the power consolidations of the modern elite may cause instability in policy at first, but eventually an equilibrium should be reached in which the decisions of the new elite will begin to have discernible effects on the society.

Figure 8-3 illustrates the composition of the modern elite. The central figures in the elite will generally be the head of state and his government ministers. It is likely, but not necessarily certain, that the head of state will have reached that position through a career in the bureaucracy or the military. A more unusual approach to central elite status may be through the emergent party system, or even through the professional modern elites, such as found in the careers of medicine, law, or related fields. Even less probable but still possible is advancement from the mass public, since the modern elite is characterized by greater permeability. The established officer corps and nonpolitical mid- and upper-level civil servants complete this rough outline of the modern elite. The ulema and the wealthy landowners still may be present, however. They continue to occupy positions of privilege in a modern society, but they have lost much or all of their political influence.

Several things distinguish modern elites from traditional and transitional elites. One of the greatest differences lies in the modern elites' worldview or philosophy. In contrast to the traditional and transitional elites, modern elites are much more likely to see the world as a place that can be radically changed by political, social, and economic policy. In other words, they see the social and political

FIGURE 8-3. The Modern Elite.

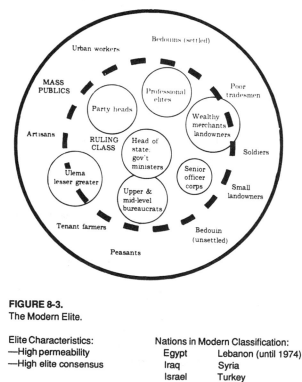

FIGURE 8-3.
The Modern Elite.

Elite Characteristics:
—High permeability
—High elite consensus

Nations in Modern Classification:
Egypt   Lebanon (until 1974)
Iraq   Syria
Israel   Turkey

order as a consequence of human activity and policy, rather than as the result of divine order or some asserted tradition. This point of view often, but not always, associates itself with a secular belief system—that is, a belief system centered on human rather than divine values. For this reason, the modern elite often finds itself in fundamental conflict with religious or sacred values. Some modernizing leaders—such as the former shah of Iran or the late Prime Minister Bhutto of Pakistan—have found religious opposition to their rule to be fierce and ultimately successful. Other modern Arab leaders—for example, Qadaffi of Libya—claim that a modern viewpoint can be supported by traditional Muslim authority and law. The ulema itself is split over this problem, some inveighing against any semblance of human-centered values or policy and others adopting a more flexible viewpoint. And many political leaders now show increasing interest in Muslim sensibilities, balancing the demands of technical innovation with new concerns for the agenda of Muslim fundamentalists.

One of the most prominent features of contemporary Muslim politics is the growing interest in the possibility of establishing modern Islamic republics, states capable of both "modern" control over environment and policy, without relinquishing the claims of Islam over social life generally. Islamic republics have been officially established in Pakistan, Libya, Sudan, and Iran; and many other countries are currently wrestling with the problematic relationship between Islam and political authority. Of those countries in the process of establishing an Islamic republic, Iran has made the most progress, but even here progress has been uneven and fraught with controversy. The specific design of the republic is likely to inject substantial conflict into elite dynamics in most Middle Eastern countries. These experiments hold the seeds of substantial transformation of the policies in question and thus are of substantial contemporary and future significance.

The triumph of a modern elite does not in any way eliminate group conflict, or for that matter even minimize it. To the contrary, the composition of the modern elite includes more groups in the political process than do the traditional or transitional political systems. Moreover, the intensity of conflict may increase as well, particularly as more elements in society make stronger and stronger claims on social services and goods. For example, traditional and transitional societies generally have low levels of public literacy. As modern societies increase literacy, they also increase the social and political awareness of groups of their particular situations vis-a-vis other groups in the society; thus the social good—literacy—carries with it the premise of higher political consciousness and hence more and greater political participation. The result is an increase in the scope of conflict and subsequent greater attention to conflict resolution. Issues and publics that are simply not relevant to the traditional regime are suddenly and irreversibly part and parcel of a geometrically expanding political process. Both mischief and progress attend this change.

International conflict can also affect these elite systems. The secular-modern regimes of Egypt, Syria, and Iraq have often found themselves individually in conflict with the transitional regimes of the Sudan and Iran, or the traditional regimes of Saudi Arabia (under Saud and Faisal) and Kuwait. Their respective beliefs are often seen as mutually exclusive and irreconcilable.

Our contemporary focus on the Arab-Israeli conflict in the Middle East often blinds us to the equally valid differences existing within the Arab and Muslim world. These differences are likely to play larger and larger roles in the immediate future, particularly as different elites make claims on the political loyalties and sensibilities of citizens in other countries. This level of conflict is difficult to resolve without resorting to widespread violence—violence that is all too capable of spilling over into other arenas of international conflict. The long and stubborn war between Iran and Iraq is a good recent example. The events surrounding Iraq's occupation of Kuwait in 1990 is an even more forceful example.

Modern elite systems—Egypt, Turkey, Syria, Iraq, Lebanon, and Israel— while sharing the characteristics of a more open and competitive structure—are clearly a heterogeneous group of nations that have substantially different histories and cultures. The specific compositions of their elites are also different although they tend to share similar outlooks on modernization.

Turkey. Under the Ottoman sultans, Turkey was the model of a traditional elite. But it was the first Middle Eastern nation to throw off the mantle of the traditional past and embrace European modernization, perhaps because it alone straddles Europe and Asia. Although many political and economic changes occurred in Turkey under the sultanate, Turkey emerged as a modern political system with the remarkable innovations of Mustafa Kemal Ataturk, who proclaimed a new, secular republic in 1923. Ataturk, supported by his political party, the Republican People's Party, mounted a strong and sustained attack on the traditional order. Reforms ranged from the general to the specific, but the major thrust was the secularization of political power, a corresponding reduction of the power of the Muslim hierarchy, and the virtual elimination of the institutions of traditional rule. Ataturk aimed at no less than the total transformation of Turkey from a weak, illiterate, agricultural nation to an industrial nation with all the attendant skills and attitudes that this implies. The very idea of a political party, even a single-party system, implied levels of public political participation undreamed of in the preceding regime.

From these revolutionary beginnings, Turkey has moved toward a complex, industrial, participatory system. The rudimentary forms of truly competitive political parties now exist in Turkey, although periods of military rule have occurred in 1960, 1971, and 1980–1981. Military-approved reforms in the early 1980s appear to have eliminated some of the fragmentary tendencies of the Turkish party system, and the system continues a slow move toward independent democratic institutions.

The Turkish political elite have made some progress toward their goals. The vision of Ataturk has yet to jell in the economic sector, and some traditional elements—particularly Muslim conservative groups—have put considerable strain on the country's political institutions. And yet progress has been made; Turkey's politics are remarkably participant in comparison with those of the transitional countries, and freer than most other modern countries in the Middle East—no mean achievement for any country experimenting in the development of democratic institutions.

Future elite conflict is likely to revolve around the demands of Muslim conservatives for some degree of restoration of the faith, the risks and opportunities following the collapse of Soviet power in the area, and the always touchy relations with Greece over Cyprus. Recently, emergent demands from Turkey's small Shia populations have been reported; and many Kurds, fleeing repression in Iran and

Iraq, have entered the country, adding to the demands addressed to the government. The Kurdish People's Party (PPK) in particular, has moved to military confrontation with the government in Western Anatolia.

As noted earlier, the achievement of a modern elite structure does *not* signify an end to internal political conflict, but rather signals a change of arena and scope of conflict. In this regard, Turkey has shown itself capable of adjusting to some serious political conflicts in recent history; and the future promises more and tougher challenges. The permeability and representativeness of the Turkish elite should be a considerable asset in meeting these tests.

The resilience of Turkish political institutions was tested in 1991. The party of President Turgut Ozal, internationally known for its aggressive economic reforms and attempts to institute market economics, lost its majority in the legislature to the party of Suleiman Demirel, a long-time opponent of Ozal. In the aftermath of the election, Demirel adopted Ozal's economic and political program, sparing Turkey from the administrative-legislative gridlock it had experienced in earlier periods. To many observers this event pointed up the growing maturity of the Turkish political system.

Egypt.   Unlike Turkey, Egypt had long been a victim of direct imperialist control and continued to be until comparatively recent times. The Egyptian revolution occurred in 1952 with the revolt of the Free Officers. This revolt, which expelled the corrupt and ineffective monarchy of King Farouk, brought to power in Egypt a junta of young army officers, most of them trained abroad. This group of officers was subsequently to demonstrate extraordinary cohesiveness, bringing a revolution of considerable scope to a faltering Egypt. Initially led by General M. Naguib, the group was ultimately headed by Colonel Gamal Abdel Nasser, one of the most remarkable leaders to grace the political landscape of the Middle East.

Under Nasser attempts were made to create a party of national revolution. Several formulas were tried, and in 1962 the efforts jelled in the formation of the Arab Socialist Union. The union was conceived as a party of national integration and ideology, bringing the masses into political contact and cooperation with the central regime. Under Nasser, the party took on some distinct characteristics that were to have profound effects both in Egypt and in the Middle East generally.

Nasser, a charismatic leader of the first order, tapped or created a reservoir of sentiment that is now called *Arab nationalism*. Essentially arguing that the Arab people were split unnecessarily and unwisely into a number of competing camps and nations, Nasser made an emotional appeal for a new Arab unity, one that would reclaim a prominent world role. Nasser's vision inspired many movements across the Middle East that were often viewed with suspicion outside of Egypt. Cynical observers were to see in Nasser's calls for Arab unity the distinct possibility of Egyptian political dominance. Others were disturbed by the coincidence of Nasser's Arab unity with his concept of Arab socialism and mass political participation. Nasser's forthright opposition to the traditional elites of Egypt did not endear him to the beleaguered traditional and transitional elites of other Middle Eastern countries.

Nasser had a particular vision of Arab socialism. This combination of politics and economics should not be viewed as socialism in any European or Marxist sense; rather, it was more a socialism of secular Islam. Its practical expression came in terms of the nationalization of basic industries, the elimination of foreign ownership, and the construction of hospitals, mosques, and schools in as many Egyptian villages as possible. There was no sophisticated understanding of socialist economics in Nasser's formula. There was, instead, a concern for the common man expressed in terms of daily needs and concerns—concerns like food, a place of worship, employment, and national ethnic pride.

The implementation of Nasser's socialism had benign political effects: mass public participation in the Arab Socialist Union, a very real improvement in Egypt's international prestige, and the integration of the professional and political classes with the military bureaucracy. But it nearly created an economic disaster: high inflation, low industrial productivity, high unemployment. But as critical as we may justifiably be of Nasser's economic policies, we cannot deny his beneficial influence on Egyptian and Arab politics. His symbolic value to the emergence of an appropriate twentieth century Arab identity is enormous.

Nasser's death and the subsequent consolidation of control under Anwar Sadat brought many substantial changes to Egypt and its elite. Under Sadat, the scope of the elite broadened as government policy became more tolerant of people and institutions in the private sector. In the mid-1970s, Sadat launched an ambitious program to create a parallel private economic structure; and he attempted to create competition between left, right, and center parties in the Arab Socialist Union. These efforts have broadened the representativeness of the elite, although their effects are still too new to evaluate completely.

Sadat's rather bold changes of Nasser's political vision did not come cheaply or without opposition. Attempts in 1978 to raise the artificially low price of bread met with widespread and angry public demonstrations, forcing the government to back down in its attempt. Nasser is still a potent symbol in the hearts and minds of the Egyptian peasantry and bureaucracy, and one is more likely to encounter his picture in a peasant home than that of Anwar Sadat. It is clear that much of the thrust of the Egyptian revolution under Nasser survives; and it is also clear that Sadat made a mark on that revolution himself, as the Egyptian treaty with Israel (1978), the dramatic break with the U.S.S.R., and the wooing of Western industry to the Nile demonstrated.

Sadat's government, however, came under increasing domestic pressure from groups dissatisfied with these changes. Palestinian organizations placed a price on his head, as did Libya's volatile Colonel Qadaffi. The Muslim Brotherhood, violently repressed by Nasser in the early days of the revolution, showed signs of resurgence, encouraged by the Islamic revolutions in Libya, Iran, and Pakistan. And Arab nationalists, unhappy with Sadat's unilateral peace with Israel, began to oppose Sadat's rule. These factors ultimately coalesced in the fall of 1981 in the assassination of Anwar Sadat by members of a Muslim fundamentalist cell in the Egyptian army.

Sadat's successor, Hosni Mubarak, has been more careful to avoid direct conflict with these alienated groups, and there is ample evidence to document a broadening of the ruling class under his rule. Mubarak allows limited representation of conservative Muslim groups in the Egyptian political elite and has avoided the personal displays of consumption and irreverence that brought Sadat into disrepute with Egyptian fundamentalists. At the same time, Mubarak has moved forcefully to reduce fundamentalist influence in the Egyptian military. Some incremental and modest Islamization has occurred, particularly in the areas of family law. Muslim political groups have been allowed to contest for seats in the legislature. And the government appears to be at great pains to avoid antagonizing the fundamentalist ulema. The prospects seem to suggest continued conflict between groups in the Egyptian elite, successfully moderated through existing Egyptian political institutions and modest electoral freedom. The Egyptian role in international affairs—particularly Desert Storm and the Mideast peace negotiations—has increased the prestige of the government domestically, an asset it will need as domestic pressures on government capacity increase.

Egypt is under enormous pressure from competing ideologies, population growth, economic stagnation, and religious fundamentalism. The elite structure of Egypt has apparently broadened and expanded in recent years to internalize some of these conflicts. It is now an asset in the confrontation of those issues and threats.

Syria. Syria shares many characteristics with Lebanon and the people of Palestine. One of the most economically viable of the Middle Eastern countries, Syria has considerable arable land, reasonable water resources, and a well-educated population. Syria has for many years exported its professional and commercial expertise, an indicator of its well developed and sophisticated elites. Syria's borders were the result of arbitrary decisions by the victorious European allies after World War I; it is also one of the front-line states in the Arab-Israeli conflict. Like Egypt and Lebanon, Syria has carried much of the financial and personal burden of the confrontation.

Syrian politics have been dominated since the early 1950s by a combination of party ideology (the Baath party) and military opportunism. Currently, Syria is run by a military-bureaucratic elite whose power is periodically confirmed by national elections. Most influential positions, including the president, are currently held by Alawite Muslims, a small and obscure sect. There is substantial resentment in the Sunni and Shia communities over this inequity, a resentment leading at least in part to broad-scale uprisings in Aleppo (1980) and Hama (1982), forcefully put down by the government. Sunni and Shia participation in Syrian government since that time has been both cautious and deliberate.

Although the Baath party, in both Syria and Iraq, has a substantial ideology of nationalism and moderate socialism, pragmatism is a strong influence in contemporary Syrian policy. The collapse of the Soviet Union left Syria exposed diplomatically and militarily. As a consequence, since the late 1980s Syria has slowly moved toward the West and the United States. In the 1990s Syria abandoned many of the hallmarks of association with the Soviet alliance, pursuing modified market economics and improved diplomatic and trade relations with the West. The education of Syrian students in the West has increased dramatically, and English has eclipsed Russian and French as the "second language" of commerce and culture.

Syria gained a measure of political stability under Baathist military rule, a stability that stands in marked contrast to the highly unstable early days of its independence, when the *coups d'etat* were literally too numerous to count reliably. A modicum of economic growth has been achieved, and internationally Syria has achieved a far greater influence in the Arab bloc than her size and power would indicate. The aftermath of the Israeli invasion of Lebanon led to a dramatic rise in

Syrian prestige in the region, an opportunity carefully exploited in President Assad's diplomacy. And Syria's key role in the U.S.–led coalition against Iraq in 1990–1991 contributed greatly to its regional prestige.

These international successes continue to be a domestic asset for the government. The expanded role taken by Syria in Lebanon since 1986 continues. A de facto annexation, once considered highly unlikely, is no longer out of the range of possibility, but Syrian objectives appear to be more limited. By 1992 Lebanon enjoyed uncharacteristic calm and political order. There are many strong ties between elements in the Lebanese and Syrian elites and some sentiment in favor of such a relationship on both sides. But it would be a venture of great risk for Syria, and would certainly bring forth an Israeli response.

The Syrian political elite has become progressively more representative in the past decade, as national elections and the promulgation of a more or less democratic constitution demonstrate. Syria is one of the most socially progressive of the Middle Eastern nations—the status of women, for instance, is traditionally higher in Syria than in the rest of the Middle East. Syria, with adequate water and growing petroleum reserves, is potentially one of the economic bright spots outside the Gulf area.

Iraq. Iraq, being both Baathist in ideology and a geographic neighbor of Syria, might be expected to share many of Syria's political characteristics. This, however, is not so. The Iraqi form of Baathism has been consistently more radical, and political conflict in Iraq has been resolved at a much higher level of violence. Since the overthrow of the monarchy in 1958, Iraq has been ruled by a series of political juntas. Most elite conflict has taken place in the military, most often in the form of bloody coups. There is also the continuing problem with the Kurdish minority in the northern mountains of Iraq. Fiercely independent and stubborn, the Kurds have fought an on and off war of national independence since Iraq gained its independence, a war often costly to Iraq in terms of lives and political stability. The Kurdish revolt following the defeat of Iraq in Desert Storm clearly tested the resources of the staggering Iraqi regime. Turkish fears of an independent Kurdistan on its borders probably gave Iraq the breathing room it needed at the critical moment. The Kurds were abandoned once again.

This problem with the Kurdish minority is not, of course, restricted in any way to Iraq. The Kurds, the largest and most militant stateless minority in the Middle East, occupy the contiguous territory of Iraq, Iran, and Turkey. All these countries have pursued policies toward the Kurds at one time or another ranging from neglect to open hostility and even genocide. The Kurds currently find themselves treated as a "nongroup" in Turkey, are under military pressure to conform to the Islamic revolution in Iran, and were subjected to a brutal resettlement strategy in Iraq, designed to move them away from the oil fields in the north and into the deserts of the south. They are the group least likely to benefit from government policy or economic development. Their plight is increasingly desperate and any viable solution seems distant. Kurdish guerrilla forces are currently active in both Iraq and Turkey.

Exploited by both sides in the Iran-Iraq war, the Kurds have been subject to violent suppression by governments suspicious of their loyalties in the conflict. Whole villages of Kurds have been destroyed and at least one Kurdish village,

Halabja, was gassed as it attempted to play Iran against Iraq. Others have been "relocated" to more secure regions. Other Kurds have moved in large numbers into neighboring countries, especially Turkey. Their numbers and influence in the Iraqi elite have declined from the admittedly marginal prewar levels.

The Shia populations in Iraq fared better at the hands of the government during the conflict. In fact, perhaps fearing Shia sympathies to Iran, the Iraqi government overtly courted Shia leaders, bringing many new faces into the Iraqi elite. Thus, while the war brought continued pressure against the Kurds, it could also be viewed as a rationale for the limited extension of the ruling class to the Shia leadership.

Government policy during this period notably emphasized the leadership of Saddam Hussein, to the point that critics of the regime characterized it as a "personality cult" of enormous proportions. In point of fact, the overrepresentation of officials with origins or connections to Saddam Hussein's "hometown" of Tikrit is clear. This clique of leaders related to each other by blood, experience, or faction is the dominant influence in Iraqi politics.

As the pressure of the war with Iran wound down in late 1988 and early 1989, Saddam Hussein reinstated many development projects that had been abandoned during the Iran–Iraq war. These projects had the potential to reinforce his popularity and stabilize the Iraqi elite. They were unfortunately squandered in the adventure with Kuwait in 1990.

The Iraqi regime has been implacably opposed to Israel and quick to blame Western diplomacy for the continued vitality of Israel. Consequently, the Iraqi elite sought closer ties with the Soviet Union and Eastern Europe, and marketed a considerable percentage of its great crude oil production in those areas. Although Iraq was by no means a satellite of Soviet foreign policy, the Iraqi elite maintained closer ties with the Eastern bloc than did nearly any other Middle Eastern state.

The strong support of American allies for Iraq during the war with Iran led to many new opportunities for contact. Many Iraqi students studied in the West and many Western corporations bid on the reopened development projects. But although there were many signs of new relationships with the West, there were few signs that Iraq was changing its views on the subject of Israel. Thus, Iraqi policy continued to have its points of conflict with the West.

The Iraqi invasion of Kuwait in 1990 and the resulting military confrontation with the U.S.-led coalition in Desert Storm severely damaged the political, economic, and military capacity of Iraq. It is remarkable that the regime survived, but it did. The Kurdish problem was unresolved and the periodic interventions by the coalition on behalf of the Kurds did not result in fundamental improvement of their plight. The Shia rebellion in the south was crushed as well. Many faces in the elite and ruling class have changed, but the basic equation, privileging Saddam Hussein and the Tikritis has changed only marginally. Western and moderate and conservative Arab regimes are extremely frustrated over this unexpected outcome. Covert efforts to destabilize the regime may increase, and it seems unlikely that the U.N. or other international agencies will soon allow the political or diplomatic rehabilitation of Iraq.

Lebanon. Until the spillover of the Arab-Israeli conflict literally tore it asunder, Lebanon was the most cosmopolitan country in the Middle East. Beirut, a city of charm and energy, was a center of commerce and finance; it had attracted a highly skilled and mobile international population. Blessed with considerable national resources, including a well-educated and ambitious population, Lebanon seemed to have a very bright future.

The Israeli invasion of Lebanon in 1978, primarily to eliminate Palestinian terrorist bases, put an effective end to the dream of the Lebanese. But in point of fact, the dream was fragile long before. Lebanon, another of those countries based on a series of unwise and shallow judgments made in Europe, was composed of at least three highly differentiated ethnic groups—Christians, Muslims, and Druze. Never integrated into a national political or economic unit, these groups lived in proximity but not intimacy. The National Pact or charter of Lebanon, promulgated at a time when the Muslim and Christian populations were nearly equal, parceled out political offices to particular ethnic groups. For example, the president was required to be a Maronite Christian while the prime minister had to be a Sunni Muslim and the speaker of the Assembly a Shia Muslim. These and other offices were apportioned on the basis of the supposed relative balance of religious-ethnic groups at the time of the National Pact. National censuses were forbidden for fear of upsetting the delicate balance between the groups.

The fiction of stable, counterbalancing religious groups served Lebanon well until it was forced, seemingly against its will, into the mainstream of the Arab-Israeli confrontation. Since the invasion of Lebanon by Israeli units in 1978, Lebanon has been plagued by a civil war that has been aided and abetted by foreign intrigue. Links between Israel and right-wing Christian groups, formalized in the aftermath of the 1982 invasion, deteriorated in subsequent years, and Syrian troops occupied much of Beirut and Lebanon, with little pretense of peacekeeping and with the open intention of exercising political control. Thus, what remained of Lebanese independence was completely destroyed in the aftermath of the Israeli invasion of Lebanon in the summer of 1982, an invasion and occupation disastrous for nearly every actor concerned. The expulsion of the Arafat wing of the PLO created a vacuum of power in the elite, leading to the rise of the Shia militias (particularly the Amal and Hizbollah), Syrian-backed factions of the Palestinians, and the Syrians themselves. Lebanon was in a state of civil war.

There have been many efforts to "fix" the situation in Lebanon and most failed. The Taif Accords, however, midwifed in 1989 by Saudi Arabia and Lebanese legislators, produced substantial progress. In effect, Syria became an active participant in stabilizing Lebanon, forcing substantial disarmament among the independent militias and establishing a governmental military presence. As a result, Lebanon by the early 1990s enjoyed a modicum of stability. Many of the Lebanese social, economic, and political elite that had fled to Jordan, the Gulf states, and Europe announced plans to return. For the first time in twenty years, there is real cause for optimism that Lebanon may "tiptoe" out of its civil war. The Lebanese elite appears to be broadening, with greater representation of the previously disenfranchised Shia. This bodes well for the establishment of effective government in this decade. And certainly the diplomatic aftereffects of Desert Storm reduced some of the international pressure on Lebanon, making it less attractive as an international battlefield. The release of all American hostages in Lebanon in late 1991 was apparently a joint venture of Lebanon, Syria, Iran, and the United Nations. The release certainly reduced the rhetorical dimension of conflict in the Middle East, hopefully to Lebanon's advantage.

Israel. In some respects, the Israeli elite is the most modern of the Middle Eastern elites; and in other respects, it is among the most traditional. It is modern in that its members are highly educated and largely of European origin. The Israeli elite has mastered the technological skills and values necessary for a modern society. For those who qualify for elite status—primarily on the basis of religious preference, technical competence, and social origin—the established political process is participatory and representative. Recent political trends in Israel have enhanced (perhaps exaggerated) the presence of the religious Orthodox and Ultraorthodox elements in the Israeli elite. Their influence as the "swing" factions in the coalitions in the Knesset have given them influence out of proportion to their numbers. They now compete effectively with the previously dominant Ashkenazi factions, and their presence in Likud's ruling coalition is critical to its survival there. In fact, the withdrawal of support by two very small parties in January of 1992 forced general elections held in July 1992. And Foreign Minister David Levy, the recognized leader of the important Sephardic faction in the Likud, was able to extract substantial concessions from the Shamir government when he threatened to resign his position just before the scheduled elections.

There are, however, large and important groups effectively disenfranchised in the Israeli system. First and most obvious are the Arabs, who number in the hundreds of thousands and who live in both Israel proper and the various occupied territories of Gaza, the Golan Heights, and the West Bank. From the government's point of view, the Arabs constitute a serious security problem and as a consequence they are subject to a wide range of political, economic, and social controls. These controls greatly increased during the Palestinian intifadah, indicating a growing government resolve to stamp out any vestige of sympathy for independence. The Palestinian intifadah eventually motivated civil disobedience and demonstrations among Israeli Arab citizens as well, leading to more problems for this poorly represented constituency. Government programs designed to end the rebellion have resulted in the imprisonment or expulsion of many younger Palestinian Arab leaders, thus limiting the development of a counterelite among the Palestinians. Observers note important changes in the Palestinian elite, with young Arabs in the refugee camps of Gaza and the West Bank displacing the more conservative Palestinians from rural and urban areas. These leaders, a product of generations of camp life, have lived lives of greater deprivation and violence than their counterparts rooted in the pre-Israeli period. They appear as well to be more interested in revolutionary Islam as a vehicle of identity and activity, a perspective presented by Hamas, a fundamentalist Muslim organization growing in influence in Gaza. Although Islamic organizations do not yet dominate the Palestinian resistance, there influence is growing. Certainly they present challenges to the PLO and Israel alike.

Moreover, reactions in and out of government to the rebellion effectively closed the Israeli Arabs' few open doors to the ruling class and contributed to the increasing polarization in the Israeli polity. It is difficult to overstate the degree of potential internal conflict that these events and policies have caused. Access to the Israeli ruling class is clearly related to service in the Israeli Defense Force, without which practically no one can gain access to influential positions in government or the economy, resulting in the de facto exclusion of Israeli Arabs from the governing elite. Direct election to the Knesset, which is rarely achieved, is the only formal route of access for this growing element in Israel.

The Iraq-Kuwait conflict exacerbated these trends. The public sympathy of Palestinian Arabs in the West Bank for Iraq (they reportedly cheered the Scuds heading for Tel Aviv and Haifa) destroyed what little Israeli support had previously existed. The Israeli left-wing went into real political decline and the Israeli peace movement, robust before the war, all but disappeared. Polarization between the Palestinian and Israeli elite increased yet again.

Disenfranchisement is not the fate only of the Arabs, however. Intra-Israeli conflict has been well documented in recent decades, demonstrating that certain Jewish groups have very little access to the ruling class. Tensions continue between the politically dominant European Jews (Ashkenazi) and the more recently arrived and less modern Oriental Jews (Sephardim) from Asia and Africa. Moreover, there are growing separations between recent immigrants from both the Ashkenazi and Sephardic communities and the second generation descendants of the founders, the Sabras. Hundreds of thousands of Jews from the former Soviet Union have emigrated to Israel. They are not well integrated into the Israeli political system and have not yet found their economic or social niche. Many African Jewish immigrants are living lives of unemployed marginality in hotels originally built for the tourist trade. Their isolation is palpable and begs for solution. In fact, Israel has been swallowing considerably more immigrants than it can effectively integrate into its system, resulting in large numbers of European and African Jews effectively in political and economic limbo. Growing levels of inflation have exacerbated these problems. And it is not clear what coalition these new immigrants will support electorally.

Finally, there are those in Israel who promote radical solutions to the Arab and Oriental immigrant problem—solutions ranging from forced emigration (euphemistically referred to as "transfer" in Israeli political discourse) to violence, both in the interest of opening up Arab lands to Jewish settlement. Some of these groups, through dramatic and precipitate actions, have made moderation of the larger Arab-Israeli dispute very difficult. A rabidly anti-Arab movement founded by the late Meir Kahane (Kach) has posed significant problems for the government as it attempts to find a moderate course between the increasingly contentious factions of the Israeli elite and polity. The conviction of Israeli citizens for the terrorist murder of Palestinian Arabs in 1985 and 1988 further exacerbated these tensions.

The Knesset elections held early in July 1992 ended Likud's long dominance of Israeli government. A significant victory by the Labor party under the Leadership of Yitzak Rabin resulted in the creation of a working coalition of Labor and two minority parties, one of the left (Meretz) and another from the right (Shas). Rabin was able to craft this coalition without resort to the splinter religious parties of the radical right, parties which had been very influential in the preceding Likud coalitions. Thus Rabin began his tenure as Prime Minister with greater independence and without the constant threat of withdrawal by the volatile and narrowly based extremist religious parties. The result has been a series of symbolic gestures from the Rabin government that would most likely have resulted in parliamentary failure for his predecessor.

Prime Minister Rabin moved quickly to heal the growing rift between Israel and the U.S. by agreeing to suspend the construction of new "political" settlements in the West Bank and Gaza. He unexpectedly traveled to Cairo to enlist the help of

Egypt in the upcoming peace negotiations. And, in an act unprecedented in Israeli political history, appointed a small number of Israeli Arabs to upper-level administrative positions. This latter act, if supported over the coming years by similar measures and policies, could broaden the Israeli political elite substantially. It might even open the door to a new politics of reconciliation in Israel, one that could bring genuine cooperation between these two long-standing adversaries. But as important as these acts may be in signaling significant changes in the Israeli political equation, history counsels caution in jumping too quickly to optimistic conclusions. The proof will be in the eating, as the old advice contends.

Future Israeli elite development will be directly linked in one way or another to the state of the larger Arab-Israeli conflict. If the peace negotiations begun in 1991 result in some form of Palestinian autonomy, then the Israeli elite will have to accommodate this reality in some way. Or if another government succeeds in a policy of massive Jewish settlement in the West Bank and Gaza, then the reality of mutually exclusive claims to land and water will have to be dealt with. It is clear to most observers that Israel has had to pay an extremely high social and economic price in this conflict. One of the most salubrious consequences of an Arab-Israeli peace would be a lessening of tension in the Israeli elite and probable improvements in its permeability and representativeness.

CONCLUSION

It is clear that political, social, and economic pressures in the Middle East ultimately affect the elite structure of politics. The Middle East is unusual in having a wide variety of elites—traditional, transitional, and modern. It is also clear that changes in the composition of an elite can ultimately cause profound changes in the policies and world view of a political system. Unfortunately, these effects are not specifically predictable.

On the other hand, we can safely predict that these changes will produce new strains and demands upon the political system, and that these strains and demands will create new and often unexpected conflicts both domestic and international. We can thus with some confidence predict a continuation of the unsettled nature of contemporary Middle Eastern politics. And without doubt, we can predict that Islam, in its various forms, will be intimately involved in that process. These factors, combined with the commonplace but accurate observation that the world is growing smaller, suggest that the political implications of these changes in elite structure will influence all our hopes and lives.

POLITICAL LEADERSHIP IN THE COMTEMPORARY MIDDLE EAST

Having discussed the ruling elites in the Middle East, we shall now focus on those individuals in the highest political offices: monarchs, generals, presidents, and so on. While effective leadership is important to the world's affluent and powerful societies, it is even more important to the disadvantaged and recently independent countries that are confronting serious internal and external challenges. Countries in which the institutions of governments are new, fragile, or discredited have a far greater need for effective leadership than those with long histories of political order and stability.

There are three basic styles of political leadership: traditional, modern technical bureaucratic, and charismatic.[1] We shall examine a leader representative of each style and show how his career exemplifies that style's essential nature. We shall then examine other contemporary Middle Eastern leaders and see how their styles of rule fit the pattern. Finally, we shall briefly examine how these leadership styles affect domestic and international politics.

The three basic leadership styles are necessarily broad and general, and do not account for fine differences, nor do they accurately predict the political consequences of any one kind of leadership; they are only rough guides. To illustrate the three types, we shall focus on three prominent figures in twentieth-century Egyptian politics: King Farouk (traditional), Gamal Abdel Nasser (charismatic), and Anwar Sadat (modern bureaucratic).

TRADITIONAL LEADERSHIP

Traditional leaders base their claim to leadership on the assertion that they are the clear and logical successors to a line of leaders that stretches back in time and that

---

[1] This leadership typology originated with Max Weber, the great German sociologist. Our use of it, however, differs substantially from his. See Hans Gerth and C. Wright Mills, eds., *From Max Weber* (New York: Oxford University Press 1964).

is legitimized by practice. They are leaders because of historical forces, and they claim the right and obligation to continue. They often imply that their leadership is necessary to maintain the social order on the right course. Traditional political orders, while conservative, are not rigid or unyielding to change; but they may be slow to implement a schedule of changes or react to changing conditions. They expect change to occur over relatively extended periods of time. As Almond and Powell observe, there is a definite promise of performance implied in the assertion of the right to rule:

> ...most traditional societies have some long-range performance expectations built into their norms of legitimacy; if crops fail, enemies invade, or floods destroy, then the emperor may lose the "mandate of heaven," as in Imperial China; or the chiefs their authority; or the feudal lords, their claim to the loyalty of their serfs.[2]

The traditional leader depends on the force of tradition, or his interpretation of it, to establish his legitimacy as a ruler. Legitimacy refers to the public perception of the ruler's right to his position of leadership and is not restricted to traditional leaders alone. The willingness of the populace to accept a particular leadership structure as right and defensible legitimizes the political process as it exists. But it is no substitute for effective policy nor can it protect an ineffective ruler forever.

Some examples of traditional legitimization may clarify the problem. There is a logic to the use of tradition as a legitimizing symbol. The shah of Iran, for instance, often publicly argued that the Persian cultural tradition demanded monarchical leadership, that the Iranian political practice for thousands of years found its most effective and satisfying expression in a monarch. As monarch, Mohammed Reza Pahlevi was therefore performing an important service for the Iranian people. The rulers of Egypt made similar arguments.

That tradition may legitimize but not stifle change is also well demonstrated in Saudi Arabia. There is no gainsaying the importance of tradition in legitimizing the Saudi leadership. But tradition has not been a logical reason for continuing a weak leader in office. The transition from King Saud to King Faisal, based on decisions within the royal family itself, suggests that this traditional elite was responsive to contemporary difficulties. Tradition was mobilized to legitimize the change and the new leadership.

The right or legitimacy of traditional leaders is often bound up in the intersection of political and religious tradition: the king or sultan may also be the defender of the faith, for example; or the sheikh may be patron of the ulema, as in the relationship of the Egyptian monarchy with the mosque university of Al-Azhar. These roles and symbols, given great weight by their persistence over time, are the most important factors in legitimizing the traditional regimes.

In the absence of competing claims, traditional leaders may find the invocation of ancient roles and symbols adequate to protect their base of power. Given the twentieth-century phenomenon of competing claims from charismatic or modern bureaucratic aspirants to office, traditional leaders have often been forced to

---

[2] Gabriel Almond and Bingham Powell, *Comparative Politics* (Boston: Little, Brown, 1978), pp. 31–32.

attempt limited reforms within the recognized tradition. And so, traditional leaders have attempted to modernize their political, social, and economic systems without sacrificing their right to rule. The Tanzimat reforms in Ottoman Turkey can be interpreted in this light, as can the White Revolution of the shah of Iran. In both cases, the traditional leader attempted to come to terms with modern technology and administrative procedures without relinquishing his monopoly of political power. It is instructive that both efforts ultimately failed.

King Farouk of Egypt

Many characteristics of traditional political leaders are exhibited in the experience of King Farouk of Egypt, the last Egyptian monarch. Farouk's rule (1936–1952) embraced a period of time that saw a fundamental redrawing of the international political order, including the rise of Soviet and American power, the concomitant decline of European—especially British—influence in the Middle East, the emergence of mass political parties, and the political reassertion of Islam and Islamic groups. Farouk's response to these changes demonstrates both the essence of traditional leadership as well as its fundamental defects.

Born in 1920 into the royal lineage founded by the great Egyptian leader Muhammad Ali, Farouk was raised in a strong tradition of royal absolutism. The line of Muhammad Ali treated the whole of Egypt as its personal possession. King Farouk proved himself to be no stranger to this tradition.

The royal family, like most of the ruling houses of Egypt for the past 3,000 years, was not of Egyptian extraction. In the case of Farouk's family, the line was founded by an Albanian adventurer, Muhammad Ali, with very tenuous ties of loyalty to the Ottoman Empire. Enormously successful at realizing the political, social, and economic potential of nineteenth century Egypt, Muhammad Ali was frustrated by European, especially English, intervention. A large, extended family buttressed by extensive retainers and officials saw Egypt as a private fiefdom run for its own benefit. With few ties to the Egyptian masses, the royal family routinely assumed its right to absolute rule and consistently opposed the extension of political rights or influence to native Egyptians.

Farouk himself was educated and socialized in a conservative atmosphere; he was exposed to periodically rabid Anglophobia and persistently pro-Italian sympathies. Farouk's tutors included the most notable ulema of Al-Azhar University, who instilled in him a serious appreciation of his role as protector of the faith. King Fuad's death placed Farouk on the throne at age sixteen, still in his minority. A regency council was formed to advise and educate him in his responsibilities as ruler of Egypt.

Farouk's father, King Fuad, saw the emergence of the first legitimate mass political party in Egypt, the Wafd. Much of Fuad's political labors in later life were devoted to frustrating Wafd aspirations to power, a policy continued by the young king. The combination of mass political activity and growing nationalism had a disquieting effect on the royal house. By complex political maneuvers, Fuad and Farouk attempted to exclude the Wafd from power. Thus, they both demonstrated one of the chief characteristics of traditional political leadership: a great reluctance to *share* political power with anyone, particularly with mass or nationalist groups. This is not to imply that Farouk was bereft of policy or ambition—indeed, there is evidence to the contrary. The point is that these ambitions never included a broadening of the base of political power.

Farouk demonstrated his traditional orientation to political power in other ways. His fascination with ceremony, pomp, and circumstance reflects the concern of the traditional leader for rituals and rites that confirm the assertion and maintenance of traditional authority. Decked out in rich uniforms for every occasion, Farouk's movements around his kingdom were spectacles in themselves: elegant livery, scores of retainers and entertainers, international celebrities. and sumptuous banquets in luxurious palaces or country estates. Grandeur was not only a perquisite of office, it was an obligation; and Farouk became increasingly enthusiastic about it.

In a similar vein, the royal house under Farouk became internationally noted for its hedonism. Drunkenness, particularly offensive to the emerging Muslim Brotherhood, sexual abandon (often reported graphically in the international press), and disturbingly regular accusations of official corruption involving minor members of the royal family were commonplace. Farouk's appreciation for attractive women became an international symbol of Egyptian royal decadence, set in the most luxurious spas of Mediterranean Europe.

There was a curious tension between Farouk's hedonism and his public attitude toward Islam. One could not call him personally pious, particularly in view of his devotion to Koranically prohibited pleasures: wine, women, and pornography. On the other hand, Farouk took his role as "defender of the faith" seriously; he made substantial contributions to the maintenance of Al-Azhar and welcomed a number of political exiles to Cairo. He also subsidized programs designed to maintain Egyptian prestige in the larger community of Muslim nations, which lacked any focus of authority since the abolition of the caliphate. These practices solidified his relationship to the higher ulema at the same time that his hedonism was coming under growing criticism by fundamentalist Muslim groups.

Despite these irritants to the prestige of the royal house, Farouk's rule and government enjoyed a legitimacy that demonstrates the strength of traditional leadership. Most analysts of the period assert that Farouk's government far outlasted its effectiveness. Aside from noting the population's predisposition to accept the traditional, there is little in the last ten years of Farouk's rule to suggest that his political, social, or economic *performance* commanded popular support for the government.

The final blow to Farouk's rule in Egypt resulted from a combination of domestic and international forces. Farouk's pro-Italian sympathies quickly ran afoul of international events in World War II, resolving in favor of his British enemies. In addition, the public became dissatisfied with his opposition to the Wafd party, and the increasingly militant fundamentalist Muslim Brotherhood was disillusioned by his personal licentiousness. Riots in Cairo involving the Wafd, extremist groups, the Muslim Brotherhood, and students became commonplace. The final blow came with the miserable performance of the Egyptian military in the war against Israel in 1948, although the full implications of the war were not to become clear to the public until the revolution of July 23, 1952. Charges of corruption and ineptitude gained widespread circulation and validity. The war became a focus of resentment against the low level to which Arab and Egyptian prestige had sunk. Farouk became increasingly unable to manipulate the forces of Egyptian politics, and instability and drift became the governmental norms.

Farouk's fall and abdication were a result of actions by the military, not the political forces that had opposed him for so long. His final attempts to abrogate the Anglo-Egyptian treaty in 1951 produced a series of ugly confrontations between Egyptian and British forces, which in turn set off a series of antigovernment and antiforeign riots in the urban centers of Egypt. The army's inability to handle these incidents further inflamed the king's opponents, and British efforts to reinforce their garrisons added even more fuel to the fire. Finally, on July 23, 1952, a group of military officers known as the "Committee of Free Officers" overthrew the government and established the Revolutionary Command Council under the titular leadership of General Naguib. On July 26, the council requested the formal abdication of King Farouk. Farouk complied, abdicating in favor of his son, and promptly departed for Italy. Farouk never recovered his influence in Egypt. His abdication itself demonstrated his inability to come to terms with the emerging political order.

> Towards the middle of the afternoon, it was announced in a broadcast from Cairo that "some very important news would be given at six o'clock." Everybody understood and prepared to listen.
>
> All round the Ras El Tin palace and along the coast road to Alexandria an enormous crowd had gathered, tense with expectation and with mixed feelings of anguish and joy. Then came the prodigious sight: the royal exit in the rays of the setting sun, on to the sea which a hundred and fifty years earlier had brought, to the Egyptian shore, the Albanian soldier of fortune, Mohammed Ali, the great-great-grandfather of the sovereign who was now taking his leave.
>
> At ten minutes to six...Farouk, in his splendid white uniform of *Admiral of the Fleet*, came slowly down the palace steps towards the sea. He was followed by Queen Narriman, carrying the new king, six months old...While the royal flag was being fetched from the palace, a cruiser in the bay fired a twenty-one-gun salute.
>
> General Naguib went aboard...Farouk appeared to be touched, behind the screen of his dark glasses. "Take care of my army," he said. "It is now in good hands, sire," Naguib replied. The answer did not please Farouk, who said in a hard voice, "What you have done to me, I was getting ready to have done to you." Then, turning on his heel, he took leave of the conquerors.[3]

Farouk's final years became a mishmash of sybaritic excess in the most expensive and exclusive resorts of Europe. Throwing himself with abandon into the gambling tables, the dining tables, and the arms of many an attractive companion, Farouk ended his life as a corpulent playboy dedicated to things of the flesh and the moment—a sad ending in many respects, far removed from the promise of leadership in the sixteen-year-old youth who had ascended the throne in 1936.

King Farouk, of course, is hardly the best example to use of a traditional ruler. He was weak and was unable to rise effectively to the challenges of his times. Indeed, he helps to maintain the myth of decadent Middle Eastern rulers.

---

[3] Jeanne and Simone Lacouture, *Egypt in Transition* (New York: Criterion Books, 1958), pp. 156–159.

Compared with the historical importance of the shah of Iran or Ibn Saud of Saudi Arabia, Farouk is something of a footnote to contemporary history.

However, King Farouk's example is important for several reasons. First, the crises of leadership that have afflicted the decolonializing world have often involved the reluctant departure of ineffective traditional leaders. To focus on strong leaders would distort our analysis. Second, the myth of decadence is not a myth. Absolute rulers, traditional and otherwise, have not shown themselves to be disinterested in pleasure or pomp or luxury. Indeed, much of the basis for their legitimacy comes from just such a claim to the perquisites of royalty. Finally, the influence of weak and ineffective leaders on world history is arguably as important as the impact of the few "great men" of our times.

We will return to the subject of traditional leadership at the end of this chapter. The crisis of confidence in traditional leadership, which undermined King Farouk just as it undermined many other Middle Eastern leaders in this century, leads to three possible alternatives:

1. Traditional political governance from a different political ruler, an apparently unlikely and short-term phenomenon.
2. Leadership based on the claims of the modern bureaucratic managers in the society, such as the military or a nascent political party.
3. Charismatic leaders who offer their transcendent leadership as a substitute for the claims of tradition or bureaucratic efficiency.

In the period after the fall of the Egyptian monarch, the third alternative materialized in the form of Gamal Abdel Nasser, a young officer in the movement that called for Farouk's abdication. Definitely a charismatic leader, Nasser was to have an important effect on Egypt and the Middle East.

CHARISMATIC LEADERSHIP

As defined by Max Weber, a charismatic leader possesses particular characteristics that set him apart from normal leaders. A charismatic leader is, in a word, unique. He possesses personal characteristics that are suited to a peculiarly intense leadership style; and he is capable of creating or participating in an intense, reciprocal psychological exchange with his followers. His actions and proposals are legitimized by reference to some transcendent source, either religious, historical, natural, or mystical. Recent world leaders recognized as charismatic include Adolph Hitler, Charles De Gaulle, Tito, Sukarno, and Gamal Abdel Nasser.[4]

Our definition and description of charismatic leadership is complicated by two factors. First, charismatic leadership is often erroneously equated with other leadership characteristics such as personal beauty, rhetorical skill, popularity, and the like. Thus, the use of the term in general circulation may distract us from the necessary distinguishing characteristics of the charismatic leader. Second, charis-

---

[4] For a broad treatment of charismatic leadership, see Ann Ruth Willner, *The Spellbinders: Charismatic Political Leadership* (New Haven, CT: Yale University Press, 1984).

matic leadership appears to be idiosyncratic to the culture in which it occurs; thus the characteristics of a charismatic leader in Egypt would differ from those of a charismatic leader in, say, France or England. The chemistry of the relationship between leader and followers changes according to the particulars of the culture and historical circumstance. Despite these difficulties, the phenomenon of charismatic leadership is real and is important in any analysis of Middle Eastern politics. Charismatic leaders have had, and continue to have, enormous impact on the politics of the region. The Sudanese Mahdi, Gamal Abdel Nasser, Ayatollah Ruhollah Khomeini, and Colonel Muammar Qadaffi—all have had, or have, the potential to alter dramatically the course of political events.

In spite of the idiosyncratic qualities of charisma, there are some general observations we can make about the phenomenon. First, charismatic leadership almost always appears during a social or political crisis—particularly a crisis in which the prevailing institutions of government have been discredited or destroyed. Examples might include the ruinous inflation in Germany that preceded the rise of Hitler or the legislative-executive deadlocks that preceded de Gaulle's second entrance into French politics. Theoretically, the public in these situations is predisposed to seek a heroic leader to provide a substitute for discredited authority.

Another expectation is that the charismatic leader will promulgate substantial and convincing images of a new order, perhaps ordained in heaven, that will raise the community to new levels of activity and accomplishment, or in another variant, restore the community to its rightful place in the world. In giving substance to the visionary demands of a disillusioned populace, the charismatic leader provides them with psychological sustenance and heightened self-esteem.

Yet another characteristic of charismatic leaders is their resonant rhetorical gift—resonant in the sense that they can raise sympathetic responses from their followers. This rhetorical gift may vary dramatically in style. Compare, for instance, the dramatic histrionics of Adolf Hitler with the icy, Olympian quality of de Gaulle's pronouncements. Whatever the style, the successful charismatic leader has the ability to move a nation by the power of his rhetoric. Indeed, in many cases the rhetoric may be more politically important than the substance of the policies articulated.

Finally, the charismatic leader leads by example. Once again, this quality seems idiosyncratic to culture. The simple, introspective life of a Gandhi can be contrasted with the cheerful hedonism of Sukarno in Indonesia or Marcos in the Philippines. But in each case, the leader in his personal life sets a standard of personal behavior that strikes the populace as desirable and ennobling.

These characteristics provide the public with personal knowledge of the leader. He has a place in the collective psychology of the nation. The leader in turn gains a larger-than-life perspective on himself, thriving and growing on the demands and support of the followers. Thus, a powerful, reciprocal psychological exchange is established, which ultimately allows a single personality to substitute for a complex of institutions.

As powerful as this reciprocal dynamic can be, there is a critical defect in charismatic leadership. That defect is the mortality of the leader himself, upon whom the whole social transaction is based. Charismatic leaders, like ordinary mortals, die, and the transition from a charismatic leader to his successor is fraught with hazard. Charismatic leaders do not appear on demand. Thus, one cannot count on replacing one charismatic leader with another. Usually, charismatic leadership must give way to either traditional rule or modern bureaucratic leadership—so nature and the human condition dictate. Let us now turn to the charismatic leadership of Gamal Abdel Nasser.

Gamal Abdel Nasser

Nasser presents an interesting counterpoint to King Farouk. Born in Alexandria in 1918 into the family of a low-level civil servant, Nasser was ethnically Egyptian, as opposed to the Albanian origins of Farouk. Educated in the new modern schools of the time, Nasser entered the Egyptian military academy in 1936. Farouk's first military job was as chief of state at age sixteen. Where Farouk was elegant and pampered, Nasser was simple and ascetic.

Nasser's physical and personal qualities have inspired many writers to attempt to capture the factors that contributed to his commanding presence. The following passages by Jeanne and Simone Lacouture are representative:

> What first impresses you is his massive, thick-set build, the dazzlingly white smile in his dark face. He is tall, tough, African. As he comes toward you on the steps of his small villa on the outskirts of the city, or strides across his huge office at the Presidency, he has the emphatic gait of some Covent Garden porter or some heavy, feline creature, while he stretches his brawny hand out with the wide gesture of a reaper, completely sure of himself. His eyes have an Asiatic slant and almost close as he laughs. His voice is metallic, brassy, full, the kind of voice that would be useful on maneuvres in the open country....

> The impression of strength remains when he relaxes. He has an air of youthfulness, together with a certain timidity. He is gray at the temples but his hard face, that reminds you of a ploughshare, sometimes takes on an adolescent look.[5]

Nasser, in short, was heady tonic to a people accustomed to foreign rule and previously convinced that government was not an Egyptian aptitude. His personal presence, reflecting both real and potential power, combined with an electrifying rhetorical style, spoke directly to the powerlessness of the masses. Nasser, it seems, became the personal embodiment of the aspirations of the people. He in turn grew in response to their fervent commitment.

Nasser entered politics indirectly. His biographies indicate an early dissatisfaction with foreign rule and political corruption, but he originally intended to reform the Egyptian military. Nasser and his associates did not come to power in the revolution of July 23, 1952, with any plan for political rule. Instead, it appears that political power and responsibility were thrust upon the officers as they began to recognize the inability of Farouk and the Wafd to work cooperatively for reform.

Ideologically, Nasser's early political views can be summarized by the formula "Fight Against Imperialism, Monarchy, and Feudalism." Only later, as he matured in the office of president, did Nasser's political views develop. These

---

[5] Jeanne and Simone Lacouture, *Egypt in Transition*, p. 453.

views demonstrated the cosmological quality of Nasser's leadership. Particularly in his promotion of Arab socialism and pan-Arabism, Nasser demonstrated the charismatic leader's claim to some cosmological source of authority. In making regular symbolic reference in his speeches and writings to the greatness of the Arab past, the Egyptian past, and to Islam and the Umma, Nasser not only provided a cultural and historical identity to the Egyptian people, but he legitimized contemporary policy in non-Western terms. In many respects, this can be labeled a triumph of form over substance for Nasser never specified the policy implications of his ideology consistently. Nevertheless, for the fragmented and uncertain Egyptian community of the 1950s and 1960s, the Nasser prescription was just what was needed.

Nasser's relationship to Islam reveals his lack of ideological precision. Although he recognized a direct relationship between Islam and Egypt's past and present, and although he appeared to be personally pious and upright, Nasser was nevertheless a secular political leader. Early on in the revolution the Free Officers came into conflict with traditional Islamic forces—the ulema, which was in league with the monarchy and was opposed to the revolution, and the Muslim Brotherhood, which did not recognize any distinction between politics and religion. In steering a course between these forces, Nasser and the Free Officers opted for a view that derived inspiration from Islam and its writings, but simultaneously honored the principle of separation of church and state. This separation was anathema to the leadership of the Brotherhood, and a nasty confrontation was inevitable.

Nasser's socialism was ambiguous and imprecise. Essentially a philosophy of equitable distribution, Nasser's socialism has been rightly criticized for economic naiveté and a devotion to publicly managed projects of dubious value. While these projects were politically palatable, their contribution to a coherent economic policy was negligible. The steel complex at Helwan is a case in point. The claims of this grandiose project could not be justified by even the most optimistic economic projections. The project was to supply most of Egypt's need for steel, employ large numbers of Egyptian workers, and ultimately contribute to the balance of payments through the export of Egyptian steel. Of these goals, only the employment of more and more Egyptians was accomplished.

Similarly, the revolution's effort to guarantee jobs to every college graduate created a swollen bureaucracy that operated on the principle of disguised unemployment. This policy often resulted in several people sharing a job that could be handled more effectively by one employee. Intolerable inefficiencies were thus built into state enterprises and made administration very difficult. Once again, the political gain outstripped the economic realities.

The differences between Nasser and Farouk are quite sharp. There is one point, however, in which their leadership styles converge. The personal presence and lifestyle of each leader supported his claim to political authority. Of course, their lifestyles differed dramatically. Farouk's love of pomp and ceremony contrasts sharply with Nasser's modest private life. Yet each to a great degree personally demonstrated in his private life the basis of his claim to power.

Finally, both leaders' careers came to abrupt ends. Farouk abdicated to a life of leisure one jump ahead of the executioner; Nasser died unexpectedly of a heart attack in 1970. Neither of them left office under "normal" circumstances—that is, as the result of regular or normal political processes. Of the two leaders, Nasser

clearly left the greater impression on Egyptian politics. As Bruce Borthwick pointed out, in spite of the difficulties besetting the regime, "Nasser had...received the
'gift of grace' that endows charismatic leaders. He and the Egyptian people were
one; his actions and his voice were theirs. They would not let him resign in June,
1967, and when he died suddenly on September 28, 1970 [6] the masses poured out
their emotions for him in a frenzy of grief."

To this day, portraits of Nasser occupy the place of honor in the simple
homes of the Egyptian peasantry. The imprint of Farouk is a historical curiosity,
and no more.

The ultimate consequences of Nasser's charismatic leadership are manifold.
First and foremost, through his charismatic claim on political power, Nasser gave
Egypt a focus of legitimate power. In a time when the existing institutions of
power were discredited (such as the monarchy, nobility, and political parties), his
exercise of charismatic power filled what would have been a dangerous vacuum.
Moreover, the cosmological qualities of Nasser's leadership, such as his commitment to the Islamic Umma, Arab culture, and the Egyptian nation, provided a
potent national identity for the Egyptian masses. His powerful rhetoric and commanding presence provided real evidence that his claims and goals were viable and
realizable, if difficult to achieve.

However, Nasser's rule had its negative aspects. His economic policies were
at best naive. His international adventures, as in the case of his military intervention in Yemen, often strained Egyptian capabilities beyond their limit. And his persistent confrontations with Israel committed vast proportions of the Egyptian economy to wartime production. Finally, his flirtation with international communism
(domestic communists were suppressed and jailed) could have generated yet another wave of foreign intervention in the Middle East.

All in all, however, Nasser's leadership was of great benefit to Egypt.
Ultimately the force of his leadership spilled over to the new institutions that
implemented the revolution and prepared the way for modern bureaucratic politics.
Thus, Egypt moved from a political process dependent on a single, fragile personality, to a political system characterized more by institutional stability and strength.

MODERN BUREAUCRATIC LEADERSHIP

Modern bureaucratic leadership is predicated on the promise of adequate short-
term performance in government. Claiming technical and organizational superiority over the older, traditional means of governance, modern bureaucratic leaders
promise to transform society through the application of management skills. In
short, these leaders believe that contemporary problems can be solved, that man
can purposively change his physical and social environment if only given the
chance and the right organization, and that these changes can lead to several possible social, economic, and political outcomes.

Although all modern bureaucratic leaders base their right to rule on their
ability to perform and solve problems, some rule within publicly accountable sys-

[6] Bruce Borthwick, *Comparative Politics of the Middle East: An Introduction*
(Englewood Cliffs, NJ: Prentice-Hall, 1988), p. 182.

tems (democratic) and others within authoritarian systems. Publicly accountable modern bureaucratic leaders recognize the right of the public to evaluate periodically their performance and decide whether to retain them in office; authoritarian, or Kemalist, modern bureaucratic leaders reject the regular review of their right to rule, arguing instead that no one has the ability to judge their leadership or its performance.[7] Authoritarian leaders often conceive of their political rule as a period of political trust and tutelage during which society learns and practices the skills and procedures that will lead to genuine publicly accountable politics. In most cases, authoritarian modern bureaucratic regimes are military in nature; publicly accountable regimes have usually emerged from a political party background. In the emerging countries, where modernization was first achieved among the military, it is not surprising that Kemalist regimes predominate.

Anwar Sadat

The immediate successor to Nasser in Egypt, Anwar Sadat, was another member of the original Free Officers. Original predictions suggested a relatively short tenure in office for Sadat, seeing him presiding over a period of transition during which more capable leaders would contest for the mantle of power. (Similar predictions had been made for the institutions of governance that had developed during Nasser's rule, particularly the Arab Socialist Union and the People's Assembly.) Both Sadat and those institutions proved much more durable than anticipated. By 1981, the Sadat regime had been in office for over ten years and had made a number of substantial changes in political emphasis and direction. Far from a caretaker or transitional leader, Sadat proved himself to be a legitimate and strong leader in his own right.

Sadat's personal history was not unlike that of Nasser. Like Nasser, Sadat was born into a peasant family and benefited from a liberalization in education policy. Like Nasser, Sadat entered the Egyptian military academy during the time when the regime was trying to develop an Egyptian officer corps. And like Nasser, Sadat participated in the Free Officer movement that led to the *coup* of 1952. It is surprising, then, that there should be so few similarities in the leadership styles and political views of these two men.

Anwar Sadat was not a charismatic leader. His claims to the loyalty of the government and the public were based on his performance. He hoped for a low-keyed, coherent managed solution to Egypt's problems of the 1970s. Indeed, to compare Sadat's political thought to Nasser's is to compare the thought of a technician to that of a dreamer. Moreover, Sadat's rhetorical style bore little or no similarity to Nasser's impassioned, moving speeches.

Sadat's personal style contrasted sharply with those of Nasser and Farouk. Comfortable in Western dress, Sadat often appeared in a conventional Western suit and tie, as opposed to Nasser's simple tunics and Farouk's elaborate uniforms. Sadat lived in an impressive villa, although it hardly compared with Farouk's palaces. Mrs. Sadat wore the latest Paris fashions and moved in the highest international social circles. Sadat was comfortable with modern political leaders around

---

[7] *Kemalist* refers to the modernizing authoritarian rule of Kemal Ataturk in Turkey that was aimed ultimately at the creation of a democratic process.

the world. He cultivated an image of international sophistication in dress, language, and personal manner.

Nothing underscores the difference between Sadat and Nasser more than their respective treatment in the American press. Where Nasser was often presented in uncomplimentary terms with thinly veiled suggestions that he was a communist or radical, Sadat was presented as a leader of quiet authority and dignity. As regular guests on American talk and interview shows in the 1970s, Mr. and Mrs. Sadat personally raised Egypt's national image by their humane, warm, and comfortable styles. Such democratic sophistication would not have occurred to a Farouk, nor have been tolerated by the mercurial Nasser. Sadat was definitely a different kind of political animal.

Sadat reversed Nasser's economic policies, particularly those toward private industry. He openly sought foreign private investment in Egypt, strengthened ties with the United States and Western Europe, and pursued a political solution to the Israeli question and Palestinian demands. Domestically, he permitted new political parties to develop, although they were carefully controlled. He subtly tried, and failed, to demythologize Nasser.

Sadat believed that his reforms had relieved much of Egypt's economic and military burdens, and to some degree he has been proven correct. The Sinai had been recovered, and commercially exploitable oil resources expanded. The West gave military and technological support, but foreign investors were reluctant to enter the mixed Egyptian economy. Ultimately the failure of the Egyptian-Israeli peace talks over the question of Palestinian autonomy gave ammunition to his enemies in and out of Egypt. As a result, Sadat retrenched on many of his political reforms, the secret police became more active, and a number of political opponents were placed under house arrest.

Some of Sadat's reforms met with widespread resistance. In 1977 he attempted to raise the price of bread, which had been subsidized at artificially low prices since the revolution; there were riots in Cairo in which mobs burned luxury hotels and nightclubs catering to foreigners and chanted "Sadat-Bey, Sadat-Bey," equating Sadat with the hated Ottoman rulers of an earlier age. Foreign corporations attempting to enter the Egyptian economy reported that in spite of sympathy at high government levels, mid-level and low-level bureaucrats did not share this enthusiasm and made life miserable for Western business managers.

In governing Egypt, Sadat had certain advantages that were not available to either Nasser or Farouk. He had a tested set of bureaucratic and technocratic institutions upon which he relied for counsel and for implementation of policy. These institutions were less efficient than many of their counterparts outside Egypt, but they were a distinct improvement over the administrative vacuum that attended Egyptian political crises earlier in the century.

Anwar Sadat's rule ended on October 6, 1981, with his assassination while viewing a military parade. The assassins were members of a fundamentalist Muslim group within the Egyptian military and reportedly had strong ties to other fundamentalist groups active in Egypt. The transition of rule was remarkably smooth, and Sadat's vice-president, Hosni Mubarak, was elevated to the presidency. The orderly transfer of power and the quiescent acceptance of the events by the Egyptian masses evidence the remarkable progress toward institutionalization of government since Nasser.

Under Mubarak's rule, Egypt recovered much of the prestige lost in the Arab world as a consequence of Sadat's peacemaking with Israel. Mubarak has been able to capitalize on Sadat's close relationship with the United States, the economic gains stemming from the military disengagement with Israel, and the aftermath of the disastrous Israeli invasion and occupation of south Lebanon. Mubarak's key role in the U.S.-led coalition that confronted Iraq in 1990 also contributed greatly to his domestic and international prestige His leadership style has proven to be relatively low-key and accommodative, with the result that many of the Egyptian groups dissatisfied with Sadat's policies or personal style now find themselves cooperating with the government. This is not to suggest that political conflict or tension has somehow been eliminated from Egyptian politics; but it is to suggest that there has been substantial improvement since Sadat's death and that the scope of political participation in Egypt has modestly widened. Since the political equation in Egypt is of critical importance to the larger political equations of the Middle East, stability and progress there generally benefit the larger system. Mubarak must continue to deal with the problems of economic growth, population explosion, Muslim fundamentalism, and international conflict that bedeviled his predecessors. But he can do so with a significantly stronger set of political institutions than any of his twentieth-century predecessors.

CONSEQUENCES OF LEADERSHIP STYLES

The contemporary Middle East presents a mélange of leadership styles. Traditional and modern technicalist bureaucratic leaders predominate numerically (see Table 9-1), but charismatic leaders like Ayatollah Khomeini and Colonel Qadaffi have had disproportionate influence. Many of the international strains and tensions in the Middle East are partially a result of divergences between leadership styles.

Traditional leaders make up the largest group in the Middle East. True to form, these leaders tend to oppose modernization or modernize in only strictly technological ways; they all resist any substantial sharing of powers. They still depend greatly on formal assertions of their traditional right to rule, undergirding

TABLE 9–1. CONTEMPORARY LEADERSHIP STYLES IN THE MIDDLE EAST.

TRADITIONAL	MODERN BUREAUCRATIC	CHARISMATIC
Bahrain	Egypt under Sadat (K)*	Egypt under Nasser
Egypt under Farouk	Iran	Iran under Khomeini
Iran (Pahlevis)	Iraq (K)	Libya under Qadaffi
Jordan	Israel (for Jewish citizens)	
Kuwait	Israel (occupied territories) (K)	
Oman	Lebanon	
Qatar	Syria (K)	
Saudi Arabia	Turkey	
United Arab Emirates	Yemen (K)	

*K = Kemalist Modern Bureaucratic

these claims with the performance of traditional rituals and the maintenance of complex interpersonal relationships with other leaders.

TRADITIONAL STATES

The enormous oil revenues of Saudi Arabia, Oman, the U.A.E., and Kuwait permit them to manage their economies and give them some political breathing time. For those traditional leaders in poor countries—Hussein of Jordan, for example—the maneuvering time is considerably reduced. In the case of Jordan and Yemen, foreign subsidies have been crucial in maintaining the existing political authority, a compromise with independence distasteful to all leaders. However, recent discoveries of exploitable petroleum reserves in the newly united Yemen may produce major changes there.

Serious challenges to existing authority have emerged in all of the countries under traditional leadership. The fall of the shah of Iran is a likely harbinger of things to come. In Kuwait a traditional ruling class traumatized by the Iraqi occupation in 1990–1991 searches for security by expelling most of the Palestinian and Jordanian guest workers that manned their institutions. Promises of greater democratization have not materialized quickly and the as-Sabah family seems intent on reestablishing its traditional political authority, even as small groups of Kuwaiti citizens petition for a greater voice in democratic institutions. In Jordan domestic and international tensions have nearly toppled King Hussein a number of times. King Hussein's attempts to mediate the conflict between Iraq and the opposing coalition severely damaged his international reputation and clearly increased political polarization in Jordan. Fortunately, the fairly new legislative and party institutions in Jordan appear to be a stabilizing factor. Oman, increasingly important in the international politics of the Persian Gulf, is bordered by a newly united Yemen to the west with unclear ideological or international tendencies, by conservative Arab states to the north, and by an unpredictable Iran across the Straits of Hormuz. Sultan Qabus has established close military relations with the United States, a relationship exercised during Desert Storm. The collective leadership in the United Arab Emirates have made similar arrangements, as have the leaders of Bahrain and Qatar. All of these states rely increasingly on the coordination of their foreign policies through the Gulf Cooperation Council.

Saudi Arabia is the dominant political actor among the traditional states of the region and plays a key role in the larger Middle Eastern system. The Saudi decision to invite U.S. troops onto Saudi soil to defend against Iraq clearly had a high risk/reward ratio. The aftermath of Desert Storm has placed the Saudi royal family under new pressures, from both the left and right. Both groups have been energized by what they observed during the coalition presence in Saudi Arabia. Groups interested in increasing democratization and social liberalization have petitioned the leadership for a consultative assembly and a liberalization of the strict Saudi social rules. The religious right has called for increased emphasis on conservative social values, opposing the liberalization espoused by the "left." The royal family cannot satisfy both camps and some increasing level of domestic political conflict is likely. In the spring of 1992 King Fahd announced the creation of a national consultative assembly, and a number of local consultative bodies. These assemblies are constituted with no power other than the persuasive quality of their advice. Nonetheless, they are widely interpreted as a first, although cautious, move by the royal family in the direction of democratization. In another significant move, the royal family agreed to broaden the pool of future candidates for king, a move that will substantially increase the ruling class in Saudi Arabia when such an eventuality occurs.

In short, the traditional states of the Middle East, rich and poor alike, appear to be subject to increasing domestic and international pressure. Most of these traditional polities are fighting a rear-guard action. The inevitable transition to modern bureaucratic or charismatic rule will be quite hazardous to these traditional leaders and to those nations dependent on their petroleum exports.

MODERN BUREAUCRATIC STATES

The second largest group of political systems in the Middle East is governed by some kind of modern bureaucratic leadership. Four of these states—Egypt, Iraq, Yemen, and Syria—are ruled by Kemalist regimes. The military or civilian leaders in Syria and Iraq profess adherence to Baathist ideology, although the two countries are ruled in quite different ways. While Mubarak apparently believes in the principal of public accountability of leaders, he has not yet entrusted substantial political authority to the parties or legislature. The Arab Socialist Union and the National Assembly, while influential, are still subject to his veto. Egypt, Syria, and the new Yemen republic seem unlikely to face serious internal challenges in the immediate future.

The government of Iraq, however, is under serious political pressure internally and externally. Although it was plagued for some time by feuding within the ruling Baathist military group, by the late 1980s Iraq appeared to be emerging as a stable and competent political regime. Encouraged by its growing petroleum revenues, in the mid-1970s Iraq had embarked on an ambitious program of economic and social investment. Simultaneously, the leadership's anti-Western posture softened, and growing numbers of Iraqi students had enrolled in European and American universities, particularly in management and technology programs. A growing disenchantment with communist influence in the Iraqi army led to a number of executions and imprisonments and explorations with non-Soviet European governments regarding trade and technology.

The long war with Iran in the 1980s accelerated these tendencies, as Iraq became increasingly dependent on the European West and the moderate Arab states for financial and military support. U.S. aid to Iraq was channeled mainly through other governments. The war was extraordinarily expensive to both Iran and Iraq, in terms of money, military and civilian casualties, and deferred public projects. Both countries, however, managed to avoid widespread domestic discontent, an indication of effective leadership and progress in political institutionalization. Saddam Hussein, during the darkest periods of the Iran-Iraq war, appeared to initiate a "cult of personality" to offset public dissatisfaction with the conduct of the war. In fact, his personal presence rose dramatically, through use of techniques often associated with charismatic leadership. The lack of a charismatic public response, however, was equally obvious, leaving us with the impression of Saddam

Hussein as an aspiring charismatic leader in search of a constituency. That said, the reins of power seemed firmly in his hands.

All apparent progress in Iraq was put at risk by Saddam Hussein's decision to invade Kuwait in 1990. This invasion, and the subsequent ejection of Iraq from Kuwait by a U.S.-led coalition of Western, Arab, and other Third World states, changed the trajectory of development for Iraq. Saddam Hussein's inept military leadership resulted in the deaths of tens of thousands of his countrymen and the rekindling of two serious revolts, by the Kurds in the North and the Shia in the South. Iraq was placed under an onerous economic embargo and in political isolation by the U.N. Security Council. U.N. inspection teams roamed Iraq in search of Iraq's programs to produce "weapons of mass destruction." All in all, Iraq and its government received heavy punishment for its transgressions in Kuwait.

Saddam Hussein's survival of this humiliation amazes commentators in East and West. Although his removal was not an official objective of the Desert Storm coalition, the rhetoric of the conflict left little doubt that this was an unarticulated goal. It was believed that the military humiliation of Iraq and attendant economic and social disruptions would lead the Iraqi elite to remove him from office. This did not occur and Saddam Hussein remained in power more than a year after the war. The survival of his key military establishment—the Republican Guards— gave him the breathing space necessary to suppress the Kurdish and Shia revolts. And given the highly integrated nature of Iraq's political elite, he was able to forestall political opposition among his influential rivals in government. Reports that the United States and Saudi governments are considering aggressive covert action against Saddam are given substantial credence.

Of the two non-Kemalist modern bureaucratic regimes, one country, Turkey, has a recent history of relatively free and open review of its leadership. Only occasionally has the military felt it necessary to intervene and suspend the political processes, and then it has always backed off after a period of adjustment. The military rule established in 1980 has been progressively withdrawn in favor of a civilian government. To date, the Turkish military has taken steps to minimize the number of parties allowed to contest elections, in the hopes of avoiding the legislative stalemates characteristic of the prior multiparty government, and has allowed an extensive experiment in free-market economics led by President Turgut Ozal. The apparent success of the reforms, and the ability of the existing leadership to deal effectively with restive political minorities, have resulted in a voluntary reduction of the military role in Turkish politics. And Turkey's aggressive pursuit of full membership in the European Community would appear to support a continued trend in this democratic direction.

The viability of Turkey's democratic system was tested in 1992 when the party coalition supporting President Turgut Ozal lost its majority in the parliament. The election of Suleiman Demirel to the prime minister's position brought an old political enemy to an important position in the government. Both Ozal and Demirel have subsequently shown their ability to work together, demonstrating an important improvement in institutional legitimacy and pragmatic political leadership. Turkey is one of the states recognized as a democratic model for the newly independent states of central Asia and competes with Iran for influence and leadership in the region.

Lebanon, in a state of civil war and occupied by Syrian, U.N., and Israeli forces, all of whom share power with private Christian, Muslim, Palestinian,

Druze, and other independent armies, is proof of just how bad things can get when domestic and international forces combine to challenge or undermine existing political authority. The pre-1976 government of Lebanon, predicated on the fiction of relatively equal and stable Muslim, Christian, and Druze populations, functioned in an effective and publicly accountable way. It was, in many respects, something of a showplace for democracy in difficult circumstances. The enormous contrast then and now suggests that when all pretense of political civility disappears, the potential for political and social disorganization is great.

The disastrous invasion and occupation of Lebanon by Israel (1982–1985) did succeed in removing the Arafat elements of the PLO in and south of Beirut, but it did not succeed in removing other Palestinian groups or their military bases. The occupation also failed to tip the equation of forces in Lebanon in favor of the Christian militias, and apparently it stimulated the political and military growth of the Shia organizations, particularly the AMAL and Hizbollah. The result was the government of Lebanon ruling less and less of East Beirut while political and military groups with ties to major international actors (Syria, Iran, Iraq, Israel, Libya, the PLO, and the United States) jockeyed for position.

Frustration with this situation led eventually to a regional conference in Taif, Saudi Arabia, in 1989. In the adopted accords, Syria assumed a major role in disarming the competing militias and supporting a nonsectarian parliamentary government. Key events included the disarmament of General Aoun's army in 1990 and the systematic reestablishment of the regular Lebanese army under governmental direction. By 1992 it was clear that this initiative had dramatically changed the political equation in Lebanon, allowing the potential emergence of genuine national political leadership, and the establishment of a "Second Republic." The dynamics of this process have begun and analysts hope that shortly a government of Lebanon deserving of the name will emerge.

Such a future will depend greatly on the ability of Lebanon's neighbors—particularly Israel and Syria—to exercise restraint in their future relations there. Israel's assassination of Hizbollah leader Sheikh Musawi in February 1992, a premeditated and well-planned military exercise, substantially raised the level of conflict between Israel and the Shia populations along its northern border. Shia reprisals, primarily a long barrage of Katyusha missiles targeted at the Galilee, prompted major Israeli military incursions beyond the "buffer" zone established in 1985. Joint Israeli maneuvers with its client Army of South Lebanon are likely to continue. And they are likely to stimulate responses from other Lebanese groups and their foreign supporters. Yet another cycle of violence has begun, placing the tenuous peace negotiations at risk again.

The leadership situation in Israel deserves discussion. The categorization of the regime as certainly modern bureaucratic, but uncertainly democratic or Kemalist, depends on whether one is talking about Israeli citizens within the normal confines of Israel (the pre-1967 boundaries) or about the administered Arab populations of the West Bank, Gaza Strip, and Golan Heights. The problem would not be so great were the populations involved not so large. We must distinguish, then, between the democratically responsible leadership of conventional Israel and their authoritarian rule over the occupied territories.

Israel has proven many times over its ability to change leadership within the structure of public accountability. Prime Minister Menachem Begin represented a conservative religious coalition, the Likud bloc, which came to power in May 1977, and broke the dominance of the Labor bloc, which had been in power since 1948. Begin's responses to Arab demands and terrorist raids were much harsher than his predecessors'; in addition he encouraged Israeli settlements in the West Bank. (We shall deal with this policy in greater detail in subsequent chapters.) However, the formal inclusion of the West Bank and Gaza Strip into the state of Israel was sufficient to classify Begin's regime as Kemalist authoritarian, since it was unwilling to extend full political rights to the resident Arab populations.

The 1982 Israeli invasion of Lebanon proved to be abortive politically, both in Lebanon and Israel. The domestic consequences of the invasion included the opening of substantial cleavage in the Israeli polity over the appropriate treatment of the Palestinians. The official government inquiry into the atrocities at the Sabra and Shatila refugee camps did not clear the leadership of the Israeli Defense Force or General Sharon of a cloud of suspicion. An active Israeli peace movement, advocating dialogue and bargaining with the Arabs emerged to question Likud's policies. The occupation of Lebanon also proved to be economically very expensive. In 1984, a dispirited Menachem Begin resigned his position in favor of Foreign Minister Yitzhak Shamir. The resultant elections were inconclusive, leading to a "coalition" government between Labor and Likud. Neither Prime Minister Peres or Prime Minister-to-be Shamir appeared able to exercise the decisive leadership characteristic of Golda Meir or Menachem Begin in his prime.

The fall 1988 elections did little to resolve the stalemate between the Labor and Likud blocs, resulting in yet another round of coalition government, an alliance of unlikely bedfellows motivated by the unexpected initiatives of the PLO in the fall of 1988 and by the U.S. agreement to begin a dialogue with the PLO. In order to present a united Israeli front to these unsettling developments, Likud and Labor (Shamir and Peres, respectively) ceased their courtship of the conservative religious parties and continued their uneasy coalition. One unintended consequence of this decision was to defer, for the moment, continued consideration of the legal regulation limiting commerce and entertainment on the Sabbath and the further limiting of the definition of Jew along lines acceptable to the Orthodox and Ultraorthodox leadership. Such restraint eventually became a casualty of partisan politics. Elections were held and the Likud, under the leadership of Yitzhak Shamir, openly sought the support of the minority religious parties to establish a legislative majority in the Knesset. Under Shamir's leadership, Israeli policy toward the PLO and the intifadah became increasingly rigid and repressive.

Government reaction to the Palestinian intifadah became extremely brutal, further polarizing the Israeli polity. Military repression of Israeli Arab demonstrations occurred late in 1988 and posed an ominous portent for Israel as a pluralistic democracy. The December 1988 declaration of Palestinian independence brought a diplomatic problem to the Israeli leadership, particularly given the PLO acceptance of U.N. Resolution 242. The Israeli leadership found itself confronting an increasingly domestic conflict for which there were no easy or palatable remedies. A large leftist peace coalition attempted to offset the growing influence of settlers, religious extremists, and the proponents of Palestinian "transfer" within the ruling coalition.

The Iraqi invasion of Kuwait changed the internal political equation in Israel. Palestinian sympathies for Iraq undermined the legitimacy of the peace movement in Israel. The government responded by increasingly repressive measures in Gaza and the West Bank; and by implementing an aggressive settlement policy in Gaza and the West Bank and by annexing Jerusalem. In so doing, the Shamir government ignored settlement in the relatively underpopulated regions of the Galilee and Negev in favor of displacing settled Palestinians and ensuring a Jewish majority in "Eretz Israel." This policy polarized international opinion and eventually led to a crisis between Israel and its primary supporter, the United States. The elections of 1992 were clearly fought on the arena defined by this emerging conflict between an Israeli government determined to annex its biblical geography and an American administration committed to a formula of "land for peace."

The elections of July 1992 ended 15 years of Likud rule. The election resulted in clear-cut gains for the Labor party, headed by Yitzhak Rabin. Rabin was able to craft a coalition comprised of only three parties—Labor, Meretz and Shas— allowing him to avoid giving a policy veto to the more extreme parties of the religious right. Rabin thus became Prime Minister with a greater latitude of action than his predecessor.

Rabin acted quickly to establish a new set of directions for the Israeli government. New settlement activity was frozen, although the units under construction were allowed to be completed. Rabin travelled unexpectedly to Cairo in an effort to enlist the Egyptian government in a more active role in the peace negotiations. An invitation was extended to Mubarak to visit Israel later in the year. Opposition to negotiations outside the Middle East were dropped, thus voiding one of the key strategies of the Shamir government.

The new government successfully defused a number of potentially damaging confrontations with Palestinian demonstrators, and tactfully handled situations with the Palestinian delegation to the peace talks, after they met formally with P.L.O. Chairman Yassir Arafat in Jordan. And in a move highly charged with symbolic significance, Rabin appointed a small number of Israeli Arabs to important sub-ministerial posts in his new government. All of these actions would have been anathema to the preceding regime, or impossible to execute given the parliamentary veto enjoyed by the parties of the religious right.

None of this is to suggest that Israel under Rabin has somehow dramatically transformed itself into a new polity with new values and objectives. Security concerns and the preservation of the Jewish nature of Israel continue to be the overall strategic objective of the Israeli government. But Rabin has evinced a greater flexibility and pragmatism than his predecessor; and if parallel moves are forthcoming from his Arab counterparts around the region, substantial progress could result from this dramatic change in leadership.

Israeli leadership is certainly conventional in its base of authority. Begin, Peres, Rabin, Shamir, and Sharon can all be described as modern bureaucratic leaders. Their survival in power is directly dependent on the consequences of their policy choices, not their charismatic or traditional appeal. We should also point out that the political leadership of Israel is aging. Shamir, Peres, and Rabin are all in their seventies and facing the end of their long careers as party and government leaders. A new generation of Israeli leaders waits in the wings. As Israel faces a range of difficult problems—economic, political, racial, international, ethical—the quality of her leadership will be of great importance. The leadership that emerges from the uncertainties of the mid-1980s to deal with the new global realities of the 1990s will have its work cut out for it.

CHARISMATIC RULE

Two Middle Eastern countries, Iran and Libya, were under charismatic rulers throughout the 1980s. Both rulers can be described as irregular, unpredictable, and dramatic; but their governments and ideologies were inherently different.

Ayatollah Ruhollah Khomeini

Ascetic and gaunt, Ayatollah Ruhollah Khomeini appeared to confirm the trite Western stereotypes of Muslim fanaticism. This predisposition to judge harshly was exacerbated by the outrage generated by the Iranian militants' seizure of U.S. diplomats and embassy employees in November 1979. Thus, it is hard to find a publicly sanctioned, dispassionate description and analysis of Khomeini and his beliefs.

Khomeini was clearly a charismatic leader. He believed that his ultimate authority was derived from Allah, an indisputably cosmological referent. His speech was laced with hyperbole and jeremiads against the West, the shah, the devil, and all corruption and debasement. His followers responded with strong outpourings of emotion. His branch of Islam, Iranian Shiism, is mystical and chiliastic. He used the Shia tenets of Islam as the basis of a new, revolutionary economic, social, and political organization.

Khomeini's opposition to the shah's regime and to Western influence in Iran was partly based on his personal history. Khomeini's father was allegedly murdered by a landlord closely allied with Shah Reza Pahlevi. Raised as an orphan, Khomeini was passed from relative to relative largely out of charitable obligation. His training, exclusively in traditional religious schools and subjects, was exactly opposite to the modern education promoted by the Pahlevis. As an adult, Khomeini was often in trouble with the regime, which restricted his movements and preaching and finally exiled him. His promotion to the rank of ayatollah was prompted, it is claimed, by other Muslim clergymen's attempts to protect him from the shah's courts and certain imprisonment or execution. Long periods of exile awaited the ayatollah, during which his son was murdered, allegedly by SAVAK. Thus, Ayatollah Khomeini has had a long history of personal and religious opposition to the Pahlevi regime.

Khomeini's political behavior bewildered most Western correspondents. Two Shia traditions may explain some of it. First, the Shia community in Iran has long practiced the right of **taqiyyah**, or dissimulation. If the defense of the faith requires it, the faithful may say or do anything that would allow them to pursue the true way, including the denial of adherence or membership. In the darkest days of SAVAK's repression, many Iranians protected themselves by exercising this right. Thus, public political statements were often contradictory or misleading. It is indicative of Khomeini's moral status with the Shia faithful that he was able to dictate the abandonment of taqiyyah during the last stages of the fight against the shah, and from a position of exile at that.

The second tradition is the low status of political officialdom in Shia Islam. Therefore Ayatollah Khomeini instinctively avoided the regular, continual exercise of political power characteristic of the "normal politician." Khomeini apparently wished instead to correct or direct politicians by exercising a moral veto when they deviated from the divine will. Khomeini's exercise of power was thus irregular and intermittent, a fact of life that confounded and confused the Western observer accustomed to administrative regularity and continuity. Khomeini's role as faqih in the Islamic Republic also confused Western observers, particularly those who simply did not comprehend institutions of mixed sovereignty—in this case, of God and man.

One also needs to understand something of the political and religious history of Iran. The doctrine of taqiyyah, for example, developed in response to the persecution of the Shia faithful by established Iranian political authority. Dissimulation, when necessary, advanced the interests of the good community. It was not a simple or universal justification for lying. The Ayatollah's symbolically rich speech similarly derived from the long Persian tradition of complex, poetic language. Much of it is impossible to translate accurately into English. An example of the difficulty is the *heech* controversy of 1979.

Heech is an Iranian word of some subtlety. It can mean "nothing" in both a literal and/or an ironic sense. Upon returning to Iran from exile in Iraq and France, Khomeini was asked by Western newsmen how it felt to return to Iran after all those years in exile. Khomeini expressed his contempt for such a superficial question with the observation, "Heech." The newsmen interpreted his response to mean that he had no feelings, emotional or otherwise, about his return and concluded that he was coldly self-controlled. Khomeini intended to convey his disgust at being asked such an obvious and superficial question. Unfortunately, Khomeini's efforts were rewarded with misunderstanding. Khomeini's behavior and justifications remained valid for Iran and largely misunderstood in the world arenas.

Khomeini's charismatic power was not restricted to Iran; it also operated among Shia minorities along the Persian Gulf and in Jordan, Syria, Iraq, and Lebanon. In addition, many fundamentalist Sunni Muslim groups recognized Khomeini's impact and wished to emulate his success without adopting the Shia disciplines. Finally, Khomeini's rabid anti-Western attitude tapped a venerable tradition of opposition that dates back to the maturation of European imperial power in the area. As a successful leader, attempting the radical de-Westernization of Iran based on the tenets of Islam, Khomeini was a living example of the political potential of Islamic revival.

In the late 1980s, as Khomeini aged and his health deteriorated, he was frequently absent from the seat of government. Nonetheless, as the Iran-Iraq war degenerated into a human sacrifice of epic proportions, Khomeini was able to provide moral support to the faction in government seeking a settlement. Without his influence, it is likely that a greater protraction of the controversy would have occurred. It should be noted that Khomeini backed the settlement at great risk to his own political reputation; for he could have been sullied by "backing down" to Iraq and Saddam Hussein.

Khomeini's political maneuvering in the aftermath of the war gives good insight into some of the difficulties of exercising charismatic power and ensuring an appropriate succession to the charismatic leader. The publication and reaction in the Muslim world to the book *Satanic Verses*, provided Khomeini with an opportunity to exercise the moral dimensions of his leadership to disadvantage his political opponents. His pronouncement of a death sentence on the author of the book, and a bounty for the "execution" of the author, prompted criticism by Ayatollah

Montazeri, Khomeini's designated successor as faqih of the republic. This reaction, and earlier statements by Montazeri critical of the policy directions of the regime, gave Khomeini the opening he desired. He demanded Montazeri's resignation, arguing that in opposing his actions Montazeri had demonstrated his unfitness to interpret God's will. Montazeri resigned, and no prominent successor of his public status was nominated to succeed Khomeini. Speaker Rafsanjani, who might have benefited from Montazeri's fall, was unable to capitalize on the situation until much later. And, in fact, the most conservative factions of the ruling coalitions were empowered in the short term by this sequence of events. Ali Khamenei ultimately succeeded Khomeini as faqih, but his less prestigious reputation signaled a de facto decrease in the institution's role.

This question almost asks itself: Why did Khomeini impeach his personally designated successor? The answer may reside in the very character of charismatic leadership, qualities in the leader that militate against the sharing of power. And it just as well may offer evidence of the implicit conflict between charismatic leadership and the institutional-bureaucratic leadership it eventually spawns. Whatever the reason, these actions appeared to make the inevitable transition of power from Khomeini to a successor more problematic and difficult than ever, a prospect that did not augur well for stability within the regime or the revolution. That the transition from Khomeini's charismatic rule to the more pragmatic bureaucratic rule of Rafsanjani and Khamenei occurred without great public disorder is a monument to the progress in political institutionalization that developed in the later years of the Iranian revolution.

Colonel Muammar Qadaffi

No less an enigma is Colonel Muammar Qadaffi, the unofficial head of state of Libya, a country with few people and considerable oil wealth, located next to Egypt on the Mediterranean coast of Africa. Qadaffi has held power since the Revolutionary Command Council removed King Idris from power in 1969. Since that time Qadaffi has consolidated and expanded his political power. His position is currently secure as head of the military group ruling Libya.

Qadaffi's power is also indisputably charismatic, although it differs substantially from Khomeini's power. Qadaffi is a radical, modernizing charismatic leader who has based his policy on unique, innovative interpretations of the Koran. Personally pious and reputedly ascetic, Qadaffi rejected the authority of the hadith and sunnah, preferring instead his own reading of the Koran as the sole authority. His personal philosophy is detailed in the Green Book, the handbook of the Libyan revolution. Qadaffi thus finds himself in opposition to the conservative ulema, whereas Khomeini's power derived from it. Although both men were anti-Western and antiimperialistic, Qadaffi is enthralled by Western technology and science.

Qadaffi and Khomeini also differed markedly in physical appearance. Khomeini appeared dour, dark, and sober, with downcast eyes, and dressed in the traditional garb of the mullah; Qadaffi is quick to flash a bright, toothy smile, and dresses in flattering quasi-military tunics. Where Khomeini's rhetoric was apocalyptic, Qadaffi's is more persuasive and personal.

Like Khomeini and Nasser, Qadaffi aspires to leadership in the larger Muslim community. Qadaffi has openly espoused the causes of numerous revolutionary and terrorist groups around the world, and offered hospitality to their leaders. Qadaffi's influence has spread to the Philippines, where Libya has supported the Moro National Liberation Front. It has also spread to Uganda, and to Egypt and the Sudan, where Libya had been openly hostile toward the modern bureaucratic regimes of Sadat and Numeiri. In 1981, Libya intervened in the civil war in Chad, ostensibly to aid the Muslim groups in their consolidation of power. The government in Chad backed away from a proposed formal union, however, and the extent of Libyan control or influence there is problematical. One of the staunchest of the anti-Israeli Muslim leaders, Qadaffi has in the past provided aid, comfort, and a base for operations to diverse groups in the Palestinian nationalist coalition. These causes, and his personal claim to a universally valid view of Muslim revolutionary government, have not been well received in the conservative or secular governments of the Middle East. The disappearance of Imam Musa Sadr in Libya in 1977 increased Qadaffi's distance from the Shia community. And increasingly visible Libyan assassination squads targeted against Qadaffi's political opposition in exile in England and Italy further blackened Libya's international image. Libya, moreover, tilted decidedly toward the U.S.S.R. in its foreign policy, although the relationship was not sufficiently strong to prevent the 1986 U.S. air raid against its capital.

The sudden transformation of the international system has resulted in the growing isolation of Libya and Qadaffi. The collapse of the Soviet Union deprived Libya of its major international protector. The stabilization of petroleum prices reduced Libya's discretionary income. And the emergence of a moderate to conservative Arab alliance in the region has effectively eliminated Libya as a major player in international events. The international support received by Britain and the United States in 1991–1992 as they demanded the surrender of two Libyan diplomats allegedly involved in the bombing of Pan Am flight 103 is a strong indicator of Qadaffi's rapidly declining international prestige.

Nonetheless, Qadaffi keeps Libya on a revolutionary course. Based on his philosophy as expressed in the Green Book, Qadaffi has continued on a course of radical democratization in the context of the original Islamic revelation. Detractors are quick to point out that Qadaffi may in fact be confusing his own role with that of the Prophet. Nevertheless, Qadaffi seems quite intent on working through a system of "People's Power" committees, unions, and boards. Ultimately these peoples' committees are intended to replace the RCC, although the RCC and Qadaffi still appear to be in control of the Libyan political process. The rising role of Muslim fundamentalist movements in the Maghreb have occurred without any direct Libyan involvement. This fact alone suggests that the international consequences of Qadaffi's charismatic leadership have declined. Qadaffi's charismatic leadership is more and more a domestic fact and not an international one.

CONCLUSION

The contemporary Middle East presents a mosaic of leadership styles with definite implications for conflict and conflict accommodation. The traditional Muslim leaders of the Middle East are conservative. Fighting a rear-guard action against increasing demands for a larger share of political power, traditional leaders are coming under increasing domestic and international political pressure. Although traditional leaders of rich or potentially rich states may be able to buy time politically, in the long run, their right to power will be undermined by the social effects of such wealth.

Most traditional regimes will be replaced eventually by modernizing bureaucratic regimes, either democratic or authoritarian in nature. These regimes will try to mobilize mass political sentiment, but keep it under strict control. Technological and economic progress are more likely under these regimes, but they are not guaranteed. They will come increasingly under the pressure of fundamentalist Islamic groups seeking to establish Islamic republics, which derive their form and mandate from the Koran and Islamic tradition.

This assault on the secular aspects of the modern bureaucratic regime may lead to instability and internal conflict, with predictably negative consequences for the systems. Modern bureaucratic leaders like Mubarak of Egypt and Assad of Syria, basing their claim to power on demonstrated policy results, will find themselves more and more challenged by credible alternative concepts of the public good and public order. These concepts, arising from a mixture of religious, political, and foreign influences, will produce potent claims for future performance, finding root in increasingly sophisticated political publics.

It is impossible to predict when charismatic leaders will appear or what the consequences of their regimes will be. They are capable of creating emotional political storms that float over the fragile boundaries of nation states. Nasser, Khomeini, and Qadaffi, all of whom enjoyed at one time substantial support outside their own countries, challenged the authority of both traditional monarchs and modern bureaucratic leaders. Their potential for destabilization and mischief or political good were great. Currently Ayatollah Khomeini's sermons reportedly enjoy a wide circulation in the Fertile Crescent, and now in the independent republics of central Asia, inspiring many active organizations. Colonel Qadaffi attempted to oust Sadat from Egypt and succeeded in ousting Numeiri from the Sudan in an attempt to extend his leadership into new areas. The recent decline of his influence does not negate the possibility of other charismatic leaders emerging. And it does not take a political soothsayer to predict the probable consequences of charismatic rule in, say, Saudi Arabia with its petroleum wealth or in Egypt with its large population and critical geopolitical position. And finally, on a much more abstract level, we must recognize the potential for charismatic leadership in the Muslim Umma generally, a leadership capable of transcending familiar national entities. Such leadership would have worldwide impact. Islamic tradition is certainly predisposed in this direction.

THE ECONOMIC SETTING

The Middle East presents a remarkably wide spectrum of economic circumstances. It includes some of the richest and poorest nations in the world and some of the most fertile and most barren land. Some of these nations have been cosmopolitan for a millennium or more, while others have only recently peeked beyond their boundaries. Some mix religion and politics in puritanical systems, and others advocate secular socialism. The Middle East's unusual diversity of conditions generally is not appreciated. This chapter and those that follow will elaborate on the diversity of circumstances, as well as the areas of commonality and the various conflicts that surface in the context of this pluralism.

Some cautions should be mentioned at the outset. Nations are complex and most short statements about them tend to be incomplete. This is understandable: The interplay of cultural, economic, and political forces are difficult to understand in the most straightforward of circumstances. When these forces are changing in character, the task of understanding becomes daunting. All countries seek political independence. But it is difficult to sort out exactly what that entails in a world of growing economic interdependence and in a geographical area where spectacular instances of instability suggests the necessity of international political cooperation. Many works—from Baedekers to sophisticated technical analyses—deal with the economic conditions of the individual countries under study. Our approach will be to deal with central themes of conflict and resolution rather than with geographic or national entities. The student also should realize that the precision implied by statistics is often illusory. Indeed, some of the available statistics purporting to describe the Middle East are in gross error due either to faulty measurement or to bias. Numbers have political uses, of course. Petroleum production figures must be viewed with caution. Migrant labor statistics are suspect. Sometimes all parties agree to ignore a changing reality. For example, the government of Lebanon consistently lacked data on the measurable economic and social characteristics of its Muslim and Christian populations. The always precarious balance between the two groups could have been thrown into disarray through political action premised on such information.

The economy of Israel has many problems common to the various Arab states, but it differs considerably in other respects. As contrasted to its Arab neighbors, its labor force is more highly educated and from a different cultural setting, its agriculture is more capital intensive, its industry contributes relatively more to national income, and it has received greater amounts of international aid. Common problems include significant migration, serious water management problems, and the need for a large and expensive military sector.

Table 10-1 indicates the per capita income levels of various Middle Eastern economies. Although these figures are not exact, they are sufficiently reliable to provide a general idea of the level of economic activity. All the countries listed have experienced some increase in per capita income, although there have been tremendous variations. In the early 1960s, Israel was clearly the leader (excepting Kuwait), having a level of per capita Gross Domestic Product ($939 U.S. in 1960) about double that of Lebanon and four to seven times that of the other adjoining countries. By 1989 the situation had changed dramatically: the measured lead of Israel increased over its oil-poor neighbors, but suffered substantially relative to the petroleum-exporting states. The remarkable differences in per capita income is a potential source of conflict, especially when it is realized that the high-income countries generally have relatively small populations and suspect defense systems.

TABLE 10-1. PER CAPITA INCOME AND GROWTH RATE.

COUNTRY	GNP PER CAPITA 1990 (US $)	AVERAGE ANNUAL RATE OF GROWTH 1965–1989
Egypt	600	4.1
Yemen	650	—
Morocco	950	2.3
Syria	1,000	2.9
Tunisia	1,440	3.2
Turkey	1,630	2.6
Jordan	1,240	—
Algeria	2,060	2.1
Lebanon	—	—
Iran	2,490	0.1
Oman	5,220	6.4
Libya	5,310	-3.0
Iraq	—	—
Saudi Arabia	7,050	2.6
Israel	10,920	2.6
Kuwait	16,150	-4.0
U.A.E.	19,860	—

Source: World Bank. *World Development Report 1992.* New York: Oxford University Press, 1992.

Per capita income figures do not show what each citizen has available to spend; they indicate how much of national income each individual would have if the income were evenly distributed. The enormous gulf between the rich and the poor found in some of the states is thus ignored, as are military expenditures. The fact that Egypt has devoted about one quarter of its GNP to military needs while, say, the U.A.E. has spent a much smaller percentage means that the gap between the two countries is much larger than indicated. Per capita income figures for the small-population, petroleum-rich countries can vary substantially from year to year. Income earned in these economies closely follows petroleum export earnings. For example, the measured per capita income in Saudi Arabia in 1983 ($12,230) fell almost 45 percent by 1986 (to $6,950), reflecting the substantial fall in petroleum prices beginning in late 1985. This does not mean that the average Saudi citizen experienced a 45 percent loss of income. To cushion the decrease in income earned, the government spent reserves accumulated in earlier years. But even the fabled Saudi wealth has finite limits. By 1989 the government was forced to adopt a more modest budget. Kuwait was more insulated from petroleum price shocks. Indeed, the interest earnings from international investments exceeded revenue from petroleum sales during the 1985–1990 period. These earnings also financed the massive reconstruction project after Iraq was pushed out of Kuwait in 1991.

The negative growth in per capita income in Kuwait deserves some comment. The figure reflects the fact that Kuwait, along with the other low-population, high-income petroleum exporters had huge increases in population in the preceding three decades. Many of the immigrants worked in low-paying occupations for Kuwaitis. Hence, the per capita income fell as Kuwait became rich!

The growth record, whether viewed from the simplicity of Table 10-1 or from a more sophisticated framework, was reasonably satisfactory during the 1960s if one ignores Egypt and impoverished Yemen. Petroleum price increases in the 1970s assured some countries of phenomenal growth and put the countries without petroleum under ever greater strain, especially those countries that had established an industrial base and needed oil.

The decade of the 1980s was not good for most Middle Eastern economies. Wars (for example, the Iran–Iraq war), virtual anarchy (in Lebanon), insurrection (the Palestinians in Israel), wildly fluctuating petroleum prices, continued high rates of population growth (adding over 1 million per year to Egypt alone), significant droughts, and clumsy government intervention in economic life all contributed to the poor record. By the end of the decade, a number of countries (for example, Egypt, Israel, Iraq) had significant debt-servicing problems, and others (for example, Syria) saw their sources of economic and military aid dry up because of the sudden collapse of the Soviet system.

THE ECONOMIC RECORD

Two overriding phenomena have shaped the economic record of the Middle East since 1950—war, or the threat of war, and the changing nature of the petroleum industry. On a more general level, the major long-run economic issue is that of resource imbalances. High rates of population increase, when placed in the context of a limited supply of water and arable land is the most obvious set of problems.

Likewise, petroleum is a nonrenewable resource; supplies are exhaustible. Economic growth in these circumstances may not be sustainable. Growing resource imbalances increase the probability of conflict within and between nations.

The Persian (Arabian) Gulf and Israel have been the foci of most major military conflicts. Israel and the countries bordering it have consumed a substantial chunk of their resources for military strength in the past half century, resources that could have been directed toward economic growth. Wars have deleterious effects beyond the pure waste of committing resources to nonproductive uses; the occasional outbreaks of war and the constant possibility of war disrupts plans and projects, discourages investment, and diverts attention from nonmilitary objectives. The disruptive effects are greater in the less-developed countries than in their richer counterparts, for the less-developed economies are far more fragile than the developed ones. A poor country is poor, in part, because it does not have the physical infrastructure—networks of communication, transportation, education, and electrical power—the right variety and amounts of economic resources, and the social and political complements necessary for sustained growth. These countries experience significant setbacks when they have to absorb outside shocks to their economies. This is exactly what happens when the local military machine is obliged to garner resources that otherwise could be used to build a stronger national economic foundation. Local circumstances, however, dictate that this statement needs to be tempered. Although the long (1980–1988) war between Iran and Iraq was enormously expensive in terms of material resources and human life, the effect on Iraq was ameliorated substantially by the receipt of tens of billions of dollars of grants and loans, especially from the petroleum-rich Gulf states. By the time of the cease-fire, Iraq had in their workforce upwards of 2 million foreigners, almost all Arab, the majority being Egyptian. Their externally financed presence meant that the Iraqi economy was able to grow throughout the conflict.

However, by 1990, Iraq was facing a set of stringent economic conditions that represented an important cluster of motivations for their invasion of Kuwait: Gulf grants had ended and debt servicing was burdensome; OPEC oil production exceeded agreed limits, lowering the price of oil and thereby depriving Iraq of foreign exchange earnings (Iraq loses about $1 billion per year for every dollar drop in the price of petroleum); and the port city of Basra would be closed indefinitely because the Shatt al-Arab waterway was clogged with mines, sunken ships, and silt.

If war generally is very expensive, so is the establishment of peace. The Camp David Accords between Egypt and Israel provides a useful case history to keep in mind as peace in the 1990s is contemplated. An essential element of the Camp David Accords was Israeli withdrawal from the Egyptian Sinai territory captured in 1967. This meant that Israel was asked to relinquish a formidable natural buffer between it and Egypt. Neither Israel nor Egypt had the financial resources necessary to construct and maintain an "electronic fence" that was to serve as a substitute for the buffer of the desert. Neither side could afford peace. It was necessary for the United States to foot the bill.

Negotiations of "land for peace" in the 1990s may involve the same sort of financial bind. All parties face severe water problems, and Israel receives a substantial percentage of its supply from the territories it occupies. It must be assured of secure water supplies. It may be that the only way to assure this is through the construction of (expensive) desalination plants.

In assessing the post-World War II record of the various countries, one must account for the dislocations caused by war or the threat of war. Egypt, for example, engaged in four wars with Israel, had a consequential involvement in a civil war in Yemen, had several confrontations with Libya, and participated (with compensation) in the 1991 effort against Iraq. In the best of circumstances the task of creating an economy capable of sustained growth is difficult; the need to be in an almost constant state of military readiness has greatly compounded the problem. Jordan has had to contend with a tremendous influx of Palestinians on several occasions, Syria has been engaged with Israel, the delicate balance in Lebanon unravelled, and so on. Israel, of course, has felt particularly beleaguered, being constantly under threat of attack, although massive international aid for many years buffered the problem. Given these conditions, the countries under study have experienced more rapid growth than one would expect. But the prospects for sustained rapid growth were dim until 1974.

One of the most remarkable transfers of wealth the world has ever seen was ushered center stage by the changes in the petroleum industry. The members of OPEC roughly quadrupled (to $12) the price of petroleum between October 1973 and January 1974, not so much as acting as a cartel, but by taking advantage of worldwide changes in supply/demand conditions. The price was doubled (from $15 to $30) by OPEC in 1979. Saudi Arabia, the leader, had accumulated more financial reserves than most other countries of the world by 1980. The other petroleum producers in the area, most notably Iraq and Iran, along with the small Gulf states, also had spectacular increases in revenue. The results of this accumulation of financial power were felt, in greater or lesser degree, throughout the world. For example, the Middle East became a more important trading partner for Japan (as measured by the value of trade) than the European Economic Community. The petroleum-producing countries had the financial wherewithal to promote economic development; their allies benefited through various direct and indirect measures, and their enemies suffered. Much of the Middle East changed forever; and because of this, the world changed.

ORGANIZATION OF ECONOMIC ACTIVITY

The three major economic goals of most countries are growth, stability, and an equitable distribution of income. There is much debate as to which of these is the most important and how the goals are best pursued once a reasonable consensus is reached on the "correct" mix. Indeed, governments and universities resound with arguments that champion a range of solutions from private enterprise to socialism. The issues have importance beyond scholarly debate; the choices are real and the stakes are high. Several countries have been proponents of "Arab Socialism," while others have monarchies that directly influence much of the "private" enterprise of any note. Others have taken a more eclectic stance, and a few are attempting to give coherence to the meaning of "Islamic economics."

There seems to be little consensus about the specific contours of Arab Socialism. The lack of a clearly defined and consistent ideology is due to several factors, including disagreements across national boundaries and espousals of an idea without any particular plan of action. What is clear is that Middle Eastern "socialist" governments came to power with a definite desire to provide greater economic growth, stability, and a more equitable distribution of income and wealth. In order to meet these goals, the leaders initiated land reforms, froze prices, and nationalized major industries. But these measures are better described as nationalistic than socialistic, especially when they are designed to lessen foreign influences in the economy.

During in 1980s, a pronounced shift occurred in the ideological stance of many of the proponents of Arab Socialism. Indeed, there was a generalized world-wide shift away from government involvement in economic life in favor of private markets. During the preceding decades most academics and policymakers favored large-scale government involvement. Their preference was rooted in various notions of the development process, from Marxist to neo-classical renditions of the failures of the marketplace in the specialized settings of low-income countries. National leaders often adopted one or another of these moorings, either from intellectual conviction or as a convenient excuse to pursue another goal. However, by the 1980s the blame for the miserable economic performance in many of these countries was placed on government, the very agent which had been seen as the driving force of development only a few years earlier. It was claimed, with a considerable number of case studies at hand, that government action stunted growth. At the same time, the U.S.S.R. was falling apart.

It is probable that some countries professed socialism because it was a convenient way for their political leaders to eliminate business opposition, or to strike an appropriate international posture; the professed ideals often faded as circumstances warranted. In 1973, three years after the death of Gamal Abdel Nasser, clearly the leading proponent of Arab Socialism in the region, Anwar Sadat declared an Egyptian "open-door policy" to foreign investment. A little more than a decade earlier Nasser had severely restricted not only foreign business operations but also private domestic investments. Nasser's relationship to the business class probably had something to do with his decisions. The abrupt change in Egyptian policy may have been based on Sadat's desire to curry favor with conservative King Faisal (d. 1975) of Saudi Arabia. Ideologies may shift dramatically with the political climate.

Iraq, considered a radical state in the 1970s, reacted strongly against the post-Nasser economic drift in Egypt. A few months after the open-door policy was announced in Egypt, and after the 1973 Arab–Israeli war, Iraq proposed that the Western supporters of Israel should be punished through an embargo on petroleum sales. By adopting this policy they proved their radical mettle to the world at large. Of course, the world at large may not have known that Iraq was selling its petroleum to the U.S.S.R., which in turn sold petroleum to Western Europe. Without impugning Iraq's motives, it is fair to say that it was able to maintain its international reputation as a "hard-line" state without having to suffer significant revenue losses from decreased petroleum sales.

Through the 1980s Syria depended on the Soviet bloc for the bulk of their economic and military aid. Especially noteworthy is that much of the aid (especially educational aid) was given by the respective communist parties to the Syrian Baath party. But then the Soviet bloc crumbled. The consequent almost total shut-off of the aid spigot coincided with a series of drought years in Syria—an agricultural system particularly sensitive to rainfall. It also became increasingly apparent that the extensive system of government ownership of industry and rigid price-fixing was becoming ever-more burdensome. The Syrian government responded to their economic crisis by drawing closer to the remaining great power, the United States. They adopted a series of measures designed to "liberalize" the economy, along with an attempt to make some of their political policies more acceptable to the United States. The 1990 U.S. call for Arab participation in the coalition against Iraq presented Syria with a unique opportunity.

After the war Syria continued to change its orientation in several ways. Among the changes was an official reinterpretation of Baathist notions of the "Arab Nation" and the role of the government in the economy. Although always stated in foggy and dreamlike terms, the keepers of Baathist ideology had spoken of some future time when there would be a pan-Arab nation free of boundaries imposed by Western powers. By 1991 they were speaking of the "Arab Nation" in the same tones as the members of the European Economic Community were speaking of a united Europe—a closely cooperating group of nations, each with its sovereignty. Likewise the past record of heavy government involvement in the economy was explained as a phase necessary to fit the objective conditions of the 1970s and 1980s; the "new objective conditions" dictated that it was time for the private sector to take a greater role.

The same kinds of observations concerning ideologically flexible pronouncements and policies can be made about those countries that profess to follow private enterprise as an operating principle. In a few countries, most significant ventures initiated by the private sector are tied directly to the government either through formal public participation or through the intervention of well-placed individuals in the government. The Iranian royal family, for example, gained ownership shares in many significant industrial ventures in that country. The royal family participated both because it desired wealth and because it perceived a need to exert control over industrialists and the growing industrial sector. In many cases this kind of intervention has had a profound effect on the functioning of the marketplace. Competitive private enterprise markets in the Western world tend to be impersonal, ideally excluding all considerations except for those of price and performance. The highly personalized industrial ventures in Iran under the shah or in Saudi Arabia, for example, should not be expected to yield the same results. It is difficult to know what to call such systems: perhaps *etatism* will suffice. In any case, they are not private enterprise systems as generally thought of in the West.

The study of Islamic economics became a growth industry after the success of OPEC and the increased interest in the formation of an Islamic state. Before this, first-rate work was relatively rare and obscure. The term *Islamic economics* covers a wide variety of issues and problems, although Western attention has focused almost exclusively on the Koranic proscription on the taking of interest and the consequent need to redesign the financial system. Since the range of inquiry is so comprehensive and the analyses so recent, many questions remain— but there are many points of agreement.

The fundamental starting point of mainstream (Western, neo-classical) economic analysis is extreme: "well-offness", utility, is maximized by an individual solely with reference to material goods (and services). Further, the theory usually posits that I make myself better off by ignoring the well-being of others. That is, it adopts an extreme individualistic and materialistic stance. While Western economists generally agree that this narrow definition defies reality, they argue that it is a most useful starting point, and that the analysis can be adjusted further down the line. However, a group of Muslim theorists feels that this abstraction from reality is not warranted: the Koranic concern for the well-being of the Umma is so central that the "complications" need to be introduced at the outset. Consequently, some Muslim theorists have grappled with the very complex issue of modeling individual utility functions that jettison extreme individualism and materialism.

There are many other issues that hold the attention of those concerned with Islamic economics. For example, there are specific Koranic guidelines dealing with the scope of inheritance, the proper system of taxation (including zakat), the nature of government expenditures, and, more generally, the proper role of government in meeting the wider material and ethical concerns of the Umma. On some matters basic principles are quite clear, but the mechanisms for goal achievement are not. The principle of the obligation of zakat is straightforward; the manner in which it is to be levied, and by whom, is not clear. On a more general level, the Koran does not express explicit hostility toward private enterprise, but its egalitarian concerns for the Umma leave open some basic questions relating to the proper extent of property rights, limits on the accumulation of wealth, and other fundamental issues.

The Koranic proscription against the taking of interest has captured most Western attention concerning Islamic economics. Most Muslim theorists are convinced that the taking of interest is indeed forbidden—after all, the Koran seems to be quite clear on the issue. However, we should realize that although the Koran specifically declares that interest is forbidden (haram), straightforward acceptance of even this involves a theological position. Some theorists argue that the words of the Koran reflect a prohibition against usury—"exploitatively high" interest rates—rather than interest per se. A strict literalist position, one that takes the word of the Prophet as immutable through time and not subject to interpretation, renders the modernist view as heretical. In any case, there now is rather widespread agreement on the need to develop an interest-free banking system.

As with any price, the price for the use of money, the interest rate, balances supply and demand forces. In general, individuals need to be compensated for deferring consumption (saving). That is, Western banks pay interest in order to encourage a flow of loanable funds. Borrowers create the demand. They are willing to pay interest because the rate of return they expect from investing the borrowed money, say, building a factory, is greater than the interest payment they are obligated to pay the bank. The bank serves the function of making this market, of bringing together people who gain from deferring consumption and those who gain from investing. Notice that the equilibrium interest rate, that which yields the same quantity demanded as the quantity supplied, also serves the economy as a whole by matching the community's desire to forgo present consumption with future rewards; that is, it helps determine the upper limit of growth.

How, then, can an interest-free system operate efficiently? How does a financial institution encourage deposits and choose among potential borrowers? Islamic institutions provide an answer: a profit/loss share system. The banks compete for deposits by indicating that the depositor gains shares, claims on potential bank profits—and they advertise what they have paid out per share in past years. Depositors in an Islamic bank do not have the contractual guarantee of a return promised by Western banks, but they do have some knowledge of the track record of the bank, and could earn more if the bank has a particularly good year. This method of gathering loanable funds is in place in several countries, including Iran and Pakistan, and seems to work well—there is no fundamental difference from interest-paying banking.

The lending decisions of the bank follow the same share principle. Instead of a firm borrowing money and having a fixed repayment schedule, the bank essentially buys shares in the activity of the borrowing company, with the provision that the borrowing firm has the ability to repurchase the shares (as well as an obligation to share profits). Since the banks are competing for the funds of potential savers, they must endeavor to deliver the highest share of profits. This, in turn, forces them to lend to those who have the highest probable rate of return. As in the interest system, competition enforces efficiency on the market.

While zero-interest banking can mirror an interest-paying system with respect to efficiency, there are several important differences that reflect Koranic concerns for equity. General Koranic ethical norms state that it is not acceptable to profit from an individual in dire straits. The share system satisfies this norm. The borrower is not obligated to make repayments to the financial institution if the investment goes sour. For example, the farmer who faces a crop loss due to bad weather is not obligated to make a payment to the bank in the same period. Rather, the bank, as partner, shares the burden. In the same fashion, the bank is not obligated to pay a return to depositors if the bank has a bad year. Both gains and misfortunes are shared.

The Islamic system of zero-interest banking, then, provides for the usual efficiency conditions of interest banking, and it fits Koranic ethical norms. Actually, the system is far more complex, and some of the details of operation and policy implications (for example, 100 percent reserve versus the Western fractional reserve system) are not fully understood. However, it is clear that the system is economically rational and managerially feasible.

The three large-population countries in the Middle East—Egypt, Iran, and Turkey—changed their economic orientation markedly over the past quarter century. The 1973 pronouncement (legislated in 1974) by Sadat of a policy of *infitah* ("opening up") of the Egyptian economy to private foreign and domestic investment was a clear political statement rejecting Nasser's policies. The movement was to be toward building "market socialism" and away from the Soviet-type material balances approach. This meant that many prices were to be market determined rather than set by a planning agency. It also meant that the private sector would be strengthened. Although the Egyptian economy grew at a robust pace for the next decade, about 8 percent per annum, the proximate causes of the growth cannot be attributed to the new policy. Rather, a surge in foreign exchange earnings emanating from forces largely out of the control of Egypt seem to have been responsible. The four major items were petroleum exports, receipts from the (newly reopened) Suez Canal, remittances from Egyptians working in the petroleum-rich states, and substantial international aid programs. During the 1980s President Mubarak slowly nudged Egypt toward more private enterprise.

A host of domestic forces consigned Egyptian policymakers to a very narrow range of options. It seems as though a policy stasis emerged. The fundamental problems of a high rate of population growth, an urban and industrial bias, and a troublesome income distribution were not matters given priority. While the root causes of this policy stasis are not fully understood, it seems that one significant factor was the emergence of a new amalgam of social forces. The technocratic class gained members and prominence under Nasser. Many of this class were members of the bloated government, and Sadat's emphasis on the private sector was a clear threat to their power. As a result, the usually cumbersome bureaucratic apparatus seemed to cease to function altogether when private investors sought government approval for some aspect of their operations. The agricultural sector was another source of resist-ance to Sadat's policy shift. Those peasants who rose toward the top of the agricultural ladder through the Nasser-initiated land reform policies would lose if there was a significant change in the system. The best off of those in agriculture stood to lose since they received substantial subsidies (and important exemptions from regulations). In counterpoint to the technocrats and new agricultural elite, the old elite class came to the surface under Sadat after many years of quietude under Nasser. They pressed for promised favors for the private sector.

The debt crisis of the 1870s led to a reordering of Egypt. One hundred years later Egypt again was in the middle of a nervous game in the international marketplace. It seems that the opening of the Egyptian economy did remove some gross inefficiencies. However, its foreign exchange earnings were subject to the volatile petroleum market (because of petroleum sales and migrant worker remittances to Egypt), and the equally uncertain political environment (the Suez Canal earnings and international aid). The basic issues of population and income distribution were largely ignored. It is consequential that the U.S. government forgave Egypt $7 billion in loans after Egyptian participation in the war against Iraq; the Egyptian economy was carrying a very heavy debt burden.

The Turkish solution to a faltering economy mirrored Egypt in that the economy was opened to foreign trade, but it differed in other basic aspects. While the primary reason for the 1980 military takeover in Turkey was to curb the alarming amount of politically motivated violence (about 180 deaths per month by mid-1980), it was clear that a grossly inefficient economy also was of concern.

The military leaders of the 1980 coup thoroughly reformed the Turkish political system by (1) disbanding all political parties and confiscating their property, (2) barring political activity (for ten years) for all of those who at the time of the takeover were in leadership positions, and barring the political activity of all those in the Grand National Assembly (for five years), and (3) initiating and guiding to passage a new constitution (November 1982). One important set of provisions in the new constitution dealt with electoral reform. In particular, proportional representation was ended and national parties needed to receive at least 10 percent of the national vote in order to have a candidate seated. This blunted the efforts of many small parties and made it possible for the largest party to govern without being saddled by debilitating coalitions.

The election of 1982 brought a technocrat, Turgot Ozal, to power and gave his Motherland Party a majority in the Grand National Assembly, a majority which was increased substantially in the 1987 elections. This cleared the way for Ozal to act decisively to bring order in the streets and coherence in the economy in order to meet the constitutional provision that stated that the economy was to be based on private enterprise. He initiated a set of "liberalizing" policies—policies designed to strengthen the free market—such as tariff reduction, foreign investment promotion, a wholesale dismantling of state-owned enterprises, a bid to join the European Economic Community, and (after the breakup of the U.S.S.R.) the formation of a Black Sea economic cooperation group of nations. Although the Motherland Party lost its legislative majority in 1991, the die had been cast; the majority in the legislature differed from Ozal in many ways, but they framed their differences within the basic market-liberalizing blueprint laid down in the 1980s. Indeed, a central feature of Turkey's concerted diplomatic effort to form alliances with the muslim majority republics of the former Soviet Union leaned heavily on the proposition that these countries would realize sizable economic benefits if they followed Turkey's pattern. As with Egypt, involved Western actors, from governments to private creditors, worried over the seeming inability of Turkey to service its debt, assisted in the effort.

During the 1980s, the International Monetary Fund, the major international organization capable of providing financing to beleaguered governments, joined the academic world in their disillusionment with extensive government control of the economy. Countries seeking financial assistance always had to meet "conditionality" clauses if their requests were to be met. By the 1980s these clauses more explicitly argued for economic "liberalization," the strengthening of the private sector. The financial weakness of the country often meant that they had little choice but to accept the conditions. However, economic liberalization often meant that policies had to be initiated that made things worse before they got better. This was an increasingly bitter pill to swallow for those countries already in deep trouble. It also seemed unfair to those who arrived at their poor status because of wild gyrations in the international marketplace rather than internally generated failings.

For example, in 1989 Jordan completed negotiations with the International Monetary Fund that allowed it to borrow from the IMF on the condition that prices of key basic commodities in Jordan be increased to reflect economic costs. This is the usual procedure for the IMF; they will approve loans only if the country institutes a program that will correct fundamental imbalances. The case of Jordan clearly illustrates why many countries object to this "conditionality." Substantial increases in food and fuel prices designed to limit imports were met by civil unrest among those elements of the population thought to be the most loyal to the government. In response to the unrest, Jordan's prime minister was forced to resign and the King promised more political participation. The political costs of economic adjustment can be high.

Iran, the other large-population country of the Middle East, took a different course. Its revolutionary government rejected moves toward a more globally interdependent economy, whether it be under the market socialism of Egypt under Sadat or the free market goal of Turkey. Although there was considerable debate in Iran about the economic roles of the state and of private enterprise, there was also rather widespread agreement that there would be no infitah in Iran. If anything, the goal would be that of removing foreign influence from the internal economy. A decade after the revolution, Iran was fitfully moderating its position on foreign investment.

Although the ideological stance of the various nations may be important, we must look beyond surface pronouncements and deeds. The remaining sections of this chapter will analyze how different circumstances lead to different policy measures, and why the same policy measures may lead to different results.

LAND POLICIES

Table 10-2 gives the geographical area of the various Middle Eastern countries. Saudi Arabia is the twelfth largest country in the world; Iran ranks fifteenth, being about one half the size of India; Sudan and Algeria are the two largest countries in Africa. In comparison, Kuwait, Bahrain, Qatar, the U.A.E., Israel, and Lebanon are very small indeed.

A great percentage of the land in the Middle East is either not arable or only marginally so. With a few minor exceptions, all of the arable land in Egypt runs along the Nile; that of Libya is contained in a narrow band of land along the Mediterranean. The Arabian peninsula has significant arable land only in parts of Oman, Yemen, and the Hijaz region of Saudi Arabia. Much of the Iranian steppe and the mountainous terrain of Turkey is unsuitable for high-yield agriculture. The vast deserts of the Middle East often have been compared with a sea; while they have an unrelenting, harsh, and beautiful power, they are difficult to control. These formidable deserts are both barriers and vast havens. However, their power to promote insularity has eroded considerably in the twentieth century. The finances necessary to overcome the power of the deserts—to cross them with roads, build air-

TABLE 10-2.   COUNTRY SIZE, ARABLE LAND, URBAN POPULATION

COUNTRY	SURFACE AREA		URBAN POPULATION AS PERCENT OF TOTAL POPULATION	
	SIZE (1,000 KM^2)	PERCENT ARABLE	1960	1990
Sudan	2,505	29	10	22
Algeria	2,382	16	32	52
Saudi Arabia	2,150	40	30	77
Libya	1,760	9	23	70
Iran	1,648	36	34	57
Egypt	1,001	2	38	47
Turkey	781	47	30	61
Yemen	528	34	9	29
Oman	300	5	4	11
Syria	185	76	37	50
Jordan	98	8	43	68
U.A.E.	84	3	40	78
Israel	21	—	77	92
Kuwait	18	8	72	96
Qatar	11	—	73	89
Lebanon	10	30	40	84
Bahrain	1	—	83	83

Source: U.N.D.P. *Human Development Report, 1991.* New York: Oxford University Press, 1991.

ports, purchase transportation systems, dam rivers, and build radio transmitters—were generated in some countries by colonial administrations and in others by nationalist modernizing forces, by means of taxes and oil revenues. Whatever the source, the deserts are slowly being changed. They will, however, continue to present severe constraints on life in the Middle East.

Agricultural land distribution and ownership patterns are generally considered to affect productivity. Obviously, they are also indices of economic justice and power. All of the countries in this survey have seen significant changes in the pattern of land ownership in the twentieth century. There have been formal agrarian reform programs in six of the countries—Egypt, Iran, Iraq, Syria, Libya, and (South) Yemen. There have been no reform programs in Jordan, Lebanon, the U.A.E., or Saudi Arabia. Land ownership and use patterns have changed considerably in Israel, but it is best to consider Israel apart since the circumstances of these changes have been unique.

Various land ownership patterns exist in the Middle East, but three types are most common. The first is **mulk**, or private ownership. The second is **miri sirf**, land owned by the state, generally with very strong *usufruct* rights (right of use without ownership) granted to the tenant. In practice, this is often little different than mulk. The third is **waqf**, a uniquely Islamic institution. One type of waqf allows for title to the land to be given to some officially recognized religious or social institution, sometimes with the condition that the family and heirs of the donor are to receive some share of the proceeds from the land either until the family line no longer exists or for some specified period of time. Another form is strictly private. A rough Western equivalent is the trust fund. And as with trust funds, a waqf may be established and administered with the most honorable of intentions, or simply to protect individual assets from the tax collector. In any case, modifications of waqf status can involve massive changes in the distribution of wealth and political power.

The following thumbnail reports on some countrie's experiences with land and agricultural policy illustrate several points beyond the gleaning of country-specific information. First, policies often have unintended results. Second, there is a wide range of ideological flexibility in the adoption of programs. Third, there can be serious international consequences to internal actions. Fourth, some policies can be very wasteful. Fifth, agricultural policies are intertwined with population and water issues. And, finally, profound political tremors can be triggered by changes in policy.

Turkey

Turkey put itself on the path of modernization with the thoroughgoing Westernizing revolution of Kemal Ataturk. Years of Ottoman neglect of agriculture, except as a tax base, were quickly reversed. At least four distinct periods stand out in Turkish agricultural history since the formation of the republic in 1923. First, during the years of Ataturk (1923–1938), the oppressive tax structure was reformed and a host of infrastructure projects were developed. The second period began after the close of World War II. The government engaged in a considerable effort to improve storage and marketing facilities as well as to introduce mechanization. Up to 1960, agricultural output expanded tremendously. Wheat production nearly doubled between 1948 and 1953, allowing Turkey to become a net exporter of this grain for a short time.

A great deal of this expansion came about by extending the area under cultivation as opposed to increasing the yields per hectare. This resulted in two deleterious effects that slowed the agricultural growth rate after 1960, the third period. Because most of the new lands were marginal, they lost whatever productivity they had during each period of drought, since there was relatively little irrigation. Second, the methods used to expand the area under cultivation resulted in a loss of soil fertility and a greater runoff of water. The fourth period has been characterized by an extensive series of irrigation projects made possible by the construction of dams, especially on the Euphrates. This has caused intense concern in Syria and Iraq, the other countries which depend heavily on the flow of the Euphrates' waters.

Egypt

The 1952 revolution in Egypt ushered in a substantial program of land reform and redistribution that proceeded by fits and starts for the next two decades. In 1952 about 1.2 percent of the largest holdings encompassed 45 percent of the agricultural land. In contrast, the smallest 72 percent of the holdings accounted for 13 percent of the land, an average of about one *feddan* (1.06 acres) per holding. Because of population pressures and a lack of alternative employment, the rental rates charged by the mostly absentee owners of the large estates were very high. The first lands to be expropriated were those of the royal family. These lands, plus the waqf lands in their possession, accounted for 5.5 percent of the total agricultural land. Land reforms also lowered the maximum feddans that an individual could hold from 200 in 1952, to 100 in 1961, and finally to 50 in 1969. At first, the larger landowning families simply split their holdings among various family members and thereby avoided being severely affected. The law, however, was gradually tightened, and by 1970 the government had redistributed 18.6 percent of all agricultural land. In 1981 the laws were modified in order to stimulate settlement on what otherwise was desert. Smallholders were allowed to own up to 300 feddan, and agribusinesses could own up to 50,000 feddan. The record indicates that the large agribusinesses have been more successful than the smallholders, partially because of their ability to move the creaky Egyptian civil service.

Syria

The process of land reform followed the same general pattern in Syria. However, due to the extreme variability in land productivity, the redistribution was based on estimated incomes to be derived from the land; therefore, larger parcels were given to those on low productivity land. As with many countries, the redistribution effort proved far more difficult than the promulgation of laws restricting maximum size. In Syria as in Egypt, the class of large landholders was more tenacious than anticipated. The reforms quickened in pace only as the political power base of this group diminished. However, a new group of agriculturists-cum-capitalists took the place of the traditional landholding elite and complicated issues of government control.

Libya and Iraq

In Libya and Iraq large landholders were rather suddenly shut out of the political decision-making process, although the situation in each country was somewhat different. Libyan agricultural landholdings were of two polar types: a small number of large estates located on relatively good and well-irrigated land, mostly owned by Italian nationals, and vast stretches of marginal land, partially (about one-third in 1960) owned on a tribal basis. The 1969 overthrow of the monarchy led to the expropriation of the Italian farms in 1970. The Libyan agricultural reform methods fit both the ideology of the "socialist" government and the agricultural situation. A mere redistribution of the poor lands would not accomplish much, if any, gain in productivity. Likewise, the average yields of the large productive farms probably could not have been retained if the farms were split up. These large units, therefore, were transformed into state farms. The redistribution of marginal lands was tied to an ambitious scheme to invest some of the country's considerable oil revenues in order to raise agricultural productivity: the building of wells, roads, and marketing facilities were included in this effort. Attempts also have been made to strongly discourage, if not eliminate, absentee ownership of arable land.

In Iraq, local **sheikhs**—generally better described as political dignitaries rather than religious leaders—were transformed into landholders in the twentieth century largely because the British attempted to transform the communal tribal ownership patterns into those of private ownership. The 1958 revolution left the sheiks without a political power base, and the carving up of their holdings was assured. State lands, the miri sirf, also provided a base for redistribution. But the state of Iraqi agriculture and the country's political instability led to highly uneven results for this potentially highly productive nation.

Most agricultural land in Iraq is dependent on irrigation to support even reasonable levels of productivity; declines in agricultural productivity occur when the central authority neglects its responsibilities in this area. The neglect lasted for over 1,000 years. The relative political stability and petroleum-generated wealth of the 1970s and 1980s reversed the process at long last. In one of the many ironies of war, it may turn out that the U.N.–sponsored blockade of food to Iraq following the 1991 Gulf war may make Iraq largely self-sufficient in food production—resources were directed to agriculture in order to stave off mass starvation.

Iran

Large-scale land reform started in Iran in 1962, and without the impetus of a true revolution. The shah redistributed some royal lands in the 1950s, but the White Revolution, promulgated in January 1963, promised for the first time a set of sweeping changes throughout the economy, including substantial land reform (the "revolution" was called "White" because it was to be peaceful). Before the redistribution, absentee landlords controlled much of the fertile lands in Iran; the peasants generally had no tenancy rights. The landowners often owned huge tracts of land that encompassed many villages. To minimize evasion of the law, redistribution was stated in terms of villages rather than area. Legislation in 1965 closed some loopholes in the law, transferred waqf land administration to the central government, and presented the landholders not affected by the 1962 legislation with five basic choices: (1) lease the land, (2) sell the land, (3) divide the land between themselves and the peasants on the basis of old sharecropping agreements, (4) form a cooperative with the peasants, or (5) purchase peasant rights to the land and continue farming. This wide range of choices clearly reflected the triangle of tensions then present between landlords, peasants, and the shah. The shah needed to reduce the landowners' power, or at least give the appearance of doing so, but the landowners' power was so great that an attempt at outright expropriation seemed inadvisable.

The results of this land reform can be analyzed fairly accurately by examining what happened in a particular village.[1] Before redistribution, about half the land in this village was in (public) waqf status, the other half being owned by a single individual. The peasants farming the waqf lands secured tenancy rights through the government. The landlord chose to split his property in half (the basis of the old sharecropping agreement), keeping, as might be expected, the most fertile land under his control. The peasants who worked this land, therefore, were excluded from redistribution policies. Other similar results followed: The largest and most fertile parcels lying outside the new domain of the landlord were worked by the family and friends of the village headman who up till then had been the manager of the lands. On gaining property rights, almost half of these village elites rented their land to the headman and became absentee landlords themselves. Also, the custom of drawing lots every three to five years to ensure that particular peasants would not be permanently consigned to the least fertile land ended, of course, when title was assigned. This meant that some of the landed peasants were put in a permanently disadvantageous position.

It is very difficult to assess the effects of these events on agricultural productivity. However, the peasants became increasingly stratified socially and economically, a new class of absentee landlords developed, and the de facto changes in power relationships with the central bureaucracy were different from those stated. Especially important in this respect was the shearing away of clerical power in rural areas. Quite obviously, some of the goals of the program were achieved— many peasants gained ownership or secured tenancy rights to the land. But in a country plagued with low productivity in the best of times, the new sets of problems generated from the reforms did much to blunt the overall positive effect.

Issues of land reform also vexed the revolutionary government. There was widespread appeal for fundamental land reform, an appeal which had been given voice by prominent members of the new government and Aytollah Khomeini well before the revolution. But there was no clearly defined program. In the year following the fall of the shah a confused picture emerged.

In some areas villagers seized large estates and farmed them on a communal basis; in other seizures, estates were broken into private plots; and in some areas disgruntled tribal leaders recaptured their feudal lord status, which had been stripped away by prerevolutionary reform. Since provincial courts and administrators gave contradictory rulings, the issue was brought to the Majlis for resolution. The attitude of members of the Majlis toward private property varied considerably

---

[1] D. Craig, "The Impact of Land Reform on an Iranian Village," *Middle East Journal*, Vol. X (Spring 1978), 141–154.

and much haggling ensued. As somewhat more "progressive" members consolidated power, proposals were brought forth that severely restricted landowning. However, several prominent clergy gave opinions that indicated that the proposed legislation was at variance with Islamic principles. On another ideological level, arguments were made that raised questions about the power of Islamic jurists on this matter. Although legislation finally passed, a number of fundamental land-related issues remained unsettled.

AGRICULTURAL POLICIES

Most countries of the world would prefer to be self-sufficient in agricultural production. Indeed, most have made considerable efforts to achieve this goal; and most have failed. The countries of the Middle East are no exception. Although all of the Middle Eastern countries are unlikely to meet the goal of self-sufficiency in the foreseeable future, the region could make considerable strides in this direction.

Total agricultural output can be increased in two general ways: an increase in the yield per unit of existing agricultural land, and an increase in the number of units cultivated. The post-World War II record of the countries under consideration is mixed. Yields for the important foodstuffs grown in Egypt (wheat, rice, and barley) increased substantially and compare favorably on a worldwide basis. This was accomplished through labor intensive cultivation and without much aid from the high technology of Western (and some Israeli) agriculture. The record of Iraq, although not as good as that of Egypt, and while suffering through a decade of war, shows the same general trend. These are the two countries that have access to long stretches of major rivers. The record of the remaining countries, except for Israel, is mixed. Both Syria and Iran have shown increases in the yields of some crops and decreases in others. The yields of wheat, for example, have decreased in Syria because marginal land has been brought under cultivation. Such poor yields, however, are not necessarily due to the chemical composition of the soil. Water is the scarce resource; its availability could markedly change the situation. Underground water deposits in Jordan, Libya, and Syria, for example, could call forth relatively high yields per unit if they could be brought into the production process at a reasonable cost. The Euphrates Dam in Syria did accomplish this. Another potential bright spot is that, except for Israel, the gains thus far have been made without heavy capital expenditures or a relatively heavy reliance on fertilizers or pesticides by individual farmers.

A Saudi experience illustrates that increased agricultural output can waste resources. In the early 1980s, the Saudi government decided that it could make the desert bloom—with wheat—through the application of a system of generous subsidies to farmers. Land, water, seed, fertilizers, and so on were provided at well below cost. Within a few years Saudi Arabia had become an exporter of wheat. It also became painfully aware of the cost of this "success" when the exported wheat was sold at the world price of $3.00 a bushel: The cost of production was about $18.00 per bushel, meaning that the Saudis were using their resources to subsidize world wheat consumption. When the government announced that the system of subsidies had to stop, considerable opposition was voiced by the wheat growers, who had invested on the assumption that the subsidies were to remain in place.

While the Saudi Arabian government was in the enviable position of being able to compensate the farmers in order to stop this wasteful use of resources, most countries are not so blessed.

It is difficult to project these production trends into the future because the ecological balance is particularly sensitive in the Middle East; the productivity gains have not resulted primarily from a wholesale transfer of Western technology, nor have they simply appeared as manna from heaven. The successful innovations have been those that have considered the particular needs of the area. Whether or not enough of these successful innovations will continue to occur is a highly problematic and important question. It is problematic because of our inability to identify the forces that lead to sustained innovation and growth. It is important because of the area's very high rate of population growth and relative scarcity of water.

WATER

By 1990 it was apparent to most Middle East policymakers and analysts that water shortages were becoming ever-more acute in most of the area. Indeed, some observers were predicting that the age of "oil wars" would be supplanted by "water wars." They may be correct; the looming water crisis is staggering.

Water is the scarcest resource in the Middle East. There are only a few significant rivers in the area. Egypt has the Nile. The Tigris and Euphrates both start in mountainous Turkey and wind through Iraq, the Euphrates also cutting across Syria. The most fertile areas of the Middle East lie in the valleys of these great rivers and in the Levant. Other agricultural areas generally must depend on rainfall.

The Nile is the lifeline of Egypt. At Aswan, the width of productive land is only a few hundred meters on each bank. The productive valley widens as one travels north, fanning out into the great Delta north of Cairo. For thousands of years the annual flooding, occurring with great regularity, provided a natural replenishment of necessary soil nutrients, as well as drainage. The Delta was long viewed as the breadbasket of the region and later as the source of cotton for English textile mills. Harnessing the great power of the Nile would give farmers a dependable source of water year round, increase the yields from a single planting, enhance the region's ability to produce double crops, and meet the nation's demand for electricity. The building of the massive Aswan Dam and the filling of Lake Nasser behind it was hailed, therefore, as a project that would alter the face of Egypt. The financing, however, was beyond the government's ability. In the mid-1950s the United States negotiated with Egypt to provide financing and technical assistance to the then new government headed by Gamal Abdel Nasser. The Egyptian government was groping for a positive course; it was trying to end the corrupt and inefficient rule of the royal family that was overthrown in 1952. As part of the move toward a nonaligned status, and because it needed to be ready for war with Israel, the Egyptian government shopped in the world arms market for military goods. Rebuffed by the United States, it signed an arms agreement with Czechoslovakia in 1955. This prompted the United States to withdraw its support for the Aswan Dam project, and implicitly invited Soviet sponsorship, with a consequent ascendancy of Soviet influence in Egypt. Consonant with its history, Egypt became a focal point for world politics. This time, however, Egyptian nationalism provided a check on the benefits to be gained by world powers.

The building of the Aswan Dam necessitated a massive movement of people from villages located where Lake Nasser would form. The Nubian villagers, well out of the mainstream of modernizing influences and culturally more akin to the citizens of Khartoum to the south than those of Cairo, were uprooted in a wholesale fashion and relocated in parts of existing towns or in newly formed villages. Since the rhythm of the river was the heartbeat of the local culture and economy, the relocation amounted to radical surgery. These people were thus forced to rely on the central government much more than previously. They had to abide by new rules as compensation was calculated, rents and land rights were established, and a new social order was set in place.

The dam had different consequences for the fellahin to the north because the river level was now constant. The water table began to rise, and as it did so, the soil became saturated with salt. By the mid-1970s, the centuries old high productivity of certain parts of the Delta had decreased dramatically. The decrease was especially marked in cotton production; cotton is particularly sensitive to the level of salinity in the soil. Keeping the Delta region productive by lowering the water table required two basic strategies: control over water use and improved drainage. Each of these efforts required the government to impose regulations and spend considerable sums of money. The government had to control the operation tightly because individual economic incentives worked against actions that corrected the problem. Ironically, the increased availability of water led to tighter water controls.

While the government controls the amount of water flowing into many irrigated areas, it cannot easily control how it is shared, a difficulty that has caused hostility between neighboring farmers. The allocation of water for individual farm use was complicated by the introduction of machine-driven pumps, and by the land reforms that significantly reduced average farm acreage and thereby increased the number of farm units to be controlled. The provision of adequate drainage presents similar difficulties. Substantial capital expenditures are needed for drainage. An individual landholder will not significantly improve productivity acting alone to improve his drainage. Yet, if all of the farmer's neighbors spend their precious capital for adequate drainage, the lone party who resists these expenditures will share in the benefits as the water table recedes. The government, therefore, must finance and control drainage in a systematic fashion.

Therefore, the boon to agricultural productivity, which was the *raison d'etre* of the Aswan Dam, has been offset by important negative side effects that have strained the scarce financial and administrative resources of the government. Indeed, some estimates placed the cost of the delta-wide drainage expenditures as greater than the cost of the dam. Many of these side effects were anticipated before the building of the dam. However, the need to feed a quickly growing population and provide adequate electricity was thought to be more important.

Both the Tigris and Euphrates rivers originate in the Armenian highlands of Turkey, are fed by melting snow, and flow into the Persian Gulf. But the rivers are dissimilar in some important ways and present different kinds of opportunities and problems. The Euphrates cuts across Syria and Iraq on its journey. It has only a few major tributaries and, therefore, is rather slow moving and has a regular flow. The Tigris passes directly from Turkey into Iraq and has many tributaries. It is liable to flood, has a swift current, and carries a large volume of water. Irrigation from the Tigris is complicated by the timing of the floods and the irregular level of the river. Flooding usually occurs in the spring, in about the middle of the growing season for most crops (except rice and barley). The land cannot simply be inundated as in Egypt. A system of catchment areas must be employed so the water can be released at the appropriate times. And here, too, provision has to be made for adequate drainage to prevent excess soil salinity.

These problems were faced a thousand years ago by the Abbasid caliphate, which exploited the fact that the Euphrates, a western neighbor of the Tigris around Baghdad, has a higher elevation than the Tigris. A canal system was built between the two rivers that allowed for catchment, irrigation, and drainage. Regular maintenance was required, as the Euphrates carried a substantial amount of silt. If the Tigris flooded, a considerable additional effort was needed to clear the irrigation system. Relatively large and continuous infusions of capital were necessary to keep the system running. Since the irrigated lands were owned by many different parties, and the benefits of maintenance and repair were spread unevenly among them, the absence of a well-defined and enforced set of rules discouraged private investment in the canal system. An effective and stable government was needed to maintain agricultural productivity on the irrigated lands. Once the Abbasids passed their zenith, the system fell into decay for a millennium.

This situation contrasts markedly with that of Egypt. Government actions maintaining adequate drainage certainly have affected agricultural productivity in Egypt, but short-term neglect did not lead to a total failure of the system—at least not until the Aswan Dam was built.

The Euphrates cuts across Syria and Iraq before emptying into the Gulf. The construction of dams in Turkey, especially the massive GAP project has caused considerable anxiety in both Syria and Iraq. Although officials from the three countries have held regular meetings on the principles and details of water sharing, considerable tension remains. The problem is further complicated by the fact that a large percentage of the farmers of Syria and Iraq who are heavy Euphrates water users have been troublesome to the central government in the best of times. So when the Syrians cut back on downstream flows in order to fill the lake behind their huge dam, it was the Shia farmers of southern Iraq who suffered.

Israeli water demands may serve as a significant roadblock to any proposed peace settlement. By 1990, Israel garnered a large percentage of its water from the territories it has occupied since the 1967 war. Especially relevant is Israeli control of the Golan, an area generally described by Israel as a military stronghold necessary to avert attacks from Syria. While this argument does not hold much water, the Golan does. The Israelis are taking water from these sources and has for a long time secured a sizable percentage of its national water needs through the National Water Carrier that originates in the northern reaches of Lake Tiberias. South of the lake, the Jordan river has been reduced to a small polluted stream. This causes obvious water shortage problems for the Kingdom of Jordan. The continued Israeli presence in southern Lebanon has a water security dimension; the Litani river is located there. Israel also pumps water from the (largely rain-fed) aquifers in the West Bank for use of settlers there as well as for general Israeli water use. By the early 1990s they were pumping water out at an unsustainable rate; the water table was so low that substantial salt water infiltration became a problem. The prospect of adding around 20 percent to its population base through Soviet Jewish immigration has heightened this problem. One cannot expect Israel to leave Lebanon, Syria, and the West Bank (and Gaza) without ironclad assurances of a secure water supply. Desalination plants may be the only feasible answer, but these plants are very expensive.

Saudi Arabia faces its own water problems. First, there was great fear during the worst days of the 1991 war against Iraq that the desalination plants would become clogged with millions of barrels of petroleum that were floating down the coast from Kuwait. Fortunately, that crisis was averted. The ecology of the Gulf is very fragile; the massive amount of petroleum transported through it poses a continual danger. Since the Gulf is an international waterway, this points to the need for international agreements on the protection of these waters. Second, several studies have indicated that the Saudis are rapidly depleting their (nonrenewable) aquifers in the central regions of the country. This suggests that comprehensive water management programs should be employed, and that research programs such as the U.N.–affiliated International Center for Agricultural Research in the Dry Areas be funded adequately.

When water sources become overburdened in the face of ever-more densely packed populations, human diseases flourish (for example, schistomiases, bilharzia, malaria), property rights need to be redefined, the role of government water policies becomes critical, and, more generally, social conflicts increase in number and severity. The water scarcity problem is a problem partially because population has been growing too rapidly.

POPULATION

Although the population of the Middle East has been increasing for at least a century, the post-World War II growth rate acceleration is of particular interest. It is one of the ironies of history that local, national, and international efforts to prolong life have led, albeit indirectly, to more suffering. Increasing the population base without increasing the food supply results in less food per person. The average annual rates of population increase in the Middle East have ranged between 2 and 3 percent in the last couple of decades; at these rates, the population will double about every quarter century (see Table 10-3).

Migration

The population increases of a few countries have come about through massive movements of people rather than natural increases in the indigenous population. The exodus of Palestinians in 1948 markedly altered conditions in Israel. Indeed, the event has dominated much of what has happened in Jordan since independence. At independence Jordan was an extremely poor country and had few natural resources. The flood of Palestinians into Jordan following the formation of Israel more than trebled the population. Already impoverished, Jordan faced seemingly insurmountable problems since the majority of the refugees were destitute. The addition of the West Bank to Jordanian "territory" added only 7 percent to the total land area but 30 percent to the total of arable land. However, these benefits did not come close to compensating for the massive influx of humanity.

TABLE 10-3. DEMOGRAPHIC CHARACTERISTICS.

COUNTRY	POPULATION (millions)		POPULATION GROWTH RATE	LIFE EXPECTANCY AT BIRTH	DEPENDENCY RATIO
	1960	1990	1990–2000	1990	1990
Turkey	27.5	55.9	1.8	65.1	63
Iran	21.6	54.6	2.3	66.2	89
Egypt	25.9	52.4	2.0	60.3	81
Sudan	11.2	25.2	2.9	50.8	93
Algeria	10.8	25.0	2.8	65.1	92
Iraq	6.8	18.9	3.4	65.0	97
Saudia Arabia	4.1	14.1	3.9	64.5	92
Syria	4.6	12.5	3.6	66.1	103
Yemen	5.2	11.7	3.6	51.5	102
Israel	2.1	4.6	1.5	75.9	67
Libya	1.3	4.5	3.6	61.8	93
Jordan	1.7	4.0	3.3	66.9	101
Kuwait	0.3	2.0	2.6	73.4	67
U.A.E.	0.1	1.6	2.1	70.5	49
Bahrain	0.2	0.5	2.8	71.0	53
Qatar	0.1	0.4	3.1	69.2	58
Industrial Countries			0.8	74.5	50

Source: U.N.D.P. *Human Development Report,* 1991. New York: Oxford University Press, 1991.

During the 1950s almost all expert opinion was pessimistic on the ability of the Jordanian economy to function in a reasonably coherent and growth-inducing fashion. Throughout that period Jordan received a substantial amount of international aid. Although it remained a very poor country, during the 1960s signs of positive movement started to appear. Many Palestinian refugees were highly skilled and experienced in commerce and industry. This "imported" skilled labor, along with considerable Jordanian efforts to improve education, especially at the postsecondary level, began to increase the country's productivity.

The 1967 Israeli occupation of the West Bank and the success of OPEC since 1973 has complicated Jordan's problems. The occupation, of course, meant that a good portion of Jordan's cultivated land was lost and that a new wave of refugees entered the country, thus putting an even greater strain on the system.

The mobilization of PLO forces in Jordan and the consequent pressure that these forces put on Israel, coupled with the Israeli policy of retaliation, led to King Hussein's decision to have Jordanian troops do battle against the armed Palestinians in September 1970. This brought home in stark and tragic relief the fact that many of the residents of Jordan held another national allegiance. The East Bank, an area showing progress amidst the abject poverty of the refugee camps, was not fully under the control of the Jordanian government.

The success of OPEC signaled another wave of population movement as Jordanians rushed to fill positions in petroleum-rich countries. From 1975 forward, about 40 percent of the Jordanian work force (a large percentage being Palestinian) was abroad. Remittances from these workers assumed rather staggering proportions by 1981, measured as a percentage of GNP (27.8 percent), imports (39.0 percent), or exports (168.2 percent). There are some difficulties associated with this influx of foreign exchange. One is the obvious heavy dependence of the Jordanian economy on the continued flow of remittances. Also, a major asset of Jordan, human capital, was depleted to the point that skilled positions within Jordan were understaffed. It is probable that several other labor-exporting countries faced selective labor shortages due to migration; the Egyptian construction industry, for example, seems to have suffered substantially. Jordan fell on hard times in the last years of the 1980s. Remittances (private and official) fell, the current account deficit increased, and international financial reserves were depleted. In addition, in 1991, Jordan had to accommodate several hundred thousand Palestinians fleeing Kuwait (and generally without their hard-currency savings), and had their Gulf aid dry up because of their support of Iraq.

The small-population, petroleum-producing countries have been the major importers of skilled labor. They include Saudi Arabia, Bahrain, Kuwait, Libya, Qatar, and the United Arab Emirates. Iraq also imported labor in the 1980s during their war with Iran. Egypt, Yemen, and Jordan have been the major suppliers. Indigenous entrants to the labor force in the rich countries often have been absorbed in government service as a matter of policy rather than need. Although this policy tends to keep measured unemployment lower than otherwise and serves to pacify potentially disgruntled members of the work force, it also results in a considerable amount of disguised unemployment since the measured productivity of these workers is often nil. Apparently notions of economic efficiency have taken a back seat to political and social issues.

The extent of labor migration has been dramatic. In 1975 about one quarter of the population of these countries were migrants; a 1985 estimate was 40 percent. As indicated in Table 10-4, some nationals are a minority population in their home country. Since most of the migrants do not bring their families, the percentage of foreigners in the work force is more dramatic. As a whole, foreigners compose over 50 percent of the work force in the small-population, labor-importing countries. This, of course, significantly influences foreign and domestic policies. For example, in Kuwait, about one quarter of the expatriates (one in every five workers) were classified as coming from Jordan, a high percentage of them being Palestinians. The government of Kuwait found itself in a rather delicate position whenever Arab states had to stand up and be counted on Palestinian issues. The generally conservative government had to guard against a reaction from the Palestinian expatriates if it took the wrong stance.

The most dramatic change in the composition of the migrant labor force was the increase in the number of Asians—mainly Indians, Pakistanis, and Koreans— working in the Gulf states in the 1970s and 1980s. There are several complementary reasons why the increased demand for labor was not met exclusively by Arabs. First, the major suppliers already had substantial percentages of their work force abroad. Second, skilled and semiskilled workers were in particularly short supply in the Arab supplier nations. Third, the Asian labor market was well organized, Asian labor was relatively cheap, and the labor force was sometimes tied to construction projects awarded to Asian firms. Fourth, Arab labor tended to be

TABLE 10-4. FOREIGN SHARE OF POPULATION IN SELECTED MIDDLE EASTERN COUNTRIES, 1975, 1985.

	FOREIGN SHARE OF POPULATION	
COUNTRY	1975	1985 (estimate)
Saudi Arabia	19.1	33.2
Libya	18.7	35.7
Kuwait	54.0	62.0
Oman	16.1	21.8
Bahrain	21.7	41.9
Qatar	70.6	83.1

Source: Middle East Journal, Vol. 38 (Autumn 1984), 632–633.

politically troublesome. Estimates for 1985 (see Table 10-5) indicate that the percentage of total migrants to the Middle Eastern labor-importing countries who came from India (8.6 percent), Pakistan (13.1 percent), and Southeast Asia (10.9 percent) was substantial. About 150,000 of the migrants were Korean. In total, about one half of the migrants in 1985 were not Arab.

The 1991 war against Iraq displaced millions of people. Several hundred thousand Kurds fled to Turkey, and over a million went to Iran in order to escape Iraqi forces attempting to reestablish control after the war. Tens of thousands of Shia in the south fled either to Iran or the fabled Iraqi marshlands after their postwar resistance was crushed. Before the war Iraq had more than 1 million Egyptian guest workers—all of these, and others, were expelled. Between 350,000 and 400,000 Palestinians were forced out of Kuwait, and several hundred thousand Yemeni guest workers had to leave Saudi Arabia after their government tilted toward Iraq.

The perceived consequences of having "too many" foreigners in a country was faced squarely by Saudi Arabia a decade before the 1991 war; they slowed the implementation of their development plans partially because of a fear that the cultural influences of the foreigners would erode important traditional Saudi values. The U.A.E. (especially Dubai and Abu Dhabi) provide a living illustration of Saudi concerns: The overwhelming majority of the population are foreigners, and it is clear to the most casual observer that much of traditional emirate culture is being swept away by a tidal wave of international commerce.

Kuwait decided to lower the foreign share of the population in a different fashion. It had a preinvasion population of about 2.2 million; only 600,000 of these were Kuwaiti citizens. After the war with Iraq they decided to stabilize the population at 1.1 million—the notion being that they needed to be a majority in their own country. Since the infrastructure of Kuwait needs close to 2 million people to function smoothly, it is not clear how this was to happen. All Palestinians were forced to leave and many other "guest" workers, mainly from Asia, were restricted in number. The government also changed the terms of (nonprofessional) guest worker employment. No longer were they allowed to bring their families with them, and the work permits were to expire after three years, more or less assuring that the foreign population would not develop roots in the country, as they had in the U.A.E.

Israel had a different sort of population influx: Jews immigrating from the former Soviet Union. They had absorbed about 350,000 people from the beginning of the influx in the late 1980s through 1991, and they estimated that 650,000 more

TABLE 10-5. COUNTRIES OF ORIGIN OF ARAB MIGRANT WORKERS AS A PERCENTAGE OF HOME WORK FORCE AND OF ALL MIGRANT ARABS IN MIDDLE EAST.

COUNTRY	PERCENTAGE OF HOME WORK FORCE		PERCENTAGE OF ALL ARAB MIGRANTS IN MIDDLE EAST (EST.)	
	1975	1985 (EST.)	1975	1985 (EST.)
Egypt	3.7	5.2	34.6	36.4
Jordan	40.2	41.0	13.6	15.7
Yemen	24.1	25.9	32.3	22.5
Oman	25.8	22.8	3.0	2.6
Syria	2.1	4.5	3.7	5.4
Sudan	0.7	2.3	2.6	4.7
Lebanon	5.0	10.9	2.9	4.2

Source: *Middle East Journal*, Vol. 38 (Autumn 1984), 639.

could enter in the first half of the 1990s—although the limits of Israeli absorptive capacity and the breakup of the U.S.S.R. have clouded the estimates. This massive influx, a potential 20 percent increase in the population, was greeted with much fanfare in Israel; after all, the *raision d'etre* of the state was the ingathering of world Jewry. The timing also seemed propitious: the Israeli psyche was in a moral quandary—large numbers of its citizens felt that the continued occupation of the territories was tragically misguided. The influx also eased the fears of some Israelis who thought that the higher Arab birthrate was leading to some future point where the Jews would be a minority in the Jewish state. It is, therefore, not surprising that the Israeli government worked hard to assure that Jews could leave the Soviet Union and that Israel would be the only haven.

But the massive influx also carried significant problems. The immigrants had to be housed, fed, and otherwise assimilated into the society. The government budget was not up to the task, so they asked the U.S. government to guarantee up to $10 billion in loans they had to raise. But the United States balked—mainly because Israel was at the same time quickening the settlement of Jews in the occupied territories, a policy against international law. Many of the Soviet Jews took over jobs otherwise given to Palestinians, thereby worsening the economic condition of these people.

Natural Growth and Urbanization

Although labor migration in the Middle East has been substantial, the high rates of population growth are more troublesome from a long-term perspective. There are different sources and consequences of population problems—the overarching problem being one of resource imbalances. Population increases and rapid urbanization are related in an integral fashion to many of the cultural, economic, political, and social problems many Middle Eastern nations are struggling with. But it is politically dangerous to attack the population issue squarely; indeed, it is the rare politician who opts to champion a policy of population control. After all, the issue strikes at the very core of family life. More often, governments simply do not enter public discussion of the issue. Some governments, notably Iraq, provide explicit economic incentives and public applause for those with large families.

Egypt provides a classic and sad case of an overpopulated country. Its population doubled in less than thirty years, exceeding 50 million in 1990. Virtually all of the jump is attributable to natural increases. Since almost all of the arable land in Egypt is along the Nile River and Delta, this narrow strip is one of the most densely populated areas in the world. Because the amount of arable land, although increasing somewhat through irrigation, is close to being constant, there has been ever increasing pressure on the land to produce more. But the additional labor can do little to add to production since the methods employed already are highly labor intensive. This combination of population increase and a constant amount of land to be worked is close to fitting the Malthusian dilemma of population increase resulting in permanent subsistence living. Egypt has avoided taking the dreary course predicted by Malthus through the application of modest technological advances, a reorganization of landholding patterns, greater availability of water from the Aswan Dam, and the shifting of crops from cotton to food. Egypt still has to import food, however. The race between productivity and population has been close. A sanguine outcome is not assured partially because the continuing high rate of population increase has led to urban sprawl that is covering prime agricultural land. Further, land reclamation has proved to be ever-more difficult, and water shortages have been felt.

Cairo holds about 20 percent of the population of Egypt. Although some of the increase in the past four decades, from 2 million in 1950 to 10 million in 1990, can be attributed to flight from the war-torn cities of the Suez Canal area, most of it has been due to people leaving the farms. Once in the cities, the rural people have not been assimilated easily or quickly. Indeed, they often form pockets of essentially rural culture and lifestyles that are surprisingly resistant to change. Projections of urban populations for the year 2000 include four metropolitan areas in the Middle East that will exceed 10 million: Cairo (13.1), Tehran (11.3), Istanbul (11.2), and Baghdad (11.1).

It is quite clear that the movement of people from rural to urban settings upsets traditional patterns, but it is not clear whether or not these changes should be considered beneficial or dysfunctional. Generally the rural migrants do not have skills useful in the urban environment. Further, there is considerable worldwide evidence that at least for the first several years in an urban setting, the individual is apt to be alienated from the urban society and has considerable difficulty in adapting to the regimen of factory life if he is lucky enough to land a job in the first place. Tardiness, absenteeism, and quit rates are generally quite high. The factory, it seems, is a particularly difficult place to adjust to. At the same time, evidence (from areas other than the Middle East) indicates that the factory is the single most effective source from which to accumulate that set of attitudes which are considered "modern." A rapid increase in the population of major cities also can lead to the breakdown of city services. Transportation becomes a nightmare as thousands of vehicles are jammed into what is essentially a pre-twentieth-century road network; electrical supply capacity is strained; the telephone system becomes virtually unworkable. On the other hand, it is easy to generate arguments to indicate that if the migrants stayed in a rural setting, per capita income and possibly agricultural production would fall: Besides having one less mouth to feed, the farmer often receives remittances from the family member in the city; this can finance technical change. Since government actions, fiscal and otherwise, have pronounced effects on the flow of labor to urban areas, one must also consider how those flows will change when particular measures are being considered. For instance, will an attempt to improve urban conditions merely lead to an increased flow into the cities and thus thwart the original effort and disrupt agricultural planning? A related urban bias problem is that usually one city is favored. For example, in Syria, Damascus garners many more resources than Aleppo; but the resource base of the country is closer to Aleppo than Damascus.

Employment

Most countries profess full employment as a primary goal. A brief account of a government's problems in attempting to meet this goal may give the reader a sense of the complexity of designing a coherent employment scheme. The first job is to figure out what percentage of the population is to be counted as part of the labor force. Middle Eastern countries have a high percentage of people who are generally considered to be out of the labor force: Between 50 and 55 percent of the working age (ages fifteen to sixty-four) population (Table 10-3). The comparable figure for high-income industrial market economies is about 67 percent. In a rough way this means that two workers in the high-income countries help "support" one person not in the labor force, whereas in the Middle East each worker "supports" another person (Table 10-3). The calculation of these *dependency ratios* gives the government a first glimpse of the magnitude of the problem it faces; but these are slippery statistics that need immense revision and more information if they are to be useful in formulating policy. For example, defining members of the labor force involves questions concerning the role of women and the minimum acceptable age of entry into the labor force, issues that are not easily resolved.

The task of the planner and analyst of the labor force is further complicated by the obvious fact that individuals are not interchangeable parts—the illiterate construction worker cannot be placed in a job for a materials engineer. An economy may have labor shortages in some areas and surpluses in others. Correcting the perceived imbalances is not an easy task, especially considering that many of the high-skill positions demand relatively advanced formal education. It is not clear, for example, to what extent the goal should be that of universal primary education, the strengthening of the secondary school environment, or expanded opportunities for higher education. Several governments adopted policies that virtually guaranteed employment to indigenous workers of a certain level of educational attainment. These policies are not limited to petroleum-rich states. For example, for many years Egypt guaranteed government employment to all college graduates. The combination of limited employment opportunities and heavy government subsidization of university education resulted in a bloated bureaucracy. Studies, including one commissioned by the government, indicated that in Cairo alone about one quarter of a million government employees had no function except to receive their salary. While this policy lowers the measured level of unemployment, there are obvious gross inefficiencies.

As Table 10-6 hints at, the economic role of females in the Middle East is much different from that of males. One could argue that placing the productive power of females in the labor force runs against long-standing cultural norms: These are arguments familiar in the West. However, it cannot be denied that the disparity in education and general social roles has enormous consequences. This is true even if the female were consigned to household chores. An overwhelming amount of evidence collected worldwide indicates, for example, that when females are literate it follows that infant mortality, low birth weights, wasting, and child stunting all fall. The rather breathless pace of social and economic change in the Middle East in the past several decades has led to substantial change in the role of women and substantial confusion with respect to what could and ought to follow.

Most observers would agree that there are significant labor problems in the agricultural sector of most less-developed countries. Typically, however, one does not find much open unemployment in agriculture; rather the problem is one of underemployment. *Underemployment* can be described as a situation where at least some of the labor force is not working to full capacity. The usual implication is that these "surplus" workers could be freed from agricultural work with little or no decrease in output. But this conclusion is not necessarily the correct one and is, in any case, too simplistic. For instance, there is a tremendous seasonal fluctuation in the demand for agricultural labor in most of the Middle East. Labor must be available on a standby basis to perform essential tasks. Another qualification is that the

TABLE 10-6. SELECTED MALE-FEMALE GAPS IN THE MIDDLE EAST.

	FEMALES AS A PERCENTAGE OF MALES		
	LITERACY RATE	MEAN YEARS OF SCHOOLING	LABOR FORCE
COUNTRY	1970	1985	1980	1988
Kuwait	65	84	78	16
Qatar	—	94	83	8
Bahrain	—	81	67	11
U.A.E.	29	—	74	7
Saudi Arabia	3	61	26	8
Turkey	49	73	48	32
Syria	33	59	47	7
Libya	22	57	26	10
Jordan	45	72	66	11
Oman	—	26	23	9
Lebanon	73	80	66	37
Iraq	36	64	66	6
Iran	43	61	66	21
Algeria	28	56	20	5
Egypt	40	49	42	16
Yemen	15	44	18	15
All Developing	54	66	53	52
Industrial	—	—	94	66

Source: U.N.D.P., *Human Development Report 1991.* New York: Oxford University Press, 1991.

labor force in agriculture is not homogeneous; custom dictates that some tasks are to be performed by men and others by women and children. Since the household (extended or nuclear) is the basis of most small farms in the Middle East, it becomes difficult to sort out the work patterns of the various types of labor. Generally, it seems that the cycle of seasonal work for men, although substantial, is less pronounced than that for women and children.

Equity considerations and efficiency also may clash when rural land use and labor deployment policies are being considered. It seems that large plots require less seasonal labor than small plots. Although the reasons for this tend to be specific to the area under study, generally we can assume that the cultivator of the larger plot has greater access to capital inputs (for example, chemical fertilizers, pesticides, tractors). A policy of creating larger plots, therefore, would free underemployed labor and make it available for other productive uses. But there are several conflicts involved in this approach; a move toward larger plots is not easily accomplished. Considerations of equity have led a large number of countries to legislate land reform programs designed to result in smaller-sized holdings. If seasonal laborers could be released from the land, one must then determine where they would be employed. Industrial growth on a substantial scale is needed to absorb this labor, and that growth has not been forthcoming in most of the countries under consideration. Also, since women and children are most apt to be seasonal workers, it presumably would be they who would be freed for alternative employment. Obviously, there would be considerable resistance to any such move.

Another problem in evaluating the labor force is that urban unemployment is open and obvious as contrasted to that in the agricultural sector. Therefore, the planner may begin with a bias and develop plans that commit more resources to urban areas than are warranted by strictly economic criteria. This tendency is buttressed both because of the politically volatile nature of the urban population and because most notions of modernity, both naive and sophisticated, link industrialization and industry to urbanization.

INDUSTRY

Because of OPEC's success, industry in the Middle East has grown dramatically. There are several prerequisites for large-scale, sustained industrial growth. Systems of communication, power, transportation, and education are needed if a modern industrial structure is to emerge and prosper. The history of all of the industrialized countries of the world indicates that this process takes a long time, that it generally proceeds by fits and starts, and that "economic miracles" have their roots in earlier centuries, not decades. But because of OPEC, several oil-rich economies are being transformed at an unprecedented rate.

Until the spectacular increase in the price of petroleum, Egypt, Turkey, and Iran were the focus of most speculation about the course of industrialization in the Middle East. They have large populations, thus providing the potential for domestic markets, as well as a longer history of significant industrial activity than the other countries of the region. Industrialization in Egypt received its first substantial impetus under Muhammad Ali in the 1820s. This ambitious attempt ground to a halt after a couple of decades and was largely moribund until the 1920s, when

Egypt received a measure of independence. Industrialization in Egypt moved slowly for the next thirty years; it finally began to receive close attention in the 1950s under Nasser. The 1960s in Egypt saw the large-scale nationalization (and weak industrial performance) of major industries; during the post-Nasser period there was a selective encouragement of private enterprise.

Iran began to industrialize more than a century later than Egypt. The years between World War II and 1960 were spent laying a foundation upon which industrialization could occur. Fueled by petroleum revenues, the growth process accelerated. By the middle of the 1970s, per capita income in Iran was about five times that of Egypt, up from less than double in 1960. In any discussion of the future of industrialization in the two countries, most observers favored Iran. Petroleum sales provided the money to purchase capital goods and to quickly train a "modern" labor force. (In 1978, one out of every nine international students studying in the United States was Iranian.) However, the Iranian revolution and the war with Iraq seriously disrupted economic activity in Iran and made the predictions of sustained industrial growth questionable.

Lebanon and Kuwait provide another set of contrasts. Lebanon has a long history of commercial and industrial development. Its relatively mature economy, its geographic position, and its tradition as the financial hub of the Middle East allowed some impressive industrial growth during the 1960s and the first half of the 1970s. Since most of the industrial establishments were centered in and around Beirut, however, the devastation of that city beginning in 1976 halted Lebanon's industrial and financial activity. Kuwait, long an earner of substantial amounts of foreign exchange through petroleum sales, attempted to diversify its industry and not rely exclusively on petroleum-related production. The Iraqi invasion of 1991, of course, put that process on hold. Bahrain has a different set of problems. The Shia of Bahrain constitute a majority of the population but are in a decidedly disadvantageous economic and social position. Since many of the Bahraini Shia have close cultural and ethnic ties to Iran, the Sunni leadership has evinced considerable concern. But Bahrain does not produce enough petroleum to finance large-scale, employment-generating industry. It is no surprise, therefore, that Bahrain has been in the forefront of GCC members calling for closer economic cooperation in ways which would ameliorate unemployment.

Saudi Arabia and Libya are more recent entrants in the race to industrialize. Even though petroleum production in Saudi Arabia started a quarter century earlier than in Libya, it was only during the 1970s that a concerted effort to industrialize began. Iraq, the other major petroleum producer in the area, also can be expected to be transformed substantially if and when sustained stability "breaks out." Indeed, Iraq seems to have the most favorable balance of resources of all the countries surveyed.

PETROLEUM

Oil has been called "black gold"—and for good reason. Petroleum has been the focus of many a country's national and international affairs during this century. Indeed, petroleum has been so important to everyday life that this has been dubbed "the age of Hydrocarbon Man."

The vital need to secure adequate supplies has been complicated by the fact that it has been exceedingly difficult to predict when supplies will run dry or be multiplied by the development of a new field. It is only with mild hyperbole, then, that European control of Middle Eastern petroleum at the onset of World War I prompted Britain's Lord Curzon to remark that "...the Allies floated to victory on a wave of oil." About a half a century later, some were predicting that the rise in petroleum prices would create a new Arab Golden Age. The clearest recent example of the worldwide importance of steady petroleum supplies is shown by the Western response to Iraq's 1991 invasion of Kuwait. Petroleum is the dominant economic influence in the Middle East, and Middle Eastern petroleum is vital to the economies of the world. Finally, petroleum has been responsible for one of the most rapid transfers of wealth in world history—a true revolution.

The Early Years

The half century preceding World War I was a time of rapid change in the Middle East. The Ottoman Empire was in disarray and decaying despite sporadic bursts of energy and direction. Turkey and Egypt accumulated very heavy public debts; one third of Turkey's government expenditures and one half of Egypt's were applied to debt servicing. Turkey was declared bankrupt in 1875 and Egypt in 1876. European interests in the area were becoming more pervasive and were setting the stage for twentieth-century events.

By the turn of the century, most major investments in the Middle East were European in origin and ownership. European domination, of course, did not begin with these investments. Western influence was substantial well before Napoleon occupied Egypt in 1798, as commerce between the two areas grew. European investments in dams, canals, railroads, and electrical systems built up gradually as the Middle East became more secure. But the surge of nationalism in the Middle East around the beginning of the twentieth century forced Europeans to relinquish direct control of some of their investments.

In the two centuries preceding the opening of the Suez Canal, Britain gained control of the Persian Gulf through a series of military maneuvers and treaties with local sheikhs. The route from India through the Persian Gulf, up through Basra and Baghdad, and then to Mediterranean ports provided a vital communications link for the British Empire until the opening of the Suez Canal. The area was again central to British interests in the 1890s because Britain wished to thwart German influences and because of the discovery of substantial amounts of petroleum in Iran.

After securing control of the Suez Canal, the British had been content to control commerce on the Persian Gulf and not travel inland; but the discovery of a large petroleum field in Iran in 1907 changed their intentions. The Industrial Revolution, although first fueled by coal, was becoming increasingly dependent on oil and other petroleum products. Petroleum products also were becoming increasingly valuable for military uses. Therefore, large consumers sought a steady and dependable supply. By 1900, the United States and Russia produced 90 percent of the world's petroleum. When the Iranian field east of Abadan was discovered, the British moved to assure their control over the area. Although the British had concessions for Iranian petroleum as early as 1872 (and then in 1889 and 1901), the rights were not considered particularly valuable. In 1908 the Anglo-Persian Oil

Company (later changed to Anglo-Iranian) was founded. As tensions in Europe heightened, British needs for a dependable source of petroleum increased, partially because the British navy was converting its fleet from coal to oil. In May 1914, about three months before European hostilities broke into widespread conflict, the British government acquired a 50 percent interest in the venture.

The finds in Iran stimulated exploration for petroleum in southern Iraq. The results of negotiations completed in 1912 allowed for the formation of the Turkish Petroleum Company (TPC). The TPC was reorganized in 1914 and again in 1920, when German interests were removed and France and the United States moved in. The participation of U.S. firms was accomplished through vigorous diplomatic activity. In 1920 there was widespread fear of an impending oil shortage in the United States. Indeed, the U.S. government even considered direct government participation instead of relying on private enterprise, but decided against it.

The agreement that formed the TPC, later renamed the Iraqi Petroleum Company (IPC), contained a proviso that limited the seeking of concessions to the area within the Ottoman Empire that was shown by a red line drawn on a map. The Red Line Agreement stated that the individual companies in the IPC would not act in a fashion that would upset the balance of company power within the red line. They were not to operate any other fields in the area and thereby gain relative power.

Although British interests had the only concessions in Arabia, there was no production there until 1934. In 1930 Standard Oil of California (SoCal) had gained an option from a British syndicate for Bahrain. Petroleum was found in 1932, and exports started to flow two years later. In 1933 SoCal gained the concession for the al-Hasa province of Saudi Arabia. Petroleum was found a few years later. In 1934 Gulf Oil and British Petroleum (BP) entered Kuwait.

The entry of U.S. firms into Saudi Arabia and the subsequent development of the huge oil fields found there threatened the dominance of the IPC, especially after SoCal joined with Texaco in 1936 to form the Arabian-American Oil Company (ARAMCO) in order to take advantage of the Far Eastern marketing network of Texaco.

The fear of a petroleum shortage immediately after World War I sparked a flurry of exploration during the next two decades. World supply had increased markedly by 1930 through various major fields coming into production, most notably in the Far East, Middle East, Venezuela, and the United States. With the increased world supply and more oil firms in the market, the "majors" maneuvered futilely to retain control of the world petroleum market.

Petroleum was in abundant supply during the worldwide Depression of the 1930s. As machines were turned off due to the Depression, so also was the demand for petroleum products: The fears of an oil shortage turned into fears of a large and continuing glut. The sustained Depression, especially in the United States, caused changes in the structure of the petroleum industry. Weak firms, especially those that were not vertically integrated, generally failed.

World War II to 1970

By the beginning of World War II, it was apparent that Middle Eastern petroleum would be vital to the world oil market. The United States, although supplying much of the petroleum products needed by the Allies during World War II, feared that its postwar position would be weak. Again there was talk of the need for direct government participation and for protecting the U.S. position in the Middle East. Saudi Arabia provided the United States with a major foothold in the Middle East. In efforts to keep the support of the Saudis, lend-lease agreements were put into force whereby the British actually extended the aid since Saudi Arabia was not eligible for direct U.S. aid. It should be remembered that Saudi Arabia was still a very poor country and received only modest revenues from the petroleum industry. The Saudis needed aid. Largely because the United States feared that the British would use their influence as intermediaries to curry Saudi favor, Saudi Arabia was made eligible for direct lend-lease aid in 1944. But there was another problem; the Saudi government wanted to increase production in order to increase its revenue. The U.S. government wanted to assure an adequate supply, but ARAMCO did not have the financial resources necessary to substantially expand Saudi production. The U.S. government first planned to buy directly into ARAMCO and then to build a pipeline to the Mediterranean in return for preferential prices and guaranteed strategic reserves. Both plans failed to come to fruition, and the U.S. government finally (1948) arranged with the financially stronger Standard Oil of New Jersey (later named Exxon) and Mobil, both IPC members, to buy into ARAMCO (30 percent and 10 percent, respectively). The entry of these IPC members signaled the end of the Red Line Agreement.

By 1948 seven Western companies controlled Middle Eastern oil: four were based in the United States—Standard Oil of New Jersey, Mobil, SoCal, and Texaco; one was British—British Petroleum; and one was a joint Dutch-British venture—Royal Dutch/Shell.

The selling price of any product, of course, is determined by the interaction of supply and demand. Although the record of the petroleum industry after World War II is too complex to be forced into a couple of equations, it is nevertheless instructive to highlight these two basic forces. The tremendous worldwide economic expansion that occurred in the decades following World War II increased the demand for petroleum products considerably. In addition, the Western nations and Japan were building energy-intensive societies and shifting ever greater percentages of their energy sources from coal to oil. The combination of these forces meant that the demand for petroleum was doubling every six and a half years.

The steady price of petroleum throughout the 1950s and most of the 1960s indicates that the supply of petroleum was increasing at about the same pace as the demand. The character of the industry, however, was changing in substantial ways. New independent firms were entering the petroleum industry, and the producing countries themselves began to feel new strength. The entry of more firms into the industry meant, quite simply, that the seven firms that controlled Middle Eastern petroleum production were slowly losing their influence in the market. Governments demanding greater revenues from petroleum exploitation were thus in a better position to bargain. For example, because of its very heavy reliance on Libyan production, Occidental Oil was more likely to respect Libyan demands for increased monies than if it had had widely diversified holdings. In contrast, the Iranian attempts at nationalization of the petroleum producers in 1951 failed in large part because of the relatively plentiful and more diversified world supply. During the 1950s and 1960s, the Middle East was also becoming relatively more important with respect to production and proven reserves. During the 1960s it became clear to close observers of the scene that there had been a fundamental change in the market: A greater percentage of world supply originated in the Middle East, petroleum supplies started to lag behind demand in the latter part of the decade, and an upward pressure on prices began to be felt.

The OPEC Revolution

The Organization of Petroleum Exporting Countries (OPEC) did not have any significant power in the first decade of its existence (1960–1970). The organization of the industry and the plentiful and diversified supply of oil blunted any thoughts about manipulating the market. However, the situation had changed markedly by 1970. During that year the postrevolution government of Libya started negotiations for substantially increased payments from the petroleum companies. Algeria and Iran had gained better concessions in 1969. Although these actions represented a breakthrough for the producing countries, they were also viewed as special cases. Revolutionary Libya, strongly backed by "radical" Algeria and Iraq, called for much greater revenue increases than previously sought and threatened outright expropriation if its demands were not met. Libya succeeded for various reasons: World supply and demand conditions, aggravated by the 1967 closure of the Suez Canal, caused prices to rise; the Occidental Oil Company was vulnerable because almost all of the petroleum for its European operations came from Libya; the companies operating in the Middle East were unable to form a common front; the home governments of the oil companies could not bring any unified pressure to bear on the producing countries; and OPEC was presenting a relatively united front. Prices were increased further after President Nixon's August 1971 announcement of a proposed devaluation of the U.S. dollar (which meant that the dollar earnings of the petroleum exporting countries would lose purchasing power). They also rose because of a continuing decline in U.S. petroleum production, worldwide inflation, and unabated increases in petroleum demand. Upward pressure on prices and calls for increased participation, partial ownership, and outright expropriation continued through 1973.

Intense negotiations between OPEC and the oil companies through the first ten months of 1973 resulted in substantially higher posted prices. These increases came without direct reference to the Arab-Israeli situation. Members of OPEC, Arab and non-Arab, were simply exploiting worldwide market conditions; they were seeking to get as much revenue as possible before their precious natural resource was depleted. The decline in the value of the U.S. dollar was eroding the purchasing power of petrodollar earnings, giving more reason to increase prices.

The 1973 Arab-Israeli war provided the catalyst that permitted the Arab members of OPEC an opportunity to flex some economic muscle and to see petroleum prices (roughly) quadruple in less than a year. Any such dramatic OPEC action needed the support of the largest producing nation, Saudi Arabia. King Faisal needed to be convinced that this bold and dangerous move was the proper policy: Saudi conservatism and substantial Saudi ties to the United States dictated against a precipitous break with past policy. However, Western, and particularly U.S., support for Israel during and immediately after the 1973 war convinced the Saudi leadership that a dramatic increase in the price of petroleum and a selective embargo by the Arab members of OPEC was necessary to change Western policy.

The embargo was lifted in March 1974. The higher prices remained. The industrial world struggled through the next couple of years attempting to adjust to the change. Of particular importance were the massive balance-of-payments problems that resulted from the price increase and the related—but not necessarily causally determined—inflation that continued to plague them. A simple example will clarify what was happening. Assume that the United States was producing the same amount of goods each year. Now suppose that the price of imported oil increased and the United States continued to import the same number of barrels. More dollars were flowing out of the United States, and less were being spent by U.S. consumers on U.S. goods. Now suppose that the exporting country spent all of those earned dollars on U.S. goods. With the same total amount of money being spent on the same total amount of goods, the straightforward result is that the oil producer had more goods and the United States had less. The only way out of this situation was to eliminate spending on imports by conserving energy and developing internal sources.

The U.S. government, however, failed to respond with a clearly defined program. Attempts to develop comprehensive energy programs floundered throughout the decade. Instead, individual actors, aided by a pliant government, attempted to recoup their losses by spending more. In terms of our simple scenario, they pumped more money into the system. More money chasing the same amount of goods results in inflation. And inflation meant that members of OPEC could purchase less with each petrodollar earned. OPEC, therefore, raised prices in order to recoup its position. The 1970s inflation in the United States was not caused primarily by OPEC actions; rather, continued U.S. inflation virtually guaranteed further rounds of OPEC price increases. Since the United States remained the most powerful economy in the industrialized world, it transmitted these problems to other countries.

Although the situation was far more complicated than the foregoing description suggests—especially important were the complications that arose from the exporting countries not spending all of the petrodollars they earned—it represents the nub of the issue. The members of OPEC had control of a large enough percentage of world petroleum supplies to call the tune. They had become a full-fledged cartel that controlled the supply in the supply/demand equations. Most petroleum companies clearly understood these shifting power relationships by the late 1960s. At least one went so far as to launch an advertising campaign calling for a more sympathetic view of the Arab cause with respect to Israel. Others sent similar messages to official Washington. They knew that they were engaged in a rear-guard action and were attempting to forestall the inevitable. The U.S. public had another point of view. Most people saw the situation as resulting from a U.S. government blunder or from oil company actions. Conspiracy theories abounded. It was as if the public could not quite believe that a group of Third World countries could have the power to foment such disorder and then "get away with it." Indeed, it was the first time that a group of Third World countries had secured such a position.

The Third World countries that had begun to industrialize but had no oil could not fully share in the jubilation. Instead, they suffered. They were not economically strong enough to adopt the Western attitude of considering the price increases to be an unfortunate irritant that caused problems but nevertheless could be lived with. The major Arab members of OPEC responded to the plight of the poorer countries by stepping up their aid programs. The Western nations had surrendered their grip on the political systems of the Third World during the preceding years of the century. Was the success of OPEC the first major victory of a future economic war?

None of the foregoing should suggest that the OPEC members all agree on the extent of the price increases. The position of any individual country depends on its particular economic needs. The countries aiming for very high prices generally have economies that could absorb all of the goods that petrodollars could buy; they have reasonably solid industrial bases and large populations. Iran and Iraq are the Middle Eastern members of OPEC that most readily fit this pattern. The price moderates, led by Saudi Arabia, generally are countries with large petroleum reserves, small populations, and less developed economies. At least in the early years of OPEC success, they did not have the ability (nor the desire) to spend all of the petroleum earnings to strengthen their economies.

Another round of significant petroleum price increases was initiated by OPEC in 1979—this time the price was roughly doubled (from $15 to $30 a barrel). Worldwide inflation since the first (1973) round of increases had eroded the purchasing power of their earnings considerably. However, several objective conditions affecting the petroleum market had changed markedly since the first round of price increases. First, there were more significant non-OPEC sources of petroleum that came on-line in the intervening period, the Mexican and North Sea fields being two prominent examples. Second, many heavy petroleum-using countries had adopted significant conservation measures. Third, the industrialized world suffered a rather deep recession during 1980–1982. These increases in supplies and decreases in demand put downward pressure on prices. It should be remembered that reductions in individual supplier output is the mechanism through which price increases can be made effective. But several members of OPEC felt that they could not reduce supplies, and therefore their foreign exchange, without causing harm to their economies. There were significant defections from the posted price and output goals, Nigeria being the most important.

During the first half of the 1980s, OPEC managed to hold together through a series of complex technical maneuvers and price rollbacks. The organization was aided in its efforts through a reduction of Iranian and Iraqi output caused by the war, and a strong U.S. dollar. Most petroleum sales are denominated in U.S. dollars. When the U.S. economy began (1982) growing at a robust rate with lower inflation and high real interest rates, the value of the dollar increased relative to the currencies of most of its trading partners. This meant, for example, that the petrodollars could buy more Deutschmarks than before, and thus more German goods. Thus, a constant dollar petroleum price translated into increased purchasing power.

Petroleum prices started a remarkable downward slide in late 1985. By the end of the first quarter of 1986, petroleum prices were close to the 1974 level (about $12 a barrel). There were several reasons for the decline: They include larger worldwide supplies from new fields and a decision by Saudi Arabia to increase its output. The Saudi decision deserves some comment.

Saudi Arabia is the largest producer in OPEC. Furthermore, it acted as the "swing" producer—it was Saudi Arabia more than any other that changed its supplies so as to have the supply-demand equations yield the agreed price. As more non-OPEC petroleum entered the world market, the Saudis decreased production. Because of a complex of unfavorable worldwide economic conditions, many OPEC producers found themselves financially strapped by the early 1980s. They responded by increasing production beyond the limit they agreed to as members of OPEC. Saudi Arabia was in an increasingly tenuous situation. Finally, by late 1985, it felt that it had to increase production. It doubled production in the following months—and at that was producing only one-half of its capacity.

The slide of petroleum prices would have occurred without Saudi action: Their decision, however, made the decline steep and rapid. Those petroleum exporters with massive debt problems (for example, Mexico, Nigeria, Indonesia) were dealt a harsh blow. So was Iran. Petroleum accounts for the overwhelming majority of the foreign exchange earnings of Iran. It is not by chance that Iran initiated a vigorous offensive against Iraq in early 1986, and threatened to widen the war to the Gulf states if the Saudis insisted on driving the price of petroleum down by producing more and by continuing to provide Iraq with financial aid for the war effort.

OPEC reached another agreement in 1988: the price of petroleum was to increase several dollars (to $18) through a complicated rearrangement of production quotas. It was impossible to increase the price to previous peaks due to increased world supplies. However, some action was needed to ease national budgetary burdens. For example, despite massive war-related aid from Saudi Arabia and Kuwait, Iraq had accumulated a staggering debt burden. Even the Saudis felt the pinch: Their petroleum revenues fell to about $20 billion in 1988 from a peak exceeding $100 billion in the early 1980s. Although the price of petroleum went up to $40 after the invasion of Kuwait, increased Saudi supplies quickly brought it back to about $18. The real (purchasing power) price of petroleum in early 1992 was lower than the mid-1960s.

Many analysts interpreted the weakened position of OPEC as the long-predicted demise of the cartel. While the spectacular successes of OPEC during the 1970s are not likely to be repeated, it should be kept in mind that it is also predicted that the production from many of the major non-OPEC fields will decrease in relative importance by the mid-1990s. The Middle Eastern members of OPEC still hold the lion's share of world petroleum reserves, and it is possible that their ability to influence the market will increase substantially before we enter the twenty-first century.

The future of OPEC is uncertain. Its past was remarkable. The powerful industrialized countries of the world are dependent on OPEC supplies. Being dependent, these countries have had to reorder their policies toward the Middle East, especially their attitudes and actions toward Arab-Israeli hostilities. Petroleum became a political tool of the first order after 1973; alliances had to be altered and new approaches to conflict resolution developed.

CONCLUSION

Increasing resource imbalance, led by rapid population growth, has a distinct tendency to accelerate a degradation of the quality of life without necessarily triggering self-corrective mechanisms. Gently put, the growing resource disparities in the Middle East are straining the capabilities of the political system. Bluntly, conflicts are bound to multiply as the system spins out of control. A major challenge, then, exists. One nettlesome dimension is that a forward-looking policy often demands the imposition of painful short-run measures (for example, placing a price on water use) that will yield noticeable benefits only in the long run while the majority of political leaders have only a short time to satisfy the demands of their populations. There are powerful political incentives to ignore fundamental problems until they cannot be avoided; that is, until there is a crisis. Lives hang in the balance.

Of course, not all instances of a degraded quality of life result from the long accretion of pressures and ignored long-term remedies: War quickly can undo decades or even centuries of change. The deliberate torching of 640 of Kuwait's petroleum wells by retreating Iraqi forces is the most spectacular case in point. Although the last of the fires was snuffed out much more quickly than anticipated (by December 1991, instead of a few years later), the manifold effects will take decades to (partially) understand. Of course, the Kuwaiti desert, the air, the Gulf water experienced immediate trauma. But more subtle effects were at work. Bahrain, some 200 miles to the south, experienced its coldest summer in a millennium; oil-soaked rain fell thousands of miles away, and it is anybody's guess to what has happened to the geological structure of the fields.

The coalition's destruction of the Iraqi infrastructure brought another set of shocks. For example, Iraqi infant mortality quadrupled in the year following the end of the war. The U.N.–imposed sanctions on imports to Iraq had another set of consequences—many more thousands died for want of medicine and hundreds of thousands suffered malnutrition, a condition that can have profound life-long implications for the young. Massive epidemics became highly probable.

The sudden and spectacular loss of life caused by the Gulf war sometimes blinds observers to the relatively gradual and potentially more pernicious effects of high rates of population growth in a setting where complementary resources are growing more slowly. The following simple linear causal chain illustrates one aspect of the problem: population growth increases the demand for food, which calls for more irrigated land, which strains water resources and leads to contaminated water supplies, which spreads disease, which decreases human productivity, which leads to lower real income. The issues, of course, are far more complicated: Conflicts about property rights surface, the health care system becomes overburdened, the educational system falls into crisis, and social conflicts generally increase.

It is the prudent analyst who shuns the opportunity to predict the specific path and shape of future Middle Eastern economic realities and ideologies. One of the central lessons of chaos theory is that the course of complex systems is impossible to predict. A related maxim from that body of theory is that there are complex causal links and feedback mechanisms between variables usually thought to be unrelated—folk culture, economics, the physical environment, the arts, and notions of the "good life" are part of the same cloth.

At the same time, humans organize themselves for purposive ends; the behavior of purposive actors count. Because of the obvious resource imbalances in the Middle East, thoughtful policies must be devised and tinkered with as conditions change. This challenge is most often focused in the political arena.

INTERNATIONAL RELATIONS IN THE CONTEMPORARY MIDDLE EAST: 1945–1990

One of the predictable characteristics of all international orders has been the concentration of power in a small number of states. Thus, at any moment in time, one can identify a short list of international actors with power and influence well beyond the capacities of most other states. It is inevitable that these states, at some point, will come into conflict with one another. And it is equally plausible that they will externalize those conflicts into their mutual relations with other states. Earlier chapters in this book, for example, have described the role played by the great powers of Europe in the establishment of the contemporary state system in the Middle East. And in this and in the succeeding two chapters we will place great emphasis on the architectonic effect of the bipolar conflict between the United States and the Soviet Union. Until very recently, the very late 1980s in fact, the way in which most of us looked at the world was determined by this contest for global hegemony.

Although one can define international relations strictly in terms of the contests between great powers for relative advantage over the others (the "Great Game," as it has been called), to restrict the analysis to these actors would eliminate much of importance. The effect of this competition on weaker states is important, particularly to those weaker states themselves. It would also be inappropriate to assume that because the so-called great powers were economically and militarily powerful that their diplomacy and decision making was somehow more rational or insightful than the diplomacy of other states. Finally, we would caution against the assumption that great power status is somehow immune to the laws of nature or physics. In fact, the inevitability of the decline of great powers is well-known fact.[1] The dissolution of the Soviet Union in 1991 and U.S. attempts to orchestrate world events from a position of *relative* decline are but the latest demonstration of this process.

[1] See, for example, Paul Kennedy, *The Rise and Fall of the Great Powers: Economic Change and Military Conflict from 1500–2000* (New York: Random House, 1987).

The international system has many features not found in national political orders. The most important of these features is the lack of a legitimate sovereign power, or even of some entity with a viable claim to the exercise of sovereign power. In comparison to the average national system, the international system is nearly anarchic—political power is at once broadly diffused among its actors and yet enormously concentrated among a few. Furthermore, international power is transitory and difficult to assess comparatively.

The actors that compose the international order have a power base that can be broken down into three areas: *economic power*, or the power to produce or acquire material goods; *political power*, or the power to coerce or influence their own populations or the populations of other states; and *military power*, the ability to gain goals through the direct application of organized coercive force. These capabilities are not distributed evenly among the actors in the international system. Saudi Arabia, for instance, possesses enormous economic power based on its extensive oil reserves, but has a population insufficient in size and technical sophistication to maintain a truly international military capability. Egypt, by contrast, has a large population sufficiently skilled to maintain a large military machine, but lacks the economic base to develop it without foreign aid. The relative international power of Saudi Arabia and Egypt, then, must be calculated on different bases, quantitative and qualitative. This enormously complicates the calculations involved in international politics, particularly since one actor's analysis of the capability of another is a core determinant of its foreign policy.

The relationships between international actors embrace a wide field of human activity. International relations occur at many levels and in many functional arenas. For example, no state can isolate itself from international trade, for to do so it would have to greatly reduce its economic activity. Thus, any nation finds it necessary and desirable to allow the movements of goods and services into its territory as varying amounts of goods and services flow out. Most states, then, are involved in some level of international economic exchange that requires cooperation with both friendly and potentially unfriendly powers. It is instructive to note that at the nadir of Iranian-American relations, Iranian oil was still being imported by the United States at the rate of some 80,000 barrels per day—a fact as politically unpalatable to President Carter as to Ayatollah Khomeini. International relations, then, possess a logic to some degree independent of the best wishes or intentions of their actors—or to put it another way, international politics and economics make strange bedfellows.

Actors in the international system pursue a combination of specific and general goals that can be lumped together under the term *national interest*. The national interest presumably directs the foreign policy of a nation, at least at the strategic level. For instance, the national interest of the Soviet Union (now the Commonwealth of Independent States) has long required a safe, warm-water port, while the contemporary U.S. national interest requires regular delivery of petroleum from its Middle East sources. Needless to say, these two national interest goals have a potential for conflict in the area of the Persian (Arabian) Gulf.

The problem in analyzing international relations strictly from the national interest viewpoint can be summarized briefly. First, nations may in fact not clearly perceive their true national interests: American involvement in Vietnam in the 1960s is a case in point. Second, power, the base of implementation of national interest, is an enormously complex entity. Miscalculations of one's own power, or the reputed power of another actor injects a quality of uncertainty into international relations. An example is Nasser's miscalculation of Israeli responses to his mobilization in 1967. Finally, international relations are only rarely dyadic—that is, involving only two nations. Although for analytic purposes we often discuss foreign policy in dyadic terms, most international exchanges involve the interests of secondary and tertiary actors. These complex intersections of national interests—both primary and secondary, immediate, and long-term—create the Gordian knots of the international process. All too often the solution to these problems is war, with its attendant human miseries and material losses.

Finally, it should be noted that in viewing the international system from the perspective of decades and centuries, one perceives dramatic changes taking place. Nations, even entire civilizations, change their positions in the relative power hierarchies of the international system, rising and falling for reasons that are often idiosyncratic or obscure. It is even possible, as was the case with the nineteenth-century Ottoman Empire, for a country to improve its absolute power—to have more financial military and human resources—and still decline *relative* to its competitors (in this case, the emerging national powers of Western Europe and Russia). As intellectually disconcerting as this may be to students of the international system, we live in a time in which just such changes are occurring. The transformation of the U.S.S.R. into the Commonwealth of Independent States (C.I.S.), the new-found political independence of Eastern Europe, the political integration of Western Europe, the dispersal of economic power to new centers, dramatic changes in policy directions in China, quantum increases in the sophistication and utilization of conventional and chemical weapons, and dramatic and unlikely diplomatic initiatives (such as the Palestinian declaration of statehood in December of 1988) force a reevaluation of basic premises upon which foreign policy is predicated.

None of the preceding should be interpreted as denying order or process in international relations. The Middle East, in particular, has seen the rise and fall of many separate international systems. The Middle East witnessed the development of an international theocratic movement during the early days of Islamic expansion, in which the world was seen as a contrast between the *Dar al Islam* (world of peace) and the *Dar al Harb* (world of war). Centralized bureaucratic empires based successively in Damascus, Baghdad, and Cairo arose. Loose relationships between competing centers of power came about as peripheral kingdoms arose in the Maghreb, Spain, Europe, Central Asia, Persia, and India. Later, a consolidation of power occurred in the decentralized millet system of the Ottoman Empire. The intrusion of European imperial power, predicated on a classic balance of power in Europe, began in the nineteenth century. After World War II, the bipolar conflict between the United States and the U.S.S.R. became the influential factor. In the 1990s, yet another international order presents itself, with concomitant challenges and changes in the international environment.

The origins of the contemporary international order can be found in the deterioration of the system that emerged just after World War II and prevailed until the early 1970s. This first order, the bipolar international system, was produced by an unusual concentration of military and economic power in two rival political systems, the United States and the Soviet Union. Perceiving each other as threats to their own national interest as well as to the larger political order, the alliances surrounding these two superpowers grew rigid and confrontational. The term *Cold War*, which applied to the early period following World War II, suggests a confrontation between the two blocs just short of overt military hostilities. During this time, the two superpowers enjoyed a nuclear monopoly and rapidly growing economies. Stymied in their confrontation in Europe, they turned to the nations of the Third World—Africa, Asia, Latin America, and the Middle East—for potential alliance partners in their crusade against international communism or international capitalism.

From the point of view of international actors in the Middle East, this transition was frustrating. Neither the United States nor the Soviet Union had well-established bases in the area. European power, while on the wane and definitely inferior to that of either superpower, was nonetheless still something to contend with. Finally, the ideological claims of both capitalism and communism did not find fertile intellectual soil in the Middle East.

Regional factors also injected themselves into the emerging international order. Primary among them was the creation of Israel in 1948 and its subsequent protection by the United States. This issue, transcending such questions as Arab unity, water resources, economic growth and development, or Islamic resurgence, provided the mechanism for the entrance of bipolar politics into the area. The unevenness of American policy toward the Arab states, combined with its unwillingness to hedge on the question of Israeli security, provided the Soviet Union with an entree, particularly into Egypt, Syria, and Iraq, the major powers confronting the Israeli state. But in spite of great Egyptian, Syrian, and Iraqi dependence on Eastern block sources for weapons and expertise, the U.S.S.R. was unable to capitalize on its advantages domestically in these countries. The United States, for its part, confused the desire for independence in these countries with a drift toward communism and reacted with hostility to Soviet gains there. Thus, the bipolar alliance system did not extend completely into the Middle East, and both Soviet and American policy goals were frustrated.

The 1960s saw the gradual erosion of the eyeball-to-eyeball confrontation between Soviet and American global power. The age of detente ushered in a period in which Soviet and American abilities to control their alliances and dictate their policies declined. The emergence of competing centers of economic and political power—Japan, Western Europe, and China—ultimately produced an international system in which the great powers of the United States and the U.S.S.R. were reduced by the growing economic powers of their allies and by the loss of their nuclear monopoly. The resulting international system, maturing in the late 1980s and ultimately transformed by the dissolution of the U.S.S.R. and the creation of the C.I.S., can best be described as an emerging set of relatively independent power centers orbiting loosely and often erratically around the United States as the last surviving superpower. Moreover, additional sources of international power appeared to be maturing, based on the growing economic and political systems of Asia, Africa, the Middle East, and Latin America. These centers of power were more and more inclined to define national interest in their own terms. All of this contributed to the complexity and potential instability of the international order. Many saw in all of this the emergence of a new international order, a topic that we will take up specifically in our final chapter.

Let us now examine the implications of these changes for the international system that is the Middle East. Our method will be to move from macroanalysis, to regional analysis, and finally to consideration of dyadic relations involving the foreign policies of Egypt, Saudi Arabia, Iran, Iraq, Syria and Israel.

In each of these sections, we will discuss three phases of international relations in the Middle East. Phase I, 1945–1948, embraces the immediate postwar period; Phase II, 1948–1974, includes the period of transition from tight bipolar confrontation to loose bipolar competition; Phase III covers the period from the 1973 Arab-Israeli war and Arab oil embargo to 1990. Phase IV, from 1991 to the present, including the dramatic changes occasioned by the collapse of Soviet power, the causes and consequences of Desert Storm, and the prospects for a negotiated peace between Israel and the Arabs will be discussed in full in the following chapters.

THE GREAT POWER SYSTEM AND THE MIDDLE EAST

In the relatively short span of forty years, actors in the Middle East have gone from a system in which their policies were largely reactive to the policy goals of the United States and U.S.S.R., through a period in which international power appeared to disperse toward other industrial states of the temperate zones, to an international system in which many Middle Eastern nations can realistically view themselves as capable of originating international exchange, politically and economically, and militarily. Some Middle Eastern actors—most notably Saudi Arabia, Egypt, Iraq, Syria and Iran—see themselves as major actors in the international arena. Decisions reached in Riyadh, Cairo, and Tehran now have repercussions in Moscow, Washington, and Tokyo.

The current system contains a number of international power centers that have substantially altered the relative influence of the United States and the U.S.S.R (C.I.S.). This is not to say that the power and national interests of these two megapowers are unimportant. On the contrary, their pursuit of their national interests is in many ways more important and more dangerous given the greater number of probable actors. The primary effects of policy shifts may be predictable, but the secondary and tertiary effects, involving other actors indirectly, are rarely predictable and controllable. For example, as the United States reduced its dependence on Iranian oil imports in the late 1970s (a primary policy decision), Japan and other U.S. allies simultaneously increased their imports of Iranian crude (a secondary effect), which, in effect, increased the vulnerability of these U.S. allies to pressure from Soviet intervention in the Persian Gulf.

Of the two great superpowers, the United States held the more enviable position of power in the Middle East. European (specifically British and French) power in the area was generally replaced by American power. The United States was historically removed from the abuses of colonial policy in the area, and many Arab leaders looked with affection toward the United States. Thus, the period after World War II saw an extension and expansion of U.S. power in the Middle East, oriented toward an alliance system aimed at frustrating Soviet moves, particularly in Turkey and Iran.

Table 11-1 simplifies the foreign policy objectives of the great powers in the Middle East from the end of World War II to the late 1980s. The table suggests some sharp changes in policy over that relatively brief period of time.

TABLE 11-1. FOREIGN POLICY PRIORITIES IN THE MIDDLE EAST, 1945–PRESENT.

PHASE	U.S.A.	SOVIET (C.I.S. AFTER 1990)	EUROPEAN (ENGLAND, FRANCE GERMANY, EC)
I (1945–1948)	1. Extension of influence.	1. Extension of influence into Mediterranean, Turkey, and Iran.	1. Reestablishment of prewar influence.
	2. Exploitation and protection of promising petroleum production in Saudi Arabia and Iran.	2. Frustration of U.S. power and prestige in M.E.	2. Exploitation and protection of petroleum production and trade relations in M.E.
		3. Support of Jewish community in Palestine.	3. Limited support of Jewish migration to Palestine.
II (1948–1974)	1. Support and protection of Israel.	1. Extension of military influence into M.E. via anti-Israeli governments in Syria, Egypt, and Iraq.	1. Maintenance and expansion of petroleum production and trade relations.
	2. Maintenance of influence and prestige against Soviet invasion; Baghdad Pact.	2. Frustration of U.S. power and prestige in M.E.	2. Maintenance of prestige and influence in M.E.
	3. Exploitation and protection of petroleum production in Saudi Arabia and U.A.E.		3. Support of Israel.
III (1974–1990)	1. Support and protection of Israel.	1. Maintenance of influence in Syria and Iraq.	1. Maintenance and expansion of petroleum production and trade relations.
	2. Maintenance of influence and prestige.	2. Frustration of U.S. power and prestige in M.E.; support of national liberation movements in Yemen and Oman, PLO.	2. Compete with U.S.-U.S.S.R. efforts in M.E.
	3. Exploitation and protection of petroleum production in Saudi Arabia and U.A.E.	3. Access to M.E. petroleum and warm-water posts.	

TABLE 11-1. FOREIGN POLICY PRIORITIES IN THE MIDDLE EAST, 1945–PRESENT (CONT.)

PHASE	U.S.A.	SOVIET (C.I.S. AFTER 1990)	EUROPEAN (ENGLAND,FRANCE GERMANY, EC)
IV (1990–present)	1. Ensure stability of region; maintenance of Desert Storm Coalition 2. Protect petroleum production in Persian Gulf. 3. Solution of Arab-Israeli-conflict 4. Support for Israel.	1. Commonwealth of Independent States seeks new diplomatic relations, trade relations.	1. Protect petroleum production, establish European Community trade relations. 2. Solution of Arab-Israeli-conflict. 3. Support of Israel.

U.S. FOREIGN POLICY

Phase I

U.S. policy toward the Middle East was not coherent nor logical during Phase I. Indeed, after World War II, the United States' concern for the Middle East grew directly as it recognized that its allies (Britain, France) were unable to play their traditional roles.

The United States also feared that the Soviet Union, the other principal winner in World War II, would attempt to exploit the political uncertainties in Greece, Turkey, and Iran. This concern led to the Truman Doctrine, a statement of real opposition to Soviet imperialism in the area, which committed the United States to direct military and economic support for the threatened areas.

As in other areas of the world, the United States found itself moving into unfamiliar political seas in order to fill what was generally recognized as an incipient power vacuum. The exploitation and importation of crude petroleum was clearly of a secondary nature in its foreign policy priorities. Critically, moreover, the United States, in honoring its commitments to the governments and policies of its allies, set itself squarely in the camp of Middle Eastern conservatism. This early commitment, as we will see, ultimately played havoc with U.S. credibility and prestige in the area.

Phase II

During Phase II, United States policy and presence in the Middle East were inextricably linked with Israel. Truman's hurried recognition of Israel, combined with U.S. influence in the United Nations, placed the United States squarely in the role of protector of the Israeli state. This, coupled with intractable Arab opposition to Israel, provided the Soviet Union with its first major successes in Middle Eastern policy. From 1958 to 1975, the U.S.S.R. was able to exploit the situation resulting from U.S. support for Israel by supplying arms and advisers to Egypt, Syria, and Iraq. Thus, the United States attempted to maintain a preeminent power position while the Soviet Union attempted to exploit potential weaknesses in the U.S. posture. It may be a tribute to the diplomacy of Middle Eastern nations that neither power managed to envelop the area within its alliance systems or to systematically dictate policy in the area.

This period in international relations saw a determined American effort to extend the tight bipolar alliance system into the Middle East and to link NATO in Europe with the SEATO alliance in Asia. The Baghdad Pact (1955) represented the greatest success of the United States in this regard. It was seen in the United States as a logical response to Soviet aggression; many Middle East leaders, however, saw themselves in danger of being pulled headlong into the ideological confrontation between the United States and the U.S.S.R. Nasser succeeded in popularizing the concept of nonalignment in the area; and the Pact, lacking full support by the signatories after Iraq's withdrawal in 1958, was replaced by direct aid to Iran. Full support of the Shah by the United States was implemented by means of a bilateral mutual assistance treaty in 1959.

During this period, Middle Eastern petroleum production was a relatively low order of priority: The U.S. oil fields until the early 1960s were more than capable of supplying most domestic petroleum needs. Thus, the maintenance of its influence, the protection of Israel, and the frustration of Soviet ambitions provided the motivation for U.S. policy. Until the late 1960s, the United States was able to accomplish all of its objectives simultaneously. The emergence of the Palestine independence organizations, however, coupled with growing international recognition of their rights and legitimacy, made the support of Israel very costly to U.S. influence and prestige. The Soviet Union capitalized on this situation by breaking relations with Israel and providing arms and aid to Egypt, Syria, and Iraq. U.S. decision makers assumed the worst, that Soviet aid meant Soviet control; and a period of very tense, even hostile, relations between the United States and these nations ensued. In short, during Phase II, the United States was able to consolidate its alliance positions with the "northern tier" states—Turkey, Iran, and Pakistan— while its relations with the core states of Syria, Egypt, and Iraq deteriorated. Strains even appeared between the United States and its client states Jordan and Saudi Arabia, at once pro-American and increasingly anti-Israeli. The maintenance of any alliance in which conflicting goals are present is extraordinarily difficult. Consequently the United States was called upon many times to put out "brush fires" in the area. The attempted nationalization of Iranian oil in 1953, the Suez Crisis of 1956, and the crisis in Lebanon in 1958 are examples. Ultimately, these foreign policy objectives were to become more clearly and forcefully contradictory. Particularly clear by 1974 was the incompatibility of maintaining and expanding the Middle East's petroleum flow to the West and the unyielding support of Israel.

Interventions in Iran. During the early Phase II diplomacy, the United States was forced to intervene directly in the Middle East. The first of these interventions was prompted by developments in Iran from 1951 to 1953, a period in which Iranian politics were dominated by the leadership of Premier Mohammed Mossadegh. Mossadegh effectively challenged the Anglo-Iranian oil agreements and moved to nationalize the company's holdings. Simultaneously Mossadegh virtually isolated the young Shah from political power, taking control of the army and moving to abolish the representative assembly, all with strong support from the Iranian public. American and British interests responded with a carefully orchestrated policy of intrigue that ultimately brought Mossadegh's downfall and the return of the shah. The shah's power, based on his increasingly effective control of the military, waxed from that period on. The petroleum production of Iran was finally organized on a consortium basis in which American and European corporations shared the profits on a fifty-fifty basis with the Iranian National Oil Company. From this time onward, and particularly during the White Revolution, the shah enjoyed generous support from the United States, who perceived Iran as playing a "policeman's role" in the important Persian Gulf. Resentment over U.S. support for the shah became an important factor in Iranian politics after the successful revolution of 1979. The U.S. labored unsuccessfully to escape the consequences of its support for that repressive regime.

The Suez War. The second major U.S. involvement in the Middle East also had long-term consequences for U.S. interests in the area. From 1948 onward, Egypt and Israel were periodically at some level of armed hostility, ranging from small guerrilla raids to larger punitive expeditions. Egypt sought American arms, the better to engage the superior capabilities of the Israeli armed forces. The successful Israeli raid on the Gaza Strip in February 1955 led Colonel Nasser to request arms sales from the United States and Great Britain. These requests were emphatically rejected.

Rebuffed by the Americans and the British, Nasser turned to the Eastern bloc for relief, concluding a barter deal (cotton for arms) with Czechoslovakia. U.S. reactions were abrupt, resulting in the July 1956 cancellation of U.S. support for the construction of the high dam at Aswan. The connection between this refusal and Nasser's independent pursuit of Soviet arms through Czechoslovakia was clearly made by the United States. Moreover, in backing out of its commitment to the dam, the U.S. threatened the very heart of Nasser's development plan for Egypt. Relations between Egypt and the United States deteriorated rapidly from this point.

Nasser reacted to this great-power action by nationalizing the Suez Canal Company in July 1956. The canal, of great importance to Europe as a trade route and defense link, had heretofore been operated by a corporation dominated by Britain and France. Their immediate response was to oppose the nationalization, freeze Egyptian funds in their respective banks, and seek a U.N. solution to the problem. U.S. interest in the proceedings was indirect until Nasser made it clear that Israeli shipping would continue to be denied access to the canal. Britain and France became increasingly restive about the failure of the United States to condemn Egypt. This frustration was to lead ultimately to the Suez War of 1956.

The events of the Suez War suggest collusion between Israel, France, and Great Britain. The war began with Israeli occupation of Gaza and the penetration and control of the Sinai up to the canal. France and Britain demanded that the belligerents (Egypt and Israel) withdraw to positions ten miles on either side of the canal. Egypt's rejection of this ultimatum prompted the invasion of the canal zone by British and French paratroops and the occupation of Port Said.

After a period of intense collective and unilateral diplomacy by the United States, United Nations troops (UNEF) were placed between the belligerents, and they were exhorted to withdraw from the territory. In point of fact, the United States placed heavy pressure on its allies, particularly Israel to withdraw. French and British troops quit the area by December 1956. Finally, in March of 1957, an agreement was reached for Israeli withdrawal from the Sinai.

The resolution of the Suez War found the United States opposing the actions of its strongest allies, Israel, France, and Great Britain. This pro-Arab action led to considerable strains in the Western alliance but did little to persuade Nasser that U.S. policy was ultimately benevolent.

The Lebanon Crisis of 1958. The third U.S. intervention in Middle Eastern affairs was generated by the Lebanon crisis of 1958, an intervention that saw the movement of U.S. marines into Beirut on July 15. The details of the Lebanese political situation that produced the American intervention were complex, involved, and confusing. The Lebanese political situation was becoming increasingly unstable, and the delicate balance between Muslim, Christian, and Druze interests had been deteriorating. This deterioration had attracted the attention of Egypt, which directly intervened in the struggle on behalf of the Sunni Muslims. The successful revolution in Iraq, on July 14, heightened the feeling of tension. At the request for aid by President Chamoun, the U.S. Sixth Fleet moved 3,600 marines into Beirut to stabilize the situation. This tactic, combined with intense behind-the-scenes negotiations, brought some order into the Lebanese conflict and helped to forestall a civil war. The action was successful, and the Lebanese regime survived until the civil war in 1975 and the Israeli-Syrian interventions from 1976 until the present. Nonetheless, this event revealed the willingness of the United States to intervene *directly* in Middle Eastern affairs if it felt its national interest was at stake—a right it steadfastly denied to its allies and adversaries alike.

Phase III

The United States—indeed, all of the recognized powers and superpowers—had clearly entered a period in which international political power was shared, a dramatic change from the era of unilateral intervention that preceded it. U.S. foreign policy in the Phase III era was conceived and executed by "postmodern" presidents, beginning with President Carter. As Richard Rose succinctly puts it:

> A postmodern President no longer enjoys isolation from other nations. The White House retains the attributes of the modern presidency, but in a changing world these resources are no longer adequate. A postmodern President cannot secure success simply by influencing Congress and public opinion; the president must also influence leaders of other nations and events in the international system.[2]

During Phase III of its Middle East policy, U.S. commitments to Israel were strained by its need for regular supplies of Middle East petroleum. The seven-month Arab oil embargo of 1973–1974 was initiated in direct retaliation for U.S.

---

[2] Richard Rose, *The Post-Modern Presidency* (NJ: Chatham House), p. 25.

support for Israel in the war of October 1973. This war, initiated by a surprise attack by Egyptian forces, was ultimately concluded by means of intervention via the U.N. As a result, the United States, by shipping arms to Israel, first prevented the collapse of the Israeli military, and then, through its diplomatic activity in the United Nations, it had rescued Egypt from probable defeat.

From the October war of 1973 until the 1991 Gulf War, the United States' attempts to play both sides of the Arab-Israeli conflict were unsuccessful in rescuing its prestige in the area. Indeed, U.S. policy seems to have alienated both sides in the conflict. Israeli complaints about U.S. waffling on aid became more frequent in the 1980s, characterized by the public complaints of Prime Ministers Menachem Begin and his successor Yitzhak Shamir. The Arab "rejectionist" states were not satisfied or mollified by U.S. economic support for Egypt or by increasing U.S. arms sales to Egypt and Saudi Arabia. More and more, the United States was pressured to consider the Arab view in the Arab-Israeli conflict. The diplomacy of the Carter administration, in particular the Camp David Accords, which led to bilateral negotiations between Egypt and Israel, was most probably the United States' only realistic option.

The Camp David agreements resulted in the cessation of diplomatic hostilities, the return of most Sinai territory to Egypt, and the opening of genuine diplomatic and trade relations between the two countries. The negotiations, however, did not engage the most basic questions regarding Palestinian autonomy on the West Bank and Gaza. The problem of Jerusalem, claimed by Israel as her historic capital, and an important religious site for Christianity and Islam as well, also proves to be difficult. However, since Egypt bore the brunt of past military confrontations with Israel, an outbreak of war became unlikely.

The early foreign policy of the Reagan administration did not hold the promise of substantial change in U.S. Middle East policy. Early administration decisions to accede to Saudi requests for longer-range and more sophisticated fighter-bombers were balanced by promises to increase military aid to Israel. As in the preceding administration's foreign policy, neither side was ecstatic about the U.S. effort to play both sides.

Reagan administration efforts to organize an anti-Soviet alliance in the Middle East were gently but firmly rebuffed in the early months of 1981. Administration concern for Saudi security prompted its approval of the sale of sophisticated radar planes (AWACS) to Saudi Arabia, a decision that produced considerable pro-Israeli objections in the U.S. Congress. The June 1981 Israeli air raid on the Iraqi nuclear facility near Baghdad prompted the administration to suspend shipment of four F-16's to Israel, which also strained relations. It is instructive that the U.N. resolution condemning the Israeli raid and calling for compensation was a joint product of American and Iraqi diplomats at the U.N. Such a collaboration would have been unthinkable a decade earlier, and certainly became unthinkable a decade later. All of these examples underscore the difficulty of maintaining traditional U.S. policy priorities in the decade of the 1980s. No less an authority on U.S.–Israeli relations than former President Jimmy Carter has observed that on many fundamental issues, the interests of Israel and the United States diverge.

The issue of Palestinian rights led the Reagan administration to offer "the Reagan Plan." The plan, which was based on the creation of a "Palestinian entity," to be nominally attached to Jordan, was rejected by Israel and alternately rejected and accepted by other Middle Eastern actors, never simultaneously and never with enough consensus to get the proposals a serious hearing. Israeli objections, interestingly, centered on Prime Minister Begin's flat refusal to consider in any way the return of areas occupied in the 1967 war that are considered part of historical Israel, particularly Judea and Samaria. This in effect announced a de facto annexation of the West Bank, a point of policy firmly opposed by the United States. Prime Minister Shamir continued this emphasis under his administration, with just as much rigidity and energy.

These growing disagreements were minor when compared with the difficulties engendered for the United States by the massive Israeli invasion of Lebanon in June 1982. What was announced initially as a limited-objective foray against Palestinian bases in south Lebanon quickly became a drive to Beirut. Indeed, Israeli Defense Forces stopped only just short of a complete occupation of Beirut and all of southern Lebanon. The United States was apparently caught unprepared by the scope of this military action and hastily created a U.S. military presence in Beirut, ostensibly to police the withdrawal of Palestinian troops from the area.

Shortly thereafter, U.S. marines were reintroduced into the Beirut area in the role of guarantor of the Bashir Gemayel government and tutor for the government's new army, composed primarily of Maronite Christian militia. The United States thus took a position opposing Israeli attempts to elevate other Christian groups, primarily the Army of South Lebanon, led by Major Saad Haddad. Both the U.S. and Israel failed to achieve their objectives. The formal U.S. presence in Beirut was demoralized by the terrorist bombing of the U.S. marine barracks with great loss of life; and ultimately by a similar attack on the U.S. embassy annex. The U.S. hope for an effective national government based on the Gemayel administration deteriorated as other groups and countries controlled more and more Lebanese territory. What hopes Israel had countenanced for the creation of a neutral or pro-Israel government dissipated in the anarchy created by the sudden removal of the Palestinians from the military-political equation in Lebanon. The primary gains from the invasion of Lebanon appeared to accrue to the Syrians, now the arbiter of political relations in Lebanon, and consequently enjoying a substantial rise in diplomatic prestige, and the Shia groups, particularly AMAL and Hizbollah, who rose to oppose first the government, then the Palestinians, and finally the Israelis.

U.S. policy at this time appeared to be more reactive than active. The events in Lebanon proved a major setback to U.S. efforts to promote a negotiated settlement between the Israelis and their Arab neighbors, and resulted in a dramatic decline in U.S. prestige in the area, a decline underscored by the Lebanese hostage crisis of June 1985. U.S. losses in Lebanon were slightly offset by the maintenance of close, even intimate, relations with Egypt and by a substantive but informal supportive relationship with Iraq. Neither policy vector was well-received in Israel and thus U.S. policy in the Middle East, yoked as it was to unqualified support for Israel, retained the internal inconsistencies apparent since World War II.

Two dramatic sets of events transformed Reagan administration policy from reactive to active. The first involved direct U.S. involvement in the Iran-Iraq war, initially in an effort to secure the release of U.S. hostages, and later as an attempt to maintain open sea lanes in the Persian Gulf. The second involved the remarkable events of the Palestinian intifadah and the subsequent efforts of the PLO to gain multilateral support for direct negotiations for the creation of a Palestinian state under U.N. resolutions 242 and 338. Each of these events needs separate discussion.

Direct U.S. intervention in the Iran-Iraq conflict occurred first during 1985–1986 as a covert effort to gain Iran's cooperation and intervention in the release of U.S. hostages held by various groups in Lebanon. The effort was directed in secrecy by an office in the National Security Council and eventually involved the U.S. government in a bizarre arrangement linking arms sales to Iran to support for covert Contra (anti-communist) operations in Nicaragua. The details of the initiative are still unclear, but the effects of the policy are known: the sale of key weapon systems and badly needed spare parts to Iran (particularly antiaircraft and antitank missiles) neutralized much of Iraq's qualitative advantage in military equipment and put the Iraqi military in a dangerous corner. With its back against the wall, Iraq responded with missile attacks on key Iranian cities and the utilization of chemical weapons, chiefly gases, against Iranian troops and its own domestic Kurdish opposition who were sympathetic toward Iran. Simultaneously, Iraq and Iran both extended their attacks on domestic shipping in the Persian Gulf, each attempting to damage the other's ability to earn foreign currency to continue prosecution of the war. These attacks, particularly against noncombatant Persian Gulf states, brought a U.S. naval presence into the Gulf.

The United States, prompted by Kuwait's threats to invite a Soviet naval force into the area, eventually moved a large naval task force into the Gulf, ostensibly to protect all shipping, regardless of source. Kuwaiti tankers were reflagged as American tankers. (In practical effect, this meant action against Iran.) The task force included most of the paraphernalia of modern superpower technology, including AWACS radar surveillance, AEGIS guided-missile cruisers, destroyers, minesweepers, helicopters, and smaller vessels. The Iranians deployed more mines and utilized small, high-speed boats for grenade and small-caliber attacks on slow-moving tankers. The Iraqis relied most heavily on air-launched missiles. The result of all this military activity was an increase in the complexity of traffic in the Gulf region, an area already congested in its sea and air lanes. This compression of traffic and activity increased the levels of uncertainty in the area, a fact that led to the May 1987 attack on the U.S.S. *Stark* by an Iraqi Exocet missile, with substantial loss of American lives. This incident was resolved by an Iraqi apology and payment of damages.

The U.S. response to this attack was to beef up its presence in the Gulf. Higher states of alert were required and more ships deployed. Petroleum continued to flow from the Gulf, protected by the U.S. navy. U.S. encounters with Iranian attacks and mines led to limited action against Iranian bases, particularly converted oil platforms. But the Iran-Iraq war ground on with appalling levels of casualties, military and civilian, culminating in the accidental shooting down of an Iranian jetliner in July 1988 by the U.S.S. *Vincennes*, a sophisticated AEGIS class cruiser. This attack, and the almost universal diplomatic indifference to it, contributed to the Iranian acceptance of a negotiated end to the conflict, through the auspices of the United Nations. A distraught Ayatollah Khomeini supported the decision to end the war, against his personal sentiments. A war that began badly, with some U.S. covert involvement at its inception, ended similarly, with U.S. covert and overt actions affecting the course *and* conduct of the war.

There are lessons to be learned from this protracted conflict and the U.S. role in it. The U.S. role in the world, while important, was no longer definitive. At the same time, it was clear that policy decisions in Washington did have effects, sometimes intended, as is the case in the Persian Gulf intervention; sometimes unintended, as the hostage-for-arms sales relationship with Iran demonstrated, for it was clearly not in the interest of the United States to tip the balance of power in that conflict toward Iran; and yet in the short run, that was the clear impact of our policy. Some critics of U.S. policy in the Gulf conflict suggested a lack of clarity in U.S. objectives; others have pointed out the essentially reactive U.S. role there. Still others have suggested that a greater multilateral presence in the Gulf would have proven useful to U.S. purposes, sharing costs and blame more equally among those benefiting from the petroleum flow. Once again, these criticisms and suggestions reinforce our previous observations about the changing nature of the international system and the U.S. role in it. (These commonplace criticisms of U.S. decision making in the Iran-Iraq war have almost eerie resonance in the criticisms of U.S. shortsightedness in the Gulf war with Iraq in 1991.) But, *ceteris paribus*, the United States was now but one of many important actors in the arena. This reality became extremely clear through the remarkable events in Israel's occupied territories.

In December 1987, Palestinians on the West Bank and in Gaza began a civil insurrection against Israeli occupation. Most of those participating in this intifadah were very young Arab youths not directly affiliated with the PLO or other mainstream organizations professing Palestinian rights. Many analysts have concluded that this insurrection was sparked by the sense of alienation that many young Palestinians, bereft of a meaningful future, have come to see as their lot in life. Israeli protestations to the contrary, there is little evidence to suggest that the early stages of the protests were conceived, organized, or executed by formal groups outside of Israel, including the PLO. In other words, this insurrection was indigenous to the occupied territories and sparked by a generalized sense of despair and frustration, particularly among third and fourth generation Palestinians in the refugee camps of Gaza and the West Bank. The Shamir administration responded to these demonstrations and riots with ever-increasing firmness. The policy of the "Iron Fist," predicated on group responsibility for individual acts of resistance or rebellion, produced daily incidents of beatings, arrests, expulsions, jailings without charge, broken bones, and many deaths, mainly among Palestinian teenagers. That these protests could continue on a very protracted basis suggests the depth of the feelings motivating both sides in the conflict. And clearly, like it or not, the Palestinian intifadah quickly became an element in the international equation in the Middle East, as the PLO attempted to control the rebellion for its own ends, as Israel tried to contain it as a domestic dispute, and as growing numbers of the international community perceived the events as a major problem of human rights.

The attempt by the PLO to benefit from this uprising led to many strains within its ruling coalition. In November 1988, the Palestinian National Council, in a move that surprised many of its friends and foes alike, declared an independent Palestinian state and asked for diplomatic recognition. The specific resolution implied recognition of Israel, but stopped short of the unambiguous statement required by the supporters of Israel. The Israeli government reaction was strongly negative, although growing minority sentiment in Israel favored a "land-for-peace" trade. The U.S. official position at this time echoed formal Israeli policy.

Later in 1988, Yasir Arafat announced plans to speak before the U.N. General Assembly in New York, for the purpose of presenting new proposals on the Arab-Israeli conflict. In a surprising move, Secretary of State Shultz refused Arafat a visa on the grounds that he represented a terrorist organization. Earlier congressionally mandated efforts to close the information offices of the PLO set the stage for this development, but even so, Shultz's refusal shocked many in the international arena, and charges were made that the action violated the U.S. contract with the United Nations. After repeated efforts to change the state department's decision failed, the meetings were moved at great expense to Geneva, Switzerland, where, in December 1988, Arafat addressed the General Assembly.

The content of Arafat's speech was astounding to all participants in the long-standing conflict. Arafat acceded to U.S. demands for unequivocal PLO positions on three points: the right of Israel to exist in peace within secure boundaries; acceptance of U.N. Resolutions 242 and 338; and a specific renunciation of terrorism generally, and of the use of terrorism as a political tool. Arafat ultimately accepted the explicit language required by the United States, as defined in multilateral discussions in Sweden, and the United States immediately moved to begin direct diplomatic discussions with the PLO in Tunisia. Supporters of Israel in the United States were hard put to explain the sudden change in American policy, and the Israeli government formally expressed its "disappointment" with the American decision. The most likely explanation for this substantive change in direction is to be found in Secretary Shultz's earlier attempts late in the Reagan administration to revive the peace process. U.S. attempts were rebuffed by a recalcitrant Israeli government, a fact which angered the administration and began the erosion of administration support.

This sudden shift in U.S. policy energized the peace process in many ways—primarily in eliminating the last practical barrier to an international consensus (minus Israel) favoring multilateral discussions of the Palestinian question. The PLO proposals for the convening of a multilateral conference in Geneva ultimately provoked an Israeli response preferring U.S.–U.S.S.R. mediated discussions of the problem. While there was no obvious solution to the problems immediately at hand, international diplomacy seemed at this juncture to be taking a more active role in bringing the conflict to some conclusion. Just what kind of "autonomy" or "independence" awaited the Palestinian people had yet to be determined. But there was little doubt that the dramatic change in U.S. policy toward the PLO created more possibilities and probabilities for change than previously existed. And the tacit approval of the Bush administration, during the presidential transition in the United States, further suggested continuity in U.S. policy for the next few years. Indeed, such prospects were realized in the U.S.-led peace negotiations begun in the fall of 1991, bringing multilateral diplomacy to bear on this difficult problem. The specifics of this process are discussed in greater detail in the following chapters.

In spite of the special relationship between the U.S. and Israel, and in spite of the presence of a highly visible and effective Israeli lobby in the United States, the realities of different interests ultimately expressed themselves. Optimistically, we can hope for a more mature relationship between Israel and the United States in the near future, one that facilitates growth and development for all states in this long-lasting conflict.

SOVIET FOREIGN POLICY

Initially, Soviet foreign policy toward the Middle East was opportunistic and reactive. It was opportunistic in that the Soviet Union attempted to exploit the postwar difficulties of Greece, Turkey, and Iran in its historic attempt to secure a year-round, warm-water port. It was reactive in that it attempted to exploit the consequences of U.S. policy in the Arab-Israeli conflict.

In Phase I of its Middle Eastern policy, the Soviet Union attempted a combination of subversion and guerrilla intervention in the northern tier nations of the Middle East. Soviet diplomatic pressure on Turkey was intense, particularly as regarded its navigation rights in the Bosporus Straits and the redefinition of the Thracian border in favor of Bulgaria. This, combined with more direct military adventures in Iran, prompted President Truman to declare the Truman Doctrine and unilaterally commit the United States to the defense of these states. Soviet ambitions in these areas were frustrated, and Soviet policy in the Middle East became more reactive to U.S. policy.

In Phase II, the Soviet Union seemed primarily interested in exploiting the difficulties raised by the U.S. commitment to Israel. Thus, in order to find a way to move her growing military capability into the Mediterranean, the Soviet Union began courting the most rabidly anti-Israeli states. Her first major opportunity came in Egypt, hard on the heels of the Israeli raid on Gaza, the French-British-Israeli attack on Egypt for the control of the Suez Canal, and the U.S. cancellation of support for the Aswan High Dam. The Soviet union abandoned its initial support for Israel, moved into the arms race in a major way, and ultimately committed itself to the construction of the high dam in Egypt. Soviet arms aid was supplemented by a vigorous economic aid and trade policy that succeeded after 1958 in orienting the trade relations of Egypt, Syria, Yemen, and Iraq toward the Eastern bloc. Extensive cultural programs were also implemented, many involving educational opportunities for Arabs in Eastern Europe and the U.S.S.R. These programs, combined with its support of nonalignment movements worldwide, succeeded in raising Soviet prestige and influence at the expense of the United States. Until the events of the 1990s reversed the trend, Soviet trained academics dominated the university systems of Syria, Iraq, and Yemen; and remained influential in Egypt.

The Soviet Union was able to turn some of these gains into tangible results. It was given the use of military facilities in Egypt, most notably an extensive naval base at Alexandria, and communication and airfield facilities at Luxor. At one point, Soviet technical and military experts in Egypt numbered close to 20,000. Similar gains were scored in Syria and Iraq, although not on such a grand scale. Its support for the front-line states against Israel and later for the Palestinian guerrilla movements, some of which received technical aid and support from Soviet allies, also contributed to the heightening of Soviet prestige in the area.

Most of the Soviet Union's overt political gains during Phase II were nonetheless intangible. Soviet attempts to influence directly the governments of Nasser and Sadat in Egypt were frustrated. The Egyptians seemed adept at taking gifts from the Russian bear while simultaneously avoiding its hug. To a lesser degree, similar events transpired in Syria and Iraq, where allegedly communist-inspired *coups* were detected and crushed, accompanied by army and university purges. When Sadat ordered the Soviets out of Egypt in 1972, American influence and prestige enjoyed something of a recovery. Syria and Iraq, in recent years, slowly reoriented themselves toward a more positive, but wary, relationship with the United States.

Phase III of Soviet foreign policy initially paralleled U.S. policy shifts. The Soviet Union aggressively supported wars of national liberation in the area. Frustrated in its attempts to consolidate its advantages in the Fertile Crescent, the Soviet Union turned to overt military aid and surrogate (Cuban) intervention, most notably in Yemen and Ethiopia, where it became involved in the Eritrean dispute. The Soviet invasion of Afghanistan raised warning signs all over the Middle East, particularly among those states formally committed to Islamic rule. The Soviet occupation of Afghanistan lowered its prestige and influence in the region, and heightened Middle Eastern awareness of its poor treatment of Soviet Muslim groups. Afghani resistance to Soviet control continued to plague the Soviet and Afghan government troops, leading many commentators to regard this venture as "the Soviet Union's Vietnam." This probably overstates the case, but the fact is that the Afghani mujahedin refused to go away and attracted greater external support. As the U.S.S.R. escalated its presence, Muslim governments throughout the area became more suspicious. Iraq is a case in point, where after considerable waffling, the Soviet Union offered substantial support for the war against Iran. In spite of this, Iraq continued its pro-Western tilt. Soviet support for Syria, particularly during the Israeli invasion of Lebanon, raised Syrian prestige and indirectly improved Soviet prestige. But Syria is determinedly independent, and it is hard to imagine a less tractable or more unpredictable alliance partner in the Middle East. The 1988 decision to withdraw from the Afghan imbroglio eliminated one of the Soviet Union's negatives in dealing with the states of the Middle East, but this did not in and of itself raise Soviet prestige in the area.

From a geopolitical perspective, the turmoil on the Persian (Arabian) Gulf presented the Soviet Union with some risky opportunities. Intervention in Iran could conceivably have produced both a warm-water port and increased access to foreign petroleum. A successful venture in Oman could have placed the Soviet Union in a position of influence at the very opening to the Persian Gulf. And success in the northern tier, bordering as it does on the Soviet Union itself, could have been exploited militarily and politically. On the other hand, the United States' response to such success was hard to envision. The movement of Iran into the Soviet orbit, for example, could have upset the international balance to such a degree that the United States would have resorted to military action. The Soviet Union had avoided such a direct confrontation with its nuclear adversary since the Cuban missile crisis of 1962. Soviet diplomacy during the worst days of the Iran-Iraq conflict was cautious and appropriate. Its attempts to improve relations with Israel reflected its growing interest in a greater diplomatic role in the region. And finally, its apparent withdrawal of overt support for wars of national liberation improved its standing in the international community.

The Soviet Union also made other international moves that were astounding in view of past policies. Under Gorbachev great efforts at internal reform were attempted, and it became clear that the Soviet regime equated declining international tension with an opportunity to put its own social and economic house in order. The 1988 nuclear disarmament treaty with the United States evidenced new assumptions in Soviet foreign policy, and the very real decision to implement a phased withdrawal from Afghanistan suggested a new realism in Moscow. Of great interest and importance to regional actors in the Middle East were new expressions of political activity taking place in Soviet Central Asia, particularly in Azerbaijan, where a regional dispute with the Armenian Republic flared into substantial communal violence. Reliable reports circulated of Soviet Muslim demonstrators carrying placards of Ayatollah Khomeini. Soviet policy toward these marginal elements were important indicators of the true intent and character of Soviet reforms. And with the benefit of hindsight, it now seems clear that the attraction of the republics of Azerbaijan, Kazakhstan, Uzbekistan, and Turkmenistan toward Turkey and Iran in the early 1990s suggest that Islam was in fact an important social and religious fact of life in those former Soviet republics.

The consensus after 1988 conceding the U.S.S.R. a role in mediating the Israeli-Palestinian conflict was further evidence of the maturation of the Soviet role in the politics of the Middle East. A joint U.S.–U.S.S.R. initiative was understood to have considerable weight on both sides of the political divide and enhanced prospects for eventual solutions to existing problems. Again, the events of the 1990s demonstrated the viability of this model, as the United States and the Commonwealth of Independent States (C.I.S.) jointly sponsored negotiations between Israel and the Arab states.

There is a substantial irony to this state of affairs. Many Middle Eastern intellectuals have long believed that the United States and the U.S.S.R. were basically identical; that they were both interested only in maintaining and extending their political and military power. For these two adversaries, accustomed to seeing each other in absolute, polarized terms, such a conclusion must have seemed outrageously inaccurate. Of course, the collapse of Soviet international power in 1990 and the dissolution of the Soviet Union in 1991 put an end to the bipolar structure of international relations and made the whole argument moot. And both states now recognize a fundamental convergence of their basic interests in international stability and relative peace.

BRITAIN AND FRANCE

As indicated in this chapter, the postwar international scene saw a substantial reduction of British and French power. Both nations emerged from World War II victorious but exhausted. Even with the direct help of the United States, these two countries were hard pressed to reassert their authority over their former colonies. Both reluctantly began a series of retrenchments.

Of the two, Britain's withdrawal from strategic power was the more graceful, the less disruptive. While the French opposed two divisive and difficult wars of national liberation in Vietnam and in Algeria, the British planted supposedly independent, pro-British regimes in their former colonies and protectorates. When things got out of hand, as they did in Iran in 1952–1953, Britain participated in intrigues designed to bring a friendly face to the throne—in this case the return of the shah from exile.

Both countries attempted to use World War I and World War II diplomacy to extend and develop their influence in the Middle East. Pursuing a course of naked self-interest, the British and the French promised, at one time or another, everything to everybody. In the end, the Middle Eastern state system, a pastiche of kings, emirs, presidents, and sheikhs presiding over geographical entities drawn by committees in Europe, emerged. In this emergence, the power of the British and the French paled in comparison to that of the United States and the U.S.S.R. Thus, they contented themselves with attempting to perpetuate their cultural and economic influence in the area under American military protection. Israel received enormous support in return for taking in the great numbers of displaced European Jews. Extensive oil resources were being developed in Iraq, Iran, Kuwait, and in Saudi Arabia.

In Phase II the British and French turned their attention primarily to trade relations. The abortive Suez War in 1956 effectively ended what predisposition they had for an overt military role in the area. After that time the orientation of the European powers became essentially commercial and focused on the exploitation of the increasingly important petroleum reserves. During this time, it also became evident that the support of Israel had become secondary to other objectives. French and British arms were sold indiscriminately in the Middle East, to the anguish of both the United States and Israel. These sales demonstrated the growing inability of the United States to control its alliances.

In Phase III of their Middle Eastern policy, the U.S. allies grew even less dependent on American initiatives and policy direction. Britain, France, and West Germany have, since 1974, sold increasingly sophisticated weapons and technology to assorted Middle Eastern governments. Even nuclear technology, over specific, energetic U.S. opposition, has been made available to such Middle Eastern governments as Iraq, Egypt, Libya, Algeria, and Iran. All of these countries have the combination of financial, physical, and intellectual resources necessary for the construction of nuclear devices. At some point in time it seems likely that one or more of this aspirant group will succeed in building nuclear weapons. This, combined with the nuclear arsenal in Israel, raises the spectre of nuclear confrontation in some unspecified future. This recognition certainly prompted the 1981 Israeli air raid on the Osirak reactor near Baghdad, a raid launched irrespective of the anticipated diplomatic fallout. Iraq's President Saddam Hussein subsequently called for aid from "peace-loving" nations to aid in the development of Arab-controlled nuclear weapons, for the specific purpose of countering Israeli nuclear devices.

Following the 1988 cease-fire, many European businesses reentered Iran, Iraq, and the threatened Gulf nations. A more unified, vital, and active Europe expanded its economic and political presence in the Middle East, yet another proof of the changes taking place in the international system. European states and businesses also continued to sell sophisticated technical equipment in the area. It is now clear that by 1990 Iraq had made substantial progress toward its goal of nuclear weapons, its success incidentally put at risk by its ill-advised invasion of Kuwait and the subsequent coalition response. Significantly, many European leaders have expressed dismay at U.S. hostility toward Libya, opinions representative of emerging differences in basic policy between Europe and the United States.

During this period, the governments of Europe became even more dependent on Middle Eastern petroleum. France, Germany, Italy, Belgium, and Holland must import much of their petroleum from the Middle East. They hastily separated themselves from the United States during the Arab oil embargo. By 1980, all of the major governments of Western Europe enjoyed privileged status in trade relations in the area, exchanging trade and technology for petroleum.

European relations with Israel have generally paralleled world opinion. Israel has found most European countries hostile toward its policies on Palestine and Jerusalem. In the U.N., they have joined the majority in opposing Israeli aggression and imperialism and have been vocal in their insistence that Israel accept Resolution 242 (1967), which calls for a return to the prewar boundaries. Not surprisingly, then, the states of Europe were supportive and encouraging of the PLO initiative toward multilateral consideration of the Palestinian question. Israel found itself increasingly isolated in the court of European public opinion and under mounting pressure to enter into a dialogue with the PLO.

Western Europe, during Phase III, began to act as though it was but one of a number of centers of world power. In 1980 and 1981, the European Common Market called for new peace talks in the Middle East that would exclude the Soviet Union and the United States. As the contemporary international system matures, we can expect to see more independent European and Japanese policy initiatives. And as we have emphasized previously, the economic interdependence of Europe and the Middle East continued to grow throughout the 1980s. The fate of Turkey's application for full membership in the European Community should provide an indication of the future of the relationship. Should Turkey finally manage to gain entry, the levels of exchange between the two regions should grow even faster.

CHINA AND JAPAN

The foreign policies of China and Japan toward the Middle East have become important in the last decade. During Phase I, both China and Japan deferred completely to the policy dictates of the U.S.S.R. and the United States. In the 1960s, during Phase II, both countries turned their attention toward the Middle East, but not in the intense or manipulative way of the superpowers or the European powers. China has historically supported Arab movements toward nonalignment and occasionally offered minimal support to wars of national liberation in southern Arabia. Its interest in frustrating the growth of Soviet power has led China to supply military replacement parts to Egypt after the Soviet Union cut them off. Japan, during this period, became a progressively larger consumer of Middle Eastern oil, upon which it is near totally reliant to fuel its industry. Japan has thus placed a high premium on innocuous, positive diplomatic relations in the area.

In Phase III, China became more directly active in its attempts to frustrate Soviet gains in the area. Overt Chinese support for anti-Soviet elements in Afghanistan was instrumental in frustrating the U.S.S.R. there. The Chinese also opposed Soviet interests in the horn of Africa. China appeared to be interested in a worldwide alliance designed to frustrate Soviet "hegemonism." The coordination of U.S.–Chinese policy in this regard has been minimal and of little importance to the contemporary Middle East, save for Afghanistan and Pakistan. As indicated earlier, Japan has seen its dependence on Middle Eastern (particularly Iranian) oil grow to critical proportions. Japan thus has had its latitude of action severely restricted and resorted to a low profile in its international policy in the area. This dependence certainly characterized Japan's diplomatic posture during the entire Iran-Iraq conflict, a period in which Japanese imports of Iranian oil grew unabated. For the Japanese, with few natural energy resources of their own, regular and predictable supplies of Middle Eastern petroleum continued to militate against taking any position of risk or exposure in the area, a point underscored by the domestic controversy over its financial support of the coalition in Desert Storm. Japanese economic activity and trade in the area continues to grow, keeping Japan ahead of Europe in its total trade balances in the region.

Chinese domestic politics turned in an authoritarian direction after the horrifying suppression of dissidents in Tianamen Square. Many of the progressive gains made in the decade preceding were dismantled. And there was resonance to these changes in China's foreign policy. China has become something of an indiscriminant supplier of arms, including middling quality nuclear technology and Chinese built Scud missiles. Middle Eastern states, including Iran and Syria, have been heavy buyers of these replacements for Soviet armaments. China is not the only non-European source of missile technology, but clearly her participation in this type of international trade was and is potentially destabilizing. For its part, China seems more inclined to independence in its foreign policy than it was in the decade of the 1980s, less inclined to accept the strictures placed on it by the industrial West. It would seem inevitable that fundamental interests of China and Japan would eventually come into salient conflict.

In summation, all great and near great power actors have recently found the Middle East a difficult arena in which to implement policy. Changes in the very structure of the international system have frustrated Soviet and American policy initiatives in the area. The growth of economic power centers outside the bipolar axis increased the number of players in the game; and the collapse of Soviet power further accelerated the trend. And Middle Eastern leaders have shown themselves to be surprisingly adept practitioners of classic diplomacy in this emergent balance of power system.

INTERNATIONAL RELATIONS IN THE CONTEMPORARY MIDDLE EAST 1945–1990:
The Regional Actors

The international politics of the Middle East have been, in the current period, highly conditioned by the realities of great power competition. The classic balance of power system that prevailed in Europe from the late eighteenth century through the early twentieth century put the region at the center of wars, intrigues, and maneuvers pitting variously England, France, Germany, and Russia against one another for influence and control. Thus, regional actors found it necessary to define their policies largely in reaction to initiatives from the outside. And calculated reaction was complicated by the realities of spying, intrigue, subtle maneuver, double dealing, and the sheer ignorance of many of the great power decision makers.[1] Informed rationality was only occasionally important in the exercise of international relations in the region. Decision makers on all sides harbored appalling inaccurate and inappropriate images of the "others."

Similar realities appeared in the heyday of the bipolar system, as both the United States and the U.S.S.R., ill-prepared for the role of international arbiters, blundered their way into and through the politics of the region. U.S. belief that Nasser's Egypt had become a Soviet satellite poisoned relations with that important state for many years. And the Soviet Union's casual disregard for Muslim sensibilities led it into a political morass in Afghanistan, a policy that carried Soviet prestige to new lows regionally.

For newly independent states of the Middle East, foreign policy was a continuing challenge, combining their highest aspirations for independence with the overwhelming reality of their relative weakness. Contemporary regional international relations can be partially understood as the attempt by regional actors to acquire the capabilities (political, economic, social) that support their independence in the international system.

---

[1] The notion that the great powers conducted their international diplomacy with high-minded rationality was certainly destroyed by David Fromkin, *A Peace to End All Peace: The Fall of the Ottoman Empire and the Creation of the Modern Middle East* (New York: Avon Books, 1989).

The Middle East is an area seemingly designed for intensive regional activity. As noted elsewhere in the text, the region's nations have many physical similarities: aridity and unevenly distributed populations, oil reserves, communications, and trade centers. Moreover, they share many ethnic and cultural similarities: large contiguous blocs of Arabs, Turks, and Persians, the predominance of the Arabic language, and the pervasive influence of Islam. Thus, there are many physical, ethnic, and cultural bridges across the national boundaries of the state system. Accordingly, there have been many attempts—public and private—to exploit these similarities.

The oldest of the regional associations in the Middle East is the Arab League. Founded in Cairo in 1945, the League initially was composed of Egypt, Iraq, Saudi Arabia, Syria, Transjordan, Lebanon, and Yemen. Although there were serious internal divisions within the League from the outset, it accomplished some positive action. Critical histories of the League invariably stress its early difficulties in coordinating the war against Israel in 1948. In this war the mutual suspicions between the Hashemites, Saudis, and Egyptians severely split the Arab forces. In the Phase II period, as mentioned in Chapter 11, the League was successful primarily in nonpolitical areas—for example, in social and economic cooperation. It has never been able to resolve the fractious politics of its Arab constituency and has survived by avoiding those difficult problems for the most part. More effective efforts at Arab unity have been pursued from the base of national power, as in Nasser's pan-Arab movement, the Baath party, and OAPEC. In Phase III, the League has been an important sounding board for diverse Arab interests.

During Phase II (Table 11-1), there were two notable attempts to achieve Arab political unity. The first was the pan-Arab movement launched by Nasser in 1958; the second was the formation of the Baath party, which was based on the philosophy of Michel Aflaq and found its most receptive constituency in Syria and Iraq. These two movements (pan-Arabism and Baathism) have often been at odds, supporters of each accusing the other of simply advancing the national interests of its leaders.

Nasser's pan-Arab objectives were couched largely in terms of national union. Based on a loosely articulated ideal of Arab unity and cooperation, Nasser's movement was considerably more pragmatic than the ideologically based Baath movement. Where the Baath depended on loyal cadres to spread its ideology and raise it to power, Nasser pursued the constitutional union of Egypt with a variety of potential partners. At one time or another, Egypt has proposed unification with Syria, Iraq, Yemen, Libya, and the Sudan.

Nasser's pan-Arab strategy produced some tangible results. The 1958 union of Egypt and Syria, the United Arab Republic, survived until 1961, when the federation succumbed to a Syrian army *coup*. Some critics argue that failure of the union was prompted by Nasser's efforts in 1959 to effect a truly economic, political, and military union—one that would to some degree extinguish remaining Syrian political identity. Others argue that Syrian nationalism simply proved too potent an obstacle for union. Nasser's attempts at federation with Yemen (1958) were much looser and much less ambitious. A proposed Union with Iraq in the 1960s was frustrated by a military *coup* and the subsequent entrenchment of Baathist regimes in both Syria and Iraq. In spite of these frustrations and failures, Nasser maintained his commitment to Arab unity via political union. Most coun-

tries of the Middle East counted among their populations groups strongly supportive of Nasser's dream. These groups were in the main not strong enough to implement his vision of unity, although they were strong enough to continually worry
their governments. These governments continued throughout Nasser's presidency
to suspect his motives, question his actions, and frustrate his international ventures.

Baathism is at once a political party and a political philosophy. It is one of
the very few indigenous political party movements in the Middle East. Based on
the work and writings of Michel Aflaq and Salal al-Din al-Bitar, it was founded in
1953 and is committed to the ultimate goal of Arab unity through nationalism,
socialism, and pan-Arabism. The Baath (Resurrection) party specifically aims to
recover past Arab greatness. Baathism found its normal constituency among the
intellectuals and military of Syria, Lebanon, Jordan, and Iraq. Since 1963, it has
successfully maintained itself in power in Syria and in Iraq. It should be noted that
in Syria, Baathist support came largely from the civilian sector; in Iraq, Baathist
power resided mainly in the military, many of whom had earlier supported union
with Nasser's Egypt.

The Baathist regimes in Syria and Iraq have been in the forefront of the
assault on Israel. Between 1965 and 1975, Iraq openly supported Palestinian separatist and terrorist organizations. Iraqi troops were moved into position during the
1967 and 1973 wars with Israel, although they were for the most part noncombatant.

Syrian policy during Phase II moved closer and closer to the Soviet Union,
particularly after dissolution of the union with Egypt. Syrian relations with Israel
and the United States were frigid, cool with the traditional Middle Eastern states
(Saudi Arabia, Iran), and increasingly friendly with Libya and Algeria. Substantial
economic and cultural ties with the Soviet Union and the Eastern bloc were maintained.

The dramatic expansion of Syrian influence following the Israeli invasion of
Lebanon (1982) moved Syria into the forefront of diplomatic activity in the area. It
seemed possible that this elevated role would lead Syria into the role of a strategic
"broker" in regional conflicts. And in fact, Syrian influence in the region has
waxed steadily since that time.

Nonetheless, the Baathist regimes of Syria and Iraq were often at loggerheads in spite of their ostensible commitment to Arab unity. Both countries have
relatively long and potent histories of nationalist feeling, and it is possible that
these factors have been a determinant in their foreign policy. Thus, they have only
given lip service to regional unity movements. For example, Iraq and Syria split
forcefully during the Iran-Iraq conflict, with Syria taking a publicly pro-Iranian
position, in spite of considerable pressure from other regional players backing Iraq.
This position put the Syrians and the Israelis in common cause, since Israel viewed
the Iraqi regime as much more dangerous than any probable Iranian government.

The end of the Iran-Iraq conflict did not ameliorate relations between Damascus
and Baghdad, and as Iraq sought ever closer ties with the United States, Western
Europe, and the moderate bloc of Arab states (Egypt, Saudi Arabia, and Jordan), Syria
burnished its already well-established ties with the Soviet Union and cautiously pursued improved relations with the United States. The events of 1991 occasioned by the
Iraqi invasion of Kuwait, of course, stood this relationship on its head. Syria aligned
itself with the U.S. led coalition against Iraq and subsequent to the war moved aggres-

sively to improve relations with the United States. Syria and Iraq still remained at loggerheads, in spite of the dramatic changes in alliance politics.

A digression on the role of Islam in the regional politics of the area is necessary here. During Phase II, Nasser's pan-Arabism, Baathist ideology, and the traditional systems of the day all stressed the importance of Islam as a common source of tradition and identity. In nearly all of the participating states, however, Islam was conceived of in politically secular terms. It was fashionable to recognize the existence of Muslim society (a society composed primarily of Muslims) as a desirable reality, while simultaneously rejecting the idea of an Islamic state (a state based on the Koran and Islamic tradition). While there were exceptions to this professed secularism—the Muslim Brotherhood, mainly, and a number of Sufi orders—there were no effective challenges to the political orthodoxy of the day. Arab socialism in particular depended on Islamic sources for inspiration, but few economists were willing to suggest that modern economies could be based on the principles contained in the Koran, the hadith, or their subsequent commentaries and codifications. This complacency regarding the role of Islam in politics, economics, and social life was strongly challenged from the 1970s onward (see for instance the discussion of Islamic economics in Chapter 10), and it would be foolish to dismiss the emergent role of Islam in the international relations of the region. Important political, intellectual, economic, and cultural links complement the established religious connections.

Islam was, is, and is likely to remain one of the major facts of international life in the Middle East. Reports of fundamentalist sympathies among Sunni groups in Egypt, Turkey, Jordan, Algeria, Morocco, the Gulf states, Saudi Arabia, and the occupied territories of the West Bank and (especially) Gaza indicate that Islamic fundamentalism has emerged as a potent force in previously secular political systems. Although these groups do not seem as radical in their views as their Shia counterparts in Iran and Lebanon, it does appear that Islam will be a growing element in the regional politics of the Middle East.

Growing fundamentalist influence in Algeria early in 1992 resulted in massive electoral victories for fundamentalist-based political groups. Unwilling to accept the prospects of a potential Islamic republic, the incumbent government and the military abrogated the elections and instituted emergency rule. The conflict in Algeria between fundamentalist Muslims and secular bureaucrats is representative of the tensions emerging in many Middle Eastern states. And the international implications of these movements emerge as other governments support or oppose restrictions imposed on fundamentalist parties, and as these groups communicate and support each other across increasingly permeable state boundaries. For Middle Eastern states as well as their Western counterparts, the distinction between domestic and international politics becomes increasingly difficult to ascertain.

One of the most promising and important regional developments was the organization of the Gulf Cooperation Council (GCC). Founded in 1980, the Gulf Cooperation Council was based on the realization that only cooperative economic policies and collective security arrangements could ensure the continued independence of the small states and sheikhdoms ranged along the south side of the Persian Gulf. These states—the United Arab Emirates, Qatar, Oman, Bahrain, and Kuwait—joined with Saudi Arabia, their larger but still vulnerable neighbor, to form an organization that would coordinate the defense policies of the region.

Among the early successes of the GCC was the standardization of key defense systems. For instance, the GCC members all committed themselves to the purchase of compatible French and British fighters and bombers. Compatible and integrated communication, command, and control systems were installed. Saudi AWAC planes provided a platform for coordinated early warning and air traffic control. A Rapid Deployment Force was organized to meet unexpected threats. A high level of military cooperation and coordination was established. Politically, the GCC was seen as a necessary response to the attempts of Iraq and Iran to establish dominance in the Gulf. The long-running war between those two states provided a continual incentive to keep the development of the GCC as a high priority among member states. The rising tide of Muslim, and especially Shia, fundamentalism also kept pressure on the Gulf states.

Saudi Arabia, by geographic size and population, was destined to play a dominant role in the GCC. In fact, the GCC became the primary instrument of Saudi policy in the Gulf. In keeping with the established principles of Saudi diplomacy, the GCC attempted to keep an arms length from entangling relationships with the superpowers or other regional powers. On this basis Saudi Arabia criticized Oman for its participation with the United States in military maneuvers in 1981.

In point of fact, the diplomacy of the GCC states adopted much of the content and style of traditional Saudi diplomacy. For instance, although the GCC states formally aligned with Iraq in the Iran-Iraq war, the constituent states still kept formal diplomatic relations with Iran. "Burn no bridges, make no enemies" could easily be the diplomatic slogan of the GCC.

Political and economic cooperation slowly followed the military-diplomatic success of the GCC. Left to its own devices, the GCC would have likely moved slowly toward regional integration. With the added goad of the Iraqi invasion of Kuwait and the ensuing war, the immediate future of the Gulf Cooperation Council seems brighter. The small, and mostly rich, states of the Gulf still live in a "bad neighborhood" with untrustworthy and unfriendly neighbors. Further integration appears to be the most likely avenue of political survival.

GCC relations with the United States have paralleled Saudi relations with the United States. That means that the GCC has often expressed reservations about the desirability of accepting the U.S. security umbrella. Historical American preferences for Israel and the astonishing U.S. attempts to trade hostages for arms with Iran during the Iran-Iraq war (the Iran-Contra affair) make the GCC states wary of publicly visible linkages with the United States. The Iraqi invasion of Kuwait changed most of those reservations and the GCC currently allows a high level of integration with the U.S. military. Linkages tested in Desert Storm remained in place afterward and the U.S.–GCC strategic alliance is one of the new facts of Middle Eastern international relations.

PALESTINIAN INTERNATIONAL ACTION

It is unfortunate, but in much of the world *terrorism* is equated with the Palestinians. It is unfortunate in the sense that the Palestinian people are for the most part no more engaged in the activities of international terror than are the members of any other nation. Nonetheless, the peculiar status of the Palestinians as a large, concentrated but stateless people struggling for some form of independence makes them particularly vulnerable to the kind of stereotyping that victimizes and dehumanizes them. That they struggle for independence against a government with a "special relationship" with the United States also makes objective analysis difficult. For the reality is that although most Palestinians are normal people who simply want to work and live their lives, terrorism has been a necessary strategy for those Palestinians organizing their drive for independence. To a people without a state, a police force, an army, or a capital, terror is the only available instrument of revolt against established state power.

Any discussion of political terrorism, regardless of how dispassionate or neutral, will inevitably raise emotional objections from those who initiate it or suffer from it. In these objections, the motives of either side in the equation of terror are reduced to the most simple and limited perspective. "Terrorists are simply bloodthirsty animals," say the objects of terrorist attacks. "No, we are freedom fighters attempting to overthrow a pitiless, merciless, repressive regime," respond the attackers, "and we must fight these monsters to the death with whatever means are at our disposal." Thus, in the final analysis, one man's terrorist is another man's freedom fighter. This fact, coupled with the widespread use of terror and political violence in our modern world, makes analysis difficult.

And yet, there are dispassionate and insightful observations that one may make about terrorists and their objectives, counterterrorists and theirs. Above all, terrorists seek the creation of a psychological mood. Terror works best in the glare of intense publicity and coverage by the mass media. This coverage can transform a small-scale and apparently random act into a gnawing sense of anxiety in the target population. We know of no government overthrown simply by the cumulation of terrorist acts. Thus, terror tactics, although morally reprehensible, can best be perceived as a sort of harassment or irritant, an activity that can claim the attention of government but rarely topple it. Reprisals against terrorists can, ironically, result in losses to the afflicted government, especially if the reprisal is not cleanly and clearly focused against the terrorists themselves. Thus, government attempts in Northern Ireland to suppress terrorism have generally created a fund of ill will among those nonterrorists who are nonetheless disadvantaged or hurt by the governmental policies. Policies of restraint are generally the most profitable in the long run, while policies of overreaction may in fact lead to substantial changes in the climate of world public opinion.

All of this has direct applicability to the situation in the Middle East, particularly as regards the Arab-Israeli conflict. Only the most studiously isolated individual is not aware of the wide-scale use of terror by the Palestinian groups confronting Israel. And Israel, particularly under the guidance of prime ministers Begin and Shamir, has made no secret of its intention to repay terrorist activity in kind, following the biblical injunction of "an eye for an eye, a tooth for a tooth." In keeping with the contemporary cry of "Never again," the government of Israel has invoked powerful symbols in its decision to utilize a counterterror strategy in its dealing with the Palestinian Arabs.

What follows in the next few pages is an attempt to place this pattern of violence and reprisal into the flow of contemporary international relations. It is not an attempt to draw moral lessons from either side's utilization of terror or violence, but simply to identify the consequences of those actions. Moreover, our effort here is not to catalogue those activities, but rather to emphasize those events that had the most symbolic importance in defining and redefining adversary roles in the conflict.

Totally frustrated in their efforts to obtain relief before 1967, Palestinians began to express their frustrations by violent means. Lacking a national base or homeland, the Palestinian movements were genuinely regional, moving from country to country as the patience and tempers of their hosts wore thin. Of the many formed, the two major organizations were the umbrella Palestine Liberation Organization (PLO) and its most powerful constituent organization, the Harakat al-Tahrir al-Falastini (Al-Fatah). Both of these organizations, between 1965 and 1975, accomplished a most dramatic change of status. From the image of bumbling PLO bureaucrats or of rag-tag, terrorist Al-Fatah revolutionaries furtively slinking across the Middle East landscape, both groups became accepted internationally as the government in exile of the Palestinian nation and are welcomed in many of the capitals of the world and in the U.N. This transformation was not accomplished without difficulty and pain. Dispersed across the Middle East, substantial groups of Palestinians inhabited dehumanizing refugee camps in Lebanon, Syria, Jordan, Gaza, and the West Bank. Others, more fortunate, occupied expatriate positions in the economies of nearly all the nations of the Middle East; they have become a valued resource, given their high level of education. Leaders of this fractured community could with good reason suggest that the Arab states had little interest in solving the Palestinian question, since to do so would reduce the pressure on Israel. Thus, it was not until the 1967 Arab-Israeli war that the Palestinian organizations found the tide of events moving, although sluggishly, in their direction.

Ironically, it was the Arab losses and Israeli victory in 1967 that gave the PLO and Al-Fatah the needed impetus. The movement of Israel into the West Bank created a new flood of dispossessed Palestinians, many of whom found the claims of the PLO and Al-Fatah attractive. Simultaneously, the defeat of the Arab armies undermined the prestige of the Arab states and their leaders, creating something of a power vacuum, at least where the confrontation with Israel was concerned. At any rate, the two Palestinian organizations suddenly found themselves in positions of preeminence in the Palestinian diaspora.

Al-Fatah, under the leadership of Yasir Arafat, became the most successful group in terms of violent operations against Israel, and in providing organized social services to its constituents. Operating initially out of bases in Jordan, Al-Fatah launched a number of attacks against Israel, attacks which ultimately prompted an Israeli retaliatory raid on a staging area in Jordan. The Israeli raid, although successful, encountered stiff Palestinian resistance, which was perceived by many young Arabs as an effective action, bringing increased attention and more volunteers to the organization. Between 1968 and 1970, Al-Fatah and other, smaller Palestinian groups engaged in increasingly violent guerrilla and terrorist activities, culminating in the hijacking of a number of jets—a Swissair DC-8, a TWA 707, a Pan American 747, and a BOAC VC-10. These audacious actions captured the attention of the international mass media, inevitably bringing the Palestinian organizations into public prominence. With this public prominence came discussion of Palestinian grievances. Ultimately, the PLO was granted observer status in the General Assembly by the United Nations.

The year 1970 marks a watershed for the Palestinian movements. Black September, the expulsion of the Palestinian guerrillas from Jordan, proved to be a serious setback to the movement. Moving to Lebanon, from 1970 to 1972, groups of Palestinians accelerated their military and terrorist activities, leading the Lebanese government to repressive measures. Palestinian units began to operate openly in southern Lebanon, in defiance of the government.

The growing role of the Palestinians in Lebanon was formalized in 1969 in a document midwifed by the Arab League and signed by the government of Lebanon and the PLO. Specific rights and areas of governmental competence were given to the PLO, supporting the war of attrition from southern Lebanon. Palestinian influence and position in Lebanon steadily improved until the PLO was generally recognized as one of the most potent political and military groups in the country. The Israeli invasion of Lebanon in 1982 radically altered this situation. The Israeli sweep placed the PLO between at least four dangerous enemies: the nascent Shia militias; the Syrian army; the Syrian backed factions of Palestinians opposed to Fatah; and the assortment of Christian family armies centered in Beirut and the adjacent mountains. The withdrawal of Arafat and his fighters, under U.S. protection, transformed the loyal PLO groups from military to diplomatic actors, with the PLO headquartered in Tunisia. Other Palestinian groups quickly emerged to continue the military and terrorist pressure on Israel.

Conflict between the various factions of Palestinians often turned violent, producing what has been called the "war of the camps." Of some international importance is the fact that the PLO itself became the focus of terror during the Israeli invasion and occupation. The horrifying massacres in the Palestinian refugee camps in 1982—carried out by Christian Lebanese militia while the Israeli army sealed off the exit from the camps and provided logistical support—created substantial international sympathy for the beleaguered PLO. Yasir Arafat has shown himself more than able to exploit this drift of sympathy, and realigned with his former foes in Jordan and Egypt, enjoy wide recognition as the only credible national leader of the Palestinian people. The departure of the Arafat factions of the PLO did not result in a net reduction of terrorist activity in Lebanon. If anything, the scope of terrorism expanded, including not just Israel, but other targets as well. Many of the terrorist actions were attributed to a shadowy organization called Islamic Jihad. This may in fact be a convenient clearinghouse for a variety of organizations. What is clear is that terrorism is widely considered an appropriate vehicle for political action. It is a fact of life, and not just in the contemporary Middle East.

Two events of 1985 and 1986—the hijacking of the cruise ship *Achille Lauro* and the coordinated attacks on the passenger lounges of the Vienna and Rome airports—demonstrate the complexity of dealing with terrorist action. In each case, initial assumptions about the origin and affiliations of the terrorists proved to be either wrong or oversimplifications. For instance, the centrality of the Libyan role in these actions was initially assumed to be clear and incontrovertible, but in the long run was shown to be problematic, with facts, motives, and organizational structure proving to be murky and diffuse. The identity of the terrorist organizations also proved to be difficult and accountability hard to establish.

A final resolution of who was responsible for the bombing of Pan Am flight 103 over Lockerbie, Scotland, may never be accomplished. But the string of credible accusations again demonstrated the difficulty of affixing responsibility. U.S.

and British authorities initially charged the Abu Nidal faction of the Palestinian movement with responsibility. Syrian involvement was eventually added, and at other times it was claimed that Iran had contracted for the bombing, in an act of revenge for its passenger liner shot down over the Gulf by a U.S. warship. Ultimately, the responsibility was pinned on Libya and U.S. and British spokesmen demanded the extradition of the Libyan diplomats charged in the bombing. Syria, Iran, and the Palestinians, by 1991, had all been exonerated in the bombing. But political pressures and realities may yet reverse even that finding. Accountability for terrorist activity is as difficult to determine in the 1990s as it was when it began in earnest in the 1970s.

Phase III Palestinian activity benefited from a growing world recognition of the fact that Jewish relief had resulted in Palestinian injustice. It also benefited from growing financial support from OAPEC members including Kuwait, Saudi Arabia, the U.A.E., and Khomeini's Iran; from the United States' growing inability to ignore Arab wishes in regard to the Palestinian question; and finally, and not insignificantly, from what was perceived as Israeli tendencies to overreact to terrorist raids on its territory. The West Bank settlement policies of Israel, in particular, convinced many governments of Israeli intransigence toward negotiated Palestinian autonomy on the West Bank.

The Palestinian intifadah beginning in late 1987 prompted Israeli reprisals and draconian attempts to suppress this insurrection. The televised images of public beatings, tear-gassings, shootings, deportations, the destruction of housing, and the like by the Israeli army did much to change international public opinion, particularly in the United States, where many Jewish political action organizations professed public distaste for the violence in Israel. American television networks and news wires began carrying information revealing Israeli repression, further contributing to a change in public opinion in the United States. Most important, protest emerged within Israel itself, further polarizing the Israeli polity and influencing the elections in the fall of 1988.

For this and other reasons, the PLO decided that the fall of 1988 was the right time for a "peace offensive" of major proportions, including a public disavowal of terrorism. Arafat's difficulties in enforcing such a line among the very complex set of organizations that make up the Palestinian diaspora was dramatized in the December bombing of Pan Am flight 103, en route from Frankfurt to New York, with a large loss of life and attendant publicity. Although the PLO was ultimately found innocent in the bombing, it was nonetheless embarrassing to Arafat and was greeted by a chorus of "I told you so's" from Israeli leaders. Nonetheless, the transformation of the PLO into a legitimate governmental organization that speaks for Palestinian interests was under way.

OPEC AND ISLAM

Regional Arab relations in Phase III were dominated by two emergent trends: first, the effect of OPEC petroleum pricing on the incomes of Saudi Arabia, Iran, Libya, Kuwait, Iraq, and the U.A.E., and others; second, the emergence of Islamic fundamentalism as a potent force in Arab politics. These two trends were in fact intertwined.

With the exception of Iraq, the major petroleum-producing countries in this region were also religiously conservative: Saudi Arabia is dominated by a severely conservative school of Islam; Iran is governed by fundamentalist Shia revolutionaries led by the ulema; Kuwait and the U.A.E. are ruled by traditional leaders who rely on the support of the ulema; and Libya is dominated by a unique Islamic fundamentalism developed by Muammar Qadaffi. These countries have utilized their substantial oil revenues to support religious goals. Kuwait and Saudi Arabia have tied loans and investments to specific Islamic reforms that they wish to see in Egypt and the Sudan. Iran and Libya have supported a variety of anti-Israel, anti-Western movements across the Middle East, both Sunni and Shia. Fundamentalist movements have gained ground in Syria, Lebanon, Iraq, Jordan, Egypt, Turkey, and Algeria, all working toward the establishment of an Islamic state, a government based specifically and exclusively on the precepts of Islam. The Muslim Brotherhood, long proscribed in Egypt since its conflict with Nasser early in the revolution, found new bases of support in Egypt and the Fertile Crescent. These movements, fragmented across many lines, nonetheless posed a singular threat to the prevailing secularism of the earlier international order.

Coordination of policy and collective action have tended to increase in the area in recent years. The early success of OPEC, and of its Arab subgroup OAPEC, led to a number of international development projects funded out of the growing revenues of the petroleum-rich states. Some of these projects had at the minimum a semblance of collective control. Joint economic ventures between OAPEC members, such as the huge dry-dock facility in Bahrain, were also examples of collective action. The successful pursuit of Palestinian rights in the United Nations has been mentioned earlier, and Arab members have occasionally coordinated the freezing of deposits for development projects seen as hostile to the Palestinian cause.

Islam itself has spawned a large number of international conferences and organizations, as a growing Islamic international community searches for ways to implement Islamic principles in banking, commerce, and social and political organization. A group of forty-two Islamic nations met together in 1980 to consider and protest the Soviet action in Afghanistan, and a small number of them actually broke off relations with the U.S.S.R. as a result. A similar meeting was held in Taif, Saudi Arabia, early in 1981. This meeting affirmed the earlier position taken on Afghanistan and additionally took a very dim view of the Iran-Iraq war, which was perceived as damaging to the Umma. The conference was persistent, although unsuccessful, in its efforts to mediate the Iran-Iraq conflict.

Nuclear Arms and Regional Politics

Finally, nuclear politics appear to have taken on a regional flavor. The Israeli nuclear arsenal has long been recognized as a major factor in any major Middle Eastern confrontation, although the specifics of those nuclear weapons are carefully guarded secrets. Arab responses to the Israeli nuclear capability have included regional support for the development of nuclear weapons, often described as the "Islamic bomb." Documented reports of cooperation between Iran, Pakistan, and Libya circulated. The Israeli preemptive strike against Iraq's nuclear reactor was thus set against a backdrop of a changing nuclear world. Complicating matters was the fact that nuclear technology was no longer the dark secret that it once was: The technology was now available for purchase, and many Middle Eastern states had sufficient financial resources to do so. The aftermath of the collapse of the Soviet Union put many sophisticated Soviet nuclear scientists on the world market.

In the aftermath of Desert Storm it was all too clear that Iraq had made substantial progress in its drive for nuclear capability, utilizing a combination of domestic and international human and technical resources. All of this suggests an enormously more complicated international system, one capable of taking the world to the edge of nuclear catastrophe from a regional level of conflict. If these trends work out as it appears they may, we will have to abandon our metaphor about the "tinderbox" Middle East and replace it with more apocalyptic imagery.

Nuclear weapons were not the only area of armament concern. In the last stages of the Iran-Iraq war, Iraq and Iran fought with chemical weapons and with independently modified ballistic missiles. The lack of effective international condemnation of these uses apparently spurred production in Iraq and many other countries as well. In 1988, U.S. accusations that Libya was building a chemical weapons facility in the guise of a pharmaceutical plant led to a confrontation between U.S. and Libyan aircraft, resulting in the shooting down of two Libyan MIG-23's over international water. President Reagan, in the waning days of his administration, publicly speculated on the desirability of a "surgical strike" to eliminate the Libyan facility. Once again, intentions and facts are difficult to pin down, since facilities that can produce fertilizers, soaps, or pharmaceuticals can easily be transformed to produce gases, explosives, and other chemical weapons. Again, the evidence from Iraq confirmed the hypothesis that chemical and biological weapons of mass destruction were technically and economically feasible in Third World countries. This, combined with the fact that a consortium of Third World nations now produce missile delivery systems independent of great power technology, suggests that the world is becoming a more dangerous place. The Middle East is, of course, a case in point.

THE FOREIGN POLICIES OF EGYPT, SAUDI ARABIA, IRAN, AND ISRAEL

In this section, we will discuss the respective foreign policies of Egypt, Saudi Arabia, Iran, and Israel. Collectively or independently, these nations have been responsible for most of the international initiatives and exchanges in the region.

Egyptian Foreign Policy

In the post-1948 Middle East, Egyptian foreign policy concerned itself with the following major issues: opposition to colonialism-imperialism, opposition to Israel, Arab unity, and, after the revolution, opposition to conservative Arab regimes.

For some 2,000 years Egypt had been the prime example of a colonized state. In that long span of time, rarely had the Egyptians been ruled by anything faintly resembling an Egyptian ruling class. The rejection received by Napoleon when he proposed self-rule to the Egyptian ulema was characteristic of the relationship between Egypt and her rulers: Egyptians were intrinsically suspicious of outside powers. All of this was to end after World War II, when Egypt struggled to free itself of European domination. Farouk's foreign policy had consisted of attempts to play one set of European powers (England and France) off against another (Germany and Italy). Since the Egyptian revolution and the rise of Nasser, however, the concept of anti-imperialism took on greater depth and meaning, until it meant to many the complete removal of foreign influence from Egypt. This rejection of foreign influence, moreover, was an issue with domestic origins and consequences—an issue to which the Egyptian masses would respond wholeheartedly. Opposition to colonialism-imperialism became as important to domestic policy as it did to foreign policy.

Nationalism and anti-imperialism are very often delicately intertwined, producing a complex fabric of action and reaction. The question is in some final sense unresolvable: does an antiimperialistic movement create nationalism, or is antiimperialism itself created by emergent nationalistic feeling? The resolution of this question must await further study. At this point, and especially in the case of Egypt, we must note the existence of a symbiotic relationship between the two forces—a relationship that has enormously complicated Egypt's pursuit of a consistent foreign policy.

Although Egypt was nominally independent of direct foreign control before Nasser's rise to power, many postcolonial problems needed resolution. These problems dominated Egyptian foreign policy in early Phase II. Among them were the relationship between Egypt and the Sudan, both former British dependencies (political union was one of the early ideological goals of the revolutionary movement); British rights to control and defend the Suez Canal; and a pattern of mutual defense agreements negotiated before and during World War II. The range of possible solutions was limited because these issues evoked powerful emotions in the Egyptian public, particularly in Cairo, where any agreement with a foreign power would be seen as suspect. The great powers insisted that these problems were but a subset of the larger bipolar confrontation of East and West.

The question of the Sudan's relationship to Egypt was solved peacefully, but not in a way that was consistent with Egypt's initial objectives. A series of elections led the Sudan ultimately to opt for independence rather than union. The other problems were more complicated and led to international tensions. The sensitive problem of Egypt's relations with the West and the problem of its security goals, conflicting as they did with Egypt's difficulties with Israel, resulted in the Suez crisis and the frustrations over the Aswan Dam detailed earlier in this book.

The Suez crisis and the Aswan Dam controversy confirmed Nasser's belief that relations with the Western alliance were going to be uneven. The United States' and Europe's response to Egypt's negotiations for Eastern bloc arms was hostile and proved that promised economic and technical aid had clearly visible political strings. Accordingly, Nasser moved more and more to a posture of nonalignment and began to play an important role in that world movement.

Egypt took a leadership role at the first major nonalignment conference in Bandung, Indonesia (April 1955). Spurred on by his distaste for the Baghdad Pact and the extension of the bipolar conflict into the Middle East, Nasser subsequently hosted many of the major meetings of the nonaligned powers and forcefully argued for nonaligned foreign policy in the region. Nasser attempted to coordinate his nonaligned foreign policy with such neutralist leaders as Nehru of India, Tito of Yugoslavia, and Sukarno of Indonesia. He attacked the Eisenhower Doctrine of 1957, and continued his unrelenting opposition to European imperialism.

In the 1960s, Egypt's opposition to Western imperialism and to Israel necessitated closer military relations with the Soviet Union, upon which it was now solely dependent for arms. This, combined with the growing number of Soviet technicians assigned to the Aswan Dam project, confirmed many Western judgments that Egypt, along with Syria and Iraq, had slipped irretrievably into the orbit of the Eastern bloc. These reactions were premature and underestimated Nasser's ability to take aid and maintain his own independence of action. The Soviet Union, for its part, was never able to consolidate its gains in Egypt and in 1972 departed on Sadat's orders.

Egypt's relationship with Israel has been paradoxical; Egypt has lost every military encounter with Israel but has won much more in the peace settlements. Israel's obviously superior military forces defeated Egyptian armies in 1948, 1956, 1967, and 1973; Israel also intervened with small tactical units in neighboring Arab nations at will during the same period. Each victory became more expensive to Israel and Egypt alike, requiring extensive and speedy military rearmament. Egyptian losses in these encounters far outstripped the losses of her allies, leading to the widespread observation that other Arab states were willing to fight the Israelis "to the last Egyptian."

Despite these consistent military losses, Egyptian prestige in the Arab world was enhanced by these defeats. World public opinion turned gradually in a pro-Egyptian direction, and Israeli interests in the U.N. began to wane. In both Egypt and the wider world, the struggle against imperialism and colonialism came increasingly to be seen as continuous with the struggle against Israel.

The political results of the 1967 Arab-Israeli war illustrate Nasser's gift at turning liabilities into assets. The war itself began as a result of Nasser's miscalculation. Increasingly irritated by the presence of UNEF forces on Egypt's territory but not on Israel's, Nasser ordered the removal of the U.N. barrier troops. Shortly thereafter, he announced his intention to blockade Israeli shipping at the Straits of Tiran. Since Nasser was at the time involved in a costly and frustrating venture in Yemen, it is doubtful that he expected the Israeli attack that occurred on June 5, 1967. At the end of the brief war the Israeli army occupied all of the Sinai, had taken the Golan Heights from Syria, destroyed most of the Iraqi air force on the ground, and occupied Jerusalem and the West Bank of the Jordan River. These losses were traumatic to Nasser and the Arab states. U.N. intervention once again brought a cease-fire and an end to the fighting. On June 9, Nasser submitted his resignation as president, citing his failure in the war. The Cairo masses refused the resignation with an outpouring of support, prompting Nasser to rescind his resignation and resume his leadership role. What in military terms could be described as a rout, became a reaffirmation of Nasser's leadership.

United Nations involvement did not stop with the cease-fire. Most important was the passage of U.N. Resolution 242 on November 22, 1967. This resolution called for the removal of Israeli armed forces from territories gained in the 1967 war, and called upon all the nations of the region to recognize each other's rights to "live in peace within secure and recognized boundaries free from threats or acts of force." This resolution was greeted with mixed emotions by Egypt and her allies.

While they approved of the return of the conquered territory, they were not pleased with the second point of the resolution, which would permanently recognize Israel's right to exist in peace. Events in the 1970s found the Arab states anxious to accept the resolution and Israel reluctant to surrender the territory. In the final analysis, Arab support of Resolution 242 became a key item in the Arab propaganda conflict with Israel. The support of the resolution was an important factor in the shift of world opinion toward the Arab and Palestinian cause.

Egypt's venture in Yemen was also frustrating. The Egyptian army was largely removed from Yemen on an emergency basis to shore up defenses after the 1967 war. From 1962 to 1967, the Egyptians had intervened substantially in the Yemeni civil war on the side of the republican forces. During this period Egyptian troop strength rose to around 80,000 in Yemen. They were opposed by Saudi Arabia, which provided logistical and communication support to the ousted imam, and by tribesmen in the Yemeni hill country. As with the 1967 war, there was no clear solution to this conflict in sight. The expenditure of many lives and dollars resulted in a coalition government, with the royalists and the republicans sharing power. The Egyptian goal, the establishment of a pan-Arab revolutionary regime, was frustrated. The Saudi goal of rescuing a traditional system from revolutionary pressure was also frustrated. The conflict between the modernizing pan-Arabs led by Nasser and the conservative traditional leaders led by Saudi Arabia was not resolved: Saudi and Egyptian relations reached a low point.

From the 1967 war until his death in 1970, Nasser pursued a political solution to the Arab-Israeli conflict. This political strategy necessitated regional cooperation, both formal and informal. Egypt's encouragement of the PLO and Al-Fatah during this period is an example of its informal diplomacy. At the time of his death, Nasser was presiding over a pan-Arab conference in Cairo designed to resolve the Black September conflict between the Palestinian fedayeen and the Jordanian army. This exemplified his formal diplomacy in the post-1967 period.

Egyptian relations with Libya, its western neighbor, were relatively uneventful prior to the emergence in 1969 of Colonel Muammar Qadaffi as the Libyan ruler. A charismatic leader, Qadaffi possessed a sense of mission and saw himself as Nasser's heir apparent as head of the pan-Arab movement. The tension between the leadership styles of Sadat and Qadaffi soon became quite apparent, although Sadat acquiesced in a proposed Egyptian-Libyan union in 1972–1973. Sadat's reluctance was probably based equally on his misgivings about the great differences between the two countries demographically and economically and his appraisal of Qadaffi's erratic and radicalizing leadership. The union never got off the ground, and it brought the two leaders into open confrontation. In 1974, the Egyptians claimed they had discovered a Libyan plot against Sadat's government. Since that time, relations between the two states have been cold, occasionally erupting into overt conflict. Libya's support of terrorist movements and her leadership role in the anti-Israeli rejectionist bloc have set her at formal diplomatic odds with Egypt. Libya took the severest stand against Sadat for his bilateral negotiations with the Israelis and reputedly placed a price on his head. As the promise of the Camp David Accords dimmed, Libya's pressure on the Egyptian leader took on more international weight. Egypt thus found itself, in Phase III, increasingly estranged from the Arab states that she once sought to lead. Egyptian diplomatic efforts during the Iran-Iraq war were largely ignored in the Arab states, confirming

Egyptian isolation. For its part, Iraq accepted limited Egyptian military aid during its conflict with Iran.

Egyptian foreign policy under Sadat and Mubarak.

The foreign policy of Anwar Sadat constituted a dramatic shift in emphasis from that of Nasser. Under Nasser, Egypt had pursued a policy of Arab unity through revolutionary action and development. Sadat sought friendly relations with all Arab states, regardless of their revolutionary status. The hostility that previously marked Egyptian relations with Saudi Arabia and Jordan, for instance, declined markedly. Sadat put great emphasis on the political resolution of the Israeli question, building on Nasser's belated conversion to this policy. Sadat's personal gifts allowed a public-relations offensive to be launched in the West, particularly in the United States, where he showed himself to be very adept at talk shows and news interviews.

Soviet influence also declined under Sadat's leadership. Soviet involvement in the attempted *coup* against Sadat in 1971, and its hesitance to supply sophisticated new weaponry to the Egyptian army, eventually resulted in its abrupt expulsion from the country in July 1972. Since that time, U.S. influence and arms have gradually replaced the Soviet presence.

Sadat's commitment to a political solution to the Arab-Israeli conflict did not prevent him from initiating the war of October 6, 1973, the Ramadan, or Yom Kippur, war. Sadat's attack on the Israeli Bar-Lev line met with short-term success but incurred heavy armaments losses to both sides; Egypt and Israel called for immediate arms deliveries. The United States responded with airlifts to Israel, which the Israeli army was quick to exploit. The Israeli army was able shortly afterward to reverse the Egyptian gains and reestablish their positions along part of the Suez Canal. The Egyptian Third Army was effectively surrounded when the Israelis crossed the canal. The threat of the annihilation of the Egyptian force brought a threat of intervention from the Soviet Union.

At this point, the Arab states proclaimed an oil embargo against the United States and its Western allies. This embargo caused the United States to exercise its influence more evenly; as a result of U.S. pressure, the Israeli army did not follow up on its advantages in the Sinai, and the Egyptian Third Army was extricated from the cul-de-sac into which it had been thrown. Subsequent "shuttle diplomacy" conducted largely by U.S. Secretary of State Henry Kissinger and his assistant Joseph Sisco resulted in a cease-fire and the initiation of many rounds of diplomacy between the United States, Israel, and Egypt. Once again, having lost the war, Egypt may be said to have won the peace.

These diplomatic exchanges, referred to collectively as Sinai I and Sinai II, resulted in the following: the withdrawal of Israeli forces back to the Mitla and Gidi Passes; the monitoring of the neutral zone between the passes and the canal by U.S. electronic surveillance; the recovery by Egypt of the oil fields in the western Sinai; and reopening of the Suez Canal with its attendant revenues. But most of all, the United States had been drawn into the Arab-Israeli confrontation in a more balanced manner. From this time on, Sadat sought closer relations with the United States and attempted to use these relations to bring increased diplomatic pressure to bear on Israel. Thus the stage was set for Egyptian foreign policy in Phase III.

Sadat's postwar diplomatic offensive reached its zenith in his dramatic November 1977 address to the Israeli Knesset. The visit of an Arab head of state to

Israel was an enormous symbolic and substantive act. His speech effectively broke the diplomatic deadlock. From this point on, Egypt engaged in bilateral negotiations with Israel, a policy bitterly opposed by the Arab rejectionists—Syria, Iraq, Libya, South Yemen, Algeria, and the PLO. These negotiations unfortunately produced little or no tangible results. They did, however, prepare the way for the remarkable events associated with the Camp David Accords, reached in September 1978.

The Camp David Accords have been described as a triumph of personal diplomacy for President Carter. During eleven days of face-to-face negotiation at Camp David, Maryland, Carter convinced Sadat and Begin to agree to a set of accords that would create a "framework for peace" in the Arab-Israeli conflict. The accords can be divided into two sections. The first accord dealt with the bilateral relations between Egypt and Israel. It involved the return, by stages, of Egyptian territory in the Sinai, and the normalization of relations, including the eventual exchange of ambassadors. By 1980 large numbers of Israelis were touring in Egypt, at least one Jewish temple was reopened in Cairo, and reports of the opening of kosher restaurants circulated in the Western press. To protect Egypt from the potential criticism of the rejectionist states, however, the first accord was linked in principle to a second accord dealing with the West Bank and the Gaza Strip. The second accord directly addressed the problem of the occupied territories and the future of the Palestinian people. The Palestinians, in the loosely worded agreement, were to be granted "autonomy" on the West Bank, although the implications of this term were not spelled out.

The negotiations that followed between Egypt and Israel proceeded fairly smoothly where the disengagement of their forces and the return of Sinai territory were concerned. Simultaneous negotiations on the second accord immediately began to stall on the question of the West Bank. Ultimately, while the first part of the accords was fully implemented, resulting in a near normalization of relations between Israel and Egypt, no discernible progress was made on the subject of Palestinian autonomy. In fact, shortly after the Camp David Accords were announced, the Begin government began to increase the number of Jewish settlements on the West Bank; and late in 1980, it announced that henceforth Jerusalem would become the indivisible capital of Israel by action of the Knesset. Apparently, Israel's leaders did not share Egypt's concepts of autonomy.

Predictably, Egypt came under intense Arab criticism for backsliding on the confrontation with Israel. Even the more conservative states of Saudi Arabia and Kuwait joined in the condemnation of Egypt. Radical groups announced the formation of assassination teams aimed at Sadat. Egypt, for its part, gained economically and socially in the bilateral agreement with Israel, but at the cost of its leadership position in the Arab world. Israel gained a secure border that was guaranteed by her most dependable international ally, the United States. The Palestinians, as usual, lost another chance for self-determination and independence.

As Egypt came more into confrontation with her Arab neighbors, she became more dependent on American aid and support. Cooperation between the two nations occurred in the economic, political, and military areas. Nasser's cherished nonalignment policy became a casualty of Sadat's pragmatism.

Ultimately, Sadat himself became a casualty of his domestic and international policies. Egyptian foreign policy under Sadat's successor, Hosni Mubarak, recaptured much of the prestige and status that had eroded in the Arab world since Camp David. Mubarak successfully sought the restoration of relations with the Arab states and cooled his relations with Israel to a diplomatically "correct" temperature, particularly after the invasion of Lebanon. Mubarak's relationship with Washington also remained strong, and growing U.S. economic and military aid to Egypt indicates that Washington perceived Cairo as a trustworthy ally. Both countries have in recent years conducted joint military exercises (Operation Bright Star) predicated on joint operations. All in all, Mubarak has been able to substantially improve his relations with his Arab neighbors (including Arafat's PLO) without threatening the close Egyptian–U.S. relationship. Egypt provided much of the venue for U.S. support of Iraq during the war with Iran, a posture palatable to all of the major Middle Eastern actors except Libya, Syria, and, of course, Iran. Mubarak engaged in "personal diplomacy" in his ongoing attempts to facilitate political "conversations" between the PLO, Jordan, the United States, and, ultimately, Israel. In this sense, he has continued the broad reconciliation policy initiated by Sadat.

Egyptian-Israeli relations were greatly strained by the Israeli effort to control the intifadah in the occupied territories. One result of the cooling in relations was strong pressure by Egypt on Arafat and the PLO for an initiative that would bring some movement on the Palestinian question. As Arafat acquiesced to pressure from Egypt and other moderate Arab states, and from the United States and the Soviet Union alike, the prestige of Egypt waxed. This growing prestige was given a great boost from Egypt's early participation in the coalition ranged against Iraq after its invasion of Kuwait. Egyptian prestige grew again as the United States pressed forward with an attempt to solve the Palestinian question through Arab-Israeli negotiations. At one point, facing destructive public rhetoric from Yitzhak Shamir and Hafez al-Assad, Mubarak threatened to make public their earlier "private" meetings and conversations. Egypt is clearly one of the premier international actors in the region. And the election of an Egyptian, Butros Ghali, in 1992 as Secretary-General of the United Nations furthered increased Egypt's international visibility and prestige. On the negative side, Mubarak's growing international prestige as a regional "moderate" may result in growing friction with the fundamentalists gaining political strength in Egypt.

The special relationship between Egypt and the United States has remained intact since the Camp David Accords and strengthened during and after the Iraq-Kuwait crisis, assuring Egypt a generous flow of American aid and the forgiveness of $6 billion of debt. One should not overestimate the influence that this aid garners the United States in Cairo, but there is clearly a relationship of mutual respect between the two countries that translates into specific policy gains for both parties.

Saudi Foreign Policy

Saudi Arabia is the one Arab country that immediately after World War II could point to a long-standing relationship with the United States. This relationship began in the 1930s as American oil companies began to appreciate and exploit the enormous petroleum reserves of this recently consolidated kingdom. In fact, the earliest relationships between Saudi Arabia and the West were exclusively the product of the oil companies' initiatives. King Ibn Saud, in desperate financial straits in 1933, required a loan of £30,000 in gold sovereigns as part of the original oil concession agreements. This loan, put up not by the U.S. government but rather by the participating oil companies, came at a critical time for the king, allowing him to maintain the loyalties of key elements in his new tribal coalition. The American government was at this time disinterested in the affairs of this remote region. The loan apparently produced enormous goodwill toward the oil companies in particular and toward the United States in general. In the future, in spite of cordial relations with Britain and concerted efforts by the Germans and Japanese just before World War II, Ibn Saud expressed his preference for America. He was to pursue this preference during World War II, in spite of his experts' counsel to the contrary and in spite of lost potential oil revenues from sales that could have been made to the Axis powers. His loyalty proved to be an enormous asset to the United States during the war and immediately thereafter.

The emerging relationship between the United States and Saudi Arabia just after World War II can be fairly characterized as *special*, a term connoting an unusual mutuality of interests and policy between the two states. U.S. interest in Saudi oil was also complemented by its interest in maintaining and expanding its air base at Dharan, a base that linked Western interests in India with the Mediterranean, as part of the larger Western attempt to contain possible Soviet expansion. U.S. payments to Saudi Arabia, both governmental and corporate, began to rise annually. The new found wealth prompted the initiation of a number of ambitious development projects from 1947 on, which in turn necessitated the movement of a larger number of American technicians and advisors to the kingdom. The development projects, which ran the gamut from communications, transportation, and electrification to public health and public education, significantly raised Saudi prestige in the Middle East. Ibn Saud's ministers fully entered into the international relations of the region. From this time, Saudi Arabia was to be one of the major actors in the Middle Eastern international order.

One of King Ibn Saud's first international ventures in the postwar period concerned the future of the Palestinians. Relying on his special relationship with President Roosevelt, King Ibn Saud sought and received assurances that no decisions affecting the future of the Palestinians and Jerusalem would be made without consideration of Arab wishes. Ibn Saud's public espousal of the Palestinian cause heightened his prestige among the Arab states. It also made for his first major disappointment in U.S. policy, as President Truman virtually ignored Roosevelt's promise of consultation in his hasty recognition of Israel in 1948.

Saudi Arabian prestige and power were clearly on the rise at the time of King Ibn Saud's death in 1953. He was succeeded in power by his son Saud ibn Abdulaziz. Simultaneously, the new king's younger brother Faisal was named Crown Prince. The new king was a far less effective monarch than his father.

The new King Saud, from 1953 onward, changed the basic thrust of Saudi foreign policy. Where his father had pursued a policy of close alignment with the United States, Saud moved into a closer alliance with revolutionary Egypt, accepting the principles of nonalignment put forward by Nasser. Simultaneously, Saudi Arabia opposed the Hashemite kingdoms of Jordan and Iraq. The Hashemite family, long influential in the tribal politics of the Arabian peninsula, had been among the final obstacles to Ibn Saud's consolidation of his kingdom. Fear of possible Hashemite reprisals from bases in Jordan and Iraq motivated much of Saudi international policy. Ibn Saud protected himself against potential Hashemite intrigue by allying himself with England, the major international guarantor of the Hashemite house. King Saud approached this problem by formally adopting in 1955 the Egyptian revolutionary policy toward Jordan and Iraq. This policy essentially involved a continuing attempt to isolate diplomatically the two countries and to support actively antimonarchical movements there. However, although Egypt and Saudi Arabia had common interests, including opposition to Israel, it was becoming increasingly clear to the Saudi elite that Saudi Arabian interests would ultimately conflict with Egypt's.

Growing dissatisfaction over King Saud's conduct of policy, domestic and foreign, led to efforts within the royal family to limit his power and to enhance the power of Crown Prince Faisal, acting as prime minister. These efforts bore fruit in 1958. The emergence of Faisal as the primary decision maker signaled what was to become an important shift in the foreign policy posture of Saudi Arabia.

Under Faisal's influence, King Saud became increasingly cool toward Cairo and increasingly cordial toward Iraq and Jordan. Encouraged by the United States, which feared growing Soviet influence in the area, Saudi Arabia ceased its attempted destabilization of Jordan and Iraq. This is the same period in which the Eisenhower Doctrine was pronounced, offering and guaranteeing necessary aid to any Middle Eastern state suffering foreign aggression. King Saud endorsed this declaration after a state visit to the United States.

Crown Prince Faisal proved to be an effective leader. His domestic reforms quickly restored fiscal stability to the kingdom. His foreign policy was more finely balanced and moderate, a foreign policy informed more by Saudi self-interest than international alliance politics. Substantial domestic policy gains were scored, all of which contributed to a recovery of Saudi prestige in the Middle East. Relations with Cairo became formal and correct, but not warm. Soon, the two countries would enter into protracted hostilities in Yemen.

Faisal's initial period of rule was challenged by dissident elements in the ruling family. These elements persuaded King Saud to place certain policy demands on Faisal that he was unwilling to accept. Faisal resigned and was replaced by a candidate from the dissident ranks. The new prime minister, Prince Talal, fell victim to jealous intrigues himself, some eight months after his rise to power. From 1962 to 1964, Crown Prince Faisal gradually reacquired his lost power and gained more, until he became the virtual ruler and Saud became a figurehead. This situation was finally resolved in November 1964 when Saud was deposed by royal family consensus and Faisal made king. Saud died in exile in 1969.

King Faisal continued the close relationship between the United States and Saudi Arabia, but the relationship changed substantially between 1964 and 1975. Faisal became increasingly bewildered and irritated by the United States' unconditional support of Israel. This developing tension between the two countries did not suffice to reorient Saudi policy toward the revolutionary Arab states or the Soviet Union. But it was undoubtedly instrumental in Faisal's decision to participate in the Arab oil embargo immediately after the 1973 Arab-Israeli war. This embargo, which shook the American economy, was indicative of a new Saudi attitude toward the United States and the U.S.S.R., an attitude that emphasized the growing independence of Saudi Arabia in foreign policy. Saudi Arabia thus moved into Phase III of its foreign policy. In this phase relations were based more and more on the grounds of pragmatism and national interest., a new posture at least partially facilitated by the increasing income generated by its petroleum sales. Thus, although Saudi Arabia participated fully in the 1973 oil embargo against the United States, it continued to maintain close economic and military relations with the United States. And Saudi Arabia, under Faisal and his successor, Khalid, attempted to substantially improve its independent military strength through the purchase of sophisticated armaments and training from the United States and elsewhere. In 1980–1981, the Saudis sought to significantly upgrade their tactical air capabilities and to purchase sophisticated U.S. radar planes (AWACs). Israeli opposition to such transfers was vehement.

The assassination of Faisal in March 1975 by a minor and mentally unstable member of the royal family ended the administration of this remarkable leader. He was succeeded in office by King Khalid. The transition was smooth and involved minimal administrative disruption. Of some importance from an elite perspective was the continued influence of Prince Fahd, whose influence on Saudi government continued unabated from the reign of King Faisal through the reign of King Khalid. Under Khalid, Fahd would assume even more direct control over the conduct of foreign policy.

Between 1978 and 1980, Saudi Arabia became even more disillusioned with U.S. policy in the Middle East. Saudi spokesmen such as Prince Fahd and Sheikh Yamani (Minister of Petroleum) were openly critical of U.S. policy. In their view, a quid pro quo between the United States and Saudi Arabia developed shortly after the 1973 oil embargo. This agreement required Saudi Arabia to increase its oil production and oppose extreme price increases by the militant members of OPEC and OAPEC. In return, the United States committed itself to an evenhanded Middle Eastern policy; it agreed to sell sophisticated military technology to Saudi Arabia and Egypt, and to pressure Israel to return the occupied territories and settle the Palestinian question. In the Saudi view, they were faithful to their part of the bargain, while the United States dragged its heels on armament sales and failed to force the Begin government to implement the Camp David accords regarding Palestinian autonomy. In the immediate aftermath of Desert Storm, in 1992, the Saudis reluctantly joined in the multilateral peace conference organized by the Bush administration, demonstrating its continuing reservations about U.S. policy

King Khalid's death in 1982 brought Prince Fahd to the throne. Fahd's stewardship of Saudi foreign policy continued a modest activism, culminating in the presentation of a comprehensive peace plan for the Middle East. Like other Saudi efforts, it was predicated on the United States taking a more active role in constraining and influencing Israeli policy. And like other efforts, the initiatives failed to bear fruit. The Saudis continued to place much of the responsibility on the United States for its reluctance to "play tough" with Israel. Another constraint on Saudi foreign policy was declining petroleum revenues, forcing harder domestic and international choices. Both of these factors were important influences in the Saudi decision to strongly commit its leadership and resources to the Gulf Cooperation Council, an organization that Saudi Arabia dominates and which demonstrated its importance as a diplomatic and military coordinating body during the Iraqi invasion of Kuwait.

The Saudi complaints about the U.S. policy inconsistencies have substance, but, in fairness, the Saudi elite probably overestimates the independence of the

American president in the conduct of foreign policy. Israeli influence in Congress and in presidential elections has been strong enough historically to make a pro-Arab stance a severe political liability. On the other hand, the United States and Saudi Arabia continue to maintain a strong military and economic relationship. Saudi and U.S. interests, at base, are predicated on a number of similar assumptions: primarily, that the political status quo is preferable to revolutionary change.

It is also clear that in the past twenty years Saudi Arabia changed from being an uncritical ally of the United States to a country pursuing its self-interest based on its growing financial and economic power. More and more, the elites of Saudi Arabia have turned away from dependent international alliances and toward independent national pragmatism. The Islamic revolution and attendant events in Iran did much to undermine Saudi confidence in the ability of the United States to unilaterally protect the Saudi monarchy and Saudi territory; and the danger to Saudi Arabia during the Iraqi invasion of Kuwait made this realization even more tangible and manifest. Saudi Arabia can be expected to pursue even more independent foreign policy in the coming years, years that will see growing internal pressure on the Saudi elite. These internal pressures, combined with the potent forces of revolutionary Islam in the contemporary Middle East, could thrust Saudi Arabia into new domestic and international conflicts.

Saudi Arabia's increasingly paternalistic posture toward its Gulf neighbors, the U.A.E., Qatar, Bahrain, Kuwait, and Oman, is also an indication of its growing international independence and regional influence. Its commitment to the coordination of regional defense and economic policy was implemented in the organization of the Gulf Cooperation Council. Saudi Arabia saw these states as part of its defense perimeter and thus sought closer relationships with them. For the most part, these efforts proved successful. All of the Gulf states exist in the shadow of two much larger neighbors, Iran and Iraq, both of which have been determined to achieve military and political dominance in the area. Both have actively courted the Shia populations of the GCC states and thus constantly raise the suspicions of these governments.

Oman became a primary focus of U.S. attempts after the Iranian revolution to improve its position on the Gulf and the Straits of Hormuz; this policy also indirectly improved the scope and quality of U.S. relations with Saudi Arabia, allowing the coordination of defense planning through the GCC without unwelcome visibility. Yemen is another sensitive area of concern. Saudi Arabia intervened in Yemen whenever necessary since 1962, and there are no signs that this concern for Yemeni stability will abate, especially given the recent unification of Yemen. Yemen is now a potentially stronger neighbor than before, with a dramatically different world view. Saudi Arabia expelled many Yemeni guest workers during and after Desert Storm, perceiving Yemeni sympathies for Iraq as potentially dangerous. Tensions remain high along their mutual border.

Saudi Arabia has taken the initiative in all of these relationships. As Saudi Arabia seeks a greater degree of partnership with the United States, as opposed to a more dependent relationship, it stands to reason that it will become even more aggressive diplomatically. These issues will be discussed in greater detail in the following chapter.

The precipitous decline in petroleum prices in the mid-1980s reduced Saudi Arabia's ability to accomplish its diplomatic agenda strictly with grants in aid or other payments. Relatively speaking, the moderation in petroleum prices and the declining rate of increase in demand during the period strained Saudi Arabia's ability to complete its ambitious development programs on schedule. Although the country still enjoyed considerable revenue from petroleum exports, less and less of the revenue could be considered "excess" and made available for diplomatic purposes. One consequence of this situation has been greater Saudi involvement in the efforts to reinvigorate OPEC and reestablish a sounder relationship between petroleum supply and demand. Iran and Iraq, desperate to improve their economic conditions, were loath to accept production restrictions, as were other non–Middle Eastern producers, Nigeria especially. Dramatically increased Saudi production, put in place as a retaliatory measure to punish those states unwilling to join in production limits, were implemented, with the effect of falling prices for petroleum worldwide. Given Saudi Arabia's growing levels of proven petroleum reserves, a factor that differentiates this country from many other producers, this policy promises to remain a centerpiece of Saudi foreign policy.

During the events of the Iraq-Kuwait conflict in 1991 and 1992, Saudi Arabia dramatically increased its petroleum production to offset losses in Iraq and Kuwait. In the recovery following, Saudi Arabia was positioned as even more of a dominant influence in the pricing and marketing of petroleum internationally. Saudi Arabia has continued to support moderate prices that stimulate continued demand for the product without instigating a search for viable alternatives.

Events in Afghanistan in 1979–1980 brought a heightened awareness of Soviet power in western Asia. This new awareness produced some cooperation between old adversaries. Iran and Saudi Arabia, for example, tried to frustrate the Soviet-sponsored war of national liberation that was launched against Oman from South Yemen, and Iraq and Saudi Arabia agreed finally during the Iran-Iraq war to divide the "neutral zone" on the border between them, a long-standing source of conflict. Healthy fear of Soviet penetration in the area had produced "discussions" between the conservative states of the Middle East and all but the most radical revolutionary states. Saudi Arabia was deeply involved in these developments. But the dramatic events that first occasioned the collapse of Soviet international power and then precipitated the dissolution of the union itself in 1991 changed the equation completely. The Soviet Union (now the C.I.S.) was now completely out of Afghanistan; and even more important, it was no longer an influential international actor in a bipolar world. This fact changed the face of international relations in the Middle East. Saudi Arabia reacted to those changes by seeking diplomatic relationships with countries she had shunned earlier, particularly Syria and Iran.

Because of her security concerns in the emerging international order in the Middle East and because of her unique role in Islam as the custodians of Mecca and Medina, Saudi Arabia has become a center of pan-Islamic activity. Many conferences have been held in the past decade in Saudi Arabia that embrace a variety of questions confronting the Islamic world. Conferences on Islamic banking and finance, Islamic law, and economic development have been held in Riyadh, Mecca, Taif, and Dharan. In these conferences, the weight and prestige of the Saudi government have been prominent. The emergence of revivalist Islam as a potent force in the Middle East may have presented the Saudi elite with a counterstrategy against the revolutionary secular governments of the region. Prestige politics of this kind are not without some hazards, it should be noted. Iranian attempts to exploit the hajj for propaganda purposes have disrupted the pilgrimage on more than one occasion and prompted Saudi police action against the demonstrators. Thus, while Saudi Arabia obviously benefits as custodian of the holiest shrines of Islam, its stewardship also raises envy and provides opportunities for embarrassment. To some degree the fundamentalist movements in Islam exacerbate this problem, a topic discussed in more detail in other chapters in this book.

Iranian Foreign Policy

Iran's geopolitical position in the Middle East has always assured it of a central role in the international relations of the region and the world. Unfortunately, this has not always worked to its advantage. It has frequently been involved in the ambitious plans of stronger nations. In the nineteenth and twentieth centuries, Russia attempted to extend its influence in Iran or gain control over Iranian territory. Britain, the Ottoman Empire, and Germany tried to frustrate Russian gains. These international pressures were compounded by the complicated domestic makeup of Iran, composed of many diverse cultures and nations. The Persian-Shia core of Iran is surrounded by large concentrations of Kurds, Azeris, Baluchis, Turks, and Arabs, all of which nurtured dreams of relative autonomy or independence at one time or another. And although Iran is predominantly Shia, there are substantial populations of Sunnis and Bahais. This makes for a political system of great complexity and potential conflict, inviting foreign intervention.

The rise to power of Shah Mohammed Reza Pahlevi in 1941 indicates the degree to which Iranian domestic politics have been influenced by international relations. The shah came to power after his father, Reza Shah, was forced to abdicate by a combination of Soviet and British pressure. In deference to the pro-German sympathies of Iran's ruling class, Reza Shah had tried to keep Iran neutral in World War II. Soviet and British leaders would have none of this, of course, and demanded his abdication.

The reorientation of Iran from neutrality to alliance with the West was accomplished during the war. A definite policy of pro-Western and anti-Soviet international relations was pursued deliberately by the shah from that time on, often causing domestic opposition to the policy. The period of stress and disorder from 1951 to 1953, engendered by Premier Mossadegh's attempts to nationalize British oil holdings, is an example of the domestic opposition to the shah's foreign policy.

From the immediate postwar period through the 1970s, the shah of Iran pursued a foreign policy predicated on close, even intimate, relations with the United States, rabid anticommunism, and the systematic expansion of Iranian military power. The shah envisioned Iran as the dominant political and military force in the Middle East, policing an area of growing economic and strategic importance. Associated with these goals were the recovery of Persian greatness and the transformation of Iran into a modern, industrial complex ruled by a benevolent monarchy. The petroleum reserves of Iran made such grandiose ambitions distinctly possible. Iran's sharing of a boundary with an increasingly powerful Soviet Union added the necessary note of urgency.

Iranian relations with the United States were not a one-way street. The United States played an important role in the shah's return to Iran in 1953.

Subsequent American aid under the Eisenhower administration, aid denied to Premier Mossadegh during his brief stay in power, helped stabilize the shah's power. Shortly after this consolidation, American oil companies successfully negotiated concessions for Iranian oil. The "love affair" between the shah and the United States was definitely reciprocal. A charter member of the Baghdad Pact, Iran was a major success in American strategy among the northern tier nations. Substantial aid and trade followed. Relations with the Soviet Union, already cool, cooled further.

The 1958 revolution in Iraq signaled the onset of strained relations between Iraq and Iran. The border became the scene of tension and frequent armed hostilities. The Kurdish minorities were exploited by each side in their attempts to embarrass or occupy the attention of the other. As the revolution in Iraq moved into its Baathist phase in 1963, relations became even more strained. Conflicting claims over territory at the Shatt al-Arab waterway to the Persian Gulf aggravated an already unfriendly relationship, as did the safety of Iranian pilgrims in southern Iraq. Both sides viewed each other's military growth with alarm. With the Soviet Union supplying arms and material to Iraq, and the United States fulfilling a similar role for Iran, the bipolar confrontation manifested itself in the regional politics of the Middle East.

Iranian relations with the United States were not unduly complicated by the Arab-Israeli conflict, at least not to the degree seen in the foreign policies of Egypt and Saudi Arabia. As a Persian rather than Arab nation, Iran did not share the rabid anti-Israeli sentiments of its neighbors, particularly Syria and Iraq. In fact, during most of the shah's reign, Iranian relations with Israel were cordial and constructive, with Iranian oil fueling the Israeli economy. Cooperation also existed in other spheres, with both countries exchanging intelligence, espionage and police technology. Iran, alone among Middle Eastern oil producers, declined to participate in the Arab oil embargo of 1973–1974 and continued to sell oil to the United States and Israel.

During Phase II, the shah committed Iran to a series of major reforms that he called the White Revolution (1963). These reforms were in part prompted by the international course charted earlier. Growing Iranian military and economic power necessitated a skilled population capable of managing the complicated machines of war and production. Predictably, the changes attendant on the White Revolution produced strains and tensions in Iran. These tensions, which included the growing alienation of the landed gentry from the shah, the outrage of the Shia ulema over the secular thrust of the reforms, and the political frustrations of groups wanting social and economic modernization, prompted increased political repression. The instrument of this political repression was SAVAK, the Iranian secret police. SAVAK became a nightmarish fact of life in Iran, presiding over a pervasive network of spies and informants, utilizing the latest in surveillance and interrogation techniques. Widely recognized in Iran as a client of the U.S. Central Intelligence Agency and the Israeli Mossad, SAVAK killed tens of thousands of Iranians and tortured and mutilated many, many more. SAVAK became increasingly linked in the public mind with the shah and the United States. These factors combined with other political forces to bring the revolution of 1978. Before the final act was played out, however, the shah managed to acquire one of the largest military machines in the world.

It would be simplistic and incorrect to portray the shah of Iran as a mere puppet of U.S. interests. Toward the end of his rule, particularly after the success of OPEC greatly increased Iran's oil revenues, the shah pursued policies sometimes at odds with the United States. This is particularly evident where oil pricing was concerned. In this policy area the shah pursued a course best described as militant, arguing for massive increases in the royalties paid the producing countries. The shah was very aware of the limited nature of Iran's petroleum reserves and wished to use the remaining production to build a postpetroleum economy. Needless to say, the dramatic increases in petroleum prices he advocated were not perceived as in the U.S. interest, or the interests of its European and Japanese allies. The shah pursued the price increases vigorously, in spite of American discomfort and pressure. In point of fact, the shah was one of the earliest supporters of OPEC and thus played a key role in ushering in the third phase of post–World War II international relations in the Middle East. The shah, even given the most conservative assumptions about his rule, contributed greatly to the changing face of Middle Eastern politics.

In Phase III diplomacy, the foreign policy of Iran was increasingly influenced by domestic politics. After 1975, rising domestic opposition to the shah's regime and to SAVAK repression prompted the shah to pursue even more drastic measures to control his opposition. Many of the opposition were exiled or fled to Iraq, whose government lent support and a podium for verbal attacks against the shah. The success of these attacks contributed materially to the ultimate decline of the shah's national prestige.

In this phase of its foreign policy, Iran became even more involved in the politics of the states neighboring the Persian Gulf. Iran sought close and amicable relationships with the smaller states of the Gulf as well as with Saudi Arabia. In spite of this policy, Iranian troops occupied three small islands near the Straits of Hormuz in 1971, thus achieving potential control over traffic in and out of the Gulf. When a Marxist-backed rebellion threatened the security of Sultan Qabus of Oman, Iranian troops were dispatched to Oman to help suppress it. All in all, from 1972 to 1978, Iran enjoyed something approaching military hegemony in the Persian Gulf. This was the high point of Iran's international power and influence under the shah.

The year 1978 saw the effective consolidation of the shah's opposition, leading to a virtual state of anarchy in Iran's cities. On January 16, 1979, the shah left Iran with his family. He would not return. Iran, under its revolutionary Islamic leaders, would enter a new age of Iranian diplomacy and foreign policy.

The foreign policy of the Iranian revolution.   Iranian foreign policy under Ayatollah Khomeini was nearly diametrically opposed to that of the shah. The United States, instead of being seen as a steady and respected ally, became the personification of imperialism and decadence, rivaled only by the Soviet Union. The foreign policy of Iran was to be based on the principles of Shia Islam, not the interests of Persian nationalism. Iranian ideology reflected an imperfect combination of Islamic social and political thought with the drives for political independence and nonalignment characteristic of Phase III developments in the region. Compounded by the irregular and intermittent leadership of Ayatollah Khomeini, it was no surprise that Iranian foreign policy would appear to its detractors as a mishmash of contradictory impulses and goals.

A low point in U.S.–Iranian relations occurred with the seizure of the U.S. embassy and the taking of its employees as hostages on November 4, 1979. The degree of complicity between the government and the students who seized the embassy was unknown, but the seizure was triggered when the United States admitted the shah for medical treatment. Many in Iran believed that the United States, so instrumental in returning him to power once before, would attempt to do so again. The seizure of the embassy was seen by these groups as one way to forestall such an effort.

The seizure and continued holding of the hostages was contrary to international law in both its symbolic and pragmatic dimensions. Negotiation proved fruitless, especially as the Iranian regime connected the future of the hostages with the return of the shah by the United States for trial. Traditional U.S. contacts with the Iranian elite had been obliterated by the revolution. In April 1980 the United States attempted a military rescue of the hostages, but it failed. More and more, the situation began to resemble a classic no-win situation for both sides. The international prestige and patience of the United States were severely tested by the seizure. Iran suffered from the U.S.-imposed and inspired economic sanctions initiated in early 1980. The resolution of the conflict came in January 1981, on the day of the inauguration of President Reagan, and some fifteen months after the hostages had been seized. Although both sides attempted to portray the outcome as a great victory, more sober judgments prevailed. As ABC correspondent Pierre Salinger concluded after his exhaustive analysis of the negotiations, it may have been a victory for the human spirit of the hostages themselves, it was not a victory for the United States. Nor was it a victory for Iran. Both sides lost considerable prestige and influence in the exchange. Subsequent events later in the decade provided more opportunities for pain and embarrassment. The Iran-Contra initiative was revealed as a bungled American attempt to free hostages in Lebanon by selling badly needed arms to Iran at the very moment that the United States was attempting to organize an international boycott of weapons sales to Iran. And the accidental shooting down of an Iranian domestic airliner over the Persian Gulf demonstrated Iranian weakness in the face of U.S. power while it simultaneously embarrassed the United States in revealing the operational weaknesses of its high-technology warfare. Iranian relations with the United States continued to be cold and antagonistic.

Although the hostage situation held the spotlight for most of 1980, other shifts in Iranian foreign policy could be observed. First, Iran became one of the rejectionist states in the Arab-Israeli conflict. Yasir Arafat met with Khomeini shortly after the latter's return to Iran in 1979, and the two pledged to work together for the liberation of the occupied territories and for Palestinian independence. The Israeli mission was turned over to the PLO. Iranian proxy groups in Lebanon carried on much of the terrorist initiative against Israel—particularly Hizbollah, a Shia fundamentalist group in southern and central Lebanon. Iranian opposition to Israel became a major premise of Iranian foreign policy.

The Soviet Union, while obviously enjoying the United States' predicament in Iran, was unable to capitalize on the Iranian revolution. Virulently anticommunist, the Iranian revolutionary elite was in domestic conflict with pro-Soviet elements, particularly in the cities and the oil fields near Abadan. As a consequence, Iran did little to reverse the shah's anti-Soviet foreign policy. The Soviet Union, with large populations of Muslims bordering on Iran, contemplated the disorder in Iran with apprehension. The Soviet invasion of Afghanistan, in 1980, brought Soviet-Iranian relations to their lowest point. Soviet withdrawal from Afghanistan did not in itself notably improve Soviet-Iranian relations. And Soviet willingness to reflag Kuwaiti tankers to protect them from Iranian attacks during the last stages of the Iran-Iraq war removed any vestige of the idea that the U.S.S.R. might be neutral in that conflict. Soviet diplomacy in the area reassured no one and renewed suspicions about the underlying motives of great-power diplomacy in the region. Iranian foreign policy continued to identify both the United States and the Soviet Union through 1991 as unwelcome interlopers.

Iranian relations with Iraq, always troublesome, turned violent following Iraq's seizure of disputed territory in the Shatt-al-Arab waterway on the Persian Gulf. For eight years Iran and Iraq engaged in a war of varying intensity: periods of relative quiescence followed by short bursts of vicious fighting. The conflict quickly spilled over into the Gulf region, with both sides attacking tankers headed to enemy ports. Both Iraq and Iran suffered substantial declines in petroleum revenues and horrifying casualties.

With its larger population base and substantial economic infrastructure, Iran was probably best situated for a protracted conflict. Iraq, given this reality, was the recipient of substantial foreign military aid. Conservative and moderate Arab states—notably Egypt and Saudi Arabia—provided money and arms to keep Iraq from defeat. Egypt channeled European and American arms to Iraq. Syria, Libya, and Israel independently aided Iran, obviously for different reasons.

The end of hostilities in the Iran-Iraq conflict was a bitter pill for the government of Iran. The prosecution of the war exacted very high costs, both financially and in human terms. Reportedly, Ayatollah Khomeini concluded reluctantly that further prosecution of the war would be disastrous; and with great pain he endorsed Speaker Rafsanjani's plan to accept U.N. mediation and end the conflict. The result prompted something of a hiatus in Iran's role as fomenter of radical change in the area—a turning inward toward domestic conflicts and problems. The diplomatic isolation of Iran, very apparent in the muted world reaction to the shooting down of its airliner over the Gulf, continued.

Iran's regional influence and international prestige received a great boost in the early 1990s, benefiting from the confluence of events in Europe and the Middle East. Specifically, the collapse of Soviet power and the reorganization of the now-independent republics (C.I.S.) created an area of fluid potential in the region. And the miscalculations in Iraq that led to Desert Storm pitted two of Iran's bitterest enemies against each other. By taking a relatively neutral position, Iran became one of the most immediate beneficiaries of Desert Storm.

Iran was able to gain politically and economically in this scenario. It has used revenue from its increasing petroleum sales to shop for arms, reportedly spending nearly $20 billion in 1992 to rearm its armed forces. One of the possible applications of this new power just might be in central Asia, where Iran supports movements of fundamentalist Muslims intent on establishing an Islamic republic. Much of the military materiel, ironically, came from the former Soviet Union.

Simultaneously, the Rafsanjani government embarked on efforts to improve Iran's relationship with the Western powers. Relations improved from cold to chilly, and the United States allowed the release of some of the funds seized during the hostage crisis of more than a decade earlier. Iran reportedly payed millions of dollars to the Lebanese groups holding American hostages, with resulting releases in late 1991 of all American hostages held there. Similar advances were made in Europe, although some problems continued to beset Iran's efforts. The death sentence imposed on novelist Salmon Rushdie, and the bounty placed on his head, for the publication of *The Satanic Verses*, a novel widely regarded as blasphemous by fundamentalist Muslims, still rankled Great Britain; and Iranian terrorist reprisals in other European states also prevented the development of "normal" diplomatic relations.

Iranian influence in the foreign relations of the Middle East is still best thought of in moral and symbolic terms, although circumstances could change quickly. The Islamic revolution in Iran, with its Islamic constitution and its stress on Islamic sources of social, economic, and political policy, is still a dramatic demonstration of the revolutionary potential of Islam in the contemporary world. Coming as it did, during widespread disenchantment with the politics of bipolar confrontation, the Iranian revolution spoke to the ability of peoples in the Middle East to organize domestic and international politics on their own terms, in their own way. And now, with the bipolar system a memory of history, peoples and movements in the region are even less constrained by external influences on their political life. Iranian influence is indirectly evident in the fundamentalist political movements in Jordan, Egypt, the Sudan, Algeria, and Morocco. These movements ultimately may have momentous consequences for the international system.

Israeli Foreign Policy

More than any other Middle Eastern state, Israel was formed in the crucible of international relations. The difficulties that afflicted the Jewish community in Europe in the late nineteenth and early twentieth century produced the international Zionist movement. This diverse group of Europeans was able, against heavy odds, to establish a Jewish state in the Middle East. In the Zionist view, this state symbolized a return to the historical site of their religion and civilization. In the view of the Palestinians living there at the time, the state symbolized an aggressive invasion of their homeland by European colonists. Neither side perceived a middle ground between these two positions. Consequently, Israel's foreign policy is also its domestic policy. Domestic security in Israel has always been a function of its international situation.

During Phase I of Middle Eastern diplomacy, the leaders of Israel were concerned with the physical establishment of the state. To accomplish this, they resorted to a variety of international efforts, legal and illegal. Above all they sought international approval for their efforts, both unilaterally and bilaterally. In this they were successful, much more so than their Arab opponents. Unanimous great-power recognition of the state of Israel came virtually upon the announcement of sovereignty. The fledgling United Nations provided the necessary diplomatic midwifery. All of this, of course, occurred in the immediate context of Arab diplomatic and military opposition.

Support in the United States for the young Israeli state was widespread. In addition to formal U.S. aid, Israel received great infusions of financial and political aid from the American Jewish community. This private aid proved to be critical for Israel. Support for Israel assumed a mantle of inviolability in the United States, particularly in election years. Opposition to support for Israel was characterized as anti-Semitic or baldly fascistic. To say the least, Arab prestige was not high.

During Phase II, Israeli foreign policy was linked tightly to its domestic policy. Domestic development depended on safe and secure boundaries; domestic development would help provide those same boundaries. In this stage of Israeli policy, the governments of Israel sought to capitalize on their diplomatic advantages over their Arab neighbors. Thus, Israel moved enthusiastically and fully into the bipolar alliance structure of the postwar period. American arms and aid flowed freely into Israel from its founding until Phase III diplomacy necessitated an American reappraisal of the relationship.

In its relations with its Arab neighbors, Israel pursued a carrot-and-stick policy. The carrot in the relationship was the supposed benefit of bilateral negotiations with Israel—the carrot ultimately nibbled by Sadat at Camp David. The stick was Israel's undisputed military superiority. The statement that the best defense is a good offense was put into practice by Israel in the Suez War of 1956 and the 1967 war. In both instances, Israeli first strikes initiated armed conflict.

Although the Israeli military actions were impressive for both their speed and effectiveness, the price was high. During this period, military superiority and preparedness began to take a higher and higher toll on the Israeli economy. This toll was reflected both in increasing levels of inflation and in the economic losses connected with the full mobilization of the Israeli military. Israel, with a small population, found it more and more difficult to sustain full military mobilization and a thriving economy simultaneously.

Repeated confrontations with superior Israeli military forces made the Arab states reluctant to battle with Israel. Instead, the Arab states chose a strategy of diplomatic confrontation and isolation, a strategy that began to pay off first in the United Nations. The 1967 conflict, in which Israel occupied the West Bank, Gaza, and the Golan Heights, prompted U.N. Resolution 242, calling for the full restoration of those areas. Israel found itself increasingly isolated in the United Nations and relied more and more upon friendly vetoes from the United States. World public opinion began to turn and resulted in a repolarization of attitudes toward Israel.

This period of Middle Eastern history also saw the beginning of Palestinian diplomatic and military activity against Israel. This activity was not confined to Israeli territory; it included many harassment actions, such as the hijacking of commercial airliners, and horrifying acts, such as the seizure and murder of Israeli athletes at the Munich Olympics in 1972. Israeli reprisals included assassination squads sent into Beirut, the imposition of punitive curfews and penalties for political agitation, the shooting down of a Libyan commercial airliner that strayed over Israeli air space, an air strike in 1985 on PLO headquarters in Tunisia, and multiple routine air strikes on PLO staging areas throughout Lebanon.

By the mid-1970s world opinion had shifted markedly toward a pro-Palestinian, anti-Israeli direction. In 1975, the U.N. General Assembly adopted a resolution condemning Zionism as a form of racism. Semiofficial "observer" status was extended to the PLO at the U.N. Israel's treatment of imprisoned Palestinian Arabs was condemned by Amnesty International, and a similarly critical U.S. State Department report surfaced in the mass media. Israeli prestige, initially created and supported by the larger world community and the U.N., was now on the defense in the same forums.

The same set of circumstances that ushered in Phase III diplomacy and resulted in a heightening of Arab prestige also signaled the growing diplomatic isolation of Israel. During this period, Israel became more and more protective of her special relationship with the United States. Simultaneously, the Nixon, Ford, and Carter administrations became more even-handed toward the Middle East. The result was an inevitable and growing political strain between Washington and Tel Aviv. The United States, more and more dependent on Middle Eastern petroleum production, found unyielding support for Israel increasingly expensive.

The Camp David agreements of 1978 demonstrate one dramatic attempt to reconcile the security needs of Israel with the economic problems confronting the United States. The first section of the agreements, implementing a bilateral disengagement between Egypt and Israel, proceeded smoothly; section two, which would have established Palestinian "autonomy" on the West Bank and Gaza, made little progress. Prime Minister Begin, after the implementation of section one of the accords, began a policy of new Jewish settlement in the "occupied territories." Israel was determined to maintain an effective presence in the West Bank, regardless of what Palestinian autonomy entailed.

The inability of Egypt and Israel to make progress on section two of the accords was aggravated symbolically by the Knesset's decision in 1980 to make Jerusalem the undivided capital of Israel. Arab reaction was predictably strong to this action. As we have seen, King Khalid called for a jihad to bring East Jerusalem back under Arab control. Coming as it did from a leader who had cultivated an image of restraint and control such a call was indeed a sign of the growing Arab irritation over the expansionist policies of the Begin government. The Palestine Liberation Organization fueled these flames of discontent by increasing its raids against Israel. Israel responded with air strikes, commando raids, and a tightening of security precautions, all of which served to heighten the sense of urgency among the Arab states.

The Israeli elections of June 1981 injected yet another note of uncertainty into Middle Eastern politics. The elections were called after the Begin government found it increasingly difficult to control its parliamentary coalition. At the onset of the campaign, the Labor bloc enjoyed a healthy lead, at least as reported in national polls, but by the end of the campaign the Labor and Likud blocs were in a virtual dead heat. This turn of events was at least partially attributable to the prevailing atmosphere of international confrontation.

Two major conflicts dominated the period prior to the elections. The first involved Israeli expansion of its role and activity in Lebanon, including stepped up counter-Palestinian raids in southern Lebanon, air surveillance of virtually all of Lebanon, and strong financial and military support for right-wing Christian paramilitary groups. Syrian action involved increased pressure on the Christian units, particularly to the east of Beirut, and the introduction of a large number of Soviet-supplied SAM antiaircraft missiles into eastern Lebanon and especially in the Bekaa Valley. Prime Minister Begin vowed to remove the missiles by force if Syria failed to withdraw them. A nasty diplomatic confrontation between Syria and Israel emerged. It is difficult and perhaps meaningless to try to determine the sequence of events that led to this confrontation. What is important is to recognize the seriousness of both sides in the conflict and its potential for widening the Arab-Israeli conflict. U.S. shuttle diplomacy, utilizing the talents of retired State

Department official Philip Habib, focused on keeping the confrontation contained, using international diplomatic pressure. In this, Habib was at least partially successful.

The second, and much more dramatic, international action involved the Israeli raid on Iraq's nuclear reactor complex (Osirak) near Baghdad. The raid, using American-built F-15 and F-16 fighters, succeeded in knocking out the reactor in what must be described as a flawlessly executed exercise. World opinion nearly unanimously condemned the raid, and the U.N. formally condemned Israel for the raid and asked for compensation to Iraq. Significantly, the U.N. resolution condemning Israel was a joint product of the U.S. and Iraqi delegations to the United Nations, a collaboration unthinkable a decade earlier. Many saw in this reaction an increasing international isolation of Israel and a growing resolve of Prime Minister Begin to go it alone, regardless of the consequences. For his part, Prime Minister Begin characterized the attack as defensive in nature, given the reactor's ability to produce weapons grade plutonium, and argued that the raid was a moral imperative to avoid another Holocaust.

Controversy over these two actions—the confrontation with Syria and the raid on Iraq—polarized Israeli politics more than at any previous time in its political history. Many backed Begin for his firm handling of the Arab danger, and as many criticized him for unnecessary reliance on military action where diplomacy might have been successful. The virtual dead heat between Labor and Likud doubtless found much of its cause in this internal division.

Instead of caution, the confused internal politics of Israel resulted in a more aggressive foreign policy. Moves toward the annexation of the West Bank and Golan Heights were initiated. And in the spring of 1982, the Israeli army began an invasion of Lebanon, ostensibly to remove Palestinian terrorists from bases adjacent to the Israeli border.

What was initially presented as a limited action soon became apparent as a full-scale invasion. Israeli troops quickly seized the southern cities of Sidon and Tyre and commenced a fast-paced move up to and into Beirut itself. The professed goal of the invasion changed to the elimination of the PLO presence in Lebanon, not simply the removal of bases near the Litani River. It appears that the architects of the invasion hoped for not only the removal of the Palestinians, but to tip the political equation in Lebanon in favor of conservative Christian groups with whom they could negotiate a favorable peace treaty. None of these goals were achieved. In fact, it is difficult to identify any positive short-term results attendant on the invasion.

From the perspective of international and regional relations, the invasion introduced serious strains between Israel and the United States, strains increased by revelations of systematic Israeli spying on U.S. intelligence agencies. This led to a substantial enhancement of Syria's power and prestige; failed to eliminate Palestinian terrorist groups in Lebanon, although the Arafat factions of the PLO were forced to leave; further reinforced images of Israel as intransigent and militaristic; created circumstances that led to the politicization of hitherto quiescent Shia groups, particularly the AMAL and Hizbollah; and ultimately failed to create a sympathetic government in Beirut.

Domestically, the invasion produced substantial internal political division over the wisdom of the invasion and the moral consequences of the action. The

Kahan Commission investigating the massacres at the Palestinian refugee camps was very critical of the Israeli Defense Forces (IDF) officer corps, and a public discussion of Shin Bet executions of Palestinian terrorists damaged governmental secrecy while simultaneously polarizing public opinion. The growing number of Israeli casualties during the three-year occupation disheartened many families. And the Israeli economy went into a tailspin, at least in part a function of the costs of invasion and occupation. Politically, the invasion was a major factor in the resignation and withdrawal from politics of Prime Minister Begin, and the progenitor of the odd sequential coalition between the Likud and Labor blocs in the face of a divisive and yet indeterminate election.

The aftermath of the Israeli withdrawal from Lebanon in the summer of 1985 saw the Arab-Israeli conflict taking on new coloration. The U.S. role in the area was visibly reduced and Israeli self-confidence in their moral rectitude challenged. The Palestinians had more faces than ever, and the prospects for a negotiated settlement appeared dim. Courageous leadership, of the type exhibited by Sadat during his trip to Jerusalem, seemed a scarcer commodity than ever. Both Arab and Jew have paid a high price for the privilege of settling disputes through violence.

The assassination of President Sadat on October 6, 1981, served to emphasize the degree to which the United States and Israel had predicated their policies on the particulars of Egyptian policy. They, most of all, found themselves in the process of agonizing reappraisal of their foreign policies. In the main, these reappraisals centered on the question of whether or not the policies of Sadat would survive his administration or would fall victim to the new political realities likely to follow.

The continuity in Egyptian foreign policy under Mubarak placed Egypt in a position of high prestige with nearly all of the international actors in the region. Mubarak complied with the letter of the Camp David Accords, reclaiming the Sinai territory lost in previous conflicts. Egypt did not repudiate the treaty even after the Israeli invasion of Lebanon, an act repugnant to most Egyptians. Egypt provided a warm welcome to the exiled Arafat and recovered a measure of its revolutionary *bona fides* in the process.

The relative calm of U.S.–Israeli relations was jarred when the Palestinian revolt prompted renewed U.S. efforts to promote a settlement. Secretary of State George Shultz personally engaged in an extensive round of regional diplomacy, alternately needling and wheedling the respective players for substantive action. Israeli leaders were successful in ignoring these pressures until the fall of 1988, when the actions of the PLO reenergized the U.S. effort. Other powers entered the discussions, and even Great Britain, long stalwart in its refusal to talk with PLO representatives, relented and opened lines of communication. This effectively left Israel very isolated and with a diminishing set of possibilities. Israeli diplomatic maneuvers centered on discrediting the PLO for continuing terrorist activity and for attempting to define a different set of Palestinian leaders with which to negotiate. International pressure in favor of some form of "autonomy" for the occupied territories was building, and the Israeli government, fragile coalition that it was, was hard pressed to find palatable and practical policies. Short-run solutions to the problem seemed unlikely, but it also seemed that a process has begun that *could* in time lead to an amelioration of the plight facing the Palestinians under Israeli control.

Public opinion in the United States, reacting to the brutal suppression of the intifadah and Israeli unwillingness to enter into substantive dialogue with a changing PLO, reflected declining support for Israel; particularly among the American Jewish community, long noted for its unwavering support, but now disconcerted by the repressive policies of the Israeli government in the West Bank and Gaza. These changes presented a serious challenge for Israeli leadership, particularly given the importance of U.S. aid in maintaining the security and economic vitality of the country. Thus, as is so often the case, clear linkages between domestic and international policy existed, complicating already complex calculations.

The collapse of the coalition government in 1988 brought the Likud back to power and ushered in another Shamir administration. The foreign policy of the Shamir government was predicated on a hard line toward Palestinian independence, increased Jewish settlement in the occupied territories, and a willingness to accept deteriorating relations with the Bush administration as the price for this set of policies. This initially resulted in growing tensions between Washington and Tel Aviv and increasing rhetorical conflict between Israel and its Arab neighbors. The continuing Israeli response to the Palestinian intifadah also added to this declining prestige.

Israel also found its foreign policies affected by the emergence of a new world order. The decline of the bipolar system devalued Israel's purely military value to the United States. And the changes in the Soviet Union allowed dramatic increases in Soviet emigration to Israel, straining the economy with dramatically growing resettlement and housing expenses.

Iraq's invasion of Kuwait proved both a blessing and a problem for Israel. Excluded from the formal coalition, Israel was not a front-line state in Desert Storm, and its losses were confined to a few Scud attacks with little loss of life or property. Palestinian sympathy for Iraq increased the latitude of the government in its attempts to control the Palestinians. Onerous curfews, the closing of schools and other institutions, deportations and increased settlement activity placed even greater pressure on the Palestinian community. It is clear that Israel's agreed low-profile role in the conflict gave it the opportunity to increase the pressure on its Palestinian population.

On the debit side of the ledger, the aftermath of Desert Storm found the Bush administration pushing hard for multilateral talks aimed at settling the Palestinian question. Implicit in the effort was a "land for peace" formula that the right wing of Israeli politics found absolutely unpalatable. Kicking and screaming, the Shamir government was forced to the conference table in late 1991 and 1992 by a combination of "carrots and sticks." Israel's detention of Palestinian staff traveling to the peace conference and its military operations in southern Lebanon in the winter of 1992 contributed further to the existing strains. The domestic political consequences of entering into these discussions prompted two religious parties to drop out of the Likud coalition in the Knesset, necessitating new elections in the summer of 1992.

The international events of the early 1990s damaged the prestige and reputation of Israel and brought her into increased confrontations with the United States. Major changes in the structure and dynamics of the new emerging international order present serious challenges to the Israeli government. And as high-technology weaponry suffuses through the area, bringing even relatively small states substantial increases in military capability, simple and direct military action becomes ever more destabilizing and unlikely to produce the desired effects. Perhaps the events of the end of the decade herald the beginning of more pragmatic initiatives from all parties to the conflict. In this political mare's nest, we dare not hope for less.

CONCLUSION

In the years since the end of World War II, the Middle East has been the scene of intense international exchange. The forces of great-power interests, emerging national self-interest, international economic interdependence, secular and Islamic revolutions, have changed the international relations of the Middle East. No longer reacting primarily to the bipolar strategies of the United States and the Soviet Union, the Middle Eastern states themselves now initiate international moves to which other powers must respond. Pragmatic self-interest pervaded the policy atmosphere of Phase III diplomacy. This attitudinal change, together with the real financial power of the petroleum-rich Arab states, signaled the emergence of the Middle East as one of the several independent power centers that make up the multipolar world.

It is clear that thinking about the world as a bipolar system yielded powerful insights from 1948 right up through the 1980s. But in the midst of that last decade the explanatory power of the model declined, and the behavior of states seemed to be less and less conditioned and constrained by bipolar considerations. We now see the end of that system and the emergence of a new, multipolar world. This change is sufficiently significant that we have added another chapter to this book, examining the possible consequences of this New World Order for the domestic and international politics of the Middle East. In particular, the following chapter examines the dimensions of the newly emergent international system; the effect of Desert Storm on that system; and the prospects for real peace between the Arabs and Israelis.

THE MIDDLE EAST AND THE NEW INTERNATIONAL ORDER

By the end of the 1980s it was clear to most observers that the prevailing international system was in the process of change. But few foresaw the rapidity and implications of that change. Systems that were assumed to be stable deteriorated in a matter of years, even months. The result was the disruption of the old order before the dimensions of the new order were clear. Many statesmen spoke glibly of the "New International Order" but few were clear about the contours and details of the new system. As is so often the case in this new age, changes occurred faster than the ability of governments to perceive or understand them.

Reviewing the signal events occurring between 1988 and 1991 gives us some idea of the direction of change. Events began with uncharacteristic agreement on nuclear weapons treaties between the United States and the U.S.S.R. With hindsight, it appears that both protagonists in the great Cold War were economically exhausted by the competition. These agreements were closely followed by Soviet retrenchment throughout the world, including its withdrawal from Afghanistan and drastic reductions in its support for its allies elsewhere.

These emerging trends assumed the proportions of an avalanche by early 1990, and in short order the Soviet Union abandoned its political and military role in Eastern Europe. "Velvet revolutions" occurred in Poland, Czechoslovakia and Hungary. The Berlin Wall fell and German reunification was permitted and then quickly implemented. The Warsaw Pact was dissolved and many of its members, including the Soviet Union, unsuccessfully petitioned for membership in NATO. The "eye-ball to eye-ball nuclear confrontation" of some forty years duration took less than forty months to evaporate. The bipolar world order was defunct.

Emboldened, perhaps, by the events in Eastern Europe, the Baltic states of the Soviet Union increased their demands for independence. And once again, events outpaced the expectations of statesmen and scholars. In fairly short order, Lithuania, Latvia, and Estonia gained a measure of independence from the Soviet center. These changes precipitated others until the chain of events eventually challenged the Soviet government itself. Decades of pent-up regional and nationalist sentiments were released. As republic after republic in the union declared its independence, the authority of the Communist party and the central government progressively declined. The reform movement headed by Mikhail Gorbachev lost momentum to the forces of revolutionary change, increasingly symbolized in the leadership of Boris Yeltsin and the political and economic centrality of the Russian Republic.

The forces of radical change were energized again in August of 1991 when threatened members of the old Soviet elite attempted a *coup* against Gorbachev and his government. The failure of the *coup* resulted in the formal dissolution of the Communist party and the progressive transfer of power from the Gorbachev government to the governments of the republics. In December of 1991 a majority of the republics of the old Soviet Union ratified a new Commonwealth of Independent Republics. This entity of confederation—a system of relative autonomy and cooperation between ethnically and historically defined regions—formally replaced the Soviet Union of old; and finally and practically signified the last gasp of the old communist order. Even the names of the players have changed. From this point on, we will refer to the former Soviet Union as the *Commonwealth of Independent States* (C.I.S., for short) in references to events occurring after January 1992 .

DIMENSIONS OF THE NEW INTERNATIONAL ORDER

Although it is very early to specify the full dimensions of the emerging world system, there are some apparent trends. In order of importance we would note the following:

1. The new world order is *not* unipolar. In other words, the collapse of the Soviet Union did not automatically elevate the United States to the level of an hegemonic power. In fact, the very pressures that caused the collapse of Soviet power appear to constrain U.S. power as well. Both are counting on reductions in military appropriations to reinvigorate their lagging economies, as are the other principal world powers. Finally, we should emphasize that the new C.I.S. is a nuclear power of great importance even in the chaotic situations attending its formation.
2. The emerging world order *is* apparently *multipolar*, a world system in which military, economic, and political power is more widely dispersed than in the previous bipolar system. And it is also likely that few countries in this system will have "across-the-board" capability. In other worlds, the new order will be characterized by the economic and military power of one actor combining with the military and political power of others in a relatively free-floating set of international combinations.
3. The movement toward *regional integration* will continue. Economic regional integration will proceed in Western Europe, North America, Eastern Europe, Southeast Asia, East Asia, North Africa, and the Persian Gulf. There are potentials for increased integration in Latin America and sub-Saharan Africa as well. These new institutions will eventually constitute power centers with consequences for the conduct of international affairs. At the minimum, their existence implies a system of shared powers and responsibilities, a system quite unlike the one it replaces.

4. In this environment, *international organizations* will become increasingly important. Multinational organizations like the U.N. and NATO will perform important coordinating roles in the international order. And *nongovernmental international actors* will also take on an increasingly important role in international affairs, organizations like Medecins sans Frontieres or the International Red Cross–Red Crescent.

5. Global political, social, and economic *interdependence* will continue to accelerate, considerably reducing the independence of governments and their actions. Resource scarcity (water, fuels) and global pollution (ozone depletion, ground water contamination) and population growth will require international cooperation for solutions. Nearly *instantaneous international communication* will keep us all aware of the human costs of disease, famine, war, and natural disaster; "national" politics will be ever more visible to attentive publics on the outside. Technology will continue to diffuse independently of the attempts of governments to restrict it.

6. *Regional conflicts* will become more active and numerous as the restraining effect of the bipolar competition fades. War and conflict will not disappear because of the changing international system, but the size and consequence of conflict will change. The arenas of conflict are being redefined by the changes at the system level. The great powers of the world will face increasing levels of regional and local risk as the dangers of global nuclear threat recede. Smaller conflicts and more of them are likely occurrences in the brave new world we all now face. The civil war in Yugoslavia is a good example of this; and the plight of the Kurds, spanning the boundaries of Turkey, Iran, Iraq, and Syria is another.

7. The *North-South conflict* is likely to intensify. As the previous system of ideological competition fades, conflict between economically and socially defined groups is likely. Demands for more equitable sharing of the world's resources is a likely nuance of the emerging world order. Global conflict between rich and poor is likely to become a political and moral, if not military, fact.

8. Finally, and in many ways most important, a blurring of the distinction between domestic and international policy confronts all major nations. The *domestication of the international* and the *internationalization of the domestic* make coherent policy making difficult. As Robert Pranger has observed, "Because the demands placed on national interests by international and domestic environments differ in ends and means, foreign policy...is more complicated than domestic policy...and requires areas of expertise not normally available in any abundance to leaders whose legitimacy usually depends on domestic political authority."[1]

THE MIDDLE EAST IN THE NEW INTERNATIONAL ORDER

These profound changes in the international system have resonant effects in the international relations of the Middle East. Many corollaries and consequences of the change had begun to emerge in the late 1980s, maturing in the early years of the 1990s. Chief among these were a new caution in Soviet relations with the area and visible changes in the U.S. posture toward the area as the Soviet threat retreated.

[1] Robert Pranger, "Foreign Policy Capacity in the Middle East," in Judith Kipper and Harold Saunders, eds., *The Middle East in Global Perspective* (Boulder, CO: American Enterprise Institute, Westview Press, 1991) pp. 20–21.

The Soviet retrenchment in Afghanistan was but the most visible of what became a general withdrawal of the U.S.S.R. from the region's conflicts. Allied states such as Syria, Iraq, and South Yemen received smaller amounts of foreign and military aid and less encouragement in the support of wars of national liberation. The PLO sensed these changes and sought "dialogue" with the West, attempting awkwardly to adjust to the new realities. All in all, a sense of uncertainty and change pervaded the area.

Analysts could also see changes in U.S. policy as a result of the reduced Soviet role in the region. The endgame of the Reagan administration began and ended with reinvigorated attempts to solve the ongoing Israeli-Arab conflict, including the previously unheard of dialogue with the PLO. And the first year of the Bush administration began and ended with attempts to restart negotiations between Israel, her Arab neighbors, and the PLO.

In spite of unsuccessful attempts to "jump-start" the peace process in the Middle East, early 1990 was a time of international optimism. The cumulative effects of the transition from the old order to the new put statesmen in a mellow mood. Many dangerous maneuvers in Eastern Europe and the former Soviet Union had been accomplished without disaster. A financial "peace dividend" appeared near at hand, providing some economic and political relief to states that had been financially strained in capacity for the four prior decades. The Iran-Iraq war had sputtered to a halt. The world appeared to be in for a period of relative progress and prosperity.

So the news in August of 1990 that Iraq had invaded its neighbor Kuwait was received in the halls of government with anger and frustration. This act and its subsequent denouement demonstrated many of the points emphasized earlier in this chapter; and depending on one's point of view, the crisis constituted the last response of the old order or represented the first response of the new. In any event, Iraq's invasion of Kuwait and the world community's response to it constitutes the primary international event of the early 1990s. Other regional events—the continuation of the intifada, the release of hostages, or attempts to begin peace negotiations between Israel and the Arabs are overshadowed by this single event. Thus the conflict was certainly architectonic to the conduct of international relations in the Middle East; and at the minimum evidence of the new international politics. It must be looked at and analyzed with care if we are to draw appropriate inferences.

THE IRAQ-KUWAIT CRISIS

The background to the Iraqi invasion of Kuwait in August of 1990 is complex. There is a long history of conflict between the two states and this was not the first time that Iraqi troops had rolled down the Basra highway toward Kuwait. There are claims and counterclaims. Iraq has long claimed Kuwait as its own, an area severed from it by the arbitrary act of the previous colonial power; by contrast, the Al-Sabah family claims to the region are old and long-standing. But in point of fact, both Kuwait and Iraq were only recently defined as independent nations, emerging from the interaction of two colonial administrations, Ottoman and English.

And there was much geographic uncertainty and strain as well. Due to the nature of the desert terrain, the borders between Kuwait and her neighbors have never been clear or well-defined. Areas of disputed ownership predate this conflict and the presence of petroleum in some of the disputed areas has resulted in areas of joint exploitation and or administration. Nomadic herders crossed these porous borders with impunity for decades, further complicating the problems of national definition. Kuwaiti control of key areas at the top of the Gulf frustrated Iraq, whose access to the Gulf through the Shatt-al-Arab waterway was all but destroyed by the war with Iran. The effect was to virtually landlock Iraq and make import and export difficult. Kuwait evinced little concern over these Iraqi difficulties.

These historical and geographic conflicts were exacerbated by the long-running war between Iraq and Iran. As one of the states backing Iraq in that war, Kuwait had extended loans and credits to Iraq. Now, as the war ended, Iraq sought further help and the forgiveness of the loans. Kuwait responded by demanding payment.

Iraq was outraged and this outrage was further fueled by its belief that Kuwait had pumped unfair amounts of petroleum from the Rumeilah oilfields, fields that dip slightly into Kuwait but whose bulk lies in Iraq. Moreover, Kuwait played a key role in OPEC decisions in the summer of 1990 not to raise the price for petroleum. Iraq, counting on a substantial increase in price to offset the costs of the war with Iran, felt that they had been "whip-sawed" by Kuwait, which both opposed price increases and deliberately exceeded their production quotas.

These charges of unfair profiteering were given some credence by the reputation of Kuwaitis prior to the invasion. It is no exaggeration to suggest that Kuwaiti prestige was fairly low in the Middle East at the time, particularly in those countries without substantial petroleum resources. Wealthy Kuwaitis vacationing in London, Cairo, Damascus, and Baghdad did for the Kuwaiti public image what earlier generations of ugly Americans, ugly Germans, and ugly Japanese had done for their own countries reputations. Public sympathy for the plight of the wealthy Kuwaiti minority was relatively scarce outside of Saudi Arabia, the Gulf states, and the European West.

U.S. restraint on Iraq evaporated shortly before the invasion of Kuwait. In a much-publicized conversation with Saddam Hussein, the American ambassador in Baghdad, Ms. April Glaspie, indicated to the Iraqi leader that the United States had no mutual defense treaty with Kuwait. The interpretation of this remark was apparently critical to Saddam Hussein's appraisal of probable U.S. reaction to his planned invasion. Inadvertent or not, a green light of sorts was presented to Iraq in the prosecution of its dispute with Kuwait. The Soviet Union, long a supporter of Iraq, was not a major partner in these discussions.

The Iraqi invasion was swift, brutal, and massive when it occurred. Well over 150,000 heavily armored Iraqi troops flooded into Kuwait. In a matter of twenty-four hours the nominal defenders of Kuwait were routed and less than a day later Iraqi troops were digging in on the borders with Saudi Arabia. Iraqi troops took up reinforced positions along the Saudi Arabian border, a presence that prompted fear in that country, and in its customers for petroleum. Indeed, the concentration of Iraqi forces on the border went far beyond that needed for the mere defense of the captured territory, raising speculation about the ultimate intentions of Iraq. At the peak, Iraqi forces in the Kuwaiti theater numbered well over 250,000 (during the hostilities these force numbers were greatly exaggerated in the anti-Iraq coalition press and briefings). The ambiguity raised by such great concentrations of Iraqi power quickly forced reaction from interested parties, particularly Saudi Arabia, the Gulf states, the United States, and Western Europe. Within a week an initial force of U.S. and Gulf area troops took up positions on the Saudi side of the Kuwaiti border and Desert Shield-Desert Storm began.[2]

Events within occupied Kuwait did little to reassure Iraq's neighbors. As many as one-third of Kuwait's native population fled, including most of the government and armed forces; those that remained behind were subjected to repressive occupation. Hundreds of thousands of "guest workers" from Jordan, Egypt, India, Bangladesh, and the Philippines also fled the area, straining neighboring states' ability to provide for them.

A puppet regime was quickly established by Iraq and the reorganization of Kuwait proceeded. As the occupation continued, reports of torture, rape, murder, and looting became regular features in the outside press. Hundreds of thousands of foreign guest workers became instant refugees. Sensationalism and exaggeration make objective appraisal of the occupation difficult, even long after the events in question. But it is clear that the occupation was brutal, if uneven in its administration and effect.

Iraqi objectives in this invasion were unclear. If Iraq's ultimate aim was the limited one of embarrassing Kuwait, securing the Rumeilah fields, and opening a water route to the Gulf, then Iraq overcommitted in its efforts and prompted a stronger response from the international community than was necessary. On the other hand, if Iraq's ultimate objectives included the annexation of Kuwait or even the seizure of the major Saudi oil fields in its eastern province, then its decision to take up defensive positions along the Saudi border signaled either a strategic miscalculation or a failure of nerve. Either way, the levels of force involved in the Iraqi invasion of Kuwait convinced the major world powers that Iraq was involved in a dangerous game that demanded a full and effective response.

The response to the invasion was not long in coming. Economic embargoes against Iraq were quickly put in place by the United States, the European Economic Community, and Japan. On August 6, the U.N. Security Council ordered a worldwide embargo on trade with Iraq. These actions were initially symbolic, since economic processes are relatively slow to respond to changes in rules. But in the long run the economic punishment of Iraq took a great toll, particularly on the nonmilitary populations. And by August 9, one week after Iraq's invasion, troops from the United States and other Saudi allies began to materialize on the border with Kuwait.

The United States took the leading role in confronting the Iraqi threat. President Bush, working chiefly through the United Nations, orchestrated a multinational response. The number of foreign troops in Saudi Arabia rose steadily in the fall of 1990, until they could in fact credibly contain an Iraqi attack. Desert Shield, as the exercise was named, built quickly, reaching a level of roughly one half million men by December of 1990. By the time of the offensive against Iraq their number had grown to in excess of 715,000 troops. Approximately one half of the troops were from U.S. forces, with the remainder drawn from Saudi Arabia, the

---

[2] Desert Shield was the name of the defensive phase of the operation. It was succeeded by Desert Storm as the coalition forces went on the offensive.

U.A.E., Britain, France, Egypt, Syria, Italy, Morocco, Bangladesh, and a symbolically important contingent of Kuwaiti troops in exile.

Iraq, during this period, continued to reinforce its positions along the Kuwaiti and Saudi borders, substantially hardening its positions with extensive earthworks, minefields, and modern trench facilities. The elite Republican Guards were placed to the north, along the Iraqi-Kuwaiti border in position to maneuver against invading forces. Diplomatic initiatives from a variety of sources, including France and the Soviet Union, failed to persuade Saddam Hussein of the seriousness of the coalition facing him, and as the new year dawned "Desert Shield" changed into "Desert Storm."

The coalition facing Iraq broke new ground in Middle Eastern coalition building. Working under the legitimizing mandate of a series of U.N. resolutions, President Bush assembled a group of the most unlikely partners. Indeed, any political coalition including Syria and the conservative monarchies of the region would have previously been considered unthinkable. For that matter, for the United States and Syria to be working partners would have stretched credibility even further, given persistent efforts by the United States to brand Syria a "terrorist state" and Syria's ongoing attempts to portray the United States as a "colonialist-Zionist" state.

For all of these states to work harmoniously with Egypt and Algeria and Turkey further stretched political credibility. And for these former colonial states to consider military cooperation with France, Great Britain, and Italy against another Arab-Muslim state would also seem farfetched. But such a coalition was indeed assembled and did indeed endure for no nation in that coalition was prepared to countenance Saddam Hussein's Iraq as the dominant military and economic power of the region. Ultimately, sixteen nations contributed ground forces to the war.

The absence of Israel from the U.S.–led coalition was crucial to its stability. The Bush administration recognized from the start the symbolic importance of Israeli nonparticipation in this unprecedented coalition. This necessitated a diplomatic "high-wire" act as the United States moved to both reassure Israel and its enemies simultaneously. This was done with mixed success, particularly within Israel, where calls for direct action against Iraq increased geometrically with each Scud missile launched against her. Although the Scuds did little actual damage, the psychological impact was great. The government of Israel paid a relatively high price domestically for its perceived passivity in this conflict.

TABLE 13-1. COALITION MEMBERS WITH FORCES COMMITTED AT START OF DESERT STORM.

United States	Bangladesh
Britain	Morocco
France	Oman
Saudi Arabia	Niger
Egypt	Pakistan
Syria	Qatar
Kuwait	Senegal
Bahrain	United Arab Emirates

Multinational Actors in the Conflict

As alluded to earlier in this discussion, international organizations were major actors in the confrontation. The United Nations, acting under the guidance of the Security Council, took an active role in confronting Iraq's hostile action. And the United States, careful to assure that its actions were either anticipated or approved by U.N. resolution, clearly legitimized its military and diplomatic response to Iraq.

Among the key U.N. initiatives were Resolutions:

660 (August 2, 1990): calling upon Iraq to immediately withdraw from Kuwait.

661 (August 6, 1990): reminding all member states of their obligation to deny financial or economic resources to Iraq (embargo).

662 (August 9, 1990): rejecting Iraq's annexation of Kuwait as illegal.

665 (August 25, 1990): inviting member states to implement the embargo and engage in necessary military action using the Military Staff Committee of the United Nations.

These resolutions and the others that followed internationally legitimized the coalition response to Iraq's aggression. But other international organizations also provided legitimation and support to the effort. NATO provided key logistical and political support, although informally, from the opening days of the crisis.[3] And other organizations joined in the chorus of condemnation: the Organization of African Unity, August 3; Gulf Cooperation Council, August 3; Organization of the Islamic Conference, August 5; and the League of Arab States, August 10. These organizations, representing the opinions of variously Arab, Muslim, and Third World states, contributed immeasurably to the legitimacy of the U.S.–led opposition and greatly reduced the value of Iraq's invocations of Muslim and Arab unity.[4] Finally, the United States and Soviet Union proclaimed joint resolutions condemning the attack, demonstrating a commonality of purpose among the world's two superpowers. The Soviet government followed these statements with diplomatic missions to Baghdad attempting to dissuade Iraq from staying in Kuwait. The government of Iraq rejected numerous efforts to arrange a nonviolent withdrawal from Kuwait.

Iraq was able to muster formal support only from Libya and the PLO. Jordan, caught in the middle between its two most important economic partners, attempted to play the role of mediator and failed in this attempt. Branded a collaborator by the coalition leadership, Jordan paid an extremely high economic and political price for its attempted neutrality. Iran, officially opposed to the annexation of Kuwait, waited to take advantage of the coming storm. The isolation of Iraq was complete.

---

[3] It is unlikely that U.S. forces could have moved into the region in such a short time without the logistical support of NATO, or without NATO's willingness to allow great reductions in its forces and supplies in Europe.

[4] For example, Saddam Hussein's repeated attempts to invoke *jihad* were blunted by the refusal of other Islamic authorities to recognize the legitimacy of his claim.

Desert Storm

The coalition against Iraq went on the offensive in January of 1991. Under the U.N. resolutions, the allies were justified, even required, to forcibly eject Iraq from Kuwait and to restore the previous government. Hostilities began with an air campaign on January 16, 1991, utilizing the latest technologies in "smart" weaponry and some of the heaviest concentrations of "dumb" technology since World War II. Air supremacy was quickly established over Iraq and what followed was a "turkey shoot" of unprecedented intensity. In the first week of the air war, over 10,000 sorties were flown, punishing Iraq day and night. Well over 80,000 tons of munitions were dropped on Iraq.

The air war was covered from Baghdad by the surviving staffs of U.S. news networks, most notably CNN. This time the world was privy to war from the perspective of the pilot and his targets. The viewing public was shown the thorough destruction of Iraqi infrastructure, particularly the communication and transportation networks. Careful censorship in the coalition staging areas kept the official images technical and clinical; while the images streaming from Baghdad and other media sources supplemented this with endless footage of death and destruction.

As the air assaults continued and Iraqi antiaircraft capability was suppressed, B-52 bomber raids were initiated, targeted against major economic and military targets, including power plants and suspected military production facilities; and increasingly against the dug-in Iraqi troops on the Saudi border. The "unknowns" regarding Iraq's rumored chemical, biological, and nuclear programs prompted an ever-broadening range of targets. The result, as inevitable as it was distasteful, was increasing loss of life among the civilians in Iraq. The totals of noncombatant losses in the air war will probably never be known, but certainly number in the tens of thousands. When combined with those who died in the coming land war, and from the effects of the war on water, food, and sanitation facilities, total Iraqi losses may have been as high as 200,000.

The duration and savagery of the five-and-one-half week air campaign was conditioned by expectations that the following air-land battle would be long and bloody. Many analysts expected the land war to run for weeks and to generate high casualties on both sides. The Iraqi army, supposedly seasoned by a decade of high intensity war with Iran, was considered a formidable adversary, particularly the elite Republican Guards held in the rear of the war theatre. Another factor for caution was based on Iraq's previous use of chemical weapons in the war with Iran. Iraq also possessed a large number of tanks and impressive numbers of long-range artillery, and sophisticated munitions for both of these systems. Further pause was given by Iraq's mining of most of the Kuwaiti oil fields and well-heads, and its progressive firing of those charges as attack became imminent.

Given these expectations, the land phase of the battle for Kuwait was something of a disappointment. Begun on February 24, coalition forces were able in short order to breach the vaunted Iraqi defenses. The heavily dug-in Iraqi forces were not able to maneuver and were systematically destroyed by highly mobile forces using more sophisticated technology. In fact, most U.S. losses in the land phase of the battle came from "friendly fire." At any rate, the Iraqi forces were quickly surrounded and a major rout of the Iraqi army ensued. Within only four days of battle, Kuwait was rid of its occupying army and was in the process of restoring its government and civil services. Iraqi troops streamed north, using whatever transport was available. The slaughter along the highway north was so complete as to be called a "turkey shoot" by knowledgeable military analysts. The Iraqi army in Kuwait was in danger of annihilation.

With the southern quarter of Iraq occupied, a cease-fire was negotiated permitting the withdrawal of the defeated Iraqi troops. Desert Storm had succeeded in expelling Iraq from Kuwait and in reestablishing Kuwait's legal government. There was great optimism in the West and considerable chaos and despair in Baghdad. Kurdish rebels in the north of Iraq and Shia groups in the south began secessionist struggles. Informed opinion awaited the inevitable *coup* deposing Saddam Hussein and establishment of a government that would attempt to negotiate with the coalition leadership.

The end-game of Desert Storm was disappointing to those who expected and wanted a thoroughgoing destruction of both Iraq's military establishment and the leadership of Saddam Hussein. But in fact, the expulsion of Iraq from Kuwait and the reestablishment of the as-Sabah government satisfied the letter of the U.N. resolutions. The coalition itself had not defined its role further and it is not clear that the political will existed for the final action against Iraq. What was a clear and signal military victory eventually transformed itself into a typical political quagmire.

The Middle East at the End of Desert Storm

As Desert Storm blew itself out over the deserts of the Middle East, the political, economic, and military contours of the region had changed. Iraq was no longer the dominant military power in the region, although its military plant had by no means been eliminated. But Iraq, still ruled by Saddam Hussein and the Baath party, had been profoundly damaged in the conflict. Disease and famine began to take its toll of the weakest in the country, mostly the children and elderly across all group and ethnic spectrums. As many as 100,000-200,000 Iraqis may have died of the war and its direct and indirect effects. Reliable figures will probably never be known.

Economically, both Iraq and Kuwait were exhausted. Neither was pumping significant amounts of oil; and in Kuwait over 650 burning oil wells created a nightmarish ecological disaster. The long-term effects on the atmosphere are unknown, as is the long-term effect of the intentional oil spill by Iraq on the northern Gulf. But the short-term effects were obvious: life in Kuwait was a bronchial nightmare for the first six months following the war. If the prevailing winds did not clear the air, Kuwait would be darkened at noon, with a reddish sun barely able to penetrate the rising plumes of smoke and gas. Great lakes of pooling oil and petroleum byproducts dotted the landscape. Fires ringed the capital city, stretching out to the horizon. Kuwaiti nationals returned to a country transformed by the events of the war, changed from a center of leisure and luxury to a country where the basic necessities could not be guaranteed. As many as 10,000 Kuwaitis may have died in the war, of both direct and indirect effects. A good number had been tortured and executed in a short but brutal Iraqi occupation.

Political life in Iraq at the end of the war was dogged by uncertainties. The cease-fire agreement did not incorporate domestic political changes into its terms. Air and land surveillance by the coalition and by the United Nations proceeded in fits and starts, with agreements often negotiated on the scene on an ad hoc basis. The search for Iraq's "weapons of mass destruction" turned up development programs of impressive size and complexity. As the government of Iraq attempted to implement a "shell game," hiding basic facilities from the inspectors, coalition leaders threatened the renewal of hostilities unless a measure of cooperation was extended.

Coalition forces were forced to offer support and supplies to the Kurdish refugees in the north of Iraq fleeing through narrow mountain passes into Iran and Turkey. Iran and Saudi Arabia were forced to give similar support to the Shia rebels in the south. In the long run, it would appear, the coalition allies had little stomach for the creation of independent Kurdish or Shia states on their own borders. In this situation, the plight of many refugees became desperate.

In summary, an elegantly executed military confrontation against a clear danger succeeded, only to produce an outcome of great ambiguity and frustration. Many of these factors were embedded in the very nature of the new international order.

Desert Storm as Indicator of New International Realities.

To what degree did the Iraq-Kuwait crisis demonstrate the emergence of a new international system? Let us apply our observations from earlier in this discussion.

First, did the event show the disappearance of the old bipolar order and the emergence of a multipolar world? Certainly it did in the absence of an influential role for the former Soviet Union. The U.S.S.R. clearly responded to the initiatives of the United States and its coalition partners. Soviet military power was not engaged in the conflict and never became an important factor in the strategic or tactical implementation of Desert Storm. The minimum standards of bipolar interest or confrontation were not demonstrated in the diplomacy or the military phase of the conflict.

Second, the multipolar nature of international power was demonstrated. States from a variety of alliances and regions were involved directly and indirectly in Desert Storm. The U.S. leadership found it both expedient and desirable to maintain a coalition of disparate members. It would be a distortion to call the operation a "U.S. effort." Members of the coalition demonstrated political independence during the crisis, often at the displeasure of the United States. The role of France, Germany, and the U.S.S.R. in last minute attempts to persuade Iraq to embark on a peaceful withdrawal are cases in point.

Third, the role of international organizations in Desert Storm were of critical importance. The U.N. played an indispensable role in legitimizing the use of force against Iraq. Without U.N. sanctions, the presence of U.S., British, French, and Italian troops in the Middle East would have precipitated powerful denunciations of neo-colonial imperialism. The domestic consequences of participation for the Egyptian, Syrian, and North African governments might have been disastrous. As it developed, however, their participation in the coalition did not result in widespread or effective domestic opposition.

In a different way NATO played a key role. It is unlikely that the U.S. could have managed the concentration of troops and materials in the Gulf in such a short time on its own. Although it acted unofficially, NATO not only released large quantities of munitions and supplies from storage, but coordinated the transportation of these supplies to the region. NATO staffers worked hard to identify the location of key technical equipment (chemical "sniffer" tanks, for instance) and make them available to U.S. procurement officers.

NATO was supportive in other ways as well. NATO staff provided much-needed intelligence to the coalition forces. And NATO command, communication, and control procedures were used to coordinate the naval blockade of Iraq and Jordan; and to coordinate the tremendous complexity of the air campaign, allowing fighters and bombers of six nations to fly in and out of Iraqi air space as many as 2,000 times (sorties) a day without mishap.

Other international organizations were important to the effort. The Islamic Conference was an important element in keeping the confrontation secular and in discrediting Saddam Hussein's efforts to link the conflict to religious issues. The Organization of African Unity was important in defusing the charge of yet another neo-colonial intrusion into the area. And the Arab League effectively kept the issue of Arab unity out of the conflict. From the start of the conflict international organizations were fully in play over the conflict. And it is very clear that their activities were responsible for much of the color and texture of Desert Shield–Desert Storm.

Regional actors also were important factors in the crisis. The response of the Gulf Cooperation Council to the Iraqi invasion was key in catalyzing the initial response to Iraq's invasion. The GCC forces sent to the Saudi border were important beyond the significance of the troops. It also signaled the marshaling of very significant international financial resources in the conflict, resources that underwrote U.S. expenses and promised political and economic support to Egypt and Syria. The crisis tested the commitment of the U.A.E., Bahrain, Qatar, and Oman to the GCC, and in the final result raised it to a new level of importance in political and economic coordination of these states.

The European Community was important in its early boycott against Iraq. And in its tacit approval of NATO's informal but key role in logistical support for the coalition. Proposals for a European-led rapid deployment force within NATO got a real head of steam from the crisis, and it appears that the European Community will develop multilateral military capacity during the next decade. This will contribute substantially to the political independence of this new regional international actor.

Nor should U.S.–Canadian regional integration be overlooked. Working largely through its NATO force commitments, Canada was shoulder to shoulder with the coalition in the crisis, particularly so politically and in the naval blockade. Cooperation between Canada and the United States is nothing new, but the vitality of this regional integration deserves some emphasis, particularly as Mexico moves into alignment with the two. At any rate, regional actors were conspicuous in the crisis.

Nongovernmental international actors were also present and involved. The International Red Cross–Red Crescent worked both sides in the conflict, handling international relief efforts, the exchange of hostages and of military captives. Amnesty International documented the outrages committed in the occupation of Kuwait. American Friends of the Middle East provided emergency relief to refugees occasioned by the war and to the endangered public in Iraq at the end of the war. Nongovernmental international agencies have proliferated in the last two decades of the century. They are increasingly relied on by governments for back-door channels to opposing powers. And they may in fact be more capable of providing relief to endangered populations than their own governments. Certainly, the Kurds have received more help in their plight from these nongovernmental actors than from their own governments. Many analysts see these institutions as key actors in the future we all face.

Global interdependence was demonstrated in the Gulf crisis in a number of ways. First and foremost, the vulnerability of the world to the disruption in petroleum supplies was obvious. To many analysts, the crisis was simply another manifestation of the world's dependence on a shrinking supply of petroleum. Second, the environmental effects of the war on the atmosphere and on the Gulf itself suggests our interdependence and vulnerability. The long-term effects of the environmental damage will not be known for some time. But it is clear that some effect was occasioned by the burning of so many barrels of oil and cubic feet of gas.

The type and quality of weaponry on both sides demonstrate the inexorable diffusion of technology around the world. The acquisition of "weapons of mass destruction" has somehow been democratized. No longer must a nation be a super-power to pretend to chemical, biological, nuclear, or high-tech weaponry. The postwar documentation of Iraq's nuclear development program showed efforts of great sophistication—"world class physics"—in the words of one U.N. inspector. Iraq was possibly less than a year or two away from the assembly of a workable atomic weapon. And Iraq had a credible armory of other high-tech weapons, including cluster bombs and fuel-air bombs. It independently modified the primitive Soviet Scud missiles for longer range and larger warheads. It is a mystery of the war why these weapons were not deployed or used to better effect. But in the larger sense of things, Iraq's armory suggests that technological diffusion is one of the prominent realities of the new world order. And only multilateral international initiatives have the muscle to deal with them.

The crisis certainly demonstrated the phenomenon of instantaneous international communication. Saddam Hussein and President Bush were able to engage in an international game of name calling in "real time." Negotiations in Geneva were presented to the world as they occurred (and failed). And the conduct of the war itself was presented in the most complete detail, in spite of the efforts of both sides to control and censor the flow of information. Charges of treason against CNN for its continuing coverage of events from Iraq only demonstrate the significance of that coverage. *Time Magazine* annointed CNN founder Ted Turner as its "1991 Man of the Year" in recognition of these new realities. Consider also the emergence of Middle East Broadcasting Center, a new nonnational "cable" news organization that is broadcasting all over the Arab world. Known to its viewers as MBC, headquartered in London, and owned principally by Saudi investors, the service seeks to imitate the success of U.S. networks in providing relatively unbiased news coverage. It now broadcasts to over 300 million potential Arab viewers without government censorship or control.

There exist now many alternative news sources and technologies (specialized news services utilizing satellite transmission, fax, phone, VCR, audio cassettes, and print). The images they produce, whether of the whimsy of a smart bomb pursuing a fleeing truck into its garage or of the horror of men, women, and children incinerated together in a concrete shelter, all affect our world view. It is conceivable that without the goad of international televised reports of their difficulties, the coalition partners would not have come to the aid of the Kurds or the Shia. As many governments have found, it is difficult to prosecute war in the light of television cameras. And there are fewer and fewer Panamas in which to indulge such a luxury.

Regional conflicts did not go away as a consequence of Desert Storm. There are still points of conflict between many of the coalition partners. Syria and Turkey have points of conflict along their mutual borders that include both people (Kurds, again) and resources (water, in particular). Turkey and Iran continue to compete for economic and political advantage in the Muslim republics of the new Commonwealth of Independent States. Saudi Arabia is still engaged in a hostile relationship with Yemen. And all of the Arab states still find themselves at loggerheads with Israel over Jerusalem, the West Bank, and the future of the Palestinians. Regional conflicts may in fact be exaggerated in the wake of the Gulf crisis, as Iraq is taken out of the regional military equation. At any rate, we may see new axes of conflict regionally. The world is still a dangerous place. In 1992 at least 30 "small" wars smoldered on around the world.

The conflict of rich against poor is also not solved in the region. In many ways, this conflict may have been intensified. Certainly, there will be many claims on Kuwait for the support it received. And the oil-rich states of the Gulf will also be under continued pressure to share their wealth with their poorer and more populous neighbors. One can make a point that the political stability of Egypt, Syria, and Jordan, all with few natural resources and fast-growing populations, can only be assured with substantial subsidies from the rich and developed nations. Failure to provide this aid will most likely result in increasing demands for a more equitable world order, demands that should hold the attention of small, rich countries with small native populations.

Finally, is there a "domestication of the international" apparent in the postcrisis Middle East? Whether new or not, all governments seem to have international policies complicated by domestic concerns. Can an appropriately "Arab" state surrender Palestinian political independence in any way without paying a high political price at home? Can a "Muslim" political leader sign an accord that will leave Jerusalem in Israeli hands? Can any government of Israel surrender significant portions of the West Bank to Palestinian control, in any form? Can the United States, for any reason, countenance a dramatic reduction in the supply of Middle East petroleum to the Western industrial system? Can any country in the region countenance the surrender of its water resources to an international or regional water authority, no matter how independent or scrupulously fair it might be? The answer, superficially at least, is a resounding No. Domestic opposition would be fierce in any of these cases.

And yet there are examples of leaders and governments ignoring these consequences and plunging ahead. Foreign policy may be severely constrained by domestic considerations, and vice versa. But the stakes are too high to allow such simplification. Leaders must live with these constraints and work around them as well. The Gulf crisis resolved the question of Iraq's attempted annexation of Kuwait. But it left most other regional conflicts alive and kicking. How they are dealt with will be a crucial indicator of the real direction of life in the New World Order.

This rough survey suggests that events are moving in the direction of a New World Order as we have loosely defined it. If this is true, these new realities should manifest themselves in the most intractable of Middle East conflicts: the four decade old dispute between Israel and the Arabs.

The Arabs and Israelis

One of the most telling criticisms of the U.S.–led coalition against Iraq was its inability or unwillingness to spell out its ultimate objectives. One analyst of the crisis catalogued no less than fifteen major reasons for the effort as articulated by President Bush. These justifications ranged from ensuring international oil supplies through the protection of American jobs to the "definition of the Bush presidency." Ultimately, of course, the coalition limited its objectives to the rather narrow goals of ejecting Iraq from Kuwait and reestablishing the as-Sabah government. This, of course, left many regional questions unanswered.

Chief of these questions concerned Israel and its occupation of Gaza, the West Bank, southern Lebanon, and the Golan Heights; and the very human question of the future of the Palestinians within these areas. Saddam Hussein, early in the conflict, attempted to link his action to the liberation of the Palestinians. Although the linkage was enthusiastically accepted by the PLO, it was universally rejected by the governments of the coalition. Nonetheless, a widespread public expectation existed in the area that the same principles that invalidated Iraq's annexation of Kuwait also applied to Israel. In other words, many in the Arab public expected the coalition to apply similar pressure and energy to the solution of the Israeli-Palestinian question. To do less would be to publicly endorse a double standard, one for Arab states, the other for Israel.

Analysts have long considered the Arab-Israeli conflict to be primary in the Middle Eastern system. No other important issues could be settled without or before progress on this issue. And, in fact, the issue has been remarkably persistent and pervasive. For this reason, it was deemed very important when President Bush in his March 1991 address to Congress included "justice for the Palestinian people" in his list of objectives for the postcrisis Middle East.

President Bush soon acted on this new initiative, sending Secretary of State Baker to the Middle East to enlist the coalition partners in a new effort to resolve the Arab-Israeli conflict. Between April and October, 1991, Secretary Baker formally visited the region at least eight times, shuttling patiently between Israel, Syria, Jordan, and Egypt. Ultimately, Syria and Israel proved to be the most intransigent of the principals involved; and, of course, the shadow of the PLO hovered over most of these discussions and negotiations.

President Bush eventually prevailed in his efforts to convene a multilateral Middle Eastern Peace Conference. The first session of the conference was held in Madrid in November of 1991. And the mere convening of such a conference indicated international diplomacy of a high and intensive nature. How was the United States able to bring these adversaries to the table, in spite of their bitter history and long memories?

It is clear in retrospect that President Bush interpreted the success of Desert Storm as a mandate to go further in solving Middle Eastern problems. Bush and

Baker took advantage of this postwar environment by embarking on a series of very high level diplomatic conversations, conversations so private that even the upper-level bureaucrats of the foreign policy establishments were in the dark as to what was agreed. One meeting between Secretary Baker and President Assad reportedly continued for eight hours with no breaks for relief or refreshment. At the end of the marathon, letters were exchanged between Baker and Assad, the contents and assurances therein known only to their most loyal and intimate advisors. In this way, domestic reaction to the negotiated points was minimized.

The most serious problem—the unwillingness of Israel to sit at any table populated in any way by the PLO—was overcome by a two-track approach. On one level, Jordan agreed to include a Palestinian component in its delegation to the conference. This met historical Israeli preferences. On the other track, the United States identified and encouraged the creation of an indigenous Palestinian leadership independent of the PLO. Although in fact such an indigenous elite already existed in the occupied territories, they were for the most part contaminated in Israeli eyes by their association with Arafat and the PLO. The fiction of an independent Palestinian negotiating team was accomplished by the expedient of selecting Palestinians of high educational and humanitarian accomplishments. The head of the Palestinian segment of the Jordanian delegation, for example, was the distinguished and long-term head of the Gaza Red Cross–Red Crescent, Dr. Haider abdul-Shafi. One by one, a delegation acceptable to even the most hard-line Israeli official was assembled. It is also clear that the legitimacy of the delegation in the Palestinian community in the occupied territories was based on their support of the intifada, a revolution that occurred beyond the direct control of the PLO.

One should not minimize the significance of this accomplishment. Much of the sympathy in Israel for the plight of the Palestinians had evaporated as Palestinian support for Iraq became apparent. Palestinians cheering the Scud missiles from their rooftops effectively destroyed the Israeli peace movement. And the Gulf crisis also provided the government of Israel with a pretext to clamp down tightly on the Palestinian community with a brutal six-week curfew. Both of these actions greatly increased the tension and distrust between the Israeli and Palestinian communities.

It is also clear in hindsight that the United States was willing to use both the carrot and the stick in motivating conference participants. Syria was exonerated in the bombing of Pan Am Flight 103, a boost to Syrian prestige; and financial incentives flowed from the Gulf states to Damascus. Israel received compensation for Scud damage received in the war and an increased flow of U.S. weapons to the IDF. The Soviet Union extended formal diplomatic relations to Israel, thereby improving the prospects of emigration for many Soviet Jews. These carrots were important in Israeli and Syrian calculations.

Among the sticks applied were these: for Syria, no postwar subsidies if she failed to come to the table, and the end of a warming relationship with Washington. In the case of Israel, the Bush administration successfully withheld U.S. loan guarantees, subject to Israeli participation in a peace conference, in the amount of $10 billion, which had been dedicated to the settlement and housing of Soviet refugees in Israel. The Israeli lobby in the United States raised a furious objection to this linkage, but the Bush administration held firm and prevailed. In the opinion of many analysts,[5] this was the first and only example of an American president since 1948 successfully standing up to the Israeli lobby.

Another important "carrot" presented to Israel was the possible revocation of U.N. Assembly Resolution 3379 (1975), which equated Zionism with racism. This resolution had long poisoned Israel's relationship with the United Nations, and its promised removal would constitute a considerable gain in prestige for the government of Israel, both at home and abroad. After Israeli participation in two early phases of the peace conference, in Madrid and Washington, the resolution was indeed revoked under U.S. leadership. And although most Middle Eastern and Muslim governments voted against revocation, the motion passed easily. Although the measure in both instances was largely symbolic, the symbolism was important; and the aggressive role of the United States in its revocation was an important article of faith between the United States and Israel at a time when many other issues divided them.

It is also important to realize that certain positions were not abandoned. Israel, for instance, not only refused to slow down or cease its settlement policy in the West Bank and Gaza, but it seemed to time the announcement of new settlements to coincide with Secretary Baker's visits. Prime Minister Shamir, moreover, never retrenched on his refusal to concede the "land for peace" formula that implicitly undergirded the conference premise. He also refused in any way to discuss the future status of Jerusalem or countenance any withdrawal from the Golan. Syria, for its part, insisted that Israeli withdrawal from the Golan was a prerequisite to peace and continued its support of Palestinian movements independent of and opposed to the PLO. It also continued to press its case that Yitzhak Shamir was himself a terrorist, involved in the assassination of U.N. peacekeeping officials and the murder of Palestinian noncombatants in the 1948 war. For the Palestinians, the intifada did not end, although its intensity was reduced. And the independent Palestinian delegation publicly voiced its sympathy for the PLO as the appropriate representative of the Palestinian nation. By and large, these reservations and obstructions were ignored by U.S. diplomats. Even a small number of gratuitous acts of terror by Israeli and Palestinian extremists failed to derail the opening session in Madrid.

In fact, U.S. hopes for the conference were both practical and visionary. In the most practical sense, U.S. decision makers placed great hope in the process of negotiation, in and of itself. The momentum of the conference itself, undergirded by the privately assured "carrots" and "sticks," would be hard to overcome. Thus, once the principals came to the table they would find it increasingly difficult to leave. International pressure, domestic public opinion, and the hopes of finding real solutions to intractable problems would also provide incentive to stay with the process.

In terms of idealism and vision, the conference structure suggested coming to terms with a wide variety of regional issues. While highly ceremonial conferences on the big issues of peace and war took place, lower-level bilateral discussions and negotiations between Israel and respectively Lebanon, Syria, Jordan, and the Palestinians were to consider many important specific questions. Among them were regional arms control, nuclear proliferation and reduction, the return of Israeli occupied territories for guarantees of peace, land and "autonomy" for the

---

[5] See for example the article by Tom Friedman, *New York Times*, October 6, 1991, p. E3.

Palestinians, water rights and distribution, regional environmental problems (of which there are many), and possible economic cooperation.

There is a frustrating aspect to these successful peace conferences. In particular, this frustration is based on the realization that successful negotiations will be played out over a long period of time. Months, even years, will denominate the success of the effort. Moreover, early gains will appear somewhat trivial in comparison to the ultimate objective of the conference conveners. In the compressed and critical space that is the Middle East, finding common solutions to long-standing problems will involve the development of common trust. This is unlikely to come quickly in the form, for example, that transformed Eastern Europe and the former Soviet Union. "The beauty is in the detail" here and the details will be long in coming.

On a more positive note, it is almost always better to talk than to make war. If an emergent consensus on the desirability of peace in the Middle East is one of the factors in the New International Order, then the nations, international organizations, nongovernmental organizations, and information media will continue to keep pressure on the principals in the conflict. And progress may in fact be made. It is important to note that the progress made so far would have been in fact unthinkable in the depths of the preceding bipolar world order. So some optimism is in fact in order. In the fits and starts of discussion between old enemies, there is some room for hope. A report of the U.S. Institute of Peace puts the situation succinctly:

> Arab and Israeli leaders will finally sign if and when they become persuaded that they have more to lose if agreement slips away. They then demand a panoply of extra "side" benefits to help justify to their domestic constituencies the concessions they have made. Only a major power, in fact only the United States can now meet this need, which helps to explain why the United States remains uniquely acceptable as the essential third-party mediator for the Arab-Israeli conflict.[6]

Let us now turn our attention to the specific foreign policy priorities of the major Middle Eastern actors.

SUPERPOWERS AND GREAT POWERS

As we have previously noted, recent events have radically changed the configuration of the international system. Nowhere is that more noticeable than in the change of status among the superpowers. The Commonwealth of Independent States does not bring to bear on international events the power and/or prestige of its predecessor, the Soviet Union. In fact, the C.I.S. is in the very process of *becoming* an international actor. That leaves the United States in position as the only surviving superpower at the end of the bipolar era. But that position is less than enviable in that the United States now confronts a world in which unknown risk replaces the known threat. To be successful as a global power, the United

---

[6] Kenneth W. Stein and Samuel W. Lewis, with Sheryl J. Brown, *Making Peace Among Arabs and Israelis* (Washington, DC: U.S. Institute of Peace, 1991), p. 31.

States will have to make prudent judgments about just when and where its fundamental national interest is at risk. To do otherwise, to jump about the globe from crisis to crisis and conflict to conflict irrespective of their importance invites a fate similar to being bitten to death by ducks: a slow, inexorable, and painful decline.

U.S. policy sees the world system as one in which decisive U.S. action, augmented and legitimized by multinational agreements and the actions of international organizations, can defend both U.S. national interests and the larger system interests as well. In the Middle East this apparently translates into a policy of frontal assault on the most intransigent of regional conflicts, the Arab-Israeli conflict.

In a less abstract formulation, this means that the United States will try to have its cake and eat it too, finding and supporting solutions that will both satisfy the security needs of Israel and solve the vexing Arab problems regarding occupied land and the rights of the Palestinian people. In the absence of a superpower adversary, the United States has both the capacity and the opportunity to exercise an "even hand" in finding a workable solution to these problems. Certainly the global and regional prestige that accompanied the success of Desert Storm enhances this potential.

Second, Desert Storm provided an opportunity for the United States to strengthen its political and economic and military relationships with the states of the Gulf. New U.S. bases have been established, forward supply depots organized, and a steady flow of new weapons systems daily increases the capability of the Gulf military. These augment previously established military relationships with Egypt and Oman . Economic cooperation, particularly with Saudi Arabia and Kuwait, is intimate and reciprocal. In short, the United States is now the full guarantor of the peace in the region of the Gulf. U.S. planes and warships regularly monitor activity in and around the Gulf.

The U.S. now presides over a grand alliance in the Middle East, composed of formerly hostile factions from the Arab system. It is anchored in the Gulf by the conservative states of Saudi Arabia, the U.A.E., Bahrain, Oman, Qatar, and Kuwait. It is buttressed on the West by Egypt, the largest of the Arab states and the most influential politically. And it includes Syria in the Levant, now one of the strongest Arab military powers. Jordan constitutes a tolerated de facto member, still doing penance for its unwillingness to join in the coalition against Iraq. All of these states at one time or another have been at loggerheads with another state in the alliance. Thus the alliance brings previously hostile nations together in a pragmatic relationship.

In a de facto sense, Israel is also part of this grand alliance, based on its special relationship with the United States. Given the fundamental differences between members of the alliance, and the historical strains between them, it will take a good deal of energy and diplomacy to keep the alliance intact.

There are, however, good reasons for doing so. The United States and the Western industrial states are still highly dependent on a regular and reasonably priced flow of petroleum from the area. Military interventions have proven very costly, even when costs are shared by the beneficiaries, as in the Gulf crisis. And the steady proliferation of weapons of mass destruction argue for a logic of mutual defense rather than going it alone. Finally, there are the intangible benefits that accrue from reducing international stress and conflict.

Middle Eastern countries outside the alliance are for the most part objects of U.S. concern. Iraq, Iran, and Libya are all to an important degree isolated by the alliance. The strategic importance of Yemen also keeps it an object of U.S. attention.

Iraq, greatly weakened by the Gulf war, nonetheless shows signs of life. U.S. policy will continue to try to keep Iraq from a major recovery, economically, politically, or militarily. The removal of Saddam Hussein and the Baath party from power will continue to be a U.S. priority and the relaxation of economic sanctions will probably not occur as long as the Baathist regime stays in power. The United States continues to support covert actions aimed at removing Saddam Hussein from power.

Iran, now in the maturity of its revolution, is still viewed by the United States as a dangerous adversary. Even the release in late 1991 of all of the remaining U.S. hostages in Lebanon failed to completely erase U.S. suspicions. Islamic political movements drawing moral support and encouragement from Iran still exist in Egypt, Jordan, Syria, Lebanon, Turkey, Algeria, and Morocco. Nonetheless, there has been a modest warming of relations between the two states. As the independent republics of the C.I.S. establish new relationships with the central Asian states of Turkey, Iran and Afghanistan, the United States will most likely recognize growing priorities there as well. The United States will continue to place a high priority on frustrating the export of Iran's Islamic revolution to the rest of the Middle East.

U.S. relations with Libya took a nose dive in 1991 as investigators finally placed the blame on Libyan diplomats for the 1988 bombing of a Pan Am 747 over Scotland (flight 103). U.S. demands for the extradition of two Libyan officials were rebuffed. It is not unlikely that the United States will sooner or later, at a time and place of its own choosing, launch another raid on Libya. For its part, Libya is a shadow of its former self. Fewer and fewer countries and organizations seek its support. Its international prestige is low and headed lower.

Western European relations with the Middle East are increasingly conditioned by its movement toward economic and political integration. The European Community is currently in the process of defining its common economic relationship with other world regions. Turkey, an applicant for membership in the EC, is unlikely to gain that status, in spite of its European geography and millions of "guest workers" in Germany and Belgium. The states of North Africa (Morocco, Algeria, and Tunisia, mainly) have been given privileged access to the EC as a consequence of their previous colonial experience. They also have many "guest workers" abroad, particularly in France and Belgium. If these two relationships are indicative of future agreements, we can look forward to EC special relationships with other Middle Eastern regions, particularly in the Gulf, where British relationships are well established and petroleum resources well developed.

EC political relationships with the region are likely to be expressed through NATO and the U.N. in the short run, and in intimate cooperation with the United States as the dominant military power in the region. Political integration will come slowest in the various areas of EC cooperation and development. France and Germany, in particular, still view each other with suspicion. The result of this will likely be conservative approaches to international policy. Like the C.I.S., the EC will be in the agony of inventing its political institutions and foreign policies for the next decade.

Japan, as a dominant financial and industrial world power, will continue to place strong emphasis on ensuring a regular supply of petroleum from the Middle East. As in the past, Japan will seek regular supply relationships with the Gulf states, Saudi Arabia, and Iran. Japan will likely continue to seek mutual trade relationships with the richest of the Middle Eastern states. It is unlikely that any dramatic increase in Japan's military capability will occur. Carefully targeted foreign aid programs, as in the decade of the 1980s, will probably continue. Japan will most likely pursue the politics of prestige in the region, with substantial success. Japan's political independence of the United States and the West will continue to accelerate. Japan's somewhat reluctant financial subsidy of Desert Shield–Desert Storm indicate the continued divergence on its basic interests from that of the United States and the EC. Given that reality, it is likely that Japan will seek stronger political and economic ties with individual Middle Eastern states. Saudi Arabia and Iran are probable targets of Japanese initiative.

Middle Eastern States

Egypt. Egypt emerged from the period with enhanced prestige. Its early commitment to the coalition confronting Iraq was of immense importance to U.S. efforts, providing both Arab and Muslim legitimacy. And Egypt's long tradition of anticolonialism further legitimized the effort. It was able to quickly commit substantial numbers of well-trained troops to the Saudi theater of the Gulf war. Its history of military cooperation with the United States, particularly its joint exercises in the 1980s and its adoption of the NATO munition standards, gave it the ability to coordinate command, control, and communication with the United States. By any measure, the Egyptian military contribution to the coalition was the most substantial of any Arab state.

Egypt moved closer to the United States in the aftermath of the Gulf war. It became an important player in the convening of the Arab-Israeli peace conference, particularly in reassuring (and pressuring) Syria and Israel. As a result Egyptian prestige experienced yet another increase and the flow of U.S. military and economic aid to Egypt also increased, as did the flow of aid from Saudi Arabia, Kuwait, and the U.A.E. The election of Egyptian statesman Bhutros Ghali as Secretary General of the United Nations also enhanced Egyptian international prestige and reflected continued great power approval of the Egyptian regime.

These increases in prestige and foreign aid notwithstanding, Egypt still faces a bleak economic and political scenario. A very high birthrate, declining revenues from overseas workers, and a relatively stagnant economy suggest great strains on its political system in the relatively near future. Regional economic integration and accelerated foreign investments would appear likely Egyptian strategies in the near future. Failure to ameliorate its economic difficulties could have political consequences of great importance. The fundamentalist Islamic parties in Egypt seem well positioned to benefit from widespread public dissatisfaction. The effects of an Iran-style Islamic republic in Egypt would be widespread throughout the region.

Saudi Arabia. Saudi Arabia took great risks in inviting the U.S. response to Iraq's invasion of Kuwait. No Arab state can routinely invite a foreign military presence, given the sensitivity in the region to its colonial and postcolonial past. And Saudi Arabia, as custodian of the holiest of the shrines of Islam, has a special obligation to protect the purity of its land. The prospect of non-Muslim Western men and women tramping casually across the holy land of Arabia was distasteful to many people inside and outside of Saudi Arabia, but particularly to the religious elites and the most conservative elements in the political elite.

Saudi Arabia risked the exposure of its citizenry to the different social and political values of its guests. A country in which the most conservative of values prevail socially—including the public veiling of women, the requirements of modest dress, and the prohibition of alcohol—could theoretically be scandalized or destabilized by the presence of large numbers of tank-topped, beer-swilling, Christ-worshipping foreign soldiers. Or at least so the argument went. The point was made by a rigorous segregation of foreign troops, even to the point of entertaining them on cruise ships anchored in the Gulf. And in the postwar environment the Saudi government reasserted its emphasis on its traditional social and political values. Nonetheless, the religious establishment in Saudi Arabia issued a number of public warnings to the Saudi government, indicating its dissatisfaction with the state of public morals and the policies of the government. The announcement by King Fahd in early 1992 that a consultative assembly would be formed was clearly a response to increasing domestic pressure from its important religious allies.

Before and after the Gulf war, Saudi priorities remained basically the same. With a small native population spread out over a large and mainly uninhabited expanse, security concerns remain paramount.

Saudi economic, political, and military relationships with the United States were enhanced by Desert Shield–Desert Storm. Saudi Arabia expanded its petroleum production to levels that ensured moderate prices globally. And its distribution presence in the U.S. market was allowed to expand, giving it a higher stake in the U.S. domestic economy. New discoveries of petroleum were acknowledged, increasing the Saudi percentage of known world petroleum reserves. Military cooperation with the United States reached new heights and there is little doubt as to the mutual assurances and guarantees existing between them. Dramatic increases in Saudi military capability are scheduled, with the majority of the new systems coming from the United States. "Nativization" of the military and related security agencies was emphasized as well.

Regional relationships also intensified. The success of the GCC in coming to terms with the Iraqi crisis enhanced its attractiveness. Military and political cooperation are understood as a high priority for countries with small populations and relatively modest military capacity. Saudi Arabia and the Gulf states abandoned their long-standing policy against the recognition of Israel and agreed to attend the Arab-Israeli peace conference as observers, further solidifying their joint relationships with the United States. Saudi subsidies were clearly important to Syria in its decision to attend the conference. And investment in Egypt contributed to U.S.-led attempts to ameliorate the economic plight confronting the Mubarak regime.

Saudi pragmatism continued to manifest itself. It played a critical formal and informal role in the attempts to settle the political questions in Lebanon, an initiative that brought it into intimate discussions and relationships with Syria. It extended diplomatic relations to Iran, in spite of its reservations about the regime in place there. And it continued modest financial support to Lebanon and Jordan. The PLO was the only obvious target of Saudi ire, and its annual support for the organization was completely eliminated.

Saudi Arabia and its Gulf neighbors continue to live in a "bad neighborhood." Both Iran and Iraq are clearly perceived as potential threats to their independence. Syria has a long history of animosity toward these monarchical regimes. Yemen has border disputes with Saudi Arabia and Oman. And the deterioration of political and economic life in the nearby Horn of Africa (Somalia, the Sudan, and Ethiopia) presents potential threats as well. Fluid and creative alliance politics will likely continue to be a major priority of the Saudi government for the indefinite future.

The Gulf States.   The foreign policies of the U.A.E., Bahrain, Qatar, Kuwait, and Oman generally bear great similarities. The coordinating role of the Gulf Cooperation Council is particularly important for these small states. By and large, their foreign policies seek security through mutual cooperation and by extension of their military and economic relationships with the United States and their economic and political relationships with the EC. Bahrain, Oman, and Kuwait have been the most aggressive in approving U.S.–basing agreements and the prepositioning of military supplies. Bahrain has agreed to extend port facilities to the U.S. navy as it patrols the Gulf. And like Saudi Arabia, the richer of these states—principally the U.A.E. and Kuwait—seek an additional measure of security by providing generous subsidies to the poorer neighboring states.

Kuwait has particular problems occasioned by Iraq's invasion and occupation. Rebuilding has been a daunting task, although many of the earliest estimates of damage costs have proven to be excessive. For example, the extinguishing of some 650 oil well fires was accomplished in less than nine months, instead of the two to three years some experts had suggested. And the damage of the Kuwaiti physical plant was very selective, also minimizing reconstruction costs. But even then, billions of dollars were needed. Fortunately, Kuwaiti oil production has recovered faster than imagined; and Kuwait's very substantial foreign investments provided income used in the reconstruction.

Kuwait will attempt over the next decade to reduce its population to roughly half of its prewar level, eliminating many of the foreign guest workers that dominated its economic and professional life; and eliminating that point of vulnerability in its security. A "nativized" and expanded military is also envisaged. These programs will permanently dispossess many foreign workers, particularly Palestinian, Jordanian, and Egyptian workers. This has exacerbated the social pressure in Jordan and the West Bank. Grants in aid have somewhat offset these effects in Egypt. Kuwait is not alone in reducing the number of Middle Eastern foreign workers—all of the neighboring Gulf states have pursued similar programs.

Syria.   Of all the states in the Middle East, Syria has made the biggest changes in its foreign policy. For years Syria was nearly a client state of the U.S.S.R., enjoying a wide range of subsidies and support. Syria's foreign policies opposing imperialism, Israel, the United States, and monarchism were supported in the main by Soviet economic and military subsidies. Its support for wars of national liberation (particularly in Israel by the Palestinians), pan-Arabism, Iran in its war with Iraq, and international socialism enjoyed similar advantage. But with the collapse of Soviet power, new international realities impinged on Syria's formula. As a result, Syria has changed many of its foreign policies to adjust to the new world emerging.

Syria's cooperation with the coalition forces against Iraq signaled a watershed in its foreign policy. Alignment with the United States, Saudi Arabia, Great Britain, and France against another Arab power would have been unthinkable in the Syria of the 1970s and 1980s. And Syria's removal from the notorious list of "terrorist states" by the United States would have been equally unthinkable. But both moves are now history; and more startling initiatives appear on the horizon of Syrian foreign policy.

Syria is moving economically, socially, and politically toward the West. Syrian decision makers have considerably opened up the economy, allowing market forces to appear. The tightly controlled Syrian currency is moving toward convertibility. Saudi financial subsidies have allowed it to find alternative supply sources for its military plant. Syrian students are beginning to study in Europe and the United States, instead of in Eastern Europe and the C.I.S. The adoption of English as the second language of choice displaces an earlier emphasis on Russian—in fact, it is difficult to find Syrians willing to speak Russian at all. Syrian universities seek formal relationships with their counterparts in the West. Academic and cultural exchanges with the West have blossomed.

Syria has benefited from its new pragmatism. U.S. and conservative Arab support has allowed it to develop a de facto suzerainty over Lebanon. Its removal from the list of terrorist states allows it to pursue closer economic relations with the West. As a result of this and of Desert Storm, Syrian international prestige has increased. But Syria appeared a reluctant player in the Arab-Israeli peace process, goaded into the negotiations by a combination of U.S. and Arab pressure. Recovery of the Golan region and Israeli withdrawal from Southern Lebanon are high priorities for Syria. President Assad has previously considered Israeli withdrawal a precondition for negotiations. But in spite of this, Syria entered reluctantly into negotiations before these stated objectives were accomplished.

Syria has not abandoned all of its prior international agenda. Forces for pan-Arabism are still influential in its politics. Syria has not abandoned its dislike for monarchical regimes and remains committed to their replacement with democratic institutions. Its competition with Egypt for leadership of the Arab world continues. Syrian relations with Iran remain warm, introducing a note of disquiet into its new relations with the West. Syria shares a long common border with Turkey and the water resources that flow across it will be a considerable future concern for Syria. In fact, water policy generally is a high priority for Syrian decision makers and is the subject most likely to lead Syria into regional compacts and cooperation.

Syria still pursues military parity with Israel, albeit with new sources of money and supply. Noting these apparent contradictions in its foreign policy, analysts suggest that Syrian policy is in the process of evolving. And given Syria's history, it would be foolhardy to predict its final contours.

Lebanon.   Lebanon has made progress toward reestablishing governmental legitimacy since the Taif Accords of 1989. Syrian troops and administrators have played a key role in suppressing the factional warfare that was the hallmark of the Lebanese civil war over the past decade. In fact, Syrian influence is so extensive as to raise the question of just how much independence the new government has.

Lebanese foreign policy priorities have largely revolved around recovering the "buffer zone" seized by Israel during its 1982 invasion. The zone, which also contains the watershed of the Litani river, is important to the Lebanese government both symbolically and substantively. Lebanese participation in the Arab-Israeli Peace Conference suggests that they have a pragmatic understanding of Israel's security needs and are ready to accept these needs as a price for the recovery of their territory. A related agenda is the eventual release of the thousands of Lebanese civilians held either by Israel or by its ally, the Army of South Lebanon. The return of Sheikh Obeid, an influential cleric associated with Hizbollah, kidnapped by Israeli guerrillas in 1989, is of great importance to the Shia of Lebanon.

The improvement of civil life in Lebanon is sufficient to have attracted real estate investment back to Beirut. But clearly, the importance of establishing stable, representative government inclusive of the major factions and religious groups is the most pressing priority. Until that is accomplished, Lebanese foreign policy is destined to be at the bottom of the Lebanese priorities.

Iran. Iran has much to gain in the new politics of the Middle East. It was an interested bystander in the Gulf crisis, skillfully exploiting the difficulties of its old adversary, Iraq, without entangling itself in the actual conflict. Iraqi planes fled to sanctuary in Iran, only to find the planes at first impounded and then eventually integrated into the Iranian air force. The revolt of the Shia in southern Iraq clearly benefited Iranian interests, but again Iran seemed content to reap such rewards indirectly. She did not move quickly to establish an independent Shia state in the south of Iraq, although Iranian public opinion would probably have supported such a move. The Rafsanjani regime played its cards conservatively and cautiously during the crisis.

In retrospect, Iran emerged as one of the primary beneficiaries of Desert Storm. Clearly, the destruction of Iraqi military power directly increased the relative power of Iran. And in concrete terms, Iran has used much of its increased oil revenues to substantially increase its armaments. Thus, Iran emerged from the Gulf crisis with enhanced military power. And its unwillingness to directly exploit either Iraq's or Kuwait's difficulties suggested an emergent maturity and realism.

Iranian prestige is very high in the Middle East, particularly among the Islamic fundamentalists. The idea of Islamic government has spread broadly since the establishment of the Islamic Republic in Iran, although the specifics of its Shia political philosophy have not found fertile ground in Sunni societies. The Muslim Brotherhood in Egypt, Jordan, and Syria, and the mujahedin in Afghanistan have different ideas about the specifics of Islamic government, as have the new Islamic republicans in Algeria. Iran has the high moral ground, even if its most ardent admirers do not intend to imitate their institutions. These facts will continue to make Iranian relations with the United States and the EC problematic.

Iran has reached out to the West in specific ways. Its role in the release of the U.S. hostages in Lebanon and Lebanese hostages in Israel in late 1991 was crucial; as a result, the United States has warmed its relations with Iran, allowing the release of impounded funds and the establishment of some modest trade and educational relations. The renewed flow of parts and technology from the United States to its economy is apparently a critical necessity for Iran. Iran has simultaneously attempted to improve its relations with the EC, although with mixed success.

Regionally, Iran appears concerned to establish good relations with the C.I.S. republics of central Asia. Iran competes with Turkey in this process and both countries have invested economically in the resource-rich Muslim republics, particularly Kazakhstan, Uzbekistan, and Azerbaijan. By early 1992, Iran had established diplomatic relations with eight of the twelve republics, including the Russian Federation. Relations with Turkey remained cool, although both Turkey and Iran have a common interest in suppressing independence movements among the Kurds. Water resources are a recurring problem, as Turkey threatens to disrupt the flow of water into the Tigris and Euphrates systems. Given all of these factors, it seems clear that Iran is destined to play a larger role in the international politics of the Middle East over the next decade.

Turkey. Turkey played a key role in the coalition suppression of Iraq. Its refusal to transport Iraqi oil to market deprived Iraq of important income; and the use of Turkish air bases in eastern Turkey allowed U.S. warplanes a much greater field of action than would otherwise have been the case. As a member of NATO, Turkey supplied logistical help to the coalition. Kurdish rebels against Baghdad were given sanctuary and supplies in the rugged mountains of eastern Turkey, and refugees streamed across the border. All in all, Turkey was as committed as any combatant member of the coalition, short of actually deploying troops in the conflict. As a result, Turkish relations with the United States improved considerably. The coalition allies endeavored to reimburse Turkey for its expenses and lost revenues. But intangible costs, expressed in the restiveness of its fundamentalist groups and the aspirations of its Kurdish minority for independence, continue to take their toll. Obviously, Turkey's participation in the coalition was not without a domestic political price. Turkey continues to seek tangible rewards for its key role in the war against Iraq.

As a nation astride the continents of Europe and Asia, Turkey has often identified itself with Europe. This has recently been evident in its attempts to achieve full membership status with the EC. Under the leadership of Turgut Ozal, Turkey has moved substantially in the direction of free market economics, accepting the economic and social costs of the attendant destabilization. Millions of Turkish workers continue to labor in Europe, and the Turkish army is the largest in NATO (except for the U.S. army). In spite of these political, economic, and military policies, Turkey has been excluded from membership in the EC. Membership will most likely continue as an important goal of any Turkish government.

Like Iran, Turkey sees opportunity in the dissolution of the U.S.S.R. and the emergence of independent states in what was formerly Soviet central Asia. Turkey moved quickly to establish diplomatic relations with the Muslim and neighbor republics; foreign investments in communications, transportation, and resource development have taken place in Azerbaijan, and commitments for similar projects have been promised to Kazakhstan, Uzbekistan and Turkmenistan. Turkey would like to be seen as a democratic role model for the emerging republics, a logical alternative to the Islamic republic model in Iran. Delegations from the republics visited Turkey to observe Turkish political and administrative practices. Relations with the Kurdish minorities continue to be problematic for both Turkey and Iran, and both have had to contend militarily with independence movements in the area.

To some degree, these actions falsify their claims as democratic or Islamic republic role models.

Turkish relations with Greece and Bulgaria continue to smolder. Although President Bush announced the solution of the Cyprus question as a major initiative for the New International Order, little has been accomplished there. It apparently has taken a back seat to events between Israel and the Arabs. Bulgaria has forcibly expelled many Turkish nationals from its territory, creating great ill will between the two states and many refugees in European Turkey. Relations with both of these countries will not likely improve in the near future. The civil war in Yugoslavia also concerns the Turkish leadership, although once again there seems little the government can do about events there.

The very cordial relationships between Turkey and the United States may be placed at risk in the coming years if Islamic fundamentalists capitalize on their electoral gains in 1991. President Turgut Ozal lost his working majority in the Turkish parliament and his own leadership may be at risk after his term expires in 1995. Surprisingly, the new Prime Minister, Suleyman Demirel, has enthusiastically endorsed Ozal's goals of increased democratization and a market driven economy. Given Turkey's key role in NATO and its geopolitical importance in central Asia and the Eastern Mediterranean basin, United States and EC policy should continue to be supportive of the democratic government of Turkey and its international priorities.

Algeria, Morocco, and Tunisia. Algeria, Morocco, and Tunisia share some of the key difficulties facing Turkey. Like Turkey, they have been at pains to establish a working relationship with the EC. And unlike Turkey, then have been somewhat successful at establishing regional cooperation, particularly in the Saharan regions where boundaries are particularly permeable. Their governments in the main cooperated with the U.S.–led coalition against Iraq. All in all, these states have enjoyed improving relations with the United States and the EC.

Domestically, however, they all face a growing tide of fundamentalist dissatisfaction with their secular regimes. Large public demonstrations favoring Iraq occurred in both Morocco and Algeria, and were suppressed with difficulty. In Algeria and Tunisia, these actions have resulted in fundamentalist success at the ballot box. And an organized Islamic opposition to the monarchy continues to gain legitimacy in Morocco. Suffice to conclude that all three states face a rising tide of organized Islamic fundamentalism. This tide threatens to change the political face of the Maghreb. Once again, the long-run implications of fundamentalist rule are not clear; but most likely their policy preferences would run counter to those of the United States and the EC.

Libya. Libya, since the U.S. air raid in 1986, has adopted a fairly low profile internationally. The U.S.–Great Britain determination that Libyan diplomats orchestrated the Pan Am flight 103 bombing over Scotland reinvigorated Western demands for more punitive action against Libya. Libya was hurt as much as any ally by the collapse of Soviet power, and remains extremely vulnerable to foreign sanctions or intervention. No major world power considers itself a guarantor of Libyan interests.

Muammar Qadaffi appears to have chosen a course designed to minimize the rationales for punitive action. As such, the foreign policy of Libya has become relatively conservative and quiet. The decline in world petroleum prices has also deprived Libya of the financial resources necessary for an expansive foreign policy. Nonetheless, we should not underestimate the symbolic importance of Qadaffi and Libya as a scapegoat for all manner of international outrage. In the case of Libya, its past reputation may be more important than the reality of its current behavior.

Israel. The emergence of the New World Order has been especially important to Israel, which finds both positive and negative implications in the new situation. On the one hand, the collapse of the Soviet Union and the emergence of the C.I.S. allowed the continued emigration of C.I.S. Jews to Israel. On the other hand, the collapse of the Soviet threat removed one of the key rationales for the privileged "special relationship" between Israel and the United States. The United States simply does not now need the Israeli military in the way it did during the dangerous confrontations of the bipolar Cold War. This new fact was made very clear during Desert Storm, when the U.S. formally kept Israel from participating in the coalition attacks on Iraq, going so far as to deny key communication codes to the Israeli air force. It seems clear that the nature of the relationship between Israel and the United States changed dramatically under the Bush administration.

As indicated above, Israel was more or less goaded into participation in the Arab-Israeli Peace Conference begun in 1991. The Shamir administration was unenthusiastic about multilateral negotiations under any circumstances and ideologically committed to a policy of "no return of land" to the Palestinians under any circumstances. The very nature of the coalition supporting the Likud government made any major deviation from this proposition unlikely, even in the unlikely event that the government would see the negotiations in a positive light. These two attitudes put Israel on a collision course with the Bush administration, which saw the surrender of occupied territory in exchange for security guarantees as the most appropriate formula for settling the long-standing Arab-Israeli dispute.

Israeli policy after Desert Storm thus exhibited some fundamental inconsistencies. Unwilling to totally alienate a U.S. administration, the Shamir government allowed itself to be bullied into participation in the peace talks; while its policy of rapid settlement in the West Bank and the suppression of the Palestinian intifada created the "facts on the ground" that would make any thought of land surrender impossible. The Bush administration succeeded in linking participation in the talks to future U.S. housing loan guarantees, the first time a U.S. president publicly defied the Zionist lobby in the United States. Public opinion in Israel about this linkage was extremely negative and many Israelis began talking about the necessity of ending Israel's dependence on U.S. subsidies.

Israeli extremist groups and Palestinian extremists in and outside of Israel did their best to disrupt the negotiations. Israeli "settlers," armed to the teeth and espousing the most nationalist of Zionist philosophy, established settlements illegally, seized Arab housing forcibly, even beat and murdered Palestinians. Settlers convicted of the murder of Palestinians received modest sentences and early parole from prison. Palestinians outside the coalition involved in the peace talks also attempted to disrupt events. The complexity of the situation was underscored in one attack by Palestinian guerillas on a bus transporting Israeli settlers, killing two. The Palestinians, attempting to disrupt the peace process, killed the two settlers while they were on their way to a rally to oppose the peace negotiations. Both the Israelis and their Palestinian counterparts have had to walk a very narrow ledge.

Relations with the United States hit a new nadir early in 1992 when the murder of an Israeli settler in the Gaza Strip resulted in the government's decision to deport twelve Palestinian leaders. The U.S. government denounced the action in strong language publicly and at "the highest levels" of the Israeli government. The Palestinian delegation to the peace talks cancelled plans to attend the subsequent second set of talks in Washington. A general polarization of attitudes between the U.S. and Israeli governments, undergirded by a similar emergent polarization in public opinion, put Israel and the United States, George Bush and Yitzhak Shamir, at political loggerheads. The United States ultimately joined in a unanimous U.N. Security Council resolution condemning Israel for its practice of deportation of Palestinians. Israel officially responded expressing "outrage and anger" about this U.S. betrayal of their relationship. Both Arabs and Israelis subsequently attended the next round of talks. Many Israeli organizations, as a result, began to openly discuss the desirability of eliminating the substantial U.S. subsidies to Israel. Public opinion in both countries continued to show declining support for the other.

Dissatisfaction with the fact of the peace negotiations prompted two right-wing parties in the Likud coalition to withdraw in late January 1992. While this did not in itself result in a loss of Likud's parliamentary working majority, it did force Shamir to move to the right domestically. As a result, the rhetoric of refusal dramatically increased in Israel. Speaking on the stump, Prime Minister Shamir vowed that settlement construction in the occupied territories "will continue and no power in the world will prevent this construction." For its part, in the same month the United States began aerial surveillance of Israel to document the extent of new settlement construction, with the implied purpose of determining what construction would have to be removed in the event of a "land for peace" settlement. Clearly, the United States and Israel differed dramatically on the premises driving the peace efforts. But in spite of all these confrontations and complications, Israelis and Palestinians continued to exchange proposals for a new system of autonomy in Gaza and the West Bank.

The change in government occasioned by the victory of Labor over the Likud coalition in July 1992 brought Yitzhak Rabin to power as Prime Minister. With his new government came many symbolic changes in the Israeli negotiating posture. Rabin's quick modification of Israeli construction policy in the Occupied Territories found favor with the Bush administration, which then dropped its opposition to the proposed loan guarantees. Rabin followed this initiative with others. Most importantly, Rabin put forward a specific calendar for the achievement of Palestinian "interim self-government" in the territories.

The rhetorical and symbolic changes in Israeli foreign policy stemming from the transition from Likud to Labor, from Shamir to Rabin, are encouraging. But these changes must be followed by substantive changes if the peace negotiations are to finally come to terms with the real problems embedded in the conflict. This observation applies with equal force to the Palestinian and Arab participants in the process. But clearly there has been some movement in the process and there now appears to be realistic potentials for progress on this most intractable of international problems.

CONCLUSION

Questions abound. Is the old world order gone? Definitely. Is the New World Order here? Probably. Do we know the details and implications of this new system? Not yet. Does this new order complicate our understanding of and relations with the Middle East? Definitely. To what can we look forward?

If our description of the emerging international system is correct, we can look forward to a rapidly changing Middle East. We can confidently predict that the changes there will have an impact on much of the world. We are still dependent on a regular flow of petroleum from the region to fuel the industrial economies. The concentration of financial resources in the hands of the petroleum producers will continue to make them important friends or foes in the world economy. That much has not changed. But the way in which we respond to risk and threat seems to have changed, both inside and outside the region.

It seems likely that the trend toward multinational responses to conflict will continue. The U.N., in particular, seems destined to play a critical role in the conflicts that emerge in the region in the near future. And the European Community, using whatever military and diplomatic resources it creates in the coming years, will also likely play an important role. The influence of independent nations seems destined to relative decline, although the action of powers like the U.S., the EC, Japan, and the C.I.S. will continue to be important.

Within the region, alliance realignment and new concentrations of power seem likely. Desert Storm clearly increased the relative regional influence of Iran, Syria, and Egypt. But here, too, regional multinational organizations seem destined to play larger roles than in the past. The Arab League, the Gulf Cooperation Council, the Islamic Conference, and the U.S.–led coalition have many substantive problems to address. Among them are arms control and the management of new arms technologies, particularly the "instruments of mass destruction," and the resolution of the Arab–Israeli conflict.

Many of the problems confronting the region are only manageable with international cooperation. The problem of declining water resources is one obvious problem; but the problems of environmental degradation, dramatic increases in refugees, the Palestinian and Kurdish aspirations for independence, population growth and attendant health and disease questions, and open access to religious sites are also complicated and persistent. In point of fact, there is no shortage of serious problems for these organizations to attack.

There is also the phenomenon of the rising tide of religious fundamentalism. There are no states in the Middle East immune to the dynamics of religious fundamentalism. The process unleashed in this century in Iran has resonance throughout the Islamic world. The critique of government that nourishes Islamic fundamentalism and brings political action is based squarely on the public perception of policy failures by secular or monarchical government. Social justice, the principles of compassion and fairness that inspire the pious folk of Islam, has not been widely achieved, even as the technology of modern communication brings that failure to the attention of greater numbers in the public. The increasing gap between rich and poor nations, and between the rich and poor within nations; the failure of governments to articulate a future other than the simple imitation of the industrial West; the obvious materialism and hedonism of many officials and businessmen—all these fuel the fires of politics and fundamentalism.

Governments inside and outside the Middle East are "lagging participants" in the politics of this new age. They are still deeply mired in the assumptions, conflicts, and constraints of the old order. One hopes—prays—that nongovernmental international organizations are now coming to terms with the basic issues in dispute. One hopes that, for instance, the Muslim ulema, the Jewish rabbis, and the Christian ministers are engaged in interfaith dialogues and discussions which can provide the basis for dignified understandings between these great faiths, that engineers, hydrologists, and specialists in dry-area agriculture are grappling with the dynamics of water conservation and allocation, that doctors and research scientists are jointly searching for the causes of disease and better systems of health care delivery; that furtive peaceniks still seek to bring Jewish settlers and Palestinian fundamentalists together in an "illegal" search for common ground, and that great international institutions like the Red Cross–Red Crescent or Save the Children can continue to deliver their services to the disadvantaged, working through and around hostile, indifferent, or ineffective government agencies.

And finally, we hope and pray that the people in these organizations will find a voice in government. Government continues to be the biggest problem in the world order, old or new. Dragging government, kicking and screaming if necessary, into a recognition of the new world realities should continue to be our highest priority. With all that has changed, "we still live in interesting times."

COUNTRY PROFILES*

LIBYA

(Socialist People's Libyan Arab Jamahiriya)

Area: 679,358 sq. mi.; 1,759,540 sq. km.
Population: 4.5m (1990 est.)
Per capita GNP (1990): U.S. $5,310

Major urban centers (1984 census): TRIPOLI (990,697); Benghazi (485,386); Azzawiya (220,075); Misurata (178,295).

Official language: Arabic

Libya is located in North Africa, bordered by Egypt on the east, Algeria and Tunisia on the west, and sharing its southern borders with Chad, Niger, and the Sudan. Most of Libya is barren desert, with the population concentrated in a narrow strip along the Mediterranean coast. Ninety percent of the people are Arabs, and nearly half the remainder are native Berbers. Sunni Islam predominates.

The economy of Libya is dominated by petroleum production. Since the 1950s, when petroleum was discovered there, Libya has become one of the world's largest oil exporters. Agriculture, which produces barley, wheat, tomatoes, olives, and dates, is far behind petroleum in economic importance. The development of agriculture is limited by the arid climate and by urban migration, which has drained the rural areas of skilled farm labor, but the government is making efforts to promote increased production of cereals, dairy cattle, sheep, poultry, fruits, and vegetables. A weak domestic market, uneven population distribution, and lack of skilled workers have impeded the development of industry, but government programs have aimed at the development

*The demographic and income figures used in the country studies are taken from the World Bank, *World Development Report 1992* (New York: Oxford University Press, 1992).

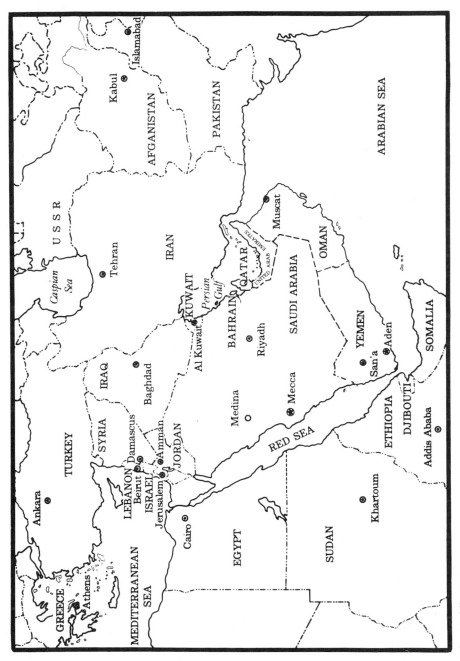

The Middle East

of various industries besides petroleum, including the exploitation of other mineral resources and the production of foodstuffs, textiles, and building materials.

Libya was an Italian colony from 1911 until it was occupied by France and England in World War II. It became an independent monarchy in 1951 under Emir Muhammad Idris al-Senussi, but a 1969 military coup led by Colonel Muammar Qadaffi set up a revolutionary republic under the control of a Revolutionary Command Council. Since then the government has been reorganized several times. The constitution, adopted in 1977, places the government under the nominal control of a General People's Congress assisted by a General Secretariat consisting of a general secretary and three other members. As general secretary, Colonel Qadaffi is the head of state. The General People's Congress is made up of 618 members representing the Revolutionary Command Council, the "people's congresses," and the trade unions and professional organizations. The General People's Committee oversees administrative functions, and its chairman functions as prime minister. The judicial system includes a special People's Court to deal with administrative and political crimes.

Libya has avowed its strong commitment to the principle of Arab unity, and has made several attempts to unite with other Arab nations. Its petroleum politics and its stringent anti-Israeli stance have often brought Libya into conflict with more moderate Arab states, and relations with Egypt were cut off in response to Egyptian peace negotiations with Israel. Although Libya concluded an "Arab-African Federation" treaty with Morocco in 1984, relations with some other Middle Eastern and Western states have further declined as a result of Libya's assassination of Libyan expatriates suspected of opposition activities, its support of international terrorism, and its military support of insurgents in Chad. Relations with the United States worsened during the Reagan administration, resulting in the breakdown of diplomatic relations. The U.S. conducted a punitive air raid against Libya following terrorist provocations in 1986. Libya's poor relations with the United States took another negative turn late in 1988 with accusations that a newly constructed "pharmaceutical" facility was actually a plant for the manufacture of chemical weapons, creating a state of tension during which U.S. Navy fighters shot down two threatening Libyan warplanes over international waters. Early in 1992 Libya faced United Nations sanctions for refusing to extradite suspects accused of bombing an American airliner, Pan Am flight 103 over Lockerbie, Scotland.

EGYPT

(Arab Republic of Egypt)

Area: 386,659 sq. mi.; 1,001,449 sq. km.
Population: 52.4m (1990 est.)
Per capita GNP (1990): U.S. $600
Official language: Arabic

Major urban centers (1986 census): CAIRO (6.05m, estimated 12m in metropolitan area); Alexandria (2.92m); al-Giza (3.7m); Dakahlia (3.5m); Sharkia (2.42m).

Located in the northeast corner of Africa, Egypt is bordered on the west by Libya, on the south by the Sudan, and on the northeast by Israel. Egypt is an extremely arid country that depends on the Nile River for its water supply. About 99 percent of the population lives along the fertile banks of the Nile, which constitutes only about 5 percent of the land area. Population densities in the settled regions are quite high, exceeding 6,000 per square mile in the urban areas. Most Egyptians are Sunni Muslims, and the small non-Muslim population consists largely of Coptic Christians.

Traditionally the "breadbasket" of the old Muslim empires, Egypt still depends on agriculture as the foundation of its economy. Industry, particularly petroleum-related industry, is making significant advances. Farming methods are being modernized by means of mechanization, hydroelectric power, chemical fertilizers, and double cropping. Egypt's most important crops are cotton, wheat, rice, sugar, and corn; its most important industries, besides petroleum, include textiles and the processing of agricultural products. President Gamal Abdel Nasser (d. 1970) attempted to reduce foreign domination of the Egyptian economy by nationalizing financial institutions and major industries, but his successors have encouraged private enterprise and foreign investment as a means of promoting economic development. One of the most difficult barriers to Egypt's economic development is its rapidly increasing population. The population increase, combined with a massive rural-to-urban migration, has made urban centers like Cairo and Alexandria some of the most crowded in the world.

Egypt was granted nominal independence from Britain in 1922, but the British maintained a military force at the Suez Canal until 1956, when the canal was nationalized. The profligate King Farouk was ousted in 1952 by a *coup* headed by the Free Officers including Colonel Gamal Abdel Nasser, Colonel Anwar Sadat, and Major General Muhammad Naguib. Under the present government, executive power is held by a president nominated by the legislature and elected by popular vote to a six-year term. The president appoints vice-presidents and ministers, and is empowered to rule by decree in the event that martial law is declared.

Egypt's foreign and domestic policies have been strongly influenced by hostilities with Israel, and these hostilities have broken into warfare four times since Israel's formation (l948, 1956, 1967, and 1973). In addition to the disputes with the Israelis, Egypt was involved in Yemen's civil war, serious confrontations with Libya, and the 1991 coalition to drive Iraq from occupied Kuwait. Relations with Israel improved as a result of the U.S.–sponsored Camp David talks leading to an Egyptian-Israeli peace treaty and the return of the Sinai in 1977. In 1981, President Anwar Sadat was assassinated by Muslim extremists and was succeeded by Muhammad Hosni Mubarak. Egypt under Mubarak has reconciled with other Arab states, especially after the 1982 Israeli invasion of Lebanon and the subsequent cooling of Egyptian-Israeli relations.

After a February 1987 meeting with Israeli Foreign Minister Shimon Peres, Mubarak called for an international peace conference to work for a settlement of the Palestinian question. The idea died for lack of support from Israeli Prime Minister Shamir and from United States opposition to Soviet participation, as well as from poor relations between Jordan and Palestinian representatives. Mubarak, however, continued to press the United States for support of an international conference, and for additional fiscal aid in recognition of Egypt's importance as a regional peacemaker. Egypt was an enthusiastic proponent of the multilateral peace negotiations begun in 1991 under U. S.–Soviet (now C.I.S.) sponsorship. Israeli Prime Minister Rabin visited Egypt in mid-1992 to solicit Egyptian cooperation in the peace process.

SUDAN

(Democratic Republic of the Sudan)

Area: 967,494 sq. mi., 2,505,813 sq. km.
Population: 25.2m (1990 est.)
Per capita GNP (1988): U.S. $480
Official language: Arabic

Major urban centers (1985 census): KHARTOUM (476,218); Omdurman (526,287); North Khartoum (341,146); Port Sudan (206,727).

Sudan is the largest country in Africa. It is bordered on the east by the Red Sea and Ethiopia. Looked at clockwise, it also shares borders with Kenya, Uganda, Zaire, the Central African Republic, Chad, Libya, and Egypt. Its outstanding geographical features are that both the White and Blue Nile rivers transverse the country, meeting near Khartoum, and that the arid northern part of the country gives way to tropical forests in the south. Sudan's international relations in the region during the first half of the twentieth century were dominated by the fact that the Nile waters flow through it to Egypt.

Approximately 70 percent of the population lives in the north and is overwhelmingly Arab and Muslim. The southern population is largely Black and adheres to tribal religions. This split has been a major concern of the government since Sudan became independent in 1956. Indeed, it was only in 1973 that a settlement was reached that granted limited autonomy to the southern provinces.

The economy is primarily agricultural. Since both productivity and total agricultural output are relatively low, per capita income is also low. However, Sudan has only a small percentage of its arable land under cultivation. It has been estimated that the land between the White and Blue Nile could, with triple cropping and the application of modern agricultural techniques, double world wheat output. This has drawn the attention of the various Arab development agencies in the petroleum-rich countries, and some funds have been granted to investigate whether the Sudan could indeed be the breadbasket of the Arab world.

In April 1985, following a period of unrest due to regionalism and opposition to the government's Islamization program, President Numeiri was ousted in a military coup, partly in response to his stringent support of Sharia provisions in the legal code. Despite Prime Minister al-Mahdi's attempts at mediation, the Sharia issue remains divisive, with southern non-Muslims insisting on its abolition (at least for non-Muslims) as a prerequisite to further unification talks, and fundamentalist Muslim factions in the new government continuing to support strict Sharia principles. The political and military strife has interfered with programs of agricultural development, exacerbating the effects of drought and famine and helping to create the largest external debt in Africa. Sudan's situation is further complicated by the presence of over a million refugees from violent conflicts in several neighboring countries.

SAUDI ARABIA

(Kingdom of Saudi Arabia)

Area: 829,995 sq. mi., 2,149,690 sq. km.
Population: 14.1m (1990 est.)
Per capita GNP (1990): U.S. $7050
Official language: Arabic

Major urban centers (1974 estimate): RIYADH (666,840); Jiddah (561,104); Mecca (366,801); Ibid-al-Taif (204,857); Medina (198,186).

Saudi Arabia is bordered by Jordan, Iraq, and Kuwait to the north. Moving clockwise, other adjacent territories include the Persian (Arabian) Gulf, Bahrain, the United Arab Emirates, Oman, Yemen, and the Red Sea. The country is mostly desert, with most of the significant arable land being in the southwestern part of the country. Two of the most important cities of Islam, Mecca and Medina, lie along the old caravan routes parallel to the Red Sea.

Almost all of the population is Muslim, the great majority being of the conservative Muwahhidun ("Wahhabi") sect. A substantial Shia minority is concentrated in the petroleum-producing areas of the northeast and therefore have been a source of concern to the government. About one third of the population and one half of the labor force is composed of nonnationals, the majority from Yemen until their expulsion because of that country's support of Iraq in the Iraq-Kuwait War. Large numbers of Saudis have studied abroad in recent years, mostly in England and the United States. It should be noted that population estimates are open to serious question.

Saudi Arabia is the world's largest exporter of petroleum and holds the world's largest proven reserves. Most petroleum production is in the northeast. Because of its premier position as a petroleum exporter, it has been the linchpin on which the actions of the Organization of Petroleum Exporting Countries depend. It has been among the price moderates in OPEC because of its large reserves and rather low capacity to absorb yearly revenues for development purposes. The petroleum company was nationalized when majority control was purchased in 1974. Agricultural output and potential are low. The extremely rapid growth of petroleum revenues during the 1970s allowed Saudi Arabia to launch a number of significant development projects.

Saudi Arabia is an absolute monarchy with neither political parties nor an elected legislature; in March of 1992 King Fahd announced the formation of an appointed consultative body, the Majlis Asshura. The king also serves as prime minister and is the country's religious leader. In the past two decades, considerable effort has been directed at creating an efficient ("modern") administration of government affairs, including a system of provincial governments announced in 1992. From the formation of the country in 1932 through the early 1960s, almost all significant affairs were handled personally by the king.

The pace of change suggests that the relative domestic calm Saudi Arabia has experienced in recent years may not last. Although Saudi Arabia has been the most important conservative Arab state in the Middle East with strong ties to the West, it has displayed more independence of action with respect to world events since the revolution of petroleum prices. Saudi Arabia exercised its influence within OPEC in order to raise the price of crude oil. Support of Iraq during its 1980–1988 war with Iran led to a confrontational relationship with Iran and Syria. Relations with Iran further deteriorated after July 1987, when an estimated 400 Iranian pilgrims were killed in a confrontation with Saudi authorities at the Grand Mosque in Mecca. Saudi Arabia joined forces with the coalition against Iraq's invasion of Kuwait, which led to the stationing of large numbers of American and other troops on Saudi soil, and culminated in its active participation in the 1991 Gulf war.

YEMEN

(Republic of Yemen)

Area: 186,364 sq. mi., 482,363 sq. km.
Population: 11.7 (1990 est.)
Per capita GNP (1990): U.S. $650
Official language: Arabic

Major urban centers (Aden 1977 est.; all others 1981 census): SAN A (277,818); Aden (291,600); Hodeida (126,386); Ta'iz (119,573).

The Republic of Yemen was created in 1990 by the combination of North and South Yemen, two previously independent states with a common colonial heritage. The unification of the two countries brought together a people separated for decades by the political interests of external states: first the great colonial empires, then regional competition (Egypt versus Saudi Arabia), and then the bipolar confrontation of the two superpowers (the United States and the U.S.S.R.)

The Republic of Yemen is located on the southwestern edge of the Arabian peninsula. It is bordered on the north by Saudi Arabia, on the east by Oman; on the south by the Gulf of Aden, and on the West by the Red Sea. It has a commanding position on the geopolitically important Bab al Mandab Straits, facing the Horn of Africa. Most of Yemen is arid, with large tracts of mountains, coastal plains, and deserts. There is a relatively large region in the northwest mountains where rainfall sustains traditional agriculture. The largest cash crop in Yemen is qat, a mildly narcotic plant much in demand there and abroad. The population is largely Arab. Most of the inhabitants are Sunni Muslims, although there is a sizable Shia community. There exists a wide range of tribal affiliations. The leadership of Yemen, while authoritarian, seems to aspire to the creation of a democratic order. The government is recruited primarily from the military cadres of North and South.

For most of the twentieth century, North Yemen was one of the most inaccessible countries in the world due to the xenophobia of its theocratic rulers. International pressures prompted an opening in 1958 when the government established close relations with Egypt, unsuccessfully attempting to form a union with Egypt and Syria. A 1962 *coup* attempt brought Egyptian intervention on the side of the revolutionary government while Saudi Arabia liberally supported the royalist opposition. Political affairs in North Yemen remained confused for the next twenty years.

South Yemen (Aden) was an important British outpost, administered first as part of India. It became a crown colony until independence was achieved in 1967. A "war of national" liberation waged by the National Liberation Front resulted in South Yemen emerging from colonial domination as a Marxist-Leninist revolutionary state. The state pursued a consistently pro-Soviet policy until the late 1980s. It provided refuge to many of the more extremist groups in the Palestinian resistance. There were serious conflicts with North Yemen, as both countries interfered in each other's politics; and a national liberation movement in Oman's Dhofar province was unsuccessfully orchestrated from South Yemen.

The union of North and South Yemen in the Republic of Yemen surprised many observers. But the union seems to have an economic, political and social logic. In the new multipolar world, neither state could count on the foreign support that had subsidized their regimes earlier. Both countries brought newly discovered resources, particularly petroleum, to the union. The few successful industrial enterprises in the South (the petroleum refinery in Aden, for example) will blend well with the agricultural strengths of the North. And both countries have had tense relations with their larger and richer neighbor to the north, Saudi Arabia.

Relations with Saudi Arabia will most likely continue as the dominant theme in Yemen's foreign relations. Saudi Arabia expelled hundreds of thousands of Yemeni expatriate workers during the Iraq-Kuwait crisis and they have not been allowed to return. Saudi Arabia is unlikely to forgive Yemen soon for its political and moral support of Iraq in that conflict. The elites of Saudi Arabia and Yemen continue to have considerable differences.

OMAN

(Sultanate of Oman)

Area: 120,000 sq. mi., 310,800 sq. km.
Population: 1.5m (1988 est.)
Per capita GNP (1990): U.S. $5,220

Major urban centers (1982 est.): MUSCAT (53,000); Salala (17,000)
Official language: Arabic

Oman, formerly called Muscat and Oman, is located in the southeastern portion of the Arabian peninsula. It shares borders with the United Arab Emirates to the northeast and, working clockwise, the Arabian Sea, Yemen, and Saudi Arabia. Being locat-

ed at the mouth of the Persian (Arabian) Gulf, Oman is of immense strategic importance, especially considering that a substantial amount of the world's petroleum
exports pass through the narrow Straits of Hormuz. The climate is very warm and arid,
and there is not much arable land.

There has never been a population census in Oman, and the available estimates are
subject to wide margins of error. Much of the population outside the capital city,
Muscat, lives in a quickly changing tribal setting. The population is predominantly
Arab and Sunni Muslim. There are, however, significant minorities, including Iranians,
Pakistanis, and Indians. The number of foreigners in Oman increased substantially dur-
ing the decade of the 1970s, filling a larger percentage of skilled positions.

Although proven reserves of petroleum are rather modest in contrast with the major
producers of the area, the income of the country is almost totally dependent on
petroleum revenues. Production started in 1967. Before the exploitation of petroleum,
the country was based on agriculture (some products being exported), some cattle and
camel raising, and maritime pursuits. Although not a member of OPEC, Oman generally adjusts its oil production to support OPEC policies.

Oman formally gained independence in 1951. It is an absolute monarchy and does
not have a constitution or legislature. The sultan rules in a traditional fashion, depend-
ing on personal retainers for advice on the affairs of state. The southern province of
Dhofar was in rebellion for many years until a truce (of sorts) was arranged in 1976.
The Dhofar Liberation Front received refuge and material support from the People's
Democratic Republic of Yemen, who, in turn, were supported by the Soviet Union,
East Germany, and Cuba. The sultan received support from Saudi Arabia and Iran,
among others. Allied with other Arab states of the Persian Gulf in the Gulf
Cooperation Council, Oman also enjoys good relations with the United States and
Egypt. The substantial interest in the fate of Oman stems largely from its geographical
position at the mouth of the Persian Gulf. The British had military installations in
Oman until 1977; the desire of the United States to fill the gap for the West was
demonstrated when the British left and intensified after the Iranian revolution. U.S.
troops have used Omani air and naval stations in military maneuvers in and around
the Persian Gulf. U. S. military equipment is prepositioned in Omani depots.

UNITED ARAB EMIRATES

Area: 32,278 sq. mi., 83,600 sq. km. Population: 1.6m (1990 est.)*
Per capita GNP (1990): U.S. Major urban center (1988 est.): ABU
   $19,860 DHABI (722,143).

Official language: Arabic

The United Arab Emirates (U.A.E.) is bordered on the north by the Persian (Arabian)
Gulf and Qatar. Oman lies to the east, and Saudi Arabia lies along the southern and

*Includes nonnationals, who compose up to three-fourths of the resident population.

western borders. The U.A.E. is a federation of seven emirates: Abu Dhabi, Dubai, Ras al-Kharima, Sharjah, Fujaira, Ajman, and Umm al-Quaiwain. The area is largely desert and the climate is very hot and dry.

The indigenous population is predominantly Arab, but the majority of the labor force are nonnationals. Although about half of the nonnationals have no formal education, as a group they have significantly higher levels of education and hold the majority of skilled posts and government jobs.

The high per capita income figures result from significant petroleum production in Abu Dhabi and Dubai. These emirates are using petroleum revenues to diversify their economies, largely through the establishment of service industries such as shipping through the deep-water harbor at Dubai, banking facilities, and the like. Manufacturing is not well developed and the potential for agricultural expansion is quite limited, although some progress has been made through the activities of an agricultural station.

The U.A.E. gained independence in 1971 after attempts by the British to include Bahrain and Qatar in the federation failed. The government is superimposed on the conservative monarchies in the constituent emirates. The rulers of the emirates compose the Supreme Council of the U.A.E., which elects a president and vice-president from its members. The fully appointed legislative body, the Federal National Council, has forty members. Since each emirate has substantial autonomy with respect to revenue and expenditure policy, and since Abu Dhabi and Dubai are the only significant producers of petroleum, relations in the U.A.E. are dominated by these two emirates. Although there have been border disputes, the U.A.E. generally has good relations with and maintains the same foreign policy posture as Saudi Arabia. U.A.E. forces were among the first to reinforce the Saudi border after Iraq's invasion of Kuwait. Foreign policy is mediated to a significant degree through the Gulf Cooperation Council.

QATAR

(State of Qatar)

Area: 4,247 sq. mi., 11,000 sq. km.
Population: 422,000 (1990 est.)*
Per capita GNP (1989): U.S. $15,500

Major urban center (1986E): DOHA (217,294).
Official language: Arabic

Qatar is located on a peninsula that juts northward from the eastern coast of Saudi Arabia into the Persian Gulf. The peninsula is largely sand and rock; the climate is warm and rainfall is sparse. The population is almost entirely Arab, but native Qataris constitute a minority. The rest are predominantly immigrants from other Persian (Arabian) Gulf and Middle Eastern countries. Most of the people are Sunni Muslims of Muwahhidun orientation.

*Includes nonnationals, estimated to constitute more than two thirds of the resident population.

Qatar was under British influence until 1971. It attempted to join with Bahrain and the United Arab Emirates in a federation, but was not successful. In 1971, Qatar declared its independence as a traditional sheikhdom, with the emir as an absolute monarch. The Basic Law of 1970 provides for a legislative Advisory Council of twenty members, three of whom are to be appointed and the rest elected. In 1975 the membership was increased to thirty; most of these were appointed by the emir rather than elected. There is also a Council of Ministers headed by an appointed prime minister. The judicial system consists of five secular courts and several religious courts.

The economy depends almost entirely on petroleum production, which has been in progress since the end of World War II. In 1976 and 1977, the government attained control of oil and natural gas production through agreements with Shell Qatar and Qatar Petroleum Company. Oil revenue is used primarily to provide broad social welfare benefits to Qatari nationals and to develop and diversify the economy. Industrial development projects include a steel plant, a petrochemicals complex, desalination plants, cement production facilities, a refinery for the liquefaction of natural gas, new electric power plants, and an enlarged port capacity at Doha. The desalinated water is being used to promote the development of agriculture, primarily fruits and vegetables. Shrimp fishing and processing have recently developed. The downturn in oil income during the 1980s stimulated an austerity program aimed at eliminating inefficiency and reducing the number of nonnative workers. Recently discovered major natural gas deposits promise Qatar a bright economic future into the next century.

In 1981, Qatar joined with Saudi Arabia, Bahrain, Kuwait, Oman, and the United Arab Emirates to form the Gulf Cooperation Council. This organization provides for economic and military cooperation as well as discussion of common foreign policy objectives. Qatari troops were early participants in the coalition action against Iraq.

BAHRAIN

(State of Bahrain)

Area: 240 sq. mi., 622 sq. km.
Population: 489,000 (1990 est.)
Per capita GNP (1986): U.S. $8,510

Major urban centers (1981 census):
MANAMA (121,986); Muharraq
(61,583).

Official language: Arabic

Bahrain is composed of one large island (Bahrain) and thirty-four smaller islands lying in the Persian (Arabian) Gulf between the coasts of Saudi Arabia and Qatar. As with the other nations of the Arabian Peninsula, the climate of Bahrain is hot and the land is largely desert.

The population is predominantly Arab, with significant numbers of non-Arabs largely from Iran, India, and Pakistan. Nonnationals compose about a quarter of the population and over one third of the labor force. Bahrain's relatively long involvement in petroleum-related activities has allowed both the finances and time necessary for Bahrainis to gain the know-how necessary to fill skilled positions in the economy. As opposed to such relative newcomers to petroleum wealth as Abu Dhabi and Dubai, Bahrain's nationals fill the majority of the skilled positions in the private and government sector. About seventy percent of the Muslims are Shia. Both this split and the large number of foreigners in the country have been sources of tension. The Bahrain government and the Gulf Cooperation Council (see the country profile on Qatar) are concerned about Iranian-backed unrest among the Shia population, especially in the wake of a 1982 plot to overthrow the government.

Although petroleum finds have been modest compared with those of several close-by countries, the economy of Bahrain has been dominated by petroleum since it was first produced for commercial sale in 1936. Petroleum production and reserves are now at very low levels. Significant efforts have been made in the past decades to diversify the economy, including the upgrading of Manama as a transit port, the building of an aluminum smelter, the construction of a causeway to Saudi Arabia, and the granting of tax exempt status to offshore banking so as to entrench Manama as a regional financial center. The Gulf Cooperation Council has actively backed these programs since its formation in 1981.

Bahrain achieved independence in 1971 after British attempts to have it join the U.A.E. were unsuccessful. The emir is head of state, and he is supposed to share power with a popularly elected legislative body. The legislature was dissolved in 1975 by the emir who informally substituted a fully appointed Council of Ministers, the membership of which is dominated by members of the royal family. Bahrain's international posture generally is the same as the other conservative nations of the area, generally favoring the West.

KUWAIT

(State of Kuwait)

Area: 6,880 sq. mi., 17,818 sq. km.
Population: 2.0m (1990 est.)*
Per capita GNP (1989): U.S. $16,150
Official language: Arabic

Major urban centers: KUWAIT CITY (the greater metropolitan area includes nearly all of the population)

Kuwait is located at the northeast corner of the Persian (Arabian) Gulf, sharing borders with Iraq to the north and Saudi Arabia to the south. It has a hot and arid climate, has no major source of fresh water, and is almost totally dependent on petroleum revenues for its income. The indigenous population of Kuwait is Arab and largely Sunni Muslim. Before 1991, non-Kuwaitis composed about 70 percent of the total population and more than 80 percent of the labor force. By far the single largest foreign nationality represented were the Jordanians (including Palestinians), who accounted for about one-fifth

*Includes resident non-Kuwaitis, many of whom have left since the events of 1990–1991.

of the total population. Most of the non-Kuwaiti population, and all of the Palestinians and Jordanians, left the country as a result of the events connected with the Iraqi occupation and its aftermath in 1990–1991.

The per capita income of Kuwait is among the highest in the world due to the large petroleum supplies. Investment income exceeded petroleum sales in the last half of the 1980s, and helped to finance the massive reconstruction effort after the pillage by Iraq. Kuwait purchased majority control of its major petroleum corporation in 1974. Kuwait has a very extensive welfare state for its citizens. As in other oil-producing Gulf countries, declining petroleum revenues and the effects of the Iran-Iraq war took a toll on the economy during the 1980s. During the Iran-Iraq war, United States concern for the safe transport of oil prompted the Reagan administration to afford Kuwaiti tankers the protection of the U.S. flag, necessitating an increased U.S. naval presence in the region.

The 1962 constitution provides for the head of state, an absolute monarch, to be selected from the Mubarak line of the al-Sabah family. An appointed Council of Ministers and a prime minister are in charge of the affairs of state. The constitution also calls for a legislative body, about one quarter of whom are to be appointed. The legislature was suspended a couple of times, and elections for it in early 1990 were widely criticized and boycotted by an increasingly vocal opposition calling for democratic reform. Postwar Kuwait has taken limited steps toward electoral liberalization.

Although the political structure of Kuwait and the attitudes of its leaders put them in the conservative Arab camp, the large foreign Arab (especially Palestinian) presence had an effect on Kuwaiti policy with respect to Israel. Generally, their relationship with Iraq was one of controlled tension, with Iraqis sometimes making the claim that Kuwait is rightly considered a part of Iraq.

Tension with Iraq erupted into an international crisis in August of 1990 when Iraq invaded Kuwait, citing various provocations including an alleged violation of agreements concerning oilfields on the Iraq-Kuwait border. The crisis came to a climax early in 1991, when a U.S.–led coalition launched a military campaign that liberated Kuwait. Severe reprisals against non-Kuwaitis (especially Palestinians) accused of collaborating with the Iraqi occupation, along with new policies against immigrant workers, caused most of the remaining non-Kuwaiti population to emigrate. The resulting demographic changes, along with internal and external pressures for political reform in the wake of the rescue of Kuwait's government, could portend important changes in Kuwaiti society.

IRAN
(Islamic Republic of Iran)

Area: 636,293 sq. mi., 1,648,000 sq. km
Population: 54.6m (1990 est.)
Major urban centers (1986 census): TEHRAN (urban area, 6.4 m); Mashhad (1.4 m); Isfahan (990,000); Tabriz (970,000); Shiraz (850,000).
Per capita GNP (1990): U.S. $2,490
Official language: Persian (Farsi)

Iran is bordered on the north by the C.I.S. and the Caspian Sea, by Turkey and Iraq to the west, by the Persian (Arabian) Gulf to the south, and by Afghanistan and Pakistan on the east. Iran is predominantly an arid country consisting largely of elevated plains, mountains, and desert. The majority of the population, about two-thirds, is Persian; the remainder are mostly Turkish, Kurdish, or Baluchi. About 90 percent of the people are Shia Muslims.

Iran was a seat of high civilization prior to the rise of Arab and Muslim power in the Middle East, and its traditions later came to influence the development of Muslim civilization. Iran remained an absolute monarchy until the revolution of 1979. Shah Muhammad Reza Pahlevi, who was overthrown in that revolution, had succeeded his father, the founder of the Pahlevi dynasty, in 1941. He survived many political intrigues during the 1940s, a *coup* attempt in 1953, and increasing unrest during the 1960s and 1970s. After the attempted *coup* of 1953 he initiated an ambitious modernizing program involving social and economic reforms, but power remained concentrated in his hands. In the White Revolution, as his programs were called after 1963, there was a major expansion of petroleum-related and other industries; oil exports and industrial production assumed increasing importance at the expense of agriculture. The programs caused social upheavals including a shift of population to urban areas. Growing unrest culminated in demonstrations and rioting; in September of 1978 the shah declared martial law in Tehran and eleven other urban areas in an attempt to restore order. Later in 1978, petroleum workers went on strike in response to the call of an exiled religious leader, the Ayatollah Ruhollah Khomeini. On December 21, the shah appointed a new civilian government and left the country on an "extended vacation." On February 1, 1979, the Ayatollah Khomeini returned to Iran and his followers overthrew the government, proclaiming an Islamic Republic on April 1,1979.

The Islamic Republic of Iran was initiated as an experiment in Islamic political and social organization. Based on the constitution adopted in 1979, the government is composed of a national religious leader (faqih), a president, and an assembly (Majlis) presided over by a speaker. The legislative majority is led by a prime minister. The legal system of Iran is officially based on the Sharia. Islam is recognized as the source of authority for foreign and domestic policy. After the revolution, the unsettled internal political situation in Iran interfered with the establishment of clear lines of authority between the faqih, the president, and the Majlis. The situation was further complicated by Iran's foreign policy difficulties, including the seizure of U.S. embassy hostages from November 1979 until January 1981, a war with Iraq from 1980 to 1988, and the assassinations of high government officials. The internal political situation has stabilized. Ayatollah Khomeini's death in 1989 raised the question of the succession of power. Khomeini was succeeded as faqih by Ayatollah Ali Khamenei. Hashemi Rasfanjani was subsequently elected president of the republic and appears to have the strongest power base in the ruling coalition.

Iran has made substantial progress in recent years in institutionalizing Islamic government. Under President Rafsanjani's leadership, Iran has moderated the more extreme policies of the Khomeini era and pursued the normalization of relations with the West. Rafsanjani's moderate faction made considerable gains in the 1992 Majlis elections. Iranian "good offices" in the release of U.S. hostages held in Lebanon provided a basis for improved relations between Washington and Tehran. Iran remained neutral in the Iraq-Kuwait conflict and emerged in the aftermath with enhanced prestige and relative power. It is now one of the strongest powers on the Gulf. Iran has expended considerable effort in attempts to attract the newly independent republics of Central Asia to the model of the Islamic Republic.

TURKEY

(Republic of Turkey)

Area: 301,380 sq. mi., 780,576 sq. km.
Population: 55.9m (1990 est.)
Major urban centers (1985 est.):

ANKARA (2.24 m); Istanbul (5.48 m); Izmir (1.49 m); Adana (780,000);
Per capita GNP (1990): U.S. $1,630

Official language: Turkish

Bridging Europe and Asia, Turkey borders on Bulgaria and Greece to the northwest, the C.I.S. to the northeast, Iran to the east, and Iraq and Syria to the south. North of Turkey lies the Black Sea, which joins the Mediterranean via the Dardanelles Straits dividing the European and Asian portions of Turkey. Most of Turkey's landmass is on the Asian side of the straits, including the Anatolian Peninsula, and is subject to extremes of climate. The majority of Turkey's population is ethnically Turkish, but there is a substantial, restive Kurdish minority in the east and southeast as well as smaller groups of Arabs, Greeks, Circassians, Armenians, Georgians, and Bulgarians. Sunni Islam is the religion of 98 percent of the population.

Turkey is the remaining core of the Ottoman Empire, which dominated the Middle East and parts of Eastern Europe until its decline and eventual dissolution after World War I. Under the modernizing and secularizing leadership of Mustafa Kemal Ataturk, Turkey became a republic in 1923. In recent times the military has occasionally deemed it necessary to intervene in government. After two such interventions, in 1960 and 1971, the government was returned to civilian control. The third military intervention occurred in 1980, when martial law was declared in order to bring domestic violence under control. Following the restoration of civilian government in 1982 and increased political freedom and recognition of human rights, relations with the West began to improve.

The Turkish economy experienced substantial growth during the 1980s. The technocratic government loosened onerous government controls on private enterprise, improved its international financial position, and generally rationalized the economic system. Turkey is an associate member of the European Economic Community and seeks full membership. At the same time, it remains an integral part of the Muslim world, thus retaining its unique status as a bridge between Europe and the central areas of the Middle East. Turkey was a major (nontroop) contributor to the U.S.–led coalition against Iraq in 1990–1991. Turkish policy is also strongly focused on the newly independent republics of Central Asia, and is sometimes presented as a model for those republics.

Turkey's constitution provides for the election of a president by the legislature for a seven-year term. The legislature has the power to impeach a president and to override presidential vetoes. The prime minister, responsible for general administration, is chosen from the majority party of coalition in the lower house of the legislature. The Grand National Assembly is a bicameral legislative body consisting of an upper house, the Senate, and a lower house, the National Assembly. One hundred and fifty of the 184 members of the Senate are popularly elected to six-year terms, fifteen are appointed by the president, and the remainder have life appointments as former holders of high government office. The National Assembly's 450 members serve four-year terms by popular election.

IRAQ

(Republic of Iraq)

Area: 167,924 sq. mi., 434,923 sq. km.
Population: 18.9m (1990 est.)
Per capita GNP (1988): U.S. $3,020

Major urban centers (1977 census): BAGHDAD (3.236 m); Basra(1.54 m); al-Mawsil (1.22 m); Kirkuk (535,000).

Official languages: Arabic, Kurdish

Iraq shares borders with Iran on the east, Turkey on the north, Syria on the west, and Jordan, Saudi Arabia, and Kuwait on the south. Most of Iraq's population is Arab, with a Kurdish minority in the northeast. The Kurds are Sunni Muslims. They, along with an Arab Shia majority located in the southeast, have been the source of considerable internal dissatisfaction with which the Sunni Arab-dominated government has had to contend.

Iraq has been a major farming region since ancient times, and agriculture still employs three-fourths of the work force even though it accounts for less than a quarter of the national income. Iraq's main crops are dates, barley, wheat, rice, and tobacco. Most of Iraq's export income and two-thirds of its gross national product come from the petroleum industry, which is dominated by the nationalized Iraqi Petroleum Company. Manufacturing industries, also largely nationalized, experienced rapid growth despite an unstable political climate and shortages of skilled labor. Iraq's other raw materials include phosphates, sulphur, iron, copper, chromite, lead, limestone, and gypsum.

Iraq became a British mandate under the League of Nations after World War I, and it achieved independence in 1932 under the Hashemite monarchy established during the mandate. Iraq became a republic following a 1958 *coup* led by Brigadier General Abdul Karim Kassem. After a series of political triumphs and defeats, the Baath (Arab Resurrection) Party came to power in a bloodless *coup* in 1968 led by Major General Ahmad Hassan al-Bakr. Iraq has struggled under the burden of domestic instability resulting from conflicts within the Baath party and Kurdish demands for political autonomy. A 1974 amendment to the provisional constitution granted the Kurds limited autonomy, and in 1975 Iran agreed to cease aid to Iraqi Kurds in return for Iranian control of the disputed Shatt al-Arab waterway. The agreement fell apart in 1980 when war broke out over the Shatt al-Arab and adjacent lands. From that time until the 1988 cease-fire, the war dominated Iraqi politics, both internally and externally. The Shia community in Iraq became increasingly restive, and the other Middle Eastern countries generally aligned themselves either with Iraq or Iran, the latter's main supporters being Libya, Syria, and South Yemen. The United States and the Soviet Union tacitly supported Iraq against Iran, and diplomatic relations with the United States, which had been severed in 1967, were resumed in 1984. Iraq's invasion of Kuwait in 1990 resulted in the creation of a formidable international coalition against it, led by the United States and including Egypt, Syria, Saudi Arabia, and the U.A.E. The coalition ejected Iraq from Kuwait early in 1991, doing substantial damage to the Iraqi military, economic, and social infrastructure. U.N. sanctions, imposed before the action, were continued after the war, severely restricting Iraqi recovery. Most onerous of those sanctions were U.N. prohibitions on the sale of Iraqi oil and the requirement that Iraq identify and destroy its "weapons of mass destruction." Despite the sanctions and a substantial loss of life among the civilian population, Saddam Hussein remained in power and sporadically obstructed the efforts of U.N. inspectors, leading to continued tension.

SYRIA

(Syrian Arab Republic)

Area: 71,586 sq. mi., 185,408 sq. km.
Population: 12.5m (1990 est.)
Per capita GNP (1990): U.S. $1,000
Official language: Arabic

Major urban centers (1981 census): DAMASCUS (1,112,214); Aleppo (985,413); Homs (346,871); Latakia (196,791); Hama (177,208).

Syria is bordered by Turkey in the north and, clockwise, by Iraq, Jordan, Israel, Lebanon, and the Mediterranean Sea. Although sizable portions of the southeastern and southcentral parts of the country are mountainous, Syria possesses large tracts of arable land. The Euphrates River enters Syria from Turkey and flows through the central lands to Iraq.

Arabs make up about 90 percent of the population and Sunni Muslims constitute about the same percentage. However, minorities (Alawites and Druze) are important and have had influence beyond their numbers. Alawites, nonorthodox Shia Muslim Arabs, dominate the government. This has been a continuing source of friction in Syria.

The economy of Syria is primarily agricultural; however, it is more diversified than most countries of the area. Although agricultural yields have been low, the source of the problem has been a lack of water; there are large tracts of potentially highly productive soil. The massive Euphrates Dam offers substantial irrigation potential and thereby should boost agricultural output. Since the Euphrates also supplies Iraq with water for irrigation, there has been considerable friction between the two countries concerning the amount of Euphrates water that Syria uses. The construction of the huge Ataturk Dam in Eastern Turkey may reduce water flows to both Syria and Iraq. Syria since 1989 has progressively loosened its hold on its economy, experimenting cautiously with the private sector, free markets, and a move toward increased trade with the West.

From independence in 1946 until 1971, Syria experienced considerable political turmoil, with the military always being involved and since 1963, formally in control. The Arab Resurrection Party (Baath party), a socialist and nationalist group with pan-Arab sentiments, first gained power in 1958. Its power was consolidated in 1971 when a group of military officers dominated by Alawites seized the government. Syria experienced more domestic political stability in the decade of the 1970s than in any previous decade of the century; however, serious unrest had to be quelled by the army in 1980 and 1982.

Syria's foreign policy has been dominated by hostile relations with Israel and by the Baathist notions of anti-imperialism which historically have tilted against the West. Its regional alliances, while sometimes spectacular (joining with Egypt to form the U.A.R. in 1958 and the 1980 announcement of a proposed merger with Libya, being prime examples), have been marked by reversals of policy toward neighbors, especially Iraq and Jordan, as events dictated. The bulk of the Arab Deterrent Force in Lebanon is made up of Syrian forces, which have been entrenched in the Bekaa Valley in eastern Lebanon. Syria remains a major force in Lebanon and seems determined to prevent the development of a regime in Lebanon that might threaten Syrian interests. Syrian diplomatic prestige in the region rose after the Israeli intervention in Lebanon. In 1987, Syria moderated its position, closing the Syrian offices of the extremist Abu Nidal faction of Palestinian terrorists. Moves toward a constructive role in the resolution of the Iran-Iraq war brought pledges of increased aid from some other Arab states.

Syria's participation in the U.S.–led coalition against Iraq confirmed that country's gradual drift toward better relations with the West. The collapse of the Soviet Union left it with little choice in the matter. Syria emerged from the Gulf conflict with substantially enhanced diplomatic prestige, and its participation in the U. S.–sponsored peace talks with Israel indicates a moderation of Syrian foreign policy.

LEBANON

(Republic of Lebanon)

Area: 4,015 sq. mi., 10,400 sq. km.
Population: 3.45m (1988 est.)
Major urban centers (1980 est.):
  BEIRUT (702,000)*; Tripoli
(175,000); Zahle (47,000).
Per capita GNP (1988): U.S. $880
Official language: Arabic (French
  used widely)

---

*Beirut's population has fluctuated significantly due to incessant warfare.

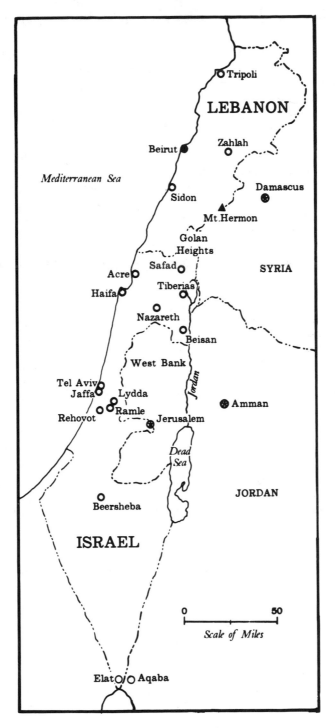

Israel and Lebanon

Lebanon is located north of Israel on the east coast of the Mediterranean Sea, sharing a border also with Syria on the north and east. The majority of its population is Arab Muslim, about evenly divided between Sunni and Shia; Christians form a very large and important minority, and there is also a small but influential Druze minority. The Christian population includes Maronites, Orthodox Greeks, Greek Catholics, Orthodox Armenians, and Armenian Catholics.

Lebanon has a long history of commercial activity, and has enjoyed a high standard of living relative to other Middle Eastern countries, serving as a center of commerce, finance, tourism, and education. While agriculture employs the majority of the work force, it contributes only a small portion to the national income. The service sector, involved in such activities as banking, insurance, transit trade, shipping, petroleum pipelines, and tourism, was most important to the economy. Industries, such as food processing, cement, and textiles, also made a significant economic contribution. Years of civil war and foreign military presence have severely disrupted the Lebanese economy.

Lebanon was a French mandate under the League of Nations after World War I, and became an independent parliamentary republic in 1941, although French troops did not actually withdraw until after World War II. According to the unwritten National Pact of 1943, the chief offices of the state were to be divided among Christians and Muslims, with the president a Maronite Christian elected by a two-thirds majority of the legislature, the prime minister a Sunni Muslim appointed by the president in consultation with political and religious leaders, and the president of the Chamber of Deputies, a Shia Muslim. Members of the Chamber of Deputies, Lebanon's unicameral legislature, are elected to four-year terms by universal suffrage. Seats in the legislature are proportionally allotted according to religious affiliation.

The delicate balance of religious groups in the government of Lebanon began to disintegrate in 1975, partly as the result of the presence of a large number of Palestinians. A substantial number of "leftist" and "rightist" groups identified with particular religious affiliations struggled for power, ultimately provoking the intervention of Israel in the south and Syria in the north. The destruction of Lebanon's fragile political balance led to catastrophic civil strife. The situation was further complicated by the Israeli invasion in 1982, the main purposes of which were to eliminate the PLO and their the Lebanon-based attacks on Israel and to establish a political order favorable to Israel. Neither objective was accomplished. In the wake of the Israeli invasion and withdrawal, the United States became involved as part of a United Nations force overseeing the evacuation of Palestinians.

The departure of the Arafat faction of the PLO did little to rationalize the politics of Lebanon. In its absence, new groups arose, principally AMAL and Hizbollah, two Shia-based paramilitary organizations. The U.S. role in Lebanon ended tragically with the bombing of a U.S. compound and the subsequent withdrawal of U.S. troops in 1984. The Syrian presence in Lebanon has grown as a consequence of the continued deterioration of central government control, with the Syrians playing a balancing role between contending factions of Christians, Druze, Sunni, and Shia Muslims, and a few independent militia cooperating with Israel.

After the Taif conference of 1988, Syrian forces began to disarm the factional forces of Lebanon. By 1992, all but the Army of South Lebanon (supported directly by Israel) had been disarmed. Under Syrian sponsorship, a new constitution is being promulgated that redressed the balance between Christian, Sunni, and Shia groups. Syrian influence is consequently pervasive, but a nascent independent government appears to be emerging. The political future of Lebanon apparently will hinge substantially on the exercise of restraint by her more powerful neighbors.

ISRAEL

(State of Israel)

Land Area*: 8,291 sq. mi., 21,475 sq. km.
Population*: 4.6m (1990 est.)
Major urban centers (1983 est.): JERUSALEM (426,000);

Tel Aviv-Jaffa** (327,000); Haifa (236,000); Ramat Gan (119,000).
Per capita GNP (1990): U.S. $10,920
Official languages: Hebrew, Arabic (English spoken widely)

Israel occupies a narrow strip between the Mediterranean Sea and its eastern neighbor, Jordan. It is bounded on the north by Lebanon, on the northeast by Syria, and on the southwest by Egypt. During the 1967 war with neighboring Arab states, Israel occupied the Sinai Peninsula and the Gaza Strip administered by Egypt, the West Bank claimed by Jordan, and Syria's Golan Heights. Control of the Sinai returned to Egypt in 1979–1981 as a result of the Camp David peace agreement between Israel and Egypt. The population of Israel (not including the occupied territories) is 85 percent Jewish, with Druze and Arab (Christian and Muslim) minorities.

The Israeli economy is diversified by Middle Eastern standards. Agriculture remains a significant part of the economy, though diminishing in relative importance. The principal crops are citrus fruits, wheat, olives, rice, and tobacco. Israel's industries are rapidly gaining in importance; these include diamond cutting, textiles, food processing, military equipment, metalware, plastics, chemicals, machinery, electronics, and computers. Israel's hostile relations with neighboring Arab states necessitate high defense spending leading to inflation, an adverse balance of payments, and a shortage of labor in certain industries. The economy has benefited from U.S. aid, tourism, and financial contributions from Jewish residents of other countries. The economy has been strained by the addition of more than 300,000 new immigrants, primarily from

*Area and population figures include the Golan Heights and the old city of Jerusalem but not the Gaza Strip or West Bank. These latter areas total 2,410 square miles with a population of about 1.5 million people. The Dead Sea and the Sea of Galilee are not included in the land area.
    **The worldwide diplomatic community refuses to recognize Jerusalem as the capital of Israel.

the former Soviet Union and Ethiopia. Tourism has suffered as a result of the intifadah and the Iraq-Kuwait War.

The majority of the urban labor force is unionized in the Israeli Federation of Labor, or Histadrut, an organization which involves both labor and management in decision-making processes. Much of the rural work force is organized in communal or cooperative arrangements including the kibbutzim, or communal farms.

The state of Israel was formed out of the region formerly known as Palestine, which had become a British mandate under the League of Nations following World War I. From the turn of the century until the end of World War II, Palestine had seen growing conflict between Jewish Zionist settlers and Palestinian Arabs, each with strong nationalistic aspirations. The United Nations attempted to resolve the conflict in 1947 by partitioning Palestine into independent Jewish and Arab states, but in the ensuing warfare between Israel and its Arab neighbors the proposed Arab Palestinian state was demolished and its territories absorbed into Israel and Jordan; many Palestinian Arabs became refugees and remain so today. Chronic hostility with Arab states erupted into war in 1956, 1967, and 1973. These hostilities and the resultant problems of national security have greatly influenced Israel's foreign and domestic policies. The 1982 invasion of Lebanon, costly in terms of lives, material, and international relations, also generated much controversy within Israel. To these problems are added the long-standing disputes over settlement policies in the occupied territories and the question of Palestinian autonomy, which was raised by the 1979 peace accords with Egypt but never successfully resolved.

Politics in Israel have become increasingly sensitive to the growing problem of the Palestinian Arabs in the occupied territories. Following an extremely close parliamentary election in 1984, the Labor and Likud blocs joined in a coalition government. A similar electoral deadlock occurred in the fall of 1988. Political opinion in Israel continues to be divided over strategies to deal with the uprising. The situation was enormously complicated by the PLO declaration of statehood and subsequent U.S. discussions directly with the PLO.

Contemporary politics in Israel are strongly affected by three recent events: the intifadah, a civil insurrection by the Palestinian population in Gaza and the West Bank; the Iraq-Kuwait conflict; and the collapse of the Soviet Union. These events cumulatively changed many of the assumptions of Israeli policy and eventually led to a growing tension between Israel and the United States over the question of a just solution to the Palestinian question. U.S. support for a multilateral peace conference (convened in 1991) and tacit approval of a "land for peace" formula ran squarely against the policy preferences of the Shamir government. The elections of 1992 centered largely on these conflicts, and resulted in the first Labor-led coalition in 15 years. Yitzhak Rabin became the Prime Minister.

Israel has no written constitution but its laws provide for a president, whose duties are largely ceremonial, and a prime minister who functions as the head of government. The government is responsible to the Knesset, Israel's unicameral legislative body, whose members are elected for four-year terms by universal suffrage. The selection of candidates is based on proportional representation of the political parties, according to national party lists.

JORDAN

(Hashemite Kingdom of Jordan)

Area: 35,467 sq. mi., 89,000 sq. km.   AMMAN (972,000); Zarga
Population: 4.0m (1990 est.)   (392,200)
Major urban centers: (1986 est.):   Per capita GNP (1990): U.S. $1,240

Official language: Arabic

Jordan is bordered on the west by Israel, on the north by Syria, on the northeast by Iraq, and on the south and southeast by Saudi Arabia. It is completely landlocked except for a sixteen-mile coastline on the Gulf of Aqaba in the Red Sea. Most of the country is high, arid plateau. The majority of the population is Muslim Arab, but there are many ethnic minorities. Sunni Islam is the predominant religion.

Agriculture, concentrating on fruits and vegetables, is the most important sector of Jordan's economy; nevertheless it is necessary for Jordan to import foodstuffs. The 1967 Israeli occupation of the West Bank, which included the bulk of agricultural land at Jordan's disposal, substantially lowered production. Industry is restricted mostly to cement making, light consumer goods, food processing, and phosphate extraction. Refugees from the West Bank have contributed to urban overcrowding and high unemployment. In order to maintain a stable economy Jordan has had to rely on aid from the United States, Britain, and from other Arab states.

Jordan became part of a British mandate under the League of Nations after World War I, and was granted full independence in 1946 as a constitutional monarchy under the Hashemite Emir Abdullah. The present king, Hussein, took the throne at the age of sixteen after his grandfather's assassination in 1951. The king shares his authority with a legislative body, the National Assembly. He holds executive authority and serves as commander of the armed forces, and he is also empowered to appoint the prime minister and cabinet, to order general elections, to convene, adjourn, or dissolve the legislature, and to approve and promulgate laws. The National Assembly has an upper house, the Council of Notables, and a lower house, the Council of Deputies. The legislature must approve all treaties and has the power to override royal vetoes. Following the recommendation of a 1974 Arab summit conference, Hussein recognized the Palestine Liberation Organization as responsible for the political affairs of the West Bank Palestinians (although not formally relinquishing Jordan's claim to the territory until 1988). The Council of Deputies was dissolved at that time, and was not to be reconvened until 1984.

Jordan's relations with other Arab states have been strained by its pro-Western stance and its "moderate" position on Israel, and disputes between Jordan and Palestinian guerrilla organizations operating from Jordanian bases have added to the friction. Jordan did, however, sever its relations with Egypt from 1979 to 1984 to protest Egyptian-Israeli peace negotiations. Because of its relatively moderate position on Israel, the United States courted Jordan as a potential arbiter in some form of limited autonomy arrangement for West Bank Palestinians. In the summer of 1988, Hussein renounced all Jordanian claims on the West Bank, thus placing any possible peace negotiations in the hands of the Palestinians themselves.

Dismay turned to overt hostility when Jordan refused to join the U.S.–led alliance against Iraq after the invasion of Kuwait in 1990. Jordan, economically vulnerable, endeavored to steer a middle ground so as neither to endanger its subsidies from the West and the Arab monarchies, nor to jeopardize its transportation industry with Iraq or the remittances of Jordanian expatriates working in Iraq. Isolated during the conflict, Jordan has slowly worked its way back into international respectability by joining enthusiastically in the U.S.–sponsored multilateral peace negotiations and by patiently absorbing hundreds of thousands of refugees from Iraq, Kuwait and the Gulf states.

GLOSSARY

Abbasids: An important Hashemite Arab family descended from Abbas, which founded the Abbasid caliphate at Baghdad in 750. This dynasty saw the highest development of the caliphate during what is recognized as the Golden Age of Islam.

Afghani: Jemal al-Din al-Afghani. A nineteenth-century Egyptian schoolteacher who became one of the first modern nationalist writers and spokesmen. He traveled widely and was important in inspiring Middle Eastern opposition to European colonialism.

Alawites: A nonorthodox sect of Islam, found primarily in Lebanon and Syria. The Alawites dominate the Syrian government under President Assad, causing considerable internal resentment and tension among the Sunni majority.

AMAL (or Amal): Acronym for a Lebanese faction favoring pragmatic, secular political strategies. They are often in conflict with Hizbollah for the loyalties of the Lebanese Shia.

Ashkenazim: The term generally used to describe Jews of European origin, specifically from north-central Europe.

Baath: The Arab Socialist Resurrection Party, a political party dedicated to Arab nationalism and socialism. Founded in Lebanon in the 1940s, Baath factions control both Syria and Iraq, sometimes pursuing mutually contradictory goals, particularly in foreign policy.

Bedouin: Refers generally to Arabic-speaking camel-herding nomads in the Middle East and especially in the Arabian peninsula.

bida: Un-Islamic innovations or deviations from tradition.

caliph: The title given to the successors of Muhammad as leaders of the Umma.

diwan: Originally, a record listing those fighting for the Umma, used to determine shares of conquered booty; later it became the rudimentary bureaucracy of the early Muslim state.

djimmi: Religious communities given special recognition in Islam, particularly Jews and Christians, the "People of the Book." They enjoyed immunity from forced conversion but had to pay higher taxes than the Muslims. Also included, eventually, were Zoroastrians and Hindus.

Druze: Mystical, nonorthodox Muslim sect, located in Lebanon and Syria.

fellahin: (*singular*, **fellah**): Peasants, or occasionally, manual laborers in an urban work force.

fiqh: Islamic jurisprudence. Literally, an "understanding" of Sharia law. Different schools of fiqh were founded during the first centuries of Islam, most prominently the Shafi, Hanafi, Hanbali, and Maliki.

ghazi: Defender of the faith, usually as a soldier.

hadith: The collected reports about the life of the Prophet, which, along with the Koran, constitute the major authoritative sources of Islamic thought.

hajj: The pilgrimage to Mecca, one of the five pillars of Islam and the once-in-a-lifetime obligation of the faithful, given adequate health and finances to undertake the journey. A successful pilgrim becomes known as "hajji" and enjoys significant prestige.

Hashemite: The family of the Quraish tribe to which Muhammad belonged, and which subsequently became influential in Muslim affairs. Traditionally powerful in the Hijaz region of the Arabian peninsula, Hashemites were established in power in Iraq and Transjordan following World War I.

Hijaz: A mountainous region of the Arabian peninsula adjacent to the Red Sea coast, including the cities of Mecca and Medina; the region in which Islam originated.

hijira: The migration of those faithful to Muhammad's preaching, from Mecca to Medina (then called Yathrib), in 622. At Medina the full fruition of the political and social aspects of Muhammad's revelation took place.

Hizbollah: An Iranian-supported radical Shia group in Lebanon, often associated with terrorist activities; rival of the more moderate AMAL.

imam: A religious teacher. Most often, the term refers to a leader of services in the mosque. In Shiism the term also refers to the leader of the Shia community.

intifadah: The uprising of Palestinians against Israeli occupation and rule in the Gaza Strip and the West Bank. The rebellion began in December 1987.

Ismailis: The followers of Ismail, the seventh imam of the Shia tradition. The sect is marked by a more esoteric and mystical emphasis than other branches of Shiism and includes the Qarmatians.

jahiliyya: The "time of wickedness" before Muhammad; also used by some fundamentalists to refer to the contemporary loss of Islamic moral guidance.

Janissary: The slave-soldiers who eventually became the core of the Ottoman bureaucracy. Highly trained in special schools, in the early years they were denied the right to have children, thus eliminating hereditary claims to administrative office.

jihad: "Striving" on behalf of Islam. Sometimes called the "Holy War," jihad refers to the obligation of the faithful to extend the Umma and protect it from its enemies, either by actual warfare or spiritual struggle.

Kaaba: A shrine dedicated to Allah, of great historical importance in Arabian history. Although of pre-Muslim origin, it was incorporated by Muhammad into the Islamic faith and associated with the prophet Abraham. Located in the Grand Mosque of

Mecca, the Kaaba is the ultimate destination of the pilgrim (hajji). Maintenance of the Kaaba is very important to the wider Islamic community and to the government of Saudi Arabia in particular.

katib: The scribes, or record keepers, employed by the traditional governments, especially under the caliphate.

Kharijite: An early puritanical movement in Islam; initially allied with Ali, this radically democratic group eventually turned against him and assassinated him in 661.

Koran: The written word of Allah as revealed through his Prophet, Muhammad.

madrasah: Schools of religion, sometimes independently supported by waqf endowments; often associated with a prominent urban mosque.

Mahdi: The messiah or redeemer in Islam, expected to come to earth in the final days to lead the faithful in their war against the infidel.

Mameluks: The slave dynasty of Circassians who ruled Egypt from 1250 to 1798. From 1517 until their destruction, they alone ruled Egypt, giving only nominal allegiance to the Ottoman sultan.

Maronites: A monophysite Christian sect located primarily in Lebanon and Syria.

millets: The religious groups given official status in the Ottoman Empire. In matters of civil conflict among members of the same millet, the conflict would be resolved by the traditional authorities and processes of the respective millet. Thus a Christian was governed by Christian laws in his dealings with Christians, regardless of his physical location in the Ottoman Empire.

miri sirf: State ownership of land with specified rights to the tenant farmer.

modernism (Islamic modernism): An interpretation of Islam that stresses its abstract spiritual values, rationality, and commitment to social justice rather than the accumulated details of Sharia law, and that argues that these basic Islamic ideas are compatible with modern social life. Modernist interpretations of Islam have been set forth by various Islamic scholars in the nineteenth and twentieth centuries.

mosque: An Islamic house of worship.

Muhammad Ali (also **Mehemet Ali**)**:** Ruler of Egypt from 1805 to 1849. He initiated major reforms in Egypt, many of which were blunted by a combination of European and Ottoman strategies. The economic and military power of Egypt was greatly increased by Muhammad Ali, who was also the first of the great modernizers in the Arab world.

Muharram: A month of the lunar year, dedicated in the Islamic community to commemorating Hussein's martyrdom. The commemoration is a very emotional event for the Shia faithful.

mujtahid: Religious leader, preacher, and scholar, the equivalent of the Sunni ulema.

mulk: Private ownership of land.

Mutawwa: Semi-official "religious police" in Saudi Arabia.

Muwahhidun: "Unitarians"; the preferred designation for the fundamentalist sect that prevails in Saudi Arabia, founded in the eighteenth century by Abd al-Wahhab and popularly referred to as "Wahhabi."

Najd: The extremely arid north-central region of the Arabian peninsula.

Ottomans (Ottoman Empire): Founded by the Turkish leader Osman, the Ottoman state gave rise to the last great Islamic caliphate. Centered in Anatolia, the empire lasted from its founding in the thirteenth century to the second decade of the twentieth century.

pir: A recognized master in a sufi tariqah or order.

Qarmatians: A long-lived communal movement within the Ismaili sect of Shiism.

Quraish: An important and powerful Arab tribe, which controlled Mecca at the time of Muhammad. As descendants of the Prophet's tribe, the Quraish have always been accorded a special respect in Islam.

Ramadan: One of the lunar months of the Muslim calendar. Fasting during the daylight hours of Ramadan is one of the five pillars or ritual obligations of Islam.

Riddah: The Wars of Apostasy, fought soon after the death of Muhammad, forcing rebellious Arab tribes to continue their allegiance to Islam.

sadaqa: In Islam, a voluntary charitable contribution, bringing religious merit to the donor.

Sanussi: A Sufi order that became very influential in North Africa.

Sephardim: Generally, the "Oriental" Jews of Spanish, African, Asian, or Middle Eastern origin. Specifically, the term refers to Jews from Spain.

shahada: The declaration of faith in Islam: "There is no God but Allah, and Muhammad is His prophet."

Sharia: The Muslim legal code, founded on the Koran and hadith (traditions of the Prophet) and codified by various systems of interpretation or fiqh.

sheikh: A term that can apply to high-level political, local, communal, or religious leaders.

Shia: Muslims following Caliph Ali and his successors, differing on various points of doctrine from the orthodox Sunni majority. Shiism, concentrated largely in Iraq and Iran, is divided into several different sects. Most Shia prefer this designation to the commonly used term, "Shiite."

Sufism: A movement pervasive in Islam, based on mystical experience. The diverse Sufi orders, each with its own tradition of mystical teachings, have cultivated the inner, ecstatic aspect of Islam, and their appeal has greatly aided the spread of Islam in some parts of the world.

Sunni: The largest, "orthodox" division of Islam.

suq: Bazaar; a place for commerce, composed of a number of merchants selling a limited variety of wares. An important setting for social interaction as well as commercial exchange.

sura: Chapter in the Koran.

tanzimat: Generally, a series of attempted reforms in the Ottoman Empire from 1839 to 1876; at least partially a response to growing European dominance at that time.

taqiyyah: Dissimulation, or the disguise of one's true religious feelings in order to avoid persecution. Widely used among the Shia in response to the many attempts to control or persecute the Shia community.

tariqahs: Specific orders of Sufism, with specified secret paths to mystical ecstasy. After the decline of the caliphate, tariqah lodges often filled many local social needs as well.

tawhid: The undivided unity of God and His authority over mankind; also refers to other, derivative concepts of unity, including social or political unity.

ulema: Muslim scholars who function as religious leaders in Islam. Unlike the Christian priests, the ulema are not organized into a clergy and claim no special powers of sanctity beyond their study of the documents of Islam.

Umayyad: One of the most powerful and important of the Arabic families at the time of Muhammad. The Umayyad caliphate was founded at Damascus by Muawiya after his conflict of succession with Ali.

Umma: The worldwide community of Islam, which ideally commands a Muslim's loyalty above all considerations of race, kinship, or nationality.

Wahhabi: Another, less preferred, term for Muwahhidun.

wajh: Group honor, "face," a concept of great importance in the maintenance of group and individual prestige.

waqf: Religious endowments, usually made in perpetuity, which support a specific institution devoted to good works, such as a madrasah, a home for orphans, or a religious building. The institution of waqf sometimes became a device for avoiding taxation.

zakat: One of the five pillars of the Islamic faith, obligating the faithful to support the unfortunate and the needy.

INDEX